ECHOES *of* WAR

SCEPTRE

ECHOES *of* WAR

WILLIAM RIVIÈRE

SCEPTRE

First published in 1997 by Hodder and Stoughton
A division of Hodder Headline PLC
A Sceptre Book

10 9 8 7 6 5 4 3 2 1

A CIP catalogue record for this book is
available from the British Library

ISBN 0 340 69606 0

Typeset by Palimpsest Book Production Limited,
Polmont, Stirlingshire
Printed and bound in Great Britain by
Clays Ltd St Ives plc, Bungay, Suffolk

Hodder and Stoughton
A division of Hodder Headline PLC
338 Euston Road
London NW1 3BH

A long war disturbed your mind;
Here your perfect peace is signed.

The Duchess of Malfi, John Webster

ONE

1

—⁂—

Holding the wreath she had made, Mrs Lammas pushed open the door of Paston church and went in. The North Sea gale swirled up the dead leaves lying in the porch, blew them inside past her legs, and those of her goddaughter Georgia Burney following her.

It was a simple wreath, chiefly of ivy with a few sprigs of holly and yew twisted in. The ivy berries hung in tight black clusters. The holly berries were red and, if they had not been cut, they too would have been food for blackbirds and thrushes half-starved by winter, Georgia thought, as she helped to heave the door shut so that the dun leaves stopped skittering about the flagstones and lay at their feet.

Georgia had come to England for the first time earlier that year, and she was learning a lot about things like ivy and thrushes – English things. She did not know Mrs Lammas at all well, but in the garden at Edingthorpe Manor they had picked the sprays for the wreath together, companionably.

During the Great War, Blanche Lammas' brother had gone down with his ship. It had been two days before Christmas 1917 and his destroyer had been torpedoed somewhere out on that stormy North Sea, which Georgia could hear thundering against the cliff three or four paddocks from the church. The ship had started to sink and they had lowered the boats, but he had stayed on his bridge – Georgia knew, Mrs Lammas had told her, cutting ivy in the grey garden. Had told her simply, without explanation, cutting with her rusty secateurs.

That had been seventeen years ago, and Ralph Michael Mack's family had commemorated him with a stained-glass window in the church which stood near the Hall where he had been brought up, and every winter on the day of his death his sister made a wreath and laid it on the sill of his window.

Inseparable, they had been, riding their ponies into the sea when it was calm, hacking along the stony stretches of the beach, breaking into a mad gallop where it was sand. On their father's stubble fields at Paston and Bacton, they challenged one another to jump the nastiest hedges and ditches. If one of them came down, the other caught the loose pony.

In those days before the war, Blanche was the belle of Norfolk. She rode pillion behind her brother on his old motorbike, which was considered a little wild for a young lady of a good county family. They went to dances in a pony-trap, for the sake of her dresses, and several men wanted to marry her or at least seduce her, but she danced with her brother as often as not.

After war broke out, she only saw him when he was ashore on leave. The last time his ship HMS *Tornado* put into Leith, Blanche went up to Scotland on the night train. Three days later she stood on the wharf and waved as the flotilla of destroyers went to sea.

'It's just here, on the south side,' she said, walking up the aisle.

Dusk was falling. The church was cold, tenebrous. But to Georgia the window when they stood before it shone with glorious colours, even in this gloom it was alive, it was triumphant.

The pictures! she exulted silently – for she had seen nothing like these glowing panes in all her twelve years. In the centre stood the Archangel Michael with his sword drawn. (Mrs Lammas said that was who it was.) He was wonderfully handsome, the girl thought. And here was the grey destroyer butting through the waves full steam ahead, and here were swans flying low over the sea, and all these visions had stories echoing if you could only hear them, Georgia was convinced of it, and stories were irresistible, echoes were everything.

And as for the words! *He commissioned and commanded the destroyer HMS Lucifer in the engagements of Heligoland Bight 29 August 1914 and the Dogger Bank 24 January 1915.* (The ship's bell now hung in the Manor kitchen. Georgia had been allowed to give its clapper a gentle touch, had heard the low beginning of its reverberative clang.) *Mentioned in despatches . . . Killed in action . . . Going down with his ship . . .* Magical words, they seemed to her, words resonant with meaning.

'Swans?' she wondered.

'Yes,' her godmother said. 'My brother's second-in-command told me that the day before they'd seen swans. They stood on the bridge together and watched them fly, and Michael was happy to see them.'

'And what's that?' She pointed to a coat-of-arms.

'That's a sheaf of wheat.' Mrs Lammas regarded the child quizzically. 'You really are a little Burmese, aren't you? A wheatsheaf is our family crest.' Her mouth stirred uneasily, fell straight. 'We've always been a farming lot.'

Nettled, Georgia pointed to things she knew about. 'That's the White Ensign. And that's Britannia.' She could not help being British, but she loved Burma passionately, considered it infinitely superior to this desolate country of schools and strangers. And now across sub-continents and across oceans, words of her father's rang to her. 'And that's called a fouled anchor. It's an anchor with a rope tangled round it, and it's the emblem of the Royal Navy.'

But Georgia's enchantment had been dispelled and she asked no more questions.

Mrs Lammas set her wreath on the stone sill below the Archangel's feet, below the glimmering words *Fear God, Honour the King*. She sat down in the pew where throughout her girlhood she had sat every Sunday morning with her family. Less than a year after the Armistice her bridegroom's family had sat there. On her father's arm she had walked up the aisle, treading on the tombstones, and even through her veil she had seen how radiant Michael's window looked in the noon sun. She had known those panes of glass stream with light that was infinitely sad but that was defiant too, and she had rejoiced and she had nearly cried, and had walked on into the chancel where Charles Lammas was waiting for her.

Mrs Lammas did not kneel down, did not appear to pray. Still, Georgia thought, she looked sad, she might like to be left alone for a minute. But the real reason why she drifted a few paces away from her was that she herself had suddenly felt solitary again.

Mr Lammas had told the girl about the Paston family in the Middle Ages and the Renaissance. They had written letters that were famous, he had said, and the seventeenth-century sculpture of Lady Katherine Paston lying on her tomb was beautiful.

Georgia stood before stone Lady Paston, but she felt too cold to admire the memorial, too cold to be susceptible to any sadness except her own.

Mr Lammas had also told her how her father had been his best man. Alex had cranked his old car to get it started, and had driven him over from Mundesley in grand style, he had told the girl, hoping these would be cheerful things for her to think about.

But now, at the image of her father in a morning-coat and a dove-grey waistcoat laughing as he cranked a car on a sunny morning, Georgia's homesickness came over her with a rush. Her misery welled up from her heart, took possession of her throat and her mouth, lorded it in her brain. Trembling with her effort to fight it down she stood by the altar rail where, before she had been born, her father had stood and joked with Mr Lammas. Daddy, Daddy! she prayed. And at these words, she burst into tears.

Footfalls came quickly toward her over the stone. She felt Mrs Lammas' arms around her shoulders. The woman and the girl stood in the twilit chancel, winter coat pressed to winter coat.

'Oh you poor little darling,' Blanche Lammas murmured. Over Georgia's Burma-sick head, her eyes glistened. 'And I'm not much better. I'm not much good at being brave either, sometimes. Now, shall we go back and have some tea?'

Exile to Europe had been a tough schooling in self-possession; already Georgia had wiped her eyes, was recomposing her face and her voice. Also, although often she felt only nine or ten years old, sometimes she felt fifteen, and she could seem it to others too. 'Yes,' she now said. 'Thank you. That would be very nice.'

They returned down the nave past the stained-glass window, which nightfall was extinguishing.

'Who knows,' Blanche Lammas said with judged playfulness, 'perhaps one day you'll be married in this church. Would you like that? Or at Edingthorpe, if you'd rather. Take your pick.'

'If I ever get married,' the girl said with polite resolution, 'I hope it'll be at home.'

Home! her heart prayed. The Irrawaddy. The Shan Hills. Daddy and Mummy. Angus. Happiness. (Angus was a terrier of confused breeding and unreliable temper but of exemplary loyalty to Georgia, and he had been the beloved friend of her hill station childhood.)

'Of course! How stupid of me. Just think how romantic!' Blanche waved her gloved hand toward an Orient now for a moment crystalline, suddenly agleam with the sumptuously hymenial. 'A wedding in Mandalay!'

2

─w─

Bewildered by her intimations, and having lost any thread of consecutive thought, Georgia plodded up-gale toward the graveyard gate where the Lammas's gardener waited with the car.

Mrs Lammas' hat was adorned by a silver hat-pin with an agate knob, but such riveting was inadequate to the occasion, she clutched it with one hand. Georgia's hair blew back from her woollen-hatted head like a burgee.

The storm blew from Norway, it blew from Denmark, it raged over the Dogger Bank where Commander Mack's destroyer *Lucifer* had engaged the enemy. The tide was rising. All along the embattled east coast of Britain, the darkening combers crashed higher up the shores, started to break against the low cliffs. The roiled sea pounded off-shore banks, it overwhelmed strands so the terns and gulls and oystercatchers rose wailing into the nightfall and were tossed inland. The tumult of cascading spume advanced up shingle spits and mud spits, deafened the evening's last bait-diggers who trudged in retreat toward their hamlets, spade over one shoulder, sack of lug-worms over the other, their oilskins and sou'westers drubbed by spray and rain.

In Norfolk the freezing wind which roared in the trees around Paston church battered all the flint churches which stood parish after parish along that coast of muddy cliffs and salt marshes and shingle foreshores, frenzied to a St Vitus' dance the blizzard-stunted sycamores and oaks and thorns. In that region of windmills, the storm shrieked in their rusting turning-gears, shook their groaning spars.

The anchorage at Brancaster was protected by the island of Scolt Head, but even inshore before the village the white waves reared awesomely around the moored fishing-smacks. All afternoon in the relative hush of low tide the men had checked their warps. They had overhauled mooring-chains, they had laid out kedge-anchors. They had rowed ashore in their cockling scows. Now at high water their smacks were exposed to the undiminished force of the gale; they chucked their tethered heads like frightened horses; they shuddered under the blows of the breaking seas.

At Burnham where Horatio Nelson had learned to sail, at Wells where he had watched luggers loading and unloading, the black tide foamed up the creeks, it flooded the marshes of sea-lavender and marram grass, it stormed against the sea-walls. Off Stiffkey, where at low tide in summer the Lammas family liked to walk their dogs on the revealed sand-banks, by nightfall the harbour bar was a maelstrom thirty foot deep; the tide had advanced two miles inshore, had whelmed the samphire flats and the river mouth and the mussel beds in one unnavigable welter of crossing pale crests and dark troughs. At Mundesley, where Charles Lammas' father Roland had lived and had his studio at Cliff House, winter by winter yards of what had been his rose garden and tennis court and vegetable garden had been lost to the North Sea. After his death, defences had been constructed on the beach below his demesne. But this 23 December the waves were over the breakwaters; though their power was reduced, they were tearing at the cliff again.

Even inland, the shifting of the balance of power of the waters was felt.

In the drawing-room at Bure Hall, twenty-five-year-old Bobbie Lammas was flirting with Caroline Hedleigh, whose golden curls were enchanting, he considered, as she leaned to pour his tea. The fire in the hearth blazed merrily; her father and mother were in another room and were also, praise God, terrific friends of his mother Gloria and his Lammas uncle and aunt; Caroline was admirably irresistible . . . Bobbie was a blithe young man, with no liking for sombre reflections or for worries of any kind, and this Christmas for the life of him he couldn't see what anyone could expect him to worry about. Nevertheless, he spared a thought for the river which ran below Julian Hedleigh's park.

Not that he interrupted his teasing chatter with that landowner's rosy-cheeked daughter, nor for long took his eyes from her rosy mouth which that winter it was his cardinal pleasure to kiss. But he brought to mind the meandering waterways that lay between Bure Hall and the sea down at Yarmouth. He thought of the brumous fresh marshes and salt marshes where you went wildfowling, the water-meadows with horses in the gloaming huddled for shelter behind leafless hedges, the reedbeds soughing. A big tide and an onshore gale down at Breydon Water would send their pulse miles inland; here in the small broad at Bure would stir the shallows around the alder carr, lift the water-lilies an inch.

At Paston churchyard gate, climbing into the back of the car while Sidney Meade held the front door open for Mrs Lammas, Georgia Burney was too cold and too lonely to be conscious of much beyond the sea's icy grey sky that was crashing over the land, and the cannonade of waves that seemed louder than before.

The car jolted forward into the murk. Georgia's fingers in her gloves were cold, her feet in her boots were cold. She hugged her coat as tightly around her ribs as she could.

Mrs Lammas' sad eyes, the Archangel with his gleaming sword . . . Images flickered in the girl's mind. Her father, when he was young and merry, laughing by a church door. A destroyer with her smokestacks volcanoing. And where was Heligoland Bight, and what had happened there? A fouled anchor. Swans on the wing . . .

Her godmother turned round to address her.

'Shall we have mince pies for tea? And there's the Christmas tree to decorate, and the kissing-bough.'

3

Georgia Burney would not advance toward you; she would not retreat
from you. She would just stand there, looking with those unseemly eyes
of hers that appeared to be of several colours or of no colour, that were
like water or air, their hues altering with the light.

She'd stand looking at you, but not necessarily seeing you. There was a
strain of insolence in that child, her schoolteachers opined when they had
faced those eyes a few times. Or if it wasn't insolence, which after all with
suitable discipline might be almost wholly corrected, it was indifference –
but here the teachers' imaginings petered out. Indifference, that far more
insidious weakness or strength which no moral authority has ever known
how to tolerate.

Her mouth didn't help, either. It was too wide, and in repose it seemed
to pout sulkily. As for her hair, it was indescribable, with all those shades
and glints in it, nobody from her mother and her ayah onward could ever
agree what to call it. Until a man she ended up nearly marrying hit on the
answer. Bronze, he said. Slightly tarnished bronze. Of her features, only
her nose was unremarkable: a bit short, slightly tilted upward – the sort of
nose you might observe on the faces of half the children at her school.
In the summer, and in the tropics, freckles specked her cheekbones.

The school was in Suffolk. It had been selected partly for the vitalising
breezes of that narrow, shallow, dangerous sea which the British in the
last century called the German Ocean, and partly for the presence of her
godparents in the neighbouring county.

Georgia's expulsion that summer from her Shan Hills childhood, from
her season of innocent vernal delights, had been timed for Alex Burney's
next home leave. Geraldine and he and their condemned daughter sailed
from Rangoon to Southampton. Their son Richard had been at Winchester
for three years, and once united, the family proceeded to Scotland. Here
the father and son dedicated the summer weeks to fly-fishing. The mother
pined for Paris, or at least London. The daughter made friends with a pony,
and learned not to complain about the cold, and struggled to keep up with
her menfolk in the matter of casting for trout (she was not permitted to
aspire to a salmon) and did one drizzly day kill a small fish.

From Scotland they descended to East Anglia. Here sailing took the
place of fishing, though you were still looked down upon if you said
you felt cold. Here Georgia could meet her godparents and, it was

hoped, begin to make friends with Jack who was older than her and with Henrietta who was younger. And here at the beginning of autumn she was what was called settled-in to her school. This process of being settled-in proved to be an abandonment, the performance of which lasted, what with the unloading of her trunk, a brisk interview with the headmistress, and a comfortless though tearful maternal embrace, less than an hour. The following evening, Alex and Geraldine Burney were back at Southampton.

Georgia was slight, but her body was strongly knit, and the first time she ran in a race she won. It was only a quarter-mile, but toward the finish she was so far out in front of the other five girls in the heat that she was seen to slow down – perhaps slow down too much, or too obviously, at any rate her house-mistress made a mental note about arrogance. So without waiting to find out if she were good at her lessons the school dubbed her an athlete. And from the start they all, teachers and pupils, called her the Burma girl.

Her intellectual work turned out to be unworthy of comment. There were two classes for each age group. Georgia was invariably either at the bottom of the upper or at the top of the lower.

With her physique, the Burma girl might have made a games player as well as an athlete – but here something went wrong.

In the locker-room before a lacrosse match she was overheard telling a girl that she hoped the other school would win. Only no one could believe she had said such an idiotic thing, and those who had heard her decided they must have misheard. Her words might have rippled away into the oblivion of generations of childish locker-room flarings of subversive vehemence, had the games-mistress not decided to question her after supper.

Yes, Georgia Burney confessed at once, standing immobile with that unnameable hair of hers, and her inscrutable eyes, and her sulky lips. She had said that. And, she added in a flat voice, when the other school *had* won she had been pleased.

Why?

Because she hated this school.

And if, the woman interrogating her enquired, she had been at the other school?

Oh, then, Georgia allowed with ready even-handedness, she would have hated *that* place and wanted *this* to win the match.

The games-mistress was not an unkind woman. The girl was in her first term. She was a long way from home. (The mistress had no doubt that the true home of those British who manned the empire was Britain, but realised you could scarcely expect a lonely child to feel this in her heart, evident though it might be to the mature mind.) It was terrible to think of a soul so young in which to know was to hate.

She told Georgia that she hoped she would come to like the school. She explained that, irrespective of one's private feelings, which unfortunately were open to error, loyalty was an indispensible virtue. She added that it was a shame she did not have a sister, and sent her away.

And that might have been that, if the wretched Burma girl hadn't then rashly converted emotion into action. She might have got away with nothing more cruel than a renewed haunting by Emma, who had died in the Shan Hills and been buried in a churchyard in Maymyo, if she hadn't contrived to get herself had up for losing the next match.

This time there was nothing the games-mistress could do. A player who deliberately fumbled the ball, who operated like a secret agent of the other side – it was doubted whether any school in England had been so dishonoured.

Georgia was doomed. The entire school ostracised her, and would continue to do so, as far as her savaged imagination could perceive, for as many years as she was sentenced to serve there. It was now, at twelve years old, that she first heard herself called a traitor. They shouted the word after her in the yard. They used it instead of her name. 'The Burma girl, the traitor.' 'What's the traitor doing?' 'Here comes the traitor girl.' The words echoed in her brain.

The headmistress, after announcing to the sullen but unrepentant culprit the punishments to be inflicted on her, wrote her end-of-term report that very evening, so unlikely was it that the remaining weeks before Christmas would bring reasons to think either better or worse of Miss Burney's character.

By day, Georgia's only solace was running. In the gym she hardened her muscles furiously, and on the track made a defiant point of winning every race for her age-group. Naturally enough, there were gallant endeavours to humiliate the outcast. But none of her competitors seemed able to match her when it came to not slowing down just because your chest and your legs hurt. Her victories were witnessed in silence, but then the girls lining the track would loudly cheer the second runner to cross the finishing line.

Cross-country running was best. A handful of the senior girls could beat her, but she always outstripped the other juniors, and then she could feel at peace.

The wintry landscape seemed to welcome her. With a lightened heart and light feet she ran the paths and lanes and headlands, vaulted the stiles, splashed through the rivulets. She liked the leafless copses, the ploughed fields. She liked the rooks cawing and the lapwings that tumbled and mewed – though she didn't know that was what they were. She liked it when she was clear away from her pursuers, liked her pounding blood and her mud-spattered legs and her solitude.

At night in the dormitory, since no one would speak to her, she was alone with her thoughts of the East.

4

Charles Lammas received his goddaughter's school report by the afternoon post on 23 December, while she was in the kitchen being restored with mince pies and tea. He read it standing by his drawing-room fire, hearing the sea wind boom around the house, glancing out of a window to where in the twilight his son Jack was pushing across the lawn a wheelbarrow heaped with holly and ivy, golden cypress and yew.

With his weather-beaten features cut in straight lines, his brindled hair and clear blue eyes, in his forties Lammas still looked like the naval officer he had been. In his well-cut but ancient cavalry-twill trousers and his dilapidated tweed shooting-coat, he resembled one of his landowning neighbours. But he was a painter.

They all seemed to be painters, the Lammas men – the ones that weren't barristers or surgeons or professors. Charles was the third Royal Academician in the last fifty years, and the youngest to be elected. There had been his father, Roland Lammas, buried at Mundesley, who had painted knights in armour riding their chargers down forested scarps, and lions padding through the ruins of Persepolis by moonlight, and small Victorian girls in frocks and sashes trying to teach Great Danes to read – subjects so out of fashion now, his son would mildly lament, that no one any longer saw how well painted the pictures were. There was Edmund Lammas, who possibly was homosexual or, according to others, a fearful womaniser. At all events, he had gone to live in Italy. And, as his cousin Charles would add, his paintings had generally fetched good prices.

Charles Lammas had had what they called a good war, and when he came out of the Navy after the Armistice he rented a studio in London. Then Blanche had, as he would put it, been mad enough to marry him. He had bought the Edingthorpe house. It wasn't grand, but it was a likeable old house built of brick and flint, with outbuildings – one of which he'd made into his studio – a stable and a paddock and an orchard, with a small wood between the garden and the North Sea winds. Soon Jack, and then Henrietta, were born. Lammas was energetic, he was sanguine, and he counted himself as fortunate as a fellow could be.

'I've been wonderfully lucky,' he'd say, fixing you with those sailor's eyes, which looked as if they ought to have been scanning an estuary for a harbour mark, but which these days scrutinised the dignified lineaments of generals and vice-chancellors and baronets, the shapeliness of society beauties, the charms of well-to-do children.

He'd be in his Norfolk studio; or he'd be in the smoking-room of his London club; or he'd be at the dinner table of one of the houses the daughters of which he was commissioned to portray.

'Got through the war without a scratch.' This was true. 'Didn't even see too many horrible things.' A drawl, what they used to call an Oxford drawl, though in fact he'd been at the Slade, and then at Dartmouth in '14.

'And now a few people seem to be prepared to buy the things I like to paint, so we won't starve, or at least not till the fashion changes.' A twist of a smile. 'Very lucky.'

There must have been other good painters in England with first-rate war records; but perhaps not many of them so naturally looked the part, played the part. Anyhow, other successful men seemed to delight in getting him to paint their houses and parks, their wives and children, and in this way he paid for Jack's and Henrietta's education. He didn't act the aesthete, which was a saving grace. Indeed, he'd only talk about his art with two or three fellow painters who were friends, with some collectors who he reckoned knew what they were up to. Of course, his profession exposed him to a lot of ignorant chatter about painting; but he was a great one for listening thoughtfully and then changing the subject with such charm that people never noticed where the deflection had occurred. If you admired one of his French landscapes, he'd tell you what fun Blanche and he had had rattling round Burgundy in their old car that summer, how the mill-pond in the foreground had been the scene of Jack's catching a perch or Henrietta's trying to collect frogs' spawn in a jar but falling in. Or he'd tell you about the architecture of the château glimpsed through the trees in the background, or about a performance of an opera in its courtyard to which they'd been invited. If you admired a portrait, he might say 'It was a lot of fun to do', or 'I could have done with more sittings', or 'Glorious stuff, that tulle'. He'd tell you what an uncommonly interesting man or woman the sitter was, give you instances of their wit.

He was well-travelled and well-read, if those were the kinds of things you wanted in a friend or a house-guest. He rode and shot, he danced. He could talk about Baldwin's canniness, or Thackeray's novels, or the Australian cricket team. Men took him for what he seemed so naturally to be, and liked him for it.

Women liked him too. The crack officer, the fashionable painter, and handsome and fit-looking into the bargain. No wonder a few ladies were suspected of having decided they wouldn't mind exploring beneath the veneer their fathers and husbands and brothers found so satisfactory.

Those well-tailored suits and that courtesy couldn't be all there was to him. So on occasion rumours rippled.

Of course, he disappointed some people – preeminently those ardent souls who would have liked him to engage with them in long discussions on the subject of contemporary art. And someone at his club once said he was just like Robert Browning, and the comparison accompanied him for years. Browning, of whom apparently it was said that when you'd met the man, who was so thoroughly the English gentleman of his time, very cheerful and pleasant, a touch too bluff, too hearty, it was difficult to reconcile this rather ordinary creature with the maker of his finest poems. Well, some people reckoned Lammas was too immaculately the officer and gentleman of *his* time, and once you'd seen the sensitivity of his best pictures this was a little disappointing.

The drawing-room was hung with part of his collection of Italian engravings and etchings, some of his favourite compositions by Guido Reni and Federico Barocci and Giambattista Tiepolo.

Warming his legs by the fireplace, he flicked through Georgia's report. French 'not bad', geography 'average'. Distantly he heard the front door bang, then the exclamations and the laughter precipitated by the entry of the wheelbarrow of greenery. Lammas liked having the house full of people at Christmas; he liked the innocent ceremony of decorating the rooms with holly and ivy. He looked up from the dull report, alone with his blazing logs he smiled. Good the sound of his trees in the stormy nightfall, good the merry voices ringing from the hall.

Mathematics 'average', athletics 'first-rate'. And then he got to Georgia's games report, to the verdicts of her house-mistress and headmistress. He snorted, muttered 'For heaven's sake'. He finished reading. Impulsively he broke out, 'The brutes!'

He stood for a moment, frowning. Then decisive, straightforward, he strode to the door into the hall, opened it, and called, 'Georgia!'

The girl had been beginning to twine ivy into the banister of the staircase. Startled by the gruff male call, she came quickly.

Placing a hand on her back, he ushered her into the drawing-room and shut the door.

His mouth smiling but his eyes worried, he cheerfully flourished her report. 'What have these beastly people been doing to you? And why didn't you tell us you were in trouble, eh?'

The child stood in the middle of the carpet, motionless. The tempest moaned around the Manor's chimneys. A log in the fireplace shifted, sparks flew up.

Carefully not allowing himself to dwell on his suspicion that the Burneys might not be the easiest parents to be the child of, Lammas waited, still smiling. But she didn't speak.

'Those letters they make you write to us every Sunday. You never breathed a word about this, you little wretch, did you? School is not too bad – that sort of stuff was all we got out of you. Didn't it occur to you that we're on your side? That your godmother and I might be of some practical use? And I'll bet you haven't written a line of complaint to your parents either.' Still she didn't respond. He waved the rustling pages. 'Now, are you going to chuck this rubbish in the fire or am I?'

After a hesitation, Georgia said, 'You do it.'

He did so. At last she stepped a pace forward. Side by side they watched the pages burn. Lammas armed her with the poker, insisted she shove the last scraps into the flames.

'Now you're not to fret. I'll sort this silly business out. If this school is really no use, we'll send you to another one. Only then for pity's sake be rebellious a bit more subtly.'

Whether Georgia had already brought her imaginable loneliness and despair under control or not, and whether she was now truly comforted, remained unclear.

5

—ᴍ—

The drawing-room door crashed open. With a billow of icy air (they must have left the front door wide to the storm) and a scraping of branches against painted woodwork, Jack staggered in clasping the bole of the Christmas tree, gasping 'Steady!' to Richard Burney carrying its other end.

Mud and lichen on their clothes, resin on their hands, their faces flushed with cold and exertion, their grins exuberant, the boys dumped the tree on the floor in a shower of pine-needles.

'Too big, you reckon? Won't fit?' Jack met his father's amused look. 'They've grown well in that plantation. We cut one of the smallest we could see. Fine tree, though, isn't it?' He noticed the flecks of mire and bark between the door and the hearth-rug, the arboreal litter on the carpet that Mrs Fox had brushed in preparation for the Christmas junketings. 'Don't worry, Papa. We'll clear up. Now, Ricky, where's that skep? On second thoughts, maybe I *will* go and fetch a saw.'

Charles Lammas left Georgia watching them cut the bottom three feet off their tree, helping them fill an old wicker skep with cobbles and bricks to wedge its foot in. He went into the hall. They'd get their tree standing. They'd even make an incompetent attempt to clear up the mess they'd made. They were fine lads. Friends at school, which was pleasing to contemplate, and good-hearted components of his house-party here. Yes, Richard fitted in admirably, he mused, haunted slightly by the boy's sister equally under his care, by her silence under oppression. He frowned, thinking how righteous teachers and children could be.

'Carpentry in the drawing-room, darling?' Blanche enquired. 'Do shut the front door. You'd think this house was freezing enough already, the boys wouldn't *need* to invite the storm in.'

She had been attempting to hurry through the hall without her armful of presents being observed, but now she stopped to be lighthearted for a moment and show her husband that her annual laying of a wreath for her brother had not dispirited her too much.

'Charlie, that *is* sawing I can hear.'

The tide was high. As the black rollers approached the coast, over the inshore shoals they reared up lumpy and ugly, they began to lose their serried formation, began to falter and slew and break. Then against the cliffs they exploded, cataracts of spray were hurled aloft past the crevices where in spring the fulmers and sand-martins nested, were whipped in dark salt blizzards onto the fields.

Two or three miles inland, at Edingthorpe Manor the gale was roaring in his uncle Charles's trees when Bobbie Lammas helped Caroline Hedleigh from his car, as he kissed her in the blustery lea of the garden wall, and then hand in hand they dashed for the kitchen door.

On a newspaper spread on a stone shelf in the larder, Sidney Meade was plucking and gutting pheasants under the approving gaze of his brother Bill, gamekeeper to a neighbouring farmer. Leaning against the wall, Bill recounted his construction of some new butts for duck-flighting down on a water-meadow near Tonnage Bridge. It was a marvel the number of mallard they had shot there on Saturday afternoon, and a few widgeon and pochard too.

Every few minutes, Sidney wrapped up his accumulated innards and feathers in a newspaper bundle, spread a fresh sheet, wiped his hands on a gory rag. He listened placidly to his brother's story of a right and left of teal shot when scarcely made out in the rainy dusk – and of course with that wind blowing he hadn't heard their wingbeats. Sidney would have his season of importance in May and June when his flowers and vegetables would win prizes at half the local gardening clubs and fêtes.

At one side of the old beech kitchen table the cook, Sidney's wife Ellen, was making a batch of mince pies to replace those devoured at recent tea-times, and keeping an eye on the clock so as to know when to put the beef in the oven, and telling Mrs Lammas about the new stuffings she proposed for the goose at Christmas lunch and the altogether different culinary treatment she planned for the pheasants that were to feed the Boxing Day dinner party.

Glad of Ellen's cheerful talk, on her side of the kitchen table Blanche was separating Christmas presents into heaps for each boy or girl, and then dividing them again between those to go into stockings and those to be wrapped up and put under the tree.

Blanche at twenty had been willowy, and she was still slender. Fit, too – she exercised her horse every day. But the principal impression she gave was of softness. She liked to dress in soft colours, that was partly it: today a coat and skirt of smoky blues and greys and greens. And the curves of her cheek and chin were soft, and her brown hair seemed to cling around her head very gently.

Now she stood looking down at the jumble on the table, a distracted smile on her lips, a frown coming and going above her eyes. With the fingernails of her left hand she drummed lightly on the scrubbed wood, showing at her wrist an Art Deco bracelet of gold and pearls, on her wedding finger her sapphire engagement ring – she liked her jewellery. Along the stone-flagged passage toward the kitchen, feet came cantering which could only be Hetty's. 'Don't come in!' Blanche raised her right hand – on this wrist she wore a bracelet of ivory engraved with dragons which her sailor brother had brought her from the China coast – to repel her Christmas-intoxicated, yodelling daughter, but did not lift her eyes from her clutter of books, toys, fripperies. 'I told you! I'm doing presents!' Outside the door the feet skidded to a halt, a whoop rang out, the feet went skipping away.

When a decision was reached (the fishermen's knives in the boys' stockings – though truly they were too old for this nonsense) the present was handed to Nanny Oldfield, who sat in the rocking-chair by the range with wrapping-paper, labels, ribbon, scissors, pen. The other member of the household wintering by the range was an aged gun-dog named Brandy, in honour of whose age and near-blindness relaxations of regime had been allowed.

For years Mary Oldfield had been too venerable to work. She was an Irishwoman, born the seventh child of nine in County Down. She had looked after British children in Penang and in Malacca – which may partly have explained her sympathy for Georgia Burney, or that uprooted child's instinctive faith in the old woman's wide comprehension. Certainly in the first days of her first Christmas at Edingthorpe the girl had let herself cry on Nanny Oldfield's indomitable and still intrinsically Victorian breast.

In the 1890s, back in Britain, Mary Oldfield had been Blanche's nanny. Her brothers' too. Then they grew up, she went to work for another Norfolk family, and during the Great War and for a few years after it for another still. Until Blanche, who was the young Mrs Charles Lammas by then, rediscovered her and brought her to live at Edingthorpe. Here she exercised a mild ascendancy over the infancies of Jack and Henrietta. Now at eighty-four she maintained certain ritual functions, such as the right to wrap up all the family's Christmas and birthday presents, which it was agreed she did better than anyone else could have done.

Baled in cardigan and shawl, tiny, crooked, bird-eyed, her sparse white hair neatly combed, she folded, she knotted, she snipped, she wrote; and she kept a watchful guard over the woman she always called 'Blanche dearie'.

Nanny knew Blanche had never really recovered from Michael's death and never would. The old Irishwoman too had sepulchred him among her griefs: he who should have come home to live at Paston Hall and farm the land, all sold now. Not that she ever spoke of her feelings. But silently she had mourned for him as she mourned for her brothers and sisters (the last to die had been Ethel, buried somewhere in Saskatchewan ten years ago), for a soldier lad who never came back from Kabul, for little Harry Ross whom she nursed through his last fever in Georgetown.

Michael's sister was never much good at Christmas, though she tried; each year it wrung Nanny Oldfield's heart to see her try. (Blanche raised her head, held out a book for Nanny to wrap up for Georgia, gazed at her with her eyes far too brilliant, pressed her lips together hard. I'm trying, Nanny darling, her look said. I can't do better than this.) A few days before Christmas the trouble would start, as regular as the brent geese that came down from Spitzbergen. It always came back, it was something she couldn't outlive. Mr Charles and Nanny did what they could, one of them would go with her when she went to the church to lay her wreath, or they'd make sure one of the children went. If she had a child with her, she didn't cry.

Nanny wrapped up *The Swiss Family Robinson* for Georgia. She was a poor little soul too, with her sister dead. Emma had not been much of a sister, it seemed. Not much of a companion for explorations or picnics

She had learned to walk a bit, before she died, Georgia had sobbed. How old? Ten. Well, hobble. And she could talk a bit. Not very clearly.

Bobbie Lammas lounged cheerfully in the larder just long enough to admire the game hanging from a rafter, to praise Sidney's labours with those birds which had been hung long enough, and to tell Bill that yes, certainly he would be of the party shooting at Bure Hall on Boxing Day.

Jack and Richard were coming too. He hoped Bill had done a good job teaching those lads some of his lore and his accuracy. They weren't bad? Excellent! And when was Bill going to come over and shoot pigeon with him? Uncle Charles's wood was full of pigeons and with these strong winds they'd fly low.

Complaining cheerfully that it was colder in the larder than out in the yard, Bobbie strode into the kitchen.

Here for a minute or two Caroline could be shown off to Mrs Meade (he insisted on taking the heavy platter of beef from her and himself putting it in the oven) and to Nanny Oldfield – not that he ever felt he knew what that ancient spirit really thought. Caroline could kiss the lady of the house; she could admire the array of presents, admire the mince pies. He could stand back a moment and appraise with satisfaction his companion's bright cheeks, the rain-drops glistening on her blown hair. He could swiftly judge that Blanche was as overshadowed as ever at this time of year, but was bearing up. (His aunt by marriage was only fifteen years his elder, and since coming down from Cambridge and declaring himself a painter there had crept into his adoration of her a certain manly protectiveness.) Then he swept his enchantress away to join the party in the drawing-room.

The front of the house was in happy tumult.

The barrow of greenery had been parked in the hall. People kept returning to it to select a particularly handsome spray of golden cypress to adorn a favourite painting, or to dispute merrily where the sprigs of holly with the most berries should go.

Raffaella Zanetti, the daughter of an antiquarian and collector who was a friend of Charles Lammas', had ensconced herself on an Afghan rug beside the barrow. She sat cross-legged in jodhpurs and jersey, and was carefully training stems of ivy around the kissing-bough, weaving in a twig of holly here, a plume of mistletoe there. She commandeered all the best bits of holly, Georgia and Henrietta complained. Raffaella just smiled. She went on bending over her work to twist and adjust, leaning back to assess how she was getting on, bowing forward again to rearrange.

Raffaella had an oval face, short brown hair and a bow mouth, and was easily beautiful enough for Bobbie to greet her with the most blithe celerity when he had Caroline with him. He hurried on, calling, 'Mama! Uncle Charles!'

The Christmas tree was up, the angel on its top with her head an inch from the drawing-room ceiling. She was a good angel, made years before by Blanche and dressed in a scrap of an old petticoat.

Henrietta was decorating the tree. She loved the brightly painted tin bells with their loops of thread; solemnly she debated which branch she should hang each one on. There were silvery baubles too, and candlesticks still encrusted with last year's wax, and brilliant enamel birds with catches under their claws for clipping onto the fronds.

The hitch was, Henrietta only decorated a limited area of the Christmas tree, low to one side, and though this patch was becoming wondrously gaudy the rest of the tree risked being left rather naked, so her aunt Gloria was attempting a little tactful redistribution.

Bobbie had been eight when his father Geoffrey Lammas was killed at Passchendaele. Since then, Gloria had in a flat in Pimlico graced by and large bravely the ranks of the widows of The Great War For Civilisation (as it was called on the back of the Victory Medals issued by the War Office). Now when her handsome son came in with Caroline Hedleigh she exclaimed, 'Darling!' Her fingers looped about with trinkets, she hastened across the still faintly pine-needle beflecked carpet to be hugged.

Charles Lammas had fetched a step-ladder from the garden shed. He had mounted it with a moist sponge in his hand, and was wiping swallow dirt from a copy of a Titian, painted by one of his assistants. Last summer a bird had got into the room and perched on the frame and made a mess down a beautifully painted tree.

Georgia had been hoisted onto the tallboy by Richard and Jack so that she might fix some enamel birds and candlesticks to the tree's upper boughs. She had leapt down with a wild shout and a fluttering skirt into their outstretched arms.

Now they had decked every picture in the room with greenery, all three were tossing sprigs of holly at the top of the Chinese looking-glass, trying to make them lodge among the gilt cranes.

6

Charles Lammas' good war had started peacefully enough. Innocently, too. In ignorance.

After studying at the Slade, he had worked in a Florentine studio for a couple of years, inducted into the Italian artistic milieu by his cousin Edmund. This gentleman was enjoying a sprightly, even raffish old age between Venice where he wintered and Rapallo where he summered, and he introduced Charles most energetically to people who collected rare books and people who might commission portraits, to opera singers and ballet dancers, to counts and yachtsmen and ambassadors, to society hostesses and svelte signorinas. Back in England in 1914 for his first London exhibition, Charles's foremost reaction to the outbreak of hostilities between the Entente and the Central Powers was that it looked like stopping him painting for a while. He would miss his dallyings in Italy, too.

When that year his brother Geoffrey had joined the Norfolk Regiment and he had joined the Navy, they hadn't known how unalike the carnages on land and sea were going to be. They had walked down to the foot of the garden at Cliff House to say goodbye. It was the finest North Sea weather: an onshore wind had scoured the sky a clear blue, a few white clouds were blowing high over the hay fields and the flint villages and churches, and the woods luxuriant with high-summer leaf. The blue offing was pointilliste with the white crests of waves, there were a few crab-boats with tan lug-sails, and farther out a majestic Thames barge coasting with tan top-sails over her gaffs.

The brothers sat on a garden bench by some gooseberry and currant bushes. They recalled all the gooseberry fools they had eaten summer after summer, and the cook bottling currant jelly. They talked about what to do with a point-to-point horse they shared, and decided not to sell him because the war would probably be over by Christmas and in the New Year they'd be racing again. Then they walked back to the house. Subsequently, they were never both home on leave at the same time.

Charles was in submarines for most of the war. In a cabinet in the drawing-room at Edingthorpe Manor, among other family medals were his Distinguished Service Order and bar, and another medal he had been awarded for saving a man's life: his submarine had surfaced and was cruising in heavy seas off Tobruk when a sailor had been washed overboard, and Charles had dived in and hauled him back. In his Edingthorpe library there was a scrap-book of his war photographs and press-cuttings, and there was a picture of him doing a swallow-dive off a ship anchored in the bay at Malta.

Jack as a small boy liked to turn over the bundles of letters that members of the family had written over the generations, read a few sentences from Antigua or Calcutta (handwriting and stamps from Cambridge, say, never had the fascination of those from the tropics), read his uncle Geoffrey's letters from the Western Front, his father's from the Mediterranean. He liked to handle the medals from the Afghan War and the Crimean War and the Boer War, pore over their inscriptions and images, touch their fading ribbons. But most of all he liked to get out his father's war scrap-book, usually during the half-hour he passed with his father in the library before bed-time, which was a childhood winter ritual.

If it were summer, after Jack's bath they might stroll out together to the paddock, lean companionably on the rail to watch the horses and ponies graze. Jack liked the feel of his bare feet on the short dry grass, and there would be stock-doves and wood-pigeons cooing from the trees, Portugal laurels in filmy flower and clematis on the garden walls.

In winter there would be a fire in the library hearth and the curtains drawn. Jack would lie on the rug and eat tangerines. There would be story-books and poetry-books and scrap-books. If he left the peels of his tangerines by the grate for a few days till they were dry, he could use them as kindling when they lit the next fire, and they burned with a beautiful blue flame.

He turned the pages of the war scrap-book. A photograph of his father at Dartmouth, holding a regatta cup and shaking an admiral's hand. A photograph, which had been turned into a postcard, of the submarine E11 steaming over a ruffled English Channel under a now somewhat dog-eared sky. Photographs of Maltese houses, and games of polo, and lateen-rigged dhows; of Crusader castles on Greek and Levantine headlands; of parties of officers duck-shooting on Dalmatian marshes.

Press-cuttings, too. Commanded by Nasmith and with Lammas as second-in-command, E11 had been the first British raider to penetrate the submarine-nets and evade the mines in the Dardanelles, the first to start sinking Turkish shipping in the Sea of Marmara, and the newspapers had been eloquent.

They had sunk merchantmen, sunk transport vessels. An American reporter who happened to be travelling on *Nagara* described how E11 surfaced alongside and gave the passengers and crew five minutes to take to their life-boats before she sank the ship and then herself slid away beneath the sea.

When *E11*'s propeller became entangled in the rigging of a foundered barque, Lammas swam out of one of the torpedo tubes with cutters strapped to his chest. 'Gallant British Officer Saves Submarine', one headline said. 'Human Torpedo', was another. They both recounted how Lammas swam up for air, dived to cut at the halyards and stays, kept diving and cutting till the propeller was free and he could bang twice on *E11*'s hull, which was the arranged signal for Nasmith to reverse the boat clear of the snag and come to the surface so his lieutenant could be pulled on board.

Then there was the story of how *E11* stole right into the harbour at Constantinople under the Turkish batteries ('below the very walls of Santa Sophia', according to one journalist) and sank *Stamboul* at anchor by the arsenal; how they got away to sea with no worse damage to the submarine than a shot through her periscope. There was a photograph of that periscope, with a semi-circular bite out of it, taken when *E11* returned to Lemnos. (The periscope itself was now in the Imperial War Museum; on one of their expeditions to London, the war-time sailor and peace-time painter had taken his little son to inspect it.) *E11* was famous throughout the Mediterranean Fleet by then, and when Nasmith and he brought her into Lemnos bay with their crew clustered round them on the conning-tower, the British ships in the anchorage were lined with cheering men.

It was all right remembering that kind of thing, Charles Lammas found. You remembered the sunshine and the salt breeze that afternoon, and the men's grins, and the hurrahs ringing over the sparkling bay, and how you'd felt just enormously cheerful that things had gone well.

That was all right. After ten years of peace you'd be sitting by your library fire with your child on the hearth-rug, and the war would be like a far sea that was always lapping on the margin of your mind. You could think how the Turks had reckoned the Dardanelles were impregnable, they'd been taken by surprise good and proper. You could recall what a splendid little vessel *E11* was, and how they hadn't lost a man.

Then other scenes came back. At Gallipoli *E11* had lain inshore, from the conning-tower Nasmith and he had seen the stakes and barbed-wire piled with British infantry. And there'd been that Australian regiment slaughtered pretty much to a man, and the next Australians to disembark had seen it all. On the beach they wouldn't line up, wouldn't obey any orders, but they went up the cliff yelling like demons and half of them were killed, but the other half took the Turkish line in one berserk hand-to-hand half-hour, and in the end had to be hauled off the dead Turks they were still bayoneting.

He'd remember the artillery barrage, how the whole peninsula had seemed to be constantly exploding, earth and rocks and trees flying in the air. Different, the way of fighting in submarines and dying in them. So quiet. So invisible. Boat after solitary boat would dive and go round the corner to the Dardanelles. Then you got caught in a net, or you bumped a mine.

He'd remember steaming on the surface all one night, and diving at the first streak of daylight and going down deep to get below the Kephy mine-field, how they scraped the boat on the sea-bed rounding Kanak Point at eighty feet but wriggled off, thank God.

The net brought you that same fear of being snagged down there, as other crews had been snagged before E11 made her attempt. The fear of being buried alive in the tiny hull down in the cold black silence, waiting to die. Nothing for it but to get her going full speed ahead in the narrows and hope, and they'd been lucky, the rending wire mesh made a hideous noise and nearly stopped the boat but she crashed through.

Other moments too. Seeing the wreck of a submarine that had gone before them – the boat had ended up beached, with Turks lobbing grenades down the hatches.

And that time a mine got caught in the bow hydroplane and they dragged the damned thing for two hours before they could shake it off. Not a comfortable travelling companion. Every now and then its mooring chains would clank against the side.

7

—⁓—

That was how the war would go on lapping in Lammas' mind. It seemed to lap right in the centre of the finest things the peace had brought him. Blanche upstairs putting their daughter to bed. The tranquil room with shelves of books he'd inherited and accumulated, with paintings. His father's self-portrait. The boy with his cheeks flushed from his bath and his scamper downstairs, snug by the fire now, his tousled head bowed over a scrap-book in the lamp-light.

Jack would have got perhaps to the last summer of the war, to the action which had earned his father his second DSO. He'd study *The Times'* report for 27 May – 'German U-boat sunk . . . British submarine success.' Then the Telegraph – 'Off Cape St Vincent . . . heavy sea running . . . no survivors.' And the official dispatch – 'The following honours and awards granted by HM the King to Officers and Men of Submarine *E35* for operations against the enemy . . . Lieutenant Lammas bar to DSO . . .'

The boy would twist around on the rug, would demand the story of the hunt. On a sheet of paper he would draw the manoeuvres his father described; he'd give the weather conditions; note the first torpedo that missed, the second that hit. Quietly Lammas would tell how he brought *E35* to the surface to look for swimmers, but there had been none. He'd watch the boy's sombre eyes as he focused on what 'no survivors' really entailed, on those individual extinctions. He'd tell him how he had waited as long as he dared, but he had known there was another U-boat somewhere not far off; he hadn't wanted the hunter to become a quarry, indeed he'd wanted to hunt again; so then quietly *E35* had dived, left the grey Atlantic waves rolling on.

Then sometimes words rather than scenes came back to haunt him. Or scenes with words which went on echoing. The padre that sultry Maltese night, that hour after dinner at Valletta on the club verandah.

Seeing there be many things that increase vanity, what is man the better?

For who knoweth what is good for man in this life, all the days of his vain life which he spendeth as a shadow? for who can tell a man what shall be after him under the sun?

Well, he was a curious fellow, that padre. Had at Gallipoli seen too much, perhaps – or had not known how to do his seeing with the requisite coldness. Faith like a rock, people said, and he was absolutely dedicated to his cure of souls, they'd add, but by '17 he was drinking too much. And certainly that night he'd let himself go a bit, the young lieutenant sitting with him had thought.

This also is vanity and vexation of spirit . . .

And the grasshopper shall be a burden, and desire shall fail; because man goeth to his long home, and the mourners go about the streets:

Or ever the silver cord be loosed, or the golden bowl be broken . . .

By then Lammas had been into the Sea of Marmara and out again, and he'd seen some pretty grim action, but he was still young enough and conventional enough to reckon that a padre who quoted the Bible at you was the last thing you wanted especially after dinner. This was at the stage when he'd forgotten about his initial regret that in 1914 he hadn't been sufficiently known to be appointed a war artist, the stage when he was enjoying fighting the war at sea, enjoying finding he was good at it. And certainly he was callow enough and cocky enough to decide that the Reverend Muir's conversation was no way to carry on.

For to him that is joined to all the living there is hope: for a living dog is better than a dead lion.

For the living know that they shall die: but the dead know not anything, neither have they any more a reward, for the memory of them is forgotten.

It was later, after the Armistice, that Lammas recalled with more tolerance that night on the jasmine-scented club verandah. It was when the living were hard at work having their dog's day that he recalled with discomfort how at the time he'd dismissed the man as hopelessly middle-aged, as irredeemably middle-class (paying scant attention to Muir's meaning, his snobbery had listened attentively to his tell-tale vowels); and, if not actually a coward, certainly with his nerves badly enough shaken for him probably not to be much use. It was when the dead lions and the dead dogs were having their names chiselled onto village memorials – Lammas' brother at Mundesley, the man who would have been his brother-in-law at Paston – that he recalled with more respect the man's harshness when he spoke of the dead.

Also their love, and their hatred, and their envy, is now perished; neither have they any more a portion forever in any thing that is done under the sun.

Muir was dead too, by then – drowned when a troop-ship hit a mine. Nicky Muir who had taken his religion so bloody seriously. Poor old Muir with no *reward*, no *portion forever*, always a touch sexless or something like that, a touch dowdy, was that it, or too damned tender always, something that made you queasy, presumably mourned now by somebody somewhere, a sister maybe.

What Charles Lammas mentioned only to a few people was that one restless day in his Kensington studio he'd flicked through a Bible till he came to *Ecclesiastes*. Thinking of those words on Muir's brandy-moistened cigar-sucking lips, he'd read on.

Go thy way, eat thy bread with joy, and drink thy wine with a merry heart; for God now accepteth thy works.

Let thy garments be always white; and let thy head lack no ointment.

Live joyfully with the wife whom thou lovest all the days of the life of thy vanity, which He hath given thee under the sun, all the days of thy vanity: for that is thy portion in this life, and in thy labour which thou takest under the sun.

Of course, Lammas didn't suppose for a minute that if God existed it would be possible to ascertain how acceptable or otherwise He rated the sinking of Turkish and German ships and the killing of their crews. But when peace came, and his grief for his brother and his happiness to be alive held equal dominion over his confused heart, the idea of living joyfully all the days of his vanity made sense.

The thought of Geoffrey in the wire at Passchendaele with his face shot away, and Alex lying half-dead beside him – Geoffrey who was an architect; who should have come home to Cliff House, come home to Gloria and their little boy. Alex, poor devil, who had gone all the way to Burma so as not to keep going back to Ypres and that wood at Passchendaele. Going back day and night in imagination, and on occasion really going back too. He'd taken himself off to his teak forests and his Irrawaddy plain rice-swamps, to his hill stations and his muddy delta settlements, rather than keep ghosting back. When Charles had asked him once if that was it, he'd said Yes immediately.

Three years the elder brother, at school Geoffrey Lammas had done a certain amount of awkward protecting of Charles, when he could get away with it. And even in 1914 the younger had still been too thoughtless to feel profoundly protective of the elder. It was when time and events were quelling the worst of his naïve exuberance, when he would come ashore at Malta or Marseilles or Gibraltar and hear reports of the infantry war in the trenches, that the likelihood of Geoffrey being killed began to keep him awake at night. And by then it was too late to do anything except write his brother the sort of sensible cheerful letters that came naturally to him.

After Passchendaele, what hurt Charles most sharply at first was the thought of his parents still alive. Their grey, shrunken, stooped figures and their upright, helpless spirits haunted him. Their agony of love that had not kept the bullets from their son followed him everywhere.

It was after the Armistice, when he met Alex Burney and came to hear of Geoffrey's last months of life and of the manner of his death, that Charles Lammas was most tormented by his brother's killing. He knew he was bottling-up his feelings, just like other survivors of that war were doing. Yet all his instincts were to keep quiet about bad things.

His intimations about his mother and father turned out to have been right. When he saw them again they appeared dreadfully aged, and somehow reduced – and indeed within ten years they had both died. But alongside his pity and his attempts to cheer them up, there had come his own terrific upsurge of delight in simply being alive. Irrepressible, unrenounceable, far stronger it seemed at first than any regret or any sorrow. There was blood pumping from his heart to his brain. There was the peace to live. There were pictures to paint. There was beautiful Blanche Mack to fall in love with. It was later, in the midst of the unwinding of his war tension and the winding up of peace-time drives which were all to do with getting back to painting and going to dances, that moments came when he was afraid Geoffrey's death was unmanning him, or unsouling him or something.

Of course, this wasn't a side known to the people who bought his canvases or encountered him at dinner parties. But it was one of the first things Blanche discovered. Sometimes the impeccable manners of the society portraitist weren't any good. Energy? At such times he was the image of lassitude. His bride would find he'd been sitting doing nothing for hours. Seemingly unable to act, or even to speak. Doing nothing except stare before him. Then he'd take to glancing nervously around whatever room it was, in a wretched kind of way. Go back to staring at Geoff's photograph or at nothing. Rub his knuckles across his eyes.

The silver-mounted photograph of Geoffrey Lammas on the Edingthorpe library mantelpiece showed him in uniform. There were also a pair of Georgian candlesticks, and a carriage clock, and generally a box of the painter's favourite cheroots. And after one of his visits to Paris arrived a picture of the Winged Victory of Samothrace.

Nothing to do with there being a Winged Victory on the back of the Victory Medal. Nothing to do with all that barbarism having supposedly been for the sake of civilisation. Nothing to do with winning or losing.

Or rather, though it wasn't to do with nations at war, perhaps it was there to hold up an idea of individual spirits' destructions and triumphs. At any rate, in the Louvre that statue had arrested Lammas. Superb, that exalted transcender, that victrix as if about to take wing, to override – and headless, that was the point.

When or where the Samothrace Victory had lost her proud stone head didn't matter. It was Geoff losing his which Charles couldn't forget. His brother trapped in the barbed-wire, held still to be killed. That beloved head so unprotected. Bullets smashing into those loved eyes, into that

forehead, those cheeks, that mouth and throat. The first shot into his
face hadn't killed him, Alex Burney said, that was the horrible thing. It
was only later, when fire went on raking the line, that his head was, bit
by bit, torn away.

Of course, Lammas had other photographs in his library. Blanche on
their wedding day. The children. But on the mantelpiece just Geoffrey
and the headless Victory with her outstretched wings. They stayed there
for the rest of his life.

8

At the same time, Charles Lammas was happy. The same time – the early twenties, the late twenties. And in the early thirties if you asked him how things were going he'd fix you with those sea-and-sky eyes of his and say 'Fine.' In his understated way, he'd let you infer that Jack and Henrietta were growing up splendidly. That being married to Blanche was the most marvellous good fortune that could have befallen him. He'd even allow, if you positively interrogated the poor fellow, if you challenged him with his worldly successes, that he hoped he was painting better as the years went by. Of course, being Lammas, the way he'd put it would be, 'My luck seems to be holding.' With a puff of bewildered laughter. With a raising of his eyebrows which meant that it was all really too extraordinary, meant also that he knew that at any moment things might change.

The simplest things triggered off his rejoicing. To walk the dogs along his wood-side with Jack on a late autumn afternoon, notice fieldfares pecking at the red berries of a mountain ash. Bitter wind soughing through the marshy, leafless wood, rustling a sere reed-bed. Lammas' survivor's joy in life would clog his throat, twist his lips. A son in muddy boots calling to a terrier. A gaunt heron standing immobile by a dyke, then slowly rising behind a screen of willow and silver birch on tatterdemalion wings, alighting again beyond the next copse. His mind would hosannah with praise, with thanksgiving. His eyes would sting. He would remember Geoffrey. Trying to swallow his tears, he would rejoice more acutely than before in the pigeons buffeted by the squalls as they swooped in to roost, in leafy water chuckling where a fallen tree had half-dammed the stream. Survivors' rewards: simple, incomparable. Scudding grey dusk. Wildfowl flighting overhead, with their colloquial voices.

He didn't grieve only for Geoffrey. Lads he'd grown up with, or been at school with. Young men he'd known at the Slade, met at balls, met in Florence. Steeplechasing friends, Dartmouth friends.

It had been such a slaughter of his generation, sometimes it seemed to Charles Lammas that his whole existence was a rejoicing in all that his dead should have enjoyed. He could not help but despise the cabinet ministers and generals and chiefs of staff who, with Christian acceptance, day by day and year by year had sent young men to attack from front-line trenches where they themselves never felt the need to set their well-booted feet. He loathed that acceptance of an order of things, of others' sacrifice.

By the Armistice there wasn't a flicker of the callow left alive in him, he loathed the old men's and the women's talk about honour and duty. So then in the peace years his contempts and his celebrations grated against each other. The war hadn't impaired his nerves. It had probably improved his character. He was right: he *was* lucky. It just left him conscious of living in honour of his dead. Small rituals kept him respectably cheerful, and at the same time revived his grief and his anger. Innocent observances. What the dead didn't have.

Blanche might finish putting Henrietta to bed, might stroll out onto the terrace, come to join him and Jack leaning on the paddock rail. She'd know what was going on. She'd remember her brother Michael lost with his ship. Her brother Claud whom she'd known far less well because he was older: when Michael and she had been galloping their horses along the beach and taking the dog-cart to dances he'd been in the Malay States planting rubber. When he'd come home he'd died almost at once, of Spanish influenza. She'd remember Charlie when he'd been her tough-minded fiancé in 1919 and she'd taken him to see the church window for Michael that had recently been completed. He'd remarked then that on occasion fighting for king and country might be the right thing to do, but talking about it almost never was. She'd know that even after ten years of peace and then after fifteen there were certain things Charlie couldn't do, without his grief for Geoffrey starting up in him. That would remind him of her grief for Michael. Then he'd start naming all his dead. A necrology. An indictment too – silent, unforgiving. John Hardcastle whom he'd shared a study with at Winchester, killed in Mesopotamia. Nigel Mallory whose submarine dived in the Dardanelles and never came up. Friends. The Farne brothers from West Norfolk, both cricketers, both killed on the Somme. Jamie Macpherson who shared his passion for Corot, with whom he went painting in Provence one summer vacation, killed at Jutland.

Or it might be winter. When Blanche had kissed Henrietta goodnight she would wait in the nursery, which was within earshot of the child's bedroom, till she was sure she had fallen asleep. This was one of *her* happy rituals, one of the good things the peace had brought her. She liked tidying away Hetty's toys, deciding which of her clothes to fold up and which to consign to the laundry basket. It was a moment when she quietly took stock of how blessed she was, when she gave thanks to life for her day, for her children's day. Then she would go downstairs to the library.

When Jack was still young enough to want to hear the stories he liked told at regular intervals, when stories were still ceremonies, his favourite

among his father's war adventures was the attack on the Ismid railway.
They were a mixed bunch, his winter bed-time tales, his library hearth-rug
tales. Adventures of Theseus and Ulysses, Hereward the Wake and Coeur
de Lion. Drake's defeat of the Armada. Captain Cook's circumnavigation.
Nelson's victories at the Nile and Trafalgar. But from the last war the only
story to hold a candle to some of Lawrence of Arabia's wilder actions was,
in Jack's view, his father's winning of his first DSO.

Other evenings when Blanche came in, the talk might be of a particularly thrilling steeplechase or cricket match analysed moment by
moment. Or they might be singing together. Or reading verse. As Jack's
childhood proceeded, after nursery rhymes Charles introduced him to De
la Mare, to Blake's songs, then Shakespeare's songs. And it worked, this
judicious choosing – he didn't put the boy off. Then they read Housman,
then Hardy.

But if on her entrance into the library Blanche discovered her menfolk
busy with dynamite in the Gulf of Ismid, she would know that a rite
of particular significance was being performed. She wouldn't dream of
interrupting, her smile would reassure Jack, anxious that his mother's
entrance into the masculine sanctum might mean the disruption of his
evening ritual. She came of a naval family too – had he forgotten? And
Jack couldn't admire his father's daring more than she did.

This time the newspapers had really gone to town. 'Deeds That Thrill
The Empire', was one headline. Then there were 'Submarine Epic' and
'Navy Hero's Exploit.' Jack had them by heart.

Some men had thought Lieutenant Lammas intolerably self-confident.
But in the Gulf of Ismid he wasn't cocky. Just tough, and successful.

It had been Lammas' idea to try to blow up the Turkish coastal
railway, and E11 surfaced offshore in the calm dusk. Nasmith brought
her in as near as he dared. Then they launched the raft they'd knocked
together, loaded it with boxes of dynamite, a pick-axe and a spade, a
flash-light, a revolver, a lanyard with a knife and a whistle, a bayonet.

Nasmith told his second-in-command he'd come back for him just
before dawn – that he couldn't risk E11 that near land in daylight
didn't need saying. That the Turks were not good people to be taken
prisoner by didn't need saying either. He took a photograph of Lammas
– a picture which later found its way into several newspapers, and then to
the Edingthorpe Manor scrap-book, where it provided Jack with a father
he had never known: young, bearded, muscular-shouldered in his singlet,
grinning in the sea with his raft freighted with gear.

As night fell, Lammas swam toward the shore, pushing his ungainly planks. *E11* submerged.

And after all, why *not* tell the story? the hero of it would ask himself, sitting by his library fireplace. It was a fine story. No one had been killed.

Whatsoever thy hand findeth to do, do it with thy might; for there is no work, nor device, nor knowledge, nor wisdom, in the grave, whither thou goest.

Blanche would know that your voice could be telling about beaching the raft, but your brain would be ringing with different words.

I returned, and saw under the sun, that the race is not to the swift, nor the battle to the strong, neither yet bread to the wise, nor yet riches to men of understanding, nor yet favour to men of skill; but time and chance happeneth to them all.

Blanche understood about the Winged Victory of Samothrace. She knew the praise of the war dead offered up by the library fire, knew the propitiation of destinies hoped for. She too prayed that Jack's and Henrietta's world might be different, their generation not fight a war.

And the raft story was all right, even though *time and chance happeneth to them all.* Even though *as the fishes that are taken in an evil net, and as the birds that are caught in the snare, so are the sons of men snared in an evil time.*

Late in the night he found a stretch of the Ismid railway line where he hoped he could work undisturbed, if he was quiet about it.

Not easy, struggling up those boulders and screes carrying boxes of dynamite without making a noise, but he did it. Nervous business, in the dim moonlight, digging beneath the sleepers and rails and burying the stuff, but he did that too.

Of course, when he blew it all hell broke loose. Terrific explosion, most satisfactory, earth and timbers and rails flying. (Bright-eyed, Jack would mime the detonation. Merrily and vigorously he would explode.) Then shouting, flares, gun-fire, and the guards were after him.

He bolted down the stony headland, trying not to break an ankle in those crevices. Turned round once and fired his pistol at one of the pursuers who was getting a bit close, but he missed. A few strides more, and he was on the beach. A last gallop, a shallow dive. He held it as long as he could, he came up and heard the shots ripping into the water, and dived again.

He swam hard, and the shooting died out. A quarter of a mile off, he rolled on his back. He floated. He gasped. He thought, Even if they launch a dory or a gig or something they won't find me by night.

Overhead, there were still stars, but they were getting paler. He thought, God I hope Nasmith comes. He thought, I hope the boat's all right.

When he'd got his breath back, he swam back up the coast, stopping every minute to listen for engines, to peer into the murk. The Gulf of Ismid didn't look like much on the charts, but it seemed limitless now. About here, or should he be farther east? Farther west? He tried not to think the gloom was lightening. He tried not to think of daylight coming but no _E11_. If she had hit a mine. If she came, but couldn't find him. Or had come, and had gone. Best not to think about sharks either.

Stop. Peer. Listen. Breathe steadily. Then swim steadily, trying not to realise you didn't know which way to swim.

In the first glimmering, he came ashore to rest on a rock. Then he set off to swim round one last headland. Nasmith might be waiting for him in the next bay. He just might be. If not . . . But swimming wearily round the point he saw what in the dawn mist he took for Turkish boats coming for him, so he doubled back, came ashore yet again.

And then the man-hunt working its way along the coast flushed him.

Knowing it was all over, he scrambled groggily back into the sea. He swam out. Out. It was light. He heard engines.

A submarine engine by God! He blinked his salty eyes, he stared. Wavelets. Mist. A conning-tower!

They weren't Turkish boats hunting him, they were the bow and conning-tower of _E11_. He swam furiously. He grabbed the lanyard around his neck, blew the whistle with all the force of his lungs.

_E11_ came up, a grey shadow against the grey. A man called, 'On the starboard bow, Sir.' And then Nasmith, calm, cheerful, 'You there, Lammas?'

He swam more moderately.

Her propeller shook the water. A rope uncoiled through the air.

9

—⁓—

Thinking of that dimly silhouetted conning-tower, of that rope falling near him in the sea, of men's cheerful voices and their strength pulling him aboard, Charles Lammas in the Edingthorpe drawing-room descended the step-ladder.

'Haul away there.' 'Here you are, Sir.' He could hear them still, as he carried the ladder out across the yard. The black gale roaring in his trees, belabouring his clothes and tattering his hair, he fumbled with the catch to the shed door. That conning-tower in the dawn Marmara haze – that had been the decisive meeting.

Not a miracle, just efficient planning, though for a few moments E_{11} had appeared pretty damned miraculous. Not a miracle, though there'd been moments of that moonlit swim and then moments in that daybreak briney opacity when *time and chance* had seemed decidedly too potent, seemed to have the game in their hands.

Closing the shed door, Lammas shivered. Far too cold to hang about in the yard musing. Also, his wife's overshadowedness each Christmas meant that under the approving surveillance of Nanny Oldfield he had adopted the rôle of master of Edingthorpe Manor ceremonies, instigator of charades and games, conductor of high spirits, commander of holly and ivy, of fancy dress and this year (it was to be a surprise, only Bobbie had been let into the secret) of fireworks. He must get back to his party.

Lammas tramped quickly back across the gravel, thinking suddenly of Alex Burney who had been lifted up not from the lapping Marmara but from blood-soaked Passchendaele mud. Geoffrey beside him had been, had by all accounts long been with horrible obviousness, beyond the need of lifting up. But the stretcher-bearers, when at last they had been able to reach that section of the slaughter-ground, had thought Alex might be worth a try.

Alex Burney with his body which had been cobbled together by army surgeons, with his leathery sallow countenance. Alex whose voice it was you remembered. Those habitual clipped accents of slightly weary good humour and defensive courtesy which, when you knew him, you understood meant that his self-contempt and his contempt for all else were solidly dove-tailed, inner disregard and outer locked immovable. Alex with his light, hard tones of bitterness which no goodness in the world would soften. Alex whose daughter Georgia, Charles Lammas observed

as he came back into his drawing-room's exuberant hubbub, was helping
Geoffrey's widow to set up the *papier mâché* Christmas stable, arrange the
little oxen and sheep, the three wise men, the baby in the crib. It was
a charming old piece of Victoriana, all soft blues and golds and greens
and whites, and like the enamel birds to clip onto the tree it had been
part of Lammas' own childhood Christmases, so now he smiled to see
it making its annual appearance.

Still, it was a shame that he couldn't help remembering that, in the
summer, he had noticed how Alex addressed his son and daughter with
manly good humour. He didn't seem to have a voice that was specially
for them.

Lammas had first heard Burney's bitterness one night at the Travellers'
Club. There were a lot of meetings of that kind occurring in 1919, men
arranging to dine with their dead brothers' friends, with their dead friends'
brothers, and Burney started urbanely enough by remarking that one of
the extraordinary things about the infantry war had been its proximity
to home. You could eat your breakfast in a dug-out, go on leave, dine
at your club. Geoffrey and he had done that. Breakfast at Ypres, dinner
in St James's or Pall Mall.

But then . . . It wasn't that he had raised his voice, he hadn't started
doing that yet.

Only something hard in his quietness when he talked about the third
battle of Ypres that July of 1917 made Lammas think, This fellow's only
just holding on. Not that Burney spoke more than glancingly of the
rain and the mud. Not that at their table at the club he mentioned the
putrefying bodies and the ubiquitous excrement. But there was a bad
lightness and hardness when he said things like, 'Of course, by autumn
our salient stuck out a bit farther than when we began.' Or, 'Of course, the
ground we'd gained was given up next year when the Germans attacked.
Given up without a fight.'

Of course. Everything in Burney's war talk was *of course*, Lammas had
noticed. The men at the parados blown to scorched chunks of meat.
The floundering thigh-deep in mud forward into machine-gun fire. As if
sanity could be held onto by taking for granted that previously unimagined
abominations were the natural course of human events.

Taking for granted, or wryly or despairingly pretending to . . . As if by
reference to an ineluctable order or a supreme law you could extinguish
at birth any flashes of hope or rebellion your soul might conceive. The
wire which the bombardment had unfortunately not cut. The wire where
Geoffrey Lammas and he had been trapped. *Of course.*

'I say, Charles, I reckon this excellent dinner deserves a glass of brandy to wash it down. You don't mind if I call you Charles, do you?'

Clipped words. That evening there had been none of the sardonic violence that he was allowing himself by the thirties. Yet it had seemed as if by speaking with that dismissiveness, using the same dry voice unwaveringly for things hellish and things trivial, you could talk the world to bits, abolish the inanity once and for all.

Shaking hands afterwards, Burney grinned. 'Well, I think Haig's been calumniated enough for one evening.'

Charles Lammas saw Alex Burney several more times that year. When he asked him to be his best man, it wasn't that none of his closer friends had survived the war. Rather, having Geoff's Ypres friend crank his old rattletrap into jerky action in the yard at Cliff House was a ghostly way of having Geoff do it, a way of honouring the dead man, a way of talking to him. If he couldn't have his brother as his best man, he didn't care who he had. So standing Geoffrey's last companion beside him in the chancel at Paston was a bit of a laying of a wreath.

So many engagements were being founded on the bedrock of dead brothers, so many marriages presided over by dead brothers, that few of the wedding guests remarked upon the circumstance.

The following year, Alex Burney left England for Burma – left in a casual, disdainful sort of way. After that, Lammas and he met whenever the Director of Forests was home on leave, which was not all that often, because he didn't seem to avail himself of all the few leaves he was entitled to, or if he did he didn't use them all for sojourns in Europe.

The first time, Burney talked enthusiastically about his teak trees, and Lammas was glad he'd found work he seemed able to let himself take innocent pride in. Apparently British forestry policy in Upper Burma was positively a success. There were an impressive number of thousands more teak trees growing in the hill forests of the territory than there had been fifty years before. Burney was intent on increasing still further this splendid disparity between trees felled and trees planted, increasing the wealth of the forests, increasing jobs and revenue.

This all sounded sensible, forward-looking stuff. So Lammas made a point of not being uneasy that, after what sounded like a dry season flirtation both torrid and perfunctory, he'd married Geraldine Radcliffe, out East in hope of a proposal. Geraldine was undoubtedly stylish. If Alex came to find her twitter and her winning ways and her extravagance unendurable, there were those auspicious forests of his where he would go alone. It sounded as if the green hills were probably already a refuge from the society of those of Alex's fellow Englishmen in the colony of whom he increasingly allowed himself to speak, not with the loyal good humour and only mild irony which were *de rigueur*, but – especially late at night, whisky in hand – with vituperation.

Of course, they corresponded fitfully. Letters came announcing the births of Richard and Emma and, as she was officially inscribed among the Mandalay British, Georgiana – this last with the suggestion of Lammas godparenthood tacked onto it. And Blanche corresponded with Geraldine, because she felt sorry for her.

But the letters didn't give you Alex Burney's self-despising scowl which increasingly seemed an integral part of his rare moments of openness. The letters were anodyne.

Even the curt page and a half composed up at Maymyo on the club's writing-paper to report Emma's obliteration betrayed little.

Our elder daughter died last month. She had never been strong. Geraldine is desolate.

Or possibly it betrayed quite a lot. Desolate . . . For his wife, awkward Frenchified English. For himself, silence.

Anyhow, the last time Alex Burney had been in England – the last time he ever came, as it chanced – Charles Lammas had been dismayed by their final conversation. It occurred toward midnight on the eve of Georgia's consignment to her Suffolk education, in the drawing-room where now she was arranging and rearranging *papier mâché* blue and white shepherds with white lambs in their arms, kings with gold and frankincense and myrrh.

'Of course there's going to be another German war, Charlie. Stands to reason, doesn't it? Versailles was a bloody ridiculous treaty. Didn't deserve to stick, hasn't stuck. Locarno was a fine idea, but it won't stick because no one will fight for it. Germany is rearming steadily, you know that as well as I do.'

No calm for the whisky in the speaker's glass: swung around in his gesturing, it was a small barley-gold maelstrom.

'This new German government are a savage bunch, you can see that, can't you? Those bloody Brownshirts slaughtered this summer. Of course, they deserved the shooting they got, but so do the shooters. Roehm, Schleicher, Strasser, Ernst, all the top brass, and – what? – five thousand others, maybe more. Civilised way to conduct a nation's political life, eh? By the way, did you hear about Schleicher's wife getting herself shot by standing in front of him?'

Burney lit another cigarette, poured himself some more whisky.

'And Dollfuss shot in his chancellery in Vienna. Quite a summer,

Charlie. Don't tell me that here in your pastoral felicity you haven't noticed. Oh, these Nazis aren't going to leave us be. You know what we ought to do? Fight them now, while we're probably still stronger than they are. Well, I'll be off back to my forests. Of course, I know they're not mine. Probably won't even appear to be for much longer.' He had glared defiantly at his host. 'But right now, the Shan Hills are peaceful.' He brooded, he sipped. 'And if we do pull out of Burma one day, the next bunch of bully-boys won't be any more enlightened than we've been, unless I'm much mistaken.'

'Shall I come out and paint those hills of yours one year?' Lammas had been as cheerfully unperturbed as he knew how. 'That'd be tremendous fun. I'll bring Blanche. Could you find us a house up at Maymyo or Lashio?'

His guest had not been placated.

'Maymyo is just about all right. You don't want to hole up in Lashio. Back of beyond. And after that there's just nowhere. Mountains. The Chinese border somewhere.'

'I thought you liked being in the middle of nowhere. Why shouldn't Blanche and I?'

Burney's mind had already lurched sideways.

'The time to be out of this lousy country will be next year. Silver Jubilee, remember? God, I can hear the hypocrisy already, the patriotic rant. Mind you, it won't be much better in Burma.'

10

Striding back to the house, Lammas shrugged his shoulders vigorously, rubbed his cold hands. He must shake off his hauntedness. He must think of Christmas things.

In the drawing-room, he took command of the revelry.

The now empty wheelbarrow must be returned to its outhouse – he dispatched Jack. The baubles and tinsel not needed to bedeck the tree must be put back in their box, and the box returned to its drawer in the tallboy – Georgia was to do that please. (He must forget her alienations, and so must she.) Logs must be fetched from the wood-basket in the gun-room. He sent Richard – in whom he was pleased to have so far discerned no discordant notes, no humours you would not expect in a fit, well-balanced, contented lad of fifteen. If Henrietta was to prove herself worthy of this evening's honour of feasting with the grown-ups in the dining-room, she was going to have to hurry upstairs to wash and change any minute now . . . But first they must all come into the hall and admire Raffaella's kissing-bough.

There was a brief distraction when the kitten Fudge, pursued hot-foot all the way from the scullery by a pink-faced and panting Mrs Meade, took refuge by climbing the Christmas tree. The tree quivered. The painted bells tinkled, the enamel birds bobbed. The trinkets swung wildly on their ribbons, and two or three fell down. The girls squealed with laughter. Ellen Meade mopped her brow with a corner of her apron. The boys grinned, and hoped the kitten would keep on climbing till it reached the angel. Gloria Lammas and Caroline Hedleigh exclaimed, 'Look, how sweet!' and 'Oh, how adorable!' Luckily Bobbie was tall enough to reach up to where in a thicket of pine-needles Fudge crouched and lashed her diminutive tail.

Then they all trooped into the hall.

Raffaella held her handiwork up so that they might admire her globe of interlaced strands of ivy with its sinuous, pale brown stems and black berries, holly with its green stems and serrated leaves and red berries. There was holly with variegated leaves too, and a third kind with yellow berries, the Manor garden being rich in trees. There were sprays of yew, with its dark, graveyard green. There were swags of golden cypress, which like the yew had reddish brown stems, only they were more lustrous, and of which the nodding fronds in the lamp-light really did look aureate. There were little red candles, which Raffaella had carefully fixed where they would not set her globe on fire. There was a clump of mistletoe.

From the landing at the head of the staircase, Bobbie lowered a long silvery tassel to his uncle Charles, who knotted it to Raffaella's bough. It was most agreeable, the master of the house found, to stand with the kissing-bough between them, she holding it, he tying a good sailor's clove-hitch. He glanced into her black, smiling eyes. Yes, agreeable to have an old friend from Tuscany who decided to send his daughter to Cambridge, so naturally you invited her to Norfolk for Christmas, it was the very least you could do. There was nothing amiss with his clove-hitch; but he unknotted it, tied an impeccable bowline instead.

'Right you are, Bobbie, haul it up. No, wait. Raffaella, would you like to light the candles? A box of matches, somebody, please. Yes, all right, Georgia, Hetty, you can light some too.'

Six foot tall, broad-shouldered, resolute-featured, looking every inch one of the youngest captains in the Navy, which is what his peers had backed him to be if he'd stayed in the service, Charles Lammas dominated the throng. Over their heads the bough rose, verdant in midwinter, spangled with candle-flames.

Now, he demanded to know, who was going to kiss whom? Any candidates? A bit sad if no one felt there was anybody there they'd like to kiss.

'Blanche, my darling!'

Encircled by smiles, he took his wife in his decisive arms, he kissed her, held her a moment. This is real and this is innocent and this is good, he was thinking, and he hoped by holding her firmly for a second or two longer than need be to instil the feeling into her too. Their festive house. The bough. The kisses. Alive. Good.

With all the confident gaiety of his twenty-five years and his handsome face, Bobbie was clattering down the stairs.

Let him by all means kiss Caroline, his uncle suddenly found himself decreeing. Let him amiably kiss his mother and his aunt and his little cousin. But the maker of the bough shall be for me.

So Lammas turned, kissed the not at all discomposed Raffaella Zanetti.

When everyone had gone upstairs to change, the front rooms of the house were quiet. Even Caroline Hedleigh, who had arrived already dressed for dinner, abandoned the warmth downstairs. She went upstairs to natter with Raffaella as she bathed, to answer her foreseeable questions about the dashing Bobbie Lammas, to shiver in the Italian girl's draughty bedroom.

Despite the cold, Raffaella spent a considerable time choosing an evening dress and putting it on, choosing a pair of earrings, choosing a necklace, brushing her hair. Caroline tidied her own locks before the foxed old looking-glass.

In his dressing-room Charles Lammas was shoving cuff-links into the sleeves of a shirt, his thoughts skittering unsatisfactorily. He had been aware, these last days, of Raffaella's eyes on him. He had admired the way she joined in the Christmas partying with charm and with appropriateness, without inflicting her personality on all and sundry like tiresome people did. Looked fetching in her jodhpurs; seemed keen on her History; dark brown wavy hair. He had no trouble numbering the things he knew about her on the fingers of one hand.

Blanche and he had little in common, these days, except Edingthorpe and the children, and though he loved the whole set-up . . . A bit dull, maybe, if that were all life ever offered again – and he'd always been too vigorous to find boredom an acceptable option. Of late years, ambition as a painter had been what kept him fascinated with each day as it came, the occasional seduction had been what kept him amused.

None of these flings had meant much, or indeed anything. Irritably twisting his bow-tie, he scowled at his reflection. The young student and the middle-aged painter, by God what a cliché! Best left well alone.

Downstairs in the hall, the unobserved candles on the kissing-bough guttered, one blew out. The grandfather clock ticked. The sea gale moaned in the chimneys, dislodged pieces of caked soot which pattered down the flues into the fireplaces. Blanche's spaniel, left to reign supreme in the warm drawing-room, woke up on a Shiraz rug. With no human kind to bully her, she hopped onto the sofa, snuggled down among the silk cushions.

The back of the house was peaceful too. Wintering companionably by the kitchen range, Nanny Oldfield in her rocking-chair and Brandy in his chewed wicker basket dozed. The Meade brothers had departed to The Crossed Keys, where Bill might continue to illuminate Sidney as to wildfowling. Mrs Meade put her head into the dining-room to check that the table was properly laid. Back in the kitchen, she took up her knitting.

Out in the yard, the gun-dogs in their kennel slept. The first spatterings of the night's rain were driven almost horizontally over the orchard hedge, its leafless hawthorns twitching and rattling.

—m—

Charles Lammas was the first downstairs, and his nephew would be hard on his heels, that was good.

When Bobbie was staying at Edingthorpe, their conversations in the drawing-room while those slower to dress for dinner were still upstairs were occasions they both enjoyed. Shadowed this evening by the dead, reached out to also by the ghostly Alex Burney with his rasping dismissals, the company of debonair Bobbie was just what he felt like. Full of comfort, that image of Geoff so triumphantly alive. Also, there was something he wanted to ask him – should, he made himself realise, have asked him before.

Lammas heaved the reproachful spaniel Honey off the sofa by the scruff of her neck.

Even amidst the general hugging and kissing which had broken out under the mistletoe there had been a moment of being haunted. That little wretch Georgia. Astonishing, and somehow not quite right, the way she'd veer from wild high spirits to silence and stillness. Leaping off the tallboy or hurling sprigs of holly at the Chinese cranes one minute. Then of a sudden absent, wan, seemingly dead to things, as if irrevocably separated off. One glance, and he had known she didn't feel like kissing or being kissed. He had drawn her aside from all that jovial embracing, the bright eyes, the teasing. He had stood with a protective hand on her thin-boned shoulder. She had not responded in any way.

He frowned, crossed to the drinks tray, poured himself two fingers of Scotch, added a whoosh of soda from the syphon. He took out his cigar case, stood tapping a cheroot against the smooth brass. When *E35* was broken up a few years after the war, the fellow who'd commanded her after him had had cases made from her periscope for them both. But on this occasion the memory of Lammas' first and last command didn't distract him. He stood, frowning. He tapped.

Bobbie Lammas came striding across the flagstones of the hall, across the rugs. He brushed aside the drawing-room door. 'Brrr . . .! Good Lord it's cold. Ah, there you are, Uncle. Beat me to it, I see.'

Slapping his arms robustly round his ribs to warm up, he advanced to the fireplace, with one foot shoving aside the now thoroughly disgruntled Honey so he could stand close to the flames. 'Rotten spoiled little dog that, don't you think? I told Aunt Blanche I thought so once. She threatened to tell my mother how often I came to Norfolk to see Daisy Rackham. Of course, I replied that I only ever came to see *her*.'

Lammas eyed with amusement his nephew's sumptuously embroidered smoking-jacket and, he judged, rather fulsomely knotted bow-tie. (His own was neat, correct, drew no attention to itself.)

'Dragons, Uncle.' A glorious sleeve was held out for inspection. 'Very handsome silk dragons. Splendidly Chinese, without being too much so. Rather fun, eh? Now, am I going to have to offer myself a drink, or will you? Winter sherry, please.'

Winter sherry was Lammas dialect for whisky. Smiling as he poured, Charles recollected those first years after the war when he'd locked his Kensington studio toward dusk and then walked to Pimlico – after a day at his easel, he'd enjoyed the exercise, enjoyed the bustle on the streets, the shops, the faces. Pimlico where in her four rooms Gloria already, in her early thirties, had lines graven around her mouth and an irrevocable bright misery set in her eyes. Pimlico where he had tried to be a father to Geoff's little boy. Then at Edingthorpe there had always been a pony for Bobbie, and a dinghy, and later a shot-gun. And now in many respects his nephew was the best friend he had, he surprised himself by thinking. The most spirited companion for days in art galleries, days in deck-chairs on the lawn, days at sea. Dear unshadowed Bobbie with his swift sympathies, with his understanding what you felt because he felt much the same. And really, that dark red cummerbund was not untasteful.

'And thinking of Miss Rackham . . .' Bobbie was propped languidly against the mantelpiece. His voice was playful. He twirled the silver cigarette-holder which had been Blanche's present on his last birthday. 'Your kissing of Miss Zanetti just now, dear Uncle, was at least as impressive as it needed to be.'

Irritated to have his comprehension of the young man's intuitiveness confirmed so promptly, Charles Lammas made himself frown.

'Thinking of Daisy Rackham, my lad, who I'm delighted to say is now engaged to marry a man who's already inherited far more money than you'll ever make . . .'

'Yes, Tony Maitland *is* dull, isn't he?' Bobbie interrupted. 'Do go on. I might add that I know precisely what you're about to ask me.' His blue eyes, just like his father's, laughing. His cigarette-holder irrepressibly jaunty. His eyebrows, his uncle considered, far too mobile, too given to mocking manoeuvres. 'I hope you're going to express yourself with suitable sobriety.'

'I was just wondering whether you were going to pluck up the courage to ask Caroline Hedleigh to marry you. Or the rashness . . .'

'Isn't she *irresistibly* beautiful?' Bobbie cried. He flopped into an armchair, laid one foot across the other knee, cast an appreciative glance at his well-made shoe, his elegant ankle in its black silk sock. 'Because if not I ought to begin to leave her a little bit alone?'

'Certainly she's lovely to look at. But . . . I've just been reflecting, slightly sadly, that I know almost nothing else about her at all. Silly, but it's true. Of course, I've known Julian Hedleigh ever since I can remember. More your father's age than mine. They were in the same cricket team. Then Geoff and I went to his wedding. We went to his children's christenings. Oh yes, I saw your charmer christened, unless I'm thinking of someone else. But then . . . One's neighbours' children grow up. When you see them, they look splendid, they seem very nice. Only . . . Well . . . I don't feel I know who Caroline is.'

Bobbie looked as amused by proceedings as ever. He raised his glass of whisky in his left hand, on which gleamed the signet ring with the Lammas crest which Alex Burney had been just alive enough to insist the stretcher-bearers take from Geoff's finger. He sipped. He appeared happy to listen indefinitely.

'You know Julian won't leave her much, don't you?' said Charles. 'They've never done anything for their daughters, the Hedleighs. Frederick will get the house and the estate. Mark may get a small farm, I suppose, or a row of cottages. I mean, certainly Julian will give the girl a decent wedding present. But it won't take her long to spend that. And, you know, dear boy, the arts . . .'

'Won't leave her anything in his will, the stingy old brute?'

Bobbie's drooping posture in his armchair had not stiffened by an inch; he was only pretending to be galvanised into indignation, his uncle guessed.

Another sip. A moment's further contemplation of his Bond Street shoe and well-turned ankle. Then, 'It's all very well you saying the arts are an uphill slog, but Grandfather Roly lived all right, didn't he? And you live exactly as I should best like to live one day. And you know that man at the Mathers Gallery has very *nearly* promised me a show. Can't remember his name. You know the chap I mean. Dreadful cravats. Dyes his hair.'

Charles Lammas had his doubts as to whether his nephew was really a painter. Still, if need arose he could probably find him a position with an auction house or a gallery. So he simply smiled. He asked, 'Well . . .?'

'Oh, your question! How awful of me.' His voice might make gestures, but his arms and legs were still utterly languid, the listener noted. 'Well . . . Well, I don't know.' Suddenly Bobbie grinned. 'I tell you what, Uncle. I'll do whatever you say.'

'My dear fellow . . .' Lammas couldn't help snorting with admiring laughter. Still, he replied firmly, 'I couldn't possibly accept that sort of responsibility.'

Now the young man stood up, and although being Bobbie Lammas he could only lounge gracefully before the fire, his long and immaculately black-trousered legs crossed, he started to fiddle with an Indian ivory statuette on the mantelpiece.

'Of course, I've *thought* about it, Uncle Charles. Even with your modest view of my brilliance I dare say you'll allow that I've *tried* to work it out. But the trouble is . . .' He confronted the man who was to all intents his father with a rueful smile. 'You see, Caroline would probably be fine married to me. Or at least, so I flatter myself. But then she'd probably be equally fine married to someone else, so long as he wasn't too ghastly. The same goes for me. And if we're not fine married to one another, or not married, or married to other people, it'll probably be for reasons we can't predict now, or do anything about. Oh dear, I'm not very good at explaining myself. Do you at all see what I mean?' The rest of Bobbie's perplexity came out through the beginnings of his wry laughter. 'So the devil of it is that it can hardly be said to matter whether I ask Caroline to marry me or not. Or it matters, but it also doesn't matter at all. Oh Lord, Uncle! I mean . . .' The Hindu goddess, forgotten in his nervously playing fingers, was dancing a hornpipe. 'Listen . . . I can put this to you, can't I? Do you honestly believe it's made much odds to Aunt Blanche her having fallen in love with you rather than with someone else? I dare say there were other men around who'd have made her perfectly decent husbands.'

Charles Lammas liked his nephew's assessment of the heart's enchant-ments, liked his bewilderment or urbanity.

'Certainly there were.' He smiled; he puffed his cheroot. 'No . . . I don't suppose it's mattered at all. Nor will it much, I expect, in your case. But there's one thing . . . We can agree that Caroline is irresistible, even if we're unsure of our wisdom in doing so. But are you?'

In an instant, Bobbie's high spirits were back. 'What a disloyal uncle you are! Well, there's only one way to find out.'

At which juncture they were interrupted by Caroline Hedleigh entering with Raffaella Zanetti, chattering.

12

—◊—

Mrs Meade bore the roast beef into the dining-room with an air of flushed, work-a-day achievement. Jack and Richard, deputed her aides for the evening, and looking very spruce and slightly self-conscious in their first dinner-jackets, followed with the dishes of potatoes and Brussels sprouts, carrots and Yorkshire pudding.

Charles Lammas stood at the side-board to carve, one of his tasks as head of the household that he most enjoyed. He liked the carving knife and fork with their ivory handles and silver butts on which were inscribed the date in the eighteen-sixties and the place in Bengal where Colonel Anthony Lammas had shot the unlucky elephant. He liked the abundance on the side-board, and everybody's healthy appetites and cheerful expectation. It was good to hear Blanche say, 'It looks delicious, Ellen,' as she always did; to hear the invariable response, 'I hope it's all right, Ma'am.' Good the way the succulent slices of beef fell away from his sharp blade; good to remember you too were hungry; good to glance around at the panelled room, at the china and silver and glass on the polished yew table, to think that the show was sustained by palette and brush alone.

Unlike the Hedleighs, the Lammas family had never been rich. No farms, no investments to speak of. For a moment, the carver's brow puckered. The problem of a remunerative profession for dear heedless Bobbie probably *was* going to have to be confronted – quite soon, possibly.

When Georgia had jumped down off the tallboy, Jack had been aware that he liked helping her brother to catch her. Then chucking up bits of holly to try to make them snag behind the golden cranes had been fun. Or anyhow, you forgot about everything except the throwing and the laughing, and how girls could never seem to throw like boys could.

But when Bobbie had hoisted up the bough, and Papa had kissed Mama, and everyone had started hugging everyone else, Jack had suddenly imagined how intoxicating it might be to put his arm around Georgia's waist, to feel her body against him, feel his lips on her face.

One look had shown him that she would not wish him to kiss her. She was sulking about something. He was in the very moment of deciding he didn't want to kiss the silly girl, when this small distress was engulfed in the awkwardness of knowing that he would never have the presumption to approach Caroline and kiss her. As for Raffaella, the act was beyond conception. And then this unease vanished into the delirious consciousness that one of them – yes, even the unforgivably poised Raffaella, after all why not? – might kiss him.

Neither of them did anything so bountiful or ruthless. They could not have done, because at this thought Jack's legs had involuntarily carried him in retreat away from the merry crush.

But when you were fifteen the problem posed by beautiful young ladies of twenty did not go away, it was there again at dinner. They might in theory be the most entrancing creatures in all the world; but in practice they made you feel horribly gauche, even obscurely ashamed of your very existence, which was unfair because after all you had done nothing wrong. Or perhaps it was not being fifteen. Perhaps it was just him, his own inadequate self. Ricky, he had noticed, had stood his ground under the mistletoe, given and taken a kiss or two like a man.

At Winchester, Ricky had slight but unmistakable ascendancies over Jack. He was nearly a year older, for a start; and a couple of inches taller; and he was captain of the Colts cricket team. It was true that Jack both sailed and rode better, but these sports had none of the prestige of cricket. He could hold his own academically too. But R. Burney (capt.) in his immaculate whites, with his cap pulled down on his tawny hair to shade his eyes, Ricky sweeping the Eton fast bowlers to the boundary had glamour – which Jack would never have.

In the holidays, though, when dinghies and Arab ponies had their importance acknowledged, the boys were equals. And today they had felled the Christmas tree together, and borne it home, so now they felt for one another the loyalty of manly comrades.

When the Manor was not chock-full of visitors, in the evenings Jack still joined his father in the library. No longer, of course, to curl up on the hearth-rug in his dressing-gown to hear stories of King Arthur or Robin Hood. These days he sat fully dressed in a chair, and read. *Far From The Madding Crowd* was the last novel he'd finished. Or he opened one of his father's illustrated books about painters. Even reduced to black and white, Giorgione and Titian, Carpaccio and Bellini would enrapture him evening after evening. Or he took down one of the beautifully bound old volumes of engravings, *The Ruins of Paestum*, or *The Ruins of Palmyra*, and his father would tell him stories from Gibbon about what had happened in these places. Or they might read verse aloud, handing the book to and fro, taking turns. Around that time, Jack liked *Crossing alone the nighted ferry*, and *The Way through the Woods*, he liked *Before the*

Roman came to Rye, and *Cargoes* – things like that. But Hardy was the writer he liked best.

It all began with his boyish hero-worshipping of Norfolk admirals. There were Sir Christopher Myngs, who led the van at the battle of the North Forland, and Sir Clowdesley Shovell who broke the French line off Barfleur. Jack's most passionate reverence, naturally enough, was for Lord Nelson – an admiration still as fervent as ever, indeed it never abated all his life. By the library fire his father had told him about the storm which blew the night after the battle of Trafalgar. Eighteen French and Spanish ships captured or destroyed in action, the threat of an invasion of England averted, Nelson aboard *Victory* dying of his wound, and the wind rising . . .

His father had read Hardy's *Boatman's Song* about Trafalgar night.

> Yet all the while our gallants after fighting through the day,
> Were beating up and down the dark sou'west of Cadiz bay.
> > The dark,
> > The dark,
> > Sou'west of Cadiz bay!

When he was eight or ten, Jack used to chime in shoutingly with the refrain. After that, for years it was a poem his father and he made a habit of reciting on the night of 21 October, if they remembered.

> The victors and the vanquished then the storm it tossed and tore,
> As hard they strove, those worn-out men, upon that surly shore;
> Dead Nelson and his half-dead crew, his foes from near and far,
> Were rolled together on the deep that night at Trafalgár!
> > The deep,
> > The deep,
> > That night at Trafalgár!

But this evening it was another Hardy poem which he had distantly beating in the back of his mind. It was the one about the old fable of the animals remembering the Nativity, about the oxen in their shelter at midnight on Christmas Eve kneeling down. Although, if the truth were known, Christmas Eve chiefly occupied his thoughts right now because of his determination to be allowed to be one of those who attended the midnight service at Edingthorpe (his worshipped elder cousin Bobbie would command this expedition) rather than, as in previous years, be made to go to Paston on Christmas morning with all the less fascinating members of the family. There was also the important factor that Christmas

Day would reveal what his parents' present for him might be. He had various hopes and fears, but no clues.

It was going to freeze again, Bill Meade had said so, Jack confided to his friend. That meant they could go skating on Hickling Broad. (Sturdy male talk of this sort was a lot easier, and a lot more pleasant, than trying to think of a remark to address to Caroline or to Raffaella – though he was aware that his mother would commend his manners if he attempted this feat.) And then it might snow, you never knew your luck. Had Ricky ever tried pulling a sledge behind a pony? And a sledge went even better – he lowered his voice, he grinned – went better still, though it might not be approved of in some quarters, behind a car . . .

After all, it would do no harm if the dashing captain of the Colts were made aware that he, Jack Lammas, knew how to drive a car, had done so more than once. Well, exactly twice – but that need not be specified. And Richard Burney was such a splendid fellow, it would never do to talk to him about poetry, and oxen, and stuff like that.

Georgia had been placed between the boys, but made little attempt to join in their talk. She was in one of her moods, her brother observed, and felt sorry, but knew from experience that he wasn't good at cheering her up. Their Burmese childhood was so far away in distance and time, he scarcely knew whether they had it in common any longer or not. And he had been in England for years, and she only a few months – it embarrassed him how unfamiliar she seemed.

As for Jack, it was one thing bewitchedly to turn the pages in pursuit of Gabriel Oak and Sergeant Troy and Bathsheba Everdene, quite another to make conversation with a twelve-year-old girl who, now she was no longer entrancing, was in her wan quietness faintly pitiable.

Still, it wouldn't be right if he found himself despising her, (after all, her brother *was* captain of the Colts). So he made stalwart conversational efforts.

Would she like to come out and walk with the beaters at the Boxing Day shoot at Bure? The beaters were excellent fellows, he pronounced heartily, and in his view shooting lunches always tasted far better than other meals, and all in all it promised to be a splendid day.

If Hickling Broad *did* freeze, she must absolutely come skating with them. Could she skate? he enquired, without reflecting that in Burma she was unlikely to have learned.

The harum-scarum Blanche Mack, who as a girl at the opening of the century had with her brother Michael galloped their ponies along the beach at low tide, galloped the Paston headlands and meadows, now, as Mrs Lammas of Edingthorpe Manor, glanced at her sister-in-law and felt relief to see her apparently cheerful.

Gloria and she were the same age. They'd jogged in different pony-traps and dog-carts through similar lanes to the same house-parties and balls in that already distant world of before 1914, when the old European civilisation had been about to collapse into barbarism but they hadn't known it. Right up to the last, civil war in Ireland seemed a more likely disaster than war against Germany and the Hapsburg Empire and the Ottoman Empire.

Two young women: one married when the British Expeditionary Force went to France, the other not. Often Blanche had brooded on this simple, enormous difference. Chance . . .

One consequence was that when, toward Christmas each year, Blanche felt her tide of sadness for Michael flowing in her heart, Gloria's visit to Edingthorpe was a reminder of all that she had and the other had not. Her husband alive. Their post-war children growing up – lucky, peace-time children. Their old house, which by what Blanche vaguely designated posh standards was shabby but which she loved for its stone-flagged kitchen and its greenhouse and its urns on the terrace. She loved everything about that house, even the creaking floorboards on the landing, even the groaning noises the cisterns and pipes in the attic made. She even loved the tatty wallpaper and the worn rugs in the bedrooms they hadn't yet been able to afford to redecorate, draughty bedrooms with rusty grates. She loved the gammy-legged dressing-tables, half the paintwork still disgracefully Victorian. It all meant peace time, and being married to Charlie, and the children growing up, so she loved it all.

Gloria did not have these things, and at times like Christmas it was important that she should not feel envious. Blanche felt nothing but fondness for her sister-in-law, and pity for her widowhood, and respect for her customary brave dignity. Still, it was unhappily true that on occasion her moods of self-pity had led to disquisitions late at night about her loneliness and her depressions and her insomnia, to bitchy comments followed by tears and appeals for understanding.

However, this evening Gloria had her brother-in-law on her left and her son on her right, and they were both making much of her; so she had gaiety in her haggard eyes.

Still, the fact that Blanche did not need to be anxious about Gloria did not mean that she should let her thoughts follow their natural course. She made herself notice with satisfaction how the boys were passing dishes, passing decanters. Darling Jack already looked just like his father ('nice legitimate lad, that', someone had once said, and made her smile); he was going to be handsome in the same regularly-cut style. And Richard with his fine-boned face, his pearly skin, his flamy hair . . . Was he going to be, was he already, beautiful? she wondered. And that wide full mouth, and those green eyes, for pity's sake. Male beauty was a treacherous quality, she wished him well. More immediately, she hoped both boys had had plenty of Yorkshire pudding.

As for poor Georgia, the ingredients must be similar to her brother's, their hostess supposed, but they'd been mixed up cack-handedly and no mistake. Improbable hair, sullen mouth, nondescript eyes – the child was a mess. Jack was making dogged attempts to involve her in conversation, she noted with swift maternal pride. She must remember to compliment him later on his courtesy to their guests.

Still distractedly hoping the lion's share of the Yorkshire pudding had gone down young throats, Blanche let her eyes travel on around her dinner party.

To be bowled over with admiration for Charlie was of course only right and proper, but really, did the Zanetti girl have to flirt with him *quite* so assiduously?

13

During the night, the storm died. Lying awake beside her sleeping husband, Blanche Lammas heard the squalls slacken their violence. From the wood, the roar of the gale in the trees slowly faded to a soughing. No more gusts of rain came rattling against the windows.

By dawn the wood, which had seemed to have a sea of wind raging over it, combers of wind crashing on its upper branches, stood becalmed, dripping. The house, which during the hours of darkness had felt as if it had been towed off-shore, anchored with growling rollers breaking against it and blizzards shrieking through its rigging, now clearly had been towed inland again to a secluded backwater, like an old wherry which after years of trading is moored at last in a rushy, uneventful creek overhung with willows, visited only by coots and grebes.

The day broke cold, opaque, motionless. The earth was sodden. Under the low sky, in the brownish air, the grey puddles on the drive lay as if tarnished, unglittering. Crossing the yard before breakfast to let his two Springer spaniels out of their kennel, Charles Lammas glanced with satisfaction at his studio's tall north window, which he had caused to be rebuilt so large that even on the murkiest days he could see to paint. The dogs bounding about him, he walked into the orchard among his apple trees. Cox and D'Arcy Spice, Egremont Russet and Costard – for years he had tended them with care, with the children's help had brought a good harvest back to the apple-loft, that was another happy peace-time ritual. He was proud of his pear trees too: Emile de Heyst, Josephine de Malines. Ducking under a low bough, he smiled at the bedraggled peacock and peahen pecking disconsolately in the drenched grass, doubtless pining for India. Never mind, he silently addressed the peacock, in the spring your tail will grow again. Coming back toward the house along a path around a thicket of rhododendrons, he met Blanche leading her thoroughbred out from the stable to join the ponies in the paddock. The handsome bay mare tossed her head, blew through her flared fine-veined nostrils. As they stood together on the weedy gravel which the hunter was pawing, they heard a mistle-thrush sing from the elm in the water-meadow hedge.

A successful marriage, most of Charles and Blanche Lammas' friends concurred. And certainly they looked harmonious, standing with horse and dogs by the rhododendron clump in the grey and brown midwinter morning.

Life had been harsh with Blanche, but everybody agreed her face had retained a wonderful gentleness of expression, her gaze seemed to fall on the scenes about her with more softness than other people's. Not only were her two brothers dead. Her uncle, a lieutenant-colonel of the Suffolk Regiment, had been killed on the Somme. The man she had been expected to marry had died of his wounds ashore at Oran. For that matter, her afflictions hadn't always been mortal. In the twenties her father had lost money badly. In the end, he sold the estate, invested the proceeds in stocks and shares, lost the best part of it in the slump, had to sell the Hall too. But although Blanche could be practically disabled by sorrow, she was almost miraculously devoid of self-pity and bitterness. There were no rough edges in the way she treated her husband and children.

She hadn't in fact been engaged to marry Tom Carraway. Or rather, she nearly had been. Nearly enough for his sisters, after his death, to give her his gold watch and chain as a keepsake. They were in a compartment of her velvet jewellery case, waiting for Jack to reach twenty-one.

A good thing if she got engaged, people had said, and smiled. If either her brother Michael or she got married, then the other one might. And marriage might steady her down. Because the dare-devil rider and the belle of the dances carried her wildness through war and bereavement unsubdued. At a time when the Pruner was lopping the Tree of Life brutally, she might have been as cruelly cut as anyone, but her spirit was not cowed, her behaviour was defiantly unaltered. All through 1914–18 she was nursing wounded men, and there were rumours about one or two convalescent officers having been her lovers before they went back to the Front. Extreme unction, one of them was supposed to have remarked. Perhaps he was Roman Catholic. She wasn't religious at all.

No, not religious . . . Unless you counted a passionate and quite unmeditated sort of pantheism – a pantheism so untutored and free of reasoning that she very likely would have had trouble telling you what the word meant, camellias and cyclamens being more in her line, or fetlocks and pasterns. She had an instinctive certainty that every stone and breath of wind was alive, every stream and every tree was divine, every shaggy pony and every glossy half-clipped-out thoroughbred and every man and woman and child was divine, each mote of dust was sublime – or else the universe was a vile mockery, but she loved it too thoughtlessly and naturally to imagine that.

Not that she would have phrased it like that, or indeed phrased it at all, even to herself. What she mulled over was whether Henrietta should be sent away to boarding-school or not, whether Jack would handle his Arab gelding better with a double bridle. Her articulacy was for decisions

about flower-beds, or enthusiasms for going to watch point-to-points
and migratory birds. Yet her tenderness for children, or for foals, for
fledgelings, for the young and the in need of nurture generally, didn't
make her unduly sentimental. Like the good countrywoman she was, she
could be cheerfully tough about drowning puppies and kittens judged
surplus to requirements. If Sidney Meade was busy doing something else,
as he had a habit of being when there was a litter to reduce, she'd do
it herself.

At any rate, she certainly wasn't a Christian. She would take her wreath
to Paston church to honour her dead brother; but she never went to a
service, except for weddings and funerals when it was the people who
mattered, not the religion.

As for christenings, she was notorious all over the county for how she'd
refuse to stand godparent to her friends' offspring, because it wouldn't be
right for a Christian baby to have a heathen like her for a godmother.
At the same time she had insisted that they stand godparent to Jack and
Henrietta, because her children should have every advantage, however
dubious, and besides, you never knew.

The exception was Georgia Burney, but that was typical of Blanche too.
Easy enough laughingly to turn down her Norfolk neighbours' suggestions,
yet she simply had not been able to summon the hard-heartedness to write
a refusal to poor Geraldine, who she was sure was lonely in Burma.

As for her wedding, that had been pagan all right. Blanche had known
what she was doing, known in her intuitive way that there was nothing
Christian about it. It had been her intellectual bridegroom, of course,
who that day had been conscious of how long nuptial ceremonies had
pre-dated and would presumably post-date Christianity. But the bride,
when she walked up the aisle on her father's arm, had known what
a deep-plied troth she was plighting, and in the presence of what
nebulous powers and irresistible callings. The sunlight adazzle in her
brother's window almost made her stop. Her undimmed grief for him
nearly stood her stockstill to weep with the living hugger-mugger in their
pews to left and right, with the nave dead hugger-mugger underfoot. Yet
when she came back down the aisle half an hour later on Charles Lammas'
arm her mind was resonant with victory. It was a victory atrocious with
sadness, because Michael's death and the deaths of all the young men
killed in the war were not to be forgotten or forgiven, but it was victory.
For a moment among the turning heads and the smiles she checked,
and Charles hesitated beside her, comprehending, loving, consonant.
She looked upward and leftward and was aware of her groom looking
with her. She saw the Union Jack and the White Ensign, she saw the

Archangel and Britannia, the grey destroyer and the white swans, and the inscription about her brother. I shall live in memory of you, silently she had promised the dead man. I shall love in honour of you. And she went on toward the foot of the tower and turned left. They came through the knapped-flint porch and out into the sun, and there was a cluster of village people standing among the graves to greet the bride and her groom.

And it worked, that marriage, most people agreed. In all important respects, it worked admirably well. Better than you might have expected.

Of course, Blanche's faith in her husband's brilliance as a painter was as unswerving as belief can only be when founded on utter ignorance of the business in hand. For that matter, his ignorance of gardening was not to be underrated. He liked the demesne to be beautiful – indeed liked to paint angles of it – but he had no time for the toil and the expertise she rejoiced in, no time for the afternoons on hands and knees weeding flower-beds, no time for Latin names for plants which had perfectly good Anglo-Saxon ones. The marsh and wood and meadows were his province. The orchard they shared. The garden was hers.

Good the way they let one another be, was the common judgement. Blanche didn't always tag along when he was in London with his friends who were dealers or painters, who were connoisseurs or curators or what-have-you, editors of *The Burlington* or *Apollo*. She was far happier exercising her horse or mucking out its stable, pruning her roses, tying back her espaliers. But when she could help him she was prompt enough. Look at that time he rode Tofthill in the Fox Hunters' Chase.

By the time Jack and Henrietta were growing up, the horsemanship in that family was all Blanche's concern – it was one of the activities Charles gave up in order to concentrate more exclusively on painting. Soon after they were married he had won point-to-points all over East Anglia on a chestnut called Tofthill that belonged to a local farmer. Then he won the King's Cup at Fakenham by a distance. After that, Norfolk people started saying that if any horse could be trusted to jump round Aintree it was Mr Benson's Tofthill, and Charlie Lammas was the fellow to ride him. Those were still the days before the idea of an artist riding a horse was enough to make a cat laugh.

Anyway, the jockey's young wife exercised Tofthill every day that winter, while he was off all over the kingdom painting portraits to pay the bills, and when she boxed the horse up to Liverpool in March he was in terrific fettle.

Lammas had made all his neighbours promise not to back him to win, because although the chestnut was a jumper and a stayer he was only a hundred quids' worth of Norfolk point-to-pointer, when all was said and done. So they asked, Could they back him for a place? Charlie said No again. So this time, without asking him, they all backed him to get round.

Thirty-odd horses started in the Fox Hunters' Chase that year, and half of them finished.

Charles Lammas rode the steadiest race he knew how, the first time round. He just concentrated on keeping out of trouble, and giving Tofthill a clear view of his fences. Even then, he was nearly brought down by a faller at the Canal Turn.

The second time round, the field was thinning out, it was easier to keep clear. The leaders weren't too far ahead of him, he had more horses behind him than in front. Tofthill pecked badly landing at Becher's, but he didn't come down. Lammas gathered him together and got him galloping again, and after that he didn't put a foot wrong, not seriously. Fifth, they finished.

For years afterwards, at his dinner parties, you might see his glance flick to the mantelpiece where, among objects more overtly graceful, was propped a horse-shoe, a racing-plate. You'd guess he was remembering the last fence, the enfilade of cheering crowds, the slow gallop on an exhausted horse up that long run-in.

14

When the brief day became too gloomy for him to continue painting, Charles Lammas washed his brushes, put on his coat and boots and cap, trudged down to the meadow.

All afternoon Bobbie and the two boys had been adding to the still unlit bonfire which Sidney Meade had begun. Onto his pile of hedge trimmings, old crates and seed-boxes, lop and top, they had heaped some rotten posts from a paddock fence which was being replaced, a broken gate, a wheelless cart, two collapsed bee hives, a holed barrel. They had fetched the remaining planks of a shed which had been decaying in a bramble thicket ever since anybody could remember, then the frame of a sluice which it was true was beyond repair, but which was also so water-logged it seemed unlikely to burn well. Now they were hauling from the wood's edge and from beneath isolated trees some dead branches the gale had brought down.

The Springer spaniels, beguiled by some enticing scent, went hunting along a ditch, then galloped to join Richard and Jack who were toiling toward the pyre with a bough from a lime tree. The darkening air, which had seemed brownly crepuscular all day, now that night really was falling had a louring, bruise-coloured look to it which might presage snow. Lammas hoped the children wouldn't be disappointed if it didn't fall till Boxing Day or later. He checked the preparations for the fireworks. Lengths of iron piping, stuck at a slight angle into the earth, from which the rockets could be launched. A worm-eaten garden table, with buckets of sand into which fireworks could be stuck. Yes, Bobbie had done everything.

Lammas heard women's voices and turned. Preceded by her Irish water spaniel, Honey, Blanche joined the party around the bonfire. She had Raffaella with her, but not Caroline, who today had remained with her family at Bure. Blanche had hoped this might mean that her nephew would dedicate suitable attention to his mother, but in fact Bobbie had passed lunch in vivacious colloquy with Raffaella. Even afterwards, in the drawing-room with cups of coffee, they had commandeered the ottoman, remained tête-à-tête chattering about Cambridge.

Maybe it was having Alex's son and daughter here, Lammas thought, stooping to show Georgia how to make newspaper spills with which the bonfire might be lit. Her white hands twisting the torn sheets into shape were muddy. Her wrists sticking out of her coat cuffs looked thin, blotchy, cold. Maybe that was why in the midst of what ought to be a pleasant family Christmas he had Alex's voice knocking in his brain. 'Of course there's going to be another German war.' And that contemptuous remark about 'all these fools in England living as if the war hadn't finished off that old way of life.' In which case . . . He lit Georgia's spill, watched her thrust her flame into the tinder at the foot of the pyre. In which case it wasn't as strange as all that, his feeling faintly unsettled by the presence of this moody girl. She was a sort of messenger – was that it? An omen child?

Charles Lammas knew that, a couple of years earlier, the British government had started to plan for the possibility of another European war within a decade – not that they'd actually *done* much. And hadn't old Marshal Foch said something about the Treaty of Versailles not being a peace but an armistice for twenty years?

He'd ask Julian Hedleigh what the Westminster tittle-tattle was. That was a good idea. He'd see him on Boxing Day, too. (Since his election in the Conservative interest two parliaments ago, that landowner had genially kept his less elevated neighbours informed about the party-political swamp.) And didn't he sit on some foreign affairs committee these days? Come to think of it . . . Lammas glanced to where Bobbie was lighting a match for Henrietta so she could launch the first rocket. Julian and he might soon find they had other things to discuss too.

A parasol of golden sparks exploded high in the black Christmas Eve. A Catherine Wheel nailed to an alder, and ignited by Raffaella with charming Tuscan exclamations, whirled madly round and round with, everybody agreed, quite splendid splutterings, flashes, fizzings, till with its dying detonation it flung itself off the tree (Jack and Richard were convicted of incompetent nailing) and into a ditch with a loud hiss. In the buckets of sand, the Roman Candles erupted into scarlet fans of sparks, blue fans, silver fans. There was a Jack-in-a-Box which emitted a shriek as it leapt up, blazing. There was a Chinese dragon, there were squibs like frogs which jumped and banged. In the thick of all this spectacle and cacophony, with people around him calling and laughing and letting off rockets, it was ridiculous to feel shadowed; but Charles Lammas couldn't help it.

After the war, it had seemed the most natural thing in the world to pick up the threads of the old peace-time way of life, set to work stitching a tissue of existence recognisably akin to the old one, loved for that very reason, valued as innocent and good. That was what most people had convinced themselves they'd fought the war *for*. Yet what if Alex Burney were right? If there had been something irrevocable about that catastrophe, something beyond redemption about that slaughter? If some entity greater than the sum of all the deaths had died?

All these fools in England living as if the war hadn't finished off that old way of life. Yes, but things didn't seem all that different from before the war. So long as you could keep earning your living, there'd be meadows where people let off fireworks, there'd be houses where dinner was brought to the table. Alex was too gloomy by half.

The bonfire was a mound of flame. In its ruddy glare, Charles saw his wife. He heard her cry to Gloria, 'Oh, do look! How lovely!' and point to a Roman Candle fountaining rainbows. Then Hetty came hurtling toward her. She listened, she replied, 'Yes, of course, darling. I'll ask him.' She called, 'Bobbie, would it be all right if Henrietta lit another rocket?'

Still, if Alex were right that the present was overcast not only by the past but by the future? If Ivor Gurney, still just alive sixteen years after the Armistice in that mental hospital of his and convinced the war was still going on . . . Yes, if that poor devil Gurney, still writing war poetry – who was it at the club who'd told him about that? – were in an abstract but inescapable sense right. If it wasn't over for good. If this peace were just a lull in a storm of wars, or a trough between two waves of war . . . What then?

Of course, there'd been scare stories, off and on. Lammas had contemplated the *possibility* of another war. However, it had seemed so fantastically improbable that the European peoples would forget the last carnage, at least in his generation's life-time, descend into savagery again. Whereas this year things *had* got worse, Alex was right, reluctant as one might be to focus on it. And if the League of Nations turned out to be a dud . . . No wonder he had not worked well today. Anxious about Blanche, of course. But also distracted. Jarred, somehow. Oh well, some days were like that. It was a mistake to attribute too much significance to them. You had days when you seemed able to perceive what you might do, and even consider you might slowly achieve it. Then you had other days when your head was murky and your heart unconfident.

Well, fool or no fool, here he was, living the old way of life as if the war hadn't finished it off, no doubt for the straightforward reason that he was incapable of living in any other way. What else could a survivor do? He borrowed his nephew's pitchfork, starting tossing embers into the heart of the fire. Perhaps the old way of life had only been injured. Perhaps it had recovered, all would be well.

Best not to imagine Alex Burney in his hatred of the world concluding that they'd fought their war in vain, the slaughter had achieved no lasting peace, now they were going to immolate their sons.

The women and girls of the party were trooping back up the dark track to the house. Lammas straightened his back, leaned on his pitchfork.

'If we pile this fire up well now, it'll burn all night,' he told Bobbie. Then he called, 'Jack, Richard! When you go, take the old table back to the terrace, please.'

15

When the contingent to attend midnight holy communion at Edingthorpe was established as consisting of Bobbie and Raffaella, Richard and himself, Jack was so delighted that he quite forgot about Thomas Hardy and the story of the animals remembering the Nativity. Tramping up the muddy path to the church he thought of it again.

After dinner at the Manor they had played charades. Scene after scene, the acting had got wilder, and Henrietta's laughter had got shriller and her cheeks had got pinker, until the culminating performance in which Raffaella and Georgia as barbers sat Bobbie in a chair with a sheet around his shoulders and gave him a shave, using a pot of Mrs Meade's whipped cream, laying it on generously with a wooden spoon and then scraping it off with a bread-knife – after which the uproar was so joyous that the game came to an end.

Then the girls had been dispatched to bed, 'So that,' as Blanche put it, 'poor old Father Christmas can get to work.' At the gun-room basin, Bobbie had rinsed the remaining traces of whipped cream from his jaw. Jack had felt excited to be going out at an hour when he was usually asleep in bed, putting on his coat and his outdoor shoes, fingering the sixpenny-bit he would give the church-warden for the collection. Still, once out in the freezing starless night he had felt different, not excited any more, or only in a sombre and romantic way.

Jack had hero-worshipped his cousin ever since, when he was four or five, Bobbie had stood pretending to be a tree and helped him to climb him, and then taught him to play football, and then swung him round and round by his ankles till dizziness brought them both to the ground. Now he didn't even want to talk to Bobbie. Nor to Ricky, even though this winter holiday had definitely cemented them as terrific friends. Nor to Raffaella, though during the fireworks and the charades he had completely lost his shyness with her.

A good two miles from the sea, Edingthorpe church stood on a low knoll. By daylight, with the dogs Jack had explored among the weather-ravaged oaks and sycamores, pines and thorns, where around the graveyard you could still just make out the form of earthworks. Ramparts, Jack was convinced. He had been delighted when his father had agreed the site was an ancient one, the long-subsided earth wall and its ditch were very likely older than the church. Now, as they tramped up the slope, in the black night the Gothic windows glimmered palely gold. The sexton was ringing the bell. Jack found it easy and happy to imagine a baby being born in a stable long ago in Palestine. Of course, he knew as well as Thomas Hardy knew that now, in the farmyards and paddocks around in the quiet darkened countryside, no horses or cattle were going to kneel down in memory of that birth. Still, it was a nice idea.

The church wasn't much more than a barn. An early mediaeval barn, not large, with roughly-hewn beams, with rudimentary pews, flint-work patched here and there over the centuries. It had an attractive air of the early Christian, Charles Lammas had once remarked to his son, and the notion must have lingered in some low stratum of the boy's consciousness, because now he felt happy that through hundreds and hundreds of years the church had stood unchanging on its knoll, repaired but never spruced up. A few gnarled oaks. North Sea winds. Graves. And now the windows shining with soft candle-light were an enchantment of an ancient simple kind, and the clanging of the bell was magical. In a dream, he followed the others into the porch.

The church window-sills had been decorated with holly and ivy, as well as with candles. The lectern had been wreathed with ivy. Near the altar stood a Christmas tree, contributed, as every year, by the Lammas family.

The twenty or thirty people of the congregation all knew one another. Before the service began there was much shaking of hands, much wishing of a happy Christmas. Of course, Raffaella Zanetti was a novelty – but Jack was so entranced by the midnight and the music and the candles that he was oblivious of the discreet admiration her Italian beauty aroused among their neighbours. He was oblivious too of the attentive way in which his cousin Bobbie ushered her to their customary pew, of the gallantry with which he equipped her with a prayer book, pointed out a fragment of a wall-painting, and apologised for the reformed, North European rite she was about to witness, but said that it probably wouldn't do her any actual spiritual harm.

Raffaella accepted these attentions with well-bred equanimity, with smiles, with bright eyes. The service began.

Jack liked carols, and now his voice had finished breaking, thank heavens, so he sang with a will. Without bothering much about whether he believed this or didn't believe that, since his confirmation he had enjoyed taking holy communion, so he looked forward to that part of the service tranquilly. He liked going up to the altar with his family and their neighbours. He liked the silver chalice, liked the ritual words, the embroidered altar cloth.

Tonight he was possessed by intimations he couldn't control or name. It might have started with a charming fable about an ox and a donkey kneeling down in a byre, but it had gone beyond that. Other stories or poems his father had read him may have come into it, though he couldn't have said which. Or they were just stray ideas that had visited him, or dreams. For the first time in his life he was obscurely aware of spiritual epochs that might be imagined to end and begin, of how at hours of absolute surrender one life of the soul might perish and another be born.

Here in the glimmering nave, out in the night fields, somewhere . . . Two thousand years ago in the Levant, or now by the North Sea . . . Jack could almost hear the old gods' despairs, see those defeated shades flitting away among the trees. Yes, it *was* something Papa had read, or had told him. Something about poplars – he knew trees came into it somewhere. And the new spirit of – of everything?

Jack came to himself with Ricky nudging him to get his sixpence out of his pocket.

On Christmas morning, Charles Lammas was free of the previous days' misgivings.

From first light, when Henrietta woke up and went scurrying to the nursery where the Christmas stockings were always arrayed on the fire-guard, the house had been merry with footsteps and voices. Then at breakfast Bobbie, never previously conspicuous for Christian devotion, had announced that he was going to drive the dozen or so miles to Bure and attend morning service there. 'A surprise attack, Uncle Charles,' he had said, and winked. Raffaella had lowered her laughing eyes to her plate.

Lammas took his sister-in-law and the girls to Paston church. His was the gentle scepticism of a man who in any country in any period would have attended the local temple and partaken of the current ceremony. He liked the architecture and the language, which were a bond with his culture's past, the shared ritual which bound him to his fellow men, living and dead. So he would no more have considered skipping church on Christmas Day or at Harvest Thanksgiving or on Armistice Day than he would have considered believing in the Creed.

Before lunch, the household gathered in the drawing-room. Charles Lammas opened a bottle of champagne, poured glasses for everyone, including half a glass for Georgia, (Henrietta had a sip of her father's). Bobbie still had not returned from Bure, but it was decided that the opening of some of the presents stacked in brightly coloured wrapping-paper beneath the tree might begin in his absence.

Lammas stood warming his legs by the fire, enjoying the sight of everybody unpacking parcels, exclaiming, thanking, going under the tree on hands and knees. Outside the window, the sky was a snow sky, but it still didn't fall. He drank his champagne. The best present of the day, so far as he was aware, was the sixteen-bore shot-gun he had acquired for Jack; it was pleasant to anticipate his delight when his unwrapping should reveal the leather gun-case. And here, at last, was Bobbie.

The young man came to lean his elbow on the mantelpiece. Deliberately casual, he accepted a glass, met his uncle's eyes. Mildly he let fall the words, 'She said Yes.'

Taken aback by the sudden thumping of his heart, Lammas let two or three seconds pass. Then he said, 'Good'. He cleared his throat. 'Well done, dear lad. I'm delighted. Now, perhaps . . . Do you think you ought to tell your mother?'

Bobbie's capacity for subdued behaviour was already exhausted. He grinned, cheeks flushed, blue eyes shining.

'Just now. Walking away from Bure church. Wonderful!' He swigged his champagne. 'What a lousy uncle you are, to look so surprised.'

TWO

1

—ᴍ—

Bobbie Lammas' announcement of his engagement to marry Caroline
Hedleigh coincided with Jack's discovery of his present.

He was on his knees beneath the Christmas tree, his mother beside
him. The jumble of bright packages had been somewhat reduced by
now, and the foundation of the pile was revealed as consisting of two
cases wrapped in green and gold paper, secured with scarlet ribbon.
(Collaboration between Upper Burma and East Anglia had ensured that
the boys' presents should be as near identical as might be.)

'Here you are, darling,' his mother had said, swiftly turning labels so
she could read them, pulling one of the cases toward him, kissing his
cheek so for an instant he breathed her faint Chanel which was one of
the tangs of happiness. 'From Papa and me, with lots of love.'

By its shape and size, Jack almost knew; he could scarcely make himself
not yet believe. With eager fingers he untied, he unwrapped. Unaware
of Blanche watching the smile break out on his face, he laid bare the
gun-case.

It wasn't a new gun, but the leather case had been polished and buffed
up, and his initials, J.M.L., stamped on it. He undid the buckles on the
straps, he clicked the catch. He opened the lid. In the longest of the
green baize compartments, the barrels gleamed, and there was a narrower
longish compartment for the ramrod, which you unscrewed so it fell into
two sections and would fit in. The stock of his gun lay in a compartment
made to fit snugly round it. There was a smaller hollow where the fore-end
nestled. There was a place to keep an oily rag and some tow.

Gazing at his weapon, Jack heard exclamations break out all around
him. He hadn't laid a finger on it yet, why did they have to make all this
shindy? And now somebody was jiggling his elbow to wake him from his
trance, was saying something which couldn't possibly matter. Reluctantly,
he turned his head to see what all the fuss was about.

Her son's arm protectively encircling her shoulder, Gloria Lammas was
smiling tremulously. She dabbed her eyes with a corner of handkerchief;
she rested her greying head against his shoulder. 'Oh, how silly of me,'
she said. 'I'm so happy, truly I am.'

Gaily, Blanche turned to Raffaella. 'Charlie asked me to marry him on
the beach at Mundesley. Howling gale. I was freezing. When I got home
to Paston, I rushed to find my mother. I'm engaged to Charlie Lammas, I

cried. And can you imagine the response I got? Don't worry, sweetheart, she said, I'll get you out of it.'

Jack suddenly decided that the way Hetty and Georgia stood gawping up at Bobbie was idiotic. Getting up from his adoration of his sixteen-bore, cloudily he had comprehended that his cousin was going to marry Caroline Hedleigh. Well, fine. Why all this rumpus about something which was neither surprising nor interesting? Even so, he couldn't help noticing with envy the manly, accustomed way in which Ricky found his moment in the hubbub, smiled, said, 'Congratulations.'

Papa would understand. Either Papa would be seeing things exactly as he saw them or, if not, he would indicate a better perspective which would instantly prove acceptable.

Inspired with this instinctive faith, Jack met his father's smiling glance. He had intended to ask some question as to his cousin's engagement, (what question, he had no idea), but the words which came out were, 'It's wonderful!'

'Glad you like the look of it. How long have you been shooting with that little twenty-eight-bore? Must be three or four years. We reckoned you deserved something better. Now, I dare say you'd like to see how it fits together. Shall we retreat with it into the gun-room?'

In which sanctuary, where they were soon joined by Richard with *his* weapon, Charles Lammas, with a glass of champagne in one hand and a tin of gun-oil in the other, began in the most natural manner to intersperse his remarks about sixteen-bores with others about the proposed marriage.

The Edingthorpe gun-room had always been a favourite haunt of Jack's. He liked the rough matting that you could walk on with muddy shoes, the chipped basin with one cold-water tap, the profusion of coats and boots and hats and sticks (the place also served as a cloak-room) including a sword-stick. He liked the tall wooden cabinet with a glass door where the guns glinted, the leather box on the table where the cleaning equipment was kept and which smelled of oil. Then there were shelves on which you might find not only fishing-rods and boxes of cartridges of various calibres, but also a South African knobkerrie, a Gurkha kukri, a Cromwellian helmet, swords from different armies and centuries. There were cupboards from which you might unearth skates, puttees, a Union Jack and a Saint George's Cross, a Sam Browne, balaclavas, cartridge belts, gun slings, a powder flask disappointingly innocent of powder, two flasks for shot with shot still in them, hunting knives, naval knives, coaching whips, a flintlock pistol. Jack would rummage there indefinitely. The walls were interesting too. A map of East Anglia which showed prehistoric sites – important because Edingthorpe was indicated as one of the few parishes where fragments of neolithic pottery had been dug up, though Jack's and Henrietta's excavations for further samples had so far been fruitless. Photographs of his father riding this steeplechase horse or that, including one of Tofthill at Aintree landing clear over Valentine's. Uncles and grandfathers in various uniforms.

Suffused with happiness at the prospect of tomorrow's shoot at Bure, Richard and Jack cleaned their new guns, not because they needed cleaning but for the pleasure of handling them. They admired their weapons' locks, compared their chasing. Lovingly they ran oily rags along their immaculate barrels.

All in all, splendid news, this engagement, Lammas confided to them with more confidence than he was sure he felt, between comments about the game-season and about gun-metal, aware that Jack didn't really know what to make of this new departure in his cousin's life.

Of course, Bobbie was going to have to pull himself together and earn some money, his uncle conceded goodhumouredly. He had already made a mental note that he must give the lad a cheque so he could go to a Norwich jeweller and buy the girl an engagement ring. Yes, Bobbie seemed to have dispensed with the convention of asking his prospective father-in-law if he might propose – but he, Lammas, could hardly criticise him for that, having been equally nonchalant in his day, and he trusted Julian and Sarah would be amiably delighted. Yes, it meant the Boxing Day shoot was going to turn into an engagement party. No, Jack wasn't to fret, his cousin wasn't abandoning them. In fact, with parents-in-law at Bure he'd quite likely end up spending *more* time in Norfolk, not less.

At which point, it was time for Christmas lunch. The two sixteen-bores were installed in the cabinet, where it was agreed they looked very handsome.

Cheerfully hungry, Jack washed his hands, calm in the knowledge that Bobbie's marriage wouldn't change anything important.

2

In previous winters, Jack had earned his lunches by walking with the beaters at Bure Hall and on other estates where his father shot. Armed with a stick, and careful to keep in line, he had trudged through woods, through fields of drenched sugarbeet, across snipe marshes, in and out of marl-pits. Shy at first, he had come to like the men's Norfolk voices and their good humour, and luckily there were always labradors and spaniels which in moments of awkwardness he could make friends with. Today was the first formal shoot to which he had been invited as a gun in his own right, and he couldn't help feeling nervous.

As the cars from Edingthorpe entered the Hedleigh estate that morning, from the slate-coloured clouds the first flakes of snow fell, were whirled against the hedges on the freezing wind. Jack scanned the fields anxiously. He saw a covey of partridges on some arable land. And there were the pegs set out at intervals where he and the other guns would stand. How wonderful it would be if, when he next saw Bill Meade, he were able to confess modestly that he didn't think he'd shot *too* badly. It would be nice to shoot as well as Ricky, too. Better, if possible.

Bure Hall was a four-square Georgian house of red brick, with a pediment and a Doric portico. The park had a herd of white cattle grazing, and a few isolated oaks. It also had a small church, some four centuries older than the present Hall – a building which the previous day had suddenly assumed an intense significance for the daughter of the house.

The party assembled behind the house, in the stable-yard. The beaters in their leather waistcoats and boots, some in coats and some in oilskins, stood leaning on their staves, conferring about the prospects for the day's sport, cursing their dogs affectionately. Some were already climbing into the wagon which would transport them to the first drive. The cart-horse between the shafts, a mighty Suffolk Punch, snorted steam into the flurries of snow-flakes.

For the guns there was a shooting-brake, pulled by a pair of sleek bay cobs and driven by the Hedleighs' groom. In addition to the Edingthorpe quartet there were of course their host, Julian Hedleigh, and his two sons. Freddie and Mark were both in their twenties, and were equipped with such confidently ringing voices and with old coats of such matchless tweed and cut that Jack had to try hard not to be in awe of them.

Mr Hedleigh he had always liked. He was a small man in his fifties, going bald, but still spare and energetic, with twinkling eyes. Jack's elders might on occasion allow themselves to be ironical at the expense of Hedleigh's political manoeuvring, of the seemingly unselfconscious and certainly passionate self-interest with which on the Stock Exchange he augmented the considerable fortune he had inherited. They might, Charles Lammas among them, jibe sometimes at the care with which Hedleigh had been positioning himself so as to be the almost inevitable choice for the next Lord Lieutenant, wonder with mild mockery whether this accession might yet be prevented. But innocent Jack liked the sparkle in Mr Hedleigh's eyes, liked his jokes. He was impressed by the fact that he was a member of parliament. Liked being invited to Bure for parties, for days in the woods or on the water. Liked the way Mr Hedleigh had lately always treated him as if he were practically a man.

The eighth gun turned out to be Major de Brissac. This meant that when Gloria Lammas and Sarah Hedleigh fell into each others' arms with moist eyes and exclamations of joy, and when Bobbie Lammas was shaking hands with his host and addressing him with a warm earnestness as unusual in him as it was briefly becoming, Jack was paying no attention at all.

Christopher de Brissac had still been at Harrow when the war broke out; but then in 1918 on the Western Front as an extremely young officer he had been awarded the MC – which explained the respect Jack accorded him when they met on his infrequent visits to East Anglia to stay with friends here and friends there. After the Armistice, he had remained in the Army, in a Guards regiment. He had been aide-de-camp to a general – Jack couldn't remember *which* general, and didn't like to ask, but he was sure it had been a very important one. He was Roman Catholic. This meant little to Jack, beyond a vague speculation as to the perhaps awkward position English Catholics might have found themselves in at the time of the Armada. He must remember to ask Papa about that. De Brissac was tall, bony, his slightly curly dark hair trimmed impeccably short and already beginning to go grey at his temples. He stood in the yard at Bure, taking from its case one of a pair of beautiful Holland and Holland guns.

Reluctant to speak until he was spoken to, Jack busied himself with his cartridge bag, his cap, his mittens.

But de Brissac too was extraneous to the fizzy nucleus of the celebration of the engagement. He turned. 'Well, young man, we're in for a white day it seems. Is that a new gun? Don't think I remember it.'

'Yes, Sir.' Jack spoke with a studied lack of excitement. 'It's a sixteen-bore.' Besides, by comparison with the intricately engraved weapon in de

Brissac's hand, his was a meagre thing. 'Christmas present.'

'And a very handsome one too, by the look of it. May I see?'

Sarah Hedleigh had been a buxom blonde, and was now solidly stately, her good will to all men founded unshakeably on her contentment to be the lady of Bure and mistress too of a pleasant house in Knightsbridge, to have a rich and eminent husband, two strapping sons and a lovely daughter.

Devoid of any ambition except social, or of any notion that others might be commendable, devoid likewise of intellectual talents and of grave defects of character, she had made a serene and loving mother of the satisfied sort. Psychological comfort being the highest good, and this in Mrs Hedleigh taking the forms of being at peace with one's conscience, with one's bank account, with one's equals and one's inferiors, of having a beautiful rose garden and a dependable digestive system, she had wished a happiness similar to her own for Caroline. Thus when it was mooted that the girl might go to one of the women's colleges at Cambridge, her mother demurred. Blue-stockings were a charmless lot, in her view. Caroline had been good at her studies at school, and the idea of reading History at Newnham attracted her; but she was still very immature and mild by nature, she didn't kick up a fuss. So her mother kept her in London and Norfolk, where she might be uninterruptedly adored and managed and indulged in.

Apart from one telephone conversation (Charles Lammas had rung up Julian Hedleigh) there had been no communication between the Edingthorpe and Bure households since Bobbie Lammas had walked his now secured enchantress back from church across the park; had in full view of her parents' drawing-room windows kissed her on her bright wind-bitten mouth; had declined to come indoors – 'We'll get all that business over with tomorrow, my darling;' had jumped into his car, waved, driven away. So now for five minutes in the stable-yard the rejoicing was general.

No one could deprecate an alliance between families of such long-standing friendship. Moreover, the flirtation had been conducted with such disarming frankness that nobody could claim to be taken aback; so really it was too late to entertain qualms.

Sarah Hedleigh was clear that Bobbie did not constitute a brilliant match; but he was a respectable one. His optimism as to his prospects was infectious, and she understood that Julian's conversation with Charles had been satisfactory. With his good looks and his charming manners you could introduce him anywhere. Her own superiority to his mother was a comfortable one.

Bobbie's prospective brothers-in-law pumped his hand, congratulated him in forthright tones and with merry eyes. The gamekeeper shook his hand also — having long ago decided that young Mr Lammas' sporting enthusiasm was going to have to compensate for his limited ability to kill the birds which, at trouble and expense to the Bure estate, were driven perfectly shootably over his head.

Caroline, when she appeared with flushed cheeks in the cobbled yard between the game-larder and the camellia, was hugged by her mother for the fifth time that morning — and it was still only nine o'clock. She was hugged by Gloria with a heaving breast and incoherent sentences. By Charles, who found in this pleasant act one certain good to weigh in the balance against his misgivings. By Raffaella, who whispered something which made them both suddenly shriek with shameless laughter, rapidly suppressed into giggles, into glances of anarchic complicity. By Blanche, gaily.

Blanche Lammas was in her element.

Remaining at home with Nanny Oldfield on Christmas morning when her husband had taken the girls to church, she had broken down completely. Forty she might be; but she had knelt by her old nurse's chair, had buried her head in that nearly dead lap, had cried like a little girl. 'I can't bear it, Nanny dearest,' she had sobbed. 'I still can't bear it, the way it comes again and again. Oh Michael my darling! Oh why? Why?'

But now the countrywoman in her rejoiced in the prospect of the day's shooting — and perhaps her Christmas paroxysm of grief had been a merciful catharsis of a kind. At any rate, she was sufficiently straightforward of heart to take simple delight in the proposed nuptials; and she was resolved to be out all day, sometimes with the beaters, sometimes with the guns.

Henrietta was too young to do a full day, though she might come out in the afternoon, her mother decreed. (The wedding-plotting women in the drawing-room would give the child a pampered morning.)

Georgia on the other hand might come with her now, if she liked. Yes? Good. (Suddenly it was of oppressive importance that her exiled goddaughter be loved actively, given an amusing day.)

3

To Jack's relief, the Suffolk Punch was pulling the beaters' wagon away down a muddy loke. Mr Hedleigh was marshalling the guns, walking round with a small leather wallet which he held out to each man in turn.

This was a significant rite, Jack paid attention. The battered wallet contained smoothly carved little ivory sticks, each with a number engraved on it. Offered the wallet in the palm of their host's hand, each gun took one of the ivory sticks, turned it over to see the number, put it back the other side up so it would not be chosen again. In this way, it was established who would stand at which peg for the first drive.

All morning, he had been hoping he might draw a number between his father and, say, Ricky. That would be splendid. Here was Mr Hedleigh. For the first time in his life, Jack took one of the remaining sticks. Turned, it displayed a black five. 'We're moving two,' his host told the boy courteously. This meant that since Jack would be at five for the first drive, he would be at seven for the second, then at one, and so on. Of more interest now was to discover whom he would have to his left and right.

The drawing-room contingent waved. The shooting-brake clattered away.

As soon as they had left the yard, the conversation in the brake switched from the engagement to the day's sport, to anecdotes of other days. Bobbie in particular appeared to have utterly forgotten Caroline. He chatted to her brothers about how he feared that if the snow fell heavily the birds would not fly well, about a shoot at Hoveton which they had been forced to curtail because of thick fog. Snow settling on their caps and shoulders and knees, the party jolted along the rutted lane through the peaceful, whitening landscape. What number was Jack? his cousin enquired. Five? Excellent. He was at four. De Brissac was at six.

They were to begin the day down by the river. This was a region of the Bure estate which Jack loved, and his pleasure at being placed next to Bobbie, and his anxiety to perform creditably in the eyes of Major de Brissac, were quickly whelmed in his enchantment at going there.

Sluggish, brown, flailed by gusts of wind to a dull glitter, the river ran between boggy woods of oak and alder, ash and thorn. Then it wound through rustling reedbeds where it was too aqueous to tread and too mirey to take a dinghy. Then out across water-meadows where geese and swans grazed, and horses, and cattle; where brick windmills, redundant in the modern age, still held up their ruined heads and broken arms; where clumps of leafless willows were buffeted to shudders by the squalls.

In one thistly meadow, there lay hard mounds under the soft earth. Here the renaissance Bure Hall had stood – built down by the water as was the custom then, Charles Lammas had explained to his son when they went to explore, just as in the eighteenth century it had been more usual to build on rising ground.

Bure Broad was small: five or six acres of lily-patchworked water surrounded by alder carr, connected to the river by a narrow cut almost over-arched by tree-tops. There was a reed-thatched boathouse. A skiff, which the Hedleighs and their friends would take out on summer days for picnics or to swim, or just for desultory sculling. A punt, for winter wildfowling.

For the first drive, the beaters were combing a low-lying wood through which a tributary which had long ago been canalised flowed sludgily, clogged now with fallen trees, its banks shelving.

Out on the meadow, the guns waited in the swirling snow. Behind three isolated poplars, an old white horse and a donkey endured, their hindquarters to the blizzard. The tributary bisected the meadow too, and half the men had crossed it by a humped bridge of now rather battered red brick. At pegs number four and five, the Lammas cousins found themselves either side of the water.

Jack laid his cartridge bag down on the lifeless grass, which the snow was beginning to cover. He shoved some cartridges in his coat pockets, he loaded his gun. Taut with expectancy, he stamped his feet which were already getting cold, peered through the white welter at the wood-side. He listened. No voices yet. No wing-beats.

Then entranced by that desolate world of woods and marshes, he forgot that he was waiting for the first driven shapes to come hurtling high over his head. The falling snow blurred all sights, it muffled sounds, it isolated him. An old vessel had sunk in the shallow stream by his side. He watched the flakes vanishing into the dark water, settling in a crust on the exposed timbers. A moorhen bobbed by.

The cold stung his ears, his cheeks, the tips of his fingers which his shooting-mittens left exposed. That horse and donkey must be cold. Poplars . . . In the church at midnight, he had thought of poplars for some reason.

Christmas, poplars . . . Next day, he had asked Papa. It was a poem, he ought to have remembered, it was Milton. Sacred springs or haunted springs, something like that, and – how did it go? One religion dying and another coming to life, anyway – he'd been right about that. Religion or mythology, his father had said. Dales of poplars, and nymphs mourning for the old gods – Papa had quoted a bit of it, they'd been walking the dogs on the common after Christmas lunch. *The parting Genius*, that was right. The ancient spirit of everything – hounded away . . . Somewhere just like this, it could have been.

'Jack! Over!'

Shocked till his cold face flushed hotly, he flung up his gun, but it was too late.

Somebody in the wood had called, 'Forward!' – now he remembered, but at the time he'd been dreaming like an idiot. And then the pheasant had been up there in the scudding snow flying fast and Bobbie had noticed he hadn't seen it and had shouted. But by the time he swung after it the dark winging shade was gone.

Major de Brissac must have seen it all, God what a fool he'd made of himself. And Mr Meade had quietly observed that if you could manage to shoot decently at the first drive it was good for your confidence, then you often got into the rhythm of shooting well.

Shots sounded all along the line, the birds were coming thick and fast. Mr Meade had told him not to get too tense, Jack recalled; but that was impossible now.

Here one came. With an ungainly motion not natural to him, he raised his gun. No, it was going over Bobbie. No, it was for him. Hurriedly he took aim, fired, missed. His boots slithering on the snowy grass he turned, told himself to concentrate calmly, missed again with his left barrel.

Major de Brissac had already shot a brace, Jack noticed, ejecting his spent cartridges, reloading. And to shoot so badly with his beautiful new sixteen-bore! Looking at the gun he held, he almost hated it for being let down by him.

Once more he instructed himself to be calm. Not to see one bird and then to miss the next – he'd shot behind it, he knew – was a shame, but not serious. He must remember to swing steadily through the target and keep following through and squeeze the trigger not jerk it. Try to miss it in front and you'll find you hit it, that was what Mr Meade said.

A pheasant was flying toward him over the trees. Jack lifted his gun. Steady. Steady. Through it. He fired. It came plummeting down, fell dead a few feet behind him.

4

—ɯ—

Georgia Burney had been separated from her parents when just young enough not to have understood much about them.

She had a vague sense that the Shan Hills, which were the land of heart's desire for her, were for her mother a weary banishment from civilisation. And that Geraldine's principal concern in life was the maintenance of her slim figure and her youthful complexion – the girl wouldn't have phrased it like that, but the suspicion had been rammed unavoidably home.

That her mother dressed too flashily for the country – Georgia was still too innocent for that to have seeped into her defensive love for that day-dreaming lady. Nor that, lonely and bored in her Burmese hill station, Geraldine conjured up romantic encounters which sometimes occurred in a box at Covent Garden; sometimes at Cowes in regatta week, or at Cheltenham on Gold Cup day; sometimes in a thronged ballroom presided over by Venetian chandeliers. Never east of Suez. Hence the pride taken in her small, firm bosom and slender waist. Hence the care taken that her cheeks should remain candid, wedding-dress white. Hence the bills from London fashion houses which her husband often found difficult to pay.

Alex Burney hadn't told her much about the nervous centre of *his* existence either. The war was over, thank heavens. They'd won, thank heavens. That was about the limit of his instruction in recent political and military history, at least so far as his female offspring was concerned; Ricky, being male, was honoured with slightly less curt despatches.

That was about the limit of his self-explanation for her too. Nothing about how when he went over the top for the first time, attacking from the Ypres salient, the worst thing wasn't men being killed beside him, after all he'd expected that, and the dead lay still, the dead made no noise. For a few moments, the worst wasn't the waiting for a bullet to hit your flesh, either. No, the nightmarish thing he hadn't imagined was that the wounded didn't always just moan. Sometimes they screamed, so that even under the barrage you heard them. One or two had writhed, they'd pleaded with him in howls, grabbed his ankles. He'd dragged them a pace or two, kicked them away. He didn't tell her how, ever since, those screaming men had been clutching his legs, tripping him.

To begin with, Georgia didn't make out much about Charles and Blanche Lammas either, or even like them particularly. Her parents had over-praised their Norfolk friends to the girl – that was probably part of it.

Almost inevitably, as a preliminary to dumping her in their charge, they'd exaggerated the alliance between the two families too. Certainly it didn't take Georgia long that August to realise that the Burney connection was less important to their hosts than the Lammas connection was to her parents. And if these people were her godparents, why were Daddy or Mummy not Henrietta's?

It wasn't her godfather's tossing her school report into his drawing-room fire that began to mollify her. She didn't believe in the efficacy of the act: it was as simple as that. Didn't believe that burning the written pages would cancel the judgements passed on her, let alone reverse them. Didn't believe Lammas understood the vileness. Didn't believe he was capable of mitigating the regime she was subjected to. She accepted that he was trying to be friendly, and the Edingthorpe Christmas gaiety was thawing her a little by then – but she didn't believe.

But Commander Mack who had still been on board *Tornado* when she went down. Georgia's imagination fastened on that rough sea, rollers breaking, spray on the wind. Grey, dead-of-winter sky. The ship foundering fast, and no one knowing where anyone was, and boats pulling away. The girl wasn't immune to that, it infected her.

Mrs Lammas in her grey, muddy garden, cutting holly and ivy for a wreath, telling the facts, explaining nothing. The girl had started to be interested in her. Then the stained-glass window that glowed even at nightfall: the destroyer, the Archangel, the white swans. Mrs Lammas' sad eyes, her not saying much. Then her hurrying steps, her hug. A real embrace, a real compassion, Georgia couldn't mistake it. The tears in her godmother's voice when she said, 'I'm not much good at being brave either, sometimes.'

On Christmas afternoon, when she had found herself alone by the fire with her godfather for a minute, Georgia had asked him why Commander Mack had stayed with his ship.

The man who, as a lieutenant in command of *E35*, had off Cape Saint Vincent torpedoed a cruiser U-boat, who had surfaced and searched for swimmers for as long as he dared but had found no one, regarded her frowningly. 'Oh . . .' he said hesitantly. 'Well . . .'

She was in one of her moods of being older than her years. In her best blue frock with white collar and cuffs, she stood at her ease on the Shiraz rug. 'They were torpedoed by a submarine, weren't they?' She looked up at him with her murky eyes.

'Yes, they were.' Lammas was gruff, but he had decided to tell her. 'But they weren't the first. What happened was, the U-boat torpedoed another destroyer in the flotilla. Michael brought *Tornado* alongside her to try to take the crew off before she went down. Of course, he had to decide in a flash whether to attempt it or not. Terrible risk, but . . . He was that kind of man.'

He spoke evenly, thinking Yes, she *is* a strange creature, this child of Alex's. Bringing things back. Seeming to cast the shadow of the future in his mind. Oh, nonsense. Funny hair. Looked as if it wasn't meant to be like that, looked discoloured or something.

'Unfortunately, the U-boat hung around. Whoever commanded her must have been brave too. And lucky. *Tornado* was hit.

'As for why Michael stayed on his bridge when he'd got his boats away . . .' Lammas frowned again at the impassive girl. 'Well, we were all trained to think that a captain ought to stay with his ship. Don't know whether that sort of attitude really survived the war or not. Still, for better or worse, that was what our generation was brought up to believe. And . . .

'Well, he'd knowingly endangered his command. Do you understand? So he took the responsibility for her loss. I don't know whether in the next war men will behave like that. Don't know either if they'll risk their ships by laying them alongside another that's sinking. But he did.'

The upshot was that the following day at Bure in the snow Georgia kept being haunted by that fight in the North Sea.

5

As a man who had stories to tell, Charles Lammas suddenly appeared to his goddaughter in a more flattering light. That his bluff, kindly manner might not be just dullness; that it might conceal an inner richness; that he might have resonances thrumming in him to which she could listen – it hadn't occurred to her.

Lammas was wrong about Alex Burney not having a voice for his children, wrong to think he always addressed them with that superficial, manly good humour with which he made nothing of most topics and kept most acquaintances at a contemptuous distance. That was his manner with them when other people were present, other people including their mother, and it was so habitual to him that for years Richard and Georgia didn't notice anything peculiar about it. When he was alone with them, often he told stories about the East, and then he wasn't dismissive.

Burney had fallen under the spell of the Arakan coast and the Tenasserim coast, fallen under the spell of the mountains of Nagaland and the Shan ranges toward the Chinese frontier and the Kawthoolei hills. His sardonic manner protected an enchantment: that was part of it. He was almost morbidly aware that his son and daughters born in Upper Burma were born already at home in exile: that came into it too.

They'd never be as British as the home-grown variety, he feared, he hoped. They were born to more tenuous loyalties and to more ambiguous identities. They were born in the realm of different genii. And he knew they'd imbibe no very great comprehension of the land of their birth from Geraldine, who was in her element only in the bridge room at the club.

So in quiet hours on his Maymyo verandah he told his children stories not from the Matter of Britain but from the Matter of Burma, which solitary Alex Burney put together himself for Ricky and Georgia – Emma never made much of what you told her. A Matter which was the fruit of his reading and his travels. Stories ancient and modern. A hotchpotch.

Right back in recorded time he reached for its origins. Myths or histories which had endured in inscriptions at the ruined capitals of Pagan and Ava, stories from the *Glass Palace Chronicle* – all about wars and dynasties, by and large, and the building of pagodas and temples. Stories of the spirit, from the Pali texts of Buddhist teaching. (He didn't want them to grow up too sniffily Christian.) Stories from Hakluyt – because the inheritance they were born to was that of Europeans a long way from Europe.

That was important to Burney, that being of the West in the East, that being precarious. Not that he talked much about how insubstantial the British East could seem to him. At the club they'd have been pretty eloquent if they'd known how often he sensed that, with a mere change of mind, with nothing grander than a new thought, the whole nebulous fabric might be dispelled. Yet the intimation gave a wry twist to his decision to live in Burma and – he was adamant – die there. It gave poignancy to the way he watched his children growing up with that landscape for their first and probably last Arcadia. Those flowering trees in their eyes. Those temple bells in their ears. That language in their mouths. Yes, in their household the master and the children, though not the mistress, spoke Burmese with the servants. Not that this was unheard-of in British families there in the twenties and thirties, but it was rare enough to be a litmus test.

So because Burney's young listeners would never become wholly Burmese any more than they would, he trusted, be too parochially British, his Matter of Burma had some calculated slants to it. He couldn't know how much of the Orient there would be in their lives to come – but it might be some mental strength to them to be aware of the tradition in which they stood. And anyhow, he'd say, the Asian discovery of Europe and the European discovery of Asia were the most rambling, most beguiling stories you could hear.

So alongside Marco Polo's claim to have travelled from China into northern Burma, and his description of two stone towers – one clad in silver and the other in gold, both girt with tinkling bells – the children also got the conquests of King Bayinnaung. They got the picture of his glory given by that other Venetian traveller Caesar Fredericke, who visited his capital, Pegu, in 1569, and said that for dominions and treasure he outdid the Great Turk.

Quite a fellow, Bayinnaung. Always at war against Arakan, against Siam, against Laos, everyone. Inveterately commissioning pagodas wherever his campaigns took him, dishing out sumptuous copies of the Pali scriptures, feeding indigent monks. It was the Buddhist clergy of Pegu who, when after his defeat of a rebel army he had several thousand prisoners cooped up in bamboo cages and had decided to set them on fire, persuaded him not to. Then he rebuilt his palace and city – his palace which was his city, in the fashion of Burmese capitals then, his city of a palace. Some of the roofs were plated with gold, according to Caesar Fredericke – according to Ralph Fitch also, who was probably the first Englishman to set foot in Burma. Fitch saw the Shwe Dagon Pagoda too. Before Burney took his children to Rangoon to visit it, he read them what the Elizabethan had written, how it was *all gilded from the foot to the toppe. It is the fairest place, as I suppose, that is in the world: it standeth very high, and there are foure wayes to it, which all along are set with trees of fruits, in such a wise that a man may go in the shade above two miles in length.*

That was the kind of stuff Georgia got in her Matter of Burma, aged eight, aged ten, sitting on the verandah of their house in Maymyo.

Georgia loved to hear about the Franciscan, Odoric of Pordenone, who discovered in Borneo a sea which ran only to the south, so that if a man drifted away he was never seen again. At Champa, he found the king had many wives, and two hundred children, and fourteen thousand elephants. Then there was the Venetian nobleman De Conti who, after twenty-five years roaming the East, was coming home through the Red Sea when to save his skin he renounced his faith and became a Muslim. Luckily Eugenius IV absolved him, on condition that he recount his adventures to the papal secretary. And all these travellers and their tales came from Rangoon to Southampton aboard a Peninsular and Oriental ship in Georgia's head, were her companions at night in her school dormitory.

No doubt the mere fact that these marvels reverberated in her father's voice was enough to make them precious to the wretched child whom none of the other girls would speak to, or at least not civilly. They brought him back to her. Brought back to her memories of his love, his voice when it wasn't tense, memories of the East, of happiness. That would have been enough.

Straightforward enough, why the first person Georgia met in Britain to strike a chord in her was Nanny Oldfield. That winterer by the Edingthorpe kitchen range had first sailed into Bombay harbour when Rudyard Kipling was still a boy, and had afterwards over the decades read *The Jungle Book* to bed-time children East and West. Nanny didn't know the mediaeval mariners' fantastic gossip about the vast island of Nicuveran, which they seemed to have fabricated out of the Nicobar Islands, inhabited by naked savages with the heads of dogs, eaters of one another and worshippers of oxen. But Georgia was catholic, all fables of the East were equal in her hearing, and her father had read *The Jungle Book* to her. Then she'd read it to herself repeatedly, till Mowgli and Baloo and Bagheera were her best friends, and her admiration for the courage of Rikki-Tikki-Tavi knew no bounds.

For Georgia, stories were the world when it was alive not dead. Stories were life in motion, they were the miracle of things happening. Stories were old worlds changing into new, were feelings that wouldn't stop changing . . . She didn't know, she hadn't worked it out. But . . . Stories were words which suggested things you half understood — and half was enough. Stories were voyages in the Indian Ocean and the China Sea, were ascents of the Brahmaputra and the Yangtze Kiang. Stories were words that went on echoing in your head till you understood a bit more and then it all changed and you forgot.

It was an important discovery that Mr and Mrs Lammas had their reserve and their stories, just like her father – which would explain how they were friends, which before had not been clear. Silence – and within it, stories. Just like her father. The pattern was satisfactorily the same. Like herself, too. So Georgia was disposed to judge leniently the curious goings-on in the Norfolk countryside in the Boxing Day snow. And the charades two evenings before had been fun. Her dreams might include Francis Drake's arrival in the Spice Islands, but they had never dared stretch to the possibility of her helping Raffaella Zanetti to lather Bobbie Lammas' chin with whipped cream and shave it off with a bread-knife.

It was a far cry from her father's days shooting, she reflected, remembering the Shan tribesmen he took with him, as she glanced at the farm labourer next to her in the line of beaters, his red face and white whiskers, his oilskins and gaiters. Still, the principle seemed to be roughly the same, and she thought the snow was magical. Luckily, so far nobody had thought to ask her if it were the first time she had seen snow, she'd been able to keep this potentially embarrassing fact quiet.

The wood with the canalised tributary flowing through it was low-lying and wet. There were a few mossy mounds, where bracken grew, and some ditches clogged with dead rush. Most of it was bog, where Georgia splashed through with the mud sucking at her boots. She knocked on the trees with the stick they'd given her, as she'd been told to do. She kept an eye on Mrs Lammas to her right, and on the farm labourer whose name appeared to be Bert on her left, so as to stay in line.

Scrambling over a fallen tree, Georgia caught her foot in ivy, tripped. With a yelp of alarm, she fell forward into some brambles, yelped again as the thorns ripped her hands which she flung forward to break her fall.

Lying among dead brambles with black swamp oozing into her clothes, shocked by the pain in her cut hands and wrists, tasting the blood that was seeping from a scratch across her mouth, she saw a pheasant. At least, she supposed it was a pheasant. It was the first she'd ever consciously seen. The frightened bird was twisting and turning through the damp stems. Then it found a gap, it flew up.

Georgia heard Mrs Lammas call, 'Are you all right?' She heard wings. The wings going away.

Pushing down with her sore hands so they sank into the mire, the girl got onto all fours. Brambles tearing at her coat, she stood up. The line had stopped. Watching the pheasant rise through the branches on its clappering wings, Bert called 'Forward!'

Georgia bent down to look for the stick she'd dropped. There was silence. The line of beaters moved on again.

Then, far ahead, a shot. A second shot.

6

Obediently, Georgia held out her dirty, lacerated hands. Blanche Lammas moistened her handkerchief with snow, mopped at the slimy mud caking the weals.

The girl was a bit wan, Blanche thought, but she didn't whimper, didn't complain. With a pulse of tenderness for that small, colourless face, and those blotchy, offered, hurt hands, she remembered how at the end of the summer holiday the child's onsets of tears had irritated Geraldine.

Snow swirled down through the dark brown trees, settled crystalline on branches, began to fur the up-wind sides of trunks. Most of the wood was deciduous, but here and there a holly or a rhododendron or a laurel blocked the view. Trembling in the gusts, they were changing from mounds of dark green to mounds of glistening white.

Blanche set a finger gently under Georgia's chin, tipped her face up so she could clean the scratch puckering her lips.

'What's the use of my giving you gloves if you won't wear them?' Scrubby little wretch, she thought, deliberately roughening the softness in her mind. Pitiful, the cold off-white scratched flesh with the cold white snow falling on it. 'If you'd been wearing them, you wouldn't have got anything like so cut. Now, where are they? In your pockets?'

Pitiful those eyes, too, blinking up at the snow. Wincing eyes . . . And yet expressionless also, as if she'd withdrawn too far behind them.

Blanche gave the chill forehead a dab of a kiss. 'Now, for heaven's sake get those gloves out. I want to see you put them on.'

Not an easy child to have the care of, she reflected, going back to her place in the line of beaters, moving forward over the marshy ground in the snowfall that was heavier now. You'd feel her beginning to like you, but then she'd remember that you weren't her mother and she'd stop. She'd begin to enjoy herself, but then something would go wrong. She'd remember that this wasn't Burma maybe. Anyhow, she'd go dead. From one moment to the next, she'd just not be there at all.

Did she realise that Geraldine's and Alex's marriage was ropey? Blanche hoped the child's mind had refused to perceive, and now far away from them would decline to imagine. Let her be protected a bit longer, her godmother found herself praying with a vehemence which surprised her. Had the girl sensed her mother's – what was it? her unhappiness, simply? Or, for that matter, her father's?

'*Honey!*' Blanche Lammas shouted with uncharacteristic anger. 'Come *here!*' Her spaniel had foraged too far ahead. Now the dog came trotting circumspectly back, circling to gauge her mistress's humour before, with unimpeachable contrition, coming to heel.

Early in the drive the pheasants mostly ran ahead of the advancing line, but now the beaters and their labradors and spaniels were halfway through the wood. As they shortened the distance between themselves and the guns, more and more birds were getting up. Occasionally one would curl back over the line, and somebody would shout '*Going back!*' Sometimes one flew out of the wood to left or right, where there were walking guns flanking the beaters, and if it came out within range you'd hear a shot. But most of the game went rocketing forward through the boughs and up over the tree-tops and over the guns waiting on the meadow.

Snow, snow, wonderful snow, Georgia thought, tramping through the undergrowth in the blizzard. She had liked it when Mrs Lammas tipped her face up, liked the gentleness of the gesture, and this time, as it chanced, no defensive feeling about her mother had intervened to make her like her godmother the less.

Snow, snow, glorious snow, she chanted silently. Snow . . . Good word. She banged her stick against a willow tump. Magical snow . . .

She had liked it when the snow-moistened handkerchief had soothed the torn sensation of her mouth and the snow-flakes had alit softly on her cheeks. She had tried to keep her lids apart so she could feel the snow settling on her eyes, but it hadn't been possible to stop blinking. For a few moments, attended to by Mrs Lammas and the snow, her mind had been lulled into a peaceful dream of – of nothing much – of kindness, and of heavenly flakes of snow falling gently. Lulled . . . The cool brilliance glittering on her lashes was nice. Her scratches were already hurting less, or she forgot them. Mrs Lammas' kiss was friendly too, and made her feel sorry for her all over again because her brother had been killed at Christmas. He had been killed, or he had decided he ought to die, and it had been Christmas, and the news had come to Paston.

Were there spirits in English woods like there were in Burma? she wondered. *Nats*, the Burmese called them. Every house had its resident *nat*. In the remote villages, there'd be a shrine for the local *nat*. In the hills every coll and gorge, every reach of river and waterfall and islet had its *nat*. Any significant rock or tree might have its ghostly guardian, you could never be sure, and they had to be placated lest they do you harm. Genii, her father called them, explaining. Demons, the Shans and Chins and Karens would tell you.

Georgia had seen *nats* carved and *nats* embroidered, some grotesque, others beautiful. With her father she had gone to Kachin settlements outside which they'd seen gory skulls of oxen and swine, and stoups of rice wine, so the *nats* could eat and drink without coming to pillage among the houses. They'd seen the short Burmese swords called *dahs* left out so the *nats* could fight among themselves and leave the villagers in peace. Her ayah and the cook had tried to frighten her with stories of enraged *nats* who might give her colic, or cause stones to rain down on the roof of the house. The thing was to let yourself half-believe for a while, give yourself the thrill of pretending you believed, let your imagination gallop ahead and then rein it in.

Her father had explained about the ancient animism which lingered in the people's hearts, the timeless terrors and the observances which refused to die away, despite Burma having been officially Buddhist since before Christ. In one mountain hamlet, he had found a *nat* shrine impudently constructed right inside the temple precincts.

Georgia had not been a bit surprised. To her it was quite natural that water and forest and air should have their spirits, that the substantial should be shadowed by the ghostly. Good, bad, indifferent – she hadn't bothered about that much. But she was alert to them. And she knew that when they built the moated fort at Mandalay they buried slaves alive beneath the turrets and gates so they would be *nats* to defend the place. She knew that Burmese armies had left gaps in their ranks so their dead should have room to fight by their side.

Would English streams and copses be so peopled with genii, be so alive? Losing interest in the dogs routing the pheasants out of the scrub, not hearing the calls of the beaters, Georgia walked into a stand of old rhododendrons that arched over her head.

The canopy of branches had kept off a lot of the snow, there was only a faint dusting on the leafmould under her feet. Tiny brown birds with jutty tails were flitting about. She didn't know they were called wrens, but she liked them, stopped to watch. It was a good house for them, she thought. It would make a good house for her, for anyone.

When she had first come to England, it never occurred to Georgia that it was a land with any aliveness. Now, for the first time, she was not so sure. Perhaps there had been genii of England, of places like this wood. The thickety canopy was a makeshift shrine. Perhaps not all the spirits had been hounded away, or killed. Some might linger here still. In hiding.

Of course, they wouldn't bear any resemblance to Burmese *nats*. But genii haunting these marshes . . . She wondered what her father would say. And

what would Ricky think? Spirits in these trees? Cold, dank ghosts they'd
be. Thin, blizzard wraiths. Condemned.

Georgia came out of the rhododendrons. The squalls blew upon her
more violently. Genii of the snow? she wondered. Genii visible in battering
welters of snow-flakes? They looked alive.

7

—ɯ—

Taking that wreath to Paston church; decorating the Edingthorpe Christmas tree with candles and enamel birds and bells; trudging over the Bure estate ... Georgia Burney was beginning to soften a little, intermittently.

All her life, she was British Burmese or Burmese British. But that first Norfolk Christmas ... Maybe it was the snow. Maybe like Jack she was beguiled by the desolate Bure woods and fens and dykes. Probably Charles and Blanche Lammas were always going to have convinced her with their kindness, sooner or later. At any rate, by the time she stumbled through a hedge at the end of the first drive that Boxing Day she wanted to consult her brother about her new apprehension that England might after all have some aliveness to it.

There had been a last flush of pheasants out of the wood's edge, a last scattered fusillade of shots. Now the guns were unloading, were slinging their cartridge-bags over their shoulders, were picking up what game had fallen near them. Further back on the meadow, along the water-side willows and beyond the poplars where the white horse and the donkey weathered the time as best they might, the pickers-up with dogs and game-bags were retrieving the birds which had come down way behind the line of guns.

Out in the unbroken buffeting of the blizzard now, Georgia shivered. There was Ricky, talking to Major de Brissac and Jack. She took a couple of steps toward them. Then she stopped. She knew what boys were like when they were talking to men about things they thought were men's things, when they were trying like mad to be men. Ricky wouldn't want to talk to her about Burma, about the genii of rivers and groves. That way he stood with his gun under his right arm and a brace of pheasants gripped by their throats in his left hand, just like Major de Brissac, listening respectfully, answering politely. She couldn't hear, but she could tell.

'Georgia!' Mrs Lammas had noticed her starting toward the men, but then stopping in her snowy tracks. 'Are you tired? Shall we stand with the guns for the next drive?'

Terribly male, the men in the shooting-brake sounded, Georgia thought. Their hard voices now chuckling at jokes she couldn't understand, now matter-of-factly knowledgeable, now cheery and making nothing of things. Still, Mrs Lammas clearly found them straightforward to fit in with. Which of the guns should they stand with this time? she was gaily debating. Anyone Georgia liked, except Charlie. She'd stood with Charlie a hundred times, reckoned she deserved a change. Who did Georgia like the look of? What about Bobbie? Possibly being engaged might make him a bit more deadly.

The girl thought of asking whether she might stand with her brother, but then she didn't. She had a horrid feeling he might not want her to.

Standing with Mrs Lammas a couple of paces behind Bobbie was fun. The snow-storm was blowing over. The guns were lined along a ride, and sunshine burst through the clouds and glittered on the whitened fen the far side of which the beaters were entering.

While they waited, Bobbie made her laugh by saying that when a girl shaved you she either cut your throat or you became great friends, so now he'd always feel safe in her hands. She could scrape away the whipped cream with a sword next time for all he cared. Then the pheasants started coming overhead. Bobbie made a play of being so surprised and delighted when he hit one, and of being so cast down when he missed, that Georgia became quite giggly. It had never occurred to her that a day's shooting might be so jolly. She picked up the ejected cartridges, sniffed the smell of gunpowder.

Now the beaters advancing toward her through the snowy reed and rush were her friends, their voices rang in the air merrily. The turbulent, dazzling sky seemed to bless the country beneath it, which in the brilliance between snowfalls lay more perfectly white than she could believe.

As for her two companions, they teased each other without drawing breath, and suddenly Georgia couldn't decide which was the more marvellous person. When Bobbie had missed three birds in a row, and the next one came winging toward them, his aunt whispered, 'Think it's Sarah.' Wide-eyed with admiration at such wickedness in a grown-up, Georgia heard Bobbie snort with laughter, watched him take aim at the plump hen pheasant, shoot it. Any potential trouble with his prospective mother-in-law thus disposed of, he turned, gave Georgia a wink which made her gasp delightedly, swept off his cap to Blanche and gave a splendidly cavalier bow. 'You watch, he'll miss the next one,' she said to Georgia – which he did, but that only increased the enjoyment of all three.

The girl's elation didn't last. When she stood with the guns, the icy wind gnawed through her coat; when she walked with the beaters, she warmed up a bit but became exhausted. As the morning wore on, the alternation of cold and weariness dulled her. Her hands and feet never warmed up, and her legs never felt rested.

She longed to talk to Ricky. Not today, necessarily, if he were busy being a man with a gun. But soon. The thought that in a fortnight the winter holiday would come to an end made her stomach feel sick.

For three or four years she had scarcely seen him. Did he ever think of their Burmese time together? she wondered with a spasm of abject desolation, hauling her legs through snow-clogged sugarbeet. The renewed flurries of flakes weren't magical any more. They were just numbing and bewildering, violent with her face, irritating inside her boots. Who was he these days? He was so English, with his gun. Did he think of the Shan Hills with her aching love for them? Did he, like her, dream again and again of when they were free to run wild in hill station gardens? Or think of Emma sometimes, buried under her cross among the other graves and the frangipani trees? He couldn't think about her trouble at school, she hadn't told him.

After the field of beet, the shoot moved to a snipe marsh. Here everybody walked in an extended line, guns and beaters alternating, dogs rummaging in the tussocks and careering through the puddles. There was no respite for Georgia's legs.

'A right and left.' 'Bring Black Horse Wood this way.' 'Going back.' 'Did you mark that woodcock?' 'Walk Grange Fen.' 'A runner.' Georgia's head was a confusion of unaccustomed phrases, words she was learning half to make sense of. But now that she was tired, the sounds merely bumped about in her wits pointlessly. 'Bring Rabbit Hill this way.' 'Did anyone pick that cock-bird of the Major's?' 'Your peg is just the far side of that ditch.' She wanted her lunch. This was just talk, noise. The only word she heard that took her fancy was 'melanistic'. A melanistic pheasant, somebody was talking about. She didn't know what it meant. Didn't ask.

Images too. She saw a keeper's gibbet: weather-tattered remnants of magpies and jays nailed up, jerking in the squalls. Then a hare shot a few moments before, ripped ears and snout and eyes dripping drops of blood as bright red as holly berries onto the shining snow.

Images she didn't see, but saw. A wreath of holly and ivy, laid on a stone sill beneath a luminous window. Only the wreath kept changing into Raffaella's kissing-bough, and changing back again. Then she'd see Mr Lammas kissing Raffaella – the way he drew her toward him, the way she came.

Apparent things once more. Ricky in the shooting-brake, his gun held upright between the knees of his knicker-bockers (plus-twos, the grown-ups called them). The way he listened earnestly to Mr Hedleigh, paid her no attention at all.

8

—m—

The telephone conversation on Christmas afternoon, which Julian Hedleigh had allowed his wife to understand as satisfactory, had given Charles Lammas no pleasure at all.

Of course, it *had* been satisfactory. Julian and he were old neighbours, were able men of the world. They would not have let matters be judged less than splendid.

Lammas had stood in the small lobby behind the main staircase, in which uncared-for room the telephone conducted its unsightly, shrill existence. He'd looked out to the corner of the yard where the bird-table stood, watched a pair of blue-tits pecking at half a coconut. Talking jovially to his brother's old cricketing friend, his principal distaste was for the necessity of discussing his nephew's prospects as a painter. For a muddle of reasons, which made him scowl at the spotted woodpecker now lording it over Blanche's offerings of rinds and cores, scaring away the poor chirpy blue-tits. Thoroughly distasteful. Every young man had to have prospects, he supposed with uncharacteristic sullenness. Yet he found he was hankering for a blissful world in which creatures as charming and funny as Bobbie might be let off.

Yes, it was disagreeable – because although Bobbie had some talent as a draughtsman, his uncle feared that his more profound dedication was to a Bohemian way of life. Because talking about money even glancingly, or indeed merely thinking about it, he'd always found irksome. Because Lammas and Hedleigh friendship and social equality might go without saying, but so did the abyss between their financial resources. Because in a family of professional men, dear butterfly Bobbie was perhaps not the most likely to be successful.

With a rush of despondency, Lammas had regarded the glamorous woodpecker devouring its Christmas repast. Because Geoff was dead. Not even buried beneath his name and his dates in one of the Ypres war cemeteries. In one of the unmarked graves, possibly. Or among the thousands of skeletons under the farm land.

Feeling obscurely ashamed, he'd heard himself concede in a cheerful voice that of course they'd give the lad a chance to make a go of painting, but then if things didn't work out it ought not to be too difficult to find him a position somewhere in the London art world.

Make light of the passions of the mind, make so light of them that they're invisible and inaudible. As to the affairs of this world, be understatedly confident. It went without saying.

Coming away from the telephone with Hedleigh's and his own expressions of friendly contentment jarring in his ears, Charles Lammas had reflected that almost any young man who married a Hedleigh girl was casting himself in the rôle of poor relation. At his library desk, he wrote a cheque to cover the not inconsiderable cost of an engagement ring that would do his nephew credit. If that young fool Bobbie had really had the drive or the passion or the what-have-you, the whatever it took as well as a little talent and a lot of training and ceaseless hard work, he would not so young have saddled himself with a bride, he'd have waited till he was beginning to be established. No, unkind, that. But perhaps true. Well, it was too late now.

He must remember to urge the lad to put off children for a few years.

He must – and this would be distasteful to a degree – the next time he was in London make a point of dropping into the Mathers Gallery. That queer fellow whose awful cravats and tinted locks Bobbie so justly despised was, it was dispiriting to recognise, exactly the pretentious and ignorant type of Mayfair gallery owner who might decide it was in his interests to hang the younger Lammas' landscapes in the hope of being offered the elder's.

Lastly and – he gave himself a shake – most importantly, he must remember to tell Bobbie that the only place in Norwich to go for a ring was Bullen's.

When he woke next morning, Charles Lammas' mood had changed. For years now, he'd ruthlessly rationed his days away from his easel. He let himself go to the Easter Monday race meeting at Fakenham, when all Norfolk turned out – but apart from that he'd pretty much abandoned the whole game. No more yachting, either. He taught his children to sail a dinghy – but that was about it. He only accepted invitations to shoot on three or four estates he'd known since he was a boy. So his annual day at Bure was a treat he was innocently determined to enjoy.

A return to old haunts, to old thoughtlessness – it was just what would do him most good, he resolved in his dressing-room, putting on breeches and stockings, checked shirt, leather waistcoat, tie. Countryside to rejoice in, an engagement to celebrate – uncomplicated, surely. And why should one not delight in Bobbie's and his girl's sensuality and optimism? He brushed his hair so robustly that his scalp tingled agreeably, admiring Salvador Rosa's etching of mysterious cloaked figures which hung on one side of his looking-glass, the Roman ruins by Marco Ricci hanging on the other. What was more, the Hedleighs were exactly the right sort of company for his mood today. The women always contented, apparently – or anyhow, he'd never given them much thought. The men city directors, landowners, politicians, buying and selling with natural ability. Not an intellectual of either sex among them from generation to generation, thank God. Yes, Caroline was enchanting, he decided, briskly descending the stairs, regarding with approval the kissing-bough, quite forgetting his recent confession that he didn't feel he knew who she was. What was more, he was hungry. He'd supplement his usual toast and marmalade with a couple of poached eggs.

In the kitchen, Lammas breathed in the scent of the hyacinths on the sill. In the gun-room, emptying packets of twelve-bore cartridges into his bag, he breathed the oil and liked that too. All things seemed good to him – the bustle of departure for Bure, Bobbie's car which was reluctant to start, Jack's excitement unmistakable in his shining eyes.

Unfortunately, Julian Hedleigh was unaware that the last thing his guest wished to talk about that morning was painting. So as they were trudging over the humped bridge at the end of the first drive, he asked him about Bobbie's artistic talents. Of course, Julian courteously recognised, Charlie had been properly modest about the young man yesterday on the telephone. But he had always understood him to have ability, the future father-in-law persisted encouragingly, and a capacity for hard work. Presumably, therefore, he had every prospect of success?

Charles Lammas' pleasure in the tumble-down brick bridge and the snow gusting through the willows was dispelled. His satisfaction that he was shooting competently was dispelled. Glancing around, he saw Georgia standing alone in the blizzard looking forlorn, which added a jab of pain to what should have been merely superficial irritation.

Bad show for a man that rich even to allude to Bobbie's possibilities of earning an honest shilling, he decided with abrupt arrogance. Damned Julian, with his family Canaletto. If he were that concerned about his daughter's welfare, let him settle on her a sum a fair bit more generous than the one he'd mentioned on the telephone.

Talking his way through Bobbie's engagement yesterday had been like eating a toad, Lammas apprehended with unseemly violence. And how was he going to have to go on crunching these slimy limbs, be nauseated again by these viscid gobbets touching his tonsils?

Turning up his coat collar as they tramped side by side, Lammas gave Hedleigh a thoughtful smile, slightly cocked one snow-smudged eyebrow.

Just as instinctively as the day before he'd played his nephew down, now he played him up.

'Yes, I hope you're right. Though of course I'm absolutely the wrong person to judge the lad. But at the Mathers they think he's first-rate.'

Bobbie have a capacity for hard work! Bobbie who was a spirit of headlong and often deliciously inconsequential enthusiasms, Bobbie with his glorious flair for turning anything that might have resembled work instantly into play . . .

Walking to his peg for the second stand, his uncle frowned. He trusted Julian's remark had not been a suave sarcasm. That would be pretty bloody uncalled-for.

Then with the crunch and creak of snow beneath his boots, with dazzling shafts of sunlight descending from rifts between clouds, Lammas' good humour returned. Now that the landscape lay under snow, the air seemed brighter than it had all through the dun autumn. In the brilliance after the blizzard, the reedbeds sparkled. The cold wind swayed the bullrushes, so the snow caked on their heads fell off with soft thuds.

The drive began, he looked forward and upward expectantly. The blustery, glittering air blew to him a dog's bark, a shout, a first shot. High seagulls tilted pale against the ominous clouds, dark in the slashes of radiance. There was a commotion in the reedbed. Something was coming his way. A fox maybe. Lammas hoped not. Julian's gamekeeper might expect him to shoot a fox, and though he knew they were marauders he couldn't help liking the creatures. Over the years, he'd deliberately shot to miss them more than once.

No, bigger than a fox. In a flurry of reeds, a roe deer leapt the ditch. With a smile, he watched the beautiful animal canter straight toward him. It saw him, swerved, galloped away leaving the first tracks on the crisp snow.

9

—ɯ—

Those woods, those meadows, those white squalls beating on the land, and then the sun coming out and glistening on a world suddenly immaculate. . . . Charles Lammas found it easy to imagine his father treading the bridle paths he now trod, dreading the future then as he dreaded it now.

In 1905, say, or 1906. Geoffrey already a student of architecture. That winter. His father shooting here at Bure. His father voting Liberal – great admirer of Campbell-Bannerman he'd been. Great admirer of Grey too, and fervent about the reduction of armaments. Here that winter they elected a government committed to cut down expenditure on arms, that winter they also launched the first dreadnought. And what else could they have done, for pity's sake? Peace in Europe depended on the nations being prepared to accept the status quo. Germany wasn't, then. Germany wasn't now.

They must have looked just the same, the flocks of greylag and pink-foot for whom the snow meant hunger. Liggers over the ditches in the same places, sluices seeping in the same way. Thorns and these half-frozen fens. His father here, thinking of his two sons growing up, and his friends' sons, seeing them already in the penumbra of a cataclysm.

It had long ceased to be conscious, if it ever had been, Charles Lammas' hope that, if the apparent man preserved an easy-going correctness, the abstract man might enjoy an autarky which others, even if they suspected it, would never condition or cramp. Instinct all along, very likely. Not that he ever talked about himself much. Though there were a few sentences of Tolstoy's which had haunted him during his war at sea, and which came back to him that Boxing Day at Bure. Lammas was of the generation who read Constance Garnett's translations when they first came out; the Russian classics were one of the great discoveries of his life.

Not the Rostov hunt, or Prince Andrei lying wounded on the field of Austerlitz. Not Kitty at her first ball, or Constantine mowing with his peasants. Sombre stuff about history being the swarm-life of mankind.

There are two sides to the life of every man: there is his individual existence which is free in proportion as his interests are abstract; and his elemental life as a unit in the human swarm, in which he must inevitably obey the laws laid down for him.

You couldn't watch the infantry attacking at Gallipoli and not understand about men as a swarm. You couldn't keep yourself sane and cheerful with dreams of the pictures you wanted to paint when the war was over, and not know about the sense of freedom which an abstract passion could bring. And then, in peace time – there had been the good hours, when at his easel his mind felt free to work on and on, to resolve this and go on and resolve that. There'd been the other hours when he'd fretted that he was painting too many commissioned portraits. Fretted that his landscapes weren't as good as so-and-so's, and someone else's still-lives were better. Fretted about bills to pay, and then in reaction resolved to spend longer on each picture because the essential thing was not to make money, what mattered was to paint a few compositions before you died which should be truly marvellous – so then, like a fool, that day you worked on late till you were too tired to work well.

There was something wrong with that bit of Tolstoy, though. During the war, it had seemed to make a lot of sense, but now he thought of it again . . . Something not right. He must remember to mull it over.

Lammas' peg for the next stand was in a narrow, muddy ride between two carrs of alder. He stood peering up into the gusting snowy murk. It was snap shooting all right, he'd hear the bird if he was lucky and then see it momentarily as it swept across the ribbon of branchy sky.

He recollected snow at sea. He'd been on watch one filthy night off the coast of Holland. Snow falling on that North Sea in which Michael was drowned, a white deluge endlessly falling and vanishing. Half-insensible with cold and weariness, that watch he'd lost himself in his longing for home and peace, in a dream of woods and meadows.

All very fine, the English countryside, unless you relied on it for earning your living. Unless you were one of Julian Hedleigh's tenants always asking to have their rents reduced, one of his labourers paid damn all. Julian made his money in the City. Kept his estate for the shooting, and because he liked being a county satrap.

Yes, but during the war men in all the armies and navies had been kept going by memories of the streets and countrysides they'd been brought up in. He had, certainly. That night off the Dutch coast, and on countless watches, he'd had a tangle in his head which was made up of places and times. Memories of landscape, and memories of landscape paintings by Crome and Cotman, by Turner and Constable. He'd carried them in his head aboard submarine after submarine. Woods and fields and tracks at different seasons, fresh water and salt seen in this light and that light. The piecings together of loveliness which seemed to be a passion of the mind there was no doing much to cure.

Coffins, those old submarines. He remembered the Dardanelles, Nasmith and him on the conning-tower taking their last look at the

Turkish shoreline before attempting the narrows. They'd caught each other's eyes for a second, and gone below. *E11* had dived.

Coffins . . . He remembered thinking of Norfolk meadows, and wondering whether he'd ever see anything again except the inside of that hull.

A year or two ago, he'd been invited aboard one of the new submarines they were building now. He'd been impressed by how big she was, how roomy. The boats of his day, of his war – sometimes they'd fitted round your consciousness damned close.

For the last drive before lunch, Charles Lammas was walking gun. He'd always liked Black Horse Wood, and it was good to be pushing through the bracken there again. As it chanced, though, he had little shooting, so his thoughts went back to ghosting him.

His heart wasn't playing up, that was good. Occasionally of late he'd felt it fluttering in his chest in a way that couldn't be right. But today his struggle through mud and scrub simply made him realise how fit he felt, how cheering it was to be active and strong.

Beautiful girl, that Raffaella, he found himself musing, one rivulet of ideas seeming inexorably to flow into another. Who was it he'd been thinking of just before that? Alex Burney, that was it. Alex who had liked English woodlands too, but had gone into exile from his native land, though not before fighting for it. Alex at the Travellers', talking about how the Somme and Ypres had betrayed the idiocy of a hundred years of meliorism.

Not that first dinner of theirs at the club, a later one. Alex talking about the fighting on the Western Front, about the insane disproportion of the means to the ends. That had finished off the myth of Progress right enough. And the black humour of it! Their religion and their poetry, all their upbringing had instilled in them that the object of life was to reach out to beauty, to refine their spirits, elevate their minds. Geoffrey, him, all of them. And then that bestial savagery. That hacking of men into butcher's meat in the freezing mud. The truth, it seemed, had been revealed.

It was all to do with acceptance, that atheist had said dryly, sipping his claret. There were horrors intolerable to face without that belief in God which made all feats possible. There were also – he had smiled with too brilliant eyes, too artificially dismissive a mouth – horrors intolerable to commit without that same faith.

War time and peace time, Lammas thought – thought rather disconnectedly, because he was puffing as he shoved through snow-weighted brushwood. Ah, here was the decoy. Trees cut back around the pool. Butts. A brace of call-duck swimming. He must remember to ask Julian to invite Richard and Jack over one afternoon. You see – he addressed the dark ripples – there *were* going to be some advantages to this engagement. Get the boys some duck-flighting.

But . . . The way war time could drub in peace time, you caught that other rhythm swelling. War time so much more tyrannous in its dislocations, more perverse in its couplings, treacherous in its variations of tempo . . .

No point in asking Julian Hedleigh for the Westminster gossip, Lammas resolved abruptly. Absolute waste of time, what with Baldwin and MacDonald preaching disarmament to the French and practising it on the British, and Julian being one of that lily-livered administration's most assiduous supporters. All these damned phonies invoking peace, he growled as he skirted an ivy-tod. Anything rather than use their brains to recognise the next war's approach, try to outwit the German cabinet while there was still a chance.

The storm was blowing over, only a few flurries of snow were harried through the trees, then just isolated flakes. Earlier, the snow which had fallen on his gun's barrels had melted, but now for minutes he hadn't fired a shot. Idly he glanced at the gun-metal glistening with tiny water-drops, saw a tuft of snow land there, watched to see if it would remain. He held out his left hand, let a single white fragment settle on his knuckle. Light, he thought, so light – seeing the warmth of his flesh cause it to begin to lose definition, reduce to chill moisture. Looking past it, he saw the flocculent particle on his gun was still intact.

They were in Cock-shoot Glade – so called because woodcock would come winging through it, and in the old days were netted there. Lammas recalled his father telling Geoff and him about it when they were boys. He stood still, his mind flinching. After the war, Roland had been so, what was it, so ashen of face and so ashen of heart too, that the temptation had been to avoid him. Geoffrey's death had not brought father and surviving son closer. If anything, it had separated them. And now . . . It was difficult to know if turn-of-the-century talk about woodcock was more heartening or more saddening. And there were things he'd have liked to ask his father while there was still time.

Scowling, Lammas advanced through Black Horse Wood in the line of beaters. The last war had come at the end of an arms race, certainly it had. But that didn't mean the next one wasn't going to be fought after a disarmament, did it? Fought, and quite likely lost rather quickly, in a scramble to rearm at the last minute . . .? Oh, he didn't know! It was just that you saw things like that snipe. You saw dozens of dead creatures, but then there was something in the way you saw that recently shot snipe. You saw something in it, and that brought back the war dead, and then there was no help for it, you saw everything crude in the garish light of death.

Alex Burney had been right about one thing, though. These Germans weren't like the Germans of 1905 or 1910 – not by a long chalk they weren't.

Those Germans had wanted their country rich and powerful and dignified. Just like the British or the French. But this gang . . . And that ass Julian hadn't a clue. Nor had the Prime Minister or the Foreign Secretary, which mattered rather more.

Lunch! That would cheer him up. Hot gammon, a glass of beer, Stilton and biscuits and apples. He trusted the traditional Bure Boxing Day lunch would not be varied.

10

—◌—

Julian Hedleigh bustled about at his sideboard, his face ruddy from exposure to wind and snow, his eyes shining with good cheer. Like a lot of ambitious, devious men, he delighted in playing the affectionate father, husband and neighbour who was allowed for a brief hiatus to forget the big world. Like a lot of men of wealth, he sometimes delighted in the apparent simplicity of his domestic arrangements. The informality of his shooting lunches was just as invariable a convention as was the elegance of his wife's dinner parties. So now the fact that Bure Hall was well-staffed was practically concealed. Hedleigh urged his guests to choose between the case of India ale and the case of stout, he opened their bottles for them. At the hearth he fussed about with logs, dusted lichen off his hands with a business-like air. When Jack and Ricky appeared, he hurried back to the sideboard to carve more gammon. 'Another slice? Excellent! Potatoes are in that dish, help yourselves.' Then overcome by pride and love he came genially around the table to kiss his daughter – part of whose being charmed by the Lammas family that winter was her awe of Charles Lammas as a man of ideas and of the arts, a man she'd heard discussed as the new Orpen or de Laszló, and whom she was feeling a little anxious about being placed next to. 'Isn't she looking glorious?' her father demanded of the party generally, with the happy innocence of a man who might never have wondered, as Lammas was still wondering, whether there were anything more to her and Bobbie's engagement than romantic carnality. Then he was off again, his attention on the table, muttering, 'Stilton, biscuits. Right. Christmas cake. Now, what was it I . . .?' He clapped his hands together. 'Apples! Knew I'd forgotten something. Where's that bag of Coxes gone?'

'Why have they all got such blobby noses?' Ricky whispered to Jack, eyeing the Hedleigh portraits which lined the walls, as they carried their plates to the table.

'I always think May is *such* a good month for a wedding,' the lady of Bure Hall confided to Gloria Lammas. 'Late May, or early June. When the roses are at their best,' she explained, reflecting with serenity that no jewellery the groom's mother was likely to wear on the day would rival her diamond necklace. Or possibly she would wear her strings of pearls with the amethyst clasp. 'Julian!' she called, sucking an annoying shred of meat from between two of her large teeth, and recollecting another of the innumerable satisfactions ahead. 'Where's that old tiara? We must remember to get it out for Caroline on her wedding day. Is it in the safe?'

'Honeymoon? Good heavens, I haven't given it a thought.' Bobbie laid down his knife and fork, let his eyes rest a moment on the Hedleigh crest engraved on the latter, took up his glass of beer. Across the candelabra in the middle of the table, he asked, 'Caroline, where would you like to . . .?'

'No, no!' they chorused all around him. 'You mustn't ask *her*! It's meant to be a surprise!'

Rather marvellous, a man in love, Blanche Lammas mused, watching the proud way her nephew carried his head, watching his eyes travel round the seated company, his eyes mischievous as ever but blazingly confident too. The power of it! she thought. The power of whatever it is he's charged with this winter and no other man here has. A touch ridiculous; a touch stupid; even a touch cruel . . . But pretty impressive, when all was said and done. With a pang of wistfulness, she turned to her husband.

'Well, I shall have to take advice,' Bobbie drawled, not betraying by so much as a flicker that his first thought had been that he'd have to ask his uncle for some money if he were going to take his bride much further than her father's park gates; nor that his second was that his benefactor understood him well, and was probably at that very instant thinking amusedly of him thinking that.

'The best advice – naturally. Let me see . . . Who have we got here who might know a thing or two about – what shall I say? – about romantic sojourns?' He winked at Blanche. 'Uncle Charles – any experience I might tap?'

Caroline Hedleigh's feelings toward her family that cock-a-hoop day were veering between anxiety that they should behave creditably and a desire to fling her arms around all their necks at once.

The anxiety she was ashamed of, but it refused to be banished. The way her mother crowed across the room about the tiara consorted ill with the quieter manners of the Lammas contingent, there was no denying it . . . Then she thought, 'Mummy darling!' and the certainty of the happiness her engagement was giving her constricted her throat – and the prospect of the family tiara being fished out of the safe and set on her bridal head *was* irresistible.

No doubt about it, her brothers at their end of the table were braying, as they had a regrettable tendency to do. Then suddenly she saw how handsome they both were, nearly as handsome as darling Bobbie, so that she ached for them to fall in love with two wonderful girls and marry them and be endlessly happy. She longed with tears prickling her eyes for sisters-in-law who should be her dearest friends.

Was her father being too hearty with Ricky and Jack? A bit school-masterish, that friendliness? What a mean-hearted daughter she must be even to formulate such a suspicion! Making sure they dug the silver spoon deep into the rotund Stilton with the napkin knotted around it, telling them which part of the estate they were going to shoot over that afternoon – they were lucky boys to have him take such trouble to give them a good day. What was more, they liked him. Paying more attention, she couldn't mistake that. Treated as men among men, they felt good and that made them like him. Treated with that unaffected friendliness, they repaid him in the same coin – and that must be nice for him, she perceived, and wanted to lay her head on his shoulder and murmur in his ear how happy she was.

She felt everything about the Lammas family must be marvellous, but that, unfortunately, didn't make it easier to know what to say to Bobbie's rather formidable uncle.

She knew his brother had been a friend of her father's. Over the years she had seen him at shoots and point-to-points, at dinner parties and weddings. Lately she'd been in and out of his house at Edingthorpe. But now that at her wedding he was going to be standing in the front pew on the right, these familiarities had abruptly and treacherously ceased to be any comfort at all.

Should she ask him about his morning's shooting? He'd find her questions uninformed and dull to answer she feared. Babble about the wedding? No, that wouldn't be right. So . . .?

Because he *was* formidable. As he had courteously pushed her chair in at the beginning of lunch, she had allowed herself to be right about that. Watching him go to the sideboard to fetch his own plate of gammon, she had wondered what it was that made him difficult to approach. The stories about his terrifically successful war? His jaw that was so stern, his mouth and eyes which were often little less so? His painting? She tried to imagine a future lunch when they would know each other far better. Laughing, she would confess, You know, when Bobbie and I were first engaged I thought you were dreadfully formidable. Hadn't a clue what to say to you that wouldn't make you despise me. And he? He would laugh too. He'd say, How awful, I *am* sorry – or something like that.

Caroline would have liked very much to talk to him about painting, but it was so perplexing to know what to ask.

She looked at the portraits on the walls, and comprehended for the first time that she had never pondered which were fine paintings and which perhaps less successful. They'd just always been hanging there. Ancestors.

She had read an article in the *Spectator* which praised the drawings Charles Lammas had made to illustrate a new and sumptuous edition of *The Scholar Gipsy*. But she hadn't seen the drawings. She was almost certain she had read something by Arnold, but she couldn't recall what.

She had, however, with her mother visited the Summer Exhibition at Burlington House, and had stood reverently in the small crowd before a canvas by Lammas – her chief interest in it at the time having been that the elegant youth reclining in a garden chair beneath the cedar tree was clearly Bobbie. The children in the skiff on the river beyond were just as plainly Jack and Henrietta a year or two ago, and there was a young lady, a girl about Caroline's own age, wearing a pretty white frock and a straw hat and also sitting under the cedar.

To begin with, the painter dedicated himself to his lunch; she bided her time. Then there was a teasing exchange between his nephew and him about idyllic places to take beautiful girls – which made her tingle, but also made her conclude that if Bobbie and he got along so gloriously well he couldn't be *that* forbidding.

So when he was halfway through his gammon, she said, 'I saw your *Cedar by the River Tarn* at the Summer Show. I thought it was marvellous. So did Mummy. It reminded me . . . It made me think of some of the French Impressionists.'

Lammas straightened his cutlery. 'How kind of you to say you liked it. But Lavery does that kind of thing a lot better than I do, I'm afraid. Charles Lavery . . . Seen any of his stuff?'

'I loved the dappled light falling through the branches.' She was gathering courage. 'And the sunshine on the river.'

'Well, it was fun to do. Of course, the children were happy messing about in the dinghy – except they kept drifting away down-stream. And, as I'm sure you know, it's never difficult to persuade Bobbie to lounge around in a chair.'

'Who was your other sitter? The young lady. I didn't recognise her.'

Lammas' eyebrows hinted at reflection. 'Girl called Daisy Rackham. She was travelling with us that summer. With her aunt,' he added.

By the time Caroline Hedleigh found herself next to Charles Lammas once more, at dinner that evening at Edingthorpe, all her shyness with him had gone. They had made the happy discovery of how to flirt with one another.

To be sure, his gallantry with her was of such suitable *gravitas*, and her charming of him was of such equally impeccable modesty, that most of the company did not realise then or ever that anything you might term a flirtation was being conducted. But Blanche did – and was glad the girl had found a way of mellowing Charlie, and wondered how long it would take her to start trying to use it to control him a little, and was glad too that he had a pretty girl to be beguiled by who would remain innocuous. Bobbie did – and resolved to tease them both that a quarter of a century – no, twenty-six years was it? – was not, when all was said and done, such a vast gulf of time. And Raffaella did – with amusement which her slyly smiling eyes revealed, with speculations which they did not.

At lunch Caroline had resentfully sensed that already her day was being appropriated by her mother and Bobbie's. But at dinner Charles and Blanche Lammas seemed quite naturally to give her back her day – the day which she couldn't help reckoning belonged by rights to her. Of course, it was Bobbie's day too. Yet somehow preeminently hers. So when at the dining table she realised that for the Edingthorpe household she was the princess of the occasion, she loved them for it sincerely and indiscriminately. From the Royal Academician to the kitten Fudge, that evening they could have no faults.

Days before, Jack and Ricky had been dispatched to the cellar to fetch some of the finest bottles of Burgundy laid down there – the Hedleighs coming to dinner, as they did every Boxing Day after the shoot, being sufficient cause to uncork good wine even without an engagement to celebrate. Jack had helped his father bring wine up ever since he could remember – it was one of the things they liked to do together, one of their rituals. And this time he had enjoyed initiating Ricky into the mystery: how you rolled back the gun-room matting, how then you heaved up the trap-hatch, propped it open with a stick. Then there was the lighting of a candle, the stooping descent of the winding stair into the black and the chill, the cobwebs and the dust, the cellar air which startled with how utterly it smelled of nothing at all. You crouched in whichever of the low arched bays Papa had indicated to you, your candle flickering on the grimy brickwork which hadn't been whitewashed for ages. You rubbed dust off tattered labels. Then in the warm kitchen the wine was stood up for a few days, and then uncorked and decanted. Jack enjoyed the whole performance. He liked the objects too. The bone handle of the corkscrew. The fluted glass of this pair of decanters, the faceted stoppers of that pair. The engraved rim of the Georgian silver wine-strainer, and its little curved spout. Now in his dinner jacket again he was pouring wine for his parents' guests – and Caroline Hedleigh, watching, thought him the nicest-looking and best-mannered boy she knew.

Somewhat taken aback by her own audacity, Ellen Meade had decided not to roast the pheasants. 'There are other recipes, Ma'am,' she had announced with respectful obstinacy, and had mentioned preparations which involved cream and onions, and apples and celery, and even one variation which called for a tablespoon of brandy. Now Mrs Fox and she were waiting at table, and she was enjoying the family's amazement that there were things you could do to pheasants beyond just roasting them, and a few moments later she was enjoying a volley of congratulations – and Caroline Hedleigh couldn't make up her mind whether Mrs Fox or Mrs Meade had the dearer face.

Radiant in her blue and pink silk dress, and so happy that she had forgotten how long she had deliberated in her bedroom over what to wear, Caroline gazed around at the candle-light glinting on the gilded frames of the pictures.

'I want you to tell me everything!' she softly exclaimed to her host sitting at her right – because she had discovered that he liked to tell her about the beautiful things he had inherited or bought. She had already asked him about the two nearest paintings, and although she had instantly forgotten the name of one artist and the century of the other she had been aware that Lammas liked the proximity of her hair and throat and arms, liked her eyes resting on him while he talked.

Of course, Bure was bigger and grander. Yet tonight in her enchantment with the Lammas family Edingthorpe Manor seemed to her . . . Oh, she didn't know! Well, it had a library, walled with serried ranks of books, books which people read. Whereas at Bure there was no library. Or rather, on the first floor there was a room which went by that name, where black tin boxes of estate records were kept but no books – for generations no Hedleigh had been much of a reader. The room's only merit, for Caroline and for Bobbie also, was that nobody visited it and there was a chaise-longue.

Caroline swung her dazzled glance past the silver-hilted court sword over one door (she'd already asked about that), past the racing-plate on the mantelpiece (it was famous all over the county), to an alcove.

'Tell me about that enormously tall glass!'

Charles Lammas stopped remembering his own engagement to Blanche, stopped brooding that it was better to fall in love and get married after a war than before one. Anyhow, it might not come for years. It might never come.

'It's a toasting glass,' he told her cheerfully. 'George III. It was my father's. Come to think of it . . .' His eyes found his son, they twinkled. 'Jack, do you think it'd be rather fun if we . . .'

Grinning, Jack jumped to his feet. And when he'd emptied the best part of a bottle of Burgundy into the glass and brought it to the head of the table, Caroline gave him such a smile of thanks that when at midnight he tumbled exhausted into bed it was still shimmering on his retinae.

Set on the table before Caroline Hedleigh, the foot-tall stem of blown glass led the eye into brilliant spiralling involutions, the slender engraved bowl which was about another foot tall brimmed rubicund and inviting.

'Go on.' Lammas smiled at her. 'You drink first.'

A smiling hush had fallen on the dinner party. Caroline laid both hands timidly on the stem, shot a bold look at her fiancé's uncle.

'The trick is to keep the glass fairly full,' he said. 'If you let it get nearly empty, when you tip it up the wine comes in a wave and cascades down your chin.'

Both their minds voluptuously possessed by the image of red wine spilling down her throat and bosom and dress, Lammas announced, 'Caroline and Bobbie! Long life and happiness!'

Cautiously she raised the glass and sipped, her eyes over the rim flicking from Bobbie to his uncle. She set it down wobblingly, with the tip of her tongue cleaned the wine from her lips.

An uproar of congratulations and good wishes broke out. Her brothers even cheered. The handsome glass was passed from grasp to grasp, refilled, handed on. Jack carried it to the sideboard, insisted that Mrs Meade and Mrs Fox drink the health of the young couple too. The spaniel Honey somehow got in from the kitchen. Infected by the merry-making, she careered around the room and startled into flight Fudge, who shouldn't have been there either.

When a semblance of peace returned, and Honey had been collared and Fudge was being coaxed down the bell-rope up which she had clawed,

Caroline asked Lammas if one day she might see his illustrations to *The Scholar Gipsy*.

'I don't know *anything*, but you mustn't mind that, please. I've read almost nothing. I've never been anywhere, never done anything. Bobbie and you will just have to be very patient, and teach me things. And I'd love you to show me what you do, if it wouldn't be too boring for you. I've read articles about you. I . . .' She laughed, quietly but not with nervousness any longer. 'I think I'd better shut up. But I wanted to say that.'

'Oh, I'll leave Bobbie to mislead you as he fancies. Certainly I'd be delighted to give you a copy of the book. Can you wait till after dinner?'

'After dinner will be perfect. How marvellous! Thank you.'

'Now. May I ask *you* something? A great favour, I'm afraid, and you must feel absolutely free to say no. I wonder – would you sit for me? I should warn you straight off that it'll take an awfully long time.'

Could it be true? Caroline's cheeks flushed, her blue eyes brightened – which faint but charming alterations caused the painter to reflect that he'd been right, she *would* be interesting to paint. Yes, he was holding open for her the door to his world of the arts. This was better than her father's and her brothers' talk about by-elections, and stocks and shares. He was holding open, in solid and delightful fact, the door of his studio. In the yard she'd walked past it countless times, but she'd never been in.

'Heavens! But isn't it a great honour to be painted by you?'

'No.' He laughed. 'No, it isn't. Just rather time-consuming.'

Thinking with trepidation (what on earth would they talk about after the first five minutes?) but also with pleasure (the whole operation could scarcely fail to be flattering) of the days and days when her chief occupation would be to be looked at by Charles Lammas, she said, 'I won't mind how long it takes.'

The only person in the dining-room whose contentment did not add to the shindy was Henrietta. All afternoon she had trudged with her mother and the beaters over the whitened countryside in the grey wind. Now too weary to be excited, her chirruping concluded for that day, she gazed at the cornucopia at the centre of the table. The Delft platter was heaped with apples and oranges, littered with handfuls of walnuts and hazel nuts. There were boxes of Elvas plums and of marrons glacés, of Turkish delight and of chocolates and of dates – but she was too tired to decide which to ask for. There was a box of preserved fruits which the Lammas children had always called deserved fruits – but she was too sleepy to be tempted even by these.

Gloria and Blanche Lammas were happy because their innocent romanticism told them that Bobbie and Caroline were in love, and their innocent snobbery adjoined that to marry a Hedleigh could scarcely be a bad thing to do. Onto this was overlaid Blanche's relief that, although the celebration must bring Geoffrey and his death alive again in her sister-in-law, she was coping admirably. No glisten in her eyes, no twist to her mouth.

Frederick and Mark Hedleigh were cheerful because Bobbie Lammas was a damned fine chap, and his uncle's Burgundy not only first-rate but liberally dispensed. Their parents were cheerful because marrying off their beautiful daughter was a rite to be indulged in (Sarah was already deciding who would feature on her list of guests and who would not), and one it went without saying they would perform with style, and after it effortlessly retain the dominance.

Raffaella Zanetti was happy with the way her acquaintance with the fashionable painter had begun, and was looking forward to getting to know him better.

Richard Burney was pleased with life because he had finished the day a brace of pheasants up on Jack, who was pleased with life because he had finished the day a brace of partridges up on Ricky. Particularly at that mid-morning stand things had gone well. Happily he brought to mind how the beaters had driven that wide slope of arable land beginning to be freaked with snow. At the foot of the decline there was a tallish hedge, the guns had stood fifty-odd paces behind it. The first covey had come whirring over, he'd swung, pulled the trigger . . . Just time to reload, then the next covey came.

Bobbie Lammas was as happy as he invariably was when wearing his smoking-jacket embroidered with dragons, and a silk shirt, and his dark red cummerbund, and a bow-tie meticulously knotted into a suggestion of carelessness. The faint stripe down his outside trouser-leg was a source of satisfaction too, and so were his father's gold cuff-links. Then the show at the Mathers Gallery was pretty much a racing certainty, honestly unless the horse fell at the last fence he hardly saw how . . . And to crown it all, Caroline would forever be twenty and forever be mad about him. After dinner, he would smoke one of his Turkish cigarettes.

Charles Lammas was cheerful because to have Sarah Hedleigh on your right bellowing about bridesmaids was not an affliction so long as you had her daughter on your left. And maybe he'd been wrong to dismiss all Hedleigh women as so placid you didn't, thank God, have to worry whether they were happy or not, neighbourly affability did the necessary trick year after year. Perhaps in Caroline there were flarings of . . . No, it was probably just his dully predictable preference for the twenty-year-old version.

Still, he'd liked her little speech about how she didn't know anything but she wanted to learn. And why the hell couldn't Julian have educated her decently? Lousy unfair treatment. He must remember that, when it came to Henrietta's turn.

Good that she was prepared to sit. He had in mind a double portrait of Raffaella and her. Where had he seen that Tiepolo – what was it called? Anyhow, there you had the fair and the dark. A blonde Venice in ermine – was it ermine? – reclining on the sea-bed with her lion. Poseidon emptying out for her a bag of the treasures of the sea. Coral, gold, jewels, dubloons and whatnot. Shadowing him, a dark sea-nymph. He still couldn't remember where the picture was.

Of course there's going to be another German war, Charlie. Stands to reason . . .

Lammas frowned. He lifted his glass of wine an inch from the polished wood, hesitated holding it there.

All these fools in England living as if the war hadn't finished off that old way of life . . .

Wishing with sudden intensity that Alex Burney could have been there to witness that at least for one evening in one house the old way of life appeared fairly healthy, he noted that de Brissac was talking to Georgia. That was good.

Strange fellow, Christopher. He didn't seem to be the marrying type. Not the usual kind of Roman Catholic, either. Read Saint John of the Cross, read Pascal, people like that.

The girl looked more animated than he'd seen her, too. Prettier. More grown-up.

12

—⁓—

At the end of dinner, Gloria Lammas and Sarah Hedleigh retreated to the drawing-room to drink coffee. Ricky and Jack went with them, and sprawled on their stomachs on the hearth-rug, and played a somnolent game of backgammon.

Emerging from the library holding a copy of *The Scholar Gipsy* in which the illustrator had just written her name and his, Caroline was commandeered by her hostess.

'Just five minutes!' Blanche promised. All day she had been meditating what engagement present to give her. Finally she had resolved it should be the ivory bracelet which her brother Michael had brought back from the China Station. After all, he'd given her other things too. That Indian fan made of peacock feathers, lots of things. But the bracelet was precious to her, she wanted to give it to Bobbie's fiancée quickly, before she lost heart and plumped for some lesser gift.

They went upstairs together, Blanche holding the nearly oblivious Henrietta by the hand.

After her conversation with Major de Brissac, Georgia had no taste for the drawing-room, she wanted to be alone. So she also withdrew upstairs – but she didn't plod like Hetty.

Christopher de Brissac knew the East. His soldiering and his curiosity had taken him to Calcutta and Cox's Bazaar. He knew the Gulf of Martaban. He'd even from Mandalay taken the rough, winding road up to Maymyo. He hadn't met her father – he'd been away in the forests at the time – but he had heard of him, and he'd met her mother at the club.

Georgia ascended the Edingthorpe staircase after the others with her head held high and with a light step, a step that had nothing childish about it. Her blue frock became her, she knew, and now Burma was close again, so close her mind could behold it complete and perfect. So close she wanted to cry, but she would not cry like a baby now.

Nearer to happiness than she had been for half a year, trembling on the brink of it, she shut her door behind her. Major de Brissac had talked to her just like he'd talked to Mrs Hedleigh on his other side, there'd been no difference at all. He had called her Georgiana with, she had judged, just the right friendly courtesy. They'd talked about the rice-boats on the Irrawaddy, and the East had been so close she could feel it, touch it, taste it. They'd talked about the lotus pond in the palace garden at Mandalay, about the pagoda bells that tinkled in the breeze.

Georgia crossed to the window, looked down to the lamplit yard, looked away beyond the outbuildings into the freezing English dark.

Charles Lammas returned to the dining-room determined to take a genial view of things. After all, whatever ensued Julian Hedleigh wasn't likely to let his daughter and her husband starve. Sitting down again at his table where now the port was circulating, he reminded himself how Julian had gone out of his way to make sure the boys enjoyed the shoot. What was more, he'd make a perfectly acceptable Lord Lieutenant one day.

But he wasn't feeling genial. The smile Raffaella had flashed him just now in the hall – Raffaella who had a poise, not to speak of an education, which naive Caroline would never match. The smile that said: Naturally, I shall make no move here and now. But you know how much I admire you; and, if we were ever to meet elsewhere . . . What was more, from the glancing smile she had elicited in response, she had known that he'd understood, he'd practically agreed. Lammas gave a shivering shrug of distaste for himself. Meaningless fidelity punctuated by meaningless infidelities, God how depressing. Cliché . . .

'No, no,' Hedleigh was protesting urbanely. 'Hitler is a reasonable man. The Germans are a civilised people. I don't think we should give in to alarm, eh, Charlie? Awfully fine port, by the way. You still buying it from Berry's? No, as I was pointing out, I think we've all come to recognise that Versailles left the Germans with some legitimate grievances. But we can redress these. I see it as our duty to put right these wrongs. By peaceful agreement, you know. Perfectly possible. Give them back their African colonies too if need be. Why not? Better than another European war.' He took the port from his right, refilled his glass, passed it to his left. 'The slaughter in the trenches was *too* appalling.' Frowning, he paused to let the sombre thought have the reverence due to it, let Geoffrey Lammas' spirit be honoured among them for a moment. 'I think all men of good will would subscribe to that. None of us wants another war, and we're right not to. Hitler doesn't want another war.'

'He's said he does often enough,' Lammas demurred, lighting a cheroot, wondering whether Hedleigh could honestly consider that people not wanting a war made it less likely. In his suddenly tired, sad mind, words lingered futilely. Reasonable, civilised . . . Slaughter . . . Men of good will . . .

Hedleigh waved aside the German Chancellor's bellicose rantings with the friendliest consideration for Lammas, with the tolerance and confidence instilled by hundreds of committee hours. 'He's renounced all claims to Alsace and Lorraine. Now, the Four Power Pact . . .'

Could Julian really take that vapid document seriously? Take any member of this German government's word for anything? Surely it was plain they were just playing for time. No, he mustn't let himself get so morose. Lammas gave himself a shake, he drank his port. What had happened to that determination of his to be sanguine? Thank heavens for wine and cheroots. That wasn't a very inspired thought, but somehow it was the best he could come up with. The débris of conversation lay about in his brain. The Rhineland . . . Era of peace . . . Locarno . . . Reasonable . . .

'After all,' Hedleigh was saying, 'Germany is a continental power. We're an island, and a maritime power. No reason why we shouldn't find ourselves in agreement. In the interests of both countries to live in peace, I should say. What do you reckon, Christopher?'

'Certainly there are persuasive arguments for conciliating Germany.' De Brissac was mild. 'The French have always had a tremendous military establishment, but we haven't. We British have never wanted big standing armies. Don't want to pay for them, don't like the look of them.'

At the other end of the table, the men of subaltern age had been in hearty discussion of a dance at Castle Acre to which they were all invited. But now Bobbie tossed back his glass of port, turned in his chair.

'War?' he demanded with flamboyance. And precipitately his uncle knew that his intrinsic optimism reinforced by this winter's romantic bewitchment would have him side with his prospective father-in-law. Making his mouth smile, Charles Lammas waited for this small betrayal.

'What war?' Flushed, exuberant, Bobbie waved his cigarette. 'There isn't going to be a war.'

THREE

1

—ɯ—

Charles Lammas and his goddaughter had breakfasted early in Nice –
breakfasted on a sunny quay, beneath an awning, on coffee and croissants.
Now their train had crossed the Italian frontier.

With his chin on his fist, Lammas gazed contentedly at the Gulf of
Genoa. The Italian government had again been making noises about
possessing itself of Nice – but with the coastline in late spring flower
and sails highlighting the sea, Mussolini was even more difficult than
usual to take seriously. *Le Figaro* and *Il Corriere della Sera* lay discarded on
the seat beside him, and both had been twittery with Hitler's arrival on a
state visit to Rome, and what a fortune the pusillanimous king had forked
out to redecorate the Quirinale to entertain his esteemed guest – but with
a breeze to ruffle the blossoming cherry trees, who cared?

Late spring, early summer, the world in the pink of health, he mused,
remembering his last visit to Italy three years before with Bobbie just
before the latter's wedding. April, May, the quick of the year, Bobbie's high
spirits, what to his fiancée he'd called his 'last escapade with Uncle Charles,
darling, before I become respectable'. Lammas smiled, thinking of that trip
in '35. Coffee and croissants, he mused in a sanguine, inconsequential sort
of way. Orchards, sails . . .

The wear and tear of his engagement had been telling on Bobbie
after a month or two, or maybe it was the pomp and circumstance of
the preparations at Bure. At any rate, when his uncle suggested that
he accompany him on his Italian sojourn, Bobbie had jumped at the
chance.

The occasion had been a commissioned portrait, then as now. They
had picked up Ned Lammas at Rapallo and gone on to the Zanetti house
in the hills north-east of Lucca three years before, as they would today.
Charles smiled again, recollecting how when he'd been in Italy before the
war it had never occurred to his callow mind that his cousin wasn't old,
whereas in fact, if you tallied up the years, he couldn't have been much
over fifty then and wasn't eighty yet – which was amusing if you'd just
turned fifty yourself and were still feeling wry about this elevation.

Enormous fun, that last jaunt with Bobbie. They had remained for a
month in Giacomo and Chiara Zanetti's house, the uncle painting a local
nobleman and his lady whose conversation and cheque had redeemed
their burgherish bulks, the nephew – well, possibly the nephew had

not achieved a tremendous amount. But he had tirelessly explored the neighbourhood in search of landscapes it would be splendid to paint if only one had time. At dinner he had always had adventures to relate: how he had got lost, or passed the afternoon in a village tavern singing, or come back in a cart pulled by oxen, or borrowed a donkey which then refused to budge. And he had drawn the gardener's daughter repeatedly. The poor girl could scarcely leave her parents' cottage to hang out the washing, without Bobbie leaping out from behind a hedge, sketch-book in hand, and imploring her to stand still just for a moment – no, perhaps with her head tilted a little farther that way – ten minutes, signorina, was all he . . . And when Raffaella returned from Cambridge he did a pastel portrait of her which her mother judged successful.

To be back in Italy, and in blossom time too. Charles Lammas stretched his arms and braced his shoulders luxuriously, gazed with approval at the Riviera di Ponente slipping by. Fishing-smacks moored along wharves, shrubs flowering in village gardens . . . In his mind he tasted grilled bass, inhaled the scent of lilac. There were good Ligurian wines too. A yawl coasting, a Judas tree in purple flower, memories of Raffaella . . .

Back in Tuscany for Easter, she had spent most of her time in the family house in Florence, had only come out for a day or two to the country, to Villa Lucia. His commission accomplished, Charles had decamped with Bobbie and Ned to the latter's house on the edge of Rapallo, where the following evening she had joined them.

Her father and mother, his nephew and cousin – none of them had by so much as an adjusted eyebrow alluded to the love affair begun at Cambridge, continued in London and Florence, concluded at Rapallo. Not one of them . . . Though possibly Chiara had not known, Charles Lammas still wasn't sure about that. And more than once Bobbie's eyes meeting his uncle's had laughed with outrageously brilliant collusion. Whether, of the other sentiments in those glances, the commiseration or the mockery had predominated had remained moot.

In depraved May . . . How did it go? Distracted, Lammas was frowning with his brow while his lips were smiling to recall days when he'd taken Raffaella to Ely cathedral, to Sandown races. That double portrait of Caroline and her had worked out well in the end too. *In depraved May, dogwood and chestnut, flowering Judas* . . . That was right. Pretty trees, not large, at Easter putting on the colour of sacrifice.

Certainly nobody had guessed that the liaison had been more than a fling – and Blanche hadn't guessed anything at all, thank heavens. At least, he didn't think anybody had. Chin once again propped on his knuckles, Lammas looked without seeing at the picturesque town at which the train had halted. His frown and his smile still cohabiting uneasily on his face, he recollected the mood of self-dismissal in which he'd brought the affair to an end.

And rightly, rightly . . . And perhaps it hadn't been anything more than a fling. Well, luckily it hadn't been a depressing cliché either.

He was bound to see her in the coming weeks, perhaps as early as this evening, and it would be interesting. She was engaged to be married, he had heard.

With this conclusion, he put Raffaella out of his mind.

2

Early in their morning's journey, Georgia Burney kept shifting from the landward side of the carriage to the seaward side and back. The Alpes Maritimes would hold her for a few minutes with their countless different greens of new leafage, with their tiny churches perched on spurs, with their peach orchards in sumptuous blossom. Then restlessly she would stand up, smooth her dress with automatic hands, cross to sit down opposite her godfather and with him be enchanted by the littoral.

'Wasn't our breakfast delicious? I hope Italian breakfasts are going to be as good as that. What's this next place called? I wanted to stop in Menton, and now I want to stop here. One year can we come slowly, and stop in all these places?'

'Well, it's either Santo Stefano or it's San Lorenzo, I always get them muddled up.'

'You haven't answered my other question. Oh, look at that fortress! How old do you suppose it is?'

'Answering your questions, young lady, is a full-time job. Fourteenth century, I should say. Yes, certainly you can come slowly along this coast one day. All you've got to do is dump Blanche and me somewhere where she can inspect gardens and I'll be happy painting. We could get Bobbie and Caroline to take you holidaying – would you like that? Jack could go too,' Lammas added, remembering his suspicion that his son, who had recently returned to Cambridge for his third term, had taken a bit of a shine to the girl.

'Bobbie and Caroline? Oh yes, glorious! We're going to see them later in the summer, aren't we? When we go back to France? Look, there's a warship! Not very big. Is she a destroyer? I can't see her flag. What nationality do you suppose she is?'

Then, without insisting on further answers, Georgia crossed back to the other side of the carriage. She sat still, silent, enraptured by the vernal hills.

Charles Lammas had taken a magisterial enough line with the Suffolk headmistress to ensure that her ostracism ended – like the story of the sinking of HMS *Tornado*, this had been one of the early knottings of the alliance between the man and the girl – but her schooling had not been a success. Her academic rating had continued mediocre. She had gone on winning races. The fact that the other pupils were forbidden to torment her openly did not make the Burma girl popular or prevent surreptitious unkindnesses. And even if there had been no repetition of the lacrosse rumpus, there was that silly episode with a golf club.

It occurred about the time that her godfather and Raffaella Zanetti were being sybaritic at Rapallo, on a Sunday afternoon. According to the staff, this was an interval of pleasant relaxation for all. For most of the girls, it was an opportunity for confabulations and gigglings. But Georgia Burney was observed by several people, on the far side of a playing field, striking herself again and again on the head with a golf club.

Headmistress and house-mistress concurred that it showed a weakness of character in the child, not to mention a deplorable instinct for melodrama, which unfortunately they had been constrained to suspect. They consoled themselves with the reflection that the contusions would soon fade. And luckily the regrettable occurrence could be dismissed when the girl denied it.

The golf club?

She'd never played golf. She'd thought it would be nice to have a go.

Without a ball?

She'd been wandering around looking for one.

And the bruises?

So feeble had been Georgia's explanations, that the only result of the episode was that she acquired, along with her other reputations, a name as the school's most bare-faced liar.

By the time she was fifteen, her requests to her godparents that she be allowed to leave school, and her written petitions to her parents soliciting the same consent, had become a nuisance. Charles Lammas had tried to convince her of the virtue of working hard and passing School Certificate and going maybe to Cambridge – thinking, as he remonstrated, of Caroline Lammas as she now was, penniless and uneducated in a cottage near Cahors with her happy-go-lucky husband.

Georgia had been adamant. 'I don't want to go to Cambridge, I want to go to Burma. Especially if there's going to be a war. I want to go home. So can't I leave school? Then you can take me with you when you go to Italy in the spring. I'll be sixteen by then. I'm sure I'll learn things in Italy.'

Fortified by a note of capitulation in Alex Burney's hand, and consoled by the thought of that exile's happiness when he should see his surviving daughter again, Charles Lammas had said yes. So here they were, their train belching coal-smoke into the azure air, approaching Genoa. He looked at her.

Her age had always seemed changeable, and it still did. You noticed the way she moved, the way she wore her clothes, and at once it was clear she was a young woman so naturally she had to leave school, such a stultifying regime must have bored her to tears. But then her impetuous chatter made her seem about twelve again. And her moods were still unstable, Lammas mused, recollecting the girl as she had been that first winter at Edingthorpe. Ragging merrily one minute, downright lady-like the next, the next again reduced to wan, silent wretchedness. She was – no, not unstable. But a shape-changer, various.

Right now, for example, the Ligurian coast appeared to have lost its magic. She had picked up *Le Figaro*, was reading painstakingly. She must have found an article about the East.

The year before, she had enquired of him, 'What are the Japanese doing in China?' Since then they had had periodic consultations about Manchuria and the Lytton Commission, about the skirmish at the Black Moat Bridge which Europeans called the Marco Polo Bridge because he'd praised its beauty. Latterly, as the Japanese armies launched attack after attack, as China lost her principal cities and her great rivers, not to mention thousands of miles of territory, and Chinese casualties began to be estimated at half a million soldiers and then more, the girl's pointblank enquiries and the man's expositions had become more frequent and more sombre.

Then in December '37 came the attack on Nanking, the massacre indulged in by the Japanese when the city fell. On the other side of the world, Georgia Burney at Edingthorpe for Christmas read *The Times'* reports as gradually information emerged from the shambles, and Charles Lammas watched her reading, imagined her understanding. Japanese soldiers using bound prisoners of war for bayonet practice. Chinese burial parties counting two hundred and fifty thousand bodies in the city, or some said three hundred thousand. Other dead who were not found till long after, or who were never found, because at night the Japanese marched columns of Chinese out to the banks of the Yangtze, roped them together in fives, shot them, pitched them into the river. This ferocity had reverberated in the Edingthorpe peace, echoed in the girl's head where she sat reading by the drawing-room fire. Arson. Torture. Mass rapes in hospitals, in women's colleges, in refugee camps.

Now she looked up from *Le Figaro*, her eyes empty. 'Chiang Kai-shek ordered them to breach the Yellow River dykes,' she said hoarsely. 'To try to stop the Japanese advance. It says . . .' Her voice petered out.

'That must have held them up all right,' Lammas responded cheerily. 'Look, Rapallo is just around that headland. We're nearly there.'

'They say the flood . . . They say probably about a million peasants have been drowned.'

He met those mutable, obscure eyes of hers, held that look, tried to infuse his confidence into her. 'Don't you worry, the Japs will never get to Burma,' he assured her, not for the first time.

Edmund Lammas was standing on the platform. White suit, Panama hat – he was as natty as ever, Charles observed with pleasure, getting down from the train to greet his cousin, watching him flourish his Malacca cane to indicate to the porter that he should load his cases into the guard's van. Damned nearly as spry as ever too, tipping the porter with one hand, hauling himself aboard the train with the other.

'Miss Burney, how do you do, I'm delighted to make your acquaintance. Now, Charlie, what have I forgotten? Getting *dreadfully* forgetful these days. Age, age, dear boy. Soon I shall be so old I shall stop believing in death. Hat. Stick. What else?'

Stiffly, the dapper old gentleman settled into his seat. He fussed with his silver-headed cane, leaned it here, propped it there. He took off his hat, set it on his knee.

'I'm *particularly* delighted to meet you since I remember your father when he was Charlie's best man. People said he was chosen for this honour because he was the only fellow strong enough to crank that ghastly old car into action, but I never believed that. Only sensible thing you ever did, my boy, marrying Blanche. I recollect getting ever so slightly tipsy to celebrate. And the *expense* of travelling all the way from here' – he waved his hand at the Rapallo cedars and maritime pines – 'to *Norfolk* . . .' He pronounced it with a tremor of fastidious amusement. 'A little too much champagne was the least I could allow myself.' He turned back to Georgia, who was beholding him gravely. 'Your father is in good health, I trust?'

The train shuddered into motion. Edmund Lammas' hat flopped off his knee, his cane clattered to the floor. Charles stooped to pick them up, thinking how splendid it was that Ned was as indomitably frivolous as ever. But he felt sad too, because his lively old rake of a cousin always reminded him of his father, who after the war hadn't had a flicker of gaiety left in him. Ned who seemed never to have entertained a thought or feeling not intended to be decorative. Roland austere, worrying about armaments and treaties, giving to charities for seamen's widows and reformed prostitutes. Maybe Bobbie had imbibed his inability to worry from Ned. Charles Lammas placed the Panama hat and the Malacca cane on the rack provided for such articles.

'I don't know, Sir, but I believe he's well,' Georgia was saying. 'I haven't seen my father for nearly four years. But now I've left school, and I'll be going back East soon. Particularly if there's a war. Going home,' she added with a soft, artless note of triumph which made her godfather smile. Georgia's conception of Home had always amused him. It appeared to stretch from the Red Sea to the Yellow Sea – and anyhow her Home had no latitude or longitude, it was a paradisal condition, a freedom, an idea. 'Ricky's gone home,' she'd recently and unguardedly remarked at Edingthorpe, and been well teased for it by every Lammas in the room. Because after leaving Winchester, Richard had joined the Army and had indeed gone out East – but he was stationed at Rangoon, which was the best part of four hundred miles from Maymyo.

'Quite right, but you absolutely *must* discover Italy first,' Charles Lammas heard his cousin genially declare. 'So sensible to leave school. One of those curious Sitwell brothers has described himself as having been educated in the holidays away from Eton, but I'm dashed if I can remember which. Age, age. Charlie, can you remember?' He patted his warm forehead with a gorgeously pavonian handkerchief. 'And why did you never tell me your goddaughter was beautiful? No need to blush, my dear, I've been judged harmless for at least a quarter of a century. Or do I mean negligible? Anyway, being flattered by me is no better than being flattered by an old woman.' He thought about it. 'Or not much better.'

Father who made himself conscientiously unhappy by worrying about unemployment, Charles Lammas was thinking. Father who died convinced the Great War had shown our civilisation to be a mockery. Ned who never married, who's never so far as I've discerned let his gaiety be shadowed by my brother's death, by all the deaths. The hook that hitches not worrying to not caring – but I may have invented that. Georgia dreaming of her East, her blessed state . . .

To revive his cheerfulness, he asked, 'That's a thought, Ned, what are you going to do if it comes to war? Italy looks bound to be on the wrong side.'

'If the next war comes while I'm still alive, you mean? Oh, you don't need to fret about me, I'll die. No call for them to shoot me if they don't feel like it. I'll just die. On my terrace, I hope. Looking at the sea.'

3

—᠁—

Inland, the marble hills of Carrara glimmering pale in the sun. Here at Forte dei Marmi, pine woods behind the beach, and honeysuckle-hedged lanes winding through the pines, and a house here and there.

No, nothing had changed, Charles Lammas thought. Nothing essential. The air among the pines resinous. An old woman in black stooping in a smallholding, mattock in hand. Her husband carrying water from the well, a yoke across his shoulders, two pails slopping. It must have been dry, if they were watering their vegetables this early in the year. Fishing-boats hauled up on the sand – there the air would be briny. Charles remembered Blanche building sand-castles on that beach with Jack, Henrietta asleep in a wicker crib beneath a parasol. They had been just about the only foreigners at Forte dei Marmi that spring, apart from the Mann family, and they had made fires on the beach and cooked the fresh fish, and the boatmen had tried to get Jack to eat the baby octopuses alive the way they did. There might be a few more people now, but not many, and the fish and wine would taste unaltered, and at evening the mother-of-pearl ripples would lap as hushingly. All was well, he told himself, overseeing the unloading of their cases. All would be well. There was Giacomo, standing by the same dusty black rattletrap in the shade of a wistaria canopy of which the station-master was no doubt proud.

Then why did he have to hear that voice? *All these fools in Italy living as if the war . . . Living as if Fascism . . . Living as if . . .* Charles Lammas frowned at the ghost's daughter, who was standing on Italian soil for the first time, glancing around expectantly at the corpulent station-master who held a red flag on a staff in one hand and a green one in the other, at equally corpulent Giacomo now ambling forward. Well, thank God for honeysuckle and pines.

Saturnine by temperament, and most convincingly passionate when it came to works of art, Giacomo Zanetti had married his second cousin Chiara in 1903. A marriage of convenience, to all intents – her branch of the family had the money, his had the title – and convenient they both found it. Her looks, her wealth and her skittishness had caused her parents to keep her on a tight rein. But as soon as she was tethered to ugly, bookwormish Giacomo, and was a contessa, all vigilance was quite correctly abandoned. She spent extravagantly. She enjoyed keeping her servants up to the mark. She indulged in occasional flurries of infidelity, which she enjoyed immensely, and of which she always repented to her confessor, who always absolved her.

'I'm as ugly as a *coda di rospo*,' her husband would remark, referring to the monkfish which had a countenance so repellent that restaurateurs often had their cooks serve them decapitated so that squeamish customers should not be put off. Yet despite his large, mis-made face, and his learning, and his bouts of gloom, he had formidable charm – which was the common explanation given for his having mistresses, and for the sheaves of invitations which were forever arriving at Villa Lucia, and for the way children and dogs trotted after him. Impossible to define, but it was something to do with the apparently absolute sincerity with which he'd take trouble to make sure you had a good time. Something about the way he'd kindle when you asked him about the arts. Or it was his low regard for himself, the way he dissembled his low regard for others. Or it was his inspired cooking, or the pleasure he took in pruning his fruit trees, or – well, charm.

It couldn't have been much fun, being used in matrimony as he had been, his friends would say. He had the odd mistress in order to keep up with Chiara, some opined – had them or didn't mind letting it be believed he had them. No, it was for no better reason than that it was expected of him, it was the done thing, others elaborated. Certainly it was a question not of one lover but of mistresses, Ned and Charlie Lammas had agreed, and had added that within that coldness of his lay a sensuality. Saturnine, cold, indifferent . . . It was the oneness of the indifference and the sensuality which Charles suspected which intrigued him.

Then the war broke out. Giacomo Zanetti had chucked up his university – he'd got his professorship at Florence quite young. He absented himself from the luxury of the marriage which was, for both husband and wife, when all was said and done so thoroughly convenient; from the children – Raffaella had just been born – who were almost certainly his; from his Villa Lucia fruit trees.

Zanetti fought right through, from the first battle of Isonzo to the Piave. Some leaves he passed at home in Tuscany; others in Venice in lonely, convivial debauchery. He was a major at Caporetto in '17 when the Austrians broke through and the Italians lost upward of two hundred thousand men, if you didn't count the four hundred thousand who deserted to the enemy. During that rout, the rabble that had been the Italian Army started to shoot their officers. Clearly the men under his command had not been of that stamp, Charles Lammas had once remarked to him, his intention complimentary. No, it wasn't that, Zanetti had replied. And then in response to the unspoken question hanging in the air, the question how it was that he'd still been alive when they reformed the line back at the Piave, he'd smiled sourly. Luck, he'd suggested. And subterfuge.

He might always have been disenchanted with himself, but you could date his disenchantment with his fellow men from the war. When peace came, he grew too ponderous of body, too withdrawn of mind and too inscrutable of heart even for the most intrepid adventuress' taste. The affluence and indolence of his marriage became more convenient than ever. Chiara was steadying down by then too.

Nineteen years after Versailles, which Marshall Foch had called not a treaty but an armistice for twenty years, and little more than a month after German forces had overrun Austria, thus extending the Reich to the Carnic Alps where in '17 Zanetti's men had broken and fled, he drove the Lammas cousins and the Burney girl to Villa Lucia.

Coming back, Charles Lammas wondered, what was it about coming back? The open Fiat lurched slowly along the lanes into the hills, shadows lengthening, breeze now pleasantly cool. Something elegiac about returning to places where you'd been happy, hoping the good times weren't over yet . . .

The year was further advanced here than in Provence, he noticed. Peach blossom over long since. The elder was in white flower, so was the hawthorn, he wanted to ask Giacomo to stop the car so he could get out and breathe their sweetness. The trees in fresh leaf hadn't yet got that high-summer dustiness. Mussolini could pontificate as loud as he liked about how the Italians needed a war to make men of them – that couldn't stop it being wonderful to be back in Tuscany on a May evening. Anyhow, at Guadalajara his goose-stepping Fascists had been kicked to hell by a rag-tag and bob-tail army of multinational volunteers, God bless them. Charles gazed around happily at the hilltop umbrella pines against luminous distances, the olive groves, the hay fields.

It *was* elegiac, he couldn't get rid of that idea. Doing things again . . . In Norfolk, at low tide you walked the dogs on the sandbanks off Stiffkey as you had as a boy with your parents and with Geoff. In Tuscany, on pale blue and pale gold evenings you came through the lanes toward Villa Lucia as you had done before the war, as you had done with Blanche after the war, and later again with Blanche and the children. (Since his affair with Raffaella Zanetti, Charles Lammas' wife and son and daughter had assumed if anything a higher importance in his scheme of values.) Poppies in the hay, he noticed. Buttercups and vetch along the road. A dog-rose. Suddenly it brought the first prickling of tears to his fifty-year-old eyes, his longing to walk off alone into the countryside. Away from the car's grinding and clanking, he'd be able to hear the birdsong.

Coming back, wanting to repeat the past, stitch the fabric of times . . . To distract himself, he decided that Ned was right, Georgia looked pretty in her straw hat.

Not that his mind ever needed much help when it came to jigging unproductively from this notion to that. This was the last village. Giacomo was telling a story about how the local priest had sold the altar-piece from a side-chapel, pocketed the money.

Georgia looking eagerly about her and saying, 'Heavens, I didn't think priests were like that,' Georgia vivacious, must have reminded him of Jack, because he found himself wondering if his son would come back to Villa Lucia maybe in twenty years with a wife and children. After the next war, Jack returning, remembering . . . Well, there was no point in speculating about what might or might not occur after he was dead. Take it extremely steady, the heart specialist had said.

Rubbish. More positive-minded men than he were working to ensure there wasn't a war, luckily. All the same . . . Mussolini jabbering about how war brought out the highest human energies, war ennobled the races with the courage to face it. The Italians in Abyssinia gassing villages, the Italians in Spain shooting their prisoners. Noble . . .

The cypress avenue, then the honey-coloured old house. In the quiet when the car stopped, Charles Lammas heard the birds singing in the garden trees, heard the insects' hum.

Something amusing about – what was it? A cuckoo here, a cloudburst, that was it. A rainy spring, ten-odd years back. He smiled, remembering.

Jack and Henrietta pretending to be a cuckoo that had caught a cold. How would it cuckoo? They'd cuckooed, they'd tishooed. They'd giggled and sneezed till they couldn't cuck or oo any longer.

Cuck-cuck-cuck-*tishoo*! Acting a charade of a bird with a sore throat and a sodden handkerchief. Cuck-*shoo*!

4

That Christmas at Edingthorpe, Raffaella Zanetti had merely needed to be herself at her most modest to impress innocents like Jack and Georgia with her poise. By the same token, for her to join in some hilarious charades in the most normal manner had been enough to win their friendliness.

On the day of the fireworks, and at church at midnight, she had allowed Bobbie to pay her gallant attentions. It would have been churlish not to. Anyway, he was entangled with Caroline – and the amorous instinct in both of them was alive and kicking and not to be taken seriously.

Raffaella had made superficial friends with Caroline, and been taken into her confidence. Well, that engagement gave a delectable *frisson* to the holiday, and that winter Caroline would have taken any girl into her confidence. Raffaella took no one into hers. Never breathed to a soul that here were mistakes she would be careful not to make, that truly Caroline was a goose to get married so young, and to Bobbie Lammas who certainly was a dear fellow, and handsome, but equally certainly was a dilettante fop.

Raffaella didn't care for dilettante men. She respected her Cambridge lecturers in History – especially the one who, in answer to a question of hers about Charles Lammas, agreed that when it came to portrait painters, Yes, Sickert and John were good, but Lammas wasn't half bad. With sad love, she contrasted them with her father, who before the war had published a few pamphlets but after it nothing, who had not returned to his university, had retreated to his wife's villa and estate. It was good that he had gone on reading, had collected paintings. But she hated to think of him letting the saturnine in his nature reign too supreme, consoling himself with fine food and wine, rather going to seed.

Giacomo Zanetti had little time for dilettantes either, a sentiment which took much of its acerbity from his knowledge that he was one. It was he who had first impressed upon her Charles Lammas' achievements.

'I'll write him a letter, get him to give you lunch next time he's in Cambridge, or invite you to his place in Norfolk. Do you remember him at all? You were a child last time he was here. One of the most brilliant men of his generation.' Considering his engrained coldness, he had been effusive. 'And it's not only your stupid old father who thinks so.'

To smile across a kissing-bough, to be kissed beneath it – what else were holly and ivy, candles and mistletoe for? To flirt a little at dinner –

surely Blanche Lammas must be accustomed to girls making much of her distinguished husband. Still Raffaella took no one into her confidence, gave nothing away. When she left Norfolk in early January, nobody at Edingthorpe or Bure had any clear notion of who had been staying in their midst. She wrote Mrs Lammas a longish letter of thanks. Caroline, who seemed unable to get over the idea that her being engaged lent her some special importance that spring, and who had declared that they *must* correspond, received no reply to her first affectionate letter, or to her second.

A week later, Charles Lammas was in Cambridge too. Of recent years, more than one college had invited him to portray a Master or a Provost, and he was back on such a task, staying at Trinity in a set of rooms in Neville's Court. Here he invited Raffaella to tea – an encounter which culminated in their taking their erotic pleasure with such an onslaught of frank carnality that before they were exhausted he had recalled his inkling of her father's combination of indifference and sensuality.

In the last three years, Raffaella Zanetti, like Charles Lammas, had embalmed their affair among her pleasant memories. Now at Villa Lucia waiting for her father to return from Forte dei Marmi with the visitors, she was in the garden idling to and fro along gravel paths with the scents of cypress and roses, with recollections and speculations.

She was a clear-headed person, and even during her first year at Cambridge had commanded a worldliness in which, fortunately, discretion matched lucidity.

During her first days at Edingthorpe, it had been clear to her that Charles and Blanche Lammas were as happily married as was reasonable to expect. Clear too that in the case of a man of his particular mettle a concomitant of this, perhaps an element essential to it, would be his allowing himself the occasional lover.

Yes, right from the start she had known a lot – from Neville's Court with January rain spatter-dashing the windows and gurgling in the gutters, from her watching his eyes comprehend that she was not a virgin (his predecessor had been a Florentine curator, but he had wanted to marry her), from that afternoon of the gas fire fluttering, and voluptuousness, and not needing to say anything.

She had known that Charles' affairs had been primarily, had been only, of sexual significance. (This was as far as he was concerned. What his women had thought did not detain her.) She had known that she had no intention of contenting herself with so little – and she must swiftly light on suitable tactics. She would enjoy the erotic with a light heart and a free mind; but she was determined to enjoy the social and the intellectual too. As for the emotional – well, they would see.

She had known that, if his wife ever came to suspect anything, it would not be she who had given the game away. (Less sanguine than her lover, later that spring Raffaella began to suspect that Blanche had noticed an infinitesimal change in his humour, some indicative something.) That he should be possessed of a middle-aged wife, a pleasant house, children – this was to be expected. But that his domestic felicity was no concern of hers also went without saying. Her twenty-year-old worldliness had been up to that, as it had been up to the resolution that if she took a lover he would be a man of achievement. That was the phrase she'd used. Perhaps her upbringing had been *too* cosmopolitan.

Sauntering in the Villa Lucia parterre, in the knee-high box labyrinth, she smiled, remembering. She had never talked about her affair with Charles Lammas to anyone – certainly not to any confidante among the other Newnham young women. But now it was going to be amusing to see him again.

She recalled days in his Edingthorpe studio when he was painting that double portrait, and how their affair had to be suspended when she came to Norfolk, and this made it almost more exciting, certainly not less. Caroline had come over from Bure for the sittings – Caroline so eager to oblige everyone, so bubbling with questions, so sweet about understanding that at Cambridge you'd been frightfully busy but next term you honestly would write. Jack or Georgia or Henrietta came in sometimes, to read or draw. Charles' studio was a work-room, but he never minded having people there who were peaceful. On occasion, to while the sittings away they'd taken turns to tell stories or sing songs.

Evenings in London theatres and restaurants. That Cambridge evening when in Clare garden they'd seen a performance of *Samson Agonistes*, and then had strolled along the Backs, and it had been plain that . . . What?

Raffaella turned on her heel at a corner of the box maze.

Oh . . . Well, they'd had this joke about them each being the ideal lover for the other, and that was great, in its way. Tailor-made, they were, reckoned to be and were. But that didn't mean you were always going to want to be a brilliant tactician and someone's ideal lover, better of course though that was than being maladroit and disappointing, and they'd each known the other too was beset by further possibilities, and anyhow by the time they were in Rapallo . . .

Luckily their lucidity had come to their rescue. Very beguiling, the Rapallo waterfront at night: cedars and gulls and yachts' lights. Charles had in the end perhaps been the more lucid of the two. And why not for heaven's sake, he was only fifteen years younger than her father, dead right that he should come to her assistance with a fillip of that incisiveness she'd always admired in him. Fitting . . . Unkind . . . Right, though.

Set free then, she'd had three years to develop a freedom of spirit which . . . Apropos of which there was something she wanted to consult him about.

She listened. Yes, from the courtyard came the sounds of arrival. She went on pacing the garden gravel, thinking.

5

—⁓—

'First I must tell you our good news. Not only is Raffaella to be married in September, but darling Pietro has got his professorship!'

Magnificently silk-swathed and softly imperious, her swags of grey hair twisted up on her head into a kind of horn of plenty from which an ivory pin, a clasp fastened with what looked like an amethyst, and a tortoise-shell comb peeped out, Chiara Zanetti drew the Lammas cousins across her drawing-room to one of the windows so they could admire her immaculate lawn and her chestnut trees in white flower in the dusk. The English lawn, as it was invariably referred to, was one of the glories of Villa Lucia.

'Isn't that marvellous?' She fitted a cigarette into her silver holder, flourished it. 'Practically his father's old post! You know that Giacomo used to lecture at the university, a hundred years ago, before the war. Well, there was this terrible commission of old sages who had to decide between Pietro and the other candidates, and can you imagine, we didn't know one of them! How he was appointed is a miracle. Although I'm so proud now, because it shows how brilliant he is.'

'Going to be a professor, is he?' Ned Lammas spoke excellent Italian, but spoke it with an English drawl – did so deliberately, the Riviera gossip had it, to distinguish himself from those other Rapallo dalliers Ezra Pound, whose accent was good, and Max Beerbohm, who could scarcely articulate the language at all. 'That's what you and I should have done, eh Charlie, instead of painting. Spend the rest of your life earning money and never doing any work. Such a sensible idea! Well, well, I'm delighted, Chiara. All the same, my dear, you're going to have to let me sit down. Age. Legs. Can't stand admiring your garden from now till dinner, I'd fall down with a thud.' In a faint aura of eau de cologne and mockery, the old dandy sat down in one of the ornate chairs, all tasselled satin and gilt scroll-work. 'Hang on a minute, though . . . What about this oath they have to take these days? We don't want any silly nonsense about the lad refusing to swear. Can't pass up a good sinecure like that. Your son has no principles, I trust?'

Lad he might be in Ned's sympathetic estimate, but Charles Lammas reckoned the elder Zanetti son one of the most cunning and dissolute men he knew. The idea of Pietro scrupling to take the oath of loyalty to the Fascist regime, which was required of university professors these days, was so ludicrous that he waited for Chiara's sally already smiling.

'I *knew* I couldn't ask Edmund!' the contessa lamented gaily. 'Talk about having no morals – I ask you! But you, Charles . . . You've always been such a liberal. I remember you in the old days, talking well of Salandra, of Giolitti, people like that.' Her eyes coruscated. 'So earnest you were – when you were young.'

'Oh, I became disappointed by Giolitti years ago.' Happy to be back with Chiara in her drawing-room with her candled horse-chestnuts across the grass in the twilight, happy to find his Italian returning to him, Charles parried amiably. 'As for this ridiculous oath . . . How many people have refused to take it? Ten, in all Italy? A dozen?'

'A venal mob, academics,' Ned Lammas interjected serenely.

'It would seem terribly bad luck for a young man's career to be blighted,' the new professor's mother maintained, her knowing eyes still glinting with mischief.

'Think of the writers who have accepted university chairs under the Fascists.' Charles Lammas' good humour was solid, his voice was easy. An old house you'd known for decades, he was thinking. Old friends. This was good. 'Oh . . . Ungaretti, lots of them.' The man might be overrated and might be a time-server – but then again perhaps he was wrong, and certainly this evening he was contented enough to be tolerant. He cast about for a dismissal of the topic which should be edged enough to amuse Chiara but blunt enough not to hurt her. 'Besides, for all I know Pietro doesn't dislike the government.'

Behind them, the party was assembling before the empty, summer fireplace, below the portraits by Pompeo Batoni and Angelica Kauffmann. In came Pietro Zanetti, with his father's pig eyes and pig jowls, in his thirties already getting flaccid. Getting rich too, on the investments inherited from his maternal grandfather, on the wine business he was developing; the university would never distract him much. Then the De Angelis couple, whom Charles Lammas had painted three years earlier, with their son on whose portrait he was to begin work the following morning – who to the artist's relief turned out to be an open-countenanced young man with a merry smile. People were entering thick and fast now, the conversation buzzed. A Dutch orchid expert, with his wife who had beautiful auburn hair. They had been at Villa Lucia all spring, quartering the hillsides and valleys in search of rare specimens. The mayor of sleepy little Pietrasanta and his wife. An American widow from Boston with a German surname who sometimes bought pictures and furniture from Giacomo Zanetti, and who right now coveted a marquetry harpsichord he was reluctant to part with, but he had invited her to dinner anyway.

'But I *like* it!' he was protesting to her mock-plaintively. 'My dear lady, you must allow me to interest you in something else.' And then, joining his wife's group by the window, and catching the last word of their conversation, 'Governments? I'm much afraid, Charles, that peoples get the governments they deserve. The French – well – what would you say? Intellectually and morally bankrupt? Emasculated? You British pompous and – my dear fellow, forgive me – cowardly. We Italians hysterical, bloodthirsty, not to mention vulgar. The Germans . . . Well, time will tell, but they don't look attractive. And getting a damned sight too close for comfort these days.'

Friends, Charles Lammas thought idly, insulated a moment by the chatter. To be back among old friends . . . The warmth of it!

He heard Ned's drawl: 'How is it that all these gallant Fascists have acquired titles? Count Dino Grandi. He never used to be. Count Ciano di Cortellazzo. *Sounds* good. Count De Vecchi di Val Cismon. Can anybody explain? Perhaps I should have new cards printed, with Count Lammas di Rapallo.' Then a voice asked, 'What's all this about eight million bayonets? The country has less than one million men under arms, surely.' And someone replied – no, it couldn't be a reply – incredulously, '*Mussolini?* But he had a Jewish mistress for years!'

Agreeably islanded in the window embrasure, and resolving not to worry that the mayor even of a place as insignificant as Pietrasanta was presumably a Fascist appointment, Charles dreamed. There was a *Sacra Conversazione* hanging in the hall which hadn't been there three years ago, he must remember to ask Giacomo about it. That cornucopia of jewellery Chiara was bearing aloft like an African woman carrying a pitcher was superb even by her usual grand standards of headdressing . . . No, it wasn't that either. Something . . . His mind went back to when he'd been a raw – very raw – Slade graduate new to Italy. Chiara, thirty, stylish, and distinctly wicked, had done her utmost to shock him – shock, or educate – with her scandalous stories, her teasing, her flirting. And now it occurred to him . . . With that urbane wisdom of hers, with that raffishness and that discretion – had she long ago thought it not unfitting that her daughter Raffaella should learn something of the world under his aegis?

On the strength of this intuition, he asked her, 'Can I send Jack out here to you one vacation? If I do, will you pack him off to all the right churches and galleries?'

'I wish you would!' the old lady cried. For that was what she had become – it made his lips tauten for an instant with compassion. 'I can't wait to get my hands on him. He was a mere child last time he was here. Oh Charlie, how good it is to see you! Three years have been too long.'

'Dead right they have.' Giacomo Zanetti had been telling Ned Lammas about how the government had been knocking Rome about. Pulling down thousands of mediaeval and renaissance houses, till the centre of the city was coming to look much like it must have done in the Dark Ages, a desolation dotted with ancient ruins. Leaving their mark. For instance, they'd razed all the buildings between the Capitol and the Colosseum, laid out a Via dell'Impero across a lot of the old Forum. Oh, fine imperialistic stuff. And they'd made five thousand people homeless so they could build their Via della Conciliazione leading to the Vatican. Christian . . . But now he laid on Charles Lammas a paw so fleshy that the knuckles had sunk to the bottom of a row of dimples; he kneaded his friend's shoulder affectionately.

'Been thinking about you a lot, damn it. Especially when a couple of years back our countries so nearly had the honour of going to war with each other. I missed that English accent of yours telling me what was right and what was wrong. Ghastly business, Abyssinia. Libya too. But we won't talk about that tonight. All the same, you should have called our bluff. The Japanese were watching, you know, taking notes.'

'Can't fight a war on both sides of the world at once, that's the trouble.' Charles smiled back at his old friend's florid, plug-ugly face, white hair, beady eyes. God damn it, he was thinking, if it came to war tomorrow I don't know that I wouldn't sit tight, try to ride it out with these friends here. 'At least, that's what the Admiralty keep saying, and I shouldn't be surprised if for once in a while they weren't right.'

'Nonsense, old man. You'd have defeated our Mediterranean fleet before the Japanese moved in the China Sea. But don't bother about what I say. Ah, here are the girls! Now we can go into the dining-room.'

Emanuela, born after the war the same year as Jack, swirled through the doorway, gaily called, 'Sorry we're late!' Hard on her heels came Georgia, whom the Zanetti sisters had taken under their wing, and who was already quite dazzled by her initiation into Italian evenings.

The last to come in was Raffaella. She stood still, brushed a smiling glance over her parents' assembled guests, and advanced to shake the Lammas cousins' hands.

6

—⁂—

After dinner, when the visitors had left, those staying at Villa Lucia dispersed. It was that see-saw time of year, wet spring one week, dusty summer the next. Tonight the sky was canopied with stars.

Intoxicated by what seemed to her the extremely grand dinner party, by the attention paid to her, and also perhaps by the two glasses of wine she had drunk, Georgia Burney was in a trance. All things seemed magical to her. The Italian cooking – she had accepted second helpings of every course. The Venetian chandelier which cast its pale, mysterious glamour over the scene. The coats-of-arms over the massive doors. The two life-size Negro page boys carved in black wood. Was it ebony? she wondered, letting the word linger in her mind. The two sculpted pages had sumptuous doublets painted scarlet and green and gold, and they too were of Venetian workmanship, Raffaella told her. They were positioned either side of the marble fireplace, and bore aloft five-branched candelabra. Then there were the damask table-cloth; the painting of a sea battle which happened to be hanging opposite her, with galleys locking oars, pennants billowing, puffs of smoke; the incomprehensible language (but everybody, when they addressed her, courteously switched to English); the bonbons . . .

And after dinner the magic showed no sign of dying away. Were orchids terribly rare? she enquired of the Dutch botanist. Absolutely not, he assured her, some species grew all over the place. For instance, there was a pretty one which the Italians called *bird in the mirror*; he'd noticed some growing in the rough grass by the drive, would she like to come and have a look? So this admirable scholar fetched a lantern.

Would Georgia like to see the fireflies? her new friend Emanuela enquired. They could be inspected at once, during the orchid expedition. So the three of them set off toward the moonlit trees – Georgia with a story echoing in her head, a far-off story of her father's about how the ladies of the Japanese court, after dark, had used to go out firefly hunting, capture the jigging sparks in the wide sleeves of their kimonos, where they would continue glimmering and going out, glimmering and going out.

From the pond came frogs' yammering. An owl hooted. Other birds were calling too, Georgia didn't know which, but it seemed part of the enchantment that the birdsong should continue after nightfall. In a few weeks, there'd be nightingales, Emanuela promised her.

Charles Lammas was too old to be aware of magic in the evening, but like his goddaughter he had enjoyed the *gnocchi verdi*, the artichokes and asparagus, the *saltimbocca*, the potatoes cooked with rosemary, the draughts of the estate's red wine. He had enjoyed Chiara's rattling away about her daughter's imminent nuptials too. Partly because the preparations for weddings, particularly country weddings, were exactly the sort of thing he liked discussion of at dinner. (Bobbie's fiancée that Boxing Day need not have feared. He would far rather have heard about her choice of church music, or her bridesmaids' sashes, than have her ask him about painting.) A wedding was an old-fashioned, happy rite of the kind which should be wholeheartedly delighted in; a wedding whether in Norfolk or Tuscany, whether Protestant or Roman Catholic, was one of the ceremonies of innocence. You assumed that the bride and groom were jumping through the hoops for all the right reasons, you assumed they were going to make one another happy – and if you had your doubts, you suppressed them for the occasion, it would be boorish not to. And partly, also – well, in the case of this particular rattling about these particular nuptials, this marquee and guest list and feast . . . Not only did it bring back amusing recollections of Sarah Hedleigh's eloquent anxiety as to whether her tree peonies with their many-fingered green leaves and their yellow flowers would be at their most superb on the day, and what about her banksia roses? There was also the continuing glitter in Chiara's handsome old eyes, which suggested to her listener that she *did* know about Raffaella's and his affair, these understandings were a comedy they might silently share.

Now his host and he were sitting in wicker ⸱chairs on the terrace. On that stage, they had lemon trees in urns, a marble table with a brandy bottle and glasses. Through an open French window, they had a view of the drawing-room card players, sufficiently distant to be inaudible. Beyond the balustrade, three shadowy figures with a lantern were vanishing. The painter had his cheroot, the collector one of those malodorous Toscano cigars from which in old age he was practically inseparable. They had the companionable quietness which will fall between old friends who have talk to catch up on, but who know they have plenty of days to come, so there's no rush.

Of course, if the war that hadn't broken out over Austria broke out over Czechoslovakia, Georgia and he would have to beat a retreat to Edingthorpe before it came to much, Charles Lammas was musing. It was nonsense to think of sitting it out with his Italian friends. Get himself corralled up as an enemy alien very possibly – and for what? He, with a wife and daughter to provide for. Maybe this time he *could* get himself appointed a war artist. If his health bore up.

All the same, there might be useful work a man who spoke the language could do here. No, ridiculous. Just a last twitch of the old longing for action, for that discipline and the sense of freedom it gave. You're a fifty-year-old painter, he reminded himself. It was probably just Raffaella's proximity after three years which was lending a tingle to his awareness this evening, was making him feel younger than he was. Pretty silly, too, to doll up as a desire to be again on British active service what was simply a contentment to be back in Italy. And now he squared up to it, his strongest feeling was one of affection for her father, who had been his friend before she was born and would still be, he reflected wryly, after she was married.

Raffaella sprawling on a Cambridge lawn, asking, 'If Papa knew about us?' and laughing. 'He'd be delighted! He'd think you were terribly good for me. Only he might be afraid I'd hold onto you harder than you'd like.'

Raffaella in a London restaurant a few days after their visit to Ely, saying how she'd dreamed of being married there: 'But, of course, you couldn't be my bridegroom, which was sad.' And he'd just been thinking that she really was rather ravishing, when he'd wondered if she'd nimbly made up this fine cathedral dream.

Heady enough, that liaison, briefly. Naturally, it had all the – all the what? – of the mutual beguilement of a middle-aged man and a very young woman. Hence the laughing at himself, which after a few months his vanity had found intolerable. Hence its having been a good idea to break relations off. But, for a while, all the – lightheartedness, yes, and the absurd charm. All the total unsuitability, and the curiously convincing suitableness. All the danger, for both of them, of letting it go too far, and the vertiginous pleasure of sauntering arm in arm along that precipice while resolutely pretending you didn't know that was what you were up to.

Now, it was her father whom it was wonderful to see again. Unobserved in the night dimness, Lammas smiled at that baggy torso slumped in its chair, those dewlaps stirring as he mouthed his cigar, that gloomy regard bending over his brandy glass.

It was her father whom there were things he wanted to ask. Giacomo who long ago had stopped merely summering up at the villa, could hardly be persuaded to set foot in Florence. 'Don't like the Florentines.' (Well, his family had hailed from Venice.) 'Don't like the visitors.' Of course he knew that any painter was tempted to take to any connoisseur who had believed in his talent and now appeared to reckon it transmuted into achievement, who bought his canvases, recommended others to buy them. It wasn't only that. The way when there weren't too many house-guests the man would go down to the stone-flagged kitchen and beaver away, in colloquy with his ally Signora Annunziata the cook, to concoct some delicacy. The way he'd labour beside her husband in the orchard, maintaining stalwartly that this was an economy, when any fool could see it was one of his few remaining pleasures.

Things to ask him. That *Sacra Conversazione* – where had he come upon it, who was it by? The Fascist censorship – was it as bad as people said, or was a lot of fuss being made about not much?

But the silence was so peaceful, both men were reluctant to break it.

'You must be pleased about Pietro's university job,' Charles Lammas remarked at last, for little better reason than that his cheroot had gone out, or from a mild readiness to point to any virtue in that disappointing heir.

'Oh . . .' Zanetti groaned wearily. With a creaking of wicker, he heaved his bulk more upright in his chair. 'Pass the bottle, would you? Thanks. You won't? All rather embarrassing, to tell you the truth. For months, Chiara was pulling strings. I mean, Pietro will make a perfectly competent dealer, but . . . Well, I can't tell you how many letters his mother wrote. The day the Minister wrote back, her pleasure was . . . excessive. And she got her brother into action, of course. He's Superintendent For Fine Arts, or something, I can't think why. Very much in with the regime. So is Pietro. I tell him he's an idiot. He doesn't listen.'

'An idiot?' Lammas wondered, reflecting ruefully that he should have guessed. 'I'd have thought, if he wants to do business these days . . .'

'Of course.' In his leaden voice, Giacomo Zanetti's contempt for his mercenary son was not despairing, it was just defeated. 'But this gang may not last, you know, and then . . . Still, at least Pietro plays along out of cynicism. He'll probably know when to change sides. I'm more worried about Raffaella's fiancé. Highly intelligent fellow. Diplomat. Vienna. Second Secretary. Rather in the thick of things, this spring. Damned cigar, always going out. Giulio Flamini, ever met him? You will.' If he had allowed himself a growl of laughter, he had also muffled it with the striking of a match and some vigorous puffing. 'Yes, very able man. But he takes his politics too seriously for my taste – though you could say that about most people. Could come a cropper, Charlie, that's what I'm afraid of. Still, I probably get alarmed too easily. Expect he knows what he's up to. Hope so. Ah, here she is. She'll tell you all about him, what a splendid fellow he is.'

Seeing his daughter come out of the French window, with more grinding of wicker the master of the house hauled himself to his feet.

'We're over here, darling, grousing about the ways of the world. Now, I really must go and see to my dogs.'

7

—ɯɯ—

Of course . . . Who else was it who was forever dismissing possibilities with that seemingly innocuous phrase? Alex Burney, that was right. The wire at Passchendaele which the bombardment had failed to cut, of course. And now Giacomo with his son who, of course, did business with the Fascists.

Why did he end up liking these implacable melancholics so much, these bedevilled men with their consciousness of ineluctable patterns of events it was useless to complain about? Why did they choose him for a friend? Charles Lammas had no time to pursue this speculation. Raffaella Zanetti had taken her father's chair.

Their affair might have had the consequence of cementing Lammas' wife and children yet more fixedly onto the highest pedestal among his values; but the moment he found himself alone with her he forgot that. Her oval face, that bow of a mouth, the way her short wavy hair bunched on her neck. How good it had been to be with a woman who talked knowledgeably about painting, who *saw*. And, quite simply, the fun they'd had. When he'd squired her about London. When they'd gone to Sandown for the Easter meeting, and suddenly there was a torrent of rain so they sheltered in a marquee and drank a glass of champagne, then the sun broke through again and they went out together into the rainbow dazzle and the smell of rain on grass to watch the next race. When at Rapallo in Ned's best spare bedroom they made love all one afternoon, the sunlight glancing through the shutters in slats that barred the floor and the furniture. Then they opened the shutters and it was already evening, the wistaria was in soft purple flower, the garden was a drowsy glen of bluey-green shadows, and a schooner was tacking in toward the bay, tacking slowly in the zephyr, the crew calling to each other as they trimmed their sails.

Giacomo lumbered away down the terrace, disappeared around the corner of the house. He had those handsome *maremmano* sheepdogs with shaggy white coats, and he was devoted to them, though what services they might require of him at nearly midnight were unclear, they having for some hours been asleep in the yard.

At dinner Raffaella had caught her one-time lover's eye. Now like him she appeared content to let moments pass in silence. Then the comedy of the situation grew upon them both, their lips began to smile, with commendable consonance they broke into quiet laughter. This was followed by a brisk confusion of questions and answers all so simultaneous that afterwards neither could have told who said what, but all along the lines of, 'Well, how's the ideal lover these days?' 'You look pretty good.' 'Fine.' 'My God it's good to see you.' And suchlike. But not very much of it, because then Raffaella leaned toward him confidentially, as if every urn concealed a crouching eavesdropper.

How well he remembered that gesture – how she propped her elbows on the table, interlaced her fingers and rested her chin on them and let her eyes dwell on his. Some confidence was imminent – mischievous? serious? her mood seemed between the two. The only girl he'd ever dreamed of leaving Blanche for. Well, she'd been worth it, wryly he congratulated himself, recalling his admiration for how she too had let herself dream of this possibility but had not mentioned it, any more than he had. Deliberately not musing too vividly on what it might have been like to sit on this terrace of Giacomo's with this daughter of the house as his second wife, Charles Lammas waited for her to speak.

'Charles, there's something I want to ask you about. Before you meet Giulio. Because of course you won't like him – not that it matters a bit. The question is: shall I get married, or not? I mean,' she smiled, she was languid, 'I'm only engaged.'

Ceremonies of innocence, he heard his mind muttering disconsolately. For someone like Blanche it was fine, with her instinctive certainty that to get married and have babies was the right thing to do, with her conviction that the raising of the next generation was of the utmost importance so naturally you dedicated yourself to it. For someone like Margherita likewise. Margherita was Raffaella's elder sister, and she was a homely creature who had married a man with vineyards near Impruneta. She had not inherited their mother's beauty – indeed, like Pietro she was of lamentably indisputable legitimacy – but their farmhouse was always a cheerful establishment to visit, and whenever you went the mare was about to foal, or Margherita had just had another baby, or the pointer bitch was expecting, or the barn was plaintive with kittens.

Ceremonies of innocence. Or rather, ceremonies which lazy minds like his were comfortable believing were celebrations of the innocence in us, but which more penetrating fellows like Alex and Giacomo doubtless . . . But he must answer her question.

'Your married life wouldn't *particularly* resemble Margherita's?'

'Good heavens no!' Her laughter pealed. 'I haven't changed *that* much. It's only three years. But perhaps I'd better explain a bit more. You see, there is an alternative. I thought I might run away to America. Go and find Mario.'

Mario had been born after Margherita and before Raffaella, and didn't resemble his father in appearance at all, but was loved by that despondent old man with fierce loyalty. Loved, and mourned. Because Mario too rejoiced in the visual arts, and had by Charles Lammas been found a job with Colnaghi's, which after a few years he had left for a post further along Bond Street with Sotheby's, who had sent him to New York – from which city he evinced no sign of wishing to return.

Temporising, Lammas smiled. 'Is your father still leaving him things?'

She raised her eyebrows in delight. 'He's incorrigible! You know his latest trick? He goes around the house writing our names on the backs of all the pictures. When Pietro does inherit this place, he's going to get a nasty surprise. I caught Papa at it the other day. You know the *Actaeon* in his study? Well, it was Emanuela's birthday, and he had the painting down off the wall. You should have seen the spiders. He was writing *Property of Emanuela Zanetti* on the back, and the date. Hadn't told her, naturally. And he never confesses these sins of his to Mama, he doesn't dare. It was lucky I happened to go in, he'd never have got it back on the wall without help.' Raffaella lit a cigarette – like her mother, she was an actressy manipulator of silver holders – and blew smoke prettily. 'As for Mario – but you know what Papa is like where Mario is concerned. He's been positively cheerful since he discovered he can sell pictures here and use the money to buy others in New York – where of course he decides they must remain. The last excuse I heard him give was that here there was going to be a war.'

'Well, there may be.'

In the silence, their confrontation was still a smiling one, although the underlying question was of a gravity they both acknowledged.

After a few moments, she said soberly, 'I knew you'd understand. You do, don't you?'

'I think so. If you stay here, you'll marry this fellow. Life will be . . . Oh, diplomatic and political circles in Vienna and Rome. Rather Fascist circles. And it may easily end in war. Or . . .'

'Or America.' She narrowed her eyes to scrutinise his face. 'Charles, you're smiling at something. I mean, I know my destiny is the most hilarious business, but . . .'

'Was I? No, it . . . I was just remembering someone else who once consulted me about whether or not to get married.'

'Or America. I've written to Mario. Swore him to secrecy, of course. But . . . He could put me up in his flat, to begin with.'

'If there's a war, he won't come back?'

'Oh no, I shouldn't think so. He doesn't have the same politics as Giulio and Pietro.' She rose to her feet. 'No, don't stand up. I like to think of you sitting here peacefully for a few minutes. Wonderful to have you here. Of course, I don't promise to do what you suggest. Mull it over. Let me know what you think, in a day or two.'

'Rather exciting, to bolt. And we won't fight our stupid European war over there.'

She stood beside him, tapping her fingertips lightly on his shoulder.

'Quite exciting to get married, too. Oh, I don't know! Sometimes I think, America, a new life! But then . . . I feel very Italian. I think I want to live things through here. Good night. And good luck with your painting tomorrow.'

Her footfalls receded over the terrace flagstones.

8

Lammas was painting in the small drawing-room, and was delighted to see Georgia when she ensconced herself on a window-seat. But already that first Villa Lucia morning he was disquieted.

Of course, there were things to be heartened by. The De Angelis son must have inherited his good looks from a grandparent, and to these were joined his parents' enthusiasms of the sort the painter sympathised with. So they chatted about fly-fishing and offshore fishing, about Russian novels and Etruscan graves, about the land-tenancy system called *mezzadria* – never about politics, Lammas being anxious lest he should discover his young friend approved of the massacre of Abyssinians to make a new Roman empire.

There was pleasure to be derived from being back in the small drawing-room, which as in past years he had adopted as a studio. Nothing much seemed to have occurred there since his last sojourn – he could have sworn the same logs were gathering dust on the fire-dogs. He liked the liver-spotted Venetian looking-glass, the circular marble table with its mosaic top which cast a shadow on the reddish brown tiles of the floor, the boule clock still telling the same time it had told in '35.

There was the familiar amusement of observing Chiara's headdress when they gathered in the bigger drawing-room. The second evening she wore a cinnamon-coloured silk fillet sewn with pearls. The third it was a purple turban with an emerald brooch and an ostrich panache.

Of solider stuff was the satisfaction of seeing Georgia fall head over heels in love with the place and the people. All things delighted her: the cuckoo-spit in the long grass, the tiny snails which as every May were climbing the stems, the wild flowers – you'd find her, hunkered down at a meadow's verge, utterly absorbed. Then there was the day the Zanetti sisters escorted her to Lucca, and she came back an expert on churches and palaces. Every morning she walked to the farm for milk, with Raffaella or Emanuela or alone with one of the dogs, and it seemed she was becoming a mighty friend of the *contadino* at the dairy and his wife and children. She rejoiced in the moths which wavered indoors, the variety of their sheens and mottlings. She would stand patiently in the sedge rimming the pond to watch the carp, and one day saw a grass-snake and another day a swallow-tail butterfly. So Lammas was contented that he'd brought her here before despatching her back to her East, though it

was a shame his commission rather anchored him to Villa Lucia, because
it would have been fun to take her off for a few days to Florence and
Siena. Still, at least the love of Italy was being lodged in her spirit –
though it was foxing to try to imagine when she might return, or what
the world might look like by then.

But even in the midst of being amused by how Giacomo Zanetti let
himself be beguiled by the gusto with which the girl devoured his peaches
and nectarines, and by the affection with which she communed with his
dogs . . . Something was wrong with Charles Lammas' mood, and there was
more to it than thoughts of war. He didn't know what. Or possibly he did.
Distastes that jarred – kept altering, but kept jarring too. Presentiments
he kept dismissing as ridiculous . . .

For a start, it was humiliating to be so predictable in his dislike of
Giulio Flamini. From the minute that suave, successful man showed up.
Gut reaction, nothing more. The most visceral sentiment of them all, and
this was dispiriting cliché and no mistake, even if the original liaison with
Raffaella hadn't been, dress it up as political antagonism as he might, try
to overcome it as he might.

Lammas didn't much enjoy being despised, either. The way Flamini, and
for that matter Pietro Zanetti too, took one look at him and concluded
liberal of the old school. Not that he wasn't in excellent company, the fiancé
and the heir being just as impatient with the master of the house, though
the former masked this for the time being behind immaculate deference.

Nor that Flamini knew about his affair with Raffaella. The painter
watched him like a hawk when he first arrived to stay at the villa. No,
it was just the fashionable contempt for the English gentleman and the
liberal, Lammas was certain of it – certain with a smile of appreciation for
his old flame's loyalty. You could pick up any newspaper in the country, it
seemed, and there'd be paragraphs oozing abuse. Britain and France were
in decline, those degenerate democracies would never put up a fight –
that kind of rant. Italy's hour had struck, Germany's . . .

Lammas found himself wishing the League had stood to it over
Abyssinia. Sanctions, for pity's sake! and they didn't even cut off oil.
The British fleet lying at Alexandria could easily have . . . No, no, silly
to get hot under the collar. All the same, to be despised by these men
who were so damned sure of Italy's martial glory, and who'd never in
their lives been under enemy fire . . .

Other disquietudes too, or facets of some malaise in him, it could on
occasion feel like. Or a discouragement you could feel properly ashamed
of, and then discourage yourself further by realising your shame was
pretty futile.

He would start with an irreproachable reflection, such as that it was all very fine lolling on the Villa Lucia terrace at evening with a glass of wine, but that if you descended from this patrician haven you'd find a lot of the nation living in ways which augured less well for the continuance of old peacefulness. But then instead of limiting himself to thinking ill of a Chamber of Deputies which could be depended on to pass any iniquitous measure, often by acclamation, his apprehensiveness would batten on his own painting, which couldn't be logical and yet which he couldn't convince himself was illogical. He, Charlie Lammas, apprehensive! Something was up. Naturally, appearing to be confidence incarnate had always been one thing, and actually being it another, but . . . Generally he'd been adept at just dripping enough anxiety into his mood to keep himself trying damned hard, but not so much as to render him ineffective with self-doubt. He'd learned that in the Navy; learned it over again every day since.

Praise heaven for work. A portrait to finish, money to earn. Discipline . . . And anyway, splendid though it would have been to take Georgia down to Florence to look at the paintings in the Uffizi, take her to Fiesole for lunch, spoil her a bit – he didn't need to leave the villa to know what was going on. He could remember perfectly well from three years ago. Those Fascist parades, the uniforms and the tramping and the flags, the shouting and singing, the revolting unison. The cult of sport being organised in every town, football and cycling chiefly, that was an opium of the people being adroitly administered. Recalcitrant journalists and trades unionists being rounded up, socialists, uncooperative souls, hauled off to gaols where they could be maltreated in privacy and at leisure. And now, it seemed, the Jews were the new undesirables. Yes – yes – but why was he fretting about painting?

An element of anxiety was part of getting down to work on any commission. That in the past clients had often been pleased and he'd sometimes been pleased; that despite some canvases he'd abandoned, if you took it over twenty-plus years the balance wasn't discreditable – this never wholly dispelled the tension, and nor should it. There was also the fact that portraits had regularly been his bread and butter, often he'd accepted more commissions than he'd really wanted in order to buy freedom to paint other pictures. Right now, for instance, there was a view of the villa in its trees which he'd done a pastel study of one evening with a view to maybe . . . But it wasn't any of these things.

In the middle of a sitting with the De Angelis lad with his chestnut hair and his determination one day to fish Scottish rivers, while Lammas was mixing a colour it struck him that he might be at Villa Lucia for the last time. If war came – particularly war between his people and these people, which to his Italophile heart would be an abomination. Giacomo might easily die before peace returned, and he wouldn't want to come here when the place was Pietro's.

If Alex Burney had been right, if their war had achieved nothing worth having. Just the collapse of some unsound empires and the shearing of Germany, the manufacture of some new countries to threaten to invade or threaten to defend, of territories to annex and treaties to break and debts to default on. If that greatest European slaughter had been also our greatest betrayal, prelude merely to a lull and then a renewal and then . . . But beyond that he couldn't foresee.

Yes, his painting came into it. If their war had been fought in vain, then his enjoying life since and his painting since were a mockery too. If Geoffrey's death and Michael's death and all the deaths . . . If the achievement was Nazi Germany and Communist Russia and Fascist Italy for God's damned sake. So much for human progress. So much for the self-sacrifice of his generation, the village war memorials, the widows, the girls who never married.

As for how he and the other survivors had settled down to trying to resurrect a performance resembling the old life, and indeed had been downright debonair for a few years. That way of life which he'd assumed was civilised, or anyhow, for good or ill they'd all fought thinking that – conducted in Britain and France and Italy, which were merely the places he happened to know and therefore liked.

As for painting. As for the training and the hard work, the fidelities and the slow understandings . . . In these bouts of discouragement it all seemed too inane to contemplate. As for the piecings together of loveliness – high-falutin nonsense.

Peace time! All the working to make ends meet, all the getting married and having babies and falling in love sometimes, the fretting about the education of this healthy new crop of cannon fodder. Best not thought about too much. Might not be good for his hand, his painting hand.

One good thing was, that first evening when Raffaella had left him alone on the terrace, he had almost effortlessly decided to advise her to marry her diplomat.

9

—⁓—

For days, gales of rain flailed the hay fields, tattered the acacia groves. The villa's gargoyles spouted cascades. The usually placid pond where the carp fattened was beaten choppy; at its outlet the sluice had to be raised, so the stream rose to winter turbulence. In the intervals between the downpours, the cold wind meant you couldn't smell the elderflower and the may.

Then the storms blew over. Birdsong resumed in the thickets, the finches' nests dried. The breakfast table, which for nearly a week had been laid in the dining-room, was once more laid in the loggia. Working on his portrait, Charles Lammas could open the windows again, let the mild air in. In the big drawing-room, the evening fires which during the foul weather had been lit again were once more discontinued, amid everyone's protestations that surely at last the season of log fires was over for this year.

Lammas had been watching to see if his goddaughter's delight in her discovery of Tuscany would desert her, if her moods would start to veer as so often they did; but she seemed to be on an even keel.

Giulio Flamini had returned to his duties at Vienna, dignified in his consciousness of their importance, leaving Pietro with nobody to gossip about the regime with, leaving Raffaella with a gleam of amusement in her eyes. Yet Flamini, present or absent, was marginal to Lammas' unaccustomed despondency. Indeed, he had quite enjoyed asking him about how Italy had done damn all for her ally Austria when the German army had lumbered across the border a couple of months ago.

The portrait was nearly finished. The sitter no longer came to Villa Lucia every day. Lammas was painting the background, which included not only a pilaster and half an embrasure but also Georgia on the window-seat, Georgia with her tilted-up nose and her freckles and her many-tinted hair, sitting with her elbow on the sill gazing out to the garden.

Every afternoon about five o'clock, when the sun was low enough for the shadows to begin to be interesting, he carried his easel and paint-box up the hillside, worked for a couple of hours on his landscape of the villa in its cedars and cypresses. After several drawings he'd settled on the view he wanted, and for a few days after the storms the distances were deeper than they had been, the sky had a fresh translucency, all the colours of the countryside seemed to have been washed clean.

The spot Lammas had chosen was in an olive grove. It was peaceful there among the gnarled trees, in the green and grey shade, and he found he liked being alone more sharply than usual. Even his cousin Edmund's company had been irking him. Oh, of course Ned's irrepressible frivolity was a perfectly legitimate way of keeping one's spirits up . . . But it could grate sometimes, and possibly contained an element of selfishness. Anyhow, it revived memories of Roland, and Charles Lammas disliked to be reminded of his own distancing himself from his father's despair after the war.

Lizards scuttled through the grass. Sheep-bells tinkled from the far hillside, and then the church bell would ring for evensong, and slowly as he painted Lammas would feel the Arcadian calm restoring him. There was a tiny butterfly which seemed very abundant and which he liked because they had no markings, were simply pale sky-blue. And one afternoon there had been a hatch of blue damsels, the olive grove was aflutter with their diaphanous wings.

All the same, things rankled which should only have niggled. That jerk Flamini so bloody cocksure, with his embassy parties to be elegantly dressed at, with Raffaella at his disposal – Lammas scowled at the idyllic landscape in which that young lady had grown up – Raffaella for his exclusive enjoyment, his use . . .

Really! he exhorted his unreliable mind, these were unbecoming thoughts. And such vitriol was out of place. Because the notable upshot of Flamini's visit had not been his succumbing to dislike of him. It had been his liking Raffaella rather less.

Easy enough to resolve to urge Raffaella to convert her engagement into a marriage. Base pride had indicated to the painter that he would not behave in any manner she might interpret as motivated by pique.

But then it had been easy also not to seek out an interview. Let her wait . . . Giulio Flamini wasn't bad-looking, he was making money, thirty-five was a suitable age. When you'd said that much you'd gone as far as the facts justified, and indubitably his virtues didn't add up to such a brilliant proposition as would reflect flatteringly on his fiancée. He toed the party line. He might rise one day to ambassadorial rank, if the regime lasted. She wasn't in love with him. She'd lately turned twenty-four, had begun to think she might get married one day. A diplomat was an unexceptionable choice. Naturally she would continue to take an interest in the arts, like any Foreign Office wife.

Taken overall, seeing Raffaella again made Lammas regret his affair with her. Sorties to France and Italy with Blanche back in the twenties – she was his real love, always would be, and those had been the grand fine times, that had been the world at the happiest he'd known it. He was musing to this effect one evening when he saw Giacomo plodding up through the olive grove toward him.

Zanetti had been out to watch the men reaping what disappointing harvest they could from one of his storm-belaboured hay fields. Now from his hill meadows dotted with free-standing oaks and walnuts he had come looking for his friend. Naturally he knew Charles was painting the villa – not for the first time. He had chatted with him while he stretched a canvas. But he hadn't seen what progress had lately been made on the picture. Now he puffed up through the whispering grasses and the lengthening shadows of the olive trees, stood looking over the painter's shoulder.

It seemed Zanetti had not come to talk about art, or about the harvest. After a few moments he grunted, sat down on the stump of a tree that had died and been felled, lit a cigar.

The setting sun was flinging aureate swathes across the countryside, Lammas worked intently. He could put finishing touches to his painting back in his Edingthorpe studio, but this was the light he wanted to capture. The sentinel cypresses so dark a blue green; radiance spangling through the gaunt boughs of the cedars. The ochreous villa and its grey terrace half in shadow now, white doves circling from shade to brightness and back to shade, the low sky palely flaming while higher up where the swifts were hunting midges it was clearest blue.

At first the quietness between the two men was companionable, then the painter forgot his host was there. Magnificent, the slowness and silence of the evening burning itself away. That was what he wanted to paint. That time which seemed to linger, to beat more slowly in the air and in his mind, then to beat more slowly and softly yet, till you could imagine it might not beat any more, might fade away. That peace which stilly commanded from his easel to the far blue hills, from the lizards up to the swifts.

The light was altering all the time, and by seven o'clock it was so different that Lammas stopped work. He got his gear ready to carry down the slope.

Zanetti was still sitting on his stump, ancient straw hat pulled over his eyes, cigar in the corner of his mouth.

'It seems we've sunk another of your ships,' he remarked. 'In Spanish waters. If things go on like this, it's going to get difficult to patch up.'

Sensing that his old friend was in communicative vein, Lammas took out his case made from *E35*'s periscope, lit one of his cheroots. That if it did come to another European war their countries might be aligned as enemies . . . The prospect was so blankly appalling that hitherto they'd made light of it. And if you didn't make a joke of it, what could there be to say? Britain and Italy had always been allies. Giacomo's and his friendship had started in peace time; but after they'd fought through the Great War on the same side, they'd had that combatants' loyalty, that knowledge the old men and the women and boys didn't have. And if now their sons . . .?

It appeared Zanetti knew what he'd come to say, his jowls were working again.

'The French and you are going to have to fight Germany, sooner or later. That is, if you want to remain Great Powers – and you do. As for us . . . I only hope we have the nous to keep out of it. Thinking of which – and it's only apparently a *non sequitur* . . .' He adjusted his straw brim so his gloomy eyes could smile shaded and direct into Lammas'. 'What do you reckon, shall we have her marry him?'

'Could you stop her?'

'Might do.' The extinguished cigar in Zanetti's bulbous lips wagged to the rhythm of his ruminations. 'Listen, I've been thinking. Our generals keep telling the Duce he hasn't a chance in hell, but he's a bellicose bastard. Vain, too. Thinks he can use the Germans, and not be used by them. And if this country goes to war, the consequences could be – well, you see, I'd like to get the girls clear away. Can't do anything about Margherita and her family. Still, at least they're sensible enough to keep their heads down. But Emanuela isn't going to Cambridge, I'm afraid. It's America for her, Vassar. And then it occurred to me, and it's occurred to Mario too, that if we all three . . .'

'Three?'

Charles Lammas hoped his shame was not visible on his warm face. There he'd been in supercilious insensitivity consigning Raffaella to a loveless marriage in government circles on what might well be the eve of a war Italy might well lose, in other words exposing her to danger. He, her old lover! Her parents' old friend!

'Yes. Mario, you, me. She won't listen to her mother. Anyhow, Chiara likes the fellow. Fancies being invited to Vienna.'

'If we try to persuade her to break off her engagement?' Lammas' voice hadn't so nearly stammered for years. 'Urge her to go to America with Emanuela, join Mario?'

'That's right.' The old man on the olive stump looked into his friend's eyes with dignity, but through it transpired the most tremulous of hopes. 'I don't like the turn things are taking here. Don't much care for the company she's mixing with, to be honest with you. Seems to me she might get caught in the wrong place at the wrong time. But if her brother and you and I all said the same thing, we just might, you never know . . . Though she's pretty headstrong.' His voice was gruff, his cigar twitched. 'I have an idea it's fairly important. I may be wrong. Anyway, Mario is writing to her.'

'Certainly I'll try,' Lammas said hurriedly. 'Like a shot. This evening. Let's hope.'

'Thank you,' Giacomo Zanetti said simply. He heaved himself to his feet. 'I knew I could rely on you.'

10

Leaving Italy for France a few days later, Charles Lammas' last exchange with Raffaella Zanetti was only one reason for his unrest.

For a start, the evening after his conversation with her father he had failed to get her alone for so much as five minutes. When all through the following day this pattern was repeated, he began to suspect she was avoiding him.

To his shame, he found he was thinking ungenerously of her. That she hadn't told Flamini about her affair with him no longer seemed a charming loyalty. Not that he could think what it *did* seem, or why she should have told him. Anyhow, suddenly it would not have been disagreeable if Flamini had known Raffaella had been his lover before. As for her enjoying her fling with the Florentine curator when she was eighteen, and now at twenty-four accepting her diplomat's proposal, the progression was dully predictable. Lammas knew he was being unfair, but he couldn't help deciding she disappointed him.

By the time two days and nights had passed since the meeting in the olive grove, he was feeling annoyed with Raffaella for preventing him from fulfilling his promise to her father. Then a thunder-storm trapped her with him in the loggia. It was one of those summer perturbations when a cold wind springs up and as abruptly dies. Black clouds thicken. Growls of thunder send everyone who is out in the fields and the garden hastening for shelter. Over the crouching homesteads and the flustered copses, Y-scrawling bolts of lightning crack the sky, and the lower air is unaccustomedly sinister with chilly whispers and damp premonitory eddies, with odours of leaf-mould and fungi.

Then nothing happens. Or rather, the same things go on happening. If the storm breaks, the débâcle occurs ten miles to the north or five miles to the south. Where you are, people take courage, and laugh. They go back out to whatever they were doing before, where the thunder seems to be less eardrum-shaking, where the lightning is still juddering its brilliance on the pale tracks, etching every stone and its shadow, but a little less luridly.

This had happened at Villa Lucia. Then they smelled the rain, which had nothing of decay about it, but was the breath of aliveness and fertility, cool and verdant and promising.

The rain advanced across the countryside, falling so hard and fast that it had the whiteness of broken water. In the garden, where now only a heartbeat or two separated the flares of blueish-pink lightning from the peals of thunder, the first large drops fell like pebbles into the carp pond, fell onto the gravel paths and terrace paving like sparrows' eggs dislodged from nests, exploded wetly. Charles strode quickly into the loggia, looked back, saw Raffaella hurrying toward him from the opposite direction, the squall whipping her hair about her face.

The sight of her hectic cheeks and tousled hair instantly dispelling his recent irritations, he said, 'I've been thinking about what you asked me. What happens here could be pretty squalid. Wouldn't America be more fun?'

'Oh, it's too late now,' she responded gaily. 'I wanted your idea of things that week, before Giulio came. You've missed the boat. Curious, Charlie. You never used to be one to stand dithering on quays till decisions were taken for you.'

In the darkened afternoon they stood side by side, looking out at the torrents which bounced up again off the flagstones in knee-high spray, sluiced away down the steps.

'You mean . . .' He was interrupted by thunder. 'You mean you've decided to marry him?'

'I mean that whatever I may have decided, or whatever I may decide, I shan't take your advice.' She finished patting her hair back more or less into its usual, more ordered waviness. 'Not any more.' She smiled at him with a twist of merriment at the right corner of her mouth which was continued at the corner of her right eye. 'You'll find out.'

In his pleasure at being briefly imprisoned with her by the rain, Lammas had forgotten that the loggia had a door into the house. Raffaella opened it, and disappeared.

He stayed where he was till the downpour ceased, then strolled out. In the quietness, he listened to the birds in the dripping trees starting to sing again, to the gutters and runnels chuckling. When the clouds broke up, and patches of sunny blue sky reappeared, he noticed the moon looking very washed-out over the sparkling fields.

The only other indicative moment he was granted was on the eve of his departure. Giacomo and he were sauntering back from an inspection of the bee hives, and they came on Raffaella in the cypress avenue.

'Help, here come the conspirators!' she exclaimed, taking her father's arm, falling into step beside him. 'But I don't mind.'

What with one thing and another, Charles Lammas was as keen to leave Villa Lucia as he had been happy to return there.

The Italian newspapers had dispirited him with their insistence that Britain had outlived its strength. Of course it was just government propaganda – but that didn't necessarily mean it wasn't true. Of recent years, the British *had* given a convincing display of feebleness, and still were.

The idea of the vast, ramshackle empire waiting to be attacked here or attacked there began to dog him. The empire as a ridiculous burden which half the British made fools of themselves by trying to carry, and which the other half hadn't yet plucked up the courage to declare they were going to put down. The empire as a fat, stupid heifer tied up for slaughter. The empire which had brought half-decent systems of justice to a lot of countries which had never known anything of the sort, but which was outliving its own justice now and no mistake. Lammas mulled it over from countless points of view, none of which satisfied him. The empire initiated by sea captains and merchants, whose world-mastering enterprise had degenerated into the placidity of thousands of administrators . . .

Well, at least the prospect of staying with Bobbie and Caroline for a few days on their way through France was appealing. But then even that innocent anticipation soured. The way things were going, how long would any of them be meandering about the continent? Staying with old friends, paying for the trip with a portrait . . . Would he be doing such things next year? In three years? Introducing your goddaughter to Italy, visiting your nephew and his wife in France . . . It all seemed increasingly precarious.

Money was another vexation, which added to the despondency Lammas was unsettled to find he couldn't shrug off. How easy would it be to earn your living as a painter in war time? Would people want their portraits painted? Would he want to paint them? There were moods in which he believed he would not. He was only fifty, he was fit. Surely the Navy would find some use for an old officer?

Still, in the immediate term, when he had worked on his landscape of the villa for another two or three weeks back at Edingthorpe, it could be one of the pictures he would show at the Summer Exhibition next year. What was more, he could ask a good price for it, because Giacomo had hinted that if it didn't sell he might buy it for a thousand or two less, which if you deducted the Academy's percentage . . . So that was all right.

Even so, he wasn't used to being plagued by such anxieties, and he didn't like it. Being dismissed as a relic by the likes of Pietro Zanetti and Giulio Flamini. He'd show them! Fretting about paying bills . . . He,

Charlie Lammas, whose confidence and success as a submariner had so satisfactorily put less lucky and less able men's noses out of joint, who afterwards in peace . . . Then there was Raffaella who had no further use for his opinions, and Giacomo whom he'd failed to help.

He found he was looking forward to getting home to Blanche. To be back in his studio would be good too. If time was running out, that was a reason for making this year's work the finest of your life. Peace, concentration! They needn't stay long in the village near Cahors.

The vital thing was not to brood on the young men who would do the fighting – on Bobbie, on Jack.

11

All through the summer term, Jack Lammas was tempted by the idea of a sortie to France. He hadn't seen Bobbie and Caroline for a couple of years – why not go to meet his father at their house? His first summer vacation was an opportunity to be seized. On his way south toward Cahors, he could stop where there were cathedrals and abbeys. The fact that his father was travelling accompanied by Georgia also had its hazy presence in his expectancy. So after May Week he set off.

Jack had grown into a young man of equable temperament and, with his shock of brown hair and his square-cut jaw and straight nose, pleasant if uninspiring looks. Everything about him seemed level, from his strong shoulders to the gaze his blue eyes gave you, to the apparent evenness of his humours. Just like his father, but without the dash, people said. And, they added, if he hadn't got Charlie's flamboyance, he had an unaffected modesty which perhaps Blanche had bequeathed or instilled.

It was typical of him that, although he was a promising draughtsman, he was convinced he hadn't got his father's talent as a painter. At Cambridge he was reading Architecture, which he hoped would lead to a successful career – success for Jack having two principal elements. The first was that he should learn to design buildings not utterly unworthy of the architecture of the past. (What these buildings should look like changed from week to week.) The second was that this should one fine day enable him to live, if not actually at Edingthorpe Manor, then in a house as like it as two pins. There was, of course, the imminence of a European war to reckon with. But meandering abbey by abbey from the Channel to the river Lot, he thought it quite probable that the nations might yet settle their squabbles peacefully; and anyway his steady nature was not one to let itself be ruffled before it was time.

It was typical of Jack too that he travelled alone. Not that he hadn't made friends at King's. But he wasn't noisy enough to join one of the parties of undergraduates planning summer sojourns together, where they would go to flat-race meetings, and play tennis, and dance with each others' sisters, and drink slightly too much. Packing his gear on the last day of term, it had come naturally to him to depart alone.

When he reached Cahors, he walked to the cathedral, carrying his suitcase. From his exchange of telegrams with Bobbie, he knew his father would not arrive for a couple of hours. In the square, he stopped at a café for a glass of beer, stood under the awning to drink it, looking across at the façade. Smallholders were selling mushrooms and plums and bunches of flowers. He gave a coin to a beggar huddled on the steps, disappeared through the west door.

That first year at Cambridge had been fun, doing the things that came to hand, enjoying them with something of his father's uncomplicated relish for life. Instead of haunting the Edingthorpe library and studio, he had browsed in Heffer's bookshop, and gone to look at the paintings in the Fitzwilliam, and read in King's library. He had gone for rambles through the Cam water-meadows and to outlying villages, sometimes alone, when he mused for hours inconsequentially, sometimes with friends, when they generally wound up in a pub for beer and bread and cheese.

He had rowed in the college second boat, and hoped next year to row in the first. He liked the good-fellowship aboard the eight, the oars swinging in time, their blades splashing and dripping. He liked rowing when the short winter days were growing cold and dim; he liked the leafless willows and frost-bitten sedge, the river ruffled by squalls, a heron rising. But then he liked it no less when summer came. Trees voluminous with May leaf, moored craft with parties of merry-makers – it was all nourishment, and his appetite for life was keen.

From his father's library to his college library, from Norfolk meadows and woods and rivers to Cambridgeshire ones . . . Going to the local university seemed such a natural progression that Jack scarcely gave it a thought. Nothing occurred to jolt his peace of mind. He missed the sea, he missed sailing, but apart from that . . . And there was the satisfaction tinged with astonishment at finding that inadvertently he had grown from boy to man, these days had the liberty to do pretty much what he liked.

Not that, being Jack Lammas, he did anything very wild. But several times he took the little train which chugged through the muddy villages and farmland to Ely.

When he was a child, listening curled up on the Edingthorpe library hearth-rug, Hereward the Wake had been one of his heroes. (Queen Boudicca, that other champion of East Anglian freedoms threatened by an alien imperialism, had been another.) His father had told him stories of how, among the forests and lagoons, the streams and marshes, local men had confounded the Norman invaders, the Isle of Ely had been a last stronghold. Then father and son had visited the cathedral, that great stone ship of the fens forever lording it over the levels which had been drained and dyked now.

So as an undergraduate Jack came back on his own, his East Anglian heart rejoicing in the arable land and pasture, the reedbeds and waterways,

the gaunt mediaeval ark stranded on its hill under the wide open sky –
came back without suspecting that the last time his father had visited
Ely had been in the company of Raffaella Zanetti. Likewise when with
friends from King's he went punting and they passed Clare, he had no
reason to be haunted by a middle-aged painter and an Italian girl with
wavy brown hair cut short on her neck who had seen *Samson Agonistes*
recited in the garden one humid, flyey evening.

Jack was still boy enough to love his father without ambiguity, admire
him without reservation – and all his life he never had Charles Lammas'
instinctive urbanity. He would have been horribly confused if he had
known of the recent vicissitudes of his parents' marriage. And now, putting
down his suitcase in Cahors cathedral and sitting in a pew, uppermost in
his heart was his looking forward to seeing his father. Or rather, among his
tumbling sentiments it was briefly uppermost, and then vanished beneath
others, and then re-emerged on top.

It was cool in the nave, and calm, and dim. An old woman knelt at
a side-altar. A pigeon which had somehow got into the cathedral took
off from up in the clerestory, broke the silence with its wings for a few
seconds, alit on another high ledge.

Jack's love of the architecture of the Middle Ages had its origin in
boyhood walks with his father and the spaniels to Norfolk churches, in
expeditions to look at memorials and rood screens, at fonts and pulpits.
He had inherited Charles Lammas' scepticism, and mixed up with it his
liking for sites which had been sacred time out of mind, his acceptance
of rituals to mark the seasons of life and to propitiate all that could not
be humanly known or controlled.

Today the student of architecture took only a cursory pleasure in
stylistic details. The thoughts in his head kept churning over and over.

The naves and chancels he had seen in the last few days – but also
how wonderful it would be to see Bobbie again. The splendid sensation
of having the summer stretching ahead, and of being a man now, and free
– but also Rose Fanshaw, who had accepted his invitation to the May Ball,
and whom by the river in the moonlight he had kissed. What a reassuringly
solid, practical undertaking architecture was – but also Georgia.

Jack got up from his pew with an impulsive action rarely observed in
ecclesiastical premises. But he didn't begin an inspection of capitals, or
a search for effigies. He fell to pacing up and down in the south aisle,
as if it were his private strolling ground, the terrace at Edingthorpe for
instance, where you could saunter contemplatively or, as in this case,
distractedly.

The Fanshaws had a house ten miles from Cambridge, and were old family friends. Jack had been over there numerous times to help exercise horses. Mr Fanshaw had just about promised him a few rides during next winter's point-to-point season. Of course, Jack reminded himself for the hundredth time, he'd never be the jockey his father had been, but all the same . . .

He glanced up. How on earth were they going to get rid of that pigeon? Scatter poisoned grain on the altar steps?

An hour still to while away before they all met at the railway station. His father would be pleased when he told him how well he'd done in the Preliminary Examinations at the end of the year.

What was it about Georgia, though – her faint aura of the oriental, the promise her stories seemed to embody? The fact that despite that exoticism he felt at his ease with her? (Unknown to Jack, Blanche had tranquilly dismissed his liking for the girl on the grounds that of recent years they'd been brought up practically as siblings, knew one another far too well to entertain a romantic attachment. Charles had not been so sure, had muttered something about a *frisson* of the incestuous.) Well, fairly at his ease. The idea of kissing her sullen, parting lips made him nearly collide with a priest ambling toward his confessional. She'd be going back East soon. Georgia, Georgiana . . .

Suddenly Jack chuckled. Maybe the bishop was a sportsman – why not, in a region like this? When no one was around, he'd let himself into his cathedral with a twelve-bore, wait till the pigeon took wing. Or better still, he'd summon the dean and chapter, all in shooting kit.

Smiling, Jack sat down in his pew again, all his perplexities banished.

12

Charles Lammas' guess that his nephew would approach him with a request for help with his honeymoon had proved correct. The consequence was that the young couple spent a month in Venice in a flat belonging to the Zanetti family, and a further few weeks in a château near Cahors.

In both cases, they found themselves in the shabbiest splendour. The Zanetti apartment near the church of San Marziale had last been regularly visited twenty-odd years before, when Giacomo had come there on leave from the Front, and the rubbish bin had filled up with wine bottles and cognac bottles and precious little else, and a number of impecunious pretty girls had found their way to knock on the door.

As for the château, it had been the inheritance of the French naval lieutenant Guy Rivac – inherited when his elder brother was killed at Verdun. Lammas got to know him when they were both ashore at Toulon around Christmas '17 and his brother too had just been killed

The farm was of too modest an acreage ever to pay for more than one tower to be rerooted. Rivac worked for a firm of ship-brokers in Bordeaux, and when his wife and he came to the château they put up in the four or five rooms they'd made habitable. Over the years, Charles and Blanche Lammas stayed there several times. Their nephew and his bride so fell for the place that they offered to take one of the damp cottages. Rivac was happy to have it lived in, and charged a rent even Bobbie could afford. So for the first years of their marriage Caroline and he had lived in that oak-clad country called the Quercy, except when on their forays to England they bivouacked in the Kensington studio which Lammas had pretty much made over to them.

On the day Bobbie drove off to meet his cousin arriving from Brive, and his uncle and Georgia arriving from Toulouse, Caroline worked to prepare for her guests with nervous determination.

Being brought up in a large Norfolk house with plenty of servants, and in a fair-sized house in Knightsbridge which was as lavishly staffed as was commensurate with Julian and Sarah Hedleigh's dignity, had not prevented their daughter from adapting to life in a cottage where if you wanted hot water you had to fill a pan yourself and stoke up the range.

That morning she had swept and dusted. She had made the beds in which Charles Lammas and Jack were to sleep, unhappily conscious as she did so that the linen was all old and had always been of poor quality.

Still, the day before she had washed and ironed the blue and white curtains and hung them up again, and they looked cheerful she thought. She went out into the thickety garden, picked some vetch and lady's smock and buttercups, put the bunch in a carafe of water on the deal dressing-table. As for Georgia, there was nothing for it, she was going to have to sleep on the sofa in the living-room. Caroline hoped she wouldn't mind. She put out sheets and a pillow and a tartan travelling-rug, so that last thing at night she could make the girl as comfortable as might be.

At midday, Caroline made herself sit at the kitchen table and eat a slice of bread and ham. Then after drinking a glass of water she set to work to prepare dinner.

Her mother had not taught her to cook – couldn't have done, she herself having never made so much as an omelette; nor had she organised lessons, for the equally simple reason that it had not occurred to her that her daughter might marry a man unable to afford a cook and a scullery maid. So Caroline had taught herself, with the help of two or three housewives in the neighbourhood who had taken her under their protection, and she enjoyed it. But today the importance of the occasion made her anxious.

Guy and Marie Rivac were coming too – which meant that at least part of the evening would be dedicated to naval warfare, which was fine, but also that they would be seven at table. At Bure Hall such a number would barely have constituted a dinner party at all – but here it was problematic, because there were only six chairs, and Bobbie had recently broken *two* wine glasses out of the eight, and the knives and forks were going to be a very odd assortment indeed. And it was all very well Bobbie lounging around this morning, saying, 'For heaven's sake, it's only Uncle Charles!' in that irritated voice which made her flush, and even brought tears to her eyes, which she knew was silly but she couldn't help it. Since the days of her engagement she had lost a little of her awe of Charles Lammas, but not much. The prospect of entertaining him had been worrying her ever since the visit had been arranged.

The drowsy afternoon was beginning to lose its harshest heat when Caroline realised that Bobbie had forgotten to fetch the artichokes she'd asked him for. She took a basket and a knife and went out.

The trouble was that the vegetable garden which some cottager had established long ago had been abandoned, so you got clumps of broom among the currant bushes, brambles tangled up with artichokes, convolvulus all over straggling raspberry canes. Guiltily remembering how many times Bobbie and she had determined to be conscientious gardeners, Caroline scrambled down a slope where wild fennel was sprouting, noticed the bramble was in flower, scratched her shin and said 'Ouch!' The other trouble was that now her stew was simmering she had begun to fear it had been the wrong choice. It was a local recipe, made with Toulouse sausage and beans and herbs, and Bobbie and she both liked it. But would Guy and Marie think it was dreadfully simple, peasant cookery? Would people want hot stew on a summer evening? What would Uncle Charles think of the girl his nephew had married? Standing in the sultry dell cutting artichokes, and recollecting how discontented Bobbie had been recently, Caroline flushed miserably for the second time that day. There was no time to lose. Sweating, she shoved through the undergrowth back up the hill.

A few yards from the cottage door stood two magnificent lime trees, and in their shade there was a trestle table. The lime flower made the air sweet. Beyond the oak spinney, you could see the stone turrets of the château. Spreading a cloth over the table's cracks and worm-holes, going to the kitchen and back for cutlery, Caroline thought the scene looked charming. Really, being embarrassingly hard-up didn't matter all that much, if you could live like this. Shadows lengthening, church bells sounding faintly from the village, the table set under the trees . . . It all appeared the rural idyll they'd hoped it would be. No – the idyll it often still was, she reminded herself.

Was that the car bumping back along the track? She listened. No, luckily not. Probably she still had half an hour. Now, the next thing was to heat up lots of water so she could have a bath and wash her hair.

For a few moments she lingered under the limes, listening to the bees. The table looked fine, she assured herself, despite the plates being the cheapest the village shop sold. As for a seventh chair, she'd fetch the one from beside their bed. And just think, all those fancy wedding presents, half of them still in boxes at Bure, and no one had thought to give them a dozen spoons.

Wood-pigeons were cooing in the spinney. Down the valley, a field of lavender was a patch of the royalest blue. Wondering what she had forgotten to do, Caroline moved around her table, straightening a napkin, picking up a glass to make certain it was quite clean.

The western sky looking glamorously gold and blue and pink. Tufts of grass on the roof of the outhouse Bobbie used as his studio. Her favourite creamy table-cloth. It *was* idyllic. Those sun-flowers, a thistle's purple head . . .

Water. Her hair. What time was it? Recollecting the simplicity of the cottage's bathroom, and hoping Uncle Charles wouldn't mind, Caroline hurried indoors.

Vinaigrette to go with the artichokes, that was it. She hadn't yet made the vinaigrette.

13

—m—

'Well, here we are,' said Bobbie Lammas cheerfully as he parked his car in the shade, noticing with irritation his wife's timid face peering from behind their bedroom curtain. She must still be prinking in front of her looking-glass.

But in ten minutes he'd organised a game of *boule* in the dusty yard behind the cottage. It was a pretty spot, with logs already stacked under a lean-to for next winter, and a clematis in flower on the stone wall, and an apple tree.

Jack and Georgia had never played *boule* before and were keen to out-perform each other, though to begin with they always lobbed their balls far too vigorously or let them fall feebly short. Also, the girl kept exclaiming that she wanted to live in a cottage this charming, or that she couldn't wait to be tucked up in bed on the sofa, and kept abandoning the game to inspect the fox-gloves and snap-dragons. As for Jack, he couldn't decide if he were most delighted to see his father, whom he had at once informed about the First he'd got in his exams; or Georgia, whom after defeating her in one game he decided it would be wonderful to be defeated by in the next; or his cousin, who in his white flannel trousers and cotton shirt, with his handsome sun-tanned face and his genius for instigating merriment, seemed exactly his old self.

Charles Lammas was pleased when he heard that Guy Rivac was expected for dinner. Having lately been too assiduously haunted by the clipped accents of Alex Burney's despair, and having failed to alleviate Giacomo Zanetti's saturnine anxiety, the prospect of a bit of old sub-mariners' gossip was invigorating. That war had, after all, been won.

Bobbie arbitrated disputed points, and with a twinkle in his eye asked his uncle what sort of fellow Raffaella was marrying, and pretended to be put off his game by Georgia's enchanting proximity. Then hospitably he brought out a bottle of *pastis* and a jug of water, and emptied his own glass several times.

Consoled by the lively voices sounding from the yard, Caroline took her time changing. Not that she hadn't mulled over which dress to wear on the occasion of the Lammas contingent's descent upon her. But she had mulled without coming to a decision. Not that she had bought any new dresses since her wedding, either – though on the rare occasions when she was in London her mother had been generous. Still, living as she did she had few opportunities to go in for much finery, and some of her loveliest dresses she had worn so infrequently that everybody had forgotten them.

Caroline was aware that her looks were her best card. Aware of it wistfully, when every now and then she decided to spend money at the hairdresser's in Cahors, and remembered the elegant establishment in Knightsbridge where in years gone by her golden curls had been fussed over. Aware of it rejoicingly whenever she seduced Bobbie, and thought that whatever else you might say about their marriage it wasn't an erotic failure – rejoicingly, and then with self-contempt. Indeed, sometimes these days she reflected that her looks were her only card – turned this supposition in the light of her new bitterness, and with revived regret that she'd let her mother persuade her not to bother about going to Cambridge. If she had only spent three years there reading, and then taken her degree, as she'd heard Henrietta was intending to do . . . Things might have been inspiringly different. So she let them finish their game of *boule* uninterrupted, and tried on several dresses.

Caroline need not have fretted about her stew. Marie Rivac declared her an accomplished French cook, and everyone agreed the local country dishes were what they liked best, and they mopped up the spicy juice with hunks of bread. Her blue muslin dress was just right for the occasion too, and showed off her figure pleasingly – she could tell from the good humour with which the veterans broke off their naval chat to talk to her.

The summer dusk was slow. When it grew shadowy, Georgia offered to fetch the hurricane lanterns, and Jack leaped up to help her with such swift attentiveness that everyone smiled and caught each others' eyes. The oblivious pair checked the paraffin, they lit the wicks and replaced the glass cylinders, hung the two lanterns from convenient low branches of the lime trees. The first bats were out, jinking by the cottage eaves and about the garden. Hesperus appeared, and then lesser stars. From down the valley a tawny-owl called, and then a barn-owl startled them all by shrieking from somewhere close in the thickets.

Guy Rivac told a story about Charles Lammas at Gibraltar – much to Jack's delight, who hadn't heard it before and still took the most straightforward pride in his father's exploits. Apparently at dinner with the Governor one evening Lammas had allowed himself to suggest that the harbour's anti-submarine defences might be defective, and the senior officers present had dismissed his idea out of hand. So what did the dare-devil do? Interrupted by protests from the protagonist of the episode,

Rivac beamed at the table of listeners. Took *E35* to sea next morning, without breathing a word to a soul, that was what he did, and then to prove his point he . . . Couldn't they guess? Brought her back in through the defences as if she'd been a German raider, and got away with it by God, much to the fury of the harbour commander.

Bobbie wasn't a bit listless, Caroline observed with relief, and didn't snap at her about anything. It was true that, when Uncle Charles declared that in the morning he was coming to his studio to see what he'd been up to lately, he changed the subject with a nervous scowl. But a minute later he was telling stories about how last summer he'd helped with the lavender harvest, he was just like in the old days.

When Guy and Marie Rivac had strolled away toward their dilapidated turrets, Caroline took Georgia indoors to prepare her bed.

Left alone with his uncle and his cousin beneath the lime trees, Bobbie Lammas' whole manner changed. He stared morosely after his retreating wife's back, shrugged, flopped back into his chair with none of his old debonair grace. He took some more Calvados. (They were pretty, nineteenth-century glasses, not much more capacious than thimbles, which Caroline had been delighted to buy cheaply in a backstreet of Cahors.) He lit one of the French cigarettes he favoured these days because they cost less than Turkish. Twice he seemed about to say something. Each time he thought better of it, went on gazing away over the darkened countryside.

Then it seemed Bobbie could restrain himself no longer. Abruptly he jammed his elbows on the table.

'It's a bad business!' he burst out to Charles Lammas. 'Damned bad, eh? And to think how gaily one went into it!'

He glanced at Jack, appeared to conclude that he was grown-up enough to be included in the discussion. 'If you want my advice, don't ever get married, or not till you're too old to be good for anything better,' he said in a rough voice his cousin had never heard before, and which made him flinch. 'If you fancy a girl, take her to bed if she feels like it, forget her if she doesn't. That's all there is to it.' He sounded vindictive – poor blushing Jack couldn't understand why. 'Take her to Paris, do anything you like, but don't marry her.' He gulped his Calvados. 'There's no point.'

Bobbie sat staring into the night. His brown fingers twirled and jigged the thimble glass on the tablecloth; it was the same nervous playing as when, years before at Edingthorpe, he had danced an Indian statuette on the drawing-room mantelpiece.

'Well . . .' He jerked his attention back to his older listener. 'Thank God I took your advice about not having children straight away. Christ! Can you imagine? Give yourselves time to see how things work out, you said. Good old Uncle Charles, full of wise advice for young fools. Well, I've seen all right.'

In dismay, Jack regarded the cousin he'd always hero-worshipped. Bobbie *looked* the same, sleeves rolled up, irritably swatting away a mosquito. Jack turned to his father for guidance. Lammas was frowning wearily. His son, for the first time in his life, thought how old he appeared.

'Of course you can put your head into my – into that shed,' Bobbie was saying. 'But I can tell you right away, you won't find anything there worth looking at. Waste of money to frame most of them. I'm not under many illusions these days. I mean, that fellow at the Mathers Gallery was right.' He scowled, set his glass down to refill it. 'All the fellows at all the bloody galleries have been right.'

'Oh, come on,' Lammas expostulated to Jack's relief, in a voice that indicated he reckoned enough of a to-do had been made about not much. 'These things take perseverance, dear lad.'

'No . . . I mean, it's jolly nice of you to be cheerful, Uncle Charles. But I haven't got your talent, and you know it. Haven't got your capacity for hard work, either. Know what I thought I might do? Join the Army. Especially if there's going to be a war. And, well . . . Something to do.'

'A bit tough on Caroline,' Lammas observed with inflexible composure.

'Oh, I don't know. At least I'd get paid. I'm sick of earning twenty quid here and twenty quid there for pictures I can't bear to look at. Did you see the portrait I painted of the Rivacs' cousin Sophie? It was awful. And we wouldn't be stuck here in this . . .'

'Guineas, my boy. Always insist on being paid in guineas. Now, that painting of the stable-yard you showed me a year or so back. Have you done others along those lines? And what about sending in something to the Summer Show?'

'It's no good, honestly. I'm through with all that. But I hope His Majesty will find a use for me.' Bobbie swigged his Calvados with a brio which augured well for at least some aspects of military life. 'For God's sake, Jack, look a bit more cheerful, can't you? Oh yes, Uncle, I know what I wanted to ask you. What's the nearest cavalry regiment to home? Damned if I'll do anything so pedestrian as join the infantry. Must have a horse.'

'Quite right.' At this flicker of his nephew's old spirit, Lammas smiled. 'Though I believe you'll find that as a cavalry lieutenant you'll have two horses, and they call them chargers. Let me think . . . the nearest to Norfolk are probably the Sherwood Rangers.'

'Sherwood Rangers? Right. You don't happen to know who the colonel is?'

Inside the cottage, Caroline and Georgia had finished making up a bed for the latter on the sofa, and had sat down to talk.

'Burma . . .?' Caroline was wondering. 'You were born there, yes, it's your home, I understand that. But couldn't you put off going back? University is such a marvellous opportunity!' She took the girl's hand. 'Go to Cambridge if you can, *make* the possibility! I wish I had. I wish it passionately.'

FOUR

1

—∞—

Charles Lammas stood on the ferry's deck in the morning sun, watching the English coast. Foulness Point and Mersey Island, the Blackwater and the Naze – it was a landfall he'd made many times, aboard ships, aboard friends' yachts, and he was enjoying this homecoming to the green, low-lying country.

Farther along the rail, Jack and Georgia were oblivious, in consultation about something or other. Anyway, neither of them would have his feeling for this sea and this island, for this sailing in from deep-sea blue to shore-sea green. In today's sunshine the North Sea *was* blue, what was more. Lammas gazed contentedly at a trawler with her entourage of gulls rising and falling and circling at her stern, looked ahead to try to make out the mouth of the Stour.

A sea he knew well, with its black and white lighthouses on headlands and islets, with its red lightships moored on shoals. His mind idled happily among voyages and regattas. The morning Blanche and Bobbie and he had taken old *Golden Eye* out of Yarmouth to cruise down to Aldeburgh for the racing the following week. *Golden Eye* was only a half-decker, but it had been a day like today, perfect regatta weather, and they'd coasted for hours with a steady on-shore breeze.

Blanche! Yes, those had been the good times, her husband thought, recollecting how a few weeks before at Forte dei Marmi he'd realised the same thing. Bobbie up for his summer holiday, at twelve or fifteen the merriest companion in the world, the dearest nephew a man ever had. Still, best not pursue that meditation, it led to . . . And it was sad about Nanny, too. She really did seem to be dying at last, a recent letter of Blanche's had reported.

His mood had changed. Glancing again at his son and his goddaughter, that was what had done it. Glancing . . . And musing once more that their English Channel and North Sea weren't his, couldn't be, because they were children of peace time and only knew about the war from stories. For them, all the wars were stories which reverberated. But he'd fought his. And so suddenly, for the first time for years, he couldn't stare at the coastal fields and villages without seeing them as a defensive position.

Those marshes and pastures in the mild sun, those church towers over estuaries . . . Ramparts. Extraordinarily stupid one must be – the way a few years of peace caused you to forget it, then there was talk of war and you remembered. A low, unprepossessing shore where the sea lapped, the sea which was a moat. A long bulwark where wars lapped, but generally didn't come ashore. And what other defensive positions had been held as consistently as this one? The Sea of Japan – yes. Not many others though.

Now as oblivious of Jack and Georgia as they were of him, Charles Lammas paced the ferry's deck as that modest vessel nudged in toward her wharf at Harwich. *Where the remote Bermudas ride* . . . How did it go? *Rocks, lee-shores, nor shoals* . . . No, wrong. That came from something else. *The watery maze* . . . It was a labyrinth in which you could voyage a long way – even he as a callow lieutenant for a few years had found it could lead you to experiences more extreme than those commonly encountered on the harbour streets of eastern England.

Of the trio returning to Edingthorpe Manor that midsummer day, Charles Lammas was the most orderly in his resolutions.

The anxieties and dissatisfactions which had haunted him in Tuscany were to be exorcised, or at least brought under severe control, and the means of achieving this was to be hard work. Of course, he hoped still to be painting when he was an old man – but you never knew, and in the meantime the sense of urgency which the seemingly inevitable approach of war had awoken in him must be put to productive effect. There was his view of Villa Lucia to complete. It must have been in 1908 that he'd gone to the National Gallery to copy Corot's *Avignon From The West*, he recalled, stiffening for the hundredth time his resolve to paint something worthy of that master's example, show he'd admired him all these years with eyes capable of learning. Then there was his portrait of Georgia to begin.

Putting her in the background of his De Angelis portrait had given him the idea. He was feeling fed up with commissions; it would be good not to have a client to deal with. And the girl was always tranquil in his studio, she'd sit immobile for hours. True, her head would never be beautiful. But there was charm in that tilted nose and those freckles. There was magnetism – was that what it was? – in her wide mouth and cloudy eyes.

'When it's finished, I'll pack you off to Rangoon on the next ship,' he'd promised her. She'd said Yes to this proposal at once. And then he had started to intuit some of his idea's more obscure merits.

Why pay a model for a few months' sittings, as he'd done often in the past, when under his own roof he had a godchild lately grown almost to be a woman? There were banal considerations of this type; but also . . . Well, he was reminded of how, when she'd first been dumped in his care in Norfolk, she had seemed not only a small, ill-at-ease deputation from the eastern empire, but a bringer back of the war too, a bringer back of Passchendaele and of Geoff being killed and her father being damned nearly killed. She'd seemed a messenger bringing him Alex Burney's gravel-voiced despairs.

A messenger, an omen child . . . Yes, ominous enough, the sense she'd unconsciously brought him, the awareness not only of the echoes of one war dying away but mixed up among them the opening chords of what might be the next, though they were still soft and not so menacing you couldn't ignore them for days at a stretch. So that now, when four years had passed and you couldn't help hearing certain tones distinctly, now when Georgia was on the brink of womanhood, Charles Lammas wanted to instil as much of the West into her as he might before despatching her back to her East.

An ill-defined wish, but a strong one. He'd work it out more clearly as he went along. If he couldn't persuade her to go to Cambridge, then – his cousin Ned had been right – they must have her discover as much of Europe as possible before she went home. So – Italy, France, England; so – books and pictures, landscapes and people. He wanted to stock her mind with impressions. The way things were going, God alone knew when he'd next see Alex. He wanted to send him back a daughter who would be as interesting an emissary to meet in the Shan Hills next dry season as she had been here four years ago. He'd spend the coming weeks painting her, but they'd talk also, and he'd take her to theatres and to galleries, and he'd . . . It would be a protracted goodbye, and he was looking forward to it.

Selfishness, in other words. Probably all this was just a way of dolling up the fact that he'd been enjoying Georgia's company more with every month that passed. A way of delaying her departure, of consoling himself for – for what? he brought himself up sharp, annoyed. Well, anyhow, with the excuse of hard work he'd spin it out a bit longer, this unexpectedly pleasing friendship with his goddaughter. They'd start their first sitting at nine o'clock tomorrow morning.

Lammas had other resolutions too. He kept parading them in the front of his mind, like a fussy officer drilling his men too long.

For a start, he was going to remember all his recent recognitions that Blanche was his one true love. He'd fall back as naturally as intention permitted into delighting in his marriage with the old light-hearted innocence. (This would involve erasing numerous pretty faces. It would involve dispelling various discontentments lately jarred into vibrancy again by Raffaella Zanetti. And he must not for a moment be disheartened by renewed contact with his wife's absorption in her running of the Edingthorpe establishment, with her chat about getting the lawns mown, and getting Henrietta and her half-Arab mare to Aylsham Show in fine fettle, and getting the rotten gunroom sills replaced which would cost twenty pounds. Of *course* Blanche talked about these things – why shouldn't she? Still, the whole business was going to call for psychological operations which wouldn't be easy.) Then he was determined to take his hitherto reliable delight in all the Norfolk summer things . . .

All Charles Lammas' resolutions were eminently sensible, and in the cheerful commotion of the family reunion he was quite optimistic about sticking to some of them. Sidney Meade, who had driven the car down to the Suffolk coast to meet them, was beaming with consciousness of the importance of his mission and his successful accomplishment of it. He felt himself to be quite an adventurer, and was looking forward to going down to The Crossed Keys and telling his neighbours about his travels. Jack was talking boisterously about how he intended to sail *Golden Eye* up the coast as far as Morston or maybe even Brancaster. Ellen Meade hurried out of the kitchen, wiping her floury hands on her apron. Charles' spaniels bounded at his legs in ecstasy, then careered madly around the yard, hurtled back with frenziedly wagging tails to have their heads rubbed all over again. Blanche stood quietly in the midst of the hubbub, brimful of her happiness to have the wanderers home. Henrietta, her skinny legs in jodhpurs and a brace on her front teeth, heaved her father's suitcase indoors. Then she pleaded with him to come with her down to the marsh, because in the early evenings the young woodcock had been flying, she wanted him to watch them with her.

So off they went, side by side, past the stables. Henrietta was perhaps obscurely jealous of Georgia, and anyhow her desire to reclaim her father was absolutely right, and her manner of doing it irresistible. When she was little, he had taken her to stand still and silent and watch that year's young woodcock fly about over a reedy meadow; so now that she was all of fourteen she wanted to offer him the same ritual to share.

They stopped among pollarded willows at the edge of the marsh. All the high summer things, Lammas thought, relieved to find how simple it was to rejoice in them. Blanche's bay hunter turned out to grass, summering in a field with clumps of dock and blown thistles. Hedgerow oaks massive with motionless, dark green leaf in the midge-speckled, slow evening. Bramble flower the palest purple.

His daughter with her jodhpurs well-stained with her pony's sweat, a curry comb poking out of her pocket. Wood-pigeons that never stopped calling.

Sauntering back, they noticed a clematis which the wind had detached from the potting-shed wall. By the time Hetty and he were tying the frail stems back onto their trellis so that Blanche shouldn't have to do it next day, Charles Lammas felt he could trust himself not to be irritated any longer by Pietro Zanetti's and Giulio Flamini's ill-masked insolence. He wasn't going to fret unduly about Raffaella's safety either. She'd know how to position herself, that one. She'd be all right. Though his daughter's grubby fingers securing clematis made him reflect that it was all very well if you had Zanetti money, but it was out of the question for him to send her to finish her education in America with Emanuela.

Still, by and large he was pleased with his equanimity. And so far as the arrogance of the Villa Lucia young Fascists went he was right. As it turned out, he scarcely gave them another thought. Or not for a couple of years. Not till one night late in 1940 the Italian Flying Corps bombers based in Belgium managed to hit a canning factory in Lowestoft and kill three people – and then his thought was ironical as well as angry, because it transpired that, out of a hundred-odd raids flown, that modest killing was their only success.

After dinner, Georgia and Henrietta decided that on a night this warm they were going to sleep out of doors. So there was a bustling to and fro with camp beds and with sleeping-bags, a debate about which lawn to choose or would the terrace be better. Then gradually the household fell quiet.

Charles Lammas knew the right thing would be to go upstairs with his wife. But he wanted solitude. Peace, the library. Half an hour to collect his wits.

'I'll come soon,' he said apologetically to Blanche at the foot of the staircase, standing beside the grandfather clock which had come from her family, had been at Paston until the place was sold.

'Come when you like,' she replied, already on the second stair, and laid her fingers on his shoulder a moment. 'It's good to have you back here.'

Lammas went to the kitchen for a glass of whisky and water, wishing she hadn't used practically the same gesture as Raffaella when she left him on her father's terrace, wishing Blanche hadn't used nearly the same words too. Then closing his library door behind him, he thought: So many things to make sense of, and so little time. He didn't know why he'd thought that, but it stayed to unsettle him.

He stood. In the glow of one lamp, the library was marvellously tranquil. He took out his brass case, lit a cheroot. Here was his most familiar ground, his sanctuary. From the hall, the grandfather clock chimed eleven. On the desk was the Chinese lacquer box where he kept Geoffrey's letters from the

Western Front, Blanche's letters from when they were engaged. There was his paper-knife with the ivory handle and the tortoise-shell blade.

So much to make sense of, and so little time. Because it was all very fine making resolutions about hard work and not worrying about things – but he'd always been a worker, and now around his consciousness he could feel doubts lapping like the seas and wars that lapped against the coast a parish and a half away. When would he next see Italy and France? Would he ever again? And Jack, who at Cambridge was already in the Officers' Training Corps? And would he himself in the next few years command the power of mind and the skill of hand and eye to paint the pictures he dreamed of, the pictures which would at last really make his mark? When all was said and done, it was saner to be ambitious merely financially, let yourself fancy you might be able to earn enough to send Hetty to America.

Restlessly Lammas crossed to the fireplace. He flicked ash into the hearth, blew a deliberately calm plume of smoke.

He let his eyes travel along his bookshelves, then on to his father's self-portrait. There Roland stood dimly, in a handsome gilt frame embossed with acorns and oak leaves, life-size in his grey coat, his right hand raised holding his brush in a gentle, hieratic gesture. Old Liberal, old believer in disarmament, old giver to charities. After the war, he'd painted that picture, with Geoff dead. Old believer in imperial education schemes, in the perfectability of mankind . . . But he'd outlived his beliefs.

The son sipped his whisky, looked up at his father who had been dead for, what, fifteen years. That bony, pale hand was beautifully painted. So were his blue-veined temples and melancholy eyes.

Charles Lammas turned, picked up his photograph of Geoffrey in the uniform of the Norfolk Regiment. He tried out ideas like, Your son wants to join the Army. Then he shrugged, frowned, set the silver frame back on the mantelpiece.

One thing he did appear to have worked out, though. That bit of Tolstoy that had kept dogging him. *History as the swarm-life of mankind*, that stuff. It took no account of the will, that was what was wrong with it.

There are two sides to the life of every man: there is his individual existence which is free in proportion as his interests are abstract; and his elemental life as a unit in the human swarm, in which he must inevitably obey the laws laid down for him.

Of course, there was still the problem that most people lived and died without bothering much about anything as high-falutin as abstract freedom. He hadn't forgotten the swarm-life of trench warfare, either, or the swarm-life of London and Paris and Berlin.

But what the hell were these famous historical or social laws, or economic or metaphysical laws either for that matter, and why should anyone reckon they existed, let alone had cogency or authority? Phenomena and ideologies kept altering, luckily – otherwise it'd be a dead world. And had poor old Tolstoy never seen a bold spirit by sheer will-power step clear of the swarm? As for interests which were only abstract, freedom which was just a cerebral impression – what good were they?

Suddenly pugnacious, Lammas finished his whisky, turned, confronted the Winged Victory of Samothrace. Her gait was so exultant, lifting her forward and up. And that way she breasted the air, her wings outstretched. Hers would have been a head to see, a gaze to meet. But even as she was, even beheaded after all these centuries ... Here was pride. Here was defiance of the swarm, here were freedom and hope.

What was that in the garden? Lammas moved to the window, the Victory forgotten in his hand. He switched off the lamp so he could see better, peered out.

A cloud must have covered the moon. But he could just make out two figures in white nightdresses. They were tussling, or dancing. Anyway, they were unmistakably happy. He caught a swift babble of whispers, a whoop of laughter instantly stifled. Then more cavorting, and giggles.

2

―᙭―

The girls wriggled back into their sleeping-bags. They went on talking for a few minutes: about the Zanetti sisters, and Bobbie's and Caroline's imminent return to England, about the projected expedition to London to see *Twelfth Night*, and the dance to be held at Bure. Then they wriggled a bit more, and rolled over, and said goodnight.

Georgia knew she was exhausted, but her mind was too alive to go to sleep. Travelling back through France she'd kept promising herself the letters from home which surely must have arrived during her absence, and when she'd run up to her bedroom on the top floor of the Manor she hadn't been disappointed. There the bundle of envelopes lay, on her dressing-table, where the house-maid always put them.

Now she lay on her back, gazed up. A wispy patch of cloud which had a sort of herring-bone pattern was drifting very high and very slow. Or it looked like a snake-skin she'd seen somewhere. No, more like mackerel mottlings. There was the Milky Way, too, and the moon past its zenith now. And there were lots of constellations, some of which her godfather had taught her to identify, but tonight she wasn't interested in stars.

Geraldine Burney wrote about her hill station tittle-tattle, had for years dutifully written letters which made up for their twitter by always concluding with a flourish of maternal emotion. Chat about the Maclaren girl's wedding, and Mrs Fielding's twins. Then some positively scandalous event which had involved several of the young men at the chummery, and had occurred after a party, only perhaps it had not occurred, she preferred to believe not, and some people were such vipers. The tennis tournament – how lamentably it had been organised, and honestly you'd have thought that after last year's fiasco . . . A picnic and bathing party at the Pwe Kauk waterfalls – naturally Alex had *refused* to come. The new administrator of the botanical gardens, and his extraordinary wife, and his extraordinary nose.

But Georgia understood about hill stations not being places where anything was intended to happen, so of course the Maymyo gossip never varied much. The great thing was, it was news from Burma. So she'd fold the letters up again, and she'd think, Mummy darling! and smile wistfully. It was good to be reminded of the chummery, which was a teak mansion called Candacraig where the bachelors of the Bombay Burmah Trading Company conducted their mysterious existence when on leave –

she'd never been in, but her mother and she had driven past in the gharry countless times. It was good to be reminded of the little church where Betsy Maclaren would have been married, even if you then remembered Emma's grave there. Good to be reminded of the Maymyo clock-tower, and the waterfalls.

Richard Burney had proceeded from Winchester to Sandhurst without his sister and he really getting to know one another again. Their childhood rampages in Maymyo bungalow gardens receded farther into the past. After a while, when they met for holidays at Edingthorpe, it felt ridiculous to go on talking about the terrier Angus, or the parrot that was called Blenheim for reasons no one could any longer explain, or their rhesus monkey who had escaped to the house next door and done infamous violence to the Blakes' wedding-present china before he could be recaptured.

Ricky had joined the Gloucestershire Regiment, who were stationed near Rangoon at Mingaladon. He didn't write often. When he did, they were short, boyish letters, consisting of chirpy accounts of race meetings and of friends he had made. The letters were quite devoid of reflection. *Dear Georgia* at the beginning. *Please remember me to Mr and Mrs Lammas*, and then *Love from Ricky*, at the end. In the middle, the Kokine Swimming Club, the Gymkhana Club. A chap he'd met who worked for the Irrawaddy Flotilla, helped run all those paddle-steamers with their Chittagonian crews, who'd taken him out in a Company speedboat on one of his patrols of the delta. Another chap who was one of the mercenary pilots of the American Volunteer Group, who'd taken him to the Silver Grill and introduced him to bourbon. (The pilot had also introduced him to the dancing girls you met there, Chinese girls and Burmese girls and half-caste girls; but the lieutenant didn't tell his sister this.)

Ricky's letters invariably reawakened in Georgia her unhappiness at the way they had become estranged without wishing to be, without knowing how to prevent it. No, not estranged, of course not. But there *was* something superficial in the jauntiness of Ricky's communications, something defensive maybe. She couldn't pretend she hadn't noticed how they could have been addressed to any acquaintance. *The Monsoon Plate, which High Jinks won by a neck . . . Posh new offices in Phayre Street, and then we went on to dinner at the Strand Hotel . . . Wet season, I'll get plenty of rugby . . .*

What was making her uneasy tonight were two longish letters from her father. Exhausted, but restless, she got up gingerly without disturbing Henrietta, walked away across the lawn.

Alex Burney might have decided he was going to live and die in Burma; but that didn't mean the place made him particularly happy, so far as any of his friends could see. Though friends was the wrong word for them. People he was constrained to rub up against.

How he disported himself when he was away up-country, none of the Maymyo crowd knew – beyond the fact that he was reputed an energetic Forestry Officer, hadn't gone slack like a lot of Westerners did in the East. And after fifteen or more years on the job, he was unmatched when it came to knowing about the hardwoods of Tenasserim and the Shan states and the Chin states.

When he was in Maymyo, which wasn't any more often than necessary, of course you saw him about the place, accompanying his wife to church on Sunday mornings, accompanying her to the club each evening, that sort of thing. His hair was white by his early fifties. His face was gaunt and sallow. In a gharry or a pony-trap, Burney sat bolt upright. If they were strolling along one of the lanes, he'd also walk bolt upright, Geraldine's hand in his elbow. You'd see them pause to admire a garden; or he'd use his stick to draw her attention to a tree that was in flower or fruiting. Wonderful place for plants, Maymyo, soil and climate seemed to conspire, and it was high enough for some European fruits to be grown too. Gardening was one of Geraldine's consolations, and he'd become a sylviculturalist, so an interest in growing things was one of the few points of contact between them that anybody ever observed.

If it was the church to which his hat and her hat and parasol were proceeding, Burney's bolt uprightness would be preserved uninflected, standing or sitting. Even kneeling, he maintained a ramrod back, and an inclination of his head that was the merest formality.

If the club was their destination . . . Well, Alex Burney had a manner of sitting in a cane chair with a tumbler in his hand, in other words doing what lesser mortals called taking it easy after a long hot day, which left you in no doubt that his limbs were bolted at those angles, and that his reserve was sturdily bolted together too. He'd discuss the colony's news with one or two of the men of his generation, and pass the time of day in a rather contained manner with their wives. He never played bridge or billiards – which was nearly unheard of. Hadn't ever been a tennis player either, the excuse being his wounds, though they didn't seem to have hindered his tramping and riding in the forests for years. He'd smoke his pipe, have a couple of drinks. When Geraldine was ready, he'd escort her home for dinner.

Of course, people knew he'd had a bad war, and some made allowances for that. The sort of war that left some survivors in the madhouse, and a lot more who – there were different polite ways of phrasing it. *Found difficulty in adjusting to civilian life* was one. And their hill station neighbours were all sorry about the Burneys' elder daughter, too. Even so . . . You couldn't blame people for concluding he was a bit of a dry old stick. Some went further, and called him a cold fish. And maybe it wasn't all that surprising that others more ribald or more lenient concocted a story about how old Burney had found himself some kind of Shangri La out in the back of beyond.

It was very big, the Burmese back of beyond. Not Ministerial Burma, or what they used to call Burma Proper, not the plains. But the Frontier Areas, those inaccessible middles of a whole lot of nowheres, generally steep and forested nowheres, zones of which, the Wa Hills for instance and remote stretches of Nagaland, were still being penetrated for the first time and sketchily surveyed when the Japanese invaded. There were the Karenni states and the Shan states. There were the Chin and Kachin regions, and the Arakan, and the entire Salween district. All in all, the Frontier Areas amounted to ninety-odd thousand square miles, which was a lot on paper and even more if you were one of the exceedingly few administrators or traders or dacoits who spent years travelling up hill and down dale there.

Even if you just took the Shan Hills, if you just took Burney's bit, it was large. Mighty few people at the club in Maymyo would have been able to tell you how many Shan states there were, let alone their names or which were vast tracts of country and which just single, Arcadian valleys. The local princes still did most of the governing – which was just as well if you bore in mind that for all those Frontier Areas there were still only forty men of the Burma Frontier Service. Then some of the states were divided into lesser fiefdoms, and the mountain dynasties near the Chinese border would have needed a whole College of Heralds to make head or tail of their intermarriages and their eliminations of rivals, and . . . Well, anyhow, one way and another the silly rumour got about that Alex Burney was more than just a rather stiff Forestry Officer.

Nonsense, naturally. Although it was true that he had friends among the princes of the Shan Hills. He had to be on terms of mutual respect with them in order to do his job efficiently.

At any rate, some buffoon at the club must have started it off by chortling that, the way Burney wandered around his fastnesses with such exaggerated devotion to duty, he must have a concubine in every valley. As for that enormous state, what was it called, Kengtung that was right, clearly the old boy kept a harem there. After his dignified figure had descended the club steps among the canna lilies and the tobacco plants at a respectably early hour, vanished with his horticultural wife on his arm into the tropical night, the wits had him a Buddhist and a ruby millionaire and a spy.

Alex Burney was ageing fast by then, and setting in his ways. Still, like a lot of lonely white men in the East, occasionally he'd talk. And not only when, on leave in England, he found himself the opposite side of a fireplace to Charles Lammas, who was acceptable because Geoffrey had been his brother. Acceptable also, perhaps, because the speaker didn't know the listener particularly well, couldn't tell when he'd see him again.

Yes, after months and months of nothing you could call private conversation, Burney would sometimes talk – as Christopher de Brissac discovered in '41. Not uncommon, among British Residents and Forestry Officers – though in Burney's case the isolation from his kind was a condition of life he'd sought. Even so, after months of travel, of trying to regulate timber extraction, of dealing with princes or chieftains or whatever they were, *sawbwas* was the Shan word, in their ramshackle but pinnacled palaces, in their wildernesses along the upper reaches of the Salween so insignificant that even the Chinese had never gone in for much massacring and annexing . . . If the bungalow verandah was comfortable; if the evening seemed conducive to story-telling; if the meeting with someone who spoke his own language felt propitious . . . And his daughter in England was also a beneficiary of this weakness for sporadic communication. So the Matter of Burma had continued to be laid down in her head, stratum by stratum.

For years, the staple of Alex Burney's letters to Georgia consisted of stories of King Mindon Min, quite a scholarly old Buddhist, though even he ordered the occasional crucifixion, and he founded Mandalay. There he had temples and audience chambers, a treasury and a lotus garden, and he ruled from his Lion Throne, his Elephant Throne, his Peacock Throne and several other thrones. Or it was his successor King Thibaw, in whom no flicker of enlightenment was ever noticed, who after his accession had eighty of the royal family butchered. They were buried in a pit in the palace grounds, but not deep enough, because after a few days the earth began to rise up and the air to be unbreathable, so a couple of the king's elephants had to be led in to trample the soil flat. A few years later, the British kicked him out – not because of his murdering, but because of a squabble about the timber trade.

Increasingly, as Georgia grew up, these stories began to be shot through with her father's wonderings about the European presence in Asia. How it had occurred – the planned, the unplanned. Tales of caution forced into daring, of reversals which turned out to be lucky escapes. Tales of highmindedness buried young, and avarice buried young – and both on other occasions rewarded with baronetcies. And Burney also let her sense how precarious the imperial cobweb could seem to him.

Of course, in those Frontier Areas of his up the Salween, the Forestry Officer was grappling with an outlying skein of the web which was of extreme filminess. But even in places that appeared solid enough, like Rangoon and Mandalay, places which if you compared the present with the recent past looked like prosperity and order incarnate, he'd had presentiments of how transient the entire performance might be. And it was this awareness, transmitted to his daughter in two letters opened that summer evening of 1938 at Edingthorpe, which at midnight caused her to set off in nightdress and bare feet across the dewy lawn with her feelings all atwangle and her thoughts shivering.

The British were forever shipping from the English Channel to the Bay of Bengal, it was the most commonplace of adventures. But Burney wanted Georgia, before she did it, to focus on what she'd be coming back to – and he knew that from more orthodox sources she wouldn't get his apprehension of the tenuous, because the orthodox line was that Singapore was impregnable and that, anyhow, the Admiralty would send the fleet.

To know what she was coming back to. (*I don't suppose you'll have the good sense to be put off. I wonder what it was we all got wrong, when we tried to persuade you to go to university?*)

To know the present condition of the cobweb. In Rangoon, if you sauntered beneath shady trees past porticoes and façades, the fabric of empire could appear made of good, durable fibres. But if in the Shan Hills you gazed out from a scarp, and all you could see were wooded ranges and clouds and eagles . . . A cobweb of which the father had tried to give the daughter an idea of the history. (*Do you remember me writing to you about how, until the second half of the eighteenth century, all the East India Company had were trading posts at Calcutta and Bombay and Madras, and the Compagnie des Indes had Pondicherry and Trincomalee? It was after India got dragged into the Anglo-French rivalry, and anyway the Mughal Empire was falling to pieces, after the fighting in the Carnatic and Bengal that all the territorial expansion got under way.*)

Thinking confusedly of Robert Clive leading his sepoys at the defence of Arcot, Georgia meandered as far as the ha-ha, jumped it, went on. India before the Honourable Company had much of an army, certainly not the strongest in the subcontinent . . . Clive after Plassey dismounting from his horse to accept the surrender of Mir Jaffir, who was being helped down from his elephant's howdah . . . She must have seen a picture, but she couldn't think where.

And if the British East really might come to an end one day? Her schooling had left her with the haziest notions of Greece and Rome, but she knew about the Mughal decline. Georgia came to a stone bench, sat down, distractedly regarded the Edingthorpe pond where in the moonlight the lilies were all shut. And if she happened to be alive when that time came? That end of an epoch, that change from a familiar order of things to . . .? If she were alive, present, at home. With Daddy and Mummy, with Ricky.

Her father had written that, if the British went on giving ground before the German and Italian dictators, the Japanese could scarcely be expected to ignore the evidence before their eyes. Of course, he hoped all would yet be well. Probably it would be. But she wasn't to believe automatically all the complacent chat she heard. In his view, letting the Anglo-Japanese alliance drop might turn out to have been a mistake. As for sending the fleet . . . Well, Whitehall might decide to relinquish control of the Mediterranean if the alternative was to lose Singapore and consequently all the British colonies in the Far East. But if the battleships and the aircraft carriers were suddenly needed in home waters . . . What did Georgia think, would whoever was cob-spider in Downing Street send the ships East then?

As for Burma, it was the gate to India. And just because in the last century Russia had ended up not invading, that didn't mean Japan might not be tempted to have a crack in this one.

What was more, Burma was well worth having in itself. The country was Asia's biggest rice-exporter, for a kick-off. Then like the Dutch East Indies it had oil, which the Japanese needed. It had rubber and hardwoods. Then copper and silver, tin and tungsten.

Georgia hadn't a clue what tungsten was. But she had no difficulty in imagining her native paradise as a realm of infinite riches which the Emperor of Japan might covet. Silver . . . And she knew about the ruby mines at Mogok. Emperors liked their finery. And the jade, and the ivory . . .

The girl didn't stop to think what a modern war might do to the country you lived in. Sitting on her bench, she was in the grip of what it might be like to find yourself at the end of things. A mere change of heart would do the trick, her father had suggested. A change of mind – nothing. If the fleet didn't sail. Or if we decided the game wasn't worth the candle. Or if the peoples of the East tossed their heads, and the Western administrators all fell off like a lot of old hats.

Georgia stood up, she strayed through the garden. A white barn-owl, the bird the Meades called Hushwing, came hawking silently over the grass.

Of course, this revolution in world affairs wouldn't occur, but if it did, she must face it at home. On the verandah, she vaguely supposed. At any rate, by her father's side.

What would it be like, if everything familiar disintegrated around you? How would you live, without the life that had produced you? You too would be inexistent, you'd find out what that felt like. The night was temperate, but Georgia shivered walking back to her camp-bed. You'd be utterly alone. Like being naked, you'd feel so defenceless. She yawned.

Then getting back into her sleeping-bag on the peaceful English lawn, she remembered reading about the Japanese Army in China. What happened to people when cities were invaded, what often happened to girls.

Her heart bludgeoning her ribs, Georgia clenched her arms about her head. She lay as still as she could, as if trying not to be noticed, trembling.

3

~m~

Jack Lammas had high hopes of the cruise up the coast with Georgia, he had high hopes of the promised expedition to see *Twelfth Night* in London, and of the dance at Bure Hall even though Rose Fanshaw was bound to be there too. It was true that his hopes would be as bewildering to clarify as they were impossible to suppress. But they infused the summer air with a wonderful effervescence, or so it felt each time Jack took a deep breath, so he pitched enthusiastically into getting *Golden Eye* ready.

More than half the long vacation still lay ahead, that was good. On the other hand, although his father's decision to paint Georgia before she left England was to be welcomed, work on the portrait was proceeding much too rapidly for Jack's taste, and Charles teased him merrily about his anxiety.

'Have to take to locking the studio door at night, eh, Georgia?' the painter asked, washing his brushes after a sitting, and he winked at his son. 'Don't want to find this young man has been at our canvas with a rag and some turps.' Then another time he said, 'Cheer up Jack, this is only a study. I don't suppose I'll start the real thing for another month.'

Making sure *Golden Eye* was ready for sea was the sort of straightforward activity Jack enjoyed. Once he borrowed the car because he had sail-bags to transport. Otherwise, several days in succession he bicycled through the familiar villages down to the river Bure. The hay had been cut, and the barley and wheat were still standing. He passed farmers and corn merchants pondering the tawny fields, saw them take ears of corn, rub them to pieces in the palms of their hands, finger the grains, bite them. Any day now, with clanking engines and clouds of dust the reapers and binders would be at work, people would come out with shot-guns and dogs. As the corn was reaped, the rabbits would bolt out of their diminishing cover. Shots would ring out, voices cheer on the coursing lurchers.

Golden Eye was a twenty-two foot cutter, carvel-built and gunter-rigged. She wasn't one of the shallow-draft vessels designed for the inland waterways, and her keel meant they rarely sailed her farther up-river than her mooring at Saint Benet's abbey.

Jack liked all the country he'd been brought up in and he liked all its rivers, the Thurne and the Ant and the Bure, but Saint Benet's was a place he liked particularly. You pedalled your bike along a muddy track through some meadows. Then there were willows that looked gaunt and feathery at the same time, broken boughs sticking out through the silvery green that glinted in the blowing sunlight. The pasture was hummocky where the mediaeval buildings had stood. You leaned your bike against the hedge, climbed the stile, walked down to the Bure past the one flint gateway that was still standing, inside which a brick windmill had later been built, though that was ruined too now. By some clerical oversight, at the Reformation the abbey had not been dissolved with the other religious houses, so once a year the bishop of Norwich came and held a service by the river side.

A fisherman might trudge down with rod and creel, or a farm labourer come to herd the sheep – no one else approached by land. The river had a little more traffic. A barge laden down almost to the gunwale with stacked sheaves of reed cut from a nearby fen. Half an hour later, maybe a trim little yacht with varnished mahogany topsides and gleaming white sails and polished brass cleats, or a trading wherry with tarred hull and tan sails.

It was peaceful, tinkering with *Golden Eye* as the afternoons waned and wildfowl congregated. There were always flocks of greylag and pinkfoot on the meadows, and that reach of the Bure had its pair of swans, with this year's cygnets half feathered but still half downy too. The river also had grebes and coots and moorhens, all of which had nested and now had flotillas of young bobbing behind them. There were mallard too, and toward evening more would come flighting in. If Jack, perhaps stimulated to greater efforts by how spick and span a passing yacht had looked, was still overhauling his rigging at dusk, he saw skeins of duck stretched in ragged chevrons across the sky, and though many continued high overhead others came swooping down. Teal came with a faster wingbeat than mallard, and he saw wisps of snipe jinking over the reeds.

Jack would be almost at peace. Or he would have been if it hadn't been for this and that and . . . If it hadn't been for a confusion of real problems and nebulous perplexities which – which . . . So he'd chuck his knife and marlin spike in the locker, jump ashore, stride briskly off in the gloaming to retrieve his bicycle.

Even real issues of the sort he'd always been contented grappling with, things like consulting the tide-table to decide which mornings would be suitable for taking the cutter out beneath the Yarmouth bridges, this summer could seem fraught with ambiguities. Georgia would be on board, so it was vital that the operation went smoothly. Of course, she'd taken part in previous Lammas sailing expeditions – but that had been in the past, that meant nothing now. He'd have Bobbie, newly returned to England, to help him get the mast down and up, that was a blessing. Although since that night in the Quercy under the cottage

lime trees, Bobbie and Caroline had joined the presences he no longer
knew how to deal with as confidently as of old. Never mind. He must
concentrate on practicalities.

After careful thought, Jack evolved his plan. He'd borrow the Fletchers'
motor launch to tow *Golden Eye* down through Acle bridge. Old Bernard
Fletcher would almost certainly give him a hand, if his arthritis wasn't too
bad. That night, the cutter could lie at their jetty – the Fletchers lived
in a timber-framed farmhouse in the marshes a mile or two up-river of
Yarmouth. Early next morning, on the last of the dawn tide – Jack's copy
of the tide-table had a cross pencilled against the date – they'd tow her
through the town, get the mast up again, and be away to sea. It had to
be a dawn tide, not only because it was easier to negotiate the bridges at
low water, but also because when they'd sailed up the coast all day they'd
need the first of the next tide in order to cross the bar off Stiffkey.

It was a fine plan, and it was made better by his father's approval. What
was more, Papa was not only cheerful about relinquishing Georgia for
a few days' sailing, he declared he too would take a holiday and bring
the crab-boat out from Morston to meet them. The two vessels could
rendezvous – well, it would depend on the wind – but off Cromer maybe.
This way, if the weather turned nasty, or for that matter if there was a
dead calm, the crab-boat's engine would be of service to bring them up
the channel to the harbour at Morston.

Still, there were hazards, of which the river with the ebb sluicing under
the bridges would only be the first. For instance, the weather. Sunshine
and an onshore breeze would naturally be perfect, especially if it lasted
all week, but such an idyll was unlikely. A westerly gale with rain would
at least not be difficult to take decisions about: they'd have to postpone
the whole voyage, in which case when the winds turned favourable the
tides would be all wrong. What if they started in tolerable conditions
which then deteriorated? Jack tried to foresee most eventualities, and
sustained himself with the thought of his father's involvement, which
he interpreted as a benediction of his friendship with Georgia. Even so,
getting the mast up in Yarmouth harbour would need care. Then the days
ahead, the approaches to Brancaster and to King's Lynn, and the return
. . . One way and another, his seamanship looked likely to be tested. And
as for the unrest which permeated his heart . . . Something was coming
to life in him, but the trouble was he didn't know what.

The scents of the happiness of previous summers hung in the air. Jack
felt he only had to sniff and he'd be on their enticing traces again.

And sometimes that was true: particularly if he avoided rationalising the procedure, it worked fine. Still, often it was more complicated than that.

Going sailing with girls, going riding with girls, going to dances. Of course it was all great fun – but it was responsible only for a small part of his lurches of mood and his tingling nerve-ends. What was more, his mother had been peremptory.

'Just remember, there's safety in numbers, my darling boy, and only in numbers.' She was right, deep down he knew it. 'Borrow the car, if you can make it start. Go to all the dances you like. But please remember not to do anything so vulgar as to monopolise any poor girl, and let me know how many evening shirts you need.'

The war came into it too – but again only tangentially. It was irritating enough, the way you couldn't go to a drinks party without having people nod their heads sagely and tell you things like, 'If it's going to come, it's going to come this year', or, 'Afraid we really are going to have to fight'. It gripped him with a depressing awareness of all the drawing-rooms of England, people clustering by thousands of fireplaces, people holding thousands of glasses of sherry and pronouncing to each other, 'We'll be lucky if we don't have to fight.'

Jack Lammas was working it out, in his level-headed fashion; or the understanding of the renewed European cataclysm was being loaded into his mind like ballast. Not only the country's drawing-rooms were disheartening. There was instruction in the churchyards too, each with its memorial to the parish's dead in the last war. Of course, the next conflict might evolve along different lines; but if it resembled the last one at all . . . You only had to take the approximate populations of the villages; then reckon up the number of those who were young and male; then count the names on each memorial. Jack at Edingthorpe had made this simple computation, and knew the figures were about the same all over the neighbourhood, he'd calculated his probable chances. And . . . Well, all his generation were the sons of fathers who'd fought through 1914–18, it was in their blood. Often these days he felt he'd been prepared for the next onset of Western fighting ever since as a child he'd lain on the library hearth-rug looking at scrap-books.

They wouldn't join up with the exuberance some people seemed to recall from the recruiting in '14. There'd be a job to be done, that was all. An inescapable job, which it was sober to expect you wouldn't survive, though you might be one of the lucky ones.

Urgencies – yes. Premonitions – yes. But mere distractedness seemed to have more to do with his strange moods. He meandered to the stable, where he teased his sister about the care with which she was washing her pony's tail. He meandered to the kitchen garden, where he picked pea-pods and split them open with his thumb-nail and ate the peas.

On occasion, determined use of his strength was the right thing. A Spanish chestnut had blown down and blocked a driftway in the wood, Jack spent all one day there with axe and saw. He came back with his clothes grimy, his shoulders aching and his hands blistered, determined to return next morning and finish the job, and in such excellent spirits that at dinner he had all the family laughing at his stories of his amateurish woodmanship.

Then it rained in torrents. Cooped up in the house, he resorted to the library. His father had books of designs by architects like Vanbrugh and Kent and Soane, handsome editions some of them. Jack lifted down this volume and that, opened them on the desk. However, today the fascination they exercised was weak. He wasted half the afternoon staring out of the window at the squalls belabouring the trees.

Later, Georgia and he went up to the old nursery, which was rarely frequented these days unless you wanted to listen to the gramophone that nobody had bothered to shift elsewhere. It was pleasant, to be lost at the top of the house, among cupboards of children's clothes and toys which had been stacked away, rain drumming on the roof and gurgling along the gutters. There was the fireguard where their Christmas stockings used to be hung. There were shelves of books which they'd all read but didn't read any more. *Treasure Island* and *Coral Island*, *The Just So Stories* and *Black Beauty* . . . Jack felt obscurely sad, running his gaze along the tattered Victorian and Edwardian bindings. *The Children of the New Forest* and *Brave Dame Mary*, *The Wind in the Willows* and . . . They were all jumbled up, Lewis Carroll mixed with E. Nesbit. Here was *Kidnapped*, which he really might take downstairs and read again.

Music! They unearthed songs by Cole Porter and Noel Coward.

'Come on, Georgia, let's dance.'

She felt light and warm in his arms, and you couldn't be sad dancing to 'You're the tops', it just wasn't possible, and then they went clattering down the stairs still singing snatches.

4

—ᴍ—

At first light, the tide turned. All along the coast, the ebb began to flow out down the creeks through the marshes. The murky sea retreated from the feet of the low, crumbling cliffs. It retreated from shingle banks, from spits of muddy sand and clean sand, from mud flats where samphire grew, from mussel beds. Everywhere the flocks of tiny dunlin and stint had a wider foreshore where they ran, took wing, flew low and fast, alit again, waded in the drying foam and the dull glisten, darting, pecking. The sea fell back down harbour slipways and harbour walls, exposing barnacles and festoons of bladderwrack. In the estuaries, the ebb united with the rivers' currents, swirled boisterously past the anchored craft.

Charles Lammas, inshore on Morston quay and pausing with his wife and daughter beside him, was pleased to see he hadn't left it too late, there was still comfortably enough water in the creek for them to be able to get the crab-boat to sea. Guessing that, down the coast aboard *Golden Eye* in Yarmouth roadstead, Bobbie and Jack were unlikely to let themselves be put off by the probability of the wind getting pretty stiff as the day wore on, he carried sail-bag and picnic hamper down to the water's edge.

Oars, rowlocks, anchor, warps, boathook – yes, the old vessel looked shipshape. Fitting the tiller into the socket at the head of the rudder, he wondered if he'd forgotten anything. Oilskins and sou'westers in case it turned foul; spare jerseys because people always got cold at sea; his hip-flask because that could have a cheering effect too. What else? Fuel. He checked it. Right. He opened the lid of the engine case, he stooped, fiddled. He fitted the crank-handle.

Dropping down the creek with the reassuring thump of the engine in his ears, Lammas felt how good it was not to be painting. Like a winter day out shooting, a summer day at sea could be just the tonic you required. An empty marsh, a winding creek with the ebb flowing low now between slopes of mud and grounded craft, a windy sky – just the trick, and though it might blow he didn't reckon it would rain much. The quiver of the helm in your hand, gulls screeching as they dived, still enough water to get down the channel – this was good for him, he could feel it. Henrietta still half asleep, but warm wearing that Guernsey, and day-dreaming happily, watching the shore. They'd spent last night with Anne Daubeney at Morston Manor, and at daybreak Henrietta had still been so fast asleep she'd taken a fair bit of coaxing from her befuddlement, and then there'd been the shoving of drowsy arms and legs into clothes. And now Blanche was getting out the breakfast – wonderful! A Thermos of coffee which smelled delicious in the briney air. And those bacon sandwiches he'd always liked. He grinned at her, and said, 'Breakfast, oh good!' thinking that it was at times like this that he loved her best. Now – when she was sitting on the thwart with the sea-wind fluttering her head-scarf, and fluttering the twists of brown hair that clung to her neck and against her cheek. Now – when they were going to be together offshore all the free, peaceful day. What was more, you couldn't beat an old Norfolk crab-boat when it came to getting about this coast, he decided with satisfaction, swinging out of the creek into the bay. Even if he did ever make some money, he'd be damned if he'd exchange this old tub for some swish modern yacht. He opened the throttle a touch, feeling the wind come onto the beam, the hull start to push sturdily through the short waves.

The sun broke through the harum-scarum clouds, glittered on the tide-race in the harbour mouth where the deep-water channel curved seaward around the end of the dunes. At least a mile of the golden sandbanks off Stiffkey had already been left high and dry. Steering out on the turbulent ebb, Charles saw Geoffrey and himself walking dogs there, remembered how it had been, when you were twenty and didn't know anything about trenches or about submarines, to go striding companionably out to that wreck which at low water lay exposed. Then he glanced at Henrietta munching her bacon sandwich, told himself that all was not lost, and now Blanche was pointing, calling, 'Look, there are the seals!' And there the pack lay, hauled out on the sand. So it was all right to remember walking with Geoff over the shoal which the sea had left wrinkled. All right to remember him calling the dogs, splashing through shallows, picking up a shell and tossing it down. All right to remember the weed-strewn slopes and the starfish drying, the crabs scuttling and the loneliness. Because Henrietta, with her half-eaten sandwich neglected in one hand, was gazing at the seals, thirty or forty of them, pale greys and dark greys and mottled greys, one or two of which were heaving and flippering their ungainly ways back into the tide. Because almost no one came here, except for a few bait-diggers and fishermen. The desolation was still good, high tide or low tide. Geoff would have liked to see the old wreck, still rusting on the sea-bed.

A seal surfaced alongside, regarded the crab-boat chugging by. Oyster-catchers swooped over the mast, their black and white chevrons looking glamorous. A tern hurtled down at the waves, flew up with a fish in its beak.

Once he was over the bar and into deep water, Charles Lammas headed east. He rigged his vessel's simple lug-sail. When he hoisted it and the boat heeled a little, he cut the engine. Quiet returned, apart from the slapping of waves against clinker-built sides, the steady bashing of the bow through the troughs and into the crests.

'Do you want to steer?' he asked Henrietta. She came aft, sat in the crook of his arm and took the tiller. It would be a reach for hours; he cleated the sheet, settled to watching the shore and the sea.

5

Caroline Lammas, aboard *Golden Eye* twenty-odd church towers along the coast to the south-east, was also contemplating the shore-sea wildfowl, and the low-lying land slipping past a mile off, and the white crests of the waves. But not for her Charles' contentment to be away from his work for a day.

She had no profession to practise, no art to be inspired by and baffled by and tantalised by. Since their sudden upheaval from the cottage near Cahors, she hadn't even had any housework with which she could make herself feel useful.

Bobbie refused to return to the Kensington studio. A quick summer holiday at Bure Hall, then he'd be off to join his regiment. He'd been to dinner with the colonel, Lord Yarborough, whom he'd declared a most likeable old boy, and who had afterwards communicated his readiness to accept him among his officers. What was to happen to Caroline he scarcely seemed to find worth discussing. It would depend on where the regiment was quartered, and anyway there was always Bure. It would depend on the success or failure of the current negotiations with Germany. She was not, please, to make a fuss.

Their last visitors at the cottage had not stayed as long as had originally been planned – this had been another of the twists to Caroline's wretchedness. Even so, entertaining them had left her limp with nervous exhaustion, and unfortunately Bobbie had sensed she'd been glad to see the back of them.

Then the demolition of their French way of life had appeared to her an unmitigated defeat. Bobbie had decided, he scowled if she protested – which seemed to her unreasonable, and bullying, and not what he used to be like at all. And when he *did* talk he was brusque, and it was all stuff about 'only serving his country, what was odd about that?' – which frightened her. If she remonstrated, if she told him how much she believed in his talent as a painter, if she pleaded with him to remember how encouraging Uncle Charles had been, he just looked at her coldly.

Packing their suitcases had been a gloomy enough occupation, but then disposing of their household bits and pieces had been worse. There was no point in taking anything with them – they were not, so far as Caroline could see, going anywhere. The very poverty of the linen and crockery that she put away for the next tenant, or for whatever use Marie

Rivac might find for them, made sobs of self-pity clog in her throat. An eiderdown, bought from a Cahors draper, with a pattern of what looked like marigolds, which had kept Bobbie and her warm on winter nights when the gales boomed around the cottage eaves. The liqueur glasses they called the thimbles.

It seemed to Caroline that, when she put mothballs among the table-cloths she had ironed and folded for the last time, what she was really doing was consigning the first three years of her marriage to the flames; and now that she was losing them, they seemed to her magical years replete with freedom and love. Bobbie working away in his studio. She coming back from the village with provisions, then sitting at the trestle table under the lime trees to read a novel, or to write to one of her girlfriends in England who wouldn't be having anything like so romantic a time. So light-hearted they'd been! In the evenings, their walks hand in hand along the lanes. After supper, chairs by the fire, and games of backgammon. Bobbie was such a riotous player of backgammon, after each throw he'd shout with triumph, or make a comic speech about his despair. And now, storage in cupboards she was afraid would prove damp – though she'd never come back to know. Now, mothballs. Now Bobbie who, when for the first time for absolute months she suggested that it might be glorious if they had a baby, regarded her with scorn and curtly asked, 'What, *now?*'

Caroline's presentiments had been accurate: coming back to Norfolk was horrible. Of course, joining the Army was a blessedly impeccable thing for Bobbie to be doing. Alarmed though she was for him, Caroline ended by being grateful for the respectable outward form which her husband's military prospects lent to their directionless and suddenly empty-feeling marriage.

Bobbie's chat with her brothers about Regular regiments and Yeomanry regiments, about cavalry and infantry and artillery . . . She hoped it fooled *some* people into thinking that certain questions were being answered. Then her father clapped him on the shoulder, jovially agreed that, 'In times like this, the arts have to be put aside I'm afraid. No question of it, you've taken the right decision my boy. Fine regiment, too, the Sherwood Rangers. Yarborough? Doesn't often get up to Westminster these days.' Luckily, too, there was what her parents had begun to refer to as the problem with Mark.

Not really luckily, of course. If Caroline thought about it, it was rather awful the way he'd get drunk and then say such brutish things. But it did distract attention from any unsatisfactoriness which might have been discerned in Bobbie and her. Anyway, the trouble was that although

Frederick was the image of cheerfulness and sound sense, as well he might be with his job in the City and the prospect of inheriting the Hall and the estate, not to mention a fat portfolio of investments and the Canaletto, Mark on the other hand . . .

Well, the merchant bank had proved damnably boring, or had chucked him out, depending on who you listened to. The titled and stinking rich young lady had married Mark Somebody-Else. There was even the suspicion that the colonel of some regiment or other, who conceivably had got wind of all the drinking or the betting too much on the wrong horses, had not been as impressed with him after a dinner or two as Lord Yarborough naturally had been with darling Bobbie.

Caroline tried to be sensible. Just because Bobbie had been a painter when she had fallen in love with him didn't mean he always had to be. People must be allowed to try different tacks, be allowed to change. And if what everyone said about Germany was right, he'd have been in the Army soon anyhow. Though she could never wholeheartedly believe that the defence of the realm justified the termination of her three years in the Quercy with her young husband. For the rest of her life, she regretted that landscape and that cottage and their freedom together.

Her mother took her to London for a few days. The Knightsbridge hairdresser was enchanted to see her again, and set about refining the handiwork of the woman in Cahors who had combed and snipped and charged next to nothing. Then Sarah Hedleigh swept her daughter off to dress-makers for fittings, and to Fortnum's for tea, and to buy shoes, and belts, and hats. Every evening they went to a party, and on each occasion there was at least one man who paid Caroline a degree of attention which surprised her.

One way and another, it all felt like a parody of her life before she'd been engaged, and she hated it, though she didn't seem able to avoid it. Then back at Bure, everything might appear just like previous summers when Bobbie and she had stayed there on holiday, but they weren't on holiday. They'd somehow drifted into dead water, they were eddying futilely around. So Norfolk was a parody of old times too.

Bure in summer, which reminded her of her wedding – why this should be disagreeable she hadn't yet worked out. Edingthorpe, where her Lammas relations were different somehow. Caroline had welcomed the idea of an escape to sea. She'd gone sailing all her life, never been put off by wind and weather. Yet for some reason today . . . The water in *Golden Eye's* bilges had soaked her canvas shoes, which was the sort of thing that always happened when you went afloat. She knew something was amiss with her because she let herself be irritated by the prospect of wet feet all day.

The wind was rising. They brought the cutter in to only about half a mile offshore where the sea wasn't too rough, and made brisk progress. Bobbie and Jack were in high spirits because of the fast sailing. Georgia was in one of her cheerful moods, taking her turn at the helm, telling them not even to consider reefing, she was racing invisible rivals and wouldn't be slowed down. Then the wind whistling in the shrouds, the bowsprit lancing at the waves which were bursting at the port bow and sweeping over the coaming . . . Caroline couldn't think what was wrong with her, not to share the others' enjoyment.

Except . . . The viburnums in the garden at Bure, with their white pompom flowers and their scent she'd always liked. The way they reminded her of the days just before her wedding. Her brothers tirelessly teasing her about how they hoped her getting married wasn't going to cause them to arrive late at Ascot. Her mother in a twitter because she wasn't sure the viburnums would be at their best, and her banksia roses were going to be over. What should dispirit her in all this, Caroline couldn't fathom. But she'd find she was thinking, I'm still only twenty-four.

Except . . . Even while Uncle Charles was still at the cottage, he'd retreated a bit into that inflexible urbanity of his, she'd been certain he had. And he didn't treat her with his old gallantry. He just set that great bone of a jaw of his, and set his eyes, and was worldly.

There was something awkward in Jack's manner toward her too these days. Sadly she recollected her engagement party at Edingthorpe, what a charming boy she'd thought he was. And now all this hearty sailors' talk Bobbie and he were going in for was a bit much, she thought, waking up to the play-acting around her, the flirtatious game in which Georgia was the tyrannous skipper and Bobbie and Jack her crew. Georgia with her spray-wetted hair blowing across her bright, laughing eyes and her mouth. Georgia at the tiller, the cutter heeled well over and pounding through the waves. Georgia issuing orders. Bobbie and Jack laughing as they manned the mainsheet and the foresails' sheets, both of them enjoying the game like hell.

Still unnoticed, Caroline watched. So merrily, this nonsense must have sprung into life around her, without her. And honestly, did she have to sit here with sodden shoes and watch this pert schoolgirl flutter her eyelashes at her husband?

It would be good to talk to Blanche one day, Caroline suddenly surprised herself by deciding with a calm clarity she wasn't accustomed to this miserable summer. Tonight it wouldn't be possible, there was going to be a terrific dinner party at Morston, Mrs Daubeney had invited the lot of them. But some time . . .

Blanche Lammas' soft gaze had met hers more than once lately. She couldn't believe there wasn't comprehension there. And Blanche would never have taken her to those London parties.

6

The rendezvous occurred off the town of Cromer as planned, rags and tatters of cloud racing across the sky so that sometimes the red-tiled houses and the flint church glittered in brilliant sunlight, then a region of shadow blew across the land and over the cliff and out to sea toward the Dogger Bank and Denmark.

Charles Lammas' sturdy crab-boat with her small lug-sail needed half a gale to get even a modest performance out of her, so the conditions suited the old vessel perfectly. But *Golden Eye* was making heavy weather of it. The spars creaked, and when she crashed off the crest of one wave into the next trough the whole hull shuddered. She was taking a lot of spray over the windward bow, and in the squalls she lay over till she shipped water to leeward too. When they let out the mainsheet to spill wind, the canvas flogged with cracking reports, and the gaff and boom jerked.

Bobbie had taken over the helm. Now the convergence of the two Lammas craft convinced Jack and him that they ought to reduce sail. Charles would undoubtedly declare they should already have done so. And if anything broke . . . Both cousins had a vision of the dismasted cutter drifting before the wind farther and farther from land.

Jack scrambled onto the foredeck, cascades of spindrift whipping his oilskins and his face. Hanging onto the gunwale with one hand and the downhaul with the other, he crawled forward beneath one foresail to lower the other. When he had an arm locked around the rearing and plunging bowsprit, he yelled aft for them to slack away the jib halyard. Foot by foot, he clawed the billowing sail down. It wasn't a big jib, but a squall blew it out of his grasp so he had to start again, lying on the tossing deck, hauling it from where it had fallen battering in the foam alongside. Then he struggled back to the cockpit.

Georgia wedged her back against the leeward sidedeck, steadied herself by jamming a foot against the mast-step, laboured cheerfully at the pump. At each pull she gave the brass handle, a jet of water spurted overboard in a most satisfactory manner.

She had enjoyed her stint as captain of *Golden Eye*, until in the mounting wind the weather-helm which the cutter developed had started to alarm her. Bobbie had said, 'Don't let her broach,' in a quiet voice. A few gusts later, she'd confessed 'I'm not sure I'm going to be able to hold her.' So then it had been a relief to relinquish command, let the men get on with it. She could still feel her arms aching.

Pumping was light work. She had enjoyed the meeting at sea off Cromer pier, the crab-boat gybing round and the two vessels heading toward Morston in convoy. Jack dousing the jib was showing off a bit, but she knew hers were the eyes he intended to impress, which left a tingle in her mind, till she forgot it laughing at him floundering with that sail. Then she listened happily to Bobbie and him disagreeing about whether they ought to reef the mainsail. She laughed with them when they realised that, if they were going to take the main down to reef it, they should have waited till the cutter was jogging tranquilly along under nothing but headsails before any fool went slithering about on the foredeck.

When the mainsail had been lowered and reefed and rehoisted, they unpacked their sandwiches. Georgia knocked off pumping for a while, ate her lunch looking across the water to the crab-boat where lunch was also in progress. Far off, the sky was bruise-coloured and a blizzard of rain had darkened the sea. Nearer, she could see Beeston church on its cliff, and the sun coming out from behind a cloud hung swags of grey brilliance in the air. The sea had far more colours than she'd known, and they kept altering. A purplish patch became almost black when the sun went in. A wave broke, and the greeny-greys crashed into white. The wind blew the crest off a comber into silver spangles, they fell back into sullenly lurching greys, heaved up into the glitter and became slaty-brown and slaty-blue.

Even under reduced sail, *Golden Eye* quickly began to draw away from the crab-boat. Georgia finished her Cheddar sandwiches, which tasted slightly of spray, ate a plum and a piece of chocolate, went back to pumping. When they passed Salthouse they'd be nearly there. It had been fun imagining they were in a regatta, and even now she no longer had the helm she saw *Golden Eye*'s spectral rivals with their sails dotting the sea. She had in mind a finishing line off Stiffkey, a race for – oh, she didn't know, but some stupendous trophy.

Silly, Georgia told herself. Then went straight on dreaming about it. She was so happy with her regatta fleet battling, that when the rain started hissing across she welcomed it as added drama, didn't mind a bit how drenched she got. Bobbie cursing cheerfully, Caroline looking cold and glum, Jack pulling faces to make them all laugh . . . Georgia was oblivious, sailing the last few miles of a hard-fought race, her head ringing with stories of storms, broken gear, daring seamanship. And were they now going to thrash across the line in such torrents of rain they wouldn't be able to see if *Golden Eye* was just in the lead or not? Georgia stared into the squall. Around in the roaring seas and weltering murk her rivals' sails crowded ghostlily, and . . .

What? What were they all calling at her, and why were they laughing?

Oh, the pump. Yes, she'd go on pumping.

7

—⁓—

Caroline was right in feeling that Blanche sympathised with her in the loss of her independent married life, and in her husband's flight from his failure in the arts into the Army. For that matter, Raffaella Zanetti had been right three years before when she surmised that the wife had guessed the husband's love affair. But Blanche Lammas only ever showed the distresses she felt for others.

You'd never have known, that sunny and stormy day aboard the crab-boat, that she had disappointments more acute than her husband's being let down by a New York collector, or her daughter's slap-dash performance over the fences at Aylsham Show. Or on any of the days that summer of '38, when it appeared that Europe must descend into war again at any moment, but all along that coast which hadn't yet reverted to being a defensive position people went on doing the usual summer things, walking dogs, going out in boats, helping small children to build sandcastles.

You could observe Blanche Lammas' reactions to set-backs of this order. In the first case: reduced household expenditure. In the second: more practice over jumps in the meadow at home, and possibly a pelham instead of a snaffle. Straightforward. Impeccable, too . . . In the sense that loyalty so seamless and efforts so selfless had something of the immaculate to them.

As for whether she, who before she was married had been wild enough to get herself what was known as talked about, had believed not in a sacrament of Christ's Church, that certainly wouldn't have been her style, but in giving your word and then sticking by it – you'd never have known. Or if she'd reckoned a fling now and then was only to be expected from a man like Charlie, shouldn't be made a song and dance about, and for that matter had granted herself an equal licence to be frivolous occasionally, only to sense that Raffaella wasn't a mere fling. Or if she'd been aware of Charles' spirit receding from her, but then far away hesitating and turning, coming back toward her.

Not if you'd seen her with him shortly after his return from Italy in '35, when they were prominent at the Bure wedding, and the presence of the distinguished painter among the groom's relations added, at least in the bride's dizzy perception, a lustre that more prosaically posh guests couldn't give. Not if you'd seen her with him three summers later, when in their crab-boat they arrived back off Morston after the tide had turned but before there was sufficient water for them to cross the bar. He was again newly returned to her from Italy. If she'd guessed he might lately have sat on Giacomo Zanetti's terrace haunted, however indolently, by the shadow of a direction not taken, of a daughter of the house not married, she didn't show it, that day or any day.

Not unlike one another, Charles and Blanche Lammas, in some respects. A part to play – that was all they asked of life.

'Oh, I'm all right,' she'd say. 'People don't expect me to do anything different. My children, the garden. These are what I'm for, everyone knows that. Horses, dogs. Other people's children and gardens. If I looked bored there'd be trouble. All I've got to do is go on turning up at dinner parties.'

That was the way she'd talk, never taking herself too seriously. That was the way you could imagine she'd probably thought when she'd had to face the possibility that what had happened to other loyal wives might happen to her, she'd be pensioned off with two teenage children to cope with. Ditched – that was the word she'd have used. And she went on defending Charles all through that year when he might have lit out to Italy or for that matter India, started a maybe wonderfully happy second marriage with a girl twenty years younger than her.

'But as for Charlie! Poor fellow, he can't do right. People who knew him in the war, can't understand why a man that able hasn't gone into the City and made a fortune. People who meet him in the country with a twelve-bore in his hand, decide it's most peculiar when they find him behind the same copse the next week holding a palette and brush. People who decide he can't be a good painter because they hear him talking about a race meeting. I can't stand any of them.'

Forthright, cheerful . . . Quite fierce too, when it came to standing up for her husband.

The rain storm blew over, revealing not the racing fleet of Georgia's imagination but a work-a-day craft aboard which men were hauling up buoyed crab-pots. The sun behind the scudding cloud-rack gave the sky a mottled look, and was well to the west now. The unabated wind was cold.

Where the tide beginning to set over the bar met the squalls whining off the land, the channel was a maelstrom of seas breaking every-which-way. Flurries of spray exploded upward among the gulls and terns and oyster-catchers alternately flogging inshore and being hurled seaward.

Nothing to do but wait. Charles Lammas anchored the crab-boat off the bar, lowered the sail. It was peaceful, with no sounds but the pelting wind, and the waves slapping against the bow, and the gulls crying. A hundred yards off, the fishing-smack which had been chugging from crab-pot to crab-pot had also anchored to wait for the channel to become deep enough. Away on the exposed sandbanks, men who that morning had beached their vessel so they could work on the hull all day were waiting for the tide to reach them. Even the seal pack hauled out on a dun slope seemed to be waiting.

Peaceful . . . and companionable. They looked good together, those two, in their sturdy vessel chucking at her warp, as they waited for the tide, their daughter burrowing in the hamper because she knew the cake was there somewhere. Blanche gave Charles a hand to furl the sail along the gaff, knot the ties. Then from his hip-flask he tipped Scotch into two tin mugs, added a splash of water. Wife and husband baled in their ancient oilskins, watching *Golden Eye* which had sailed on up the coast and tacked, now storming back toward them and looking rakish, heeled over as she sliced through the waves with canvas taut and spume flying . . . You wouldn't have thought those two had a care in the world, beyond getting their family party up the harbour and ashore before nightfall so they could all have baths and be in more or less respectable shape for Anne Daubeney's dinner table. But Blanche Lammas had already understood how her generation of European women looked like being uniquely damned. How it could seem they'd been singled out for a trial more cruel than their mothers', their grandmothers' or great-grandmothers'.

A banal matter of when you chanced to get born. Yet that generation of young women who had their lovers and husbands and brothers fight in the Great War, and then had their sons grow up to be of fighting age when the . . . Well, nobody knew what was occurring, what was about to be enacted. But . . . The second campaign at Armageddon, it could loom like.

Charles Lammas knew, and no one else except Nanny Oldfield knew, that there were nights when Blanche couldn't sleep for thinking about Jack. Not only couldn't sleep. It was as if she had asthma. She'd lie on her back with her chest heaving. She'd choke for the air that she couldn't breathe, which for reasons you could call nervous she had difficulty dragging into her lungs.

Reasons . . . To do with nerves strung intolerably tight, or heart-strings. To do with warfare, and young men, and love.

Reasons . . . A brother. A fiancé, whose gold watch and chain she had been given by his sisters, who were her companions in that doubly tortured generation, her sisters in that dread which should have been outlived but twenty years later came back. A son, for whom she had put aside that watch and chain for his twenty-first birthday, and who now might be killed before he reached that age.

You wouldn't have known. A gull flew up with a fish in its beak. 'Look, Henrietta!' her mother cried, pointing. Because a black skua had swooped in pursuit. From the crab-boat they watched the quarry jink this way and that, beat its wings in an agony of fear, the hunter harry it with relentless agility. Then panic worked, the gull disgorged its prey. The skua broke off the chase, dived for the falling sliver of still living food.

Versed in fear for their men, that generation of women. Versed in grief, and in stoicism. Not hardened. Just experienced.

And then, after years of peace, to have the horror return with undiminished virulence. In Blanche Lammas' case, after twenty years of taking an ivy wreath to one of the coastal churches each Christmas, laying it on the sill below a stained-glass window. After years of watching over her son, seeing him grow to be a man.

1914–18 had been such an overwhelmingly male affair, she didn't fret much about her daughter. Naturally she knew about a few women who'd been killed. Edith Cavell, for instance, a nurse in occupied Brussels whom the Germans court-martialled for helping prisoners of war to escape. She admitted the offences, and was executed. She'd been a Norfolk woman, Blanche couldn't fail to know about her, with her memorial statue put up in Norwich after the war, in front of The Maid's Head near the Cathedral. NURSE PATRIOT AND MARTYR, the inscription read. But that war had been such a slaughter of the young and the male that it was Jack whom his mother feared for, and Bobbie who was as good as a son to her, not Henrietta, or Georgia.

Then there was the slatting of *Golden Eye*'s sails as she came head-to-wind alongside, and Blanche Lammas leaped up from her thwart to make sure the cutter's slamming boom didn't clout Henrietta on the head. Conceivably Bobbie, who took a jaundiced view of wedlock these days, might have intuited how the impending war had caused her husband's inconstancy to fade into insignificance. Certainly Jack showed no sign of yet having worried about his mother's anxieties for him. The day had whetted his appetites, he was in rather zestful form.

The exhilaration of stormy sailing, the political news, Georgia's hip and waist in that dress she'd worn last night . . . He didn't know, his head was a jumble as usual. But something . . . A jumble of the immediate and the fantastic. *Golden Eye*'s rigging had stood up to the day's wear and tear, that was good. What was that fable about a bird his father had told him? The halcyon, that was right. It bred at the winter solstice, in a nest that floated on the sea. Jack glanced around at the foaming breakers, imagined a brilliantly plumaged halcyon that charmed the waves to make a calm hollow for her nest. Georgia was bundled up in seafaring garb, you couldn't make out her figure, but all the same . . . Safety in numbers. Going to be a war. Bound to be. Rose, Georgia, who cared? Still, better check the gooseneck, that could be a weak point, and after today's jarring . . . And the jaws of the gaff, and the shrouds. Marvellously elegant drawing-room at Wimpole, who was the architect?

On the in-coming tide, the crab-boat chugged up the channel. Aboard the cutter towing astern, Jack cheerfully stowed sails, so that when they reached the harbour and dropped anchor she'd be ready to be left for the night. *In the wild October night-time*, that was how Hardy's Trafalgar poem began, and it was going to blow hard tonight too, high summer didn't mean you couldn't expect gales. It'd been fun, hearing that read in the library on Trafalgar nights before he'd been sent away to boarding-school. *And the Back-sea met the Front-sea, and our doors were blocked with sand* . . . Of course, Hardy had written finer poems, but that one wasn't half bad, and it brought back autumn evenings and the library hearth and . . . Georgia, Georgia. *Pull hard and* . . . No, no. *We heard the drub of Dead-Man's Bay, where* . . . Come here, come and kiss me, Georgia.

At the helm of the crab-boat Charles Lammas was watching the bait-diggers trudging homeward, half-a-dozen tiny figures scattered over the wilderness, making their ways toward land now that the sea was rolling in behind them. He steered close enough to the wreck bedded in the shoal for Henrietta to be able to see the rising waves crash over its rusty flanks. He told her how after the ship ran aground and started to break up, men from Morston and Stiffkey used to come out with horses and carts to salvage timbers, anything that might be useful. Even at night, with lanterns on the carts, going a mile or two out to sea, working till they had a load and the next tide shepherded them inshore.

Those sands, those snaking creeks, that loneliness. Geoffrey and he walking the dogs. But this time in his mind's eye he saw other figures too striding there, and not just the men with horses and carts who had come and gone, and the bait-diggers who still came and went in their thigh boots with their forks slanted over their shoulders. Others . . . His father and mother, old, afraid for their sons abroad fighting. In the evening gale, in the mind's miasma, toiling over the immense sands. Blanche and Michael, and then she without him, intolerably alone.

Blanche would understand. Possessed with sudden violence by his love for her, he looked to where she was chafing Henrietta's cold hands between hers, heard her say, 'Whitebait for dinner, I'm told, we're in luck.' That gentleness with which her hair clung to her temples. That curve of her cheek – inexpressible, never to be renounced. The soft glance she threw him. She'd understand.

Confusedly aware of a return to her with greater love than before, Lammas gazed again at the sands, at figures who strode, others who . . . His parents after the war, stricken with a palsy of the spirit that finished them in a few years. Brothers. Ghosts who appeared and disappeared, walking at low tide in the blizzard light. Then Blanche and he himself, Blanche and the survivor. They who as they walked told each other about their dead, but who were triumphant in their being alive. Who as they splashed through puddles made plans, and stopped in the middle of planning to kiss, and tramped on deciding things and imagining things.

There, where the sea had rippled the sand, and left shells. By the rusting hulk. Beneath the most open, blustery, brackish sky you could aspire to. Between the farmland in the distance one way, and the other way – well, in due course Scandinavia. With seals and terns for company. Blanche would understand. She'd walk here with him when Jack was away at the war, and she'd understand.

Odd, how your heart could be sick with foreboding and at the same time hosannah with love. As for that girl, that Raffaella – bloody ridiculous, how susceptible he must be.

Lammas headed into the harbour mouth. Scanning the shore, he picked out Morston church tower. Far ahead, a windmill which had lost its sails held out four bony arms.

8

—m—

Charles and Blanche Lammas were both looking forward happily to the evening at Morston, for reasons some of which overlapped.

Pleasant, the ritual of leaving the crab-boat on her mooring in the creek, of lifting sail-bag and hamper into the dinghy, rowing to the shore up which the evening tide was encroaching. Pleasant, the landing among buoys and warps, among luggers and scows, the dinghy's bow bumping the shingly mud, Henrietta jumping blithely overboard with a splash and a slither to haul them in.

No one on the quay. No one by the sail-shed. The western sky was an effulgent haze of yellow and blue and rose. Miles away over the shoals where the sea would be breaking now, a few rafts of charcoal cloud floated. Behind them, an explosion of red and gold hung magnificent in its silence and slowness. The cold wind had scoured the sky, except that very high were blowing a few wisps of the tattery gale-clouds called mares' tails. You could hear halyards being blown against masts, that sailors' lullaby of cordage rapped lightly and incessantly against timber. Apart from that, just the skirling wind, the tide chuckling, larks trilling high over their miles of green and grey marsh, gulls cawing low over the creeks. Down-sun, the eastern sky had no haze. There, every wading bird was etched with brilliant precision. The acres of sea lavender bloomed with the clearest purple.

Blanche Lammas surveyed with satisfaction her party trudging up the track, which everyone's feet took automatically because it led to the Morston Manor meadow, and had been taken summer by summer after crab-boat expeditions. It was redolent, the mother liked to feel, of her son's and daughter's happy childhood. The Ayrshire cows; the tussocks and thistles; the lights already lit in one or two of the Manor windows. Beyond, the stocky tower of the unlit church. Henrietta giggling, pretending to try to push Caroline so she trod in a cow-pat, or was she really trying? Bobbie in retaliation telling Henrietta that an uncommonly bulky Ayrshire ambling their way was a bull, who would take the greatest pleasure in wedging his horns under her backside and hoisting her into those nettles, where he would then amuse himself by trampling on her a bit.

Anne Daubeney's husband had been killed at Jutland, and after the war their only child had died in the same epidemic of Spanish influenza as

Blanche's brother Claud, home from Malaya to visit his family at Paston Hall. Claud Mack not yet forty; Rupert Daubeney ten.

Blanche remembered Anne right at the end of that now almost inconceivable pre-war idling away of practically griefless time. She remembered her laughing, saying, 'Don't fret, I'm not going to ask an atheist like you to be Rupert's godmother. But when you get married and have children, you can ask me if you like. I'd love to try to save some little soul of yours.'

She remembered how years later Charlie and she had within a month seen Claud buried among the family graves on the south, landward side of Paston church, and come to Morston to Rupert's funeral. She'd been pregnant. And a few months later she'd driven back to Morston, without Charlie on this occasion, but with Henrietta in a carry-cot on the back seat of the car. She'd sat with Anne Daubeney in her drawing-room, and found she was unable to speak.

Intolerable with the presences of the dead, that room. Intolerable with John Daubeney lost with his ship, and Michael Mack lost with his. With Tom Carraway, whom the Daubeneys had hoped would marry Blanche when the war was over, who in a hospital at Oran took three weeks to die of his wounds.

All the way from Edingthorpe, Blanche had been exhorting herself to be brave. But when she found herself in the drawing-room it was hopeless. Claud who'd sailed from Penang to Southampton, come to see his brother's memorial window, to try to put a little heart into his bereft parents. Who had met his sister's husband, patted his little nephew Jack on the head, given him a Malay silver bowl inscribed with verses from the Koran. Rupert who'd been the apple of his mother's eye before Jutland; and after it . . .

Hopeless. After a long silence, Blanche had managed, 'Do you remember you once said . . .?' and couldn't go on, so with her brimming eyes she gestured to the carry-cot which she'd placed on the sofa between them.

She'd wanted to try to explain why she'd come that day without Charlie, but then an instinct which had felt coherent enough became a muddle. She'd wanted to apologise for her own lack of faith, though she couldn't think why. Above all, she'd longed to get a few strangled words out which might explain that of course she knew that no child of hers could compensate in the slightest degree for Rupert, or for the post-war children that John and Anne might have had, but all the same she . . . Well, here was the carry-cot. Here was the offering.

She'd been unable to articulate any of these things. It had been atrocious, she'd never forget it, that silence. Anne and she on the sofa. The dead. The baby.

Anne Daubeney had been heroic. Smiling through her tears, she had asked, 'Do I understand? I hope I do.' She had leaned over Henrietta, with the back of her fore-finger had touched her cheek very softly. 'How silly of me, I mustn't cry on my goddaughter. Listen, Blanche honey. Can I ask you for one thing? Would you bring her over here, to be christened at Morston? I don't suppose Charles would mind, would he? And I . . . I should like that very much. Do you remember, in the service for the burial of the dead, there's a bit about *In the midst of life we are in death*? Well, if we christen your baby here . . . I like to hope that, *In the midst of death we are in life.*'

So Henrietta Lammas, swaddled in creamy lace, was carried up the path to Morston church, that small, bleak, flint bastion, past Rupert Daubeney's diminutive grave where his mother had planted primroses. Her godfathers were Colonel Fletcher from the Acle marshes, and Major de Brissac from — from many places, but on this occasion he'd dashed down from London, where he'd been staying at his club, and that evening returned there. The other godmother was Sarah Hedleigh.

Now, fourteen years later, Blanche Lammas crossed Anne Daubeney's field thinking contentedly of how her old friend would be pleased to see her godchild looking so bonny. (The plate to straighten her front teeth was a pity, but it would be coming off in the autumn.) Henrietta had been admirably unperturbed by Bobbie's nonsense about one of the Ayrshires being a bull. Now she was trying to cajole Georgia into shouldering her share of the family's clobber as well as her own, saying, 'Anyway, you can give your kit to Jack. He'll carry anything of yours you like, if you kiss him.' (Perhaps there *was* jealousy there — Charlie had said he feared there might be.)

Never mind. So long as between them they lugged all the gear as far as Anne's yard, it would be churlish to complain about their skirmishing. And it *was* agreeable to have such a sweet, skittish daughter to show off. In a few years she'd be quite a charmer, Blanche was already allowing herself twinges of proud apprehension. And Jack grown into such a splendid young man, and doing well in his Cambridge exams, which pleased his father no end — it would be nice for Anne to see Jack too.

Charlie was in a cheerful mood after his day at sea, dinner was certain to be merry. It always did him good to desert his easel briefly, she knew it did. Though it was becoming increasingly difficult to lure him away.

Still, suffused today with consciousness of the renewed cohesion of their marriage, Blanche returned unworriedly to being protective. People had said that years ago Charlie was dreadfully cocky. Well, she didn't know. Maybe he had been. But these days! He drove himself too hard: it was as simple as that. As for people who muttered that he was arrogant, or consumed by ambition, and people who thought that to be an achiever was fine but he was too damned perfect altogether . . . For these she reserved an implacably blithe dislike.

All the same, Blanche mused as they trooped into the yard, Caroline was going to have to learn to handle Bobbie a touch more intelligently if she reckoned to . . . A man like that could take some challenging.

'We're here, Anne!' she called to the drawing-room window, breathing the honeysuckle on its trellis. Sheltered, the yard, by flint barns, by flint garden walls – otherwise the scent would have been whipped past her on the gusts.

Darling Bobbie, ploughing through a difficult patch, but . . . More spirit Caroline needed. More boisterous, tougher spirit.

9

—꿍—

Like his wife, Charles Lammas took pleasure in trudging across a meadow
to a house where they'd been welcomed year after year, where in the
walled orchard he knew the individual apple trees. The low-built, flint
and brick manor, where in Anne Daubeney's snug little drawing-room
a coal fire was burning cheerfully because though it was summer the
nightfalls were cold. The yard with its barn door which he noticed had
been freshly painted. With its honeysuckle, its roses. How good were
familiar things! And the two cannons, which had seen service during the
Civil War at the siege of King's Lynn, and been bought somewhere or
other by John Daubeney – although they brought back the image of little
Rupert scrambling over them, pretending to fire them at intruders into
the yard. But what had set the cat among the pigeons in Lammas' mind
this evening was his recognition of his susceptibility.

Extraordinary, the way you stumbled upon a word, and it brought into
focus a scene that before had been fuzzy. A word . . . You recalled a girl
with brown hair bunched short on her neck, and making love in Rapallo
in a bedroom that looked over the sea – and a word came to you. It was
as straightforward as adjusting your telescope, suddenly seeing a ship you
hadn't made out before. Either that, or . . . Perhaps the distance wasn't
blurred. It was that you had a contemptible ability to observe yourself
living in the world for decades without seeing what you were up to,
without learning what manner of creature you were. And then, a word.
So he was absurdly susceptible! It was as simple as that. And not very
creditable.

That evening Charles Lammas was divided. Half of him rejoiced in
coming back to Morston Manor after a day at sea, just as he rejoiced
in his periodic returns to other houses and other friends, Bure Hall for
instance, or Villa Lucia. The bustle of arrival. Wet shoes taken off in the
porch, oilskins hung up in the cloak-room. Anne's smile of welcome, her
grey eyes. Chatter about a terrific catch of whitebait, and in the kitchen
there was also apparently a great dish of crabs. Then feet thumping up
the stairs, the running of baths, Blanche chivvying the girls to get a move
on please. And it *was* good after a hot bath to change into clean clothes
by a bedroom window you'd liked for years because of the view of the
orchard, and the dour church on the first knoll in from the sea.

And at the same time the other half of his mind was saying: So that's it! Perfectly plain, once you've found a word for it. All your life you've been falling for people and places, letting yourself be enchanted by this, beguiled by that, seduced by the other.

It explained a lot, he reflected with amusement, downstairs again and warming his legs by the hearth, vaguely recollecting a phrase of Byron's about a sea-coal fire, recognising as old friends the Chelsea figurines on Anne Daubeney's mantelpiece, noticing the propped-up invitations with several of which he was familiar from his Edingthorpe mantelpiece. Yes, he who'd always reckoned he was a fellow pursuing quite distinct directions, had if you looked at it differently, had all the while in fact been . . . Well, his life beheld as merely a chance sequence of bewitchments was certainly sobering.

Returning to the manor which had been John Daubeney's always reminded him of Jamie Macpherson, who also had been killed at that indecisive battle of Jutland when the German naval gunners outclassed the British, and Beatty said 'There's something wrong with our damned ships today,' but in the evening the German fleet steamed for home and the British were left in command of the sea.

Jamie and he had been susceptible all right, in France before the war. Now he thought of it . . .

He stooped, with the tongs put another chunk of coal on the flames. How they'd fallen for things! Passionate about Chardin, then the next day mad about Corot. Heading south from Paris, in love with every village spire and bridge. In the end he'd had to leave Jamie in Aix because he was so enraptured he refused to budge. On his own, he'd meandered on to Italy, and fallen head over heels for Vicenza and Asolo, for Verona and Mantua – not to mention all the girls Chiara Zanetti had introduced him to, particularly Lucrezia Venier, which was a shame really because she was about the only one who . . . Chuckling, the fifty-year-old survivor of these beguilements contemplated his life as that of one who'd never had the trace of a moral principle, had merely lurched from passion to passion.

Why, at the start he'd even been – what was the right word? – intoxicated by the war. Wondering if that were true, if that were the accurate way to put it, recollecting his enthusiastic 1914 self, he crossed to the window to draw the curtains. Night had fallen. You couldn't see the yard, or the church beyond. The wind must have risen again, it was howling.

Stimulated by the war? Passionate to fight it, certainly. A seduction of a kind, which later with scant originality he'd regretted. Then to be intoxicated by peace time, and now lately have come to suspect this had been a fraudulent charm too, though no worse than fraudulent.

He was gullible to a degree! But cheerful this evening. So he didn't castigate himself for spineless immorality, but mused instead how instinctive appeared to be the wish to instil into others' heads some knots of the tangle he'd always carried about in his own.

The delight he took in watching Jack fall under the spell of these English woods and estuaries and skies, for no better reason than that as a boy he'd fallen under the same spell. Watching the attention with which the lad rigged the old cutter, the way he bicycled home and with the same enthusiasm pored over books of reproductions of Constable and Cotman. For that matter the delight, which he had recently resolved to take more deliberately, in etching Georgia's impressionable mind before he sent her back East.

Here came footfalls, here was Anne. With any luck she'd report that the dressed crabs were already on the sideboard, the whitebait on the range already sizzling.

10

—·ɯ·—

At dinner, Caroline's efforts to join in the general merriment were woeful simply because they were efforts. She was so eager to be charming in Bobbie's eyes that Blanche resolved to take pity on her. She must not be repelled by the soft glances of appeal her nephew's wife directed at her across the table. She must take action, or other family parties might not just have a couple of wobbly moments like this one (although she was almost sure Anne hadn't noticed), they might be spoiled.

The hitch was that after dinner people dispersed about the house in talkative pairs and threesomes, so it was difficult to find a cranny where they would not be overheard. Still, determining not to take this excuse to postpone an interview in which she had little notion of what it might be useful to say, Blanche remembered the billiard room. She hadn't been into it for years, but she supposed it must still be there.

'Come with me just for a few minutes,' she said to Caroline. 'There's something I think we should talk about.'

The room where, Blanche now recollected, Tom Carraway had engaged in epic contests with John Daubeney had become a laundry. The billiard table was still there, shoved aside and draped with a sheet. Its former place had been taken by an ironing-board. Where once had stood a round table with a decanter and ashtray, now Anne Daubeney's maid had her mangle, and a stove where irons were heated. Still, there were a couple of chairs.

'Look what this place has become!' Blanche Lammas exclaimed, her sadness inaudible in her puff of exasperated laughter. 'Oh well, never mind. Do sit down.'

She sat too. Resting one elbow on the swathed edge of the billiard table, she passed her fingertips slightly wearily across her forehead. The star sapphire of her engagement ring coruscated. Her gold and jade bracelet slid half an inch, settled against her cuff.

Caroline wasn't interested in Blanche's wrist, she was tremulously aware of her own, of its ivory bracelet carved with dragons, that had been brought back by Michael Mack from the China Station and given her by his sister twenty years later at Edingthorpe on Boxing Day. And now Blanche appeared troubled by something, or anyway she didn't speak. So Caroline smiled hesitantly, to show that she appreciated this invitation to retreat among these piles of folded linen under the rack of billiard cues.

'It was the first night they stayed with us at the cottage,' she began. 'Something happened, I just know it did. After dinner I went indoors to make up a bed for Georgia, and then we sat talking, and . . . I don't know, how could I, no one told me anything. But they must have said things out there . . .' Caroline smiled again, but nervously this time, hoping to indicate she wouldn't dream of criticising her listener's husband and son. 'Bobbie didn't come to bed for hours, and when he did he really smelt of drink and didn't say a word. And the next day . . . After that, he wouldn't go back into his studio, wouldn't even talk about painting. I asked Uncle Charles. He said he'd always thought Bobbie had talent, but probably there was going to be a war. He said he really liked the picture of the château farm-yard.' Caroline's eyes lit up. She gave her blonde curls a shake. Her old vivaciousness flickered across her face. 'Do you remember? The oil painting of the byre gable, with the cart shafts, and some harness hanging up. There was a plough in the shadows, and a sunny patch with bantams pecking about.'

'Things can't have gone suddenly wrong in one evening,' Blanche Lammas demurred, wondering if the girl honestly expected her to believe Bobbie had got fed up with painting and with her from one day to the next. She didn't care terrifically for Caroline casting herself as a victim, either.

'No, of course not.' Caroline swallowed. 'Not much fun, though – to have your whole way of life abolished one summer. Our married life. What we'd wanted. Everything we'd done.' She faced the elder woman timidly, but held her gaze. 'I don't think I'd deserved that.'

'I'm sure you hadn't,' Blanche assured her with warmth, wishing she could do so without recalling Gloria, whose marriage had been curtailed with a savagery which . . . But she must concentrate on the young woman before her.

Still, for all she knew Geoffrey's and Gloria's marriage had been this sort of fiddle-faddle. Incomprehensions, inadequacies. . . . Till the collision of empires condemned him to – to a death better not thought of too much. Or the butchery in that Passchendaele mud, and his name carved on memorials there and in England, lent his courage a . . . No, she must concentrate. Lent . . . Mocked his courage with a loathsome glory which Charlie still couldn't speak of calmly, which wasn't glory, was an offence to the soul. Which she couldn't want him to speak of calmly. Made him snarl unprintable things about justifying the ways of God to man. What was Caroline saying? Honestly, it might be kinder to tell her straight out that she'd get nowhere with Bobbie by being insipid.

'Naturally I know your loyalty is to Bobbie. As far as Uncle Charles and you are concerned, my job in life is just to make him a satisfactory wife.'

'Oh, we're not as bad as that.' Blanche smiled, to try to make herself forget how her nephew's decision to join the Sherwood Rangers had triggered in his mother such noisy, damp hysterics, followed by such self-pitying suppression of them, that he'd just about given up visiting her. 'Not *quite* so unimaginative, I hope!'

'I won't pretend I haven't noticed he's unhappy.' Caroline was knitting her fingers, but she kept at her confrontation stalwartly. 'He'd never have chucked up his painting if something wasn't wrong. Wasn't wrong deep inside. He wouldn't always want to stay up late drinking with people he scarcely knows, always be dashing off to parties.'

'Oh yes he might! Easily! Parties are a lot of fun. I hope you always go with him, make sure he sees you're having at least as good a time as he is.'

'I don't always,' Caroline confessed. 'I get so exhausted. Mama took me to London, and we went to parties. But Bobbie wasn't there. I hated it.'

'Yes, that jaunt was probably a mistake. Oh – I don't know . . .' The wild girl from the Edwardian years was, a generation later in the respectably elegant middle-aged shape of the Royal Academician's consort, raising her pretty head, looking about the billiard-cum-laundry room with mocking incisiveness. 'Why aren't you pregnant?'

Caroline blushed painfully. 'I . . . I wish I . . . But Bobbie doesn't want us to have a baby.'

Blanche raised her eyebrows. She went close enough to saying, 'For pity's sake, girl, just fire away and have one,' to dangle the idea in the air between them. But then she changed her mind. She suggested instead, lightly, 'Well, I think you ought to go to lots of parties, where Bobbie can see what a success you are. You ought to play him at tennis and get such a lot of coaching that you always beat him. I don't know, but – learn how to tango and become famous for it, always with other partners. Now, let's go back to the fire, and smoke a cigarette together. This room used to be so jolly, but these days it's . . . Look at those damp stains!'

'Is that all you can say?' Caroline almost wailed. 'Oh, I had hoped . . . No, no, what more could you have said?'

The two women stood, they faced one another.

Then the ripples began to die away.

'Just imagine some of the places Bobbie may be posted to. Sierra Leone, Tanganyika . . . You and he will have a glorious time. Where are the Sherwood Rangers now?'

Caroline couldn't help smiling. 'Nottinghamshire.'

'Well, that won't last long. It could be Jamaica . . .' Her husband might, at Villa Lucia six weeks before, have worried about the empire as an overweight heifer tethered for slaughter. But for Blanche Lammas now it was an arena where her adored nephew could disport himself, and quite likely by so doing salvage his marriage to this really very sweet girl. 'Palestine, the Gulf . . . Lots of dances, lots of riding. Bobbie will play polo, he'll ride point-to-points. All his brother officers will fall in love with you. Then you can have a baby. Bobbie rides well, Charlie and I taught him.'

11

―᙭―

Judging by the peals of mirth sounding from the dining-table next door, Charles Lammas' peace by the drawing-room fire wouldn't last long, but all the same he found it agreeable. The crab and the whitebait had been first-rate; so had the Moselle. And now to retreat from the hilarious rumpus, which of course would be chiefly of Bobbie's inspiration; to light a cheroot, collapse into an armchair . . . Perhaps it was being fifty. What a hubbub they made! Perhaps it was age.

Too somnolent to be other than contented, Lammas stretched his legs. The leaping, murmuring flames in the hearth had a soothing influence too. *I like a sea-coal fire* . . . Something like that. Time he read Byron again. Where had all the women of the party vanished to? They couldn't *all* be clustered around Bobbie, laughing at his imitation of his father-in-law at the hustings or his mother-in-law opening a fête. Nothing like a day at sea to put you to rights. Good heavens, had that shriek of delight come from his daughter Henrietta's throat? Nothing like a dinner of fish that had been caught right here, a mile off the old wreck.

Lulled by these platitudes, Lammas drowsed. He dreamed he was swimming somewhere. He was exhausted but he had to swim on, he didn't know why but it was desperately urgent. Warm, grey sea. And the water was horribly frightening, which was odd because he'd always been a strong swimmer. But this sea now . . . With failing muscles, he floundered forward, but it was no good, something was catching him up. The air was glittering murk, he couldn't see a . . .

This also is vanity – he heard that. Whatever was chasing him was very close now. He tried to look back over his shoulder, but his neck wouldn't turn. *For the living know that they shall die.* Ahead suddenly the sea was a cauldron, he'd be sucked down. No! Christ, what was coming up? The sea boiled, a conning-tower broke into the air. Cascades of water crashed back off the hull, he was going to be drowned, he tried to yell for help but no sound came. *For time and chance* . . .

'On the starboard bow, Sir.' 'You there, Lammas?'

They were raising him up, he was going to be saved! A rope to hang onto. Up he came, out of that warm ghastly sea, up!

Then something happened, he was falling back, he . . .

Shaking, Lammas woke. Dear God, what was all that horror? Quickly he picked up his cheroot. It had gone out, Anne's carpet didn't appear to have been singed, that was all right then.

He hoiked out his handkerchief, mopped his chilly forehead. Damned Nicky Muir again. And that sea! *So are the sons of men caught in an evil time.* Something unwholesome about that Muir fellow always. Sexless, or religious, or half drunk, or – something wrong with him. Mind you, some of the padres were fine men. Muir didn't know how to handle being afraid, maybe – a bit of a coward? Well, he was dead. Didn't seem to want to lie down, though.

Matches. Lammas relit his cheroot, frowning at the way his fingers trembled. He looked around at the small, comfortable, provincial room.

Encouraged to more wicked audacity by his wife being cloistered in the old billiard-room with his aunt, Bobbie Lammas let himself rip. As Julian Hedleigh in a draughty village hall, trying to convince an audience of a dozen farm labourers and marsh-men and their wives that they ought to vote Tory, he reduced his younger listeners to yelps of laughter. Even Anne Daubeney, who had always privately considered Hedleigh as fake as they made them, smiled happily. It was brilliant, they all agreed, the way Bobbie switched back and forth at lightning speed between his impersonations of the hearty politician, his pomposity only held in check by his wiliness, and a local poacher rather the worse for beer and heckling fearlessly.

Still Caroline didn't reappear. Bobbie's election harangue started to be laced with asides about how, honestly, the lord lieutenancy was in the bag. Then he acted the fawning but dogged Conservative party agent. Then back to the truculent poacher. And the candidate's asides became more and more daring, all about how, honestly, he hadn't reckoned to wait this long for his knighthood. Two City companies of which he was a director contributed annually to Tory funds, and he'd always voted according to the Whips' instructions – what on earth was the hitch? Had the Prime Minister no conscience?

Jack laughed unrestrainedly, his handsome young face ruddy from the weather at sea, his powerful shoulders shaking, tears in his eyes. Then his thoughts distracted him, he fell quiet. But a minute later, Bobbie as Sarah Hedleigh opening the Bure gardens to the public in order to raise money for the restoration of the organ in Norwich cathedral brought his attention back to the dinner table. Less dilatory than Mr Chamberlain, her son-in-law had made her Lady Hedleigh for the occasion. Jack chortled with delight when she announced that she was going to *throw* her garden open, with a gesture more indicative of casting shrubberies, flower-beds, lawns, ponds and all to the winds, and in tones more appropriate to the sacrifice of her gold and silver for guns for the defence of the kingdom, while at the same time giving an under-gardener hell for the condition of a yew hedge.

Jack had always rejoiced in his cousin's talent as a mimic — rejoiced quite unenviously, because he knew he couldn't act. He'd never been offered even a minor rôle in a school play. Whatever efforts he made, he remained solidly himself. But tonight, although Bobbie was in diabolical form, other presences too were having their way with Jack's heart.

Jack could hear the wind roaring through the trees now, and rattling the panes. He imagined *Golden Eye* out in the moonless bay tugging at her anchor line. On the promontory, the terns would be asleep in the dunes, in hollows of marram grass and shells. Sand would be blowing against the door of the old lifeboat-house.

If *Golden Eye* dragged her anchor in this storm, if she went aground . . . Jack was visited by a horrible vision of his beloved cutter lying on her beam-ends being crashed against the beach, beginning to break up. No, no, that anchor had held her in gales as fierce as this. Still, in the morning he'd go out and check that she was all right. If this wind didn't die down a bit, they'd have to stay in harbour here, there'd be no sailing on to Wells or Burnham in this weather. How many days away from the studio would Papa allow Georgia?

In France, Georgia had loved it when Bobbie flattered her and teased her, she'd responded with the most cheerful coquetry, and Jack hadn't minded in the least because she treated him in the same manner. And now today she'd flirted with them both indiscriminately, and it was a game he found rendered her more attractive not less. Here she was again, tilting her head a little on one side to catch his glance in that way she had. And the movement of her mouth when she smiled at him was . . . He didn't know what it was, but he kept looking at it.

What was more, lately he'd got the distinct impression that Papa looked with benign amusement on his liking Georgia so much. *How* much? He'd have to decide some day. No he wouldn't. Why bother? Get it wrong, whatever he decided. The thing was to take her in his arms, kiss that pouting smile. If you fancy a girl, take her to bed — that was what Bobbie had said. Take her to Paris, do what you like, but don't marry her.

Georgia's flushed cheeks, her tilted-up nose, her confident eyes . . . No wonder Bobbie found her attractive. It went down awfully easily, this Moselle. Kingfisher colours, a halcyon was supposed to have, and a nest rocking on the sea. *That surly shore*, that lee-shore.

His cousin's outburst beneath the lime trees in the Quercy had shocked Jack. But tonight . . .

Perhaps it was the wine he'd drunk, or all the recent talk about Hitler and the Sudetenland, or the excitement of rough sailing, or his mother's moderately innocent remark about there being safety in numbers. Maybe the ghosts of his heroes Horatio Nelson and Thomas Hardy had something to do with it. Or Bobbie's and Georgia's playful awareness of one another as forbidden fruit and therefore probably excellent. Or what was fairly blatantly that young man's cousinly lesson in the enjoyment of feminine charm. Or the girl's revelling in the admiration of both cousins possibly in order to encourage the quieter one.

Anne Daubeney's presence in the dining-room ensured decorum, but then she adjourned next door to talk to Charles Lammas. It was not until Caroline reappeared to repossess her husband, that any new sobering influence came into the room, and then Bobbie didn't pay her much attention. He was in the middle of a story about Venice, which involved warning Georgia that although Uncle Charles these days appeared a respectable sort of fellow, in fact downright staid, the last time he'd been in The Serene Republic he'd met a lady who'd known his uncle there before the war, and had some ludicrous anecdotes to recall.

'Bobbie!' Caroline interjected primly. And then she blushed, because of the dismissive, laughing glance he gave her; and because this was exactly the kind of conflict she'd been resolving to avoid.

Jack lolled in his chair, thinking about Nelson in Naples with Emma Hamilton. The trouble was, he knew perfectly well he wasn't made of the same stuff as Nelson, had no potential as a romantic hero. He didn't even have Bobbie's natural gallantry. He'd never be a great seducer of women – it might be a pity, but he just wouldn't be. Bobbie might have had amorous adventures left right and centre, ('Oh, Bobbie's girlfriends!' Blanche had more than once exclaimed), and might if his marriage got dull resume his former dallyings. But Jack would want to marry a nice girl sooner or later, and would try hard to make her an admirable husband – he just knew he would. However, not yet.

Upstairs, Morston Manor was a warren of creaking corridors and crooked staircases and small, Spartan bedrooms. In the bathrooms, pipes groaned and murmured. In tonight's tempest, broom cupboards and linen cupboards kept swinging open unexpectedly. Above again, the attic rooms had truckle beds and dusty rafters and peeling wallpaper. Jack was lodged up there; but he didn't know if Georgia was sharing a room with Henrietta or not. Music would have suited his mood – something by Gershwin perhaps, or what was that song Astaire sang that he'd liked?

Listening to girls' voices through the wall, he took off his jacket, took off his tie. No electricity up here under the roof. He'd placed his candle on a low beam, the reverberations of the storm made it gutter. Really there was no call to fret about *Golden Eye* with that big anchor down, and in the harbour the holding was good.

The girls had stopped talking. Those footfalls were one of them going away. Cheerfully, but with his heart thumping, Jack strode to the little attic door, which for simplicity could have been the door of a shed. Grinning at the fool he was making of himself, he lifted the iron latch. He asked the dimness beyond, 'Georgia, do feel like dancing?'

She giggled. 'How do you know I'm not your little sister?'

'I don't. I can hardly see you.'

She'd placed her candle on the threadbare dressing-table. In the looking-glass, it had lit a golden shimmer. Apart from that, all was gloom. A water-tank in the corner whispered. The window was a black square. The bed was a grey oblong.

'And are you sure dancing is what you want to do? Mind your head, there's a rafter. Dancing is just a word, it can mean anything. Anyway, what are you up to, barging in here? I might have been taking off my clothes. I bet you wish I had been.'

'Come and dance. You can take your clothes off later. You just have to imagine there's the most fantastic band playing.'

A few moments before, in his head Jack had been hearing 'Dancing cheek to cheek', and then it had been 'I get a kick out of you'. But now, when he put his arms round Georgia's waist, silence fell in his mind. Anyhow, no dance started like that. And she wasn't already swaying into motion as she would have been if it had been one of their dances at Edingthorpe up in the old nursery.

Her waist felt warm and supple. In the candle-light, all he could see of her face was one cheekbone outlined with pale, almost silvery gold. Thinking how ridiculous it was to have wanted this for so long, he pulled her toward him, he kissed her mouth.

Her arched back, her breasts against his chest, her lips beginning to kiss – he'd forgotten she was Georgia. It was the sensation which he knew he'd never forget.

She must have heard something, because she murmured, 'Shhh.' Then, 'Do you suppose Bobbie and Caroline are kissing like that?'

'What? Oh . . . No, I don't, actually.'

'What a good new dance we've learned.'

A few moments later, he asked, 'Do you think we'd be happier lying down?'

'Good heavens, Jack, what a suggestion! Well, yes, I dare say we would be. Tiny bed, though.'

In the blank daybreak Georgia, with a flutter of giggles and kisses, turfed Jack out of her bed.

Neither of them had slept for more than a few minutes now and then. Both were in such high spirits that it was going to be difficult in others' company to keep from laughing aloud out of sheer joy in life.

Still blowing a gale, Jack noted as he brushed his teeth. There'd be no sailing today. But he didn't care. What was so wonderful was that Georgia, like he, was only playing.

12

_____

After twenty-four hours, the gale blew itself out. The party at Morston Manor dispersed – Blanche and Henrietta to their horses at Edingthorpe, Charles and his model to the studio there, *Golden Eye* to sea with a reduced crew. They sailed on in sunshine, with an easy wind which kept backing round to the south so the cutter reached steadily over small, lulling waves.

Jack's heart was so high it was . . . It was up, up, all over the bright sky. It was up with the taut white sails, it blew joyously with the soughing breeze where the burgee fluttered and terns flew.

Bobbie and Caroline seemed to be being cheerful with one another, so that was all right, or if they weren't he didn't notice. As for him, when they sailed past the marshes he kept thinking of Georgia half undressed wriggling in his arms, thinking of pitch darkness when the candle was out, of a water-tank that mumbled and sighed, of a bed so narrow they had to cling close so as not to tumble out. Georgia three-quarters undressed, Georgia kissing and whispering, Georgia playing – that was the feeling which most happily convinced him. Play . . . Ideal, enchanted play.

But when they had sailed past Holkham beach, and decided to put into Burnham that evening, briefly Jack forgot Georgia. Burnham! Where Horatio Nelson was born and brought up in the parsonage just inland. It was practically holy ground, in Jack's mythology. Burnham, where as a boy on those creeks the future victor of Aboukir Bay learned to sail, learned about winds and tides. Where he returned as a captain on half pay after bringing *Boreas* back from the Leeward Islands, for years farmed his father's glebeland, wrote letters begging their Lordships of the Admiralty for a new command. A ship – any ship!

Jack sailed inshore, musing vaguely about Nelson at Antigua, at English Harbour, going to dine with Commissioner Moutray and his pretty wife. Then Nelson at Nevis visiting the mansion called Montpellier, where he proposed to Frances Nisbet and was accepted. Nelson . . . Georgia, when the stormy day began to break, and in the attic window's greyness he could see her again as well as touch her. Nelson at Naples going ashore to visit the Hamiltons at Palazzo Sessa . . .

A few days later, back at Edingthorpe, Jack walked across the yard to the studio, carrying a copy of *Twelfth Night*.

13

—ɯ—

Charles Lammas had teased his son about his anxiety caused by the progress made in the portrayal of Georgia. But his joking had been truthful when he'd said that he had started by drawing her head two or three times, and then over a month had made several small oil studies of the girl in different poses wearing different dresses. His dealer in Bond Street would know how to dispose of these for small but useful sums.

Now he was down to work on what he assured Georgia was 'the real thing at last, and then I'll let you go home'. He had her standing at an oblique angle to the tall Venetian mirror, which was one of the most glamorous trophies he'd ever brought back to Norfolk. (Giacomo Zanetti had produced it years ago, in thanks for some drawings of Emanuela and Jack when they were five, romping and confabulating on the lawn under the chestnut trees.) Georgia wore her first ball-dress, the one she was going to wear to the dance at Bure Hall. And as the summer passed, and increasingly assumed the aspect of an idyll, Lammas found he'd stopped teasing Jack about coming at night to tackle the canvas with a rag and turpentine.

An idyll? Well – for those three, for the painter and his son and his model. And not only in retrospect, either. There was more to it than just the summer weather, too, and the scent of mown grass which drifted in, and tea on the verandah along the studio's south wall where the buddleia was in purple flower and frequented by what could appear to be half the butterflies in the parish, red admirals and commas, peacocks and tortoise-shells and cabbage whites. More to it than Georgia's light blue dress. (Cambridge blue, not that dark Oxford blue, Jack remarked with what was intended to be manly, amused approval but which, because he was young and enchanted, came out with a bubbling laugh of delight.) More to it than the way she stood with her shoulder to the glass, her head slightly turned, with that hesitation, that air of the girl newly a woman and the young woman still a girl; than her tarnished bronze hair; than her obliqueness to the viewer and her other shadowy obliquity in the edge of the lustrous mirror. Though these were what the painting was all about. Or all these were parts of the idyll, but the whole was greater than the amassed parts. And of course it was idyllic for three different muddles of reasons. Remained potent, for that matter, until the widely distanced ends of all three lives; remained dying away but still resonant, in times when that sort of elegant portrait seemed a ghostly presence from an abolished world.

It wasn't really a verandah. More of a lean-to outhouse with an open front. Blanche sometimes used it as a potting-shed. But there were wicker chairs, and when after a sitting they'd made tea on the studio stove it was pleasant to carry it out and sit where you could watch the butterflies on the buddleia.

That studio wasn't really the treasure house Georgia Burney had discovered – though the great gilded mirror was a handsome object and must have been worth something. To Charles Lammas, that barn of his was a workshop. It was where he produced, and where often he sold. It was where each morning he started work with cheerful determination, and then all day enthusiasm flared up and sank down and flickered again. It was where hours went by in apparently the most perfect peace you could imagine, and he was aware of being on his own spiritual ground and at the same time given over to his utmost tension, in which his resolve to do good work and his dissatisfaction with his talent vied with each other and wore him down.

There were days when his control was good. Hour by hour, he dripped just enough dissatisfaction into his mind to keep his concentration taut. Then even if by late afternoon his head ached he didn't much care, because tiredness was natural, and he recognised some aches which meant the right tension had been there so maybe the work done hadn't been slack. Anyhow, a walk with the spaniels for an hour would bring calm.

There were also days when the dissatisfaction became a damned sight too like self-hatred. Then he couldn't regulate its flow, and the nervous tension produced on canvas nothing worth having. The tramp afterwards with his dogs along lanes and hedgerows turned into a lonely wrestle to exorcise his despair at time passing and at his own stupidity. He'd walk farther afield, often not come back till after dark, till he reckoned that the malaise of today probably wouldn't infect tomorrow.

Yet when the good working days came one after another . . . Though Lammas didn't call them good days. He'd smile cheerfully, say things like 'Not bad, I hope', or, 'Well, you know, one slogs along'. When he seemed to have hit upon a rhythm, and the trick was scarcely even to be aware of it, to make the most of it while the going was good, not get wrought up because it couldn't last, and not relax either. Those times meant that the world wasn't just bearable – for moments together it was glorious with beauties perceived and intimations realised. For entire days, even when you were fifty years old, you could understand how people had spoken of places that were Arcadian, times that were a Golden Age. That was, if you took care not to think about it either too contentedly or too nervously, this propitious season you'd blundered into, or achieved, or awoken to, or whatever it was you'd done. That was the secret, in his case. If you could manage not to despair too much, or too little . . . Well, anyhow, it felt as if there were a balance in his refractory brain which sometimes he could strike and sometimes he couldn't. And it was while he was musing on this, during one of his sittings with his goddaughter that summer, that he suddenly comprehended why those melancholics Burney and Zanetti had chosen him for a friend.

Alex after the war had taken pretty much the first career that came to hand. So long as it was a long way from England and Belgium and France. So long as it would pay him enough to keep his family respectably, do things with that correctness – not just send Ricky to Winchester, be perfect even down to the formal good humour and the small kindnesses – which was often characteristic of the implacable melancholic. If the forests of those Frontier Areas of his would enable him to keep up appearances, and would occupy his thoughts for a fair stretch of his days, then they'd do fine. And Giacomo had settled for activities below his powers too. Had after the war written no more art history. Had bought and sold a little. Had grown too heavy and idle even to go in for much dissipation any longer; so now he played the genial landowner and father and connoisseur.

While he, Charlie Lammas, stood before his easel with his palette in his left hand and his brush raised in his right, with his goddaughter posing with exemplary patience, his son in a chair reading aloud to them the first act of *Twelfth Night* because they were off to see it at Wyndham's Theatre the week after next. He stood in what were for him the right place and the essential attitude, concentrating on the work he loved, or at least couldn't contemplate renouncing.

The difference was that he could often control the level of dissatisfaction in his mind. Or that was part of it . . . Along with a streak of hearty ordinariness which he had, but men like Alex and Giacomo could only assume. The way he really *did* lose himself in the enjoyment of life. Wasn't pretending. Genuinely delighted in the most ordinary things. Club dinners, race meetings, country weddings, chat about politics or cricket. They were distractions that really distracted – and the more ordinary the better. Palliatives that really did mitigate, had the desired superficial effect. And thinking of country weddings . . . The invitation to the nuptials of Raffaella Zanetti and Giulio Flamini had just arrived.

A very posh invitation. Thick, gilt-edged card, ornately printed – Chiara had begun as she clearly intended to go on. With, written in pencil in Giacomo's hand across one corner: *Vedi che non ci siamo riusciti.* You see, we've failed.

'I'm a lucky devil and no mistake.' That was the way Lammas would formulate his awareness of the summer going well. And of course at the best his would be a fifty-year-old, work-a-day kind of idyll, nothing to get lyrical about. All the same . . . Though he finally did seem to be past anything better than labouring at canvas after canvas for with any luck a decade or two yet – reduced to watching, to listening, to being amused. Because it *was* amusing. Not only the tingle of the erotic in the air between his son and his goddaughter. The whole business of painting this kind of picture too.

It had been after Georgia's last fitting with the dress-maker. Blanche had said, 'Charlie, she really *does* look rather fetching. Why don't you come up and see, before she puts her old rags back on?'

In the bedroom where the fitting had taken place, Georgia had paraded her sumptuous light blue dress a little gingerly, given her skirts an experimental swirl. And Lammas had thought: Right, that's how I'll paint her.

Now the picture was well under way, and he had no regrets about choosing this dress and this pose by the mirror, and the whole thing amused him. Lavery had painted this sort of portrait on the eve of the last war, and so had William Orpen. He'd learned from them, and from Augustus John, and others too. And now here he was, almost certainly on the eve of the next war – and from the tangle in his mind he'd picked out this unashamedly charming thread.

Now . . . When he had time, which was the one element absolutely vital for an idyll so far as he was concerned. When he had no fussy client to content. When he had before him, not an impatient and vain sitter, but a model who was so patient he had to remind himself not to exploit the sweetness with which she'd stand till her back and legs *must* be aching. A model whom he'd made a bargain with, whom he could keep posing for as many weeks as he fancied, so long as then he put her on the next ship to Rangoon.

Time. Time. Keeping at it. Never allowing yourself the skimped or the slapdash. Never letting yourself solve the painting's problems with evasive methods which you knew deep down wouldn't stand up to the only criteria that counted – whatever they were, but when he wasn't tired he knew them when he saw them. So much easier said than done. Probably best not talked about either. But – thinking, Just a fashionable portrait painter, and chuckling to himself at that as he often had. Thinking that he reckoned Duncan Grant was overrated, but Harold and Laura Knight both had tremendous ability – and knowing that it didn't matter a damn what you thought in that superficial sort of way, so long as underneath you were concentrating like the devil. Thinking, A hell of a sight better a fashionable portrait painter than an unfashionable one, and smiling again. To concentrate, to give the picture all the time it needed, not to die – that was the trick. Not to lie dying, like poor Nanny now.

What Jack and Georgia got up to in private was their concern. Charming, though, the decorous manner in which she stood to be looked at. Charming, the rueful way he sometimes let himself glance up from his Shakespeare to her posing there.

Twelfth Night being read, and all this splendid sentimental education going on before your eyes, and time to try to paint something truly good. A bit of sexual education too, imaginably, and why not?

War coming. When would there next be girls in their first ball-dresses posing in summer studios, for pity's sake? Paint them while they lasted. Could be a long time before the survivors got back to having much fun, and the Venetian mirrors got back to having these sorts of reflections. The next ship to Rangoon. Time . . . He'd take his time.

14

—ɯ—

The Edingthorpe kitchen had lost two of its presences. Last winter the gun-dog Brandy had died, been buried in the garden, and an oak planted where it could draw vigour from his goodness. The wicker basket he had chewed with his remaining yellow teeth, and the old rug in it, had been burned.

Or rather, Brandy had not simply died. When his dying had become too horrible, Charles Lammas had fetched his twelve-bore. They had gone out together into the garden for the last time, into the lightless December afternoon, only on this occasion not after rabbits, and not pigeon-flighting either. They went at less than walking pace, because Brandy could only hobble painfully along.

Still, Lammas felt he ought at least to get out of sight of the kitchen windows, because when this last short foray together had been decided upon, poor Ellen Meade had become distressed, had said, 'Oh I'm sorry Sir,' and started snivelling into her apron. But out on the back lawn near the rookery Brandy could go no further. He wagged his tail a bit, feebly. He lay down on the damp ground.

Lammas tried standing behind the animal's back, but that seemed somehow awful, and Brandy kept trying to turn his head to look at his master. So he stepped round to face him. He couldn't bear to destroy his old dog's head, so he put the muzzle of the gun close to his neck. Holding the dog's gaze with his own, and wondering how much he understood, he said, 'Goodbye, Brandy old fellow,' and pulled the trigger. From the bare trees, dozens of startled rooks flew up, wheeled black and clamorous in the grey air.

Now half a year had passed, and Mary Oldfield was in her bedroom, dying unobtrusively.

Charles Lammas and Georgia Burney always came to talk to her for a few minutes when their sittings were over, and Jack and Henrietta were forever dashing up the stairs to see if she wanted anything, dashing and then tip-toeing the last few yards along the landing in case she were asleep. Not that she ever minded being disturbed by those two. And anyhow she seemed to pass most of her days and nights halfway between waking and sleeping. If it was Henrietta, she'd murmur 'Hello my pet,' and shift her hand on the counterpane to indicate that the girl should perch there for a minute. If it was Jack, he'd stand looking massively tall and robust over the minute old woman who took up only half the bed. She'd think of something those arms and legs of his could usefully bring. Or she'd smile, and then her eyes would close, and he'd come away.

The person who spent far and away the most time by Mary Oldfield's bedside was Blanche Lammas, who up in that little room with its faded Victorian pink and white wallpaper went back to being Blanche Mack. Naturally she had other things to do. But she passed as much time as she could up there, nursing her old nanny through her last illness, her last few months. Not that she had any chronic disease. Just a mass of minor ailments, none of which was actually going to kill her, and what Doctor Bennett called 'Simply old age, Mrs Lammas.' That was it. The mortal weariness of having been eighty-seven for a whole year, and now being eighty-eight, having to go on tiredly being that, hour by hour. Just time, that was what was killing Mary Oldfield.

So there they were together, day after day in the summer storms and the summer calms, 'Blanche dearie' and 'Nanny darling' just as they had always been.

Nanny Oldfield would recall Paston Hall before the war. Only twenty years since the Armistice . . . But the estate had been sold, and then the Hall, and Blanche was the only one of the family still alive, so that along with the place, the love and the fun they'd had could also seem to have vanished into thin air.

But Nanny remembered. She knew the magical time it had been for Blanche, when Michael and she had cantered their ponies over the stubble fields, and then a few years later cantered their horses there. Hacking along the paths hedged with hawthorn and bramble, jumping the banks. Riding past the church and over a couple of salt-bitten meadows down to the sea, at low tide galloping along the glistening beach.

The old woman was so weak, often it was difficult to tell how conscious she was. Blanche would settle in a chair by the window, darn a pair of socks. To care for the woman who had cared for her; just to be there if she needed anything . . . It didn't bring Michael back, because he was always there. Nanny had looked after him when he was a baby too, and when she died another thread in the yarn would be cut, and Blanche sometimes wondered who there'd be left to talk with about the old days. Anne Daubeney, yes. Not many old friends seemed to be left – and she was only in her forties.

As for what Nanny dreamed of, in that halfway-house of hers between waking and sleeping, between life and death . . . Her childhood in County Down in the middle of the last century, possibly – but if so, she'd buried it too deep for talking about. She'd worry sometimes about her sister Ethel's children, grown up in Saskatchewan. 'Some of them must be old enough to be dead now.' She'd repeat the story of her brother Percy's short life as a mighty Orangeman. This she invariably concluded with her faint voice thrilling with pride: 'And, Blanche dearie, there was shooting at his funeral!'

Then Blanche discovered that the old woman liked to be read to. Liked to hear the stories she had read to children in Malaya and Norfolk. So she fetched *The Wind In The Willows*, she fetched *The Jungle Book*. It was peaceful, sitting in the pink and white bedroom, reading. Nanny would doze. Then she'd wake up, say something about how she'd used to take the Ross children down to the harbour at Malacca to watch the schooners. Or about later, when the Colonel was posted to Georgetown, and there were pepper plantations, and little Harry took sick.

Once when they'd been talking quite merrily about a gymkhana at Paston, Blanche took her courage in both hands. She leaned over the bed, she smiled. 'And, Nanny darling . . . You did hint to me, long ago.' After all, she'd been her confidante in the Tom Carraway years. And to speak might be some slight comfort at last. 'Wasn't there once someone? I'd love it, if you'd tell me. A soldier, who went to the Afghan War?'

But Mary Oldfield couldn't have been as close to this world as, a moment before, she had appeared. Either that, or the young man who never came back from Kabul had been sepulchred deep enough, she wasn't going to talk about him now.

15

The three in the studio didn't allow their idyll to be tainted by the extinction in gradual progress up at the house. Nor, certainly, would Nanny Oldfield have wished them to.

The studio had been a small barn, built of flint and red brick in the Norfolk manner, with gables and reed thatch. Charles Lammas' large north window was the only structural innovation, apart from the chimney necessitated by the iron stove he installed. Then a coat of white paint, the repairing of the door, the putting up of picture rails, the appearance of a dais and an easel – the place had become a studio while remaining a barn.

Then things had accrued, till by the time Georgia first knew it, that room was a treasure house.

A lay-figure wearing a saffron dress with slashed sleeves stood by a bookcase – wearing also, for some reason, a tricorn hat. A dapple-grey rocking-horse, banished from the old nursery, had half-a-dozen sumptuous stuffs laid across its worn saddle, had the tatters of a bridle cock-eyed on its head, one stirrup still dangling from a threadbare tassel. Against the chimney-piece, pikes and lances were propped.

Georgia would stand in the hospitable peace, marvelling. The bureau, with its pigeon-holes shadowy and enticing. The bookshelves and the paintings on the walls – among them a White Ensign, long since flown on E_{35}, bearing witness to the painter's war. A still-life set up on what had been a card table: a Chinese tea-pot, Christmas roses, apples, a napkin. On an easel near it, the painting, half finished. A toy theatre, which looked as if it had once been left out in the rain. A bamboo hat-stand adorned with bonnets and boaters.

Things. The beauty of things, and their mysteriousness. Things arranged, things just dumped any old how. Things in themselves. Each school holiday, Georgia used to haunt that studio. She never wanted to paint, as the Lammas children did. For her the panacea had been to be among those objects. Then gradually she came to know that studio as a treasure house not only of the inert but, so it seemed to her, of immaterial riches too, as a place where songs were sung and ideas debated and stories told.

Charles Lammas was working with the right tenseness and tranquillity, he just knew he was, and, though there was a long way yet to go, the painting was beginning to come together as he'd wanted it. Georgia's dignity already at sixteen; the way having her hair up made her look both older and very young; the great mirror with its shadowy sheen . . . Nothing like being really taken with your subject, he mused. Nothing like the determination that gave.

He'd wanted something, some still-life, lowish in the foreground, and after trying various ideas had settled on a small marquetry table with a jade lamp he'd always liked. Then he hadn't been able to decide what she should be standing on, till he remembered that Shiraz rug in the drawing-room and suspected those soft reds and blues and golds might go well. So he'd sent Jack to roll it up, carry it across the yard, and they'd spread it for Georgia's feet – and it *did* go well. So now he was working on that too. He wanted the faintest suggestion of that sumptuous pattern. And one way and another, his blood was up. Cautiously; cannily   But – he couldn't help hoping his view of Villa Lucia was one of the best landscapes he'd done. And if this time next year at Burlington House it were joined by this picture of Georgia . . . Something to make people meandering around the Summer Exhibition stop, and catch their breath – that was what he wanted. Oh, well . . . Probably a more reasonable way to phrase it would be to acknowledge that this was as good as he was capable of.

The open window. The sound of wood-pigeons cooing from his trees. Then Henrietta leading that frisky Arab of hers clip-clop across the cobbled yard. Awareness of outer things had exactly the right importance these days: enough to steady the poised mind, but not distract it.

Lesser thoughts glimmered around his central idea in a manner he liked. Without slackening his concentration, he thought of Alex and Giacomo who – why hadn't he focused on this before? – probably despised him a little for that streak of ordinary obtuseness which was such a valuable ingredient in his nature, but were nice enough not to show it.

This was the way to think of things – glancingly. Old friends, this and that. Guy Rivac going every morning to his ship-broking office in Bordeaux, off with Marie whenever they had a free week to that château which was more dilapidated every year. Splendid fellow, Guy. And, God damn it, if Ned intended to wait for, for whatever was coming, at Rapallo looking out through his cedars to the bay, he himself would . . . He'd take his stand right here. Working at this composition, at this unashamed elegance he'd felt like choosing, this wonderful charm. They'd find him brush in hand, painting the sash at his goddaughter's waist.

Vedi che non ci siamo riusciti . . . Smiling wryly as he rubbed out those pencilled words of Giacomo Zanetti's before taking the invitation to Blanche. He'd already known he wasn't going to suggest they went. A Tuscan September was always worth sousing your wits with; the wedding at Villa Lucia would be a superb occasion; there'd be amusement in watching Raffaella marry her Fascist . . . But he'd rather be here, painting Georgia.

All the same, the magnificently thick, creamy invitation, with its gilt edges and its embossed script, had brought back to him not only the quantity of jewelled combs, brooches, egret feathers and what-have-you which Chiara Zanetti could contrive to fasten onto her head all at once. Back at work on his canvas, on the one thing never to think of glancingly, he was reminded of the disreputable virtues of clandestinity, what an excellent policy it often was. Jack and Georgia now, for instance.

Something was happening . . . You only had to cheer yourself up by listening to the ripple in their voices to be sure of that, only had to notice their brilliant eyes. Thank heavens he wasn't required to know more than that. And the gaiety they left in the air – why should he try to resist it? Disappearing on their bicycles for picnic suppers on the river down at Saint Benet's abbey. Going out to the paddock at nearly midnight, to catch up the horses and go riding bare-back. Off next day to the cinema in Norwich to see *The Thirty-Nine Steps*.

It couldn't last. He was going to have to pack her off to Burma. Good thing, probably. Educative. But even so, while here they were . . . Another reason for taking his time over this picture.

Come to think of it . . . One vacation soon, he ought to suggest Jack went to Italy. Chiara had promised she'd send him to all the right churches and galleries. Quite likely she'd detail Emanuela to escort the lad round Florence.

As for Jack – occasionally he wondered what he'd reply if, when he was back at King's and the point-to-point season began, Mr Fanshaw wrote to enquire if he'd come over for a couple of mornings a week to exercise horses. But apart from that . . . We might all of us be *born in moral stupidity*, as he couldn't recollect which novelist he'd read lately pointed out, *taking the world as an udder to feed our supreme selves*. But he that summer was emerging from moral stupidity by finding Georgia inconceivably more fascinating and important than he found himself. What was more, his days and nights were a whirl, and his head was a whirl, so he only thought about his emergence and his fascination in the most deplorably lighthearted way.

And really, thinking was the wrong term for the intermittent, blissful impressions kaleidoscoping dizzily in his grey matter.

From breakfast outside the kitchen door, where a table was laid in a corner of the yard beneath a climbing white rose, Jack's days were all one long, swift vibrancy. Or rather, the start of his days should be fixed earlier, in the high-summer daybreak, when after Georgia's and his night-long tussles, caresses, dreamings, he huddled on his dressing-gown and made his wary way to his own room.

Hours in the library, purportedly reading, but actually staring out of the window. Late afternoons, when his father was left to walk his Springer spaniels alone, and to marshal the right spirit for effective action next morning alone. Jack would commandeer his mother's bay hunter, Georgia would take a similar liberty with Henrietta's grey Arab. The pair of them would go a thunderous gallop along a field, with the sea shining a mile off, with the wind singing in their ears and their hearts racing.

Dinners with the French window open onto the west lawn and the ha-ha, onto the slow dusk where by the far oaks and chestnuts you'd notice rabbits hopping about. His mother, being a dedicated gardener, couldn't be doing with rabbits. The advantage of this was that sometimes at the dining-table she'd ask, 'Jack, can't you *do* something about the little brutes?' This was splendid, because then, in a tweed coat or in a dinner jacket depending on what kind of evening it was, he could slip a couple of cartridges into a shot-gun and go out to stalk his prey, which was an admirable way of passing the lull between meat and cheese. If he was lucky, in the gloaming he could steal along the lime walk stealthily enough to get within range of the nibbling rabbits before he alarmed them. Once by this method he'd even killed a right and left – Mama had been delighted with him. If he startled his quarry too soon, or if he missed, she would demand of the company, 'What on *earth* is the point of having a son, if he can't defend my flower-beds?'

And at the still centre of all this active happiness was his father's studio. All his life he'd gone down there, when work was in progress, had sat down to read. But now, when he went in and closed the barn door behind him – now Georgia was there, in her ball-dress of Cambridge light blue, motionless.

It didn't take him long to read them *Twelfth Night*. The first three acts during their morning sitting, the last two in the afternoon. After that, he'd go in carrying whatever book he was immersed in. *Far Away and Long Ago* was one he read that summer, so Argentina in the last century kept swimming into his exuberant consciousness; *Seven Pillars of Wisdom* was another. It was so quiet in the studio, the time measured out with the barely audible taps of Papa's mahl-stick against the edge of the canvas, that occasionally Jack remembered that progress on this picture meant the end of Georgia in England, meant the end of summer, his going back to Cambridge, the end of everything. He'd watch his father's right hand, and think of that. Watch as Papa hesitated, looked quickly from Georgia to the canvas, made his light deft stroke. Think of the composition coming together, the surface acquiring finish . . . and time running out, and a Peninsula and Oriental ship. When he came home at Christmas he'd go duck-flighting with Bill Meade on the fens down by Tonnage Bridge, and he'd go to the Boxing Day shoot at Bure and afterwards the Hedleighs would come to dinner, but Georgia would not be here. She might never be here again. In a few years, he'd be told she'd married someone in Mandalay.

Luckily, having Georgia now was far more absorbing than not having her later — so Jack never fretted about progress on the portrait for more than a minute. The three of them might chat about whether the stream needed to be dredged. Or Papa would ask him to read aloud that Bedouin attack when Lawrence contrived by over-excited use of his revolver to shoot his own charging camel through the back of its neck. Then if it wasn't the stream being dredged, it'd be whoever had come to dinner last night. Either that, or how the formidable Barton Turf village cricket team might be withstood next Saturday by the eleven drummed up from Crostwight and Edingthorpe and Ridlington, hamlets with no great cricketing tradition as could be deduced from the fact that Jack had been invited to bat at number four. If it wasn't Lawrence and his dead camel being galloped over by the rest of that mad charge, it was the time when he tried to blow up a train but the detonator didn't work, so he had to sit on the sand while the interminable Turkish troop train jolted by, and hope to God they didn't stop to investigate, and no one took it into his head to take a pot-shot at him.

Then quiet would fall again. Jack would read. He'd raise his eyes, look at Georgia posing by the mirror and know she knew he was looking at her and she liked that.

Her feet in their little satin dancing shoes on the Shiraz rug. Her waist, that sash. He could have gazed at her forever. Her breast in that ruched dress, her shoulders rising from it. Her hair up, so her nape was revealed for the first time, and the full curve of her throat. Then Jack would realise that his father had noticed this contemplation and would drop his eyes back to his book.

16

Georgia Burney was quite sure she was not in love, knew it for a fact with blithe disregard even for the possibility. But Jack was a darling, and he was good-looking enough and vigorous enough to excite her, and flirting with Bobbie had whetted her appetite, and she loved the whole game.

Dancing up in the old nursery was a game, riding bare-back after dinner was a game. Flirtation and seduction and consummation were games. Secrecy was a game. Wearing her glorious dress and posing by the shimmering mirror was a game. The whole summer had a breath of the ideal blowing through it, as if there were no before and no after – at any rate, no after in the West. Ideal . . . As if nothing you did, or said, or felt, could possibly have any consequences. As if, whatever happened, nothing would ever happen. That was it, that was the magical thing. Nothing seemed to contrive to *be* very conclusively – not enough to matter.

So long as they took care she didn't get pregnant, and took care not to get found out. For as long as the summer lasted, as long as the painting of her portrait lasted, the mood lasted – for as long as the moment stretched out . . . All Georgia's consciousness being suffused with the promise of her release to return to Burma, she had no difficulty in finding the World a happy place, and the Flesh gloriously intoxicating. As for the Devil, he led his limited existence in the frowzy mythology which had been one of the many reasons she had hated that school in Suffolk, and which now she'd left behind.

At Villa Lucia, mixed up with Georgia's falling in love with Italy at first sight, had been her sense of an aliveness between Charles Lammas and Raffaella Zanetti. Almost, she had been jealous. After all, *she* was his female accomplice in that venture. And as the days went by, the memory kept cropping up of odd things about Raffaella at Edingthorpe sitting for that double portrait, things she hadn't made anything of at the time. But now, in the full flush of her own first affair . . . So when Bobbie, lounging at the drawing-room fireplace, picked up the wedding invitation, shot his uncle a mocking smile and enquired, 'Are you going?' with a jolt Georgia knew.

That year, she was aware of a world of erotic intrigue. Aware through channels she couldn't have named . . . But she seemed to be porous, the way understanding seeped into her. She couldn't have told you how she knew Bobbie would be unfaithful to Caroline when he got around to it, but she knew. The world was instinct with sexuality, or she was, or it was the same thing. Anyway she was instinct with knowledge, all her nerves were learning all the time. Only she never finished decoding all the information that came in, so whole days would seem marvellously suggestive but she still couldn't have told you suggestive of what.

Now that Georgia was confident of leaving England soon, she had no trouble liking the place. She liked eating supper aboard *Golden Eye* while they sailed back along the Bure to the mooring by the ruined abbey, white sheep dotting the darkening meadow, skeins of teal whirring down onto the ruffled river. If you weren't going to do it again after this summer, it took on quite a different lustre. The smell of river water, different from the smell of the sea. The twilight breeze crossing the fens. So times that for Jack were the essence of the life he'd inherited and he loved, for Georgia had the piquancy of withdrawal. She enjoyed sailing the cutter past the willows at nightfall now, because she could imagine the others doing this next year without her, she could see her own absence. She liked going to bed, dreaming of the erotic encounter to come, knowing it didn't matter if she drowsed because when the household was asleep her lover would steal to her room and wake her. She dreamed of her other lover too, the man she would fall in love with.

He was very vague, as yet. She imagined him British; she imagined him in the East; but apart from that . . . In uniform, certainly. But, then – the way things were drifting, all the men were going to be in uniform soon. Still, she enjoyed making up stories about him. He might be aide-de-camp to the Viceroy in Delhi, or a pilot, or in Intelligence, she mused. He might be married. What would that be like? For that matter . . . Suppose he wasn't British. He might be one of the princes of the Shan Hills. Why not? He might have his own state, where she would elope with him and reign and never come back.

Then the Edingthorpe corridor floorboards would creak, Jack would push open her bedroom door. And really, right now to have the erotic without the romantic was highly satisfactory. Georgia was calmly clear about that. She mulled it over, posing by the Venetian mirror, listening to *Twelfth Night*, listening to the tap of the mahl-stick against the edge of the canvas where her image was gaining definition, gaining richness and depth, where her return to the East was coming closer. *Tap. Tap. Tap.*

> If music be the food of love, play on;
> Give me excess of it, that, surfeiting,
> The appetite may sicken, and so die.
> That strain again! it had a dying fall . . .

When Georgia first heard those lines, she had no idea that words could be so potent and melodious. She had the cloudiest notion of what they meant. But that didn't matter, she could think about that later if she felt like it. The great thing was the rhythm that beat in her head more magnificently than words had ever sounded there before.

Then at once, as she stood there to be painted, and a bit more of the passage's meaning dawned on her, she wished it wasn't Jack who was reading it aloud. She became conscious of her face. The way Godfather Charles had posed her, with her head slightly turned toward him, she couldn't see herself in the glass. But she was sure her cheeks had coloured, her eyes had brightened. The chair into which Jack always flopped was to one side, she could only see him if she turned a fraction which she wasn't meant to. But she felt she knew when he was looking at her and when he wasn't, and he was now, she was certain of it, and she hoped that his glance was strictly frivolous.

At Villa Lucia, she had liked going into the small drawing-room where her godfather was painting. Partly because for years she had been at ease with him when he was at work. Partly because Francesco De Angelis had a shock of chestnut hair, and it curled on the back of his neck in a way she liked. She had sat in the window seat, and then her godfather had said, 'Don't move, Georgia, there's a good girl.' After that, he'd had her sit with her elbow on the sill for several mornings in a row. She'd got used to being looked at to be painted, had got to like it. And now it amused her to reflect that, when Francesco saw his portrait hanging in his parents' house, he saw in the background that English girl who'd been staying.

Now in the Edingthorpe studio she wasn't in the background. She was the subject, she and her reflection with her. She was wearing her first ball-dress, and she was the centre of attention, and she liked that.

She remembered how mysterious the studio had appeared when she had first discovered it. How she had come quietly in here carrying – what had it been? – *The Swiss Family Robinson*, yes, that was right. She had gone softly to a chair, determined to be so invisible and so silent that she'd be allowed to come back again – and a lay-figure had been sitting in that chair, she remembered now, one of the enigmatic old lay-figures with some gorgeous stuffs laid against its polished wooden breast. So she'd had to search for somewhere else to sit, and she'd settled in that small green chair which had then become hers, become where she always sat to read, holiday after holiday.

Now here she was again, standing in her satin dancing shoes on the Shiraz rug. About to go away . . . But here, she and her light blue dress and her reflection.

This time she had to hold her head still, so she could only see a section of the big window and her godfather at his easel and the corner where the pike with its rotting pennant leaned. She was aware of all the room's presences, of paintings that had hung there for years, others she remembered well but that had been sold. She knew the paintings framed and unframed, the paintings stacked against walls. She was aware of the canvases that had been taken off their stretchers and rolled up for transport abroad. Without seeing them, she saw the compositions which had made her godfather groan with stoical laughter, declare they would be the death of him. She knew the pictures he had given up on, would never finish now.

Posing, she felt the presence of the lay-figures too, and the desk with its pigeon-holes full of curious odds and ends, and the plaster casts of hands sculpted by Canova, and the Venetian mask. She didn't bring them to mind, but they were there. The White Ensign which had been flown on *E35*. The rocking-horse, brought down from the nursery years ago. It generally had an armful of silks chucked over its tatty saddle.

Often they chatted, they joked. She hated her freckles, and her godfather Charles knew she did. He'd tease her about how he was making splendid progress painting them, painting them good and big. There'd never in the history of portraiture been cheekbones so freckled as the ones he was giving her.

Then there were other times. Silence fell in the studio. In Georgia's head, scene after scene of *Twelfth Night* was performed. Sir Toby Belch got dreadfully drunk. Sir Andrew Aguecheek challenged Cesario to a duel, and scared himself out of his wits.

Georgia posed, and felt the painter's eyes looking at her body, at her dress, at her reflection. She felt how posed on her neck her head was. She felt his gaze flicking thoughtfully to its outside, to her face and her hair; and at the same time, on its inside, figures were acting and speaking. Feste came on stage. He sang, *Come away, come away, death,* and his words echoed and died away and then came echoing back again.

17

The evening Charles Lammas took his son and his goddaughter to *Twelfth Night* he was feeling pleased with both of them. He had been on his own in London for several days, roosting in his old Kensington studio, and he was enjoying himself.

After weeks down in the country, after weeks working hard at an ambitious painting, London was a tonic and no mistake, especially now that the summer was almost over, a number of his friends were reappearing in town. What was more, he was pleased with his portrait of Georgia. He'd get back to it refreshed, and so with any luck after a further month's concentration on it . . . But today he had a lunch appointment at his club.

He often lunched or dined at the Travellers'. He liked the library, with its windows looking down over Carlton House Gardens. He'd go to earth there to write letters, or leaf through back numbers of *Apollo* or *The Burlington*. Then in the morning-room or the smoking-room he was always bumping into some fellow he'd been in the Navy with, or whose sister's portrait he'd painted back in the twenties, or who recollected watching him ride Tofthill in the Fox Hunters' Chase – and they would invite him to lunch at White's, or to dinner at the Garrick, all of which was highly agreeable.

One way and another, it was easy to get through quite a lot of time most convivially. Money, too, of course . . . But Lammas had long been used to the fact that most of his friends had incomes more ample and more dependable than his. Nor, when it came down to it, had he ever been able to regret not having stayed in the Navy after the Armistice, or not having gone into the City, or the Diplomatic Service, or something.

Best of all, this time his first saunter along Bond Street had proved satisfactory, which it didn't always. When he opened Peregrine Bracknell's door, the first thing he said as he stood up behind his desk and held out his hand, was, 'Just the man I wanted to see! I've got a cheque for you, Charlie. Quite a decent one.'

It turned out that his still-life of the Christmas roses and the Chinese teapot had finally fetched the highish price they'd been asking. Not only that. Of the three of Charles Lammas' Norfolk landscapes which dominated one wall of the gallery, one was as good as sold, and another . . . Bracknell lowered his voice with delight. Another – well, judging by the succession of the Tate's buyers who'd been trooping in to look at it over the last few weeks, their interest appeared to be the real thing.

Lammas decided on the spot that his doubts as to Perry Bracknell's abilities as a dealer had been unjust. For the foreseeable future, he'd stick with him. What was more, with this cheque in his pocket, and with the prospect of others . . . Naturally most of the money would go on simply keeping the Edingthorpe establishment running over the next few months, on keeping Jack at Cambridge and Henrietta at school. But he might allow himself . . . Had Perry still got that pen and ink drawing of a seated woman by Tissot which he'd shown him back in the spring? It hadn't sold yet? Admirable! He'd take it with him right now.

Bracknell sold the drawing for a price calculated to influence the painter's loyalty to his establishment, put a stop once and for all, the dealer trusted, to the talk there'd been a year or two back about how Lammas might be thinking of selling through the Mathers Gallery next door. What was more, as they agreed to have lunch at the Athenaeum the following day, he mentioned that Lord Furze-Holt intended to commission a portrait of his daughter. 'She's going to be twenty-one. Either that, or she's engaged. Can't remember, off hand. Both, maybe. Anyhow, I recommended he approach you, and the old boy seemed quite happy to take advice. So with a bit of luck, when you get home to Edingthorpe there may be a letter waiting for you.'

Charles Lammas strolled away down the pavement in excellent spirits. It was true the cooking at the Athenaeum was never up to much, but it was a club he'd always liked. His father had been a member – and the cellar was good. It was true that he had been enjoying not painting commissioned portraits. But . . . Hell, the great thing was to be in business at all, be in action. Fine chap, Perry Bracknell, he'd always said so.

Unfortunately, he had remembered his father, and walking past the dealers' windows he couldn't forget him immediately. Roland had sold his pictures through galleries in this street and in streets that ran off it. But there wasn't anything by him hanging on a wall here now. The Tate Gallery had bought three or four of his canvases, too. These days, they didn't hang them any more.

The son shrugged his shoulders, walked more purposefully. By the time he'd stridden past his father's old club, and entered his own next door, he was delighted with the drawing he'd bought. All his life, he had entertained the same degree of love for Tissot's work as he had for Whistler's. To buy one of his oil paintings would always be out of the question – but this pen and ink study had irresistible charm.

Carrying it, he went into the smoking-room. He rang, ordered a glass of champagne. Then choosing an armchair near a window, he took his acquisition out of its cardboard folder, held it on his knee for calm inspection.

Yes, it *was* beautifully done. Absorbed, happy, he sipped his champagne without taking his eyes off Tissot's draughtsmanship. Chic – that was the word. He'd hang it . . . In that alcove in the dining-room, perhaps, opposite the chalk drawing of a woman's head by Shannon. Or up in his dressing-room, where he'd clustered a few favourite things.

Something had saddened him about the club, though – what was it? They'd told him Alex Burney had resigned, that was right. Alex who had been a member of the Travellers' since before the war, for God's sake, Alex who'd come here with Geoffrey on leave from the Front. Well, apparently he'd chucked it in, written a letter of resignation. And instead of coming out with the usual twaddle people invented when the truth was that they couldn't afford the subscription any more, he'd said he wasn't coming back to England and therefore could have no conceivable use for a London club. Not just not coming back for five or ten years. Never coming back again.

The unease awoken in Charles Lammas by Alex Burney's resignation from the Travellers' Club had, as its only tangible consequence, his being seized by the desire to give that self-exiled man's daughter a present. With the excuse of her having posed for weeks with a patience that was downright angelic. With the further excuse of her impending departure. And he'd always enjoyed buying women lovely things. Tailors' shops bored him. But he liked the brilliant gowns hanging up in women's dress-shops; liked the mannequins and the rich, soft stuffs and the fripperies.

So dawdling about Mayfair in early September sunshine, trying not to think about that morning's *Times* which had been all about the German threat to Czechoslovakia, he looked in the shop windows. He hesitated. He recalled a picture he'd painted of a room in a fashion house, with a seamstress stitching, a girl changing, armfuls of sumptuous dresses. Hats for weddings, hats for race meetings; high-heeled shoes, muffs, feather boas; looking-glasses – glorious! He'd like to see that picture again, in the end he'd been happy with how it had turned out. However, it hung in a Scottish castle, and when he'd next be north of the border he couldn't imagine.

He idled on. He spun out the pleasure for as long as he could. Even so, at the end of an hour he had purchased a Parisian silk scarf, which he had them wrap up in shiny green paper and tie with a scarlet ribbon. Back in Kensington, he left the packet on his studio table, with a card on which he had written, *For Georgia, with love from Godfather Charles*, so the girl would find it when Jack and she arrived from Norfolk to dump their bags and change for the theatre.

Then all that afternoon Charles Lammas dashed about town, and he enjoyed every minute of it. To a studio in Tite Street, to see the watercolours a friend had recently brought back after six months in the Levant. To Hatchard's bookshop, in order to buy a novel by an American called William Faulkner which people had begun to tell him was powerful stuff, a novel with the peculiar title *Absalom, Absalom!* – and naturally he lingered too long among the shelves, and came away having bought five other books too. Then across the road to the RA, to confer about borrowing back his *Ely From The North* for the Retrospective Exhibition that Bracknell hoped to organise, perhaps next year. Finally back to the Travellers', to collapse into a chair in the smoking-room before heading off to the theatre. The evening editions of the papers were dispiriting, all about whether the German government was likely to back up its idiotic pretensions with military force; but the club champagne tasted the same as ever.

It was dusk when he walked through the bustling streets toward Wyndham's Theatre, his sanguine mind warmed by two glasses of champagne and the prospect of a fetching Viola. Damned terrific, too, if the Tate really . . . And it was excellent to be able to give your son and your goddaughter an entertaining evening. What was more, Jack was growing up just the sort of young man he had hoped for. So much so, indeed, that Blanche teased him about it. 'Of course you're delighted with him, he's just like you!' Then swinging along through the crowd, Lammas chuckled. 'Poor Jack,' Blanche had added, 'he's even got your square-cut head! and that terrible plough-share of a jaw of yours!' More practically, there was no reason why the lad shouldn't make a successful architect.

Henrietta . . . Her father didn't feel he knew about Henrietta yet. Mad about riding, which was splendid of course, but . . . Somehow, she hadn't yet declared herself. It was going to be interesting to wait and see.

Outside the theatre, people were milling about. Glancing to his left and his right, Lammas ascended the steps, went into the foyer. Good, there Jack and Georgia were, waiting for him.

Quite disproportionately contented with the pair for not being late, he advanced toward them through the smartly dressed throng. The boy was as tall as he was these days, and very grown-up in his bearing, the proud father noted. And the girl's eyes were brilliant with excitement at her first evening at the theatre. Well, you couldn't have a finer initiation than *Twelfth Night* at Wyndham's, and the reviews had been good – he was pleased with his choice. She had knotted her new scarf around her neck so it fell prettily across one shoulder. And here she was, coming forward to him, saying, 'Godfather Charles, my present! It's *wonderful*, what have I done to deserve it?'

'Been extremely patient and sweet, that's what you've done. Glad you like it.' No question of it – this summer's long goodbye to his goddaughter was being the amusement he'd hoped for. Intriguing, too. 'Right, here are the tickets.' He smiled from one to the other of his young companions. 'Shall we go in?' They looked good together, side by side. Pity. Never mind.

18

—⚏—

Everything conspired to make Georgia's heart beat joyously, from the elegant men and women chattering in the ornate foyer, to her own reflection in one of the mirrors which showed that, even beside the stylish lady in the black dress who happened to be reflected with her, tonight the girl from the Shan Hills could stand comparison with anyone.

As for her Parisian scarf! She knew that, after glancing at her reflection so swiftly that she trusted she had not been observed, she must turn away again. But she couldn't resist rearranging the swag across her collar-bone, simply for the pleasure of touching that heavy silk with her fingertips.

And her eyes . . . Often they had disappointed her. She had envied girls of whom you could say that their eyes were green, or blue, or any colour. But hers! All colours, no colour. But tonight her eyes glittered like two diamonds, Georgia decided boldly, wheeling back to Jack and her godfather who were discussing the cast-list. You couldn't say what colour diamonds were – but they shone.

She was given a programme, but she held it absently. After all, she knew all she needed to know about the play, she had *If music be the food of love* drubbing in her inner ear. She heard it resound again and again, opulent with promise, unrenounceable. *If music be the food of love, play on; Give me excess of it* . . . Exciting, that demand which pulsed in her brain; and threatening. *Play on*, she thought, as an usher opened a door which in her bedazzlement she had not noticed, as her godfather gestured that she should precede them through it. *Give me excess of it.*

Gallery, boxes, stalls . . . The words were part of the magic, and no doubt their meaning would become clear if that were necessary. Her godfather Charles told her the names of the actors and actresses, commented on who had been an enchanting Rosalind at the Aldwych last winter, whose Coriolanus had been powerful but his Antony disappointing. Since Georgia had never set foot in a theatre before, the names and reputations meant nothing to her. She assumed that this brand of conversation was a preliminary part of the ritual which it was quite right to go through, and she supposed she'd get the hang of it in due course if she wished to.

Charles Lammas had taken a box. His goddaughter followed the usher toward it, (to her, this personage appeared almost supernatural in his combination of deference and dignity, not to mention how fantastically buttoned and braided and epauletted he was), already aware that, if you could play the game of making love, you might play the game of being in love too. The usher escorted her along a curving corridor set with identical, small doors, all painted the same creamy colour, with the rims of the panels picked out in gold. When he halted by one of these, and held it open for her with an infinitesimal inclination of his shoulders and head, and what struck Georgia as the friendliest of smiles, she glanced over her shoulder at the father and son following. Her step made buoyant by this reminder of her lover's good looks, she went into the tiny, elegant room.

Really they were just loose-boxes, her godfather remarked with a laugh, one almost expected a hay-net to be provided. But Georgia's first thought and, she was sure, Jack's too, was how intimate the dim, cramped space felt. Between these painted panels, beneath this low ceiling, there'd just be room for a double bed. That was it – a four-poster! One of those beds enclosed by decorated walls, which they used to have in castles and palaces – she'd seen pictures of them.

She moved forward to the elegant little chair waiting for her. She sat, leaned her elbow on the purple-covered sill.

Georgia gazed at the auditorium lit by tiers of brass lamps. From the grey street outside, she could never have suspected the existence of this horse-shoe of glittering lights, the fulsome chandelier lording it up there, the blue and gold and pink moulding around the proscenium arch. That was what it was called, Godfather Charles said. She tasted the word. Proscenium . . .

'Nice little theatre, Wyndham's.' He had said that too. And now Georgia brought into steadier focus the painted curlicues, the polished brass and the glowing shades, the plush, she saw he was right, she discovered a wonderful smallness. Now she brought under some mental order the hum of voices and the effulgence and the expectancy, she found it was like being inside a precious cabinet.

A minute or two until the performance would begin. His father insisted Jack take the other chair at the front of their box – his ostensible reason being that he'd seen the play 'dozens of times' and could perfectly well watch it from behind them, his true motive being the amused pleasure it afforded him to see those two shoulder to shoulder. Georgia looked down at the people making their way to their seats in the stalls. Then the opening chords of an Elizabethan song made her glance toward the footlights. Without her having noticed, three musicians had come onto the stage. It was amazing how unobservant she could be, in the very minutes when she had felt she was sopping up impressions as never before. Anyway, there they were, one with a flute, two with stringed instruments she didn't know the names of, and they had started to play. They were in front of the massive, dark blue curtains which must be going to be pulled up any minute now, hoisted up or drawn aside, she wondered which. The musicians' doublets were green and red, they reminded her of the ebony page-boys in the dining-room at Villa Lucia.

The Edingthorpe studio had been all the theatre Georgia had ever known. It was the place where stories were read and told and songs were sung, and it was a place where things had their mysterious personalities. Now momentarily its image visited her – and it seemed a very shabby barn. And so provincial! She forgot it in a trice, in her new conviction that she was always going to be wearing evening dresses and flitting about the West End from this theatre to that, making an appearance at a restaurant here or a dance there.

In too happy a rapture to listen to the musicians, she watched two exceedingly handsome young men who were laughing together in a box on the other side of the theatre. She was sure they had noticed her admiringly. *Give me excess of it, that, surfeiting, The appetite may sicken, and so die.* Well, why not? The idea was vague to her – but sharp enough to make her heart thump. Potent words: excess, appetite. Sicken, die.

Now that she came to notice it – every one of the boxes opposite was a minute stage, scenes were being acted out in each one. A gentleman showed a lady to her seat, she raised her opera glasses. In the next framed aperture, a whole family had squashed in together, for the ones behind it must be terribly difficult to see much. In the next again, there was a fair girl of about Georgia's own age. She wondered if the fair girl often came to the theatre, or if it was the first time for her too. Further along, the two dandies had stopped laughing, they were looking her way.

That strain again! it had a dying fall . . . Georgia couldn't wait. She knew the performance must start soon. But suddenly she was fed up with all the preliminaries, she wanted the thing itself. In her echo-chamber of a head, snatches rang in any old order, began to mean things they hadn't meant before. *Sicken, and so die* . . . Nothing could be relied on to mean the same thing twice – and the play hadn't even begun yet. *So full of shapes is fancy* . . . Still, Georgia Burney was going to pass her life in the London theatres, that much was certain.

The house lights dimmed. In the hush that descended on the audience, either the musicians played more vigorously or they could be more distinctly heard. The curtains stirred, they were drawn aside. There was Duke Orsino, sitting with his head leaning against his hand.

An hour later, when the blue curtains swung back to conceal the stage, and the house lights came up again and a clatter of applause broke out, Georgia had forgotten that halfway through the performance there was going to be an interval. Never mind, it was only an interruption, it would pass.

Later she would have time to think in a more measured way about the revelation which that wall of dark blue velvet with golden fringes and tassels had been drawn back to disclose, and now had hidden again, but soon would open to discover once more. She would try to understand how for an hour that illuminated stage had *been* her consciousness. But now her hearing still echoed with the play's voices. Georgia was longing for the house lights to go down again. All she desired was that the interval should pass quickly, her enchantment remain intact for the second half.

She turned to Jack, her cheeks pale from her abstraction, her eyes as diamantine as she could have wished.

The usher reappeared, this time carrying the bottle of Lanson which Charles Lammas had ordered. He set the tray down on a little console-table, and withdrew. Lammas uncorked the cold bottle, in jovial spirits on account of the evident success of the entertainment so far as Jack and Georgia were concerned. He handed them their brimming glasses. And then, to the surprise of all three, their door opened again.

'Thank heavens, I've got the right box!' Christopher de Brissac's tall figure loomed between the obscurely painted walls. His drawl became a snort of laughter. 'Not easy, working it out from down there in the stalls. Didn't any of you see me? Well, first tier, seventh from the stage, I told myself, and here I am.' He eyed the tray. 'Glad to see you're looking after your party properly, Charlie.'

'Christopher!' Lammas stood up, so did Jack. 'What a splendid surprise. I didn't know you were back in this country.'

'Here on leave. Going out East again in a couple of months. No, don't call for a glass for me. I'm with a bunch of people, I must get back to them. I just noticed this handsome pair, and I thought, I'm dashed if that isn't Charlie and Blanche's boy.'

'Good evening, Sir.' Smiling broadly, Jack shook de Brissac's hand. 'Do you remember my father's goddaughter? This is—'

'Certainly I remember Georgiana Burney, though I've seen her parents more recently than I've seen her. Miss Burney, good evening.'

Stooping toward her where she sat by the sill which gave onto the glittering auditorium and the interval hubbub, de Brissac shook her hand. She saw the smudges of grey in the brown hair at his temples, saw something bony about the shoulders in his dinner jacket, saw his eyes were green.

She said, 'Good evening. You've seen my father and mother?' Her voice quickened. 'You've been in Burma?'

'Absolutely. Alex and Geraldine are both in good form, and I shall give you the rest of my Maymyo news when we meet in Norfolk. You're all going to this jamboree of the Hedleighs' later in the month aren't you? Excellent! Look, Charlie, I'm staying at Bure all that week. If you don't invite me over to Edingthorpe, I'll come anyway.'

Turning to leave, de Brissac caught Georgia's eyes once more. 'That little devil of a dog of yours . . . What's his name? A Border terrier crossed with a Jack Russell – or something like that. Angus, that's right. Getting a bit grey around the muzzle these days, and his temper comes and goes, but he's fine.'

19

—꿰—

The day after Charles Lammas' return from London to Norfolk, he was walking from his studio across the yard toward the house when he had his first stroke. The doctors had warned him that he might have a heart attack, but it was a stroke that knocked him down first.

Of course, he didn't immediately know what it was. He didn't understand anything. He found he had fallen down, he was floundering on the gravel, and his brain had suddenly become so feeble that he could make no sense of anything at all.

As it chanced, nobody else was in the yard, or looking out of a window onto it. Lammas tried to stand up, but he couldn't. The left side of him worked normally, but the right didn't. He tried to crawl toward the kitchen door. But with his left arm and leg which knew how to crawl, but his right which didn't, he dragged himself in a curve. After a bit, he found he'd blundered into the greenhouse.

Getting a grip on a shelf with his left hand, he hauled himself onto his left knee. He reached up to a water-pipe. By terrific bracing of his good leg and heaving with his good arm, he stood up and leaned against the wall. He looked at dusty glass.

Then he must have fallen down again. He was on the brick floor. Blanche was there. She was kneeling beside him.

20

◆

Julian Hedleigh had resolved back in the spring that it was time to give another ball, and as the great day approached he was more and more contented with his decision. The immediate cause for festivity was his wife's fiftieth birthday. It fell on the last day of September, and scores of invitations had been sent out for that evening. But all the other reasons why a ball would be a satisfactory move were jostling in his mind in a semi-conscious condition – partial consciousness being the most pleasing form they could possibly take.

For a start, balls had recently been held at Houghton and at Raveningham, and one was planned at Hoveton House for Christmas. So the honourable place of Bure Hall among the great houses of the county, although not precisely at stake – that, it would never be – could not possibly be damaged by some lavish reaffirmation. What was more, it would be timely, because the aged Lord Lieutenant was in declining health. Then too there was Frederick's political career to launch. Although only thirty, the heir to Bure Hall was already making a success in the City. And it was the father's intention that, when he himself should decide to rest after many years of duty at Westminster, there should be no doubt in those minds which counted that the next Conservative member for this particular Norfolk constituency should be the son.

So it was in a mood of contentment with his own intelligence that Julian Hedleigh gave his orders for the entertainment which was to be given, and let his wife understand that when making her dispositions she need not stint. The stock market's lurches and tumbles since the war had reduced many great fortunes, and had practically ruined a few people Hedleigh knew. Farming had been unprofitable too. Just think of Blanche Lammas' father having to sell Paston. That had sent ripples through the county – and no son left alive to pull the family situation round. But the Hedleighs had weathered the slump, and this last year had been a good one.

Not only was a ball now absolutely the right card to play. There were also personal satisfactions the master of Bure Hall could look forward to. As September passed, and the risk of a European war became more acute each day, he couldn't help realising that he was going to be in a position to speak authoritatively about international affairs with his less well-connected neighbours.

It was true that the Prime Minister had a tendency to take initiatives in foreign policy after practically no cabinet discussion at all. For instance, a fortnight before the ball which was to dazzle half East Anglia, when preparations at Bure were in full swing, he flew to Berchtesgaden to talk to the German Chancellor after telling only about half-a-dozen colleagues what he was up to, and certainly without the knowledge of a back-bencher like Julian Hedleigh. It was enough to make a fellow wonder why he'd sat on the same foreign affairs committee for five solid years, and had never voted against the government on any issue that mattered, but only once or twice on trifling concerns, which was a recognised way of showing that you were a man of independent judgement who couldn't be taken for granted. It was a question, Hedleigh found, as so often in politics, of being extremely wise extremely soon after the event – and by the time Chamberlain flew back to Germany and met Hitler again, this time at Godesberg, he was getting quite adroit at it.

There was only a week still to go before the ball. On the front lawn at Bure the marquee was being put up, and Hedleigh in London spoke discreetly to one or two old friends about the delicate diplomacy being employed to solve the problem of the Sudetenland. It was unfortunate that no one had actually defined the borders of that troublesome territory, and reports as to its relative Czech and German populations changed all the time – but Hedleigh wasn't alone in being ill-informed. What was more, he had conferred with Lord Runciman after that emissary's return from Prague, and our ambassador at Berlin, Sir Neville Henderson, was an old acquaintance, so he had plenty of political insider's gossip with which to regale London and Norfolk drawing-rooms.

No doubt about it, by the evening of his wife's birthday he was going to be in possession of new precious nuggets of information, mined that very week in Whitehall. The Czechs had just mobilised. Julian Hedleigh was not privy to the discussions between the Prime Minister and the First Lord of the Admiralty, but he knew that they were taking place, so he spoke with quiet moderation about the readiness of the British fleet. The day on which Duff Cooper's argument prevailed, and Chamberlain authorised the mobilisation of the fleet, Hedleigh went to Asprey's to collect the magnificent salver which was to be his present to Sarah, and which had been being engraved with his coat-of-arms. Life, after all, must go on, he thought, walking back to the House of Commons with the silver salver wrapped up under his arm. He was there the following day, listening to the Prime Minister speak, when that statesman received an invitation to join Hitler, Deladier and Mussolini at a further meeting in Germany. The next morning, Chamberlain flew to Munich. Hedleigh took the train to Norfolk. He arrived tired from many late debates in the House, but at once energetically set to work to make sure that all his orders regarding the ball had been carried out.

Of course, it was dreadfully sad about poor Charlie Lammas, but apart from that the county news seemed by and large good. Anyway, what with Hedleigh's meditations on the crucial negotiations being conducted in Munich, and the necessity of interviewing in rapid succession his bailiff, his head gardener and the hired caterer, he had no time for friendly distress.

Almost everyone of the slightest consequence had accepted, Sarah Hedleigh told her husband as they strolled in the garden just before dark to check that it was as faultlessly prepared for the morrow as it should be. Not that any of the guests would *see* the immaculate lawns and flower-beds, except by the flickering light of the flambeaux which would be burning on either side of the drive and along the terrace. But Hedleigh agreed that his wife had been dead right to rally her gardeners to make particular efforts in these last days. When night fell tomorrow, and the first cars swept between the park gates bearing those favoured few who were invited to dinner before the dancing began, both host and hostess would feel sustained by their irreproachable garden spreading all around the house, unseen but there, perfect, like money in the bank.

The Lord Lieutenant was too ill to come, and his wife had written a letter of the most pleasing friendliness, but apart from that . . . Proceeding on their tour of inspection, Julian Hedleigh listened to Sarah's report of those who would be of the company tomorrow. His authority had never been impaired by his small stature, and now ruddy-cheeked and bright-eyed he walked with a sprightly tread. The caterer seemed confident that his team were all set to produce a banquet which would be the talk of the county for weeks to come – but Hedleigh addressed him a little sharply, just to be on the safe side.

Husband and wife entered the marquee, which was connected to the drawing-room French windows by a canopy. She showed him the stoves which had been installed within the canvas walls in case the evening should be cool. They approved the band stand, the polished dance floor. He cast a benign eye on the women putting the finishing touches to the flower arrangements.

The Beauchamps were coming, and the Gurneys of course, and the Macleods, Sarah told him – good, good. Freddie had *promised* to speak to Mark, *try* to make him see sense. The Cokes were coming. Bobbie was going to join his regiment any day now. As for Caroline, they would have to see. Just a family dinner party this evening – plus the Fanshaws, who were staying in the house, and Christopher who'd been here for three days though he was always disappearing over to Edingthorpe. Now, Julian must forgive her, but she just *had* to go to the kitchen to check up on a few final things.

He would come with her, the master of the house genially declared, holding open the door which led to the larders and sculleries and pantries, thinking how ably Sarah always gave her instructions, it would be a pleasure to listen to her. Yes, he remarked gravely as he accompanied her down the flagged corridor of the kitchen wing, they were living through momentous days. The fleet mobilised for the first time since . . . The French were no use, that was the real problem, in his view. So the Buxtons were coming, and the . . . Good!

21

Charles Lammas lay in bed in his dressing-room. At first, the blankness in his head was so total that he was only alarmed by it dully. Then the first revulsion to haunt him came from memories of the war. That floundering on the earth. A man stricken witless, reduced to that animal jerking of useless limbs . . . Too familiar.

Now there were two invalids upstairs at Edingthorpe Manor. Blanche tended them both, walking from one room to the other along the creaking corridor.

Mary Oldfield had been born when Palmerston was Foreign Secretary, and now as the summer passed she was declining irreversibly. She lay between living and dying, images of empire and images of children guttering in her brain. Bombay when first she saw it as a sixteen-year-old nursery maid, the ship sailing in among the islands, and the harbour flecked with lateen sails. That time in the bungalow at Georgetown when she'd been reading to the children, she raised her eyes and there was a krait – right there, a couple of steps from where little Harry was lying on the mat listening.

Farther along the landing lay Charles Lammas, who had been born soon after Bechuanaland became a British protectorate, and just before Cecil Rhodes launched his incursion into the land of the Ndebele king.

Right from the start, when she came upon her husband struggling feebly on the greenhouse floor, Blanche Lammas was calm itself. A quick intake of breath, a quickening of her tread as she hurried toward him . . . But by the time she had knelt, and laid her peaceful hands on his shoulders, her voice was calm. 'It's all right, Charlie, I'm here. Oh, my darling.'

Of course, it wasn't all right. She just murmured the first soothing sounds that came into her head. Even at the time, he was foggily aware of being comforted by her tranquil voice, aware that her presence made things better. And he remembered, afterwards. Remembered the love in her simple words, spoken over again. 'It's all right. I'm here. Oh, my darling.' Remembered how she had knelt with her hands on him, in those first moments when she thought he might be dying then and there, this might be the end of their being together.

When Blanche realised he probably wasn't going to die immediately, she went to the kitchen window, called to Mrs Meade to find Jack. Together they hoisted Charles to his feet again. With his son lifting his nerveless right shoulder and arm, and with his right leg dragging, the disabled man was helped up the stairs. When they had made him as comfortable in his bed as they could, Blanche drew up a chair, sat down.

By then, all the household knew what had occurred. Georgia had changed out of her ball-dress at the end of the sitting. She had arranged it carefully on its hanger, come out from behind the Chinese screen in her every-day clothes. She was sitting in a deck-chair in the verandah, reading *As You Like It* and watching the butterflies on the buddleia, when Jack found her. 'Papa's just had a stroke,' he said, 'but he's alive.'

Henrietta was out riding. When Jack heard her Arab's hooves on the cobbles, he went down. She only had a vague idea of what a stroke was, but she dismounted and ran indoors, leaving her brother holding her restive pony in the yard. Up in her father's dressing-room, Henrietta stood, white-faced, her heart juddering. She stared at Papa who suddenly could do nothing for himself. She looked at his right eye which drooped stupidly, at his mouth which was drawn all wrong, looked dead. She stepped toward him. Choking with sobs, she buried her face in his chest.

Even Charles Lammas, in his physical and mental prostration, was beginning to understand. For the first few hours, Blanche never left his bed-side. She wanted to be there when he began to focus on how damaged he was. On how he couldn't speak properly. On what it meant, not to be able to use the hand he painted with.

To begin with, Lammas was aware only of weakness. He lay. He felt utterly unmanned. Sometimes he wept from sheer impotence, he couldn't help it, the tears just oozed from his eyes.

Outside his dressing-room window, he could see the upper boughs of a mighty chestnut tree which stood on the lawn. Hours passed, the window began to be dusky. After a while he could no longer see the green horse-chestnut foliage which September was making tawny. Then Blanche stood up, she drew the curtains, switched on a lamp. She sat down again.

Doctor Bennett came. He said it was possible that Lammas might make a full recovery. As soon as any life returned to his right side, he must try to move his hand. Even to stir his fingers would be something.

Memories visited his half-alive mind, blurred there. He was a boy in a clearing among winter trees, and his father was telling him how the woodcock came winging through that glade, so it had come to be called ... But he couldn't remember. Then something about sitting with Geoff on that bench by the gooseberry bushes, and not selling a horse because the war was going to be over by Christmas, they'd go point-to-pointing again. But it got muddled up with a message someone had written on a wedding invitation. He wanted to remember what the words were. He wanted to understand what something meant, but he couldn't remember or understand anything, and tears dripped down his cheeks.

His bed stood beside the wall. That evening, he found he could lift his right hand. He tried to control his fingers sufficiently to trace the pattern on the wallpaper.

Georgia was less demonstrative than Henrietta. In those first days, when it was clear Lammas was recovering, but not clear how complete or how durable his recovery was likely to prove, she kept her inner self to herself. After the idyll of the last few months in Tuscany and the Quercy and Norfolk, and after her rapture at the theatre, this summary half-killing of her godfather stopped certain innocences of hers in their tracks – no question of it. Bad luck for the idyll, and bad luck for the man. But good that she was learning fast, and learning discreetly, behind those murky eyes of hers, under her murky hair. Learning about idylls, and about men, and vulnerability – at Wyndham's theatre, in the Edingthorpe dressing-room.

She had not betrayed to Jack that since that meeting in the box during the interval she had been bearing Christopher de Brissac's image in her mind like an icon – and had calculated that the differences in their ages couldn't be much greater than that which Charles Lammas and Raffaella Zanetti had found superable. What images she elevated for romantic adoration were her concern. Likewise, what she did with her body. So duplicity entered her first affair quite naturally, she was amused to discover. And when she came to perch on her godfather's bed, she couldn't help reflecting that his stroke might delay her departure for Burma.

In Jack's case, when he was manhandling his father to his feet in the greenhouse, the summer's exhilaration came to an abrupt end. But then in some respects it got going again. His optimism told him that Papa would live, was already pulling through. His sense of his new maturity rejoiced to take up the challenge of finding he was temporarily the man of the family, and providing what support he could for his mother and his sister. His sense of the dramatic reminded him that his new responsibilities might not be temporary.

So far as his affair with Georgia went . . . It never crossed his mind that Henrietta's godfather, a man only ten years younger than Papa, and whom he recalled at Bure a few Christmases ago shooting with a beautiful pair of Holland and Holland guns, might be his rival in the girl's affections and desires.

True, there had been a delectable tension in the air, when Georgia had to stand still to be looked at, and every touch of brush on canvas brought nearer the end of the affair. But there was so much to do now, with the household turned topsy-turvy by Papa's illness, and by the time Jack had started to let death sink into his mind, had started to grasp what it might mean to lose his father, there was the ball at Bure to get ready for.

As for Jack's and Georgia's nocturnal escapades . . . They were both a bit muted of spirit the night after the seizure – but they met as usual. And in the days and nights which followed, they found their erotic exuberance unimpaired. Neither de Brissac's return from the East, nor Lammas' blood-clot in the brain, cast much shadow at all.

After a few days, Charles Lammas could enunciate his words so that not only his wife could understand him. The paper on the dressing-room wall was a floral design by William Morris, and for minutes together he would move his right hand over it.

But quickly his arm and his mind tired. Those were the loathsome times: limbs incapable, brain incapable. He felt like a hulk lying awash in a sea of death, a hulk that sooner or later would founder completely. Sometimes that horrifying sea washed right over him, but he hadn't the strength to cry out. His soul if he'd ever had one was already part of that infinite, lapping inanity. He was too torpid even to suffer very coherently.

Time would pass, and again he would feel up to looking around, feel up to listening and sometimes trying to talk. He looked at those favourites from his collection of Italian etchings which he had hung in that room, Marco Ricci's Roman ruins on one side of his looking-glass, the mysterious cloaked figures by Salvador Rosa on the other side. He'd often imagined that he'd go through his final illness in this dressing-room of his, and now he'd think that this was either the beginning of that or a foretaste of it, come years before he'd expected. There was a view of the Rialto by Marieschi which he could also see from where he lay, so he'd look at that, and at the chestnut tree outside the window. And whenever he had the strength, he played the clumsy fingers of his right hand along the lineaments of the iris flags of the wallpaper. To learn how to control eye and hand again, to live once more! not lie here debilitated, with nothing meaning anything. To learn how to work problems out again, learn how to concentrate not for minutes but for hours – that was life.

In the times when his mind felt stronger, he'd wonder about his collapse.

One day you were painting a picture you hoped was going to be one of your best, or you were strolling cheerfully about town, and the next . . .

Then Lammas would remind himself of the Gulf of Ismid. This wasn't the first time he'd been down struggling in an inane sea that felt like it might be his tomb. Never giving up, that was the trick. A hell of a sight easier said than done. Keeping at it, keeping fighting for yourself even when . . . He'd been man-hunted. He'd gone splashing forward through that brackish haze with rifle bullets ripping into the water around him. He'd kept swimming, he didn't know where, but he'd kept at it. And E_{11} had come. He'd been raised up. So now . . . And Lammas would force his hand back to the wallpaper.

But more often, he worried about money. It gave him the measure of his new weakness of spirit. Letting that useful mind of his bother itself for more than five minutes at a stretch with the hitches of getting and spending . . . But possibly his mind was not henceforward going consistently to be as useful as it had been. At any rate, he fretted. Not causelessly, but fruitlessly.

Perry Bracknell had sold that still-life, in the short term they'd be all right. After that, if it took weeks for him to get back to painting, if months and months passed before he next sold anything . . . Lammas didn't worry about Jack, except to reflect that he'd be lucky if he concluded his three years at King's, but at least the Army would pay him. It was Blanche he'd worry about, and Henrietta – because Jack on a subaltern's pay certainly wouldn't be able to look after them. And he himself had long back decided – had indeed had no choice but to decide – that he'd pay for the children's education first, think about Blanche's and his old age later.

Henrietta must finish her schooling, that was the immediate priority. If necessary, he'd sell Damiano Mazza's copy of Titian's Aegean evening bacchanalia. It had been a wedding present – but never mind. There was his Sassoferrato too, which his father had left him. But he would come to the end of things he could sell, and he didn't want to have to sell the house and move into a cottage. Yes – once the tissue of a life began to fray, it could ravel pretty damned fast.

Courage. There were those three landscapes hanging in Perry Bracknell's gallery right now. But if he were never up to doing good work again . . . The marketplace was often stupid, which could be trying; but then it was also often ruthless – which when he'd been fit and sanguine he'd thought was fine, but might be inconvenient now. And if he never recovered his form – if he never felt again that balance of excitement and doubt and determination which had made life sweet to him . . . This having his confidence all shot to bits was new.

And if he had another stroke, as Ronnie Bennett had warned him he might . . .

On the day of the Hedleighs' ball, a letter arrived at Edingthorpe from Lord Furze-Holt. Blanche brought it upstairs, along with the *Spectator* which had just arrived and had an article about Philip Wilson Steer and Charles Lammas as two painters of East Anglian landscapes.

Furze-Holt wrote that he wished to commission a portrait of his daughter Elizabeth, on the occasion of her engagement. That Peregrine Bracknell had spoken of Lammas' abilities in the most glowing terms, and he himself had admired his work in such-and-such a house and such-and-such an exhibition. That he would be delighted if . . .

Charles dictated to Blanche a brief reply, saying he much regretted that ill-health prevented him from undertaking this picture. And to think that this summer he'd been feeling disdainful of commissioned portraits, had let himself feel arrogantly free!

Blanche asked if she should read him the *Spectator* article. He was beginning to feel weak again, but he mumbled, Yes if it wasn't *particularly* abusive. Blanche had not with the passing of the years become an expert on painting, but she had developed a ruthless understanding of those who presumed to hold opinions about her husband. So now she said No. The writer cavilled a bit, and ingratiated himself a bit, and tried to sound as if he knew what he was talking about. It was the usual sort of arts journalism.

The article carped, it flattered, it didn't mean anything. But for the first time since his stroke Charles Lammas had remembered the beauty of the English east coast, remembered those marshes and tides and skies, and he'd remembered the passion with which he'd determined to give his life to the attempt to do that desolate loveliness justice on canvas. When his wife finished reading and looked up, his eyes were full of tears.

Before they set off to Bure Hall that evening, everybody trooped upstairs so that Nanny Oldfield and he might in turn admire the girls' finery, and be bidden goodnight.

Georgia was the last to go to her godfather's dressing-room. Lammas had been reflecting that Furze-Holt clearly hadn't wanted to pay John's prices, and wondering if he'd approached Sickert or would now. But when the girl came in he managed to concentrate on her. There was something he wanted to say. Since he'd fallen down in the yard, this was the only mental act he had performed which you could reasonably call a decision, and he wanted to communicate it to her.

Here she was, in her ball-dress. And one glance at her told Lammas that she was alert to what her appearance in that light blue might signify to his mind.

She stood by his dressing-table, where his hair-brushes lay, and where he'd had Blanche prop up his Tissot drawing where he could see it. Georgia said, 'We're off to Bure in a few minutes.' And then she wavered.

That indescribable hair he'd mixed his colours again and again to get right. That sash. The whole picture. Her aliveness.

She came toward him, stooped to kiss his cheek. She straightened up. 'Goodnight, Godfather Charles. Tomorrow morning I'll come and tell you all about it, shall I? Who asks me to dance – if anyone does. How awfully badly Jack and Henrietta behave. Everything.'

'Listen, Georgia.' He must do this right. 'I've been a bit knocked about by this thing. But it needn't affect you. You're free. Free to go to Burma, I mean. You must set off whenever you like.'

'Absolutely not.' She never hesitated. 'We'll wait till you're better. Then we'll go on with our picture. I'm not going to abandon you.'

'You're a darling girl; but . . .' The way she talked about *our picture*, he'd forgotten that. 'You see, the fact is, I may not get better. Or not for a long time, or not better enough. So you understand . . . You're to consider yourself free, please, young lady. Now . . . Off you go, and strike lightning into all the men at the ball – I mean the alive ones.'

'I'll wait for you to get better. Honestly I will.' She must have been taking her decisions too. Certainly tonight she was more than his equal in clarity of heart. 'I'd like to.'

Lammas had said what he intended to say. Now, for the time being, he was finished. With his eyes, he gestured that she should leave him.

Georgia held his gaze for a few moments, and went out.

22

The dusk was darkening when the guests for dinner began to arrive at Bure Hall. Jack was still feeling relieved that he had managed to start the antiquated Lammas car without getting grease on his evening trousers or oil on his cuffs. Now as he drove his family party in through the gates and the shelter-belt, he imagined the pheasant and woodcock roosting, thought of that isolated pond at the top of the park where on winter evenings the Hedleighs and Bobbie and he had stood in the butts, waiting for the duck to come flighting in.

Long past, his boyish nervousness that first time he'd been a gun at a Bure shoot. His father's musing that snowy day had been realistic: almost the only benefit to accrue to anybody as a consequence of that Hedleigh-Lammas marriage had been that Jack had received more shooting invitations than he would otherwise have done. As practically a member of the family, he'd shot partridge on the open land of the estate, he'd shot pheasant in the woodland. The beaters had got to like him, the gamekeeper had got to like him – he was a far superior shot to his cousin Bobbie.

Better still, Freddie and Mark, when either of them was in Norfolk at winter weekends, had taken to ringing up Edingthorpe, getting him over for some duck flighting. Three or four of them would pile into the car, go jolting over the farm tracks to Black Horse Wood to that old decoy, or to a flooded marl-pit up by the Grange where you stood behind a screen of hawthorn and silver birch.

Jack had not been to many balls. Even so, this wasn't the first, he was far from being as wrapped in excitement as Henrietta, who was in a torment of apprehension lest the car journey should be crushing the skirts of her pink and white dress, and was so awed by her first evening party that she hadn't yet realised she was going to have to think of things to say to people.

Still, Jack had a manly consciousness that he was his father's representative. At least for this evening, his mother and his sister were in his care. Georgia too – he was longing to dance with her. Also, he wanted to talk to Bobbie about whether he thought the Sherwood Rangers might conceivably have a use for him, and if so how one went about securing an interview with the Colonel, Lord Yarborough. Come to that, possibly Christopher de Brissac might be disposed to offer him friendly advice – de Brissac who, it was a bit daunting to recollect, had been the age Jack

was now when on the Western Front he'd won his MC, and now recently
had been promoted Lieutenant Colonel.

At Munich, Chamberlain, Hitler, Deladier and Mussolini had conferred
late into the previous night, and in the early hours of this morning an
agreement about the evacuation of the Sudetenland had been signed –
this Jack knew from the wireless, and from the late edition of *The Times*
with which the post-boy had bicycled to Edingthorpe Manor. He didn't
suppose that, this evening of all evenings, Mr Hedleigh would have time
for an exchange of views on these negotiations with a mere lad like him.
But you never knew, he might. His father's having been laid low stimulated
in Jack a notion that he might find that he was increasingly being treated
as a man among men.

Beside Henrietta in the back of the car, Georgia's tremulous spirits rose at
the sight of the lanterns at the Bure park gates. To left and right in the
gloaming, the white cattle sleeping under the oaks and beeches looked
ghostly.

Then as the car came up the curving drive, which that night had been
transformed into a colonnade of flambeaux, the girl felt ushered toward
a house she had thought she knew but was now a palace flickering
mysteriously. The terrace too was lit by swaying yellow flames, and
so were the garden walks. The great marquee glimmered palely. Figures
were coming and going on errands, or already in pursuit of pleasures. The
moon was up, every window of the Georgian façade was ablaze, and as Jack
drove the old Austin sedately forward between the flambeaux which would
crackle and flare all night, Georgia felt called to a stage on which she would
know how to act.

Or perhaps she would not be up to it. Unseen, her too-wide mouth
pouted.

Oh, but she would! Tonight Georgia scarcely had to rally her confidence
for five seconds. Her energetic body was already poised to walk onto that
stage. Every nerve of her consciousness was already testing the air in those
candelabra-lit rooms ahead.

All you needed to begin with was a dash of modesty, she reminded
herself. That, and a modicum of self-possession, a secrecy behind your
eyes. After which . . . That moments of social glory would not one night
be hers never crossed her exuberant mind – and perhaps as soon as this
evening. After all, Emanuela Zanetti wasn't here – Emanuela who would
undeniably have eclipsed her. So now . . . Georgia was so accustomed to
wearing her ball-dress, that she jumped out of the car without giving its

condition a thought. She followed her godmother to the room where they would take off their coats, her eyes darting this way and that.

A suite of bedrooms had been put aside for the ladies to prepare themselves in. Here coats and mantels were hung in wardrobes and heaped on beds, hats and muffs soon occupied all the brass hooks, and there were very nearly enough looking-glasses, and two of the Bure Hall maids bustled about with pins and homely chatter. Georgia stood still while the Hedleighs' old nanny, who liked her, ran a critical eye and a fussy hand over her dress and her hair.

On the walls were watercolours of Indian ghats and rivers, of temples and palm trees. Georgia was happy to stand motionless. Nanny Hazzard was a friend of Nanny Oldfield, although she was nothing like so old, only sixty or seventy. She asked about 'poor dear Mary', she asked about 'Mr Charles'. Twitching the girl's skirts, she told her how, as it chanced, she had been over at Mundesley that day in the spring of '16 when news had come from the Dardanelles. Yes, she'd gone over to Cliff House with old Mrs Hedleigh, Mr Julian's mother, to visit old Mrs Lammas. She'd been there when word had arrived about how that submarine had not only got into the Sea of Marmara but got out again too.

Old Mr Roland Lammas, now, he was always very stiff, you couldn't tell much about what he was thinking. But Mr Charles' mother . . . When she read about that boat getting safe back to Lemnos bay. When she heard that her younger son wasn't just alive, he had single-handed blown up a Turkish railway line. He'd blown up one of their supply lines for that campaign, and our king was going to give him a medal for it . . . Poor dear lady, she hadn't been able to help herself, Nanny Hazzard remembered, giving Georgia's back a pat to dispatch her downstairs. Thinking of that submarine steaming in among the great battle cruisers with their rails lined with men cheering like mad, little *E11* with her two young officers and a dozen young sailors on their conning-tower, grinning in the sunshine beneath their half-shot-away periscope . . . Mr Charles' mother had burst into tears right there, in the hall at Mundesley.

Georgia waited for a minute, for Blanche and Henrietta to be ready too. She watched anxious ladies and assured ladies titivating in front of the mirrors. She breathed their scents which, all competing with one another in the small bedroom, were rather oppressive. Powder-puffs, combs – Georgia liked the paraphernalia. She liked the anticipation tingling in the air, the promise of revelry, the promise of challenges to take up. To see, to be seen . . . All summer she had been looking about her; for weeks she had been posing. These were activities which suited her mood. A dance, a dance . . . The words vibrated in her head.

Christopher de Brissac had promised he would dance with her. It had been in the studio. These last days, he had come over to Edingthorpe a lot, to talk to Blanche, to sit with her by her husband's bed. And once he had asked Georgia if she would show him her portrait.

Ever since Wyndham's theatre, she had been telling herself stories about Lieutenant Colonel de Brissac. Because all her life stories had been spinning themselves in her brain, and because he knew Burma, and . . . Accompanying him across the yard, even Georgia had not been so light-headed as not to remind herself that it was also because she knew next to nothing about him, so she was free to invent practically the whole man. Invent him different from minute to minute, if she so fancied. And freedom had become more and more vital to Georgia Burney all summer, in France, in Italy, in England, in the all-promising gleam of her imminent return to the East. So now by the end of September it was exceedingly important indeed – chiefly because it was an absolute freedom she carried hidden in her head. It was the power to think what amused her, rehearse events just as they stimulated her passing tastes.

De Brissac had opened the studio door for her. She had gone in, carrying her freedom in her head with alert happiness, not bothered a bit that it was only abstract. His height, his bony shoulders, his green eyes, she was thinking as they stood together before the easel. Slightly hooked nose, brown hair going grey at his temples. But these were appearances you took for granted, like the well-cut clothes and the quiet, reserved manner. And as for the invisible man . . . Well, she wasn't Burney's daughter and Lammas' goddaughter for nothing. She already thought it was fine for men to be a bit inscrutable, just like the more intelligent girls.

They had stood together, looking at the portrait which Charles Lammas had wanted to spend another month working at. With de Brissac silent beside her, Georgia had been stabbed by awareness of how her godfather had not flattered her. Her freckles she'd always hated; but even apart from them . . . Her figure might, charitably regarded, be almost a woman's, but equally it was still half a scraggy child's. Mouth which sulked. Forehead low, broad. Eyes which gave back no light. Hair up, but somehow clumsily so.

To distract her companion, Georgia had demanded, 'At the ball, are you going to ask me to dance?'

He had turned, surprised. Had started to say, 'Ah, if you—' but then had corrected himself. 'Certainly I shall ask you, Georgiana. But as for what you may reply . . .'

Now Nanny Hazzard gave Georgia's back a second pat of dismissal. 'Wake up,' she said cheerfully. 'They're waiting. Be off with you.'

23

Waiting in the hall for his womenfolk to return, Jack Lammas chatted to the Hedleigh brothers and to a few of the other younger men who, he was pleased to discover, apparently quite naturally included him in their friendly conversation. It was true that some of these young gentlemen were wearing tail-coats and white waistcoats and white bow-ties, and others sported the most sumptuously elegant smoking-jackets, while only the less fashionable wore dinner-jackets and black bow-ties like Jack. But one of the enviable embroidered jackets was Bobbie's with its Chinese dragons – and where his cousin was, Jack could never feel irredeemably ill-at-ease, even though this summer Bobbie's eyes had often had a cold glitter, and he tended to laugh too heartily and too long, and then fall moodily quiet.

Still, the hunting scenes on the walls were familiar, and the stags' heads and the flintlocks and the college oars were old acquaintances of Jack's, and the first thing Frederick Hedleigh had said when they shook hands was, 'Have you heard the news? It's going to be peace. Can't have Hitler getting in the way of our partridge shooting this autumn, can we?' So he felt in command of the situation – or he did for a minute, till he noticed he *had* got mud or grease or something on one trouser leg. However, on the black material it hardly showed.

When the guests had regathered in the hall, they passed through into the drawing-room – undergoing as they did so the double trial of being loudly announced by the major-domo, and then exchanging a few words with their host and hostess.

Jack may have been unsophisticated for his years, but he knew a little about never drawing attention to oneself, never appearing out of one's depth, stuff like that. So he followed his mother and the girls through this introduction competently, taking a grown man's pride in his clandestine lover's figure and her dress. He knew this wasn't the moment to hope for indiscretions about the real import of the Prime Minister's return to Heston airport earlier that very day, with not only a resolution of the Sudetenland problem, but also an Anglo-German agreement of some sort. (Of what sort, he had no idea.) So he answered Sarah Hedleigh's enquiry about his father's health briefly. He told Julian Hedleigh that yes, he'd be off to Cambridge in a few days. He walked on into the drawing-room.

His sister was really far too young to be at the ball, and had only been

invited because it was her godmother's birthday party. This meant that
she had to be embraced by that solid lady as if her presence were wholly
unexpected, kissed as if she had just returned safe and sound after years
in some malarial colony. All of which – the clutch to a brooch-embossed
bosom, the big-toothed kiss, the guffaw of love – was merciful, because
the astonished Henrietta found herself launched into the party without
having to say a word.

Georgia, on the other hand, when she heard others being announced
and a few moments later was announced herself, was jerked abruptly out
of her dreams of social success. 'Miss Georgiana Burney!' came a roar. 'Miss
Henrietta Lammas!' All very fine, crediting yourself with effortless *savoir
faire*. But she'd forgotten this whole performance, which should have been
banal, and to be taken with nonchalance. So she flushed like a schoolgirl,
stammered some idiocy.

Blanche Lammas could have unselfconsciously enjoyed any ball at any
house on any night, except this one on this night. She couldn't forget
Charlie – not for more than a minute or two at a stretch. Charlie who
was no more than fifty, but could only think intermittently. Could
scarcely struggle out of his bed, let alone paint a picture or dance a
waltz. And Blanche was haunted too by a ball here at Bure on the eve
of the last war.

You wouldn't have guessed that she was thinking of a dead brother and
a dead lover, or of a husband who'd been vitality incarnate as lately as
last week. She moved gracefully into the drawing-room, her soft gaze
searching the party to see if Anne Daubeney had yet arrived. The image
of a debonair lady, Blanche Lammas appeared – stepping forward escorted
by her handsome son, who thank heavens when he'd reached six foot had
stopped growing, she'd never liked bean-pole men. Still charming to look
at, not a thread of grey in her brown hair, everyone breaking off their talk
to greet her . . . You wouldn't have known she was thinking of anything
more momentous than what a relief it had been when the dentist had
consented to take that horrible brace off Henrietta's teeth before her
first ball.

The Hedleighs had invited sixty people to dinner, and then a further
three hundred guests were coming to the ball later. The dining-room at
Bure Hall was big, but not big enough for this evening, so four tables
had been set on a low dais at the head of the marquee. They had been
laid with the family's finest linen and silver, china and glass, and now
the household servants and the extra staff hired for the evening, all

immaculately turned out for the great occasion, were waiting for the gong to be struck.

In the drawing-room, two footmen moved discreetly through the throng, bearing silver trays laden with glasses of champagne. When everybody had arrived, host and hostess were free to leave the door. They moved separately from this chattering group to that, tactfully disengaging themselves whenever their progress was held up by others' excessive friendliness.

Sarah Hedleigh was not without her anxieties. Unfortunately, they were chiefly to do with her own family, which was most provoking, because like so many people with no abilities she had elevated The Family to the loftiest position in her scheme of values. So now to have two of her three grown-up children behaving unsatisfactorily . . . Not that she would ever let this become evidence to impugn her own virtues as a mother. But it was essential that tonight the Hedleigh triumph should not be marred by any suspicion of faulty character at its very core – tonight with practically *all* the best families in Norfolk represented, and distinguished contingents from Suffolk and Cambridgeshire too.

So Mark absolutely must *not* drink too much. She had given Frederick the firmest orders to keep his brother in check. And as for Caroline . . . Always going for long walks on her own, or locking herself into her bedroom, or bursting into tears when it was least convenient. And in the run-up to the ball she'd *refused* to enter into the spirit of the thing.

Of course, if the darling girl's husband proved *hopelessly* unsatisfactory, or was killed fighting for king and country, he would need to be replaced. But they would cross that bridge when they came to it, that young man's mother-in-law resolved, catching sight of the bed-ridden Lord Lieutenant's nephew who, it suddenly occurred to her, might benefit from some intelligent handling on her part. And anyhow, marvellous Mr Chamberlain had prevented the war. They had listened to him today, on the wireless. It was *peace with honour*. It was *peace for our time*. Although, it had to be remembered, a son-in-law killed in action was always preferable to a socially or financially disappointing one. As a pretty war widow still in her twenties, Caroline would be far more likely to make a better second marriage than as a divorcée. Meditating on this, the lady of Bure Hall surged toward the Lord Lieutenant's unsuspecting nephew.

Julian Hedleigh was a cautious man, but that evening he could not resist his contentment at the way things were turning out for him. That his wife and he should give a ball on the night the government of which he was such a stalwart supporter secured peace in Europe. That the tireless political endeavours, of which all that month he had been a vocal advocate,

should be crowned with success today of all days . . . The situation was one
he would know how to turn to his advantage. He had already dispatched
a telegram to Sir Nevile Henderson in Berlin, congratulating him on the
diplomacy with which he had smoothed the way for the satisfaction of
the German government's demands and the resolution of the crisis.

Of course, there was bound to be a bit of a rumpus, both at Westminster
and in the country. One or two resignations from the cabinet, conceivably.
The First Lord of the Admiralty, Duff Cooper, might resign – but Hedleigh
had never been *absolutely* sure how reliable he was, and anyway if there
were gaps in the government's ranks to be filled it would be interesting
to see who the Prime Minister chose.

As for here in Norfolk . . . The crucial thing was that no unpleasantness
should ruffle the cheerful harmony tonight. Julian Hedleigh made a rapid
reckoning of those men he had invited who might be so cussed as to object
to the lopping of some land off Czechoslovakia and the sticking it onto
Germany. Charlie Lammas, for one. Really, in some ways the poor chap's
absence was fortunate. Christopher de Brissac . . . He was a splendid fellow
too of course. Old Catholic family. Guards regiment. (Hedleigh shared
the common English assumption that to be born into an old recusant
family was rather romantic, and certainly not socially disadvantageous;
whereas to *become* a Roman Catholic would be ludicrous, and in the worst
possible taste.) Still, he'd heard Christopher murmur something the other
evening, murmur it with the utmost mildness naturally, to the effect that
he'd been trained to believe that steady giving way might more plainly
be termed defeat.

Luckily six of the richest men in the county, all in tails and white
waistcoats, had gathered around the master of the house – had done
so quite naturally, because his own position in the top coterie was an
indisputable one. So Julian Hedleigh was at once presented with the first
of his evening's opportunities to be disarmingly modest in victory, and
so wise so hard on the heels of the event that any listener might be
forgiven for concluding that he had enjoyed access to counsels which,
until the Munich Agreement was safely signed, he had very properly not
spoken of.

'Certainly, we shall have a vigorous debate in the House. The memo-
randum which the Prime Minister has signed is not perfect. But I firmly
believe that it represents the best arrangement which, under the present
political conditions, it is realistic to hope could be reached. Still, some
of our friends on the Opposition benches will have hard things to say, I
have no doubt. What is more . . .' Hedleigh allowed a frown of troubled
sincerity to crease his forehead. 'There will be men of our own party . . .

And let me say right away how whole-heartedly I regret this. Above all now, when surely the need for unity has rarely been greater. Yes, there will be some from our own ranks . . . Not many, I hope. The Prime Minister has loyal friends. And now in the hour of his success, when he has come back to us from Munich with the most solemn assurances, with a pledge of Anglo-German friendship which . . .'

As for the resignation of the President of Czechoslovakia, it could have been designed for Julian Hedleigh's use.

'Regrettable.' Spoken with a manly, forthright tone. 'Most regrettable. But as I think you will allow, we had to be prepared for this. From his point of view, I absolutely understand. But for the general good . . .' His voice serious, calm. 'We've known war, my friends. And now I have no fear of being wrong when I say that we must be resolute for peace.'

A ball here when the guests had included Michael Mack and Tom Carraway . . . That last spring before the war, it had been – Blanche Lammas remembered. A marquee on the lawn outside the drawing-room French windows, then as now.

She had been twenty. She smiled faintly, remembering – because not all the past was sad. That had been the Bure ball when quite late into the night she'd been dancing a fox-trot with Michael, and then they'd strolled away somewhere together – into which rooms she couldn't recollect. Anyhow, away from the dancing, arm in arm, idly, through rooms where they were alone. She'd leaned her head on his shoulder, and he'd wondered, 'If Tom Carraway asks to marry you, what are you going to say?' And she had known without having to think what the answer to that was. She'd walked on slowly, with her brother's arm hugging her now, and she'd said, 'Tom's terrific, but it's you I love most of all. I won't get married unless you do.' And Michael had laughed softly, and they'd gone back and danced another fox-trot.

Now a generation later in the same house, the major-domo struck the gong to announce dinner. Couples began to form to go in. Bobbie Lammas hastened through the party, with splendid gallantry offered his aunt his arm.

'I'm starving,' he declared with all his old gaiety. 'And if I don't eat something soon, all this champagne . . .' Then his eyes fell on the pair immediately in front of them, which consisted of his wife and the Lord Lieutenant's red-faced bachelor nephew. Bobbie lowered his mouth toward Blanche's ear, whispered, 'He keeps a mistress in a little house in Cromer. Quite a young, pretty girl.'

Lit by scores of candles, to Georgia Burney the marquee seemed a silvery pavilion from a history book or a fairy tale. If the lion and the unicorn had made their entrance with her, she wouldn't have been all that surprised. The band playing softly, the starched servants standing ready, the festoons of flowers . . . Georgia was scarcely aware of the polite boy still at Eton who had been deputed to take her in, and now was helpfully searching for her place at one of the tables arranged in an E-shape.

Her first dinner party at Villa Lucia had dazzled her – but this! Georgia wondered if Christopher de Brissac would be seated anywhere near her. No, he was among some grand-looking people at the central table. She was with a younger set, at one end of the E. Then – poise, she reminded herself. Self-possession when it comes to demeanour, and even more when it comes to what you think. The Eton boy was pulling out her chair for her. She gave him a charming smile, and said, 'Thank you.'

24

—⁂—

Before leaving her husband's dressing-room, Blanche had drawn the curtains. Now Charles lay with his shoulders and head propped up on three pillows, sometimes imagining the revelry at Bure Hall, sometimes thinking of Nanny who was dying farther along the landing. But more often, he was beset by memories and fears which were so vacuous they left a taste of nausea, and then signified just enough to be obscurely horrifying, and then were meaningless again.

Beyond the glow of his lamp, the wallpaper's iris stems and flowers were crepuscular. The clock ticked softly.

He had two books on his bedside table. One was an edition of Matthew Arnold, because the editor who had commissioned him to illustrate *The Scholar Gipsy* a few years ago had been inspired by the modest success of that project, and had written to ask whether he would attempt *Thyrsis*. So that morning, when Charles Lammas had been able to move the fingers of his right hand on the irises with more dexterity than the day before, he had felt encouraged. Perhaps he really was recovering, and this would be an excellent first job of work to get down to. What was more, as soon as he delivered the illustrations he would be paid.

So he had wanted to read *Thyrsis* again, and he had enjoyed the opening page or two, had begun to imagine what he might draw. He recalled how he had tackled the last moments of the other poem. Those *cloudy cliffs* where the Atlantic beat, and the *shy traffickers* came down . . . His drawing of that had had aliveness, he'd forgotten but now he remembered. And the seafarer who landed on the beach, *undid his corded bales*. It had been fun. So now he had read on. But then he had felt groggy again. The second half of *Thyrsis* hadn't meant anything.

The other book was a Bible. Not because the sick man had started to feel Christian. Because in a confusion of dreams the night before he'd seen damned Nicky Muir again, and among horrible apprehensions that had been the most loathsome. Blinking, kind, weak eyes. Brandy-moistened lips, which sucked a cigar. The Reverend Nicholas Muir on a club verandah on a hot night. Old Nicky. Damp, tender mouth. Tender eyes. Leaning toward him. Abominable.

Charles Lammas had woken up in the blackness. Muir was dead, thank God, he'd reminded himself. A troop ship, he remembered. A mine. Lost at sea.

Long hours afterwards, when the light broke and the Edingthorpe household came to life, Lammas had asked for the Bible as well as for *Thyrsis* out of a blurry determination to put up a fight. Against Nicky Muir, disintegrated in the Mediterranean, or against something that ghost brought with him. And anyway, one thing he was clear about. Those sentences from *Ecclesiastes* were superb, and he wanted to get them back from bloody Muir who'd appropriated them.

This also is vanity and vexation of spirit . . .

And the grasshopper shall be a burden, and desire shall fail; because man goeth to his long home, and the mourners go about the streets:

Or ever the silver cord be loosed, or the golden bowl be broken . . .

Lammas was lying disabled; but he glanced up from the page combative once more. To hell with Muir, English like this could survive a few jerks like him, and the great thing was to rescue it from that corrupt mouth.

For to him that is joined to all the living there is hope: for a living dog is better than a dead lion.

For the living know that they shall die: but the dead know not any thing, neither have they any more a reward; for the memory of them is forgotten.

Also their love, and their hatred, and their envy is now perished; neither have they any more a portion for ever in any thing that is done under the sun.

That rang magnificently and it rang true, you ought to be able to lay a few lousy ghosts with an exorcism that fine. Or . . . Or the living went on kicking the dead aside as best they could.

But by night, Charles Lammas was weak again. Figures came to him, and moments, and went away.

Raffaella, who had been married a few days before. Well, he'd never make any girl a lover again, that was sure. Henrietta who had leapt from her saddle, come tearing upstairs, flung herself on him still wearing her riding hat, so its hard rim had thudded against his chest.

Roland who . . . A story somebody had told him long ago, about his father as a child. Roland had been a small boy when the railway was first built between London and Norwich, and in the East End he'd seen the slums and they had made him cry. Travelling between a well-heeled district of London and a pleasant house on the coast, there had been that interval, and the child at the carriage window had never seen anything like it, he'd burst into tears.

The slums were still there. Roland aged eight, or something like that, had not been able to bear the sight of those miles of hovels, smoking chimneys, ragged underfed people, grime. All his life he had given money to charities for slum clearance. But the slums were still there. Over-sensitive, unmanly boy. Better be like the Hedleighs. Men had fought through 1914–18 like heroes, most of them, and they'd come home to a Britain that wasn't a jot better than the country they'd left. Twenty years later and some governments later, there'd been slumps and there'd been unemployment. The General Strike too – he remembered discussing it with Julian, and how aggressively the man had talked. There were still millions of British people living in hovels and not getting enough to eat – but you wouldn't have known it from the entertainment being offered at Bure Hall that night.

That was one of the things about living in eastern England – coming in and out of London through the slums. Lammas wondered whether when men next fought for their country the survivors would come home to one that was a better place to live in. Not if Julian Hedleigh and his Conservative cronies had much to do with it. But perhaps . . . And at least this Munich surrender meant we had a respite to rearm in.

The society he'd lived in couldn't detain Lammas' faltering ideas for long. He started to recollect how, if he'd had what people called a good war, and Alex Burney's had been nightmarish, Julian Hedleigh's had been . . . Well, by comparison it had been downright splendid. On the Staff most of the time. He could remember the clipped way Alex spoke that word. Staff.

Then his brain lapsed into apathy. When, late at night, a little mental vigour returned, he came to himself thinking: it's too late. It. Whatever *it* was. But too late.

Charles Lammas lay in the penumbra of his lamp, too dispirited to lift his hand, play his fingers on the wallpaper. He listened to the clock ticking, and it seemed to him then that he knew time wasn't doing that in his head any more. Some mechanism was breaking down, or he'd lost the rhythm of it.

That metronomic tick-tock was a lot better than no time. But it was outside him; while inside . . . He felt too stupid to understand – but he must have been keeping step with some time of his own all these years, without knowing that was how he was living. And now he seemed to have got the beat wrong. Or the music had its intermittences, or something. Yes, maybe that was it. Maybe now and then there was no tune to keep time with.

Not the hush that sometimes fell in his mind when he was painting. On the hillside above Villa Lucia. At home in his studio. Not that peace when time pulsed slower and slower, it almost died away, and you might believe that if you concentrated you could capture the sight which you loved on canvas so it would be there afterwards.

Not that. Something you should have understood before, about it being too late. You went back to the Gulf of Genoa in May and you remembered being there with Blanche, and it was too late. You could tell yourself it wasn't, but it was.

Back on the English coast, too. Back in all the returns. Last month in the crab-boat coming up the channel that stormy day, his heart had been suffused with renewed love for Blanche. But that evening, in the middle of Anne Daubeney's merry dinner party . . . He'd known you couldn't recapture anything. And now it was getting late for painting too. Even supposing he pulled through, did a few workmanlike things for a year or two. Getting late.

Then he must have fallen unconscious again. The next thing he knew, he was listening to a tawny-owl, which had not been calling before.

He thought of the night outside, the owl's silent searching flight. Moorhens asleep by the pond. The dark studio. His portrait of Georgia on the easel, not finished yet. A fox crossing the rough grass under his apple trees, maybe. Bats on the wing – it wasn't too late in the year for bats.

He would have liked to range farther – up to Edingthorpe church on its knoll, down to the cliff where the sea lapped. But his mind hadn't got the old life in it. His thoughts died away, till he hardly knew he was lying there.

25

The roast-beef had scarcely begun to be carved, and the steaming plates carried from the sideboard to the tables on the dais, before Julian Hedleigh felt that he could set his mind at rest as to any repercussions the Munich Agreement might have at the ball tonight. He should have known, he reminded himself cheerfully. Nobody whom Sarah and he might have invited would be so ill-bred as to be disagreeable about politics.

The beef – he reloaded his fork – was first rate; that caterer fellow really did appear to know what he was up to. The claret was from his own cellar, therefore unimpeachable. And with the whole nation rejoicing that the Prime Minister had come home with peace achieved . . . Well, nearly the whole nation – but you'd always get a few cantankerous blockheads. What was more, Asprey's had done a fine job with that salver.

Hedleigh liked to believe that his wife had everything a lady might reasonably desire – and certainly she was not unaccustomed to magnificent presents at Christmas and for her birthday. Yet even Sarah's eyes had lit up when she'd seen that noble piece of silver, he recalled with equable pleasure. So satisfactory, too, to see your own coat-of-arms engraved on things about the house.

By the time the tables had been cleared (they would be laid again toward daybreak, for a lavish breakfast), Julian Hedleigh had settled down to enjoy the ball with that innocence with which he often delighted to be seen to forget the cares of state among his family and friends.

Sprightly for his age, pink-cheeked as one of the pippins that were grown with such commercial success on his acres of orchards, he opened the dancing with Sarah. Watched affectionately by several hundred of their neighbours, with the band, which had been brought from London, playing just for them, they whirled across the polished and chalked dance-floor with, everyone agreed, wonderful lightness for a couple who might hope soon to be grandparents. The moment the strains of that waltz died away, and the master and mistress of Bure stood smiling, a subdued rataplan of applause broke out around the marquee, and then dozens of gentlemen hurried to invite ladies to dance.

The floor quickly filled. Christopher de Brissac commandeered Sarah Hedleigh for the second dance. Julian had thought for an instant that it might be a charming gesture to ask Blanche Lammas next – but she always had plenty of partners, so he plumped for Lady Waveney, and after her for

the Lord Lieutenant's matronly daughter, even though red faces really did
seem to run in that family.

After several dances, Julian Hedleigh exclaimed merrily, 'Heavens! I'm
getting too old for all this cavorting,' and left the floor. 'Time for a
breather,' he declared boisterously. 'And I must make sure the boys
and girls are having fun. They're really the bunch one gives a dance
for, after all.'

That was the kind of thing a lot of his acquaintances liked in Hedleigh.
The way at a shooting lunch he'd wait at table himself, and then sit down
to chat with the rawest lad present. The way at an evening party, when
you expected to find him puffing a Havana cigar with friends of his own
generation, and talking about the committee stage of some bill or other,
in fact he'd suddenly be master-minding a game of charades with those of
his guests who were thirty or forty years his junior. And now he slapped
Jack Lammas on the shoulder. With twinkling eyes, he remarked, 'You're
a lucky fellow to have all these maidens flocking around you. Dance
with all of them, my boy – if only to gladden the heart of an old gaffer
like me.'

Then on he went to Henrietta – leaving Jack quite convinced that
he'd been right always to like Mr Hedleigh, and with no recollection of
having wished to ask him about the sheet of paper the Prime Minister
had flourished at Heston airport earlier in the day. Henrietta must just
let him get his breath back, their host was apologetically requiring of her,
and then . . . Why, his wife's godchild, and the youngest belle at the ball
– of *course* he was going to ask her to dance. How was that half-Arab mare
of hers, in terrific form?

It was true that Blanche Lammas had never been short of dancing partners.
And tonight especially it seemed she was going to have to insist most
pathetically if she were to be allowed even a brief rest. For the first few
dances, Bobbie and Christopher handed her to and fro between them
almost as if by prior arrangement. Blanche hardly had time to be haunted
by those Edwardian balls in Norfolk houses to which most of them had
gone not in cars but in pony-traps.

Then other friends asked her to dance. Bernard Fletcher – and he
mentioned that Jack must come and shoot over his Acle marsh next
winter, so she was pleased he'd have some fun when he came home
for Christmas. Basil Fanshaw – and he said he was going to ask Jack
to ride a horse of his in a couple of point-to-points. So Blanche was
pleased about that too. Then she smiled to find that these days she

only went into society in order to secure amusements for her children.

Round the dance-floor they swept, stately but gay, and Blanche remembered that Jack had taken the Fanshaws' daughter Rose to a May Ball. So she asked Basil, as he courteously twirled her around, 'I hope he brought your girl back safe and sound?' And Basil said, 'Oh yes, she'd had a splendid time.' That was good, Blanche thought. Because when Georgia was bundled off East, and that flirtation or whatever it was died away, and Jack was back at Cambridge . . . Yes, Rosie Fanshaw would make a charming girlfriend for him – and if her papa lent him thoroughbreds, better still.

Then Blanche Lammas recollected how alone she was, taking thought for her children. She remembered why tonight people were being particularly friendly to her. The sight of her sister-in-law Gloria talking to Anne was sobering too. Blanche recalled pre-war dances when Gloria had been engaged to Geoffrey Lammas, and Anne had been engaged to John Daubeney, and she hadn't been engaged to anyone. Not to Tom Carraway. Certainly not to Charlie – he'd been in Florence as often as not in those years, she scarcely knew him. Later she'd gone to memorial services for both Geoffrey Lammas and John Daubeney. And these last days, she had felt herself very close to being a widow too. So when the dance was ended, she asked Basil Fanshaw if he would please take her somewhere she might sit down for a minute.

Once in a chair, Blanche Lammas gave herself a shake. Julian Hedleigh was waltzing with Henrietta, to general delight. All evening, the child had been in seventh heaven – which could not fail to kindle her mother's heart. What was more, she'd had it so drummed into her that tonight she must behave in the most grown-up manner, that for the first hour she'd hardly dared open her mouth, and she was still the image of enchanted modesty. And even if Charlie died before his time . . . Even if he died tonight, if he beat Nanny to it . . . They'd been lucky, Blanche reminded herself firmly. Come spring, they'd have been married twenty years. But what was going on in those curious eyes of Georgia's?

Her goddaughter might have prided herself on her concealment of her recent turbulence from Jack. But unknown to her, Blanche Lammas, less naive, had swiftly surmised that something was up.

A week or two back, she had begun amusedly to suspect that midnight assignations might be being made under her roof – right up under it, on the top floor, where the children had always had their rooms. And she had been worldly enough, or perhaps just as ruthlessly egotistical as most mothers when it came to a first-born son, to think that if Jack found the girl pretty . . . Yes, she *knew* Georgia was in her care, she *would* feel guilty, but the sheer life in those two was irresistible. Well, she'd pack the child off to Geraldine as soon as Charlie no longer wanted her in the studio.

Then they'd come back from that expedition to London, and something had been different. All summer, ever since Georgia had been allowed to leave school, she'd been merry as a grig. But now, suddenly . . . Blanche had been reminded of how she'd been when she first came to England, four years ago. The way she'd be bonny one moment, the next go dead on you, just be going through the motions of life. So you were left with a sullen mouth to look at, and a couple of dim eyes.

In the old days, her godmother had felt sorry for her. But now, seeing Georgia in the laughing, chattering cluster of younger dancers, and noticing her fall quiet, recognising that absence which was suddenly there in her look . . . It occurred to Blanche to wonder if there were an element in the girl it might be unwise to trust. Well, she'd ship her back to Geraldine.

At dinner, Georgia Burney had awoken to the fact that the boy from Eton was good-looking – indeed, with his fine features and his green eyes, which reminded her of her brother Ricky, he was possibly rather beautiful. She had then discovered that he seemed happiest when talking only to her. So she had become her most vivacious self, and only chattered occasionally to other young men for the sheer satisfaction of finding her green-eyed admirer always ready to renew his attentions. When Jack, a few places away across the table, gave her a quizzically enquiring glance, she winked at him conspiratorially, and plunged straight back into her game.

Then the dancing began, three hundred more guests arrived and were announced, and the camaraderie among the younger set became merrier still. They waltzed, they fox-trotted, the music changed and they changed partners. Jack danced once with Georgia, but when he asked her a second time she said 'No,' and shot him a look of disarming sensuality, and whispered, 'I'll see you later.'

Caroline Lammas had been feeling tearful all day, because she couldn't help remembering her wedding, which had been the last time there'd been a marquee at Bure, and now something intangible had altered. She knew it was stupid, but something horrible she didn't understand was oppressing her, she felt frightened by invisible changes she was sure were happening in the air all around her, behind her back, in other rooms, in people's hearts. Still, she put a brave face on it, she danced with everyone who asked her. As for Bobbie, it appeared that all his old Norfolk girlfriends were overjoyed to see him, because in the three years he'd been in France they'd rather lost touch, or because mostly they too were now married. He danced with all of them, with inexhaustible flamboyance. Daisy Maitland, who had been Daisy Rackham when Charles Lammas painted her under a cedar by the river Tarn, danced with her old flame with more animation, several people observed, than she had displayed for a long time, not since before giving birth to a son to inherit her husband's fortune.

When Julian Hedleigh gave a sign to the band-master, dozens of couples took the floor together and danced a Cumberland Reel. This was executed with such spirit that by the end some of the younger revellers' dancing was almost romping, and one or two of the older ladies who were watching frowned, but most of them smiled. Jack always enjoyed reels, and then they danced Sir Roger de Coverley, and then Strip The Willow, and the idea of Georgia's and his sexual complicity was always there beneath the tunes the band played. The flower-swagged marquee, the magnificence of some of the ladies' dresses . . . A secret understanding, pleasure promised but postponed . . . Jack discovered how much he was enjoying holding different girls' hands and waists. During a complicated manoeuvre in the next reel, he passed Rose Fanshaw, with whom he had already had one dance which had been a source of light-heartedness to them both. He held her gaze, smiled, called confidently, 'You'll keep the next waltz for me, won't you?' 'Yes,' she flung at him over her shoulder as she was whirled past, 'if you ask nicely.'

Long before the Sir Roger de Coverley, Georgia had half-forgotten that a man more than twenty years older than her had promised he would ask her to dance. A man who, when visiting his friend Charles Lammas' sick-bed these last days, had found time to impart to her his Maymyo news.

It had turned out to be rather disappointingly superficial news. Her mother and father were in good spirits. Six months ago, when Alex had been back from his forests for a week or two, they'd had a drink together at the club. That sort of thing. Better than nothing – but all the same . . .

What had inspired her had been her hope that Christopher de Brissac might have remembered her as she was when he came into that theatre box. The ornate auditorium in the lamp-light, so small that it was like being enclosed in a rich cabinet. The interval babble rising from the stalls. She had been sitting with her elbow on the plush sill of the box, wearing her new silk scarf, and he had come in. She had lifted her eyes to his – and that night they had been shining. He had stooped, had shaken her hand. *Certainly I remember Georgiana Burney* . . . She had brought it back, lying in her bed at Edingthorpe late at night, waiting for Jack. She had rehearsed the scene repeatedly, to elicit from it all the conceivable flattering interpretations. That was how she wanted him to have carried her away in his mind. Too much to hope. But . . . Her head and shoulders framed by the box, silhouetted against that glimmering horse-shoe-shaped auditorium with its magic made of paint-work and brass-work, of fashionable people (it never occurred to Georgia that anyone there except herself had not been exceedingly fashionable), of music and champagne and curlicues. There beneath the radiance of the chandelier, before the curtains which drew back to reveal a world where everything was make-believe.

Georgia was standing in an uproarious huddle of people of her own age – it included both her Etonian and Jack – when she became aware that Lieutenant Colonel de Brissac was making his way through the throng toward her. Away from the friends he naturally moved amongst: the Hedleighs, Lord and Lady Waveney, Blanche Lammas and Anne Daubeney, Sir James and Lady Bosky, the Cators, the Fanshaws. Away from the fine young ladies whom Georgia had been vaguely conscious of him dancing with, creatures quite out of her girlish sphere. Not only Lady Waveney, known in the county, on account of the slow-flowing river which had lent its name to that peerage, as Duchess Sludge, but also her eminently marriageable daughter. Susanna Fitzwilliam, too – who was reputed to ride to harriers like a demon, and certainly twiddled her cigarette-holder and knocked back her champagne like one whenever de Brissac was within ten yards of her. *All* the Misses Barclay, even – very correctly – the plain ones.

It was at this moment, with de Brissac coming toward her through the party, that the girl from the Shan Hills by some sixth sense knew that her godmother's eyes were on her. She went dead quite naturally, on the instant.

Here he was, arrived at a suddenly hushed group the youngest of whom was his goddaughter Henrietta Lammas. Smiling faintly, he said, 'You see, Georgiana, here I am. Will you dance this one with me?'

If he were surprised by her sudden lack of sparkle, he didn't show it. The next thing that Georgia knew was that her blood was clanging her heart like a bell, but she had to dissemble everything.

It was a waltz, and there were lots of other couples on the floor, that was a relief. Christopher de Brissac was swinging her through the dance with controlled elegance, and she found it wasn't difficult to keep her demeanour immaculately inexpressive and at the same time let her mind exult with joyous abandon, till all she knew was that the music had taken over and this motion was all she would ever desire.

He asked when she was sailing for Rangoon. She replied that she didn't know, but soon now. As for her pleasure when he rejoined that he also would be shipping back East before long – it was as nothing beside her satisfaction with herself for not exclaiming that her godmother had been wondering in whose charge to put her for the voyage, so wouldn't it be wonderful if . . . Anyhow, Georgia had always assumed that it would be a lady, not a gentleman, who was asked to keep an eye on her. And meanwhile he steered her decorously around the floor, and her light blue dress must be fluttering out just a tiny bit, she could feel it – though the whole performance wasn't like dancing with boys a year or two older than she was. It was much more staid. And now it was over.

Christopher de Brissac said, 'Thank you, Georgiana.' He offered her his arm. 'Now . . . Where may I take you? To your godmother? To the friends I snatched you from?'

26

The following winter, Jack Lammas was invited to dinner by the Colonel of the Sherwood Rangers. His cousin Bobbie, who had caused the invitation to be issued, warned him that Lord Yarborough 'owns about half of north Lincolnshire. What's more, he only talks in grunts, but you mustn't be put off by that.' His father told him to keep an eye out for a painting by Hans Eworth which he was almost certain was hanging at Brocklesby Park. 'About 1550. A Turk riding a charger. Don't walk past it on the stair without noticing.'

The day fixed upon was in mid-December. Jack drove from King's to Brocklesby Park before going home for the Christmas vacation. In the Officers Training Corps at Cambridge he'd passed a thing called Certificate B, which he understood meant he'd probably get a commission sooner or later. But he wanted it to be in the same regiment as his cousin, and he knew that, at least in the case of this particular Yeomanry regiment, the Colonel chose the officers he wanted, and the War Office then tamely ratified his decisions. A commission would take a few months to come through, Bobbie had warned him. But that was how the system worked.

A park which stretched away for impressive distances, a house which looked vast . . . But probably it was just his being a little nervous, Jack reminded himself. He drew up his dilapidated car on the gravel sweep, carried his suitcase toward the imposing entrance, remembering his cousin under those lime trees in France. *Damned if I'll do anything so pedestrian as join the infantry. Must have a horse.*

Up in his bedroom, changing out of his tweed suit into his dinner jacket, he looked out of the window. His modest vehicle had vanished – no doubt tidied away in a stable-yard.

The other person staying in the house was Lord Fortescue. At dinner they chiefly talked about riding. Bobbie had been right about Lord Yarborough conversing in grunts, but Jack instinctively liked him for his horseman's spare frame and his weather-beaten, wizened face. And if the Colonel wished to discover if he had any sense in his head and would make an officer, Jack was happy that the discussion should be of this order. So he answered questions about the Fanshaw horses he was helping to exercise that season, about the first point-to-points he'd ridden. All evening, there was no talk about the regiment.

After dinner they played poker. Jack had never liked card games, but he was relieved that he'd been taught how to play. They played for marvellously low stakes, so that the undergraduate should be able to engage with the two magnates and Lady Yarborough fearlessly.

The following morning, his car had reappeared on the gravel. Lord Yarborough was master of the local hunt, and after breakfast they were meeting in his park, so before driving away Jack lingered a few minutes to enjoy the scene. Frost on the turf and on the trees, rooks cawing. The riders in their pink coats, the whippers-in. All these splendidly turned out thoroughbreds, the pack of hounds . . . Back in 1914, people must have tried to get commissions in regiments on winter mornings like this, Jack supposed. Oh Lord, what was that picture Papa had . . .?

A few days later, at Edingthorpe he received a letter from the Colonel to say that he would be pleased to have him in the regiment. The Adjutant wrote too. Yeomanry regiments usually had an adjutant seconded from a Regular regiment, to stiffen them up a bit, and the Sherwood Rangers had Gerald Grosvenor of the Ninth Lancers. He wrote to tell Jack that the War Office had been asked to process his commission. Also, the regimental tailor was Sandon, in Savile Row. The hatter was Herbert Johnson.

Jack Lammas went to London for fittings; he came back. But somehow Christmas wasn't the same without Georgia, or Norfolk wasn't the same, or maybe it was something quite different that was wrong with him. She had sailed from Southampton at the end of October, in the care of Mrs Harvey whose husband was something to do with shipping in the China Sea, on the same Peninsula and Oriental liner as de Brissac.

Jack went wildfowling with old Colonel Fletcher and afterwards, in his timber-framed farmhouse in the marshes, by a blazing fire drank the first glass of whisky of his life. He went to a few dinner parties, to a couple of dances. On Boxing Day he shot at Bure, and afterwards the Hedleighs dined at Edingthorpe.

His father had recovered from his stroke, but it seemed to have aged him fifteen years, and Jack found that depressing. Georgia had remained in England until her godfather was strong enough to do a last few mornings' work on her portrait, and he had then declared it finished.

Noticing how quickly his father tired, and how that old sure-fire confidence of his had gone. Finding one wall of the drawing-room suddenly bare, and being told that his sister's education and his had necessitated the sale of the Titian studio's evening bacchanalia, Theseus sailing away on the Aegean horizon, Ariadne's naked body glimmering like ivory where she drowsed. The quietness of his mother's approval when she first saw him in his brand-new uniform . . . Jack was dissatisfied, he was restless, he was a lot of things he didn't understand.

No one knew whether there was going to be a war or not – which he found meant that he didn't even know what he ought to be trying to concentrate on. Missing Georgia was futile and demoralising. But then when he forgot the ache she'd left in him, and then later realised how he'd forgotten her, that was demoralising too. It had been a game, just a marvellous game, he kept reminding himself. And he knew that was what it had been for her and how it had begun for him. But why did he feel so bruised inside?

Jack discovered he was looking forward to getting back to King's for the spring term. Architecture, a career! And if the war came . . . Afterwards if he were alive he'd need a job.

FIVE

1

—ɯ—

Those four years when his daughter was away in England, Alex Burney was talking to her all the time. The letters he wrote weren't a tenth of the musings he silently addressed to her.

During his descents to the heat and the dust of Mandalay. On his rarer visits to Rangoon, down in the Irrawaddy delta, which was just as sweltering hot and more humid. Walking with that bolt upright gait of his along the shady sides of those dignified colonial streets, his hat pulled down over his haggard, tobacco-leaf face, he'd be wondering about Georgia and about himself, wondering as if in her hearing.

Up at Maymyo also, three thousand feet above sea level, where the climate was pleasanter for a European. Not that Burney was the sort of English bore who in the tropics makes a fuss about high temperatures and high humidity. He seemed as impervious to climatic extremes as to everything else. But on the verandah of his teak bungalow, he'd be trying to make sense of what was occurring in the East, and always as if for Georgia's benefit. Or when he was riding up hill and down dale in those Frontier Areas where the only other travellers were traders and smugglers, missionaries and dacoits, and on a clear day you could see the snow on the mountains in China.

Disappointment with his marriage probably had a lot to do with Burney's taking an absent daughter as the companion of his solitude. Of recent years, his and Geraldine's being man and wife had become about as empty a formality as you get.

She never left Maymyo, never came with him even to Mandalay, which was only forty or fifty miles off – Mandalay where the Royal Palace was still standing, though it was called Fort Dufferin these days. Still there, the pagodas and the lotus garden; still there the king's audience chambers, the queen's tea-room and her summer pavilion. Shabby, but preserved . . . Thanks to Lord Curzon, who when he was viceroy came there in 1901, gave orders for the government offices to be moved out, the palace maintained as nearly as possible as it had been in royal times.

For that matter, when Alex Burney was at home he slept in a spare bedroom. Generally, in the room that had been Emma's. After the child's death, Geraldine had tidied away her odds and ends. No point in being sentimental. So now it was just any hill station spare bedroom. Teak bed, teak dressing-table. Cane chair. A Shanghai jar for water, a ladle. Pewter basin, pewter jug. A mosquito net.

Poor Geraldine Burney. Nothing for it but to oblige herself to learn that this encroaching coldness was what marriage came down to. Poor Geraldine, poor mem-sahib – with nothing to do but grow roses, and slowly give up pining for Paris; nothing for it but games of bridge, and chit-chat. All she had were a husband so abstracted that the word *husband* was a mockery, and a son who visited infrequently, called her 'Mother darling', and was bored by her. One daughter buried in the local Church of England graveyard when she was ten. The other who long afterwards may have acknowledged that her mother's departing this world redeemed a lot of the silliness of her living in it, but who when she returned to Burma that winter of '38 certainly had not yet come to any such magnanimous conclusions.

Geraldine Burney was wrong about Alex's adoption of a separate bedroom. His sexual abstinence was not confined to his relations with his wife – as she, wretched woman, supposed. And it wasn't simply a case of the creeping dead-aliveness which was that type of marriage. Not that he didn't make the most of the rotting away of any real feeling between them, as an excuse for his increasing detachment. Any camouflage, so long as it was effective. The fact was, he had syphilis – which his wife died without contracting, or knowing about.

One of the houses he frequented in Mandalay belonged to an Army doctor he liked and trusted – or rather, whom he knew superficially enough to feel at his ease with. Of course, there was an Army cantonment at Maymyo too, with the medical staff you'd expect. But Burney would slope off with his secret to Mandalay. The doctor lived right in the heart of that sprawling town, his patient could walk there quite easily from the Upper Burma Club.

Another reason for Alex Burney's ghostly communings with Georgia was that he didn't get on with Ricky much more comfortably than Geraldine did.

Odd, really. After all, they appeared to have a fair amount to share. Soldiering. The East. That streak of sensuality you'd notice in all the Burneys, something about the mouth and the eyes . . . A concupiscence which was in tremendous health in the younger generation, withering away in their parents.

Blanche Lammas had been right, looking down her dining table at Richard Burney that Christmas when he was a boy of fifteen. With his wide, curling mouth and his green eyes; with his hair not banally red but, depending on the light, seamed with tawny lights and flamy lights; with skin that would have been more suitable on a girl . . . Life might have been more straightforward for him if he could just have been handsome, but he was beautiful. And, then, having that power to corrupt which the beautiful naturally possess. Being one of the toughest lieutenants in the Gloucestershire Regiment. Being equipped with conspicuous energies and appetites, and having only recently turned twenty-one . . . He was what was known as quite a handful.

The Gloucesters were stationed at Mingaladon, by the airfield. When Ricky was free during the day, you might find him at the Rangoon Gymkhana Club playing tennis with his brother officers, or with friends who were in government service or worked for the trading firms. When they played mixed doubles, he always seemed to be partnered by one of the prettier young ladies of the colony – daughters of the Governor's aides, daughters of colonels, daughters of company directors. When evening fell, he might be at a dinner party in one of those households, or in livelier form at the Mess. And however he started the evening, he'd often adjourn later to the Silver Grill or one of Rangoon's other late-night haunts, go drinking and dancing with girls who weren't always white or respectable.

All in all, Ricky Burney was living in a decidedly end-of-empire style. Certainly he was both more sophisticated and more dissipated than his old school-friend Jack Lammas, to whom these days he rarely gave a thought. And you might have hoped that this would chime with his father's sense of how vulnerable the British East was. A father amused by his son's wildness, indulgent of his snatching at the hour, at that civilisation while it lasted. A son cheerful to be so affectionately watched, eager to discuss the looming crisis in world affairs with the older man . . . Several people allowed themselves to hope that sort of comradeship might develop.

Ricky didn't think of it like that. Not that his was a frequent presence on his parents' Maymyo verandah, nor that when he showed up his father was invariably there too. But when at least three components of that fissile family were gathered together . . . Ricky would lounge elegantly in a rattan chair, a young man as callow and as suave as Britain in decline was making them – and the difficulties of defending the Eastern empire against Japanese aggression would run off him like water off a duck's back.

Nothing to him, the bleak perspectives his father couldn't help staring down. That there appeared to be damn all that British diplomacy could do to deter Japan from lining up alongside Germany and Italy. That with Washington isolationist and Tokyo opportunistic, if we found ourselves fighting three enemies at once it might not be possible to send East a fleet strong enough to beat the Japanese without leaving Italy paramount in the Mediterranean and, worse, Germany in a position to take control of the North Sea . . . Ricky was as jaunty a young officer as he was a night-club voluptuary, and as conventional in his views as any of the upper-class mamas whose dinner parties he graced could have desired. Singapore was impregnable. And if the Japs did come through Siam and try to invade Burma, we were ready for them. Let 'em come. He was raring to have a crack at the little bastards. They'd learn.

Nothing to Ricky, that while the strafing of our ambassador on the road from Shanghai to Nanking might have been an accident, the obstruction of Western business and the harassment of the occupants of the European Concessions were evidently systematic. As for the Treaty Port system in China, which his father and all the older generation seemed to take dreadfully seriously. A system which, they grumbled, once dismantled would almost certainly be gone for good . . . Ricky found a Treaty Port a hard thing to get steamed up about, indeed was not entirely clear what sort of treaties were involved. And anyhow, such talk was unbecomingly defeatist.

What about Westerners being killed during the Sino-Japanese fighting in Shanghai? the father might enquire of the son. And all the other times when Britain and Japan teetered on the edge of going to war but just didn't? In December '37 when they attacked our gunboats on the Yangtze, and HMS *Ladybird* and HMS *Bee* were damaged, and USS *Panay* was sunk. Washington hadn't at that time really got a policy for reacting to that kind of thing, so they dithered. Ended up accepting an apology and two million dollars' indemnity. London dithered too. It wasn't obvious what you could do except dither, Alex Burney would point out. If the Americans wouldn't come in with you to reestablish the old order on the China coast, which had been quite a convenient one for both of you. If you hadn't got a two-hemisphere fleet, so on your own you couldn't fight a two-hemisphere war . . . What did Ricky think?

It appeared that Ricky didn't think anything which allowed of despondency. Not after the attack on those gunboats on the Yangtze. Not the following month, when a couple of British policemen in Shanghai were murdered by Japanese soldiers, and again Mr Chamberlain talked about sending the fleet. Not in the autumn of '38, while on the other side of the world Georgia was posing a last few times for a prematurely debilitated painter, and on the Pearl River a Japanese force seized Canton, thus arriving mighty close to Hong Kong.

And Alex Burney didn't know how to convince with his intimations this son of his who hadn't yet seen any action, but who was enjoying being a young military man of indomitable spirit. Alex who had been known to murmur curt recollections about how he'd never known whether the likes of Geoff Lammas and he had been good soldiers or not. They'd pulled their weight, he trusted. Been mentioned in despatches once each, as it chanced. But no glamorous medals. Then the Third Battle of Ypres. And whether stumbling toward the German guns until half of you had been killed and half of the rest of you half-killed – if that made you a good soldier . . .

Facing that sallow countenance, you had Ricky. Who may have looked a bit too much like Adonis, or for that matter even Ganymede, but who turned out later to be a terrific fighting man. Who heard that grating, clipped voice. Who couldn't help overhearing those laconic speculations – but didn't match them.

The father might say something about how of course if the Japs *did* go for Hong Kong we'd never be able to rescue the place. To which the son would respond, generally with a glass of pink gin in one hand and a cigarette in the other, and with his cockiness taking the form of an arrogant drawl, that naturally if the situation got *badly* out of hand it would become necessary to do something about it. Crown Colony, damn it, after all. Worth a mint of money, too.

And Alex Burney was never heard to snap anything like, 'For Christ's sake, why don't you think before you open your mouth?' Usually he'd end with a gruff remark along the lines of, 'That's the spirit, my lad.'

A few days later, he'd have vanished into the hills.

2

—ᴍ—

Alex Burney didn't come from the grand side of his family. The Jacobean house in the East Riding of Yorkshire belonged to his cousins. Rufford Hall, it was called.

As a boy, he stayed there a few times. Not often, but enough for those chimneys and those mullions to stick in the back of his mind as the incarnation of elegance. Enough for that walled garden to become his idea of a verdant sanctuary.

Rufford was never going to be his, there was no point in getting too fond of the place. The last time he went was during the war. His great-aunt Patricia invited him to spend a few days with her when he was next on leave. By then, Alex's experience of trench warfare was too extensive for him to find inspiration in the long gallery hung with pictures brought back from the grand tour, or the park dotted with fallow deer, or the lake dotted with lilies.

No solace, the conversation of great-aunt Patricia, whose intelligent marriage half a century before had enabled her to send all four sons to Eton, dedicate her existence to the repair and rehanging of the Rufford tapestries. No solace, his cousin Alfred, with his belly straining his waistcoats, with a frill of white hair on the back of his beefy head, terribly concerned about the way the war was going, concerned about what was going to happen to farming. Not even much solace his niece Maisie who made eyes at him.

The next time Alex Burney was in England, Geoffrey Lammas had some home leave too. Alex accepted his invitation to spend a few days in Norfolk. Better than listening to more talk about how his relations' war effort might have to include ploughing up the park at Rufford and sowing it with wheat. So he got to know the village of Mundesley, and Cliff House which was built of flint and not large, but had a commanding view of the North Sea.

Of course, there was no way he could have imagined that he'd be back after the war as Geoffrey's brother's best man. That leave, Alex Burney and Geoffrey Lammas only had time for a week on the Norfolk coast. But when they were back in their quarters behind the lines, and later when they went up to the front again, Alex had precise pictures of what his friend meant by home and peace time, what life he intended to live if, when peace returned, he were still alive.

Geoff was going to practise architecture in Norwich. Gloria and he and their little boy were going to live in one of those villages along the coast, or a few miles inland. He'd keep a sailing boat on one or other of those waterways. They'd have horses, and a pony for Bobbie and for the other children who might be born. They'd go riding between those flint churches along those wood-sides, riding along that shore.

Alex had no such specific visions, and only vague determinations. When he was a child, they'd forever been shifting from pillar to post, always in rented houses. Then his father died. His mother took a cottage in Twickenham.

No such beloved visions; only cloudy ideas. And anyhow, after Passchendaele he subsisted in a fog of pain. Then when he was fit enough to be moved they shipped him back to England, for months he was in a hospital in Kent. That was the period when his body was being got back pretty much into working order, but unfortunately you could not make a similarly cheerful judgement about his nerves. He found his mind had become horribly treacherous. No ability any more to think what he had determined he would think, avoid thoughts of other matters which were better neglected. Such as a head being shot away. Such as the life which Geoff had dreamed of living when the war was over. That was another idea it proved unhelpful to return to, but impossible to forget for long.

So it was always there, that conception of a life on the east coast of England which Geoffrey Lammas had carried with him month after month, coming and going along water-logged trenches. And when Alex Burney recovered sufficiently to leave the hospital in Kent and travel to Norfolk, where at Cliff House he again met old Mr and Mrs Lammas and Gloria, where he gave the young widow that signet ring. When after the war he returned again, in order to stand in Paston church with his scars invisible under his morning coat and a wedding ring in his fob pocket . . . The conception was there, irremovable. When later he'd come to stay at Edingthorpe Manor with Charlie and Blanche who were doing all the things Geoffrey had longed to get back to . . . It gave a rasp to the way he talked. *All these fools in England living as if the war hadn't finished off that old way of life.*

Late in the war, Alfred Burney ploughed up half the Rufford Hall park and grew wheat on it. Then, soon after putting it back to grass, he died of Spanish influenza. A few years after, another of the Yorkshire Burneys died without producing an heir, and in the Shan Hills the survivor of Ypres realised he might be going to inherit after all.

The spell of the Shan Hills began to lose a little of its potency. After all, he'd only taken to Burmese forestry because he needed a career. Well, for that reason, and also in order to get clear away from where the war had been fought, and for what.

Now he permitted himself to dream that after years in Burma he might get home to be buried in an English churchyard. Yes, he even slipped back into considering the country as home – even thought of Rufford as home, though it never had been. The fact that the place was only a dozen miles from that east coast which had been Geoffrey's had its suggestiveness too. He let himself confess how weary he was of a job which largely consisted of a struggle to reduce double-dealing and theft. How weary he was of hill station society; weary of the Shan princes and their henchmen; weary of solitary journeying.

When a few years later somebody else died, and from a Hull solicitor Alex Burney received notification of his inheritance, he had his first spontaneously affectionate thought of his wife for many years. Geraldine would revel in being the mistress of Rufford Hall, a position which had always carried a fair bit of social clout in the East Riding. What was more, she would be so busy being a great lady that with any luck she'd leave him in a degree of peace.

Then the letters about the debts started to arrive in Maymyo. The last two masters of Rufford had both, it transpired, borrowed money left right and centre. And before them, beef-faced beef-brained Alfred, who had talked so relentlessly about agriculture, had lost impressive sums by that pursuit. Alex Burney had always been perfectly competent when it came to financial matters. Now at his desk in the bungalow he worked through the sheaves of communications about the values of cottages, about yields per acre, about the interest on loans. But then another mortgage came to light, and then another.

Certainly his salary as a Forestry Officer was not going to reverse the family rout. And naturally he had told Geraldine of what had seemed their extraordinary good fortune, and naturally she had shown off about it at the club. So now her disappointment at having the prize dissolve in her grasp was aggravated by humiliation before her bridge-playing friends. The upshot was, she made that sojourn of his at Maymyo even more distasteful than usual.

For a while, Burney hoped he could stave off the end by renting Rufford out for a good number of years. Twenty, if need be. Any period – if it yielded the possibility of his bequeathing the place to Ricky. For himself, he was quite ready to end his days in Burma. But his son . . .

Then it turned out that wasn't going to clear the debts either. The next time the Forestry Officer was back in the civilisation of Maymyo, he wrote instructions for Rufford to be sold. The Hall, the cottages, the farmland. Pictures, sculptures, tapestries – the lot. If anything remained, when the family's debts had been settled and the lawyers paid, it was to be divided between Richard and Georgia, deposited in their names in the bank in Hull.

It was during the same afternoon at his desk, that Burney wrote his resignation from the Travellers' Club, giving as his reason that he was never going back to England.

By the time he'd resolved his business affairs, it was evening. Standing up from his desk, suddenly he couldn't think of anything left to think of. Except for the futility of the whole Rufford episode. Lives, deaths. Debts, letters.

Tiredness, probably. Foolishness, certainly. He tipped a splash of whisky into a glass, went out onto the verandah, stood looking spiritlessly at his wife's japonicas. A rickshaw going by under the rain-trees . . . So this was going to be it, then. Between the club and the cantonment and the botanical gardens. With the Chinese temple one way and the English church the other. With the muezzin calling . . .

Then he remembered Georgia. Her return to the East, to him – that held promise, possibly.

3

—〰—

Georgia Burney's departure from England was overshadowed by Nanny
Oldfield's death. Standing in Paston churchyard for her funeral that
autumn afternoon in spattering rain, with a dozen other people all in
mackintoshes, with gulls being blown past the tree-tops, suddenly the
girl had not been able to bear the sight of the open grave.

The mound of soil, the sexton's mattock and spade. The coffin. Nanny
in it. Nanny being dumped down into that black, cold, wet hole, and left
there forever. Georgia had burst into tears, and that had started Henrietta
crying. Blanche Lammas had pressed her lips together tight, and stood
very still, her eyes glistening.

But by the time her ship was passing Cape Trafalgar on a stormy
nightfall, days had passed since Georgia had last felt discomfort at the
idea of Mary Oldfield being consigned to Norfolk mud. In the fancily
gilded saloon, she raised her tea cup carefully as the liner rolled, paid
attention to Lieutenant Colonel de Brissac. He was giving Mrs Harvey
and her the sort of brisk account of Nelson's tactics that 21 October which
he judged might prove acceptable to female ears. Georgia looked out at
the tumultuous Atlantic, at the Iberian coast now almost too tenebrous
to discern. She told her companions about her godfather reading Hardy's
poem to Jack and her by the library fire.

All the voyage out, Georgia's spirits rose by leaps and bounds. *I'm going
home*, she chanted silently. *Home* . . . The same word which, whispered
night after night in school dormitories, had made her misery clamp onto
her brain till her eyes oozed tears of self-pity. Now it rang exultantly.
Gibraltar, then Malta, then Port Said. *Going back*, she rejoiced. *Back* . . .
To her East. Also, it could feel, back in time. Back toward her state
of heart before she'd been expelled from her original happiness. Back
to hill station frangipani trees; to before she'd ever been lonely; to . . .
She didn't know, but she wanted it.

Fleetingly, the Mediterranean reminded her of Emanuela Zanetti, of
walking with the white sheepdogs to the village for milk, eating nectarines
for breakfast. But her immediate fellow-feeling was for the ship's Lascar
crewmen, who looked so cold on deck in the dirty weather, and who
also were heading homeward. Perhaps when they got back to the Bay of
Bengal some of them would jump ship. *When you've heard the East a-calling*
. . . Only it was supposed to be Cockney, or . . . But it was something like

that, Godfather Charles and she had read it in the studio. *If you've heard the East* . . . Some of the Lascars might not be able to resist it. When they got back to the palm trees, and the temples, and the bazaars' spicy smells. They'd vanish away to their villages.

To the tropics . . . Georgia repeated the phrase like a charm. *Tropics* . . . Pregnant word. *Back East* . . . An incantation. A promise she'd been making to herself for upward of four years and now rehearsed triumphantly. She was away, the ship was steaming steadily, she was free, they weren't going to stop her now. Leaning at the stern rail when the weather was calm again, Georgia contemplated the liner's wake as if that drawn perturbation were a sign of deliverance.

At Port Said, she felt on her skin the first playing of what she recognised as the warm breath of the East, and she remembered Nanny. She was the same age as Mary Oldfield had been when she sailed to India as a nursery maid with the Ross family – though for Nanny the adventure had been a going, not a coming back. Georgia was too excited and too hazy to ask anybody how the voyage would have been made in 1866, find out that the Suez Canal had not been finished for another three years. So she watched the Egyptian shoreline, and thought fondly of her old ally Nanny Oldfield watching it when she was a girl, setting forth to earn her living in the British East

Then in the Red Sea the heat of the sun felt to Georgia like a promise already beginning to be fulfilled. The Lascars looked more cheerful, too, now that their brown faces were no longer greyish-blue along the bones from the European winter cold. Watching the feluccas and the dhows, Georgia forgot Nanny – who had indeed known Suez, but on her way back to England nearly twenty years later. Who on her outward voyage had marvelled at Table Mountain from the sea, and the shores of Madagascar.

The tropics . . . Georgia desired in her head only those words which echoed with promise. *The tropic of Cancer* . . . Mysterious, haunting words. And whatever they meant – she'd checked on the chart outside the purser's office, she knew she was going to cross that line soon now.

As for whether she'd ever return northward up the Red Sea . . . It was such an unattractive possibility, it never crossed her mind.

East of Socotra, Georgia started to worry about whether she had remembered Burma right. For instance – up-river from Mandalay, where the Sagaing Hills came down to the Irrawaddy plain, their knolls pinnacled with pagodas, where your ferry steamed in to the right bank, and there . . .

It was all so long ago. She had been very little when Daddy took Ricky and her – she was almost sure Ricky had been with them. But there stood the vast ruin of what was going to have been the greatest pagoda of all – or had she not really seen it? Had she just heard it talked about, probably been shown a photograph? The Mingon Paya, it was called. Only a third of the elevation had ever been built, but even so it reared up on that wooded bluff like a hill of bricks. A ruin, cracked by an earthquake, which had hurled down mighty blocks of masonry – they lay in the scrub like smashed cottages – but hadn't come near demolishing it. Or had that been a different picnic expedition? Burma was studded with ruined pagodas.

Still, Georgia was pretty certain about the Mingon bell. Her advantage here was that she *knew* she'd seen a picture of it, a photograph of an Edwardian party visiting the bell. But she could *also* recall standing beside her father while he explained how the Irrawaddy Flotilla engineers had managed to rehang the monstrous thing – which was the biggest bell in the world, or was there a bigger one in Moscow had someone said? Anyhow, the shackle from which the Mingon bell was suspended was taller than a man.

In the Arabian Sea and then in the Indian Ocean, Georgia thought less and less about the people she'd left behind her. Jack was a darling, of course . . . But if she brought to mind her fling with him, these days it was with an uneasy sensation of relief. Thank heavens she'd got away with it. Not that she was clear what she meant by that – but the feeling of having escaped lightly was acute.

Dangerous play, over now. And as nothing beside the satisfaction of observing her consequence in Mrs Harvey's eyes enhanced by her acquaintance with the Lieutenant Colonel. As nothing beside the abstract joy of imagining a wild passion with him, or with someone like him, while all the time enjoying the security afforded by their scarcely knowing one another, the protection of his correct urbanity with her and of her correct modesty with him.

Georgia did not think much about the people she was going toward, either. Ricky would be on the Rangoon waterfront. Possibly her parents would have journeyed down the country to greet her too, she didn't know. Apart from that . . . Certainly she had not imagined the frigidity of their marriage, or the position she had come ghostlily to hold in her father's heart. Nor was she meditating on his letters, on his premonitions of political moribundity and military débâcle.

In the household up at Maymyo, at the very worst she supposed the parrot might have died, she ought to be prepared for that sort of unpleasant surprise. But her trouble was more cloudy. For no sooner had she settled the question of the Mingon bell more or less satisfactorily, than a dozen similar doubts beset her. Then she began to be anxious about whether the whole country would live up to her expectations, such was the difficulty she found in deciding what she really knew and what she didn't.

All Burmese statues of the Buddha were in temples, or in the image-houses clustered around pagodas. So why, then, did she seem to recollect a hillside overlooking the Irrawaddy – above Prome, or below? somewhere thereabouts – a rock scarp, out of which figures of Gautama had been sculpted? Painted white, some of them, and others sheathed in gold-leaf, by reverent souls. Lots of them, all sizes. Forty or fifty, maybe. Gazing serenely over the great river and its egrets . . . Or had she dreamed them up? Perhaps she had dreamed that approach, with the thumping splash of the stern-wheeler. Dreamed the river islands with their groves and pagodas and heronries. Dreamed the rice boats with their lateen sails gliding down that great region of fresh water endlessly rolling south to the sea.

Now that Georgia brooded on it more energetically, not *all* Burmese statues were undercover. Near the abandoned capital, Amarapura, there was that gigantic image of the Enlightened One sitting near a long, rickety bridge across the lagoon. But those others, hewn out of the Irrawaddy cliff – had she truly seen them? Disconcerted, she rehearsed the things she knew beyond a shadow of doubt.

Maymyo things, chiefly – realities of which she might feel reassuringly certain. The individual trees in their garden, she wasn't likely to get them wrong, and the tree-house Ricky and she had built long ago. The trees in the Blakes' garden over the fence, and in the Maclarens' down the lane. The bazaar. What was to be found in each shop, one by one.

Yet the instability of what she thought continued to dog her. All those bitter nights in England, dreaming of Burma, conjuring up magnificence and happiness . . . And then your ideas got all skewed, the whole business of knowing seemed too difficult for words. You could tell yourself stories till the cows came home – but afterwards . . .? And another thing: was she going to be able to remember how to speak Burmese? It had never occurred to her that she could forget it; but four and a half years . . . She tried out a sentence or two, gingerly.

Luckily the ocean had its beguilements. While Mrs Harvey was ensconced in a deck-chair beneath an awning, knitting a scarf for Mr Harvey with a view to his Yellow Sea winter nights, Georgia stood at the ship's rail. She was contented indefinitely, watching for flying fish, catching her breath each time she saw that iridescent flight. And one glimmering morning, when she came on deck the liner was forging through a school of whales.

4

—⁂—

Strange fellow, Christopher. He didn't seem to be the marrying type. So far, Charles Lammas' musings at Edingthorpe that Boxing Day dinner party might have been those of any of de Brissac's acquaintances.

Not the usual kind of Roman Catholic . . . Read Saint John of the Cross, read Pascal, people like that. A reflection that only half-a-dozen friends could have made. Adding, perhaps, if they were not of his Church, that a taste for theology was just as rare among Protestants and, so far as they knew, among the Orthodox. Adding conceivably, if your interlocutor were Lammas, who was one of the exceedingly few souls to whom de Brissac ever confessed to any feeling about himself, that a surprising amount about that man was fortuitous.

To down-play anything in his friend that might have appeared striking, Lammas might have said that. Out of loyalty. To protect him against suspicions of unbecoming weakness of character. Or, for that matter, against suspicions of more than respectable spiritual complexity.

Fortuitous . . . De Brissac went straight from Harrow to Sandhurst and then into the Coldstream Guards, because there was a war being fought. He was Catholic because his family had always been of the old persuasion – quite beyond reformation, as he would put it. He stayed in the Army after the war because his elder brother inherited the controlling interest in their Northumberland shipping business. He went to India in 1919 because he happened to meet old General Holm-Mere, who decided he was an excellent young man and wanted him as his aide-de-camp.

You could say things fell out as they did pretty much by chance. Or you could say events proceeded very ordinarily because there were no pressing reasons why they should not.

De Brissac sailed for India that first time without having asked Lord Fitzwilliam if he might propose to his daughter Charlotte, because as a young officer he couldn't afford to marry her. Or, others opined, because she would have come with such a resounding dowry that he'd have been a bought man. Or because he wasn't really in love; or because she was Church of England; or because India would be more fun for a bachelor. At any rate, this particular chance was later a fount of much satisfaction to Charlotte's young half-sister Susanna, who on the eve of the next war could flirt with him at balls like the Hedleighs' far more flamboyantly than if he had for years been her brother-in-law.

At Simla when he was twenty-three he became Captain de Brissac, because General Beaumont esteemed his social graces and his horseman-ship just as sincerely as General Holm-Mere prided himself on doing, and because at hill stations and summer Seats of Government if a brace of generals wanted a young man promoted the thing was done. Still at Simla, he didn't get married to Amy Lockhart because she was already married and, although she was far unhappier, half the club agreed, than Our Lord ever intended a pretty girl to be, she lost her nerve about divorcing her boor of a husband. Or, according to the other half of the club, because the fact that Lockhart was an oaf didn't mean that de Brissac wasn't a . . . Here opinion became hopelessly multifarious. Still, the gist of it was that her lover persuaded Amy to lose her nerve. He, as the saying went, put her back.

Of course, there were things that couldn't be accounted fortuitous. That Military Cross, won on the Western Front in the last months of the war, when he was still practically a boy. Won at night in no-man's-land, when his three men and he had crawled close to the enemy front line. According to the citation, they surprised some Germans who were out doing the same sort of scouting. Surprised them when they were lying doggo in a bomb crater, and de Brissac used his bayonet several times, effectively.

His religion, too. Because being born into a Catholic family was one thing, but sitting up late to read saints and religious poets was another. And yet there they were, on his shelves: poets whom almost nobody else read, like Southwell and Vaughan – and he was one of Hopkins' earliest readers. Then Saint Augustine, Saint Teresa, Saint Thomas Aquinas . . .

His upbringing probably accounted for his reticence. He'd been brought up to make nothing of the savagery for which medals were awarded, just as he'd been brought up to make nothing of the honour they conferred. So he did make nothing of these things. He'd been brought up to make nothing of religious differences, and to keep his religious experiences to himself, so he did. His friends' nubile goddaughters too. Because waltzing at Bure Hall, Georgia Burney may have congratulated herself on how impeccably she concealed the fact that her heart was palpitating, her wits were scrambled and her resolution was steeled; but naturally Christopher de Brissac wasn't fooled. Still, he wasn't a roué. So he just let himself be enchanted and amused, and made nothing of it.

Making light of things . . . Just like, although he might have taken to reading Blaise Pascal because of man's condition being *inconstancy, boredom, anxiety,* he was only ever heard to quote the worldliest axioms and the most superficial jokes. He was as deft at fobbing off questions about his faith as Lammas was at deflecting dilettante conversation about art when it looked like getting earnest. Pascal's remark about how he could understand a young man like Alexander setting out to conquer the world, but Julius Caesar should have been too grown-up . . . That was a favourite of de Brissac's, when it came to changing the subject.

Even so, standing on deck with Mrs Harvey and Georgia as the ship steamed up the Gulf of Martaban, he was not too urbane to let himself join in the girl's delight.

Radiant, dry season sunshine. The heat tempered by the wind of the ship's passage. Georgia with her straw hat shading her eyes, Georgia gazing at the green, low-lying coast as if it were the promised land . . .

It was as if she had been holding her breath for four and a half years – when the ship came into the mouth of Rangoon river, she let out a soft sigh not of satisfaction but of excitement.

Standing beside her at the rail, in his white suit and his Panama hat, de Brissac heard. He looked at her. She turned her head, met his eyes.

5

—ɯ—

The ship was steaming up Rangoon roadstead. Passengers lined her rails, pointing out landmarks and vessels, chattering. Fore and aft, the Lascar crewman were getting warps ready for mooring.

Georgia had enjoyed holding her distinguished companion's gaze. (As for what his distinction consisted of, she was as vague as she was unquestioning.) But quickly she turned back to scanning the shore.

From the sea she had picked out the Shwe Dagon pagoda when it was still only a golden speck shining on the smudgy horizon. Then she had been conscious of people beside her calling out when they spied it, people exclaiming, people explaining. While it was still tiny in the distance Georgia only glanced at it now and then, with a glance that was both a promise and a holding off, because she knew that once she let her mind possess the Shwe Dagon fully she would be home, the anticipation would be over.

So while the waterfront was still indistinct, she let her thoughts go darting ahead past the docks and the Mawtin Street jetty, past the Chinese quarter, on to the Strand Hotel with its Doric capitals where they'd probably have dinner tonight. Oblivious of the Lieutenant Colonel and of Captain Harvey's good lady, Georgia's victorious spirit went skipping up Dalhousie Street, down Phayre Street, and her eyes glittered with a colourless radiance.

It was as if she had a flying carpet, the way her mind glided out through the ragged edges of the city, where the Bengali clerks would never dream of establishing their families, but where the poorest Burmans lived in shacks of wood and wattle, fowls scratching under their Jack-fruit trees. Then further afield to the Royal Lake and the race course. Back to the street dominated by the Madrassi chetties, who lent money at perilous rates of interest and into whose debt it was essential never to fall – she recollected her father admonishing Ricky rather sternly.

It was late afternoon, but Georgia's flying carpet paid no more heed to time than to space, so she saw the monks come out of their monasteries for their morning walk to ask for alms. Her spirit swished past those files of saffron-robed men with their begging-bowls slung on cords from their necks – and everywhere she flew, her mind hosannahed *I'm back, I'm back!*

Of course, she knew the rice-trading season in Rangoon would not get under way for another couple of months, though inland the crop would have begun to be reaped and carted and threshed. But that didn't stop her conjuring up the pandemonium when the mills along Puzundaung Creek should get to work winnowing the harvest, didn't stop her conjuring up the clouds of rice-dust that would hang over that shore, and the tons of paddy husk which all season would spout from the shoots into the tideway where it would wash to and fro and clog the shallows and foul the slipways. She had all Rangoon to repossess, wet season and dry, Buddhist and Hindu and Christian – so from her swooping carpet she saw coolies unloading rice into godowns, and the boats' up-country skippers hunkered down on their raised sterns to smoke cheroots and watch the work. The rice season of five years ago and of next year were all one to her, they lapped into her happy mind as one time. Chittagonian firemen stoking up, black with coal-dust. Scottish engineers, Chinese carpenters. The Burman girls who stitched the rice bags. The English assistant from one of the big firms who hurried by, rice-dust thick on his hat and moustache, shouting to one of his brokers to get afloat, there were more paddy boats to meet, deals to be struck.

All Rangoon to repossess – which was an earnest of the country lying beyond it, which Georgia had lost and now refound. (In the excitement of her approach to the coast, she had forgotten her doubts about whether she had remembered her native land accurately, or whether things might have changed, or prove disappointing.) All Rangoon, with its waterfront a lot clearer now. And though the rice trade was still in abeyance, the roadstead was busy with other vessels. A ship of the Henderson line – she recognised it – putting to sea. Tramp steamers at anchor. Native craft with their lateen sails furled along their curving gaffs.

It is called Dogonne, and is of a wonderful bignesse, and all gilded from the foot to the toppe . . . It is the fairest place, as I suppose, that is in the world . . .

Georgia was a child again, on the verandah in Maymyo when Emma was still alive, and her father was telling about the Elizabethan voyager Ralph Fitch. She was alone at a school in England, and his voice was reaching her all the way from Burma. She was standing by the ship's rail, and the Shwe Dagon pagoda was here, was now, but for another minute she kept it just as a glint in the corner of her left eye, as if she had a chip of gilded glass burning there. It must be magnificent now, tapering above the roofs of Rangoon – but not yet, not quite yet . . .

It standeth very high, and there are foure ways to it, which all along are set with trees of fruits, such wise that a man may goe in the shade above two miles in length.

Her knuckles white on the rail, Georgia made herself wait a few

moments more, her consciousness peopled with all the pilgrims who came
to this shrine, her heart swelling with pride to be of that company. From
all Burma they had come, time out of mind, from the river Chindwin and
the river Salween – but also from farther still. From the Brahmaputra they
had wended their reverent ways here, from the Yangtze and the Mekong.
On foot and in carts, then by sampan. Across the seas in schooners and in
dhows. Taking off their shoes when at last they reached the vast guardian
leogryphs, entering the sacred precincts on naked soles. For four cycles of
time . . . Because here were immured not only eight hairs from the head
of Shin Gautama, but relics of the three previous Buddhas also. And here
she too came now.

Georgia turned. For one blissful moment, with the golden pagoda
against the azure sky full in her gaze, all happiness played its brilliances
in her mind. She was entering into her kingdom, she was home. She stood
bewitched. All time came lapping into her mind. It brimmed, sparkling.
It stayed.

Then at her elbow she heard Christopher de Brissac's dry curiosity.
'What are you going to do, I wonder, in Burma?'

He had not intended to interrupt her trance. But he had noticed that
Mrs Harvey too had observed the girl's clenched fingers and parted lips
and bright eyes. He had wished with a gently uttered enquiry of his own
to rescue her from what were about to be her chaperon's purposefully
brisk declarations about disembarkation.

The trouble was, his question didn't ring gently in Georgia's ears,
which were still enchanted by the voice of a traveller dead more than
three centuries before. She wheeled round at him with hurt jolted into
her eyes. Anger too, he was distressed to see.

'What am I going to *do*?' she demanded, dumped back vulgarly by him
into the commotion of the ship's arrival in harbour, and letting enough
contempt rasp in her tone to make him glad that Mrs Harvey's attention
had been caught by the harbour master's launch, chugging by looking
spick and span. He could just imagine the lady's, How *dare* you speak to
the Colonel like that?

All through the voyage, Christopher de Brissac had found it beguiling
the way this girl flirted with him whenever she dared. How should I not? he
had mused, and alone in his cabin had smiled wryly. Equally, he had been
grateful for Mrs Harvey's presence. It had meant that Georgia's instants of
coquetry were few and swift. It had meant that in the ship's ball-room he
had invariably asked the protectress to dance first and her charge second,

and then had restored the latter to the former rather than taking her to stroll on deck and admire the effulgent Indian Ocean night. It had meant also that he had sauntered agreeably in the moonlight with one or two other young ladies, whose only advantage over Georgia Burney was that they'd been out of the schoolroom for a few years not a few months . . . and weren't Charlie's and Blanche's goddaughter, on whom it would be impossible ever to lay a finger.

But the thing now was to slacken this tautness in the girl quickly, before it was remarked upon.

'Yes,' he said easily, as if not aware of that hectic tinge in her cheeks it was so vital to dispel. 'You haven't told me, but I bet you've thought about it. Now you're back again . . . At tea the other day, Mrs Harvey was suggesting you trained as a nurse, at Mandalay Hospital maybe. I shouldn't dismiss it out of hand, as an idea, if I were you. Might come in useful. Or is it *all* going to be tennis parties?'

It seemed Georgia's fire was not to be quenched so amiably. To his relief, she shot a quick look at their companion to ascertain her distractedness; but then she confronted him once more, defiantly.

'Oh, I don't know. I'll do what I please. I'm free now. Why did you barge in on my thoughts?'

'To try to protect you, Georgiana.' He smiled. 'From our friend. Whose good sense and good intentions, by the way, in my opinion you underestimate.'

'Oh, how gallant of you!' Earlier in the voyage, she had sometimes called him Colonel with sibylline skill. Latterly, she hadn't called him anything. 'Well, I'll tell you one thing I'm going to do. Right away, tomorrow morning. Go to the Shwe Dagon.' She tossed her head to indicate the golden spire which rose glittering beyond the town. 'You can come with me, if you like. If you'll let me think my own thoughts, peacefully.'

Comforted to find the glisten of hurt had left her eyes, de Brissac thanked her. 'I should enjoy that very much. And I promise I shan't speak till I'm spoken to.'

'Good. Then I'll tell you the story about the bell. Mrs Harvey,' she called, 'do you know the story about the Shwe Dagon bell? It's a lot more interesting than that launch you're taking such a polite interest in.'

'I'm sure it is,' that lady concurred tolerantly. 'Do tell us, if the Colonel would be interested.'

'It's called the Maya Ganda, which means the great, sweet voice. It's enormous. I mean, you can get half-a-dozen people standing in it. I've done that.'

Georgia was suffused once more with the joy of her return. She'd forgotten she had any interrupting of dreams to forgive.

'Well, after the second Burmese war, the English tried to carry the bell off to Calcutta as a trophy. They got it on board a boat on the river. But she can't have been much of a boat, because she capsized. The bell went to the bottom. Somewhere right here, it must have been.' She tapped her foot on the liner's deck. 'Of course, they tried to raise it, but it turned out that English engineering wasn't any better than English seamanship.'

As confident as if now she had the entire Coldstream Guards to stand about her, the girl flicked her laughing eyes between her two listeners.

'The bell stayed down in the mud on the river-bed. For years. Till the Burmese persuaded the Governor or the Viceroy or somebody that they should be allowed to try to fish it up. And after a terrific amount of work, they did. Carried it back to the pagoda in triumph. I'll show you it, tomorrow.'

6

—⁓—

Christopher de Brissac had often given thanks for the Army – given thanks for its simply being there. Whenever he couldn't think who he was, or why: there was the regiment. Whenever he couldn't imagine what use his being anyone at all might serve: there was his faith, and there was the regiment.

In his twenties, de Brissac's not getting married felt to him as largely accidental as most other events or lacks of events. Then in his thirties the accidents seemed to acquire a bit of pattern to them. The meaninglessness of his sentimental eddyings had on occasion struck him as downright coherent. Which would have been fine, if he had not, during this voyage to the East, begun to regret it with spasmodic sharpness, and waste a lot of time dismissing his regrets.

Aden was the worst. It was Armistice Day. The ship was in harbour, and of course the Anglican padre held a service, and . . . Well, the stupid truth was that Christopher discovered he'd been pacing the same stretch of deck for half an hour simply in order to see Georgiana Burney's face when she came away from the awning after the service, try to read in those opaque eyes what Armistice Day might signify to a girl who wasn't going to be seventeen till the end of the month. By which time she'd be leading a nice dull existence up at Maymyo, and he, thank God, would be at Singapore, and busy.

For days he'd been humiliated by that sentry-go of his at Aden, infuriated by his mind parroting on about how he was twenty-plus years older than her. There was the other parroting, too, about how she wasn't even beautiful. Nose too tilted, mouth too big – on it went, the rigmarole. Give him soldierly tasks to fill his days, not these stray inanities that kept dogging him. Give him the defence of the empire to help prepare, not *inconstancy, boredom, anxiety*. He'd been lucky, last time – a few months' active service in Flanders, then it had all been over. This time he was going to be in it right from the start through to the finish, or for as long as he lasted. And if there were going to be hedonism on the eve of the devastation, and even if there were going to be passions . . . Better make a fool of yourself with someone nearer your own age, someone only a little less jaded.

By the time Mrs Harvey and he were listening to the girl's story of the Shwe Dagon bell being sunk and raised, arrival at Rangoon meant arrival where he'd regain his peace of mind. Tomorrow evening, the ship sailed for Penang.

Nose too tilted. Mouth too . . . Fine story about the bell, though, and told with fine unpatriotic verve. Georgiana with her freckles he liked, and her name he liked, and her sulky mouth he liked. Well, he'd be shot of her tonight. And dinner with those depressing Burneys – with any luck that would cure him.

De Brissac's prediction of the anaphrodisiac properties of a dinner party at the Strand Hotel with the Burneys and Mrs Harvey having proved correct, he found himself back aboard ship feeling rueful and with as yet no desire for sleep.

He'd always liked the Strand – Doric portico and teak staircase and all. This evening the mulligatawny soup had been excellent, and a prawn curry cooked that well was a dish for a rajah all right. Alex had ordered some very fair white Burgundy. Even so . . . When the ship called at Penang – if he went ashore at all, he'd dine at the Eastern and Oriental on his own.

Of course, the girl's rejoicing to be back in Burma had been irresistible enough. Glancing this way and that with her eyes aglitter . . . A sense of triumph, she'd exuded. But right now, what was he going to do to calm these jangled thoughts of his? Uninvited thoughts about how Charles Lammas had clearly grown to value his goddaughter enormously, so perhaps there *was* something ominous – no, something propitious – about her. Coerced thoughts about how middle-aged soldiers were fools if they let themselves be enchanted by young girls.

A book. A drink. A chair on deck, where he could survey the harbour, and the lit waterfront, and that pagoda of hers. To visit it tomorrow with Georgiana would be delightful, even if the rest of the family tagged along; but then . . . Why did everyone call her Georgia, when her real name was so pretty?

Christopher took an edition of Donne from the books in his cabin. On deck, he selected a chair from which he could brood on the Shwe Dagon glimmering in the moonlight, sent a boy for a whisky decanter and a jug of ice. When his drink had been brought, he sent him off again for the cigar box. But then, even with good Scotch and a cheroot; even with Donne to read who'd been a lousy apostate, and indeed a poser from font to coffin he'd often suspected, but who wrote so damned brilliantly line after line after line . . . Even with all these aids which usually were efficacious . . . Well, for a start it would help if he opened the book.

He began to read, turning back and forth in the volume to find the poems he wanted tonight, glancing up to the harbour which by midnight was a shining bay of tranquillity, catching sight of the luminous pagoda. So his thoughts about how all those Burneys seemed dreadfully awkward with each other, or about how unfortunately transparent had been Geraldine's determination to bring her subaltern son to the attention of a senior officer, got mixed up with *Batter my heart, three-personed God*. His disappointment that the girl had been too superficial, or too self-absorbed, to appreciate Mrs Harvey's sterling heart, slid into *Death be not proud*; slid out again as the suspicion that it was family life which Alex and Geraldine Burney put one off so decidedly, not love affairs.

All through the voyage, when Georgiana had seized her moments to flirt with him she had only been playing. This was satisfactory, and unsatisfactory. Yes, and all the same – dancing at Bure, she'd been over the moon to be in his arms. Dancing on board this very ship, she'd been over the moon. And he . . .? And more potent than any waltzing was this complicity they'd slithered into.

Better read. Far better. Donne's tireless sparring, that was what he'd always quickened to, and the way his words were so gristly, and . . .

> At the round earth's imagined corners, blow
> Your trumpets, angels, and arise, arise
> From death, you numberless infinities
> Of souls . . .

The superb posturing of the man! And his attack! But why, then, had he looked up from the page? Better read on, read on . . . Preferably without reflecting that his duties would almost certainly bring him back to Burma before long, and it would be disagreeable to watch lieutenants trying to seduce her. What regiment was stationed up at Maymyo? The Yorkshires, that was right. And young fools from the Bombay Burmah Teak Company . . .

> But let them sleep, Lord, and me mourn a space,
> For, if above all these, my sins abound,
> 'Tis late to ask abundance of thy grace,
> When we are there . . .

Still, one minute this evening had been spent as he could now be pleased he had spent it. One.

He'd been prompted to it by memories of Simla. And especially if she hadn't got the nous to do something sensible like learn to patch up wounded men. If it really was all going to be swimming parties, and fancy dress parties, and that mother of hers showing her off, in other words touting her around. The girl would get bored pretty quick, and the next thing after getting fed-up and restless would be convincing herself she was in love. That was hill station ennui for you. That was what young hopeful lives came down to.

So he had snatched his chance between the Doric columns while everybody was shaking hands and saying goodnight. 'One word, if I may. Don't get engaged, Georgiana. I mean – not for a few years. It would be a mistake.'

She had faced him with frank amusement. 'Do I have to wait as long as you? I'll see you tomorrow, at the pagoda' – she hesitated, and then whispered – 'Christopher.'

SIX

1

'It's going to be such a dispersal!' Blanche Lammas had said at Norwich station, kissing her goddaughter goodbye. 'I just know it is. Everyone off to the ends of the earth, and no one knowing when they'll be coming back.'

She said the same thing over a year later, the day Jack went to the war. Not actually at the station. In the car, on the way. 'Such a dispersal'. When they were on the platform, and he had to get into the train, she found she wasn't very good at saying anything.

It was one of those mid-winter days that never really get light, and it had been sleeting. Straight and slim in her overcoat, Blanche watched her husband and son shake hands. She heard their goodbyes. Then it was her turn, and she went to his arms like a girl, and she clung there a few moments. Then she stood back. She managed to say, 'Off you go, my darling.' He jumped up into the carriage. She stood, with her blue eyes glistening.

A dispersal, and not knowing what was going to happen to anybody. Blanche knew, in her visceral way. Like she knew that, whichever countries were fought over by whatever armies and which were let be, no deity was going to intervene to stop the savagery, though here and there men might have mercy on one another.

Of course, there had started to be talk about the bombardment of civilian populations. But a woman of Blanche Lammas' stamp was never going to have made a fuss about the discomforts of war time, even if those discomforts turned out to include bombs through the roof. So her sympathy was for the anxieties of those left behind at Edingthorpe and Paston and Ridlington – two young fellows of the Meade clan were in the Norfolk Regiment. She worried about the Fanshaws, who had a boy at Dartmouth. She went to tea at Bure Hall, and listened to Sarah Hedleigh's anxieties for Frederick, for Mark who really did seem to have pulled himself together. She thought of Geraldine Burney, who had Richard in the Gloucestershire Regiment in Rangoon – though the Far Eastern colonies had drowsed through the last war unaffected; and surely Burma was such a backwater, though people said it was wonderfully beautiful, so that with a bit of luck . . .

To Charles, it might be the crisis of the greatest empire the world had ever seen, which now for the first time faced Great Power threats simultaneously East and West, and found itself horribly over-extended and unprepared. To Blanche, it was life going back to being made of countless separations, of nothing but goodbyes, which naturally people were brave about but which were none the less atrocious for that.

Not just British goodbyes and scatterings to the far winds. She lay awake at night and thought about Guy and Marie Rivac, who had two sons in Admiral Darlan's fleet, and neither of them twenty-one yet. She weeded her flower-beds thinking about Giacomo and Chiara Zanetti.

Charlie could growl as sourly as he liked about how the Italians had got the government they'd desired and got the German allies they desired and deserved, so that, if they did pluck up the venality to go to war, the disasters that befell them would be their own bloody fault. About how Pietro wasn't even in their goose-stepping Army, he was down in Rome doing something administrative and nefarious. Blanche was content to let her husband make the family's political distinctions. *She* would never discriminate between one mother and another, if they had sons or daughters in countries on the verge of war.

Emanuela had been packed off to Vassar in the nick of time, and Mario was in New York. That still left one married daughter in Tuscany and another in Vienna, and she hated to imagine Chiara's anxiety for them. (Blanche had often thought bitterly of how one of those daughters had come to Edingthorpe, and seduced Charlie, and probably tried to tempt him to chuck up everything for her. But with the advent of war, she put her rancour aside as firmly as she could.) And even Pietro . . . She didn't mention it to Charlie – but she remembered those holidays at Forte dei Marmi. And that year when Henrietta was still in her carry-cot, and the Zanetti girls were such gorgeous ragamuffins . . . Making driftwood fires to cook the fresh mullet – how she remembered it! Charlie and Giacomo sitting on that up-turned dinghy, drinking jugs of white wine and talking about pictures. Mario always trotting around after the fishermen, or up some tree or other. And Pietro had been a dear boy, the way he helped Jack, who was ten years younger, to build sand-castles.

It was chiefly the British dispersal which haunted Blanche, naturally enough. That already dotted-about people seeming, that first winter of the war, to be going in for a busy and possibly terminal bout of departures for just about everywhere under the sun. Norway, France, Egypt, India. So that the knowledge in Blanche Lammas' bones – and in the bones, she never doubted, of decent women up and down the British Isles and the length and breadth of the empire – was of a scattering so violent that it was hard to feel confident about what sort of life would ever be pulled together again.

The day Jack set off from Norwich to the war, his father and mother drove home to Edingthorpe Manor in silence. Blanche took off her coat in the hall. Henrietta was away at school, so luckily she didn't have to bother about her right now. She went through to the kitchen. To see if a pot of tea might be possible, perhaps; but she wasn't thinking. And there she found no one, as it chanced. And there she stopped. Without putting the kettle on the range. Unable, it appeared, to take any action, for a while.

Her blue hyacinths and her white hyacinths were arrayed on the window-sill, and they smelled sweet. But she stood gazing obliviously past them, out to the yard. Great-tits and blue-tits were hopping about on the bird-table, pecking at the cores and rinds put out there. It began to sleet again. When a covey of partridges whirred over the orchard hedge, in the blizzard she could scarcely see them. Then Charlie crossed the yard, coat buttoned up to his chin, cap pulled hard down on his grey hair. A couple of minutes later, he trudged back from the wood-shed, pushing a barrow of logs for the library fire. She shivered. It was lonely in the kitchen, with Ellen Meade back in her cottage. Where was Janet Fox? Oh yes, she'd had to take her little girl into North Walsham, to the dentist, poor child. And Mary Oldfield, who would have understood, had been dead for over a year.

When Blanche Lammas thought about people, it was their eyes she saw. Pairs of beloved eyes, with the thoughts coming and going in their depths. Beloved heads, with their miraculous aliveness in them. So now she thought of Jack in the train, with his kit she had helped him pack – or rather, which she had packed without much assistance from him, but attempting to have him at least understand what she had put where. Jack who had only done two years at King's, and then had joined the Nottinghamshire Sherwood Rangers Yeomanry, who were camped in the park at Brocklesby under the winter rain, and now was going overseas. To Palestine. She thought of his eyes looking out of the train window at the East Anglian landscape in this January dusk she was gazing at too, his eyes watching the sleet blow across hamlets and fields. His eyes thinking. She would have loved to know whether that letter she'd seen him drop into the postbox at the station had been addressed, as she suspected, to Georgia

Afterwards, all through that long dispersal, Blanche was shadowed by how she'd begun her years of waiting at the kitchen window where the hyacinths were in bloom. Knowing she was going to lose Jack to the war was one thing. Remembering her brother Michael; steeling herself . . . But then the day she truly lost him was not a day you could ameliorate. There was nothing the spirit could do. So sometimes as the war went on it felt as if she had never stirred. All that lengthening war time, the sleet had been driving the blue-tits and robins and finches away from the bird-table. She'd been watching her husband shove his barrow through the blizzard, thinking he looked fifteen years older than he ought to.

A pheasant calling *cock-cock-cock*, flying up from sleety bracken to roost in a sleet-lashed elm. The kitchen clock which ticked. She standing at the beginning of a new war, which for a long time everyone had wriggled like mad to dodge, but which had caught them all now, so that everywhere men were going away. Her own head and eyes, which as night fell she met reflected in the window, looking back at her. Her head alive with the images of other heads. Her eyes looking back, but seeing others' eyes who were scattered all over the world. As far away as Singapore, where Christopher might be imagined to be conducting a fashionable existence. Or the China coast, where the previous spring that nice Marianne Harvey had no sooner reached her husband at Tientsin than the Japanese Army completely barricaded the British Concession there – and the French Concession too, for that matter.

But right away, Blanche's consciousness was all for her son, jolting through the nightfall toward quarters where she hoped somebody would have lit a stove. And when her attention left him for a moment, it didn't circle half the globe to fret over her friends in the threatened empire in the East, but settled much nearer home, on Mrs Fox having to take her child to that grim old Mr Ironside. He must be easily the clumsiest dentist in Norfolk, really it was hateful to imagine the man being rough with Maggie's eight-year-old mouth.

All the same, the world was being criss-crossed with anxieties like hers – she knew it was, she could sense it going on, sense the atmosphere electric with cares. You couldn't read the living thoughts in people's minds, any more than you knew what horrifying things might already have happened to them and the news not yet reached you. That didn't mean – Blanche was fierce about this – that the earth was not a little blessed wherever loving thoughts lit on a head, looked into beloved eyes.

However, she must pull herself together, put the kettle on the range to boil. Also, she must not always be thinking of that Christmas at Paston when the news came that *Tornado* had been sunk. And she had left Charlie alone in the library with his thoughts too long already. He and she were going to have to live through this side by side, and a good start would be tea by the fire.

2

~m~

That first winter of the new war, it wasn't that you didn't expect the usual winter things to happen, or didn't expect to do the old seasonal things as well as the new war things. But – at least, so it seemed to Blanche Lammas at Edingthorpe Manor – familiar things had a loathsome warp in them. It was always the same warp. But you were hopelessly bad at guarding against it. So you were caught unawares time and again, felt that stab of dread.

Some things she could forearm herself against. The Sherwood Rangers Yeomanry were still at Brocklesby Park, and the Lammas cousins were billeted in a farmhouse on the Colonel's estate, when Charlie and she took her wreath a mile through the lanes to Paston. She had known that ritual of hers would this year not simply be sad with its old sadness, so she managed to appear quite cheerful.

There were a few women in the church, decorating it for Christmas. Women who had been girls at Paston when she was a girl there. Old women who remembered Christmases before Claud and Michael and she were born. They had a hand-cart of greenery in the nave, and they were glad to see her, and she was glad to see them. The pulpit and the altar being made beautiful with holly and ivy, as they had been at the winter solstice time out of mind. This was heartening, in the face of the new war. The familiar grave-stones paving the aisle. The rood screen. Lady Katherine Paston's sculpted tomb in the chancel. There was comfort in the steadiness of these things, Blanche found; or she resolved there was going to have to be, now more than ever. Despite bitterness about the old sacrifice, and fear about the new. Good, the friendship of these women, some of whom had been married in this church, as she had been. These women who had men of their families inscribed with Michael on the parish War Memorial on the north wall, their dead alongside her dead. Some of whom had sons and nephews in uniform now.

Wreath in hand, the Miss Mack of the Edwardian dances chattered by the hand-cart. Then one of her old neighbours started flapping a feather-duster at the lectern, while another took a besom to the dead leaves in the porch. Blanche set her circlet of ivy at the Archangel Michael's feet. Good, the North Sea wind soughing through the trees outside, the afternoon glimmering through the emblazoned panes. And though her neighbours might be a bit subdued this winter, they didn't complain. Comforting, somehow even the familiar knots in the wood of what had used to be her family pew. Still undefeated, perhaps, she obscurely sensed, the White Ensign and the grey destroyer and the white swans. And anyhow, certainly it was best not to meditate too sharply on the pride you took in the dead, and in the living.

The trouble was not new things like the black-out and the petrol rationing. Blanche Lammas would never have dreamed of grumbling about such nuisances, or of stinting her scorn for those who did.

But the way its being war time again put that warp into the doing of the most commonplace peace-time things . . . She couldn't even walk under the lime trees in the garden and notice the snow-drops coming up, without being reminded of Jack last Christmas being pleased to see them.

The humblest things. Going up the ladder to the apple-loft, to fetch a basket of Coxes and Egremont Russets. The smell of the shelves of fruit in the cold loft. Swallows' nests, the birds flown to Africa. Cobwebs. A broken window shrouded with sacking. Blanche filled her basket. But then, taking a few apples which had begun to rot, and tossing them onto the lawn for the blackbirds and thrushes . . . She remembered Bobbie as a little boy, trying to chuck rotting apples so they cleared the ha-ha. Then years later, how he'd schooled Jack in apple-throwing.

The simplest winter rituals. And was there going to be *nothing* she could do without being reminded of her son, and of their nephew whom Charlie and she had always loved practically as if he were their son? Then spring would come, and summer. Was everything she ever did going to remind her that the world was back in war time? Back in the war time which the Great War had been persevered with in order to finish for good and all – so they'd proclaimed. *Never again* . . . Blanche would turn from whatever it was that had given her that feeling of being back in an old nightmare, of not being able to wake up from a hideous dream which she had thought was over but was not. She would tell herself to be sensible. Then immediately she would have to command herself not to reflect that what she meant by being sensible was, more accurately phrased, being stalwart about not facing facts.

She would turn to whatever was the next thing to do. Yet everything she did was either a new, war-time thing, (she had joined the Women's Voluntary Service as soon as it was formed), or an old, peace-time thing that now haunted her with memories of a war which had not been conclusive, and of a peace it turned out had just been a lull when people let themselves hope. So even keeping so busy that she shouldn't have had time for unhelpful thoughts didn't work.

Familiar, winter things. Sometimes, to the habituées of the Manor kitchen, it felt that even the making of a pigeon pie was nearly enough to reduce you to tears, when you thought of all the Edingthorpe lads who this winter wouldn't be eating it. The Meade boys with the Norfolks. Mrs Fox's nephews in all three Services – though Petey was greasing axles at the airfield at Coltishall, so he was nice and near home, he came over on his bike sometimes. Bobbie and Jack at sea somewhere between Marseilles and Haifa, where what with German U-boats . . . When Petey Fox *did* see fit to pedal through the ruts and mud to visit his aunt, he was swiftly feasted on such abundant helpings of the Manor's pigeon pie, and sent back to the airfield with his bicycle panniers so stuffed with plum cake and short-bread and flap-jacks, that a less stolid young man might have surmised that he was doing duty for others beyond the reach of such practical love.

Even the plucking and gutting of a goose could treacherously stab you with misery. Blanche went into the larder, and there was Sidney Meade plucking a greylag, just as he had scores of times, and his brother Bill the gamekeeper telling stories. They would be off to The Crossed Keys soon, and everything was just as it always had been and always ought to be – only neither Bobbie nor Jack had shot that particular bird.

It seemed that old stories were not funny any more, either. Because Bill Meade commenced courteously to tell her his shellduck joke, no doubt under the impression that he had not told it to her most years since she could remember. And Blanche had always enjoyed old Norfolk stories, and this was fine one, and she liked all the Meades; but this time . . .

It was all about a fellow who didn't know the first thing about wildfowling, ('must 'a bin a Lun'ener, Missus Lammas,') who shot a shellduck. He was walking back, carrying the duck, when he met a marsh-man. So to pass the time of day, and to be friendly to one of the locals, he asked how he'd best be advised to cook it. And the marsh-man said . . .

Blanche stood in the icy larder. She listened. She saw Bill Meade start to grin, as he always did at this point in his narrative, because of how funny it was that a man might not know that there was absolutely no point in shooting a shellduck because, even if you somehow magicked it soft enough to get your teeth into, you'd never want to fill your mouth with brackish mud.

She listened, she even smiled. But Jack was there too, aged about eight, the first time he'd heard the story. ('Well, yer tek an' git an ole brick. An' yer put that ole brick in the oven, along o' yare ole shellduck.') She could see Jack, who'd come to watch the game being plucked. Sitting on that table and swinging his legs, his eyes shining with the delight of listening.

A brick! in the oven! ('An' when yer kin git a fork into that there brick, yare ole shellduck'll be fit to eat.')

Luckily the cat Fudge jumped up, and began to mosey among the goose-feathers. Blanche scooped it up in her arms. Holding it so tightly that the poor creature wriggled, she took it back to the kitchen.

Blanche Lammas' immediate concern was the expansion of her vegetable garden.

They only had a dozen acres around the Manor, and the wood consisted of three or four of those on the seaward side of the property. Then down by the stream and the lily pond there was a stretch which was too boggy to cultivate. Indeed, during the winter rains it generally flooded.

That still left two paddocks, the orchard and the garden. So with her husband and Sidney, Blanche set to work to see what they could achieve as market gardeners. For a parish like Edingthorpe, to be self-sufficient would just be a beginning. After that, they must see how much surplus produce they could grow for people who lived in towns.

The back lawn near the rookery, where the old gun-dog Brandy had been shot, they dug up straight away, and planted with potatoes. In the orchard, they dug patches between the trees wherever sunlight would fall, so that past the plum trees you might come upon a few yards of broad beans, through the branches of the medlars glimpse peas coming up. Digging the tennis court and planting it with carrots and lettuces and parsnips was a particularly happy inspiration because, being netted all round, it was already rabbit-proof.

The paddocks were more of a problem, because right from the start of the war people muttered that thoroughbred horses were going to be an impermissible luxury. Blanche made no bones about her determination to keep her bay hunter and Henrietta's grey half-Arab alive. She went further, and announced that she would try to look after other hunters and point-to-pointers that would be in danger of being put down when paddocks were ploughed and riders went to the war. Logical or not, she'd retort if anybody demurred: had we all become brutes, that we began shooting our horses the minute times got difficult, without trying to find a better solution?

The solution was not easy to hit on. There must be boys and girls in the neighbourhood who would be competent to exercise and care for horses, Blanche was confident – and on her bicyclings about the villages at once recruited Sally Barlow from Witton, who'd always yearned to have a real thoroughbred to ride.

However, the parish of Witton produced not only Sally, who was fifteen and red-headed and would muck out stables valiantly, but also a farmer who declared that anyone could have his horses who wanted them, but they'd better be quick about it, because any day now he was going to ring up the knacker, and these animals would be meat for the kennels. So arrived at Edingthorpe a gelding that had won races at Hethersett, at Bawdeswell, all over the county.

He was a handsome, chestnut horse, and the household all became unguardedly attached to him. That little scrap of a girl Sally galloped him along headlands in a half-out-of-control ecstasy, and dreamed of landing over the last fence at Cheltenham neck-and-neck with the favourite. But Blanche Lammas frowned anxiously, and set off on her bike to discover who had stables not being used, because at the Manor she only had two loose-boxes.

Above all, there was the problem of feed. Poland had not yet been defeated, before she had gone to Briggate Mill, as she went every autumn, and ordered a good quantity of crushed oats and bran. She ordered sacks of wheat too, because she was resolved to enlarge her poultry enterprise, and to breed duck on the pond. And if that year she bought from the mill not merely enough feed for the coming winter, but such a cornucopia as would cram every meal-bin in every outhouse around the yard – well, that was simply to be provident; like Charlie laying in such a store of coal that you could scarcely get into the black shed to quarry the stuff.

Come summer, the horses could grow fat and out of condition in the paddocks – if the animals were not too many for the modest acreage, and if what ground there was had not been given over to pig-farming. But when the hard weather came again, would her old ally the Briggate miller be allowed to sell her corn for idle race-horses? Would she be able to stock her hay-loft with a new wagon-load of bales? The embattled mistress of Edingthorpe Manor persisted doggedly in her hope that, if she market-gardened with such energy that she was nourishing a whole street of towns-folk, (but somehow it never worked out quite like that), and if her dove-cote and hen-run and duck-pond provided suppers for all her poorer neighbours, (in this she was more successful), she might be allowed to keep her horses.

Right from the start of petrol rationing, Blanche bicycled indefatigably. News of the war might reach her from the coast of Norway or the River Plate – but she thought about it in a world reduced to her range as a bicyclist. The market town of North Walsham was only three miles away, so that was easy. A similar distance the other way was Happisburgh, where the parson's wife and the lighthouse-keeper's wife and she gave first-aid lessons and rolled bandages. Yes, her Great War experience as a nurse proved useful.

In clement weather, occasionally Blanche went farther. To Bure Hall, for instance, which was a dozen miles at least, what with all the lanes' meanderings – and where on her first visit after Jack and Bobbie had sailed for Palestine she arrived slightly late for lunch, on account of having to stop several times to pump up a leaking tyre.

Pink-cheeked from pedalling in the frosty air, she came up the gravel sweep which the Bure gardeners so assiduously raked and weeded. With mud-splashed hems to her skirt, she dismounted before the front door, and was embraced by Sarah Hedleigh at her most magisterially affectionate.

'Dearest, the next time I shall *insist* on sending Phipps with a car for you.' Like most landowners, the Hedleighs never seemed to be much incommoded by petrol-rationing. Something to do with putting it all down on the farm accounts.

Blanche had known when she accepted the invitation that to lunch at Bure right now would not be a lot of fun – the cause being her nephew's wife's presence there. Rather like having Gloria down from London to stay at Edingthorpe that Christmas; and thereafter extending, because you knew you had to, a fairly open invitation – so that she came quite often, early in the war, before such gadding about was discouraged. Lately, Gloria had gone in for spiritualism.

Yeomanry regiments like the Sherwood Rangers were still so old-fashioned, that married officers might be followed by their wives even when posted overseas on active service – a privilege not invariably commented upon favourably by other ranks. Bobbie Lammas had not availed himself of this right.

Dumped back in Norfolk, almost as if she had never been married, Caroline was trying to be calm and useful. These were endeavours in which Blanche attempted loyally to back her up. But there were wobbles of Caroline's morale, and tears. It could all get rather distasteful, if you were as determinedly loyal to Bobbie as Blanche was.

Luckily, there were evacuated children to cope with. But then the expected devastation of London did not occur. As the months passed, more and more children and their mothers migrated back again.

Her neighbours teased Mrs Lammas about how her reaction to the outbreak of hostilities was an all-out effort to save the lives of race-horses. But she didn't care. Maybe she'd end up having to put them down, she would allow. For that matter, if Charlie's gloomier jokes were accurate forecasts, maybe she'd end up shooting them in the lane to make a barricade, so he and the other village men could ambush the first posse of German soldiers who dared to encroach on Edingthorpe soil. In the meantime . . . The horses might be superfluous, but they were alive, and to her eyes glorious, and that was enough for her.

Her friends teased her again when she took to going about in a pony-trap, as she hadn't done for twenty years. This time, Blanche was uncompromisingly defiant.

A thoroughbred, good only for galloping three miles over the birch fences on Fakenham steeplechase course, storming home up the run-in through a cheering crowd . . . Blanche Lammas might concede that there could be two opinions as to how essential to the war effort such a creature was. But a stalwart cob or pony, which would pull a trap for miles . . . A Connemara or an Exmoor, which in the autumn grew a thick coat, so it could winter out rough in a meadow, all you needed to do was chuck a bundle of hay over the fence morning and evening. It would take a specially convened meeting of the War Cabinet to persuade her that the country's ponies were not pulling their weight.

Luckily, they still had the old pony-trap – the same one in which Michael and she had jogged between the hedgerows to dinner parties and balls before the last war. When Paston Hall had been sold, it had been one of the things which Blanche had salvaged from the family débâcle, brought over to her new home at Edingthorpe, like the grandfather clock and the Chinese screen.

It was true that she had not looked after it as well as she ought to have done. It had been backed beneath a catalpa tree behind the house, and had a tarpaulin swathed over it and lashed down, and thus it had been left to weather the winters and the ascendancy of the internal combustion engine as best it might. At least she hadn't had it broken up for firewood, Blanche congratulated herself, as a lot of people had burned their old pony-traps and dog-carts and gigs.

Sally Barlow and the champion point-to-point horse were not the only arrivals from Witton. They came accompanied by Sally's shaggy pony, for which asylum at Edingthorpe Manor was besought in exchange for hours spent mucking out loose-boxes, and filling hay-nets, and toting buckets of water – besought, and naturally granted. And it was with this animal in mind, that Blanche and her skinny, red-headed groom undid the tarpaulin's lashings and hauled it off the trap.

Time had not been kind. Several rotten spokes. Mould under the seats. Ironwork showing signs of rust. The solid rubber tyres beginning to rot.

With a jolt of pain, Blanche remembered the trim, brightly painted vehicle of her girlhood. How gaily they'd gone bowling through the lanes! Always off to a picnic on the shore, or a gymkhana somewhere! And even years later, that summer holiday when Jack and Henrietta had got the poor old trap into action, it hadn't been as tatty as this.

Action! Activity, not memory – that was the trick. Not too much imagining of the future, either.

Sidney Meade must carpenter some new spokes. He must file down the rusty iron, and reblack it. Then the entire household must pitch in, sandpapering the woodwork and repainting it. And at least the shafts appeared to be still sound. Red, blue and yellow had been the colours in the old days; and red, blue and yellow they should be again. Sally must come with her to the harness shed immediately; they were going to find out what driving reins and traces and collars had been put away in the chests. There would be lots of saddle-soaping to keep them busy. A car was all very fine; but if you hadn't got any petrol to pour into its tank . . . Now, Sally was please to stop worrying about her pony straight away. So long as he pulled the trap, he would earn his keep.

3

—ɯ—

After his stroke, Charles Lammas did not go into his studio until he had regained control of the right side of his body. Then one morning, when he brushed his hair in front of his dressing-room mirror, however critically he scrutinised his right eye it looked exactly like his left. The right corner of his mouth had no trace of that horrible slackness. Lucky – amazingly lucky.

He put his hair brush down on the chest-of-drawers beside the little bottle of *eau de cologne* and the other familiar things. The framed photograph of Blanche, taken at Paston Hall during their engagement. The tortoise-shell box where he kept cufflinks. The tiny yacht which Jack, when he was fifteen, had carved from a piece of yew for his birthday present.

Smiling to recollect the solemnity with which Mr Prentice the photographer, summoned all the way from Norwich, had erected his tripod on the front lawn, watched with stern amusement by Blanche's father and unfortunately bayed by an over-zealous terrier of her mother's, Lammas set his right hand down flat on the chest-of-drawers beside his left. Blanche patient and smiling, though concerned about the purplish brown cloud-rack which suddenly began blowing in from the sea; Mr Prentice bustling importantly about, diving in beneath his apparatus' black hood; that idiotic dog bouncing and yapping, till he himself had hauled it off and shut it in an outhouse until the rite on the lawn had been enacted, and they could all return to normal and go for a trudge along the cliffs . . .

He gazed down at his hands. An anxious frown puckering his brow while his lips were still smiling to recall Mr Prentice practising his art, he played all ten fingers lightly on the polished wood. He must decide. He looked up at his mirror, confronted himself a moment without either frown or smile. Action . . . He tapped his fingertips, stilled them. *Coraggio*, he thought, remembering Giacomo Zanetti, who believed in his talent. He turned from his reflection, glanced at the Tissot drawing propped up. Go for it. That's what Giacomo would say. *Dai, coraggio*.

Musing that it was easy enough for the dilettante to exhort the practitioner, Lammas went down to breakfast. There was that idea of illustrating *Thyrsis*, to be a companion to his *Scholar Gipsy*, too. But first, Georgia.

Charles Lammas was lucky, all his life he'd generally woken up feeling optimistic – and breakfast was a meal he'd always enjoyed. Pale October sunshine glinting in the kitchen windows, the smell of fresh coffee, a breeze in the oaks when he crossed the yard to unkennel his Springer spaniels. Seeing his gardener and odd-job man, he called, 'Light the stove in my studio, Sidney, would you?' Then back to the kitchen, deciding that the zest for life imparted by the morning's blowing sunlight justified a couple of poached eggs.

The table looked cheerful, set with silver and china, set with honey from their own hives and marmalade of Ellen Meade's making. Blanche and Georgia were already seated, and merrily choosing a crust to feed to that spoiled little creature Honey – who if only because of her name had to have a trace of butter and honey smeared on her morsel each morning, and begged for it very charmingly.

So now he sat down in excellent spirits, taking from the Delft platter a pear that, at this time of year, came straight from his own orchard, and again remembering his old Italian friend. Those breakfasts under the loggia. The pleasure Giacomo took in having his own peaches and nectarines to offer . . .

To recover, to be alive! That was the main thing. That was the *only* thing. Life, rather than . . . To be here at the kitchen table, with crockery glinting in the dresser, with poached eggs on their way, and that jug of peacocks' feathers on the mantelpiece. As for not knowing how long you'd recovered for – well, you never knew that, and the trick was to go back to never giving the unworthy matter a thought. And right now, the sun streamed in and made lustrous the peacocks' tail-feathers' eyes. It made lustrous the brass of the ship's bell which had been *Lucifer's*, and which the children had always loved to ring gingerly. He glanced at his model eating her toast, remembered how when she'd first come to England he'd let her stand on a chair so she could swing the clapper, ('Gently!') and awaken the reverberative beginning of that naval, storm-outclamouring clangour.

Right now, life. Right now, breakfast beneath these familiar beams, and then work. How did it go, that bit of *Lavengro*? Years since he'd read it. When George Borrow was with the gypsies on Mousehold Heath, and he was downhearted, and Jasper Petulengro said . . . To cheer him up, Petulengro said: *There's night and day, brother, both sweet things*. That was it. *Sun, moon and stars, brother; all sweet things; there's likewise a wind on the heath*. And here came his poached eggs. Lammas said, 'Thank you, Ellen,' and picked up his knife and fork.

He was nervous, though. Or why else did his mind keep reminding him that he'd already put in a lot of work on that portrait, a few more sittings ought to be enough? Why else these thoughts about how, when he'd finished this picture, he'd then slowly get back into action with some less ambitious compositions?

The air was mild for October, and as he walked through the yard Lammas thought, Trafalgar weather – for during the battle the wind was light, the gale didn't blow till nightfall. Then he thought, just as inconsequentially, about the autumn ploughing, and the partridge season getting under way – he'd been invited to shoot at Bure, he'd been invited to Hoveton and Woodbastwick. But these thoughts just flicked across his consciousness, and deep down his anxiety about his portrait never slackened. Not determination to paint as well as he ever had or better, as he would have felt in vigorous times. Anxiety about whether he could finish it professionally. He reached the studio, put his hand on the cold iron of the latch. Courage . . . Often, after setting aside a picture for a week or a month, with refreshed eyes he'd seen its defects at once, got to work confidently to put them right.

When he stepped into his studio, it looked wonderfully unchanged, and his spirits lifted. The stove lit, and already hot to touch. The coal scuttle refilled. Georgia already changed into her blue dress, perched on the dais and – what was she playing? – he peered – draughts! Playing draughts, her left hand against her right it looked like.

She smiled at him, and quickened her play. The counters clicked on the board. 'Don't fret,' he told her. 'I haven't mixed my colours yet. No rush.' So she went on playing, and a white piece hopped over two black ones and reached the far side and was made a king, and Lammas started fiddling with tubes of paint and selecting brushes.

No doubt about it, there was a lot to be said for familiarity. The great north window bathing his easel and that whole area of the room with light. That venerable dapple-grey rocking-horse. His lay-figures. His bureau with its shadowy pigeon-holes which Jack and Henrietta and Georgia had always loved to forage in, and unearth the Lalique pen, or that old silver snuff box still with some aromatic dust in it. Or the bundle of tawny letters from the great-uncle who had gone ornothologising in the Shetland Isles, in South Africa – all over the place. Or that other bundle in the hand of the great-aunt who had escaped marrying any of the local gentlemen, decamped to Florence for what by all accounts were fifty uncommonly happy years.

Familiar actions might be a source of strength too. Charles Lammas rummaged in his paint-box; he took out this crumpled, stained tube and then that. At this rate, he'd find he was in action before he'd worried enough to make much difference. He picked up his palette. The utter

calm in this old barn of his. The garden around. The sea not far off. Eden,
so far as he was concerned. The stillness of things, and the steadiness of
north light, and the peace he'd often sensed in his head. He turned to the
portrait on his easel. Dear God, was it *possible* that after working on it for
weeks it was still so far from resolved? No, no, he mustn't think that. It
was resolved; it just wasn't quite finished yet. 'All right, Georgia. Ready
when you are.'

He commissioned and commanded the destroyer HMS Lucifer . . . *Dogger Bank,
Heligoland Bight* . . . The early sun making golden that brass bell had
reminded him of the ship it had come from, and reminded him of his
brother-in-law who had taken her into those engagements. So he had
those words singing away once again at the back of his mind. He had
Lavengro too. *There's night and day, brother, both sweet things; sun, moon and stars,
brother; all sweet things; there's likewise a wind on the heath.* He was aware of
Georgia too, walking to stand on the Shiraz rug by the Venetian mirror,
turning, taking up her pose, asking, 'Was I about like this?' And then
how did it go? *Life is very sweet, brother, who would wish to die?* Only poor
old romantic Borrow insisted on feeling discouraged, so Petulengro told
him he'd get the boxing gloves out, he'd show him how sweet it was to
be alive.

Lammas stood with his chin in his palm, facing his canvas. The wind on
the heath, and how lucky he was not to be lying six feet underground in the
graveyard up there on the hill, below the round tower which was Norman
or some said Saxon, but he wouldn't see it, and with a far view of the sea,
but he wouldn't see that either. Blanche and Jack getting a headstone cut.
His obituary in *The Times* – they were probably brushing it up right now,
with word of his stroke getting around. But more immediately, there was
the necessity of not being dismayed just because he'd been unwell and
was feeling unconfident.

Yes, might as well focus on it. Gloom knotting in his chest, he *was*
unconfident.

Then there was the other necessity, of not convincing himself there
wasn't really such an awful amount to do on the painting, it was merely
a question of tidying up a few details, and then . . . Though that was
probably what he *would* end up deciding – why duck it? And . . . (All
the while, his gaze had been travelling about the composition, following
its lines of coherence and beauty.) And the work was . . . He went on
glancing back and forth between his subject and his canvas, went on
measuring with his eyes. The design of her hands was good and tight.
And the distance between the green lamp on the table and . . . Courage!
The way the line of her dress at her shoulder ran up her neck and into

her hair by her ear. A lovely passage, that. He picked up his palette-knife, tapped his other hand with it. He pursed his lips, looking, looking. A few nasty edges still to be put right, but he could do that. And her partial reflection in the glass needed . . . Still, all the same — the case was not hopeless. 'Right, dear girl. Here we go. Head a fraction more away from me, please. Now, these freckles of yours . . .'

She laughed exasperatedly, she pouted, she pretended to growl like a dog. 'FRR-RECK-KLES!'

So he set to work, and the familiarity of the place and the activity felt good, the professional routine felt good. The fire in the stove rustled, and when they paused for a minute so that Georgia could kick her stiff legs and flap her stiff arms, he opened the black iron door and shovelled some more coal in and clanked the door shut again. Outside, the six white fantails flew in an arc above the Manor, alit on the stable roof. Peace, and a job of work to do . . . But after an hour he felt tired.

This was new. Before, he'd been able to keep concentrating all morning, and after lunch put in a couple of effective hours too.

Yet today . . . Well before Mrs Meade crossed the yard carrying a tray with coffee and, for Georgia of whom she was fond, a thick wedge of almond cake, Lammas had a weariness in his head that was new. Not the tiredness that after a day's work was natural, and he'd never disliked — on the contrary had often rather welcomed it, as a sign that at least he'd been trying hard, so maybe something worth having had been done. Not that lassitude with a hint of sensuality to it, which a tramp with his dogs would partly dispel and partly make yet more pleasurable, so he strode home with a keen appetite for his bath and his glass of whisky and his dinner.

Very faint, as yet. But a distractedness he hoped was not a presage of states of mind to come. He kept having to tell himself to concentrate — whereas before, concentration had been a temptation he indulged in whenever nothing got in the light. An apprehensiveness he hoped wasn't a presage either.

He fell back on an old trick of his when a painting became difficult enough to be perhaps beyond him to finish, and assured himself that all that remained were technical problems to solve. So, therefore, with resolution, with workmanship . . . But he didn't feel resolute, and workmanship was a notion that had suddenly become vague.

He put down his palette and mahl-stick and brushes. He sipped his coffee. Watching Georgia bite into her cake, he said, 'Give me this week. Then I'll let you go. Promise.'

She swallowed. 'I told you, I'll stay as long as you need me. We want our picture to be as perfect as it can possibly be.' She took another mouthful, chewed it. 'I mean, allowing for the sitter's funny face, and her funny hair, and . . .' She gave him a swift, smiling look. 'You keep at it.'

'No, honestly.' Lammas felt such an unexpected comber of unhappiness beginning to break in his mind, that he sat down beside her on the dais among the cups and the opened letters and the paint-rags. 'Just a few things to tidy up,' he declared cheerfully. 'Three or four mornings, perhaps, if that's all right.'

It came back to haunt him, during the last year of peace, that minute of wretchedness. Like a freak wave, which out at sea must have been building up, though he hadn't seen it – or possibly he had, foggily. That grey breaker crashing down in his consciousness, so he could hardly keep on his legs. All that year, after Georgia had gone, when he stubbornly went on trying to paint good pictures, and earn his living. And the next year, in the beginning of the war.

At first, Charles Lammas' life resumed largely as it had been before he collapsed in the yard, and then crawled into the greenhouse.

He did the best job he could, finishing his *Georgia In Her First Ball-Dress*, and signed it with a pang of guilty relief. A fortnight after she'd sailed from Southampton, when he was sure the paint was dry, he applied retouching varnish. Then the picture went into Norwich, to the framer. Feeling liberated, he tackled *Thyrsis*.

He knew the images from the poem which he wanted, and his weary spirit ached for the simplicity of working on paper with pen and ink, and then for the meticulous labour on the wood-cuts. Weary, and slightly cowed . . . He, Charlie Lammas! If he didn't think about it, it would pass. And he'd always been able to draw. At the Slade, donkeys' years ago, he'd won a prize, and surely now . . . Hand, eye. Practice!

He'd draw Arnold's *signal elm*. He'd draw his *wet field*, his *vext garden-trees* and his *volleying rain*, his English summer. Lammas smiled, choosing his nibs, and smiled again to recall how pleased his father had been about that prize. What was more, he knew which elm down by the meadow he was going to spend this morning drawing, and he could already sense how he'd enjoy it. Later in the poem, there was that girl, too, by a boatman's door, unmooring a skiff.

The press which specialised in such handsomely produced, limited editions was in Cambridge, and Lammas was always happy there. As usual, he stayed at Trinity, where three of his watercolour drawings hung in the Master's Lodge. They put him up in Neville's Court – in the same set of rooms where once Raffaella Zanetti had come to him on an afternoon of rain-squalls.

That oak panelling and that four-poster bed brought back her twenty-year-old body, her love-making which had impressed him with its combination of sensuality and indifference. He recollected how that had made him think of her father.

But the Raffaella of a few years ago remained only a memory. Some tempo in him had altered since then. He was living in a different – a different . . . He wasn't sure, but in a new time, or according to an altered rhythm, something like that. Without thinking of it further, he walked out across the town to his meeting with the fellow who ran the Egret Press.

At Trinity high table that evening, the conversation among Charles Lammas' friends was all about Roland, whose *Ruins of Persepolis* had recently surfaced in a London sale-room. From boyhood, Charles had been accustomed to being the son of a well-known father, and had long adopted a minimising loyalty. ('Yes, well – bias on my part, no doubt. But I've always reckoned . . . Skilful . . .') Of later years, he'd grown used to being the son of a father no longer anything like as well-known as he had been. ('Out of fashion now, and no mistake. Oh, well . . . It'll happen to us all. And *some* of us will come back.') So now he mildly joined in the talk about Roland's portrait of Lady Tennyson with a wolf-hound. No, it had been painted after the poet's death, he happened to know – in 1899. But the wolf-hound had belonged to the great man. Karenina, the dog was called. Was the painting still in the family? He was ashamed to say he didn't know, but he hoped it was.

Someone chipped in with a remark about von Herkomer's portrait of Roland Lammas, which was in the collection of the Royal Academy. Someone else mentioned charcoal drawings by Roland which he'd come upon at the Victoria and Albert, and an oil painting the Ashmolean had. There must, a third voice supposed, be pictures of his in half the city collections in the country.

Charles said Yes, in his quiet manner. Manchester City Art Gallery, Birmingham City Art Gallery . . . But then at once he told them the story of how, when a lion had died at London Zoo, they'd been most obliging about delivering the carcass to his father's studio so he could do some drawings. But the carriers just dumped it down in the hall, where the lady coming to tea . . . And, after a few days, the smell . . . Then, the labrador . . . And the house-maid . . .

So the talk was deflected. However, Charles went on remembering how honoured his father had been when museums wanted to buy his canvases. How it had been Liverpool too, and Cheltenham and Aberdeen, and others he'd forgotten. For that matter, his paintings had been bought for Sidney Art Gallery, and for Melbourne and Auckland too – but who knew whether they still hung them?

In the short term, Lammas' financial situation did not deteriorate sharply. Several pictures he had painted in the twelve-month before his stroke remained in his studio, and now were sold. The last of the landscapes hanging in Peregrine Bracknell's gallery in Mayfair went. The next time he was in London, the dealer took him to lunch at the Garrick, where over roast partridges and Burgundy they bumped into a number of old friends, and everything appeared just as it had used to be.

Shortly after that, the Director of the Tate Gallery wrote to him, and a member of the committee visited him in Norfolk. The upshot of this particular Edingthorpe studio tea was that two of his coastal scenes joined his father's four canvases in the gallery overlooking the Thames. Not in the vaults, either, initially. Side by side on a wall, with a notice which read: Recent Acquisitions.

By summer, Lammas had sufficient funds to pay for Henrietta's last two years at school. Then, remembering his own last summer before the previous war, he gave Jack enough money to go to Italy for a month. Whether anybody beyond himself – Perry Bracknell? Blanche? – had noticed that the work the family was living on had all been done before his stroke, he was unsure. Anyhow, at the Royal Academy's Summer Exhibition his portrait of Georgia and his view of Villa Lucia both sold.

That July of Jack's sojourn in Tuscany, Chiara Zanetti fulfilled her promise to his father to 'pack him off to all the right churches and galleries'. She had Emanuela conduct him around, or had him escort her – as anyone could see was the most sensible arrangement. Had they not as tiny children romped together in the shallows at Forte dei Marmi, and once famously come to blows over a toy yacht, so that it had required *pots* of ice-cream to cement a truce? It was high time, Contessa Zanetti proclaimed, that they got to know one another again, and the Uffizi would be just the place, followed by a little restaurant around the corner.

It was the following winter, when Charles Lammas was coming to grips with the futility of his efforts to get passed fit enough to do anything that might effectively damage his country's enemies – that was the bad time for him. That first war winter, when he was also coming to grips with his being just as cooped up in their neighbourhood as his wife. Blanche had never known him so uncommunicative. Just a few outbursts along the lines of, 'Christ, fit for action! They won't pass me fit to sit behind a desk!'

Remarks about how he hadn't reckoned to be reduced quite so young to the category of useless mouths to feed.

A bad time for Lammas . . . He who'd always tackled everything with terrific confidence, and now found that even a politician like Hedleigh appeared more useful than he was. He who now, instead of charging off to paint the French or Italian countryside, or to stay in Scottish castles while he portrayed their occupants, had to struggle to take a genial interest in his wife's campaign to save the local horse-flesh from the knacker.

When any of his friends *could* tempt Lammas into conversation during that period, he'd make contemptuous comments about how blithely he'd always pitched into whatever interested him. Or the contemptuous comments would be about the high expectations he'd so lately been fool enough to entertain. Havering between Naval Intelligence and an appointment as a War Artist, for heaven's sake! And he'd had silly notions about how, with his French and Italian, and his Navy training, the Foreign Office might . . . The truth, however, was otherwise, with his heart. Had you ever read that letter of Horatio Nelson's to the Admiralty, written from Burnham Thorpe, where in humorous desperation he beseeches their Lordships for the command of a cockle-boat? Well, that was about his situation now. Were you aware that it was only with ludicrous difficulty that he'd got onto the reserve crew of the Cromer lifeboat?

Of course, he never mentioned the Distinguished Service Order, awarded to him twice. He didn't mention either that he'd approached Hedleigh to find out if anybody on that Foreign Affairs Committee felt like pulling strings on his behalf – though a few people got to know about that.

Lammas would allude with aggressive cheerfulness to the fact that he knew a few fellows who'd always found him intolerable, and now were amused to watch him digging up his back lawn to plant spuds because he was good for nothing better.

If you liked him, it was rather a grim sight. He'd work beside Sidney Meade all afternoon, and then Meade would go home to his cottage, and Lammas would continue in the dusk for as long as he could see what he was up to. Brown earth, brown trees, grey winter nightfall. The man labouring with his spade. Or he'd be in his spinnies with an axe, or outside his wood-shed cutting up logs. With no patience for those who told him a man with his heart trouble ought to take it easy.

As for his fears about his painting . . . He'd make remarks about the war's effect on the art market. But his painting as the high hope he'd dedicated himself to . . . He didn't talk about that. Not that he gave up going to his studio, working for a few hours each morning. Yet none of his really ambitious pictures date from that time. He did a series of small still-lives, and managed to sell some of them gradually, for modest prices.

4

—◊—

Blanche Lammas did not dislike the way in which the war largely restricted her to the immediate locality she could traverse with her pony-trap or her bicycle. A country-woman born and bred, the impossibility of saying when she might next get to London was not a matter likely to preoccupy her. Back in her childhood, often, she seemed to be. Clip-clopping a mile or two to Witton to arrange to prolong the life of a race-horse, Blanche remembered a mossy lawn there, a white mansion which had been the seat of the Wodehouse family, and dances she and her brothers had gone to in the first years of the century, when they were little more than children.

Magical, the dark Witton woods had appeared to her then, and the glimmering house enfolded by rhododendrons and Portugal laurels, and the gravel sweep where the broughams rattled up and unloaded cargoes of chattering guests. From the hall they ascended the double spiral staircase, and up in the great parquet-floored and pillared drawing-room they danced. Blanche remembered the Eton jackets which Claud and Michael and all the boys wore. She remembered her own white dresses and those of the other girls, and their open-work bronze stockings, and their bronze shoes with rosettes.

From the alcoves, the chaperons in their dark gowns and their Indian shawls watched. The three musicians – had they always been three? – bowed away at their fiddles. Lady Kimberley, Blanche recollected as if more than thirty-five years had not elapsed, had a tolerant, lazy smile. In the centre of the drawing-room, the piebald galaxy of boys and girls danced the Gay Gordons and the Dashing White Sergeant, and right at the end they charged into the Posthorn Gallop, which was the wildest and most joyous and dizzy-making dance of all. Then the next thing you knew, the butler was announcing that Mrs Mack's carriage was at the door. Shyly you took Lady Kimberley's hand, you said thank-you for a lovely party. Then you were on your way home, part of a procession of candle-lit carriages bowling along through the dark woods.

That first winter of the war, Charles Lammas did not find memories much sustenance, but the rituals of the countryside were sometimes a strength to him. He shot on the estates where he had always shot. Better still, he went back to doing a fair bit of rough shooting over the local marshes and commons and heaths, as he had when he was a boy, and as later he'd done with Bobbie during his winter holidays, and later again with Jack.

Bill Meade was gamekeeper on the Dilham estate, and Lammas found solace, or anyhow found distraction, in their sallies along the upper reaches of the river Ant. It was the absolute dead of the year. In the swampy carrs, the alders had not yet started to form their buds, which at the beginning of spring lend those dun East Anglian wood-sides a purplish haze. The water-meadows were cold and desolate. The pollarded willows had not yet begun to sprout new sappy wands; the grown willows stood with their cracked trunks and fractured limbs, looking gaunt.

Greylag and pink-foot grazed on the lifeless grass. Blackbirds hopped on the ivy, and pecked at the clustered berries. The two men and their dogs would walk the hedgerows down to Tonnage Bridge, maybe, and shoot a rabbit or two as they came, stuff them still warm into the game-bags slung over their shoulders. Then it was amicable to discuss where to stand for wildfowl that evening, and the war gave added dignity to the ancient and honourable sport, because it stood to reason that every household round about must have a brace of mallard to roast as often as possible.

Deciding which houses they would later bike past homeward, and for whom they would open their mud-stained and bloody-feathered bags, the painter and the gamekeeper would trudge to the positions they'd picked. In those copses, if you were canny you could shoot a pheasant going up to roost, and then still be in time for the duck when they came winging down.

Lammas was beset not only by his sense of futility, his being summarily relegated to the ranks of the country's old dodderers. He also had to make some sort of peace with the idea that as a painter he might already be in decline. A peace that might be inwardly wretched, but outwardly must be good-humoured, and dismissive. 'Oh, well, time will tell. Feel quite fit these days, luckily. And now, with the war . . .' So far, so good. 'These days, I've got more important things to do.' If only that were true!

However, sometimes duck-flighting with Bill Meade or with other neighbours, with farmers, with marsh-men, he would forget his aching sense that something had broken in him, the bold spirit with which thousands of times he'd set to work at his easel was ailing now. Watching old Bill in his lichen-hued clothes taking up his position fifty yards off behind a tree in the twilight; hearing him quiet his dog; watching him stand motionless minute after minute to scan the dimming sky. He himself doing likewise . . . But then it would come back, that faltering of the old spirit he'd had. His mind would be flooded with loss.

Didn't matter, of course.

Charles Lammas could not imagine his life without his painting. For God's sake, he'd been a painter before he'd joined the Navy, hadn't he? Properly considered, it was the Great War that had been the interlude. Or . . . Well, perhaps . . . And anyhow, that didn't mean he wasn't certain he ought to be back in the Service now, ought to be *doing* something. Get him back under the authority of the First Sea Lord – and he'd recall a blasphemous joke of his from Dardanelles days – *in whose service is perfect freedom*. It didn't mean either that he could be rid of that feeling of having been living in a civilisation that was no such thing. A mockery – and he'd been part of it. That was all the life he'd had, married to Blanche, painting, bringing up the children.

Those afternoons, he didn't go rough shooting with anyone. He didn't join his wife and her village friends in their ratting in the stack-yards either. Blanche had always been an enthusiastic ratter. At nightfall they'd go to the yards, shine their torches so you could see the scores of rats which would have come out and be scampering up and down the stacks to gorge on the grain. Then there would be good sport when the rats bolted and the terriers went after them.

When the day started to grow murky, Lammas would put on his shooting-coat, take his gun from the cabinet where, among the other family guns, Jack's sixteen-bore of one Christmas and his twelve-bore of a later birthday waited gleamingly. With his cap pulled down over his eyes, and his pockets laden with cartridges, he'd go out to his own small wood to shoot pigeon for Edingthorpe's kitchens' pots and for the pies which Mrs Fox and Mrs Meade made in his Manor kitchen.

Something useful to do. Somewhere lonely to be. Even in snow he'd go out, if it wasn't falling so thickly he couldn't see. And certainly often in rain, all through the month they called February fill-dyke. He'd stand in a glade among his firs and oaks and ashes, wait for the pigeon that would come flying up-wind over the wood, then swoop down toward the tree-tops searching for somewhere to roost.

He'd remember pigeon-shooting with Geoffrey when they were lads. How could he not? And then shooting here with Bobbie, and Jack. He'd think of Alex Burney, away in the British East which was still at peace. Alex resigning from the club, because he . . . And Georgia, in Maymyo for more than a year now, whose letters were so merry, and . . .

A winged scrap of grey came whipping between two blizzard-belaboured ash trees. Lammas swung, fired. The bird came tumbling down among the snow-flakes, bounced off a branch, landed with a soft bump – but there'd been another, and he hadn't seen it till it was too late to get a shot.

He must concentrate. Sky a sort of pewter colour. What had he

been . . .? Oh, Georgia's letters. He'd been sadder since she had gone
– that was the truth of it.

Snow getting in his eyes. And supposing after the last war he'd joined
the Diplomatic Service, would things now be . . .? Pigeon. He fired. Too
slow. He swung farther, killed it with his left barrel.

5

The first local man to be killed was young Noel Jarvis from Irstead, in April. He was a lieutenant aboard the destroyer *Hardy* when Captain Warburton-Lee took the flotilla up the West Fiord at Narvik in a snow-storm to attack the German ships.

Charles and Blanche Lammas went to his memorial service in their pony-trap, now restored to its former spick and span condition. After weeks of wind and rain, the morning was blue. In the yard at Edingthorpe after breakfast, helping Sally to groom the pony and back him between the brightly painted shafts, Blanche felt confusedly wretched at the loveliness of the hoar-frost glittering on the buildings and the garden trees.

The sweet smell of hay, and then the acrid tang of litter where a horse had staled, and then the scent of polished saddlery. Birds' tracks criss-crossing the white rime on the lawn. Things which should have been good in the most straightforward way. The girl whistling between her teeth as she groomed. Woodsmoke pluming up from the chimneys into the windless dazzle – Sidney was lighting the fires. Cat-ice on the water-butt – how its sheens cracked when you dipped your bucket, how the glistens tilted and were rinsed away.

Silly, her confusion, Blanche knew. But that didn't help you feel anything coherent about things which had this war-time warp in them – and yet were still good, surely, good in themselves. Down by the pond, the way the heron stood under the cedar because there the shallows hadn't frozen, he had a chance of stabbing up a perch.

No, she would not begrudge that grey fisher a tiddler or two from her stew-pond. But the thought got muddled up miserably with her recollection of Noel Jarvis winning the marathon at Swanton Abbott fête one summer, and with her thoughts of his parents. Then she remembered that the Hedleighs would be at the service – bound to be. The evacuated children had all left Bure Hall now, though there was talk of a London school being sent there. Funny, it had been, how Sarah had made a point of never betraying an ill opinion of those East End scamps' ignorance or dirtiness, but had constrained herself to no such broadmindedness when it came to the mothers who had accompanied some of the infants.

Clattering through the familiar parishes, Blanche wondered whether Charlie sitting beside her and driving the trap would let himself be a little invigorated by such a heavenly morning. Of course, he never complained

. . . or not much. His telling her less and less about what he truly thought was one of the ways in which all winter she'd taken the measure of how depressed he'd become. But money embarrassments . . . The Titian studio's Aegean evening had been sold at Sotheby's, for rather less than they'd hoped for; and it was not an expedient which could be repeated. Then the humiliation of his endless medical check-ups, and the Navy not having any use for him because of his heart which apparently really *was* rather dicey, and because of that stroke he'd had.

The pony's brisk trot, his breath which puffed in the frosty air. The harness that jingled, the wheels that rattled and crunched . . . Blanche found it impossible not to be inspirited and made wretched at the same time. She felt so stupidly muddled that she kept silent, instead of cheerfully pointing things out to Charlie as she had intended. The hoar-frost spangling the oaks in the park at Honing, a sparrow-hawk that stooped. That man uncoupling his team, and the boy, his son perhaps, who scrambled up to ride one of them home, but he was so little that his legs stuck out sideways in the most splendid posture. However, distracting Charlie sufficiently for him to take pleasure in anything was uphill work these days.

Beside her, he flicked the reins, and he glanced over the fields; but he didn't talk. Yes, she thought – probably the sinking of German warships and merchantmen only made Charlie's sense of his uselessness worse. Captain Warburton-Lee, who people were saying was certain to be decorated posthumously for that attack; Lieutenant Jarvis, killed doing his duty beside him . . . Charlie who was different these days, somehow was just going through the motions. This morning she'd watched him in the yard, talking to Sidney about whether this late frost had come at just the wrong time for the fruit trees. He hadn't really cared. She could tell.

The small, flint church stood among frost-white oaks and beeches. The Irstead verger was clanging the bell. And there were Mr and Mrs Jarvis, looking ashy but dignified. Blanche went through the church door, which Charlie held open for her. At least she had a letter from Jack in her pocket – a merry letter, all about how the regiment was camped among orange groves, and in what manner the horse-lines were organised, and what a lousy map-reader Bobbie was turning out to be. There was Caroline, two pews ahead, between her father and mother.

Looking at how prettily Caroline's golden curls rippled over her velvet collar, (her mother's cheque-book lay behind that natty, Knightsbridge coat — certainly not her husband's), Blanche shoved a hand into her own pocket, touched her son's letter like a talisman. If the service got too moving, she would think about that camp by the Levantine shore. He'd been sailing, Jack wrote. The secret was to have something extraneous to think about, and to think of it tenaciously, and hope whatever it was stayed as extraneous as at first it had seemed.

She was awful about crying in church, Blanche knew she was. Always had been. She'd even cried at a couple of weddings. And funerals! Even at the funerals of people she hadn't known particularly well. But to her it was unforgivable that *anyone* should be hauled from this life — no, not the old, that was different — but anyone young, like Noel. And if you really listened to the service for the burial of the dead, if you let those sentences take their effect, have their way with you . . . They had not, it seemed, been written to anaesthetise. And then if you allowed your mind to hesitate on the difference between this dignified service, and what being killed in action meant. *Hardy* had sunk the ship flying the German Commodore's pennant, but then her bridge was hit. Then another shell exploded in the destroyer's engine room. She was beached. The survivors struggled ashore, carrying Warburton-Lee's body.

Blanche reminded herself that, if Mrs Jarvis in the front pew could preserve that calm demeanour through the memorial service, so undoubtedly must she. Also, before she told Caroline about her news from Palestine, she must wait to hear if Bobbie had written. Now — think of the orange groves, and the regimental trumpeter blowing Reveille, and those horse-lines.

Her mind was mazey . . . And into its crannies an old horror was seeping like gas. She stood in Irstead church beside her husband — who was impassive, inevitably. They sang, *The Lord is my Shepherd*. Only twenty-five years . . . and had people forgotten *everything*? All this talk now, about how 'it isn't going to be like the last time.' About how 'the generals have learned'. But no one explained how an army might take ground except by attacking across it.

Horse-lines. Reveille, Last Post. *In pastures green, He leadeth me*. And Jack sailing a dhow along the Levantine coast, and *death's dark vale*, and horse-lines.

The Sherwood Rangers had seen no action to speak of, yet. But their peaceful camp made Blanche think of the Polish cavalry, who beyond question had also had excellent arrangements for picketing their mounts, and then last autumn had charged the German tank divisions. They'd galloped into the attack, and a few minutes later the battlefield was a shambles of disembowelled and dismembered horses and men. She tried not to imagine what that must have sounded like.

No doubt the Sherwood Rangers would be mechanised before they were required to go in for any very serious warfare.

Blanche held the letter in her pocket firmly, but without indulgent clutching. She observed the back of Mrs Jarvis' head. She sang.

After the service, Caroline Lammas slipped her hand into Blanche's arm. 'I had a letter from Bobbie this morning,' she said with a smile, its timidity better concealed at the back of her eyes than on their recent meetings, and drew his aunt away across the frozen sward to the river. 'They seem to be having a terrific time. Swimming, and going into Haifa in the evening sometimes, and . . . But he says Jack's map-reading isn't up to much.'

Charles Lammas remained by the lych-gate, talking to Julian Hedleigh about the set-backs of the campaign in Norway. Hedleigh was still a loyal supporter of the Prime Minister, but he agreed that the debate about the progress of the war, which the Opposition were demanding, was going to be a tense one.

The two women stood beside the quietly flowing water in the crystalline sunshine. Blanche watched a grebe dive and come up, remembered how when she was a child she had once announced to Nanny Oldfield that she wished she had hair the colour of a grebe's head plumage. Or had she said, When I grow up I'm going to have . . .?

Liking the bonny way Caroline smiled, and the steady way she referred to the evening dissipations in Haifa, Blanche took out her own letter. 'Here, dear girl, have a look at this. Much the same sort of stuff, only according to Jack it's Bobbie who can't read a map.'

Caroline crackled pages. She let one envelope drop, stooped quickly for it. With busy fingers and bright eyes, she compared the two cousins' communications.

'Well, *one* of them led his troop to the wrong hill,' she exclaimed gaily. 'But which one?'

Blanche watched her turn a sheet over to read the other side. Twenty-seven, she must be – was that right? – but as beautiful as ever. Hadn't even got her mother's slab teeth. Poor girl, it was a hundred to one she lay awake dreaming of babies. Still, at least her husband wrote to her sometimes.

'And whichever one of them it *wasn't* . . .' Caroline glanced up under her eyelashes – full of fun, for all you could tell. 'Seems to have got into a frightful pickle on parade.' She turned from this letter to that, frowning cheerfully as she read. 'It says, Lieutenant Lammas. He shouted *Left!* when he ought to have shouted *Right!* or something, and cantered off the wrong way. I tell you what, I reckon they've invented a comic character called Lieutenant Lammas, who gets everything into a mess. Well, luckily the sergeant immediately bellowed *Right!* and the men knew he was the one to pay attention to. So then Bobbie, or Jack, had to gallop back to get in front of his men again. And the Colonel . . .' She looked up, met the older woman's regard. 'Which one do you think it was?'

'I think . . . I think something quite different. I expect they're both very slightly better officers than they make out. But . . . Why don't you appropriate the Bure pony-trap? That's what I was thinking. You'd be so much more independent, Caroline, and you deserve to be, and you ought to be. We've gone back to using ours. So have lots of other people. Look at the carts and gigs here this morning.' She gestured with her eyes to the dispersing congregation. 'Commandeer one of your father's cobs. Get out about the countryside.'

'I'm pretty busy with the Voluntary Service, you know,' Caroline said, and flushed.

'I know you are, dear girl. Believe me, I didn't mean that. I meant what I said. A bit of freedom, that's what you need. And think how much more useful you could be with a pony-trap rather than just a bicycle.'

'You think I don't *know* how absurdly I'm tied to Mama's apron strings?' Caroline's mouth was too much a conventional rose-bud to express bitterness, but it trembled. 'I haven't got a shilling to call my own, I suppose you're aware of that. But do you imagine I don't understand?' Her voice rose with a choking rasp. 'If you think I don't know!'

Almost everybody had left the churchyard, except for the parson and the bereft parents. From the lych-gate, Sarah Hedleigh waved encouragingly.

Blanche faced that crescendo of protest, and she thought about that cottage near Cahors, and about Haifa. She said, 'I understand. I mean, I hope I do. I want to.' She hesitated, watched Caroline fishing out her handkerchief. 'But doesn't Bobbie, surely . . .?'

'Oh yes, he gives me an allowance from his pay. As much as he can afford. I don't spend it. I keep it – for – for when the war's over. We're bound to need it, to get going together again. Either that, or . . . Or when he comes home, I'll give it to him.'

Caroline dabbed her eyes. Then she got the letters into their wrong envelopes, and that had to be sorted out. She tossed her curls to indicate the figures by the gate.

'It's all right,' Blanche said. 'We can be as slow as we like.' She took her arm, but stood still. She kissed her cheek. 'When you've got your trap in action, come and see me. I know it's quite a long drive for a pony, but that's why I'll insist you spend the night with us.'

Caroline nodded. When she could speak, she said, 'They're calling. We'd better . . . I hadn't seen Noel for years, but in the old days he was always at Barton regatta.'

'Don't forget. I'll be waiting for you.'

6

⸺

Afterwards, Blanche Lammas would say it was the first winter of that war which nearly finished off her husband, but he was already beginning to cheer up by the time they sat down to dinner on 14 May 1940. That was the day Eden broadcast his appeal for Local Defence Volunteers.

Charlie Lammas was into his car, and off to North Walsham police station to join up, while the minister's voice was still crackling out of the wireless in the kitchen. The next day, at a pow-wow at The Crossed Keys, which had a bowling green and therefore in summer was the most popular pub in the neighbourhood, he was chosen by his fellow men as their area commander. A few months later, when they were renamed the Home Guard and were getting a touch more organised, he was a battalion commander. And already in June he'd been down at Osterley Park in Middlesex to attend a course. That was the training school run by Wintringham, who had commanded the British contingent of the International Brigade during the Spanish Civil War. Lammas came back to Edingthorpe with all sorts of new ideas about camouflage, and destroying tanks, and guerrilla skirmishing. He set to work to jazz up the defence of his patch of Norfolk.

Decidedly, Local Defence was a good sphere for his energies. Action! that old deadener, that friend of flattering illusions. Right from the start – now that at last the German attack on the West had begun. On the morning when Eden made his appeal for Volunteers, Rotterdam was still holding out. But by that evening, a thousand people had been killed in the bombardment, and the city had surrendered.

The next day, up and down Britain the first groups of Volunteers began to assemble to make plans and drum up support. On the other side of the North Sea, the defeated Dutch Army laid down its arms.

A bicycle ride from the English coast, Lammas chatted to those of his neighbours who'd been equally quick off the mark to join up. Not difficult, that week, to agree about the desirability of a nation being ready to defend its territory. With the German Army across the Dyle, across the Albert Canal, across the Meuse, and the invasion of Belgium by most reports in full swing. *Again.* With Rommel and his armour having successfully attacked through the Ardennes, and broken the Allied line, so that now to the north the French First and Seventh Armies and the British Expeditionary Force were cut off.

The BEF. Couldn't they at least have called it something different, this time?

All right, action might be a deadener, Lammas thought, distractedly gazing out of the pub window at the apple trees. But that didn't mean it was not essential. And what was wrong with a bit of deadening? He felt better already – and so, he reckoned, did most of the men in the bar. What was more, if his experience in submarines was anything to go by, a gloomy, fretful man was usually ineffectual.

Action might sometimes be the friend of flattering illusions. It was true that the Dutch had resisted the Germans for only a few days, but that didn't mean they had not been right to stand up against the aggressors. And remember the Finns, last winter! Forty Russian divisions, or was it forty-five, against the Finnish Army of a couple of hundred thousand men and boys – and they fought magnificently, and held the invasion up for months.

On the other hand – if you stopped gazing out at the orchard and the green and the rooks. If you joined in the talk with your fellow defenders of the island . . . Charles Lammas chuckled, and called to the landlord for pints of bitter for a couple of recent arrivals, a bailiff and a dairy-man, who hadn't yet got mugs in their hands. No – hang on a minute. The dairy-man would prefer a pint of mild. First-rate beer it was too, he thought, and smiled at this spasm of local loyalty at such a time. Brewed from Norfolk barley, in a Norwich brewery.

Well, Sonny Hannant was here, who had fought on the Somme, and since then had been a lengths-man, which meant he was responsible for the hedges and ditches along a given length of the neighbouring lanes. Norgate the builder, who had ridden into Damascus with Allenby's cavalry, but had put on weight since then, and made money, and now tended to philosophise in a melancholy vein. Old George Morter, who had fought in the trenches too, and now had a smallholding – what in Norfolk they called a pigtle. The Meade brothers of course, and the Honing schoolmaster, and a couple of tenant farmers, and a lad still at school. What was more – all over the country, groups of men were probably eyeing each other, and laughing, and saying, 'Well, naturally, with the defence of the kingdom in these hands . . .'

The landlord offered his pub as a headquarters, because it had a telephone, unlike most houses, and his wife or he was usually at hand to answer it. Everybody was cheerful, and had suggestions about who else might join them, and who had vehicles or guns. No one thought France would fall. Lammas offered his car, and fat old Norgate and he drove off into the May evening to see whom they could recruit.

7

If the enemy came, they would be defeated by British Regular divisions, half of whom were now in France, or not at all. Therefore the Territorials remaining in England must take over as many of the Army's less essential functions as possible, and any units of Irregulars which might now be formed must do the same. When the first groups of Volunteers had begun to organise themselves parish by parish, their reasoning so far had been clear enough.

The likes of Charles Lammas and the other coastal commanders were not much interested in the raising, far inland behind them, of what amounted to private militias. If factory workers banded together, or miners, or railway-men, well and good. But if the Germans penetrated as far as the Midlands, that would mean the game was quite likely up. Certainly it would mean that the defence of the south and the east had failed – not to mention that they themselves, as commanders of shore garrisons, would presumably be dead. Because right from the start, they all agreed it wouldn't just be a case of guarding bridges and stations and what-have-you against sabotage or surprise attack. Not just a case of being the Army's eyes and ears – sending out patrols to watch for ships on the horizon, gliders and parachutists in the sky. They might be such amateurish garrisons that the name Irregulars was as yet too complimentary for them. But if the attack came against their sector, they didn't reckon to go in for much tactical falling back.

Before Churchill made his speech about fighting on the beaches, so far as Lammas could make out that was what most of his able-bodied neighbours intended to do – and those who were unsure weren't prone to talk about their perplexities. The Prime Minister's pugnacity, and the orders from above which began to come through, confirmed what most of them had already grasped. The counter-attack by Regular divisions would with any luck win the day. But the invaders must lose as much time, and as much equipment, and as many men as possible right away.

The first problem was weapons. That May week when the Germans advanced two hundred miles and the French Air Force was extinguished, not to mention the RAF losing a hundred of the bombers they were operating in France, Charles Lammas went into his gun-room before setting off for his second meeting at The Crossed Keys.

Oilskins and waders, fishing-rods and gaffs and creels – it was a room he'd always liked. Bobbie and Jack had been happy here too, he thought, glancing at the game-bags and cartridge-bags hung on their pegs. These old decoy ducks on the window-sill, along with the pair of flintlock pistols and the photograph of E_{11} steaming into Lemnos with . . . Lammas leaned toward it, a smile crinkling the crowsfeet at the corners of his eyes. Yes, with that bite shot out of her periscope. With Nasmith looking young and cheerful, and he himself grinning like a boy.

He turned to the gun cabinet, suddenly piercingly aware of how this room was redolent of old wars, and redolent too of peace-time attempts to give his nephew and his son the sort of country upbringing he'd had. Framed photographs of Blanche's father in uniform at Khartoum, one of her uncles at a durbar somewhere on the Deccan plateau. Photographs of Geoff in a college eight, Jack a generation later in another.

Lammas smiled again, reflecting that there'd never been much risk of Bobbie doing anything so exhausting as to row in an eight. And how old had Jack been when he'd insisted on putting on that old Cromwellian helmet – five or six? Naturally the helmet had obliterated his head entirely, and then he'd demanded to have the Ironside's sabre belted round his middle, and it had bumped along the ground and tripped him up.

A small boy who wanted to be lifted so he could reach down from one of the dusty shelves that Syrian dagger with the garnets in its hilt, or the Gurkha kukri. A boy who on hands and knees would burrow into cupboards like a terrier, emerge triumphantly with a pair of fen-runners he'd then have to try to strap on, or a bandoleer, or a holster. Years later, two young men back from duck-flighting, two cousins who joked as they companionably cleaned their weapons together . . .

He must pull himself together. What guns could the family muster? The only rifle he possessed was the little .22. What some people called a rook rifle, though this particular one was mainly used by Bill Meade, who borrowed it sometimes when he had a fox taking too much interest in his breeding pens. Handy little weapon, of course; but as an anti-tank gun . . . Oh, and there was the air rifle – but that didn't count.

As for shot-guns . . . His own Jeffrey twelve-bore, which had been Michael's. Bobbie's pair of Purdeys, which had been Roland's. Facing the cabinet with its rack of gleaming stocks and barrels, Charles Lammas frowned to recall how for the first years of his marriage his nephew had kept his guns at Bure, but just before the Sherwood Rangers had gone overseas he'd turned up at Edingthorpe with a mass of kit he wished his uncle and aunt to keep for him. Then Jack's twelve-bore and his sixteen-bore. The little twenty-bore, which was a perfect boy's gun, and which Blanche had shot with occasionally. A beautiful Victorian .410, with very long barrels, with hammers, with ornate chasing. Nothing else.

Pretty things. But not much, to take on professional regiments landing on Mundesley beach, parachuting into the fields. He swung his gaze around the room. A few daggers and swords. A knobkerrie. Where had that old sword-stick got to?

He peered in among a tub of umbrellas and walking-sticks, pulled it out. If he remembered rightly, you unscrewed this silver band around the cane, which . . . He twisted it. Nothing happened. He gave a wrench, it turned, he unscrewed the hilt from the cane that was also a narrow sheath. He drew the rapier, held the blueish grey steel up to the light. It glinted dully. All over the country, this week people must be getting out these elegant old toys, and thinking: ludicrous!

Lammas opened the leather box where the cleaning gear was kept. He'd oil the sword-stick, and while he was about it he'd oil some daggers too.

It was peaceful, working methodically there, with the ram-rods carefully leaned in a corner of the cabinet, and all the family's multifarious hats on hooks. A rag in one hand and a naval dirk in the other, he went to the shelf where the cartridges were kept, started to count the boxes of fifties of this calibre and that. Seemed to be a good number. All the same, he'd ring up Rosson's in Norwich, make a biggish order.

The rook rifle he'd retain for himself. The lighter shot-guns he'd keep in the house. At least, if the countryside were overrun, and German uniforms were seen in this yard of his, anybody at the kitchen window who wished to take a pot-shot should be able to do so. Even with the .410, you could make a mortal hole in the first man round the corner of the stable.

There was no reason why his twelve-bore, and Jack's, and Bobbie's pair, should not be made available to those men of the local platoon who hadn't got guns of their own. Who were not farmers, who were neither gamekeepers nor poachers. This could turn out quite funny, it suddenly occurred to him. This evening at The Crossed Keys, when it became clear who had a shot-gun and who hadn't. Old Davey Strike from Smallburgh Fen, who'd been taking pheasants out of everyone's coverts since at least the Boer War – what sort of weapon would he show up with, and how many more would he have left behind under his cottage thatch?

Well, these sparsely populated East Anglian farming parishes might be insignificant from some sophisticated points of view. But they'd know how to defend themselves a bit better than the towns, where nobody had a gun, and most people would need teaching how to use one. And thinking of

African wars, wasn't Blanche's papa's old revolver stuffed away at the back of his desk?

Chuckling to imagine the platoon which he would marshal for parade that evening under the pub's apple trees, Lammas went through to the library, poked about in his drawers. Sure enough, there his father-in-law's pistol was, a heavy Colt swathed in an oil-moistened cloth, where years ago he'd carefully put it away – and a couple of dozen rounds too, as luck would have it.

At those first gatherings at The Crossed Keys, the men with shot-guns were the lucky ones. The rest carried a splendid selection of pikes ancient and home-made, pitch-forks, coshes, crowbars. Sonny Hannant paraded with his scythe over his shoulder, George Morter with his axe. Then in July the first shipments of American .300 rifles arrived for the Home Guard, and began to be distributed in small numbers to local commanders, though at first with only ten rounds for each gun.

Charles Lammas was in charge of platoons all over the neighbourhood by then, but he regularly went out at night with one or other of the patrols. Men would finish their day's work, go home to eat something, then in small groups scatter over the countryside in the gloaming. In order that they all got some nights' sleep each week, they organised a rota.

That summer of 1940 was hot, usually it was pleasant to be out. Everyone agreed the Germans would choose to cross during darkness and make their landfall at first light. So as the nights wore on, the men on Paston cliff peered out into the opaque distance over the darkly wrinkled sea. The brackish wind made the grasses whisper. You might hear horses grazing, or a barn-owl shriek.

Everyone agreed that the invasion would also be airborne. Hadn't the Germans in May taken that place in Belgium – what was it called? – with gliders? Mr Lammas might know. Great Belgian fortress, quite impregnable. Eben Emael? *How* did you say it? Lord, what a . . . Well, Paston now – that was the right sort of name for a place to have. At any rate, forty gliders had appeared silently over the fortress one night, and . . .

So they'd talk about that. Or about the prolific rumours. One man knew for certain that enemy agents had been surprised while they were preparing an airfield somewhere up in Lincolnshire. There was no doubt Fifth Columnists were active everywhere, another was sure. It was the folk you'd never dream of suspecting, they were the ones to keep a damned sharp eye on. As for these curious lights people had been noticing at night

– they were the first Germans to be dropped, burning their parachutes. It stood to reason. No parachutes had been found, had they? Still, at least their first crack at getting across the Channel had been scuppered by our side. Down off Hampshire, that had been. A whole lot of their dead had been washed ashore. Common knowledge, that was. Yes, on the Sussex coast too.

Charles Lammas liked the companionship of those nights watching. No one had expected Poland to throw back the German onslaught – but France! In a matter of weeks, the country had been reduced to some sort of lousy German satrapy. He still had scarcely comprehended how quickly and utterly it appeared that a great nation could cease to exist – let alone anything you might call a civilisation. Yes, definitely the fellowship of one's neighbours was heartening. Funny, often, too, luckily. So that when all the Our Island Kingdom talk in the papers got too bloody embarrassing, rather like the King and Country talk last time, you only had to remember the east coast parsons and you cheered up at once. Of course, every Norfolk child knew that the county's mediaeval churches were the finest in the land. But the competition now between clergymen keen to point out that *their* noble flint tower would make the best observation post! One of the first things Lammas had done had been to arrange for a look-out for in-coming aircraft to be kept from Edingthorpe church tower. The very next morning he'd been telephoned by the parsons of Mundesley and Bacton, both in the grip of a suddenly zealous patriotism, both eager to remind him how well their churches stood. The Smallburgh parson was a disconsolate man these days, his church's tower having collapsed in the seventeenth century. But the incumbent at Happisburgh, with the mightiest church in the district and the loftiest belfry, standing right over the shore – this happy man's superiority to his ecclesiastical brethren was so obvious that he had no need to mention it, and strode about his village with an air of sublime unconcern.

But Lammas was dogged by anxieties. He didn't brood only on Britain's sudden isolation, either. Or on the Nazi provinces across the sea. Or on the way in which the Italians had waited till France was clearly beaten before they declared war and occupied Nice, and what gloomy ironies Giacomo Zanetti might pronounce, if one ever got to see one's friends again. He fretted about petty things too – far more than he would have allowed himself to before his stroke.

Home Guard commanders had begun to receive an allowance to cover expenses, but it fell way short of the real cost of running platoons.

Silly to feel embarrassed about being hard-up. Yet if Lammas cast his mind to the other commanders he knew . . . A couple were landowners.

One was a solicitor. Another owned a fleet of trawlers. Not one lived by so fragile a skill as his, by that skill of the mind which could seem the most tenuous fibre ever spun. Silly, also, to feel even mildly irritated when his neighbours, just because he lived at the Manor, expected it to be he who forked out pounds shillings and pence every time something had to be paid for.

Well, fortunately his heart hadn't packed up. His stroke had been a slight one, and he hadn't had another. What was more, Kenneth Clark, who had been made chairman of the War Artists' Advisory Committee, had written a very nice letter suggesting that, even if he weren't fit enough to be sent overseas on a special assignment, he submit any work that the Committee might find suitable to buy.

8

That year along the North Sea coast, the terns and oystercatchers were not much disturbed when they bred in the sand dunes and on the shingle spits. Indeed, as the longshore-man, Ted Eales, remarked to Charles Lammas while he was showing him the gun emplacement at Cley mill, men who mined and wired the shore and then withdrew probably caused less disruption than the holiday-makers, who this summer had not come.

Ruffs, which bred in the damp meadows. Curlew, which liked the estuaries and the mud spits, and uttered a shrill wail that the men of the platoons sometimes heard at night when they were out guarding a bridge. Snipe, breeding on the fresh marshes, as every year. Charles Lammas had been brought up to have an eye for these creatures, and he was aware of them now, the summer that the east and south coasts of England were being hastily prepared for defence. The birds skimmed away, and got mixed up in his head with the problem of getting enough sand-bags for the machine-gun positions on Cromer pier, and vanished into his general sense of not knowing what was going to happen next.

Those were the overriding feelings of that time: having been precipitated from frustrating inaction into having far more to do than he could get around to, and, after France had fallen, not knowing where and how the enemy was going to strike. And still the woodcock would come, nesting in the thickets beneath his Edingthorpe trees. Nettle-beds in flower. The stream half-clogged with rippling weed. And the young woodcock which, when Henrietta and he went down to the pasture as they had summer after summer, came flying over the lush land, croaking their harsh cry. Hetty would tense slightly, breathe 'Look!' Under a lime tree, the horses would shake their heads to gain an instant's respite from the flies, and swish their tails and stamp their hooves.

Lammas would stand there, thinking that, despite all the boisterous talk now being indulged in, there wasn't much disguising the fact that the British Army's campaign in France had been disastrous. Less than a month's fighting, and a conspicuous lack of defeats inflicted on the attacking German Army, and then they'd scrambled back to this country. Bailed out by the Navy of course. (His loyalty to his old Service would flare up predictably.) Maybe a hundred thousand men, the Admiralty had reckoned they might be able to rescue from Dunkirk. But in the end they'd fetched away upward of three times that, with a bit of help from fog and rain, and help from fishermen and yachtsmen. Even so, the beaten Army had left all its equipment in German hands, not to mention the best part of forty thousand poor devils as prisoners of war.

That was after Lammas came back from his training at Osterley Park, and his head tended to feel rather jammed with the difficulties of organising the Home Guard units in his area. (Behind this first line of defence, on the probable invasion beaches, all down the eastern centre of England now ran the second line, of anti-tank obstacles and trenches, to protect London and the great industrial regions. Behind again, were the reserves.) Of course, it was wonderful that even that first platoon they'd formed at The Crossed Keys was part of a plan developed over the summer by the Commander-in-Chief Home Forces and the Chiefs of Staff. That the activities of Sonny Hannant and George Morter, of the farrier from Crostwight and the rat-catcher from Ridlington, were to be coordinated as cogs in a machine which the War Cabinet had approved – this could only be inspiring. All the same, when it came to ensuring that a fuel depôt in North Walsham actually *was* guarded, and one cliff patrol knew how to communicate with other patrols . . . Knowing damn all about what was going to happen where and when could make your head ache too.

The Luftwaffe were already attacking British vessels in the Channel. One fact. The Germans now had every Danish, Dutch, Belgian and French harbour facing the British Isles, and if they could gain air supremacy over the sea the necessary conditions for launching a mighty invasion would all fit into place. Another fact. They might invade with a force of, initially . . . with a second wave of . . . While the defenders . . .

But there was so much you couldn't know! You might hope to get a rough picture of movements of shipping between Calais and Boulogne. But were small ships being got ready behind the screen of islands dotted along the Dutch and German coasts, and in every inlet from Flushing up to Heligoland? Was a fleet of big ships going to come steaming out of the Baltic through the Skaggerak?

So it was good to forget all that for a few minutes, go with Hetty to check up on the strength of the bat colony in the apple loft. Forget, or half forget. Because even if it wasn't much use worrying about what might come steaming out of the Skaggerak, (if Churchill didn't know, you weren't likely to be the man who found out and had the honour of telling him), there were still all these nitty-gritty problems within a ten-mile radius to tackle. Norgate had helped him choose the sites for the first pill-boxes, and his firm had started to build them, but now they were running out of concrete. What civil servant in what office must they get hold of to explain that this work must be given priority, and the issue of materials for it be authorised?

In June and July, the British Government considered an attack on the east coast the most probable. It was true that reconnaissance and aerial photography had not revealed fleets of transport vessels being prepared in the Scheldt harbours. But no great movement of shipping south through the straits of Dover, which would be necessary before an invasion of southern England could be launched, had yet been observed either.

The First Sea Lord advised the Prime Minister that he thought a force of a hundred-odd thousand men might get ashore without being intercepted. The question would be whether their Air Force could overcome our Navy and Air Force, which otherwise could cut the invaders off from supply and reinforcement. Also, whether these storm-troopers fought their way quickly to London.

Because of the danger of the Luftwaffe, no capital ships were stationed south of the Forth or east of Plymouth, but flotillas of the Navy's smaller ships patrolled the narrow seas. Where air attacks started to be made on fishing vessels, the local commanders in the Humber and the Wash, at Yarmouth and Harwich, armed them with machine-guns so they could fight back. And no sea-worthy craft was too humble to be made use of. After all, hadn't little ketches and sloops sailed over to Dunkirk? Many the German fighter aircraft had dived for, with their guns spurting. Many had been sunk, or left to drift away freighted with dead men and dying men. Others had sailed home, each perhaps with ten or twenty rescued soldiers.

Direct attack on fortified harbours seemed unlikely. All the same, to Charles Lammas' south-east, Yarmouth and Lowestoft were being made ready for defence on both their seaward and landward sides. While to his north-west, the sea-front hotels at Cromer were requisitioned, their bedrooms sand-bagged so that from them fire could be trained on the cliff-tops and the beaches. Up there, the local commander was Giles Whitchurch, who in peace time had devoted his attention to the Norfolk Archaeological Society. He lived at Weybourne Mill, and he was a big shambling fellow, with a grizzled beard and aquiline nose and handsome brown eyes. Lammas liked going with him to inspect the preparations to demolish Cromer station, or inspect the block-houses at the crossroads. Or they'd tramp along the Weybourne headlands, and Whitchurch would talk about the excavation of a Roman fort or a Saxon burial ground, and make dour remarks about how, off and on, the country had been overrun.

Then one day, Whitchurch was in the merriest spirits. Off his neighbourhood, the deep water came in quite close – Weybourne Hoop, it had
always been called. Well, he'd been rummaging in some archive or other,
and he'd come upon a rhyme from Napoleonic War days.

> He who would old England win,
> Must at Weybourne Hoop begin.

Good, eh? he chuckled. Well, of course, Charlie could imagine – the next
day at the Volunteers' meeting in the village hall, he'd told them that
jingle. You should have seen their faces, when he pointed out how Admiral
Raeder, whose Intelligence officers had no doubt brought him this couplet,
was probably this very minute assuring Hitler how convenient the Hoop
would be for bringing ships near to land. Oh, Weybourne had been singled
out, no question of it. The first panzer division ashore would be the one
they had to stand up and fight by their slip-ways and boatsheds here.

About then, Lammas brought his crab-boat out from Morston and down
the coast to where he could use her more often. There was a brisk wind,
and all afternoon he sailed past the villages, church tower by church tower,
past the dunes and cliffs and marshes which a couple of years before he'd
sensed might return to being a defensive position, and which now were
one long barbed-wire entanglement. At evening, he beached his vessel
half an hour's walk from home. Crab-boats were built to be hauled up a
shingle bank by a team of horses or men, or these days, if you were lucky,
by a tractor. Anyhow, the summer appeared to have settled in warm and
blue, for the time being the old boat could lie to her anchor perfectly well.
And she'd be useful for getting about these low-lying ramparts. Yes, at the
rate things were going, he was more likely to be in the front line here at
Edingthorpe, than Bobbie and Jack cantering about in those Palestinian
orange groves of theirs. All about Crusader castles, Jack's last letter had
been. And about ruined temples. Smiling to remember the schoolboy
sprawled on the library hearth-rug, who'd always wanted stories about
Arabia Petraea and the Roman legions' campaigns, Lammas plodded up
the dog-legging cliff path, mud yielding under his boots.

As the summer wore on, thoughts of Jack as a boy no longer always
made him smile. Doing the old, peace-time things with Henrietta didn't
always restore his good humour either. Nor busying himself helping Giles
Whitchurch position machine-guns on the Sheringham sea-front.

Not that Lammas too often failed to keep up the *appearance* of cheerfulness – but the thing itself was elusive. For that matter, the keeping up of
appearances was something he increasingly mocked himself for. *Appearing*

to be a good painter. *Appearing* to maintain his family, his household (he was going to have to find Mrs Fox another employer, he just knew he was), live in a certain style.

It wasn't like after the last war, when in his tremendous joy at being alive he'd done all the innocent, country things, and he'd known he was living in honour of his dead. It wasn't like when Blanche and he were first married, and everything they did they did grieving for their dead, but they did with joy too, by God yes, with rejoicing.

Live joyfully with the wife whom thy lovest all the days of the life of thy vanity . . .

Joy! When had he last felt that? These days, often he knew he wasn't living in honour of anyone. Going through the motions of the only way of life he more or less knew the drill for. And these anxieties of his, or depressions, or whatever the right word was. The indicative thing was that they were part of a growing range of things he never talked to Blanche about.

When eels began to move in the rivers that summer, and nets were being laid in the Ant and the Bure and the Thurne, Lammas took Henrietta to an eel-man he'd known all his life who had his tarred barge moored near Ranworth. Geoff and he had done that years ago, and he'd done it with Jack last summer. It was peaceful to row out there in the late dusk, when the Saint George's Cross on the church tower had been hauled down for the night, and the wildfowl were going to sleep in the alder carrs.

Even after dark, there was more traffic on the waterways than in the past, so the big eel-nets which stretched across from bank to bank were not much used any more. These days they had a smaller net called a fyte, which was made of tapering hoops – willow, generally – and you laid it slightly below the surface.

It was peaceful, paddling their dinghy to and fro with a lantern, helping their old friend with his net. Peaceful the night, when the eel-man brewed tea in his cabin, and you sat on deck and heard the breeze in the reedbeds and watched the river flowing by. Sometimes an owl flapped soundlessly past.

But Lammas, sipping his scalding tea, kept fretting about how these days the most idiotic things sufficed to put him in a foul temper. An official who made difficulties about supplying concrete for pill-boxes. Janet Fox and the Meades, whose innocent minds it apparently never crossed that he might have problems paying their wages.

Then he saw the tan sail of a wherry, looking ghostly as she glided on through the night. Taking advantage of the favourable wind, probably, to make her passage down to Yarmouth before the tide turned.

He stood up, for an instant back with his brother in that vanished, deathless world when they were boys. He called to the wherry-man which side of the river to steer. He showed Hetty how to haul in their net's lines a bit, so the deep-laden hull swept by without the fyte snagging and getting torn.

9

—⚊—

Charles Lammas had wanted to get over to Bure Hall while Frederick was there for a few days on leave, after being rescued from Dunkirk aboard a fishing-smack from the Naze. But he was so busy, that it was not until early July that Blanche and he were able to accept the Hedleighs' invitation to lunch.

While Mr Chamberlain was still Prime Minister, he had recognised Julian Hedleigh's years of loyalty to Party and to Government with the knighthood that Bobbie Lammas had long before mockingly awarded him. At the outbreak of war, during the debate in which Conservative, Liberal and Labour politicians, the overwhelming majority of whom had for years been disposed to go to any lengths to let the German dictator have his way, now revealed themselves ready to go to any lengths to stop him, Hedleigh was shocked by the fierce manner in which the Prime Minister's cautious speech was received. There were times when to temporise was simply prudent – surely they all knew that? As for the dramatic moment when Mr Greenwood rose to speak on behalf of the Opposition, and from the Conservative ranks Mr Amery called out to him, 'Speak for England!' Well, the new knight was outraged. He growled to the Honourable Member beside him, who had so far forgotten himself as to join in the cheers ringing from all sides of the House, that in his view the Prime Minister had spoken for England with sound sense, and he only hoped he would long continue to do so. Loyalty to their chosen chief had always been a Tory virtue, and he'd be damned if he neglected it. What was more, he happened to be in a position to be almost certain that an ultimatum had been issued to Germany only the previous evening, and it would be opportune to wait for the response to this before taking any rash step.

By the following May, during the equally fiery debate over the recent military and naval reversals, in which Sir Roger Keyes, wearing his uniform as Admiral of the Fleet, spoke to such stirring effect, Hedleigh's attitude to attacks on the Government had become one of dignified stoicism.

Not that he stood up and addressed the House. In all his years in the Commons, his interventions had been few. Even after his appointment to the Foreign Affairs Committee, he had only spoken on questions concerning his East Norfolk constituency, which were almost invariably to do with agriculture.

But this time his fury at Amery's disloyalty, and at the even more painful condemnation of the premier by David Lloyd George, was tempered by resignation. When Amery, from the benches behind the Government, began to quote Cromwell's words to the Long Parliament, 'You have sat here too long for any good you have been doing,' Hedleigh's pink-cheeked countenance expressed a manly recognition that these were rough knocks, but one had to learn to take them. 'Depart, I say, and let us have done with you,' Amery adjured the Front Bench. 'In the name of God, go!' Applause thundered. Silent among Mr Chamberlain's abashed friends, Hedleigh's face bore a frown of troubled responsibility. 'And this haranguing fellow is a Privy Counsellor!' his pursed lips seemed to be saying. Still, his thoughtful eyebrows pointed out, when all was said and done the Government had a majority of eighty-one, so with a spot of luck . . .

The next day, when the House divided, Hedleigh was neither among the thirty or so Conservatives who voted with the Liberal and Labour Oppositions, nor among the twice that number who more tactfully abstained. Even the following day when all the talk was about the possible formation of a National Government, Hedleigh was of a quiet equanimity to put heart into the most harrassed Whip. After all, even if Mr Chamberlain did decide to lay down the burden of his high office, the Conservative Foreign Secretary, Lord Halifax, was far and away the strongest candidate to succeed him.

Two months later, when the Tory Back Benches were grudgingly getting accustomed to supporting the party-switching Mr Churchill, Sir Julian and Lady Hedleigh received their guests at Bure Lodge. It was a pleasant house, by no means small unless you compared it to the Hall, and it stood in that part of the estate down by the river, all oak groves and marsh and meadow, which Jack Lammas as a boy had found a mysteriously magical region.

During Queen Victoria's reign, the Lodge had been the abode of a Hedleigh maiden aunt of evangelical fervour, much involved in the sending of missionaries to civilise various bits of the empire. She was followed beneath those red-brick gables, as if by decree of a mockingly even-handed Providence, by the present owner's Uncle Louis, who was devoted to whisky, and to bloodstock, and to what were least unsatisfactorily termed actresses. Then a heart attack felled genial Uncle Louis. Felled him in circumstances the family never referred to. Dispatched him – according to Ned Lammas, discoursing irreverently on his Rapallo terrace – to, if God were good, a Hereafter where the decanters were always full and the girls half-undressed. The next occupants were a tenant farmer and his family, which was convenient, because when Julian Hedleigh abruptly needed the place they could be required at short notice to depart to a cottage.

'Just while this *beastly* war is going on,' Sarah explained, pressing her skinny goddaughter to her matronly chest. 'My dearest Blanche, you can't *imagine* the condition this house was in. No running water . . . And some of the things they'd left behind! Well, naturally Julian had everything set to rights before we moved in, but all the same!'

'Morning, Charlie. Splendid to see you.' As spry at sixty as a fortunate man could be, Hedleigh strode forward across the small drawing-room where the missionaries, and later the actresses, had been interviewed to ascertain their suitability. 'Henrietta.' He shook hands with her also. 'Heaven help us all, I believe you're going to be as beautiful as your mother. What's more, they tell me you ride as well as she does. Is that true? Yes, this place was rather a mess, Charles. In reasonable condition now, though. Nothing like increasing the value of a property. Got a school up at the Hall, that's the trouble, as I mentioned to you on the telephone. London school. Isle of Dogs. Children, teachers, the lot.'

The headmistress, Miss Harding, I consider to be an admirable person. But her assistant, Miss Crane!' Lady Hedleigh's teeth banged shut.

'Glass of sherry, old boy?' Their host signalled to a servant with a silver tray on which the cut glass coruscated. 'Now, you were a terrific Navy man, and over lunch I want your opinion of this business at Mers-el-Kebir. But straight away, your Edingthorpe news. All well?' And he beamed at Henrietta, to include her in the conversation, in that affable manner he'd always had of putting his youngest guests at their ease. 'First things first, no? First one's Norfolk friends, I always say, and then the rest of the world.'

Charles Lammas reflected that Julian knew that at Edingthorpe not *all* was well. The last time he'd been there, he had noticed that the drawing-room lacked the Titian studio's great painting of a Naxos bacchanalia, with Theseus' ship sailing away, and abandoned Ariadne drowsing naked. 'Sent it to be cleaned?' he had supposed. 'You're dead right to take good care of it. Marvellous picture. Come to think of it, our Canaletto . . .'

Smiling inwardly to recall his cheerful, 'Had to sell it, unfortunately,' and Hedleigh's, 'Oh I say, what a shame,' Lammas shook hands with the others who would make up the lunch party. There was ancient Lady Long-Furlough, whose husband had been equerry to more than one Viceroy, and now was loudly commiserating with Sarah Hedleigh for poor Mark in Delhi at the hottest time of the year – he *must* escape up to Simla. There were Judge Fenby and his wife. And there was Caroline, her husband's uncle discovered with a jolt of liking for her. When a few minutes later he found her seated beside him, he was amused by the pleasure this afforded him.

Of course, she made him recollect that double portrait, which was bad. Not bad because the other sitter had been Raffaella Zanetti. Bad because it reminded him that he no longer tackled that sort of ambitious picture. On the other hand – if Lammas didn't think about that, but let himself enjoy Caroline's resumption of her flirtatious admiration of five or six years ago. If instead of plunging into the discussion of how important it was to plough up as much grassland as possible, he told her about how he'd gone to try to persuade the Ranworth eel-man to join the Home Guard. If he stopped thinking how splendid it was for Julian, that the war-time economic policy of the Government he supported now included subsidising the conversion of pasture to arable land at the rate of a couple of quid an acre, and instead enjoyed telling his story about rowing out with Henrietta past the reedbeds. If he told her about finding the eel-man unperturbed by the war; his hulk well-provided with firearms; his readiness to shed enemy blood just as firm as his refusal to join any organisation whatever, or to cooperate in the defence of parts of the kingdom beyond his patch of fen and his reach of the river. Charles felt warmed by the smiling way Caroline listened to him, till he recalled what wretched luck she'd had with Bobbie, who had let his discontent with his career become discontent with their marriage.

No, that wasn't fair on Bobbie. That depressing night under those Quercy lime trees, with the hurricane lanterns glimmering, he'd faced his unsuccess as a painter squarely enough.

Yes . . . But even so, there was an element of truth in it. If the lad had been getting flattering commissions, and flattering offers from gallery owners, he wouldn't have been so keen to chuck it up and join the cavalry. (With a shiver of distaste, Lammas recollected the Mathers Gallery, and his own attempts to circumvent the caution of a man with odious cravats and dyed hair.) Then Bobbie's marriage would probably not have irritated him, and Caroline might have had a baby or two, and one way and another matters would now be a lot more satisfactory.

He had not been impressed by his nephew's after-dinner outburst against marriage. Since then, the suspicion that Bobbie might deep down be a weakling had consorted unhappily with recollections of how from childhood he'd been the most delightful of companions. Bobbie so debonair, always joking, always affectionate – he'd been cheered up by him a hundred times. Even so, a man ought not to offload onto his wife his dissatisfaction with his own shortcomings.

Charles Lammas had finished telling his brother Geoffrey's daughter-in-law about the Ranworth eel-man, and had given up trying to stop thinking of her in those terms. Lady Long-Furlough was still spelling out hill station anecdotes to Lady Hedleigh, who was silently thanking the Lord God of British imperial arms that in Delhi or in Simla her darling Mark was a fair distance from the nearest front line. What was more, it might well be, her motherish heart decided, that he had put his worst dissipations behind him. Blanche Lammas had just discreetly assured her daughter that certainly they would leave after lunch in time to take the horses to the farrier as planned. Henrietta was still worrying whether this excellent intention would really result in a mercifully brisk departure, when Sir Julian exclaimed with statesmanlike sobriety, 'A tragic necessity! Horribly sad,' he went on, audibly weighing his words, and pronouncing them with the gravity he knew was correct when mentioning the loss of human life. 'A sad day indeed, when our guns are turned on French ships. But Admiral Somerville had his orders.' Then remembering that he was not addressing the chap from *The Times* but a lunch table where ladies were present, he lightened his tone a little. 'What do you think, Charlie? Could it have been resolved in some better way?'

'Well, without knowing exactly what Admiral Gensoul told the French Admiralty, it isn't easy to say. We don't know their deliberations either. But at Alexandria, diplomacy seems to have done the trick. There the French disarmed their ships themselves. And of course, there's no doubt that to stop the Germans . . .'

For the last few days, ever since the news from Mers-el-Kebir had come, Lammas had been feeling sick at the thought of British Naval gunfire killing French sailors. Sick, like he'd feel if he bit into something rotten. It had made him think of Guy Rivac, and going ashore in Toulon together that Christmas of 1917, and what a wild time it turned out you could have in the dives and the hotels there, despite your brother and Guy's both having recently been killed, what a damned good wild time. It had made him pray that neither of the Rivac boys had been killed in that shelling. Made him hope it with such urgency and such nausea, when he thought of Guy and Marie in Bordeaux occupied by German invaders hard at work setting up their disgusting little tyrannies, that . . . So that, rather like Britain being at war with Italy, it was a thing too putrescent to bite into. But you bit into it in all your waking hours, because you had to; and you went on organising the defence of this east coast of yours; and you went on answering appropriately when at lunch people asked you questions.

So Lammas reminded the company of Admiral Darlan's orders to his captains on 24 June to ensure that their vessels should in no circumstances fall into German hands. For that matter there was the French – what was the right word for it? not armistice, in his view – the French capitulation, signed at Compiègne two days before that, which provided for the demobilisation of their fleet. Naturally, though, you couldn't trust anything the German Government signed.

Lammas reminded himself that he didn't actually *know* that either of Guy and Marie's sons had been at Mers-el-Kebir – though he knew one of them had been earlier in the year. Robustly deciding that one boy was probably in the Caribbean, and the other at Dakar maybe, or at Casablanca, he led the discussion of whether, once Admiral Somerville had decided that time was running out and he had to open fire, we might have wrought more destruction than we did. A couple of their battleships were disabled. Of *Dunkuerque* and *Strasbourg*, which were two of the most powerful capital ships afloat, the former went aground, but the latter escaped, and lesser ships with her.

Reports were still changing, but it appeared probable that well upward of a thousand French sailors had been killed. Lammas only touched on that briefly, in his most abrupt manner. But he went on thinking about it, and it got mixed up with other unsettling presentiments, and the taste of something loathsome remained.

Mers-el-Kebir was the port of Oran. He looked across the table at Blanche, imagined her being reminded of Tom Carraway, who in the last war in a hospital there had taken three weeks to die of his wounds.

Another trouble was that Caroline's faintly flirtatious attentiveness reminded him of when she'd first been engaged to Bobbie, and what fun that Christmas had been. Jack and Ricky hauling that fir into the drawing-room, scattering mud and bark and needles all over the carpet. Bobbie who couldn't make up his mind whether to ask the girl to marry him or not.

Quite perceptive the lad had been in his uncertainty, his uncle recalled with an ache of unstoppable love. Trust Geoff to have such a flamboyant son. Leaning against the fireplace, wearing that smoking-jacket embroidered with dragons, and a red cummerbund. Flourishing the silver cigarette-holder Blanche had given him. Jigging that Indian statuette in his fingers, and talking. Bobbie wasn't *all* weakness, hell no.

Lammas recalled the urbanity with which Julian Hedleigh and he had smoothed over any awkwardnesses about that engagement which might have arisen, and how thankful he'd been that these worldly wisdoms were so dependable. Unfortunately, this brought to his mind how more recently, when that marriage had come to appear shaky, he had appreciated once more the Hedleighs' *savoir faire*. Yes, yes ... But such worldliness could also be unkind.

On the spur of this last thought, Charles Lammas dropped out of the conversation about the sad end of French Naval glory, and whether the damage done to Anglo-French friendship were likely to prove critical.

'Caroline ...' He lowered his voice, gave her his gaiest smile. 'I'll tell you what I've *really* been thinking about. The winter when you and Bobbie got engaged – do you remember the kitten climbing the Christmas tree?'

'Oh!' She flushed. 'Yes, of course I do! Jack and Ricky putting the tree up, and all of us helping to decorate it, and ...' Her voice had a catch in it. 'Sticking holly and ivy on the pictures. Raffaella and her kissing-bough.'

Caroline's cheeks glowed. Her blue eyes said, 'Bless you for remembering that now,' so unmistakably that Lammas stopped wondering whether she would have been more successfully married to somebody quite unlike his nephew. Tony Maitland, for instance, who was so uncomplicatedly rich, and who had married another of Bobbie's girlfriends. Daisy Rackham, that was right. The girl who had come to France with them one summer, sat for him under a cedar by the Tarn.

'*I tell you what, Uncle. I'll do whatever you say.*' '*My dear fellow, I couldn't possibly accept that sort of responsibility.*' The rags and tatters of old friendship.

'Wasn't it all fun? Don't you worry, dear girl, when Bobbie and Jack come home we'll have those sorts of Christmases again. Shooting with your father, then dinner with us.'

'Will we, I wonder?' she asked him, with a grave voice, with shining eyes.

'I hope so,' he replied with quiet firmness. 'People go through ups and downs. There's a lot of good in Bobbie. It'll come to the fore.'

'Of course it will! But ... But I'm afraid that, for him and me, by then it'll be too late.'

'I haven't stopped hoping. But it needs guts, I know. The great thing is not to give up.' The poverty of it! But what else should he have said? Then he recalled something. 'Keep swimming. There was an occasion, once ... Years ago, off the coast of Turkey. They fished me out of the drink after they'd given me up for lost, and I was sure I was a goner.'

'I remember every second of that Boxing Day dinner party in your house.' Just as Caroline was showing a bravery she had not had as a fiancée, so now she deflected their exchange, and yet did not really deflect it, with a sophistication which Charles Lammas supposed must be the fruit of her last couple of years' distresses. 'You told me about the pictures on the walls, and I instantly forgot half of what you said and got the rest muddled up, and I thought all the Lammas family were glorious.' She held his gaze, and repeated slowly, smiling: 'Utterly glorious.'

Fancy that! he thought. Conventional, uneducated Caroline, with her rather banal beauty, with her husband in the Haifa flesh-pots! And he said, 'That toasting glass – remember? Jack filled it with Burgundy. We drank to Bobbie and you.'

In both their minds' eyes, the tall engraved glass glittered again, she raised it brimming with red wine.

After lunch, Blanche Lammas whispered to Henrietta, 'Don't worry. We'll get to the farrier. Now, be a darling, and talk to your godmother for five minutes. *Five* – all right?' Then she followed Caroline, who had stepped out into the dappled garden.

Blanche had noticed the animated conversation between her husband and Bobbie's wife, and needed to know nothing of the actual words to know their tenor and guess some of their effects. She had wished to back that talk up with renewed friendliness of her own. But that was easier intended than done. She would never be able to impress Caroline as Charlie effortlessly did, nor charm her as he always could. So outside, under the Lodge's rose arbour, she wavered.

However, Caroline had not strayed far. She was pausing too, by the sun-dial, and now turned her head.

Blanche approached her. She asked, 'Well, did you commandeer your parents' old pony-trap? Was my idea any good?'

Caroline smiled too. 'Oh, yes!'

'But you haven't driven over to see us.'

She replied with the same amused simplicity. 'No.'

'Well . . . I'll just say again that I hope you will.' Blanche checked, clearer now about the question she wanted to confront, but hesitant. Then her eye caught the younger woman's wrist. 'Oh, how nice. You wear that bracelet. My brother Michael brought it back from China – but I expect I told you that.'

'I wear it a lot.' Caroline lifted her hand, so the ivory bracelet could be seen to advantage. Her mind still suffused with Charles' sympathy (she had escaped outside in order to keep her first impression of their conversation intact for as long as possible), she said, 'It was a lovely engagement present.' Then, with a flick of her glance to the door to be certain her mother was not pursuing them, she added reflectively, 'You two must have had a fine time together, after the last war.'

'After our war . . .' Blanche Lammas took her time. Could Caroline really be broaching her question for her? No, it wasn't a question. But a feeling, or a ray of – of something! 'Charlie and I, in the twenties . . . Yes. We were extremely lucky. You're right. We had a terrific time.'

'Lucky?' Caroline wondered.

Leaving aside their obvious good fortune in having both been alive after their war, in having loved one another, in having two children, leaving aside those cardinal happinesses which she had rejoiced in and Caroline might in time or might not, Blanche grappled her courage to her. She said, 'Charlie was a fantastic man to be with, in those days. You see him now, a bit the worse for wear. But then . . . At regattas, at steeplechases, at parties – he was such fun always! And when it came to his painting . . . Amazing energy, yes, and ability to keep at it for hours, but other things too. I remember watching his eyes looking at his subjects and his canvases, sometimes with very quick glances, sometimes concentrating for a long time, and . . . Well, I'd never met a man like him. And it wasn't just the extraordinary way he always seemed to know what he was going to do next, and have lots of ideas about how to go about it. But . . .' Caroline's eyes were smiling. So Blanche went on, 'He really did seem to know who he was. I remember thinking I was very lucky. He was lucky too, that a little success began to come when he still wasn't all that old.'

'He's a remarkable man,' said Caroline evenly.

'I'm sorry, I didn't mean to show off. I meant to answer your question. And . . . Oh, I don't know. But – with that tremendous confidence in everything he did, sometimes he seemed to know who he was going to be. Though now . . .' Blanche's mouth was warped with unhappiness for him, but she finished. 'In some respects, he was wrong. This last year or two, he's been very different.'

'I didn't think you were showing off.' Caroline's voice was soft. 'You've explained what I asked you about. What I'd imagined.' Her puff of laughter got tangled up with her sadness. 'Oh, my poor Bobbie! Only knowing what he *doesn't* believe he can do, only knowing he *doesn't* know who he is!'

'Dearest girl . . .' Pressing her lips into a disciplined line, and blinking away her incipient tears, Blanche took Caroline's arm. They strolled toward the sanctuary promised by a yew hedge. 'You're right not to bother about whether he paints after the war or not. Charlie has always said it ought to be possible to get him a position in an auction house or a gallery.'

'Yes.' She smiled wryly. 'Yes.'

'For that matter, he may decide to stay in the Army.'

After a few more paces, Caroline suggested, 'Do you think we ought to rescue Henrietta from my mama?'

10

—〰—

All winter and spring, when Charles Lammas had been depressed, Jack's letters had often heartened him. Bobbie's letters too, and Georgia's. But although his nephew's and his goddaughter's scrawlings for Edingthorpe consumption were consistently cheerful, they were also ambiguous in their ways. While Jack ... It was true that often he sounded as if he were still about eighteen, and that boyish tone of voice was reminiscent of the letters his father and just about every other lieutenant in the Army or the Navy had written home at the beginning of the last war. Still ... Jack's blitheness was so open, so unshadowed!

Off he went to Acre, with *The Historical Geography of the Holy Land* in his saddle-bag, not to mention *Seven Pillars of Wisdom*. He wrote gaily about how the massive walls jutted out into the sea, how the Crusaders had besieged the place for a couple of years. Next he'd gallivanted off with his cousin and Timothy Farne in the latter's car to the ruins of Samaria, up in the hills near Nablus. He wrote about how these days it was called Sebasté, and there was an Arab village on one side of the hill, where they used the remains of a huge Crusader church for their mosque.

Bobbie also wrote home about that jaunt. But there were too many things he never mentioned in his letters, such as his wife and his parents-in-law – and, indeed, the question of where these days, if anywhere, his home might be.

Bobbie, of all people, to write guardedly! But it was true, and it was sad. So it was altogether more satisfactory to read Jack's version of how they'd clambered over the Roman ruins where Salomé had danced before Herod and John the Baptist was beheaded, and not far away had found Jacob's well and let down a bucket for water. Or how in Jerusalem he'd bought Henrietta an Arab bridle and posted it off to her.

Even so, today for some reason ... Charles Lammas had always enjoyed going to the farrier at Crostwight, and just because there was a war on didn't mean you could neglect the condition of your horses' hooves. But the lunch party at Bure Lodge seemed to have left him in a filthy mood – though maybe it wasn't that at all. Anyhow, not even the thought that, far away in Palestine, a cavalry lieutenant and his troop farrier had put their heads together and come up with a mounting for their Hotchkiss gun ... He rode sour-faced in the drowsy afternoon sun.

Blanche and he, Henrietta and the Barlow girl, were each riding one

animal and leading another. (His womenfolk's campaign to save the local
horseflesh from the knacker had so far been, Lammas considered, amply
successful.) They rode up the grassy path to the forge, ducking their
heads because the elms' branches needed cutting back. Then there in
its thickets of elder and dog-rose was the old smithy, with its sagging
ridge-pole and the tufts of grass sprouting between its tiles. There stood
Grimes, in his dark doorway, wearing a leather apron. Henrietta had
been riding ahead. She jumped off her grey half-Arab mare, she called,
'Here we are, Mr Grimes!' The farrier shoved away the door-post with his
ox-like shoulder, he said, 'Good afternoon, Miss. Afternoon, Mrs Lammas.
Afternoon, Sir.' But Lammas was so jaundiced today that even this scene
and this ritual jarred.

Sarah squawking about 'while this beastly war is going on'. Jack writing
that *if we get sent to Libya, things should liven up*. Admirable enthusiasm, of
course – and he remembered too well how you never wrote anything
that might distress your mother, you didn't write the sickening things.
He remembered also how in war light-heartedness quickly came to be the
second virtue, after courage; how you kept joking . . . But wasn't some of
Jack's chatter a bit callow even by subaltern standards? All that silly talk
about how when you were excited the tendency was to shoot high. And
Giles Whitchurch too, chuckling about how the old men and the boys of
Weybourne were going to have to hold their boatsheds against the first
armoured division ashore. My God, had none of these people got a clue
what modern fighting was like?

Carefully loosening the scowl which had gripped his eyes and mouth,
Lammas dismounted.

The smithy at Crostwight stood behind a disused marl-pit, now choked
with hawthorn and elder. There were a couple of stalls where horses could
wait their turns, and iron ring-bolts in the outside wall for tethering.
Grimes' cottage stood among clumps of lilac, and there was a paddock
because the farrier was also something of a horse-coper, and had a
fund of stories about gypsies' tricks for passing off broken-down nags as
crackerjack mounts. He was a poacher too, though by unspoken accord
for years he had let Lammas' wood at Edingthorpe alone.

Usually Charles Lammas enjoyed leading his horses into the open
front of the smithy one by one, standing by the forge to watch Grimes
shoe them. He enjoyed lending a hand to stoke up the fire or ply the
bellows, liked watching the methodical way the farrier unclinched the
nails securing the old horse-shoe, prized it away, then cut and filed

the edges of the hoof. He liked the stories about the copers on Holt
Heath who used to make a spiritless horse swallow a live eel just before
they showed off its paces, with the consequence that, for a minute while
the buyer was watching, the brute showed liveliness. Then there might
be the story about the poacher who one night on the Salhouse estate
was nearly caught by the gamekeepers, but who dropped into the river
where the reeds grew good and thick. He stood with not much more
than his nose above the winter water, while the men decided to wait for
him right there.

Lammas liked the way the farrier told his slow stories, with the blows
of his hammer marking time. He liked the way it was left unclear whether
Grimes himself had been one of the copers in question; whether it had
been he who had stood up to his chin in a reedbed, with Salhouse
pheasants sodden in his game-bag, with water doing his gun no good,
spoiling his temper, spoiling his cartridges.

But fortunately today everybody else pitched merrily into unsaddling
the horses and tethering them. Grimes had more than enough helpers
and listeners. With the pretence of taking an interest in the fruit forming
on the cottage's apple trees and pear trees, Lammas strolled away.

Weeks of trying to convince his Defence Volunteers of the ferocity with
which an attack on the country would be carried forward – that was one
thing that had been jangling his nerves. Trying to drum into their heads
what the German Army had been up to in Poland, in the way of burning
and murdering and raping, and what they'd do here. The labour camps.
The hostage-taking. The punitive raids. Drumming it into Sonny Hannant
and Davey Strike and the rest of them, that if glider-borne troops landed,
or parachute troops landed, you set to work shooting as soon as they
were in range, you killed as many of them as you could before they
killed you.

Well, at least they finally *were* mounting batteries of coastal and anti-
aircraft guns to defend Weybourne Hoop – doubtless to the accompaniment of Whitchurch's remarks about how in 1588 defences had been built
there in case the Armada showed up. A Territorial battalion of the Norfolks
was there too. Good. Because it was true – ships could come in so close
there you'd hardly need flat-bottomed barges to put an army ashore.

At least he was busy, too. What with having to find time to paint,
because otherwise the family would be without even this precarious
income, and yet making sure that all the road signs and mile posts in
the district were removed. What with getting more pill-boxes built, and

raising more platoons of Volunteers, and helping to get Conscription organised. (He scowled, recollecting how as lately as April the Liberal and Labour Oppositions hadn't displayed the guts to vote for Conscription. One had to be grateful to Hore-Belisha and the Conservatives for pushing the measure through.) Busy . . . Which poet was it who described action as the struggle of the fly in marmalade? Must have been writing after breakfast. These days when he was just going through the motions . . .

Not that it mattered. An accurate shot would put an enemy soldier out of the battle just as satisfactorily, whether or not the man who aimed straight thought he was just going through the motions of living his life.

Lammas strolled farther among the fruit trees, wondering about the tiredness, or dejection or whatever it was that he'd been succumbing to of late – since the war began – no, longer – since his stroke, or since Raffaella, even. Often it was mere disgruntlement that was wrong with him. Today, for instance. Now, with German armies everywhere triumphant and Britain the only European Power left in the fight, all he was capable of were peevish thoughts about Jack who wrote chirpy letters. A fine way to love the boy! Dear God, when a lad who by rights ought still to have been at university couldn't even write home light-heartedly about the bloody awful historical moment he'd grown to manhood in, without his stupid father getting grumpy!

Jack writing about overcast, stifling days when a scorching wind called the *khamsin* blew out of the desert, and clouds of dust swirled endlessly, and sweat rinsed down your face, down your arms and back and legs. Jack who spent his pay on Arab harness for his sister, bought her camel bells, and sent them off. No parcels had arrived from Palestine yet – but doubtless they would. All very fine, letting yourself think gruff thoughts about how you might shortly find you'd just about finished going through the motions of your life and were going through those of your death, and it wasn't just a going through of motions either. But Henrietta, Jack's *Dearest Hetty*, who if this invasion came would . . .

Charles Lammas sat down on a bank, distractedly started picking sprigs of groundsel. You could get disheartened about how predictably you really *did* like the people you'd grown up amongst, really *were* contented lunching with the Hedleighs and the Fenbys year after year. You could get irritated with the people who this summer were going in for a hell of a sight too much of the Our Island Fortress twitter, while at the same time refusing to grasp how savagely they were going to have to fight if an invasion were to be slowed up – probably because they were the sort who, when it came to it, would not fight. But then you remembered your daughter. You wondered if you really expected the country's schoolchildren to get themselves slaughtered, and then you thought of German soldiers getting their hands on Blanche and Henrietta and the Barlow girl – and you went on jerking up groundsel out of the earth.

Georgia came to mind too. Because whether the Führer ordered the invasion of Britain to go ahead or not, and whether his armies were repulsed here or not, it looked increasingly likely that Japan would strike southward. That was another thing that people here could be annoyingly complacent about. People in the East too, according to Alex Burney's last letter – Geraldine conspicuous among them, but in consonance with what sounded like every empty-headed bridge player from Bombay to Hong Kong.

The Japanese had asked Marshal Pétain's government for military, naval and air bases in French Indo-China. Then, while negotiations were proceeding, they'd occupied strategic points along that coast, regardless. Of course, Upper Burma was a long way from where the first attacks would be launched. But with Holland and France overrun by Germany, and both of them possessing now virtually indefensible colonies which Japan coveted . . . And if embargoes were enforced against Japan, she'd pretty much *have* to attack.

Recollecting that Mrs Fox fed groundsel to her canaries, Lammas picked it less violently, collected a small heap. He wondered what Alex made of this Burma Road business. It was the main overland route for supplying arms to China, and the Japanese wanted it closed, and the British had blustered for a bit but then complied.

Closed it for three months . . . But it wasn't any use being pleased with yourself at drinks parties on account of how we'd cleverly agreed to close that road for the three monsoon months when it would anyhow have been largely impassable. Because the Japanese Government would have picked up the signs they'd been watching for, right enough. They'd have learned that Britain didn't want a quarrel with a third enemy. It was the old, old story about not having a two-hemisphere fleet.

Lammas remembered Georgia as a girl in his studio reading, telling him how stories reverberated in her head. She was a young woman now, eighteen she must be, and in her last letter to him from Maymyo she'd written about that same feeling, written about stories that rang, words which echoed and died away.

Putting the bunch of groundsel in his pocket for Janet Fox's canaries, he stood up, sauntered back toward Grimes' forge. Goddaughter, he thought, liking the two words together, the word they made. Godchild. Echo girl.

11

It was evening before all the horses had been shod, and the party were riding home. There was no wind. Swarms of midges swayed in the air over the winding lane.

Far away, thunder growled. Maybe that was it, maybe it was the electricity in the sky, Charles Lammas mused, or it was just that his moods were ridiculously volatile these days – at any rate, his humour had cleared. He hacked along cheerfully, glancing over the high-summer hedgerows to where at a wood's edge rabbits were hopping about in the last of the westering sun.

He rode with his reins in his right hand, the leading-rein of the saddleless horse in his left. Sometimes the animal bumped against his left leg. Then a big grey horse-fly alit on its flank and he knocked it away with his crop before it could sting, and it came back so he knocked it away again.

It couldn't really be the electricity in the sky, though he'd always been exhilarated by thunder and lightning. Anyhow, the rumbling was so distant that he couldn't tell if the storm were brewing over the land or the sea.

Henrietta and Sally were chatting away merrily about snaffles, martingales, cruppers, Lord knew what. It was pleasing to think of all these horses tightly shod, hear their clinched metal clippety-clopping on the road.

Coming past Crostwight church, he told Blanche about how lately there had been a tremendous collision of wills, because Jane Kersey was marrying her young man there on Saturday, so of course her father wanted the bells rung before the wedding service. But the parson had refused, because all over the country orders had gone out that church bells were only to be rung as a signal that the German invasion had begun. Well, old Kersey was set on having his Jane married in the finest possible style, and didn't reckon to let Herr Hitler's shennanigans cast a pall over the proceedings. So the parson told him he'd have to speak to Mr Lammas, who was in charge of all those kinds of matters around here.

Charles had chuckled, telling Blanche how Ben Kersey had stood there, insisting on 'Just one bell for our Janey, rung nice and loud when she comes up the path.' And now . . . He smiled again, to remember how Kersey had eventually conceded that, if Mr Churchill honestly believed it to be in the national interest, he supposed he – but it was a funny old world. Now Lammas urged his horse into a trot, and the others followed suit. He recalled the bells at Gibraltar being rung on Armistice Day, and how he'd imagined these Norfolk church bells being rung for the peace which had come at last, and he thought pugnaciously that he hoped to live to hear bells pealed for victory again one day. He looked over the meadows and wheat fields, and his mind was aflutter with ideas.

Julian Hedleigh had been right – Henrietta *was* getting to be as beautiful as her mother. She had Blanche's willowy figure, her brown hair which clung softly around the curves of forehead and cheek. Henrietta was a country girl of the same stamp too, with that passion of hers for horses, for all living things. Always befriending an unwanted puppy, supervising a hatch of ducklings, adopting a lamb with a broken leg.

But Lammas had stopped brooding on what might happen to his daughter if the war went the wrong way. He didn't worry either, as on occasion he had, that he'd found Georgia Burney the more interesting of the two girls growing up in his household, and possibly Henrietta had sensed this. Inspirited by his string of horses trotting along the lane, he thought how lucky he was in Henrietta, and how splendid it was that she was keen as mustard to pass her exams and go to Cambridge – because in the new England after the war there was going to be no more nonsense about intelligent boys getting an education and intelligent girls not.

Yes, things would have to change, this time. In all manner of ways . . . but university places for young women would be a start. Look at poor Caroline, equipped only to be the not particularly interesting breed of wife. Whereas Henrietta was going to get a degree. Couldn't decide right now whether she wanted to read Classics or History, but either would be terrific – and there'd be tennis parties and river parties and May Balls. Then, whether she got married young or not, and in his view if she put that off for a few years it could only be a good thing . . . When the war was over, he'd urge her to go to Italy, he resolved abruptly.

Lammas slowed his pair of horses to a walk, and then with the cavalcade making less clatter he heard the wood-pigeons again, and the thunder. To the east over the sea, he saw the first flash of lightning. But here where they were coming onto Ridlington Common, in the last of the sunshine he seemed to see all his ideas picked out with brilliant clarity.

Henrietta would spend three years reading hundredweights of whatever she fancied. She would go back to Forte dei Marmi, where in her carry-cot she had slept in the shade of one of those pines which made the sea air resinous, where a few years later she had learned to swim in a doggy-paddle style of her own improvisation. She would go winding up into the Tuscan hills on a warm evening like this evening, jolting in the old Zanetti car through the olive groves where the shadows were lengthening. She would come to Villa Lucia, and it would be as if the war had never been. Everybody would be alive. Nothing would have altered, or nothing important.

Well, conceivably ... But Lammas' awareness was flitting so lightly, that in two or three heartbeats he'd brought to mind poor old Marshal Balbo shot down the other day over Tobruk by his own anti-aircraft gunners; Jack writing about how he'd *crossed the railway line which in the last war Lawrence spent so much time trying to blow up;* a story of Grimes' about a landowner who with a couple of farm-hands had laid an ambush for a poacher and caught his own gamekeeper. He'd recollected how Hitler might have ordered Edith Cavell's memorial in Paris to be demolished, but her statue outside the Cathedral Close in Norwich still stood. Perhaps more than three heartbeats. He'd noticed how the thundery haze in the east was darkening, so the lightning writhed with a more startling silver over the woods. Then a sparrow-hawk caught his eye. The next moment he hoped that, if the storm did break, this promising-looking field of barley didn't get too knocked about by the battering rain-squalls. And thinking of Tobruk, it had been splendid last week how, thanks to aerial photographic reconnaissance, aircraft flying from one of our carriers had hit Italian naval targets there.

Yes, yes ... But there *was* a thread which ran through all his musings today. What was it? Extraordinary, this way he seemed aware of his brainpan, he could *feel* his ideas fluttering: quick, vulnerable.

Something about Tolstoy which he'd never been able to work out to his satisfaction, and the innards of a submarine, and ...

'That's it!' he whispered, and leaned forward to pat his horse's neck.

He could see Tolstoy's paradox about freedom clearly at last, or thought he could. How inescapably we were determined by causal chains, and yet how essential to us the sense of our freedom was – because without it, we couldn't claim much for our responsibilities, and our virtues, and our loves.

All his life, it appeared to Charles Lammas now, he'd been trying to blunder his way through this impasse. In his Navy days. That night a couple of summers ago, when they'd just got back from Italy and the girls had taken their sleeping-bags out into the garden. That night when abstract passions and abstract freedoms hadn't seemed much good. Then today at the smithy he'd ... Damn it, old Tolstoy was brilliant, though, the clear-eyed way he kept seeing that no action we took could be free of the conditioning nexus, but that didn't mean the sense of freedom didn't keep welling up in our hearts. And *that* – which let us go in for our moralities and our arts, our loves and our hates, our life – *that* was the illusion to be dispelled if the truth were to be arrived at.

Well, he'd never have made a professor of philosophy. Didn't have to try, luckily. The others were chattering about whether they'd reach Edingthorpe before the downpour caught them, and deciding they wouldn't, and debating which short-cut to try. The horses' hooves beat gaily in his ears. In the gathering storm-light, Sally Barlow's mop of hair was a dully smouldering red he liked. Thank heavens for appearances. Thank heavens even for the nebulous doubts which accompanied the application of paint to canvas. Soon now there'd be that swirl of chill wind over the land which presaged a cloud-burst, and the smell of rain. Good!

The first drops of rain fell, and seemed very slow, and very big. The birds were still singing. At the next clap of thunder, Henrietta's horse shied. Lammas joined in the moment of anxiety, when the grey mare's hooves slid sideways and she staggered and might have come down. He joined in the merriment when his daughter brought the dancing horse back under control.

Gusts of rain whipping into his face, Lammas let his horses break forward. The eight hooves pounded. The led horse curvetted and tugged. To hell with ideas – right now it was terrific to be charging up a headland on a fine thoroughbred rather than lying in the churchyard.

The storm soaked his shirt and his breeches, made the reins slithery to hold. Then a willow was blazingly illuminated. Both horses were frightened by the thunder-clap, but he got them galloping steadily again. He caught up with the rest of the family, hacked on through the deluge into Edingthorpe in his highest spirits for years.

12

—⁂—

To begin with, Lammas kept his son's war letters in the Chinese lacquer box on his desk, along with Geoffrey's letters home from the Western Front, and Blanche's letters to him from her last months as Miss Mack. *I expect this war may fizzle out before long*, Jack had written cheerfully soon after he arrived in Palestine. But then it did not fizzle out, and his letters mounted up. Bobbie's and Georgia's letters to Edingthorpe accumulated too, so the overflow were kept in an old walnut writing-case.

The night after the ride back from Crostwight in a thunderstorm, Charles had the writing-case open and reread a few pages. That summer of the Battle of Britain, the apparent imminence of a German landing meant that as a coastal area commander he never had time for luxuries like reading until after supper, and only then if it wasn't his turn to go out on patrol.

Sheets covered with his son's handwriting, his nephew's, his god-daughter's. Other hands too. Alex Burney in Upper Burma and Mario Zanetti in New York both corresponded occasionally. Christopher de Brissac wrote too, usually from Singapore.

Often Blanche would come into the library with him, to read or to talk. But that night, he was alone with the letters and his thoughts.

Still feeling exhilarated by his stormy gallop, Lammas sat down at his desk, switched on the lamp. His mind had gone on fluttering with ideas. Géricault's painting of a horse frightened by a storm . . . Riding home with sodden clothes, squalls battening on the twilit countryside and the sky cracking and flaring, he'd remembered that picture. In an Edingthorpe meadow he'd *seen* Géricault's horse, seen his storm-light on the animal's hide. Then helter-skelter notions about how, just because his experience had tended to chime with Tolstoy's cataclysmic view of war, that didn't mean there wasn't a fair dose of Clausewitz in the German Government's recent thinking.

Lammas pulled a bundle of letters toward him. The Sherwood Rangers had been mechanised. Bobbie had been down in Cairo. Something to do with gunnery. Bobbie's letters were a lot less innocent than Jack's, and some of those worldly observations and scandalous asides now would . . . Well, with any luck they might stop his mind harping on how damned right Tolstoy had been to explode all that optimistic rationalism. Give him Bobbie in Tel Aviv with the High Commissioner's daughter and *a very beautiful young married Frenchwoman to chaperon*. Bobbie in Cairo at the Gezira Club with an officer of the Black Watch and the Greek consul.

That was the way the new war came lapping into Lammas' head, on quiet nights in his Edingthorpe library. Letters. Musings. Distractedness. That summer when the war really was lapping around the English coasts, and you didn't have to be clairvoyant to intuit how you lived enmeshed in infinite chains of infinitesimal causes. That August, when British Intelligence confirmed that Hitler had ordered Operation Sea Lion for the invasion, and large numbers of craft began to pass southward through the Straits of Dover each night, to assemble in the Channel ports from Calais to Brest. When therefore it became clear that the south coast was to be attacked, as well as or instead of the east. When after France collapsed, in Britain it might have appeared logical to feel trapped in a hopeless situation beyond our ability to battle our way out of. But in fact most people seemed to cheer up, and point out that the French had been bloody useless allies anyhow. Hell, there was even a certain satisfaction in the prospect of a straight fight to the finish with Germany. And the first Canadian contingent had turned up to help, that was good.

There was the wireless in the kitchen, with its bulletins about Fighter Command and the Luftwaffe shooting it out in the skies. About Bomber Command attacking the assembly ports on the French coast. About British destroyers and motor torpedo-boats in action against the would-be invaders' ships. And in the library, there were letters. Familiar voices, from Palestine, from Burma.

In August – when the greatest air battle was fought on the 15th. Fought on a front of five hundred miles, with a lot of squadrons fighting twice that day and some of them three times. When by night the tally of aircraft shot down was seventy-six German to thirty-four of ours. Not that anybody had those figures at the time. Both sides overestimated their successes tremendously.

In September – which was the month when the Luftwaffe switched from attacking Fighter Command's air fields and sector headquarters and radar stations, and began to bomb London. September was when the invasion had to go ahead before the equinoctial gales, or be postponed till the next year, and on the 5th reconnaissance recorded an increase of the armada of barges at Ostend. On the 6th, German bombers struck at ports on the English south coast, and the 'Yellow' invasion alarm was issued, which meant *Probable attack within three days*.

That was the month when Hitler kept postponing the decision to invade, or sometimes postponing the date on which he would decide. Naturally, no one in Britain knew that. At Edingthorpe it turned out also to have been about the time when Jack wrote home: *This invasion of yours seems to be hanging fire. Why don't you go ahead and have the damned thing?* A remark which – weeks later, when this missive arrived – caused that lieutenant's father to snort, and his mother to protest, 'Charlie, you were young once. Long ago.'

On the 7th, while the Luftwaffe were unloading bombs over the London docks and the surrounding slums, the code-word 'Cromwell', which meant *Invasion imminent*, was issued. That night, Eastern and Southern Commands' forward coastal divisions were at action stations, and a lot of Irregular commanders, including Charles Lammas, called out the Home Guard by ringing the church bells. At Whitehall, the Chiefs of Staff knew that barges appeared to be moving to forward stations in the Channel, and German Army leave had been cancelled. At Edingthorpe, Sonny Hannant, George Morter and Davey Strike knew, because Mr Lammas was explaining it to them, that this week moon and tides were favourable to a landing.

The next morning, the invasion was expected from hour to hour. Then all that week, in the Manor kitchen Mrs Fox, the Meades and Charles and Blanche Lammas listened to reports of the bombing of London, where over a thousand people had now been killed. To reports of raids on other cities. Reports of the days' air battles, in which the German bombers were suffering heavily, and their fighters again and again failed to win the clear victory they were after.

On the 15th, the last great engagement of the Battle of Britain was fought. Lammas sawed up firewood all afternoon, came in at dusk to be told by the scone-bakers and broth-simmerers about the onslaught of more than two hundred bombers and seven hundred fighters – *could* they have been that many? he wondered, scrubbing his hands under the tap – against English cities. Still, Janet Fox hastened proudly to let him know, our lads had been giving it 'em back all right. (Petey had always been her favourite nephew, and his hard work greasing RAF engines at Coltishall lay behind Goering's set-backs if anything did.) At the time, the British claimed a hundred and eighty-six German planes shot down that day. And though after the war it turned out that the attackers' losses had been fifty-six to the defenders' twenty-three, Mrs Fox had the essence right – Fighter Command was winning. And that night and the following day, Bomber Command attacked the shipping prepared ready at Antwerp, Boulogne, all along that coast.

One way and another it wasn't a period when Lammas had much time for rereading letters. Then that autumn, when the bombing of Britain went on night after night, and German submarines were attacking Atlantic convoys, for a while Italian activities in the Mediterranean meant that no correspondence from the Sherwood Rangers reached Edingthorpe.

When Jack's next letter did arrive, it began: *Dear Mama and Papa, judging by the BBC, the bombers seem to have taken to roosting in Pratt's Wood.* The boy wasn't far wrong, Bill Meade reckoned, when that afternoon Lammas and he trudged off there to shoot pigeon.

Bobbie's letters were always a tonic. Remarks jotted down in Cairo, about a fellow who'd been at Eton with the Hedleigh brothers, and now was off to join the Somaliland Camel Corps. An account of a sixteen-year-old girl called Antoinette, *always at the* plage, for whom *I entertain a, for me, surprisingly virtuous affection*, and for whom he'd been to the bazaar to buy a phial of lily of the valley. Then a rattle of anecdotes from Palestine, about Susanna Fitzwilliam who was *here with her uncle's entourage*, and *playing around with Tony Fairfax;* but who then, according to a later scrawl, *broke her collar-bone in the ladies' race, poor girl.*

Jack's . . . Well, his letters were *meant* to be read in that Edingthorpe library – that was the great thing about them. Of course, he didn't say so. But his mother knew, and his father knew. His sheets of paper were intended for the Chinese box, or the English walnut writing-case, or the folder that someone had had made out of an old Indian Army sabretache, just as plainly as he was intended for that house, if he came safe home.

That house, or another in the neighbourhood like it. First Cambridge again, to get his degree. Then a Norwich architectural practice. Just like his Uncle Geoffrey whom he'd never known. Jack with his oarsman's shoulders and his even temper and his even gaze. Jack and most of the young men in all the countries at war, who wanted nothing more complicated than to get back to the ways of life they happened to know and therefore liked, get back to houses and to work like their fathers' and uncles'.

'It's going to be such a dispersal,' Blanche had said. But early in the war, the dispersed writers of letters addressed to Edingthorpe Manor were none of them in battle, and could sound marvellously like their old selves.

Those were library evenings when it was companionable for his parents to read Jack's account of climbing Mount Carmel, or sailing a dhow off Acre. He not only appeared unlikely to come to much harm; he was manifestly having the time of his life. Dancing in a club in Jaffa. Then off with the Transjordan Frontier Force on Arab mounts through a defile till they reached Petra, where the temples and the amphitheatre and the tombs were not built, but sculpted out of the red mountain-sides – steps, columns, façades, chambers, everything. And the whole city dead, apart from the wind. Dead, apart from the lizards and rock pigeons.

Charles would watch Blanche reading about how next day Tim Farne and Jack and their Frontier Force companions had ridden on to the

Crusader castle at Kerak. He would think of how sometimes she would lie at night struggling to drag the air into her lungs just like before the war. For reasons of nerves strung intolerably tight. Reasons of heart-strings played upon by events, by the world's proceedings, by what seemed to be destiny, in ways scarcely to be borne. She having sat it out like this before. Having kept busy, and cheerful, and waited.

He'd watch her in the library lamp-light, as she read, or knitted socks or jerseys, or rolled bandages. He'd think of the gallant way she was forever biking off to Happisburgh to teach that First Aid course. The equally gallant way she kept changing out of her work-a-day clothes each evening, tidying her hair, putting on one of her Art Deco bracelets maybe, or the coral necklace Michael had brought her back from the East.

Blanche had always liked her hard, glittering things. Never possessed anything approaching the arsenals of precious metals and precious stones which fortified a Sarah Hedleigh or a Chiara Zanetti, of course. But she liked the few gold bits and pieces she had, and the few emeralds and rubies and amethysts; and in war time she went on wearing them with just the right dash, her husband thought.

Those evenings, Jack was there, unmistakably. Bobbie too – returned a London boy in Norfolk for his holidays, returned happy. But Jack, as a tousle-headed child sprawled on the rug to read *Peacock Pie* or *Alice* . . . When Charles looked at Blanche across the hearth, he could see the boy lying between them. Then Jack a few years older, with a novel by Hardy, or a volume of Kent's designs, or Soane's. Jack who'd remember the nuthatch which used to come to his father's library window, and knew the wagtails that were always flitting on the lawn, and who'd remember the year a flycatcher made her nest in the old iron lantern over the stable door. Charles would watch Blanche when she glanced up from her knitting, and he'd know she was seeing the boy there, seeing him with an ache of such headlong love that it was better not to speak of it. Of course, they did speak of their son, all the time – but lightly. The protective longing, the love that undid you because it was irrevocable . . . That they did not talk about.

Right from the first departures overseas of that war-time dispersal, Charles Lammas was conscious that this was only the beginning, those voices were going to recede a lot further off. In one way, or another. Or in ways not yet imagined – though the imagination could be damnably active. While Bobbie's letters, and Jack's, and Georgia's, with their stories and their jokes and their enquiries after the Edingthorpe dogs, were still barely to be differentiated from their old peace-time chatter . . . Sooner or later, those letter-writers were going to go deeper into the war. Those voices were going to change. Would reach him, if they reached him at all, from . . .? But then in his mind he might hear Jack's footsteps in the hall, his voice calling something. Or Bobbie whistling one of those songs he liked – 'I'm putting all my eggs in one basket', or 'Dancing cheek to cheek'. Lammas would frown, glance round distractedly at his bookcases.

In 1940 the Sherwood Rangers had seen little action, beyond helping to quell a riot or two in Tel Aviv. But the next spring – the spring when Germany invaded Yugoslavia and Greece – the address which Jack gave at the head of his letters altered.

It had been Notts S.R. Yeomanry, Palestine. Then the designation Middle East Force had been added. Now it became B Battery, Notts S.R. Yeo, 15th Coastal Regiment, M.E.F.Z.

Most of the regiment, including Bobbie's squadron, had been sent to Libya – where Rommel had just arrived to take command of the German forces. But B Squadron, which now was B Battery, had gone to what Jack called *the land of* Z. Which omega of a country it was not difficult for him to hint, and his parents to guess, was Crete.

13

—⁂—

Georgia Burney's first letters from the Shan Hills to Norfolk were addressed to Dear Godmother Blanche and Godfather Charles, and were all about how glorious it was to be home, but even so she missed the Edingthorpe spaniels horribly.

Here at Maymyo the monkey had died, and been buried under Mummy's most splendid japonica. But the parrot Blenheim and the terrier Angus were alive and kicking. Mummy and Daddy sent their love. It was *wonderful* to see Ricky again, but he was *quite* outrageous — so she wouldn't write about him.

Henrietta honestly had been a darling to let her ride her grey so much these last years. She knew she'd said thank-you before, but she wanted to say it again. They were please to give Ellen and Janet her love too. Did Honey still have a bit of toast and honey from the breakfast table? She hoped so.

As soon as Georgia had been dispatched back to her cloudily golden Orient, to that mystical condition Home about which the Lammas family had so resolutely teased her, Blanche put aside the faint suspicions of the girl she had felt, went back to thinking of her only affectionately. Even so, it was Charles who replied to Georgia's first exuberant communications — Blanche added a line or two at the foot of his letters. And soon, as the girl's letters began to change, her godfather was her only Edingthorpe correspondent.

At least, he was pretty certain he was. Georgia enquired after Jack sometimes, just as she enquired after Blanche and Henrietta, after Bobbie and Caroline, and sent him her love in the same sentences. It really did appear to her godfather that a clean break had been made between his two companions of that idyllic summer, when the girl had posed for her portrait, and Jack had come into the studio and read them *Twelfth Night*. So, slightly wistfully, in his letters to Georgia he made brief mention of Jack's comings and goings that last year of peace time, Hunt Balls and May Balls, Christmas partyings and Tuscan expedition and all. When the Sherwood Rangers went overseas, he told her where — so in her mind she could follow him a little, if she wished to.

As Georgia's letters changed . . . And as they went on changing. In number, for a start. She wrote Charles Lammas maybe four or five letters in '39, the next year twice that, and the next twice that again. By early '42, when Kuala Lumpur was abandoned to the advancing Japanese in January, when Singapore fell in February and Rangoon in March, Georgia Burney had, so far as it proved possible later to ascertain, stopped writing to anyone except her godfather, and to him she was scribbling her messages every few days.

Even more strange, she continued writing to him after she'd disappeared – continued her ghostly communing. Because disappear she did, for all that in England you could know. From that March and April, when the unopposed Japanese Air Force was bombing the towns of Burma – Meiktila and Prome and Mandalay, Thazi and Maymyo, Lashio and Taunggyi – which, being chiefly built of wood, caught fire easily.

After those weeks when hordes of refugees tried to escape to India – including Geraldine Burney, who set off in one of the trucks jammed with Maymyo civilians, with, among other worldly appurtenances, Blenheim in his wicker cage. After that night at the end of April when Burma Corps, or what was left of it, pulled out of Mandalay, and crossed the Irrawaddy by the Ava bridge and a ramshackle fleet of ferries, and at midnight the bridge was blown . . . After the retreat was over, if you hadn't got out to India, you must still be in there, alive or dead – and Japanese-occupied Burma was an oubliette.

No news trickled out. The diminishing British survivors were immured in war. Not only the British. A few other Westerners. Rather more Anglo-Burmese. Some Indians – those the Burmese didn't take the opportunity to slaughter. Any Chinese unwise enough to fall alive into Japanese hands. For that matter, the indigenous peoples of the country also: Burmans, Mons, Chins, Kachins, Karens . . . All were immured.

But Georgia Burney went on writing to Charles Lammas. Or rather – not to him, that was impossible; but for him.

They were not, in the normal sense, letters, her writings intended for his eyes, or for his spirit. A jumble of outbursts, attempts to set records straight, bewailings. Invocations of his spirit, summonings up of his understanding and his love.

Sheets of paper found in abandoned bungalows. An exercise book from the Saint Michael's Girls' Protestant School in Maymyo. Bits of different notebooks. And printed pages resorted to in less comfortable periods of the occupation. A Mandalay station time-table; scraps of paper filched or begged from Japanese soldiers; some sheets of music . . . She'd written all over them all, in a minute hand, with her hoarded pencil stubs. Writings, writings – many of which she'd begun with *Dear Godfather Charles*, as if somehow they might be wafted to him if the enemy occupation ever ended, or if she lived long enough to smuggle them out to India, or somebody else did after her death. Whispers from the oubliette.

So that was how Charles Lammas came into possession of his god-daughter's war, of her spiritual changings. At the time when Georgia was briefly controversial, he had – dumped on his lap, where he sat by his library fire – the truth. Fragmentary. Passionate. Shot through with her longings to know the simplest things – who was still alive, and where; how to get food for tomorrow. Shot through with her pride, and, in equal measure, with her self-hatred. Written often in circumstances so loathsome, and in the intermittences of sufferings so atrocious, that . . . Well, their first effect was that Lammas wept. It was true that with age and ill-health he was increasingly given to tears. But the contrast with the letters she had written him before the occupation, before the ruin of that happy state of the soul she had unthinkingly called Home, was dreadful.

So by the end Charles Lammas had two parcels of his goddaughter's outpourings of her heart and mind to him. There were the letters which, while Britain was already at war in the West but not yet in the East, started coming thick and fast, and changed in spirit too, seemed to come from someone who was changing all the time. Then nothing, from '42 until '45. And then, after the silence, out of the silence . . .

He kept her writings in a drawer in his library desk – kept her voice there. Kept his genie there . . . If, as he once remarked, she was really one of the jinn from the mountains of Kâf, one of the good jinn who are supremely beautiful. Which she certainly was not when that brigade liberated Maymyo.

Only her side of their correspondence survived the war. His letters to her before Burma was lost had vanished by the time the country was reconquered. The subsequent letters which, in the hope she were alive in some prison camp somewhere, he tried to get to her through Red Cross channels, never arrived.

14

In 1941, Georgia's letters from the Shan Hills still had their old light-heartedness. She could sound just as young as Jack, writing from *the land of Z*. But tangled up in her merry chatter about not much, there were other elements.

Lammas already knew her Maymyo society, and it wasn't the cast of characters which changed much, nor what they got up to. Some Anglo-Burmese families, who sent their children to the government English High School (those of undiluted British blood were generally shipped to England for their education, as she had been), whom her mother did not frequent but with whom Georgia had made friends. Young officers of the King's Own Yorkshire Light Infantry, stationed at Maymyo, and always game to leave the cantonment for a swimming party at the waterfalls, or for mixed doubles on the club's tennis courts. Young men who worked for Steel Brothers, or for the Bombay Burmah Teak Company – no less keen on dining out.

The hill station year had its rituals that didn't vary much. The golf tournament . . . Here Georgia Burney was abrasive, wrote to her godfather that she reckoned golf was the most suburban, middle-class, worst-sort-of-British fiddle-faddle ever invented, what did he think?

Fancy dress parties . . . Here she always seemed to be in the thick of things. She was Scheherazade on the night of the Maclarens' dance, when Amy Foster got engaged but Roberta Gillway was sick, threw up frightfully poor sweetheart in Mrs Maclaren's bed of lilies. The next time, Ricky was on leave. Georgia went as Emma Hamilton, with her father looking very distinguished as Sir William Hamilton, she recounted to Lammas, and her brother as Lord Nelson – Ricky whom she hardly saw all evening, he was such a tearaway success, with his empty sleeve she'd pinned up, and the black patch she'd fastened over his eye, though she wasn't sure if Nelson wore a black patch.

Then at Christmas for the play . . . To be quite honest, she didn't think plum pudding tasted right in the tropics, but this was a view so heretical she would only mutter it to her godfather, who was not to betray her. Well, anyhow, last Christmas they'd acted *The Importance of Being Earnest*, and she'd been such a wow as Cicely that she'd been asked to play the part again when the performance was revived in honour of the Governor's next visit, expected in June. But she wasn't having that.

She was holding out for the part of Gwendolin next time. A lot more dashing, didn't Godfather Charles agree? *I am glad to say that I have never seen a spade.* That was the line she wanted. By the way, had he *really* dug up the Edingthorpe tennis court?

Charles Lammas smiled, to remember the girl aged twelve on her first Norfolk winter holiday, rummaging in the nursery dressing-up chest for what finery caught her fancy for the charades. It was good also to think of stiff old Alex Burney being coaxed into making an appearance as Sir William, with his daughter as wild Emma, no doubt in sumptuous glad-rags, and his son as her lover. Nice for him, Lammas hoped, if he could be amused enough to do that. Who was it who'd painted that portrait of Emma Hamilton, the one she'd liked, she'd hung? George Romney, that was right. Stylish on his part; stylish on hers . . . and sexy.

No, the principal figures in Georgia's cast remained predominantly the same ones – though a few of them might be surmised to have taken to playing double rôles sometimes, gone in for a bit of shape-changing. About her mother, she was amiably wicked. One of her earliest letters from Burma had been all about what a shame it was that her father never took his family with him on his tours of duty. Other Forestry Officers elsewhere had been known to. His predecessor here had, she'd learned. With four elephants to carry his wife and children, their tents, their cooking gear, all the paraphernalia. Could Godfather Charles *imagine* what fun? Off for a couple of months up-country, with the mahouts, with the syce and the horses, with a whole entourage. High on a swaying howdah beneath a parasol, from village to village, into the forests for week after week . . . Had her godfather read *Elephant Bill?* She was halfway through it right now. And she didn't care how long it took – and Daddy could leave Mummy behind at Maymyo if that was what he preferred . . . But sooner or later, she was going to persuade him to take her on his next up-country tour.

She did, too. That expedition was part of the idyll which Georgia's last peace-time year became, and her godfather was glad for her. Glad too for Alex, that the last time he set off into his green, crepitating fastnesses toward the Chinese border, into those outermost and filmiest skeins of the imperial cobweb, he had his daughter beside him on his second horse, and her kit roped beside his on one of the pack elephants, and the syce following behind with two spare mounts instead of one.

Lammas thought about that tour of duty again and again, afterwards. He rejoiced that in the nick of time father and daughter had allowed themselves that idyll, had been allowed that. The following year, when he didn't know what had happened to either of them, but the likelihoods were fairly grim. When Japanese officers were being driven around comfortable, pretty Maymyo in cars left behind by the routed British. He thought of those forested mountains, where no roads ran, none that a car or a tank or a truck could use, and where if you emerged on a scarp the only imperial presence would be an eagle soaring. Away there, Charles Lammas supposed, sitting in his English library, probably the retreat of one empire and the advance of another had made mighty little difference at all.

Even before then, Lammas was feeling isolated, and annoyed with himself for letting it discourage him sometimes. That was one reason why he responded so alertly, when it became clear that Georgia had a spate of things she wanted to write to him about, and another spate of questions she wanted him to answer. That was what lent sharpness to his gratitude for the sullen-mouthed and murky-eyed little emissary from Burma that Alex had offered him, made him hope he'd sent her back as an interesting emissary to receive. Lent sharpness to his pleasure that Alex and she had found the sense to escape up-country together, and to his envying them, and to his missing her.

Isolated . . .

Well, at least Alex Burney continued to write occasionally, supplemented his daughter's effusions. But Charles Lammas was cut off by the war from a number of old friends. From Giacomo Zanetti, whose acerbic judgements of Italy's unprovoked attack on Greece would have been worth listening to, and of how after a week the defenders' counter-attack had already been driving them back. From Guy Rivac, one of whose sons *had* been wounded by British Naval gunfire at Mers-el-Kebir, and died a few days later.

Cooped up in his neighbourhood as he was, Lammas enjoyed it even when he managed to get as far afield as Acle, which was fifteen or twenty miles from Edingthorpe, and where Bernard Fletcher was in charge of Air Raid Precautions. It was just like the old times, to sit by his fire-side for an hour – only the chat would turn not only to familiar local things, but also to the new airfields being constructed all over the county, and the motor torpedo-boats operating out of Yarmouth. And all the while . . . As the war went on, what had been the staples of a pleasant existence contented Lammas less and less. Things that should have been the same, war or no war. Old friendships.

It had been good to be alive in England that first war summer. That July when Hitler offered to make peace, but by the time the Foreign Secretary had got around to formulating his brush-off, the BBC and the newspapers, quite on their own initiative, had dismissed the idea. That summer when the possibility of giving up the fight was not something the War Cabinet ever discussed. When the American ambassador was reporting to Washington that Britain was finished, and all round the world most of the bloody experts were yowling the same dirge, but here when everybody should have despaired they cheered up. That terrific pride rearing up in people. That determination not to be shoved around.

But now, with the trawler captains making money hand over fist. The farmers too, they were having a good war and no mistake. Now, with the papers jingoistic, and the news generally depressing, and often horrifying. There were days when to be united with Blanche by discussion of vegetable patches, and by unvoiced anxiety for Jack, didn't seem much. (The horses had been put down at the start of the second war winter, for lack of forage. The ponies remained in one paddock. There were pigs in the other.) There were days when Charles Lammas couldn't banish his sense that he was living among the remnants of his old zests – and then it was good to open one of Georgia's envelopes. It was good to read about Sister Caterina, who was a recent addition to her Maymyo cast. About Christopher de Brissac, who in his letters also made mention of Georgia, and who appeared to be one of her shape-changers. Almost as amorphous as she was.

Sister Caterina was one of the Italian nuns in the Roman Catholic convent. There were others too with whom Georgia Burney had made friends: Sister Maria and the Mother Superior (who was not at all forbidding, Charles Lammas smiled to read), Sister Paola and Sister Teresa. By the time that in the West the German Army had conquered Greece, and everyone was wondering whether the Axis were next going to attack Malta or Crete, or even conceivably Cyprus, in the somnolent British East young Sister Caterina and Georgia had clearly struck up a tremendous alliance.

Still young, she was. In her early twenties. And with wonderfully beautiful black eyes, wrote her enthusiastic friend, who had always envied girls the colour of whose eyes was without ambiguity. Indeed, Caterina was always so bubbling over with merriment, and she had the most beautiful wrists and ankles you could imagine, so one was tempted to feel it was a shame she . . . And so young, she had joined the Order, Godfather Charles would hardly believe it, so terribly young! But she came from a dreadfully poor family of course. And she was in love with her Church, truly she was, you couldn't not see that. In love with her Saviour, in the most ecstatically spiritual way – you only had to watch her when she was praying before an image of Christ.

Yes, she'd gone with Caterina to her church, Georgia wrote. Well, she sat in a pew while her friend prayed. Godfather Charles wasn't to fret, she wasn't getting too religious. At least, she didn't think so – and he'd always encouraged her to visit churches, hadn't he? This was just like going to Paston church with the wreath for Michael Mack's window. Or like going to Edingthorpe church on Christmas Eve, or on Armistice Day, or for Harvest Thanksgiving. Or like going to Knapton church to see those wonderful ranks of carved angels in the roof. Had he been to Knapton recently, to see the angels?

Anyhow, to go back to what was far more interesting – Caterina wasn't just mad about her religion, she was mad about everything else too. The trees in the botanical garden when they flowered, the Shan children you met in the bazaar . . . Caterina and she loved the same sorts of things, or they loved them in the same way. Even so, with those luminous black eyes – if Godfather Charles saw her he'd want to paint her, that was for sure – and with that sweet nature, it *did* seem a waste that . . . But you had to remember that she was contented as she was. Come to think of it, that was an idea – after the war, would Godmother Blanche and he come out to Burma? Mummy and Daddy would love to see them, and then he could paint Caterina if he wanted to. Perhaps they'd have to ask the Mother Superior if that would be all right. But she didn't see why it shouldn't be.

Fizzy talk about her new friend, mixed up with *The Importance of Being Earnest*, and mixed with how funny it had been that Mummy hadn't *wanted* to come up-country with them, because of all the gossip and the bridge evenings she'd have missed. That was how the last of the peace in the British East came sounding into Charles Lammas' head, that spring when Georgia was writing her letters at an increasing tempo and writing them longer, and with each morning's *Times* and each evening's BBC News it became more probable that the New Zealand and Australian, British and Greek troops on Crete were going to be attacked. (Letters from the Far East and from the Middle East were still usually reaching England, though often after long delays. Jack's last communication from *the land of Z* was dated 13 May, speaking of the asphodels which had been magnificent in the olive groves, and of the oleanders which were coming out. He asked for more socks. He asked if they had heard from Georgia.) That spring when one night the German bombers achieved their first slaughter in the Lammas' neighbourhood. It was at Horning, on the river Bure. At the Ferry Inn that evening they couldn't have been as scrupulous with their black-out as they should have been, or maybe they were just unlucky. At any rate, the pub was full of people. Farm labourers. Marsh-men, wherry-men. Some

RAF fellows who'd decided to go for a drink there that evening, instead of at The Crossed Keys. The old boy who worked the ferry. It was a direct hit. Twenty of them were killed.

Fizz on the subject of how glorious it was to talk about Italy with Caterina – how she brought back those Tuscan morning walks to the village to buy milk, and Emanuela, and the white *maremmano* sheepdogs. (Georgia did not mention Francesco De Angelis with his chestnut hair, in the background of whose portrait she could be seen, sitting by the window.) But then in a flash she'd be writing about historical figures, or characters in novels or plays – writing about them all without varying her tone of voice, she didn't seem to recognise different orders of reality.

All those stories forever ringing in her head . . . Georgia lived them over and over again, the same each time and different each time, and she told her godfather about her relivings of them.

Stories from her father's Matter of Burma. Stories from Shakespeare – when she sailed from England, her godfather had given her his India paper edition, for the sake of their good studio times together. Then Catherine Earnshaw, Hetty Sorel, Tess Durbeyfield . . . they seemed to be alive in her head. Came and went, with nothing dreamy about them.

Girlish fizz about de Brissac too – Lammas was into his third year of reading that. The Lieutenant Colonel was her absolute hero, of course. (This was first proclaimed in her earliest letter, the one about their visit to the Shwe Dagon pagoda. But it was repeated, at intervals, right up until their transmutations had made such language hopelessly inappropriate.) He was *never* in Burma . . . This too was rehearsed, till it altered to the complaint that he was never in Burma enough. Then jokey confessions about how she was head over heels – which she always wrote as heels over head – in love with him, she couldn't possibly lie to her godfather about that. But the great Lieutenant Colonel lived *surrounded* by the most fashionable beauties, so what could a poor girl do? All the same, she'd refused a *charming* captain in the Yorkshires – Godfather Charles was not to breathe a word about this to Mummy. And when C de B *was* in the colony she locked herself in a kind of purdah, absolutely kept her silly face for his eyes only, in the hope that he might take pity on her breaking heart, or at least notice that she adored him. Why, his ship's docking at Rangoon meant that up here at Maymyo she *immediately* stopped going in for any form of jollification. But, alas . . . Blind as a bat and deaf as an adder, de B.

Georgia clearly rather enjoyed these frivolous confessions of hers. Flaunting her adoration of his old friend was, Lammas mused more than once, another form of flirtation, after all.

And yet, tangled up with the hill station twitter and tangled up with King Mindon Min who'd held his court at Mandalay, Blaise Pascal – because, it transpired, Christopher had given her that philosopher's *Pensées*. What did Godfather Charles think of Pascal's famous wager? His argument that, although there was no evidence for God's existence, it was rational to believe. Because if you committed yourself to a life of faith in God, and it turned out to be justified, you inherited the Kingdom of Heaven; and if it turned out to be false, you hadn't lost much, if anything. Christopher had been explaining this audacious wager to Caterina and her. She thought she'd understood it right.

Times when Georgia babbled merrily. Times when her head echoed with stories and with marvels, and her echoes reached her godfather. Times when her lithe, happy mind made him reflect bitterly on his own fireless thinking. But she was not the first of his dispersed voices to recede farther away.

15

—◦◦◦—

All through late May, in the kitchen at Edingthorpe Manor they kept turning on the wireless to hear how the Battle of Crete was going.

In the first day's fighting, the defenders held the airfields at Maleme and Heraklion, and the Navy wrought havoc on the German convoys. But after that the news was always bad. Positions were lost. Counter-attacks succeeded for a while, and then failed. Ships were sunk by German dive-bombers.

Then the news was of retreat across the island. Of flotillas sailing from Alexandria to evacuate Allied troops by night from the southern beaches. Of ships carrying rescued soldiers attacked by dive-bombers and fighters.

After five nights' evacuation, the flotillas could no longer get through. The defeat was over.

At Edingthorpe, for ten days they waited for word. Then the post-boy bicycled up the lane with a telegram. Handwritten. Dated 10 June, and stamped at Norwich on the 11th. Blanche was crossing the yard, and took it from the boy.

Regret to inform you of notification received from Middle East that Lieutenant J.M. Lammas reported missing 1 June 1941. Any further particulars will be forwarded as soon as received. Under Secretary of State for War.

Blanche stood, holding the telegram. She stood very still. Then she went to look for her husband.

16

—◊—

That day, Charles and Blanche Lammas did not talk to each other much. They had waited during the Battle of Crete, when the bad news from the Mediterranean had come mixed up with news of the German victory in the Western Desert, and the only British success had been the sinking of the battleship *Bismarck* in the Atlantic. They had waited after Crete had been lost, when it remained true that hopes and fears did not require the embellishment of conversation, and some facts and figures about the campaign began to be known. Over two thousand British and Commonwealth sailors had been killed at sea. But in those last May nights the Royal Navy had taken seventeen thousand soldiers off the evacuation beaches. Once, to be courteous to a vilely sympathetic neighbour, Charles allowed himself a brusque: 'Naturally, I hope the lad's all right.' But otherwise he was only heard to fall back on loyalty to his old Service, and growl that it was still the same old story. The Navy had rescued the Army after another of its disasters.

Then, after that first telegram, there was still nothing for it but to wait. Janet and Ellen both sobbed copiously when Charles Lammas told them that Jack had not made it back to Alexandria, but then they stopped; and when they'd pulled themselves together, they didn't say a lot. Sidney said, 'That's a bad business, that is', and 'Oh dear oh dear, poor Mrs Lammas'. Then he coughed a bit, and used his handkerchief, and went down to his runner beans. The house was very quiet, that day.

Missing . . . So much it might mean. So little it told you. Blanche did not cry – she whose eyes had glistened at Mary Oldfield's funeral; and who at Noel Jarvis' memorial service had needed to try extremely hard not to weep, had touched Jack's talisman of a letter and had sung 'In pastures green.' She went about her day's work with a firm step.

At lunch-time, they went through the motions. You could hold on tight to the fact that *reported missing* was not *reported killed in action*, was not that yet, and might never be. You could each hear the other's murmurous spirit holding hard to that – but there was no call to discuss it. Nor what the battle-fields of Crete must be like now, which for days they had been unable not to think of. Gliders crashed in the olive groves, German dead and British dead sprawled around them. Parachutists hooked up obscenely in the trees – preserved from the hungry dogs, these dead, but equally swarmed over by flies. Suda Bay, where the dive-bombers had set ships on fire, which were wrecks now. Where bloated corpses washed on the tideline. The bombed-out streets of Chania. Burial parties getting to work, in the reek of putrefaction. Shambling columns of prisoners being herded along, half-starved, desperate for water. The gunning-down of any Cretan who resisted his island's invaders. The rounding up of villagers as hostages and shooting them.

In the afternoon, Charles Lammas went to his studio, but he couldn't work. He fiddled about with this and that. Later, a car drew into the yard. He went out. It was Anne Daubeney, with her grey-flecked hair, and her grey-flecked eyes.

'Charlie . . .' Her gaze held his steadily. 'I've heard. Never mind how. Well, through the Kelletts, actually. He's the new colonel, after Yarborough. But of course you know that. I heard, so I . . . Here I am. Is she . . ? And you. Oh, my dear Charles.'

Faced suddenly with Anne who had lost her husband young and her son as a child, faced with her eyes and with her love for Blanche and for him, Charles Lammas' control of his own eyes came closer to wavering than it had during the entire war. He looked away to the orchard, frowned as if the prospect displeased him.

'Blanche is fine. I mean, she's bearing up fine. We expect that he's been taken prisoner, you know. Most likely outcome, I think. In due course, the Red Cross will . . . If he wasn't too badly wounded, he'll be all right. Now, let us give you a cup of tea. Not sure exactly where Blanche is, but she's around the place somewhere.'

They moved across the gravel toward the house. Charles added, 'Oh, yes . . . one thing. Your goddaughter is still at school. End of her last term, actually. And we've decided not to tell her anything till we've got more certain news.'

Anne Daubeney nodded. She put her hand in his arm as they walked.

Blanche seemed nowhere to be found. They went upstairs. For a moment Charles thought she might have gone to be miserable in Jack's bedroom – but she was in theirs. She was sitting at her dressing-table, looking at something she was holding in her hands.

When she heard their footfalls, she made as if to put away whatever it was. But then she thought better of it.

'Anne,' she breathed, looking over her shoulder at them. And then, as they approached and could see the gold watch and chain in her fingers, she glanced from her husband to her friend and back.

It was the watch and chain that Tom Carraway's sisters had given her, which she had always kept in one of her jewellery boxes to give to Jack when he was twenty-one. But when that birthday had come, the Sherwood Rangers were already overseas.

17

Charles Lammas left Anne with Blanche, went downstairs. For days and days he'd been what people called sensible. But now . . . That word: *missing*. Anne coming to find them. How she'd stood before him in the yard, looked at him with those grey eyes. Then Blanche at her dressing-table, getting out the gold watch that the Carraway girls had – which last winter Blanche had written to Jack in Palestine to tell him was – which Jack who . . .

Lammas' brain was in a whirl. Of course, in company he'd go on being imperturbable. Would be unable not to. Too late to teach an old dog new tricks, thank God. But he wasn't in company, and he didn't want to be. He strode out of doors with his thoughts coming pell-mell, not making much sense, making such a lot of sense that you took damned good care not to see the whole picture and not understand too clearly, only then of course you did anyway.

The post-boy was there again. Lammas checked his striding, took the afternoon's letters, flicked through the envelopes. Nothing that might be about Jack.

Nothing of much interest, except . . . That was Peregrine Bracknell's handwriting. He opened it, glanced. Perry wrote that he honestly couldn't see how they could make a success of a biggish retrospective of Charlie's work, under the present dismal circumstances. So they'd have to put it off. But not indefinitely. As soon as this lousy war was over, it would be the first show he put on.

Oh, and a letter from Georgia. Watching the boy pedal away, Lammas put Bracknell's letter in his pocket, shoved his finger under the flap of Georgia's envelope, ripped it open with unaccustomed impetuosity. Then he stuffed that too into his pocket, unread. He tramped off at random toward the water-meadow.

Being sensible about things . . . Since the Battle of Crete, his mind had been frozen around that idea. Since he'd had this long-awaited, new experience of having his son in a battle. Unfortunately, on the side that lost.

A block of ice, his mind – frozen around Jack, who must firmly be supposed to be alive. Around Blanche, who by day must have the comfort of his strength of heart whenever her eyes sought his. By night also, when she lay with all her nerves winched so tight they were hard. Around

Henrietta, whose last letter from her brother had been as cheerful as ever, on the subject of how he wished he'd been with them when the Meades and she went ferreting in the Worstead Park warren. Around Henrietta who at school was concentrating on passing her exams, one hoped, and not giving too much idle thought to what shot and shell did to young men's bodies. Not thinking yet – would please God never have cause to think – of Jack not Jack any more. What had been Jack a blood-mired thing, the worse for several days under the Cretan sun, the worse for dogs and crows and rats, tipped with others into a pit.

But now the block of ice in Charles Lammas' head was melting and no mistake. Anne would stay with Blanche for an hour or two, that was good. Indeed, he'd ask her if she could stay for supper and spend the night. And now . . . Out of sight of the Manor's windows, he let himself swing over the stile with a violence which nearly demolished that rickety structure, strode on with his ideas pelting.

Now . . . John and Anne Daubeney had been good friends of Tom Carraway's, had hoped that after that war Blanche would accept him at last. As she might have done, Michael being dead – only Carraway was dead too.

Now . . . That was a blackbird he could hear fluting from those alders. But the snag was, this hedgerow reminded him of coming here when Jack was a little boy to find nests for him to learn about. Coming along here in May, with the spaniels of fifteen years ago. Blackbirds' eggs, greeny-grey, mottled. Thrushes' nests mud-lined, their eggs bright blue with a few black spots – which made them more visible to marauding jays and magpies. Wrens' nests in ivy stumps. Telling Jack he could look for as long as he liked, but he mustn't touch, because the mother birds wouldn't like that and might desert. Those vanished, post-war years of his tremendous survivor's joy at being alive, at having everything Geoffrey had been denied. Having summer come, and a small son to take out to look for nests.

Now this. Still, it was a relief of sorts that Blanche's entire soul was so given to her ceaseless willing that Jack should be alive, that he didn't think she'd done much imagining of what might yet happen to him after the good news came that he was a prisoner of war – if it did ever come. How long was the German Army taking, these days, to make lists of its prisoners, get the lists to the Red Cross in Geneva? On the 1st, he'd been reported missing. Had not been on the last ships to leave Sphakia the night before. Ten days ago.

Lammas reached the wood, swung on his heel, came striding back along the meadow's side. Buttercups in the grass, and lady-smocks, and marsh orchids, he noticed vaguely, and a sunny June late afternoon. One way and

408   ~~~ William Rivière ~~~

another, perfect wedding weather, he snorted, and scowled at the bees flying in and out of his wife's hives, where Jack had often helped her with her
apiarist's tasks. Yes, birdsong so loud that a man could hardly hear himself
think his jumbled foolishness, and perfect bloody wedding weather, and
. . . We were back getting these same old War Office communications.
Reported missing, or *reported wounded*, or *reported killed in action*. And the fact that
all over Europe casualties were being reported, and a lot more casualties
were never getting reported, so that your son was a . . . If anything, it
made your sense of utter impotence worse. The fact that this renewal of
the old war had been seen coming and had been eminently avoidable, but
had not been avoided . . . So that now Anne was up in their bedroom,
talking to Blanche in her soft voice. It made your sense of the futility of
your life worse. And if Jack . . . It would finish Blanche. Finish her.

To and fro along the meadow hedge, with the blood thumping in his
head till it ached. Well, he was out of everyone's sight, which was a relief
for an hour.

Back and forth – with his brain that felt like an ice floe breaking up,
so that in retrospect that cold seemed to have had a merciful dulling
effect. Because it *was* intolerable. If you remembered the last war's dead. If
you remembered Armistice Day, and the hope. If you remembered: *Never
again* . . .

Blanche Lammas had been right, that frosty day of Noel Jarvis' memorial
service at Irstead. News of British Naval actions always made Charles
wince, deep down. From the first engagements of the war. From when
Warburton-Lee led his destroyers up the West Fiord at Narvik to attack
the German ships, and was awarded a postumous VC. Whenever ships
commanded by men of Lammas' generation were in action against the
enemy – particularly when they were in successful action.

Then for a while his Home Guard command kept him so busy it was
a palliative, staved off his sense of uselessness. But with the Battle of the
Atlantic being fought . . . And now this afternoon his thoughts came
so helter-skelter that even his longing to have been one of Admiral
Cunningham's captains in the eastern Mediterranean could not be a
straightforward one, but got entangled with his old naval lieutenant's
hatred of non-combatants' acceptance of young men's sacrifice. Hell yes,
he remembered that all right. Old men's Christian resignation, as they sent
troops to attack. The civilian population even managing to congratulate
itself on the fortitude with which it decided that these casualties were a
tragic necessity . . .

Lammas got fed up with striding to and fro in the meadow pointlessly. He went down to the stream, strode to and fro there instead, and his mind went on doing things he didn't want it to.

He'd remembered T.E. Lawrence, unfortunately. Remembered Jack reading *Seven Pillars of Wisdom* for the first time, sitting in the studio and turning the pages with that boyish keenness to find out. But then, thinking of his son who might already have been shot trying to escape, or who might be in some foul camp dying of his wounds or of dysentery . . . He'd remembered Lawrence in Damascus going into those Turkish barracks full of prisoners and dead and dying. Dead in whom the rats had gnawed red wet galleries. Swollen dead. Dead gone yellow and blue and black. Dead liquescent with decay. The wounded on their stinking pallets, no less fly-crept than the dead, muck dripping down to stiffen on the cement floor. Norgate had ridden into Damascus with Allenby's cavalry, when he was a pink-faced boy of twenty, and Lammas had asked him once whether Lawrence had been exaggerating or not. Norgate had said No, they'd stumbled on some unpleasant scenes.

Lawrence in those Damascus barracks with his stretcher party, carrying down the corpses, some of which could be lifted easily, though others had to be scraped up with shovels piecemeal. Jack who might have succeeded in slipping away into the hills when the Germans encircled the last few thousand British abandoned on the coast. Jack who otherwise, if he were alive, would have been marched in a column of prisoners to . . . Where? What? His father's attention jigged unprofitably from this to that. Pretty, all the clumps of agrimony growing along the banks of the stream, below the silver birches. Perry Bracknell who . . . He hadn't been up to London for weeks, but next time he got up he'd have a chat with him. But not now. Mustn't leave Blanche even for a day till they knew Jack was alive. Yes, yes – but in all this mental welter there was something else. Something at the back of things.

Charles saw Blanche and Anne come sauntering down the lawn toward the lily pond. He was so restless that, without thinking, he paced vigorously away in the opposite direction, after a wide sweep around the garden approached the house on the terrace side.

Alex Burney's clipped way of saying: *of course*. Giacomo Zanetti, who had the same awareness of patterns of events you were never going to have avoided. They came into it, those two.

Alex at the Travellers', sipping his claret, making his atheist's dry observations on how there were horrors unbearable to endure without that faith in God which made all things possible, or anyhow made more things possible. There were also, he had elaborated, setting down his wine glass with a too artificially dismissive smile – there were also horrors intolerable to commit without that faith.

Giacomo talking about how when the Italian Army broke at Caporetto the men started shooting their officers. *Of course*. About how the Duce was determined to pitch the country into a new war. *Of course* . . . Though Giacomo didn't often actually say *of course*, because usually they spoke Italian together, even at Edingthorpe. He chewed his cigar, he shrugged his fat shoulders. He said, *Naturale*. He said, *Ma certo*.

Below the terrace wall, the viburnums and the veronicas had been in flower for weeks. Often in May a cold wind had blown off the sea; but now the air was still, and the terrace smelled, Lammas supposed distractedly, like Arabia Felix must have done.

He stood irresolute, wondering what else was lurking at the back of his mind.

Missing . . . That word. It kept whispering. Lost. Not known about. So that two women, two friends, who stood by peaceful water on a summer evening . . . That was it! Looking at water! He'd stood, oh, a few years back . . .

Absently, Lammas dropped into one of the wicker chairs. He forgot about the air smelling like Arabia Felix.

He'd been out shooting – that was it. At Bure, after a snow-fall. In Black Horse Wood. And he'd pushed through some brushwood, and there had been the old duck decoy. Trees cut back around the black water. Snow-whitened earth. He'd stood, looking at the brace of call-duck swimming, looking at the ripples. And he'd thought about how war time could beat in your head in peace time, you caught that other rhythm swelling. And now . . .

He frowned at the viburnum flowers. Now peace time was the distant, faint rhythm. Now he was back with war time the dominant beat. War time so much more tyrannous in its dislocations, more perverse in its couplings, treacherous in its variations of tempo. So that . . . Well, you had hill station chatter and a War Office telegram in your pocket at the same moment.

Yes, when it came to perverse couplings . . . Lammas took them both out, weighed them in his fingers. Georgia would have no idea that her old friend had been reported missing, was perhaps already dead. Bobbie would know. Bobbie had quite likely already spoken to the last men of the regiment who had seen Jack on Crete. He'd know what shape his cousin had been in when last seen. But Georgia . . .

Her godfather spread out her letter on his knee. Maybe it would absorb his mind for a minute. He began to read.

18

—⁂—

Georgia's thoughts came just as pell-mell as her godfather's. She wrote about how seventy-odd years ago the Resident at Mandalay, whose name was Sladen, had travelled up the Irrawaddy as far as Bhamo, her father had told her. Then Sladen had taken the mountain trail into Yunnan, where the mule caravans plodded, and he had explored and he'd made plans for a railway. Of course, now there was the new Burma Road, built by two hundred thousand Chinese coolies, which ran three hundred and fifty miles from Kunming in Yunnan to Lashio in northern Burma. The road all the political rumpus was about. But Sladen's railway had never been built, and the mule caravans still crossed into China along the old trail.

Georgia wrote about how there were a few Japanese in Upper Burma. Photographers and barbers, chiefly. Navy spies and Army spies, respectively – that was the club joke going the rounds. Then, straight after this twitter, the girl wrote about what sounded like a long conversation, conducted on her parents' Maymyo verandah, between her father and Christopher de Brissac and her, all about the embargo on the sale of scrap iron and war materials to Japan, which President Roosevelt had imposed last dry season. Nearly half Japan's trade was with the United States was that right? – and her balance of payments was precarious. Would sanctions really have an effect on Japanese belligerence in China? or mean that war against Britain and America was *more* likely?

Charles Lammas read on, reflecting that it didn't sound like the sort of discussion in which hill station young ladies customarily joined. But, then . . . It reminded him of her last letter. In which one minute de Brissac was a dazzling figure, made much of by half the elegant ladies in the British East, whom the girl was reduced to hero-worshipping. In the next breath – Georgia's transitions were swift – he was Christopher. He sought her out whenever he was in the country – possibly even made a point of coming at every opportunity. They attended the same dances. He either invited her to join his party on excursions, or he took her on excursions. (This was left, presumably deliberately, imprecise.) He gave her books. Not novels. French, philosophical books, for heaven's sake. She had introduced him to her friend Sister Caterina. The unlikely trio were, apparently – Lammas smiled – in the habit of confabulating on such subjects as Blaise Pascal's thinking it reasonable to bet that God existed.

Jack was still there, aching in his head. Jack. Blanche's stricken eyes.

The oppressive, unbearably heavy feeling in his chest was still there, as if behind his ribs he had an anvil. Lammas made himself take Georgia's second page.

Nebulous, she seemed. And the more opaque and various, the more marvellously alive – because she switched straight from wondering what might follow if Japan extended her control of Indo-China from the north to the south, into telling her godfather about the first man who had been Agent for the Irrawaddy Flotilla Company. Back in 1862, according to her father, Dr Clement Williams, stationed with the Thayetmo garrison . . .

But Georgia broke off this story, (oh, it was too long, she'd tell him when the war was over), to report that the monsoon had reached Rangoon. Up here at Maymyo, they were over three thousand feet above sea level, so the heat was never plains heat. But down at Mandalay . . . So when the rains worked their way up-country, it would be a relief, though of course Mummy would complain and complain about the humidity. Anyhow, next dry season, Christopher and Daddy and she were going to take the ferry from Mandalay Shore up the Irrawaddy a short distance to visit the huge Mingun pagoda which King Bodawpaya had ordered to be built – but when he died, it had been abandoned. It had the most gigantic bell. Had she ever told Godfather Charles about the Mingun bell? Bigger than the one at Rangoon. The greatest bell in all the East. The Reverend Caldicot was coming with them, who ministered to all the Anglican communities up and down the Irrawaddy and the Chindwin. He had the most fun job in Burma, after Daddy's, she thought. She wanted Caterina to be able to come with them, but apparently the Mother Superior was likely to be sniffy.

Charles Lammas read on, that day of the first War Office telegram and the wedding weather. He still had that latest instalment of Georgia's – of whatever it was in her, a flowering it could seem like, an exuberant happiness indubitably – ringing in his head, three days later when a letter came from the War Office Casualty Branch in Liverpool.

I am directed to inform you, with regret, that a notification has been received from the Military Authorities in the Middle East that your son, Lieutenant Jack Michael Lammas, The Nottinghamshire Yeomanry, was reported missing on 1 June 1941.

No further information is available at present, but the Missing and Prisoners of War Department of the British Red Cross Society has been acquainted with the circumstances, and . . .

Any information received . . . Should news reach you . . . I am, Sir, your obedient Servant . . .

The following year, when Georgia Burney and her father were both unaccounted for after the Japanese conquest of Burma, Charles Lammas remembered those courteous War Office communications. One way and another, what with the British Army and the German Army and the Red Cross, in Jack's case that word *missing* was always going to have acquired more specific meaning in a while. After a few weeks . . . Enough weeks to reduce his mother to a gaunt-eyed wraith.

But the next year, when in East Anglia it was the usual cold rainy spring, and in the Irrawaddy plains the dead lay in the hot season dust and were uncounted and nameless. When the living were corralled up, or were left at large, left to the mercy of Japanese platoons and renegade Indian platoons, the mercy of deserters and freedom fighters and dacoits. Then when the rains began to fall, which in peaceful times had caused Geraldine Burney to complain about the humidity, but this year caused her son Richard, fighting his way out of the country toward Manipur among the survivors of the Gloucesters in Burma Corps, to be glad the torrents and the quagmires bogged down the pursuing Japanese. When all across the Irrawaddy plains the carcasses of people and animals sank into the dark mud, were kettle-drummed by rain, in that warmth and wetness became one with amorphous warmth and wetness. Then, when everybody still in Burma was *missing*, and the word could mean any vile thing you cared to imagine. *Missing, presumed interned.* Or: *Missing, presumed dead.* Or: *Missing, presumed* . . . Then, Lammas recalled the previous summer, when at least the uncertainty had been one you expected to see resolved before long.

But at the time, that June, with Jack's merry voice abruptly silenced, and Georgia's still carrying strong and clear . . . In those weeks, Charles felt all manner of wretched things, and one of them was that his anxiety for his son was somehow taken from him, or warped, or something, by his tireless anxious watching over Blanche and her fears.

Unfair. But that didn't stop it being true.

Not that Blanche was selfish in her love for their son. Not that she cracked up, either. She couldn't help the alterations to her countenance and in her eyes – but her conduct remained calm, and her voice only rarely betrayed her.

No . . . And it wasn't that Charles had forgotten that day at Morston, when he'd brought the crab-boat up the harbour channel past the wreck and the sand-banks and the seals, and his whole being had felt suffused with renewed love for his wife, he'd known his susceptible heart was back beside hers for good. But he also couldn't forget how that evening at Anne Daubeney's house he'd had that horrible dream, and he'd known that for Blanche and him all might be acceptably well, but something was irrecoverable, it was too late.

Oh, certainly he and she were anchored side by side now, till death came along and cut their warps. Especially since his stroke, and now with Jack missing. It would be Blanche who came up to his dressing-room, sat by his bed while he was dying – and quite right too. The only thing was, he still had a lot of work to put in on her income after his death.

Charles would recall that day when he'd fallen down in the yard. How he'd dragged himself into the greenhouse, and lain there. Then Blanche, who knelt down beside him. Her hands. Her voice.

Yes, but even so . . . When he tried to bring Jack wholly to mind, love him as he'd used to do . . . Dog-tired, his imagination felt. When he was alone – in Blanche's presence, it was hopeless – and he brought to mind why Jack had been born, who he really was. It was too late for something, or something was too late.

As if, so far as his wife and his son and daughter were concerned, he'd shot his bolt. Was that it? So he felt guilty – but also, in a sense, relieved. So that, although whatever occurred he'd go on loving them in the same way . . .

What a feeling to discover, at this miserable time! Still – yes . . . If any new note were ever struck in him – and it probably wouldn't be, and if it were it'd be a broken-down, prematurely old man's most hazy presentiment. But if . . . It would be elsewhere. Other. Remote.

In the library, eye to eye with Roland Lammas' melancholy self-portrait, Charles would remember how after the last war he'd shied away from his father's despair. Had been too taken up with living joyfully all the days of his vanity to pay much attention to Roland's decline toward death. He'd turn to the mantelpiece, where a framed photograph of Jack in uniform had joined the one of his uncle, and the Winged Victory.

19

—m—

Charles Lammas' head felt jarred with dissonance, those midsummer days and nights. What with Georgia's voice and Jack's silence, what with the BBC and the newspapers. Blanche's voice, too: its occasional trembling. Anne Daubeney's quiet voice. She came over to Edingthorpe a lot, at that time; was good at just being there, loyally.

Public voices that clanged, private voices that whispered. When the nights were the shortest of the year, Lammas went out on patrol at dusk with the others of their original platoon, because according to their rota it was his turn. And because Blanche had insisted that he was not to change duties with anyone on her account. She would manage to sleep or she would not, with or without him beside her. And because he hoped that in the quiet and solitude of the dark hours on Paston cliff, slowly his consciousness might feel less jarred.

If he gave himself a lonely stretch of cliff to patrol, the discord in his head might die down a bit.

It turned out that these were nights of momentous events. The first evening, when Norgate and Lammas with their guns over their shoulders were trudging through the lanes to join the others, they had both just heard on the News that Damascus had fallen.

Defended by Vichy French troops, not Turkish, this time. Attacked by a British force and a Free French force. But these differences didn't stop Lammas again recalling Lawrence who had stepped in his soiled robes and bare feet into that barracks become a charnel-house; and it didn't stop Norgate reminiscing about how they'd taken the place twenty-four years ago. Some magnificent Australian cavalry they'd had with them, and the Arab Army on their camels and their fiery little horses. Then Lawrence in a British Army Rolls-Royce escorted by Indian cavalry, and . . . But by God they looted, Mr Lammas, those devils of Arabs and Druze. No holding 'em. He hadn't by any chance brought a drop of Sir Julian's . . .? Well now, he wouldn't say no.

There had never been great reserves in the Edingthorpe Manor cellar, and what remained Charles and Blanche were keeping so as to be able to give Henrietta a dinner party or two, and maybe to cheer up Christmas a little, and above all for when Bobbie and Jack came home. Their war-time, plain meals were washed down with what people used to call Adam's ale. But the cellars beneath Bure Hall, which had for years enjoyed the benefit of Julian Hedleigh's buying and for that matter his father's before him, contained a plenitude of French wines and brandies and Scotch whiskies which . . . Well, when after about a year of hostilities it suddenly occurred to Hedleigh that nearly all his friends were less comfortably positioned, and that the nations' belligerence was resulting not only in boring meals (though not, naturally, at Bure, where the beef and pork and mutton were always abundant) but also in empty decanters, that good-hearted magnate launched himself upon some systematic giving. A contribution to the Allied endeavour which some of Sir Julian's neighbours were disrespectful enough to mock behind his back, muttering that his dishing out of his vintages and his malts did a damned sight more for the defence of the realm than his trotting in and out of the lobbies at Westminster. Others' amusement was more sly. It was the pleasure the man took in being such a decent fellow that they found risible, and how while he was slapping you on the shoulder he always contrived to mention cheerfully how many Home Guard platoons he'd raised from men on his Bure estates.

The first time that Julian asked Charles if 'this rotten war' was meaning that he found drinkable Scotch hard to come by, and added that if so he'd be delighted to send Phipps over with a case or two, Lammas had been a touch surprised. Still, he had replied automatically that at Edingthorpe they had all they required, thank you. But Hedleigh was not so easily rebuffed – and he knew that not only war-time shortages but also his old friend's reduced income might lie behind the Manor household's austerity. So he asked Sarah, who always knew about things like that, when old Charlie's birthday was, and had Phipps drive him over to Edingthorpe with the car well-stocked.

Two cases of Glenfiddich. Two cases of Glenmorangie. Two cases of some other fire-water so precious that Lammas had never heard of it, and his genial visitor could not help alluding to the fact that it had never been sold 'on the open market'.

'Now, don't be cross, old boy. I know perfectly well this war's a bloody . . . Just unload it, Phipps. You see, Charlie, Father bought gallons of the stuff, and if I live to be a hundred I'll never drink it all. Nor will Freddie, and it'll be much better if Mark doesn't try. And I know you like a glass of whisky in the evening.'

The next time Lammas was at Bure, Hedleigh insisted on taking him down to the cellars. Holding up a lantern, he led the way past arch after arch, each recess racked with hundreds of bottles of Bordeaux and Burgundy. Then on to the reserves of port, of champagne. He talked boisterously about what a mistake it would be to let all this good wine go down German throats. He made Lammas agree that 'it'd have to be quite some war' before his cellars were noticeably depleted, mentioned a number of their friends whom he'd cajoled into letting him cheer up their fire-sides.

So it was that Charles Lammas had taken to bringing a hip-flask with him when he went out with the platoon at night. And this evening, as they tramped along the lane with its verges waist-deep in cow-parsley and its hedges latticed with honeysuckle, Norgate's memories of Palestine and Syria were interrupted while he accepted Lammas' little silver flask, took a swig of the Honourable Member for East Norfolk's Glenmorangie.

The second evening, on the News they'd just heard of the German invasion of Russia – of Germany's surprised, it appeared, ally Russia.

So much for a quiet night when the clamour in your head might fade away, Lammas thought, trying to explain to George Morter and Sonny Hannant what manner of calculation had perhaps lain behind the Nazi-Soviet Pact, and what might lie behind its breaking. So much for hoping that for a night the world might stand back, leave you in peace with your private anxiety. Then there were tasks to portion out. Who would go to Edingthorpe church tower, and who to the towers at Paston and Bacton, and who to the cliffs. Then Norgate pronounced that Bonaparte had tried invading Russia, and look what had happened to him. And at any rate, it appeared now that the attack against this English coast of theirs might be postponed for a while, what did Mr Lammas think?

That night, sometimes a wind would blow off the sea, and later as mysteriously as it had started would die away. Then an hour afterwards, once more it would tatter the cliff-top grasses, and sough chill and briney for a while. The cloud-rack was high and diaphanous, and you could see a good many stars, and a few constellations – Vega, Cassiopeia. When the moon went behind the cobwebby vapour, you could still see it, and when it came clear again the shadows of the furze-clumps were sharply etched, and so were men's shadows with their guns sticking up over their shoulders.

As they tramped on their companionable sentry-go along the cliff, Norgate said, 'So them Russians are catching it now.'

Lammas said he'd been thinking exactly the same thing. Thinking of their own watch kept tonight. Men guarding the bridges at Coltishall and Wroxham and Acle. Men keeping watch on the dunes at Waxham, on the sea-wall at Palling – all over this district of theirs. And, at the same time, on the other side of Europe, in what had been Poland, in a country already fought over once in this war . . . Aerodromes being dive-bombed.

418 ~~ William Rivière ~~

Towns shelled. Villages set on fire. The panzer divisions going forward on a front of – could be the best part of a thousand miles, couldn't it, the front?

When Norgate began to puff a bit, and yawn, he sat down on a bank. Lammas went on pacing a few hundred yards along the cliff one way, and then a few hundred yards back. Not with his violent stride of the day the telegram came. As steadily as he could, in the hope of calming his mind. Thinking of Jack, with the same blurry pain that was always there. Thinking of all the people who tonight had sons who'd been reported missing. Thinking of how the night before, when he'd been pacing here with his .300 over his shoulder, and toward first light the birds had begun to sing, they'd started the war on the Eastern Front. They'd started that carnage. And here Norgate and he had talked about King Feisal and General Allenby, and how from the ridge overlooking the oasis of Damascus the British and Arab cavalry had looked down and seen the city had not been destroyed but shone pearly in the morning sun, its quiet gardens green beneath the river mist. He went on pacing, and he went on thinking – as since the fall of Crete he'd been unable not to – about how Jack might already have been killed, and Blanche lying awake willing him to be alive not know. And he, on sentry-go here, willing that same aliveness just as futilely. Or . . . This war didn't look as if it were going to be over in a hurry. God only knew how far into the future he might be trudging here, rain-cloud or moon-glimmer, and Jack might be being killed that moment, and Norgate and he would look up and east into the pre-dawn pallor when they heard the bombers flying back from their night raid.

Lammas' feeling of being powerless had never eaten into him with such acidity. From a titanic collision like that between Nazi Germany and Communist Russia, to the unknown fate of one lieutenant who happened to be your son . . . And it wasn't only his mastery of any events whatever that had been reduced to insignificance, so that he supposed his freedom just about extended to the decision whether to turn back toward Norgate now, or pace on and not turn till he reached that thorn tree, but his capacity for decisive action didn't impress him as going much beyond these mechanical motions.

Julian Hedleigh who dashed about his constituency, dispensing bon-homie. The Ranworth eel-man, who'd refused to join the Home Guard. The ferry-man at Horning, who'd moored and unmoored his vessel from either side of the river, morning noon and night for decades. Shipped his neighbours and their horses and bikes to and fro between the village and the mirey way through the carr. Generally gone to the Ferry Inn for a glass of beer in the evening. Then . . . Would it have been better if Blanche and he had had more children? If they'd had several sons in the war? If they'd had no children? No, no.

These Paston fields were where Michael and Blanche had galloped as boy and girl, and then as young man and young woman. Then before the next war Jack and Georgia had careered with drubbing hooves along these same headlands, and there was a tinge of the incestuous in them too. Different . . . The same . . . Had Blanche, watching them galloping this shore at low tide, watching them ride neck-and-neck at these hedges, remarked on the reembodiment?

In the moonlight, Lammas could see across a couple of fields to the barn, to the trees around the Hall where his wife had been brought up, to the church tower. It was not difficult, walking these dim meadows with the sea washing at the cliff's foot, to imagine the riders of thirty or forty years back. Not hard to hear the thunder of their hooves, see those silhouettes, hear their voices calling. Not hard to find them mingled in your head with those two other riders of three or four years ago, who'd charged at the same banks and ditches with the same abandon, called to each other with the same gaiety. Scrambled their horses down the shelving cliff path. Ridden them into the shallows. Who had, for a summer, wanted none other than . . . And who now . . .

Lammas woke to the fact that he'd gone far past the thorn tree, swinging along as if he were shod with seven-league boots. He checked, turned. Made himself walk back soberly.

Haunted, and powerless. What was more, if Hitler were really making his most ambitious bid so far for the famous *Lebensraum* he'd shouted about so much . . . Early days yet, of course. Have to wait and see. But if the war was going to be fought this summer and autumn on the Eastern Front, then here on this coast his own principal enemy would be his sense of the uselessness of his comings and goings. The uselessness of his thinking and feeling too.

Well, this was a problem which would prove temporary. Because if the Germans were victorious against the Russians, which they very likely would be . . . Then if the Reich were undefeated from the Norwegian Sea to the Gulf of Sirte, and from the Gulf of Finland to the Sea of Azov, the assault on the English southern and eastern coasts which the Wehrmacht would be able to launch would be such that no British Army could repel.

Haunted, and powerless. And now, when there was nothing he could do for Jack . . . Not even get himself shot fighting the same tyranny. Not even bring his mother any scrap of comfort. Now it was Georgia who haunted him. Or, of all his haunters, her ghostly presence was the only one that brought hope.

Because there *was* something going on in her. A flowering . . . Or a coming to hitherto undreamed-of aliveness. Going on in her, in that voice of hers. What was more, if he weren't badly mistaken, Alex and Christopher were aware of it too.

20

Charles Lammas walked back toward Norgate, worrying about Henrietta who would be home from school next week, and who, if no word of Jack came, would have to be told he was missing. And the longer no word came . . . Norgate was lying on the dewy turf, looking even bulkier all baled up in his coat, asleep.

Lammas smiled, walked on, listening to the sea. Henrietta who, when she'd been told he'd had a stroke, had rushed upstairs, flung herself on him without taking off her riding hat, so its hard rim bumped his chest. Henrietta who'd be lucky if she heard her brother were behind barbed-wire, or in a cattle-truck being taken from one camp to another. Yes . . . But through all this inability of his to think anything effective, let alone do it – Georgia. The freedom with which his goddaughter combined and recombined her stories, and broke them off, and scampered through a dozen enthusiasms, and apparently guilelessly was several speakers at once. Unusual, no?

Sister Caterina did not come from Tuscany. Sister Caterina came from – to Georgia Burney's intoxicated imagination – over the hills and far away. Or, to her godfather's more sedate understanding, as he had read her latest bulletin of Mandalay and Maymyo metamorphoses, the young nun had been born in Urbania, in the Metauro valley. Which was certainly, if you set forth from Tuscany, over the Apennine chain and down into the hills on the other side. As he knew very well, having gone there with Giacomo Zanetti in the spring of '28.

Georgia's account of her new friend's childhood home came interwoven with what she'd been up to and what she'd been reading. With what her father and de Brissac thought about Chiang Kai-shek. What de Brissac had told Caterina and her about Anselm's argument that it was implicit in the very idea of God that He existed. What Roberta Gillway thought about the *terribly* handsome Agent for Burmah Oil. But her godfather liked her unselfconscious interest in all her different strands. He rejoiced in the freedom with which her mind went darting on – now, with his own mind clamped onto its inanity. He envied – no, he was bewildered by, as if he'd forgotten such confidence were possible – the way Georgia never doubted for a second that with flickers of her attention she might illumine this, transform that, resolve the other.

Now briefly Georgia Burney's voice rang in Lammas' head as it ought to have done. As if in a world without wars, without *reported missing*. He kept an eye on that Yarmouth flotilla – but they vanished swiftly in the gloom. He sauntered. He paused, looking out over the sea. He heard Georgia's voice telling gaily about how Sister Caterina had grown up in one of the paved streets behind the ducal palace in Urbania. Telling about a tumble-down arcade, a courtyard with a well. Telling about the poulterer next door – the squawking! the feathers! The rumble of the ox-carts' iron-rimmed wheels. The carpenter's wife who was so mad she wanted to make a pilgrimage to Jerusalem, but Father Gervasio stopped her. So she went on taking in washing, went on darning, and telling people that Father Gervasio was no more Christian than the Protestants. They asked her what manner of creature a Protestant might be, but she couldn't answer, and then one day she declared she was going to walk to Padua to pray in Saint Anthony's basilica, and the next day she was dead. Beside the well. With her washing half done. Her head in a puddle of suds.

Naturally, the voice in Lammas' head being his impetuous goddaughter's, the delights of a Metauro valley childhood were always getting interspersed with how Caterina *longed* to get back there. But it was impossible to say when she might, or even whether she ever would. Didn't Godfather Charles think that was dreadful? How *could* her Church be so dictatorial? Or she would break off to complain that Sister Caterina and Lieutenant Colonel de Brissac got on so flamingly well together that on occasion honestly she felt jealous. Felt left out in the cold. The way they'd pitch into chat about the Pope's Swiss guards at the Vatican, or about his summer palace out at – she couldn't remember the name of the place. The way that in solemn discussion of His Holiness they might check, and Christopher would wink at Caterina, and explain, 'The bishop of Rome, Georgiana, to you.'

Then the girl's attention would go veering off to how the Mother Superior required all the sisters to learn English and Burmese. How she had been trying to help Caterina with both these, in exchange for Italian lessons. So that after the war, when she went back to Villa Lucia, she wouldn't make *quite* such an idiot of herself. How funny their miscomprehensions could be . . . But never so hilarious as when Caterina persuaded Christopher to venture upon a phrase or two of Italian. Really that was one thing he was *never* going to be good at. Still, lucky he wasn't perfect.

Effusions about how brave Caterina was about buckling down to her duties here, and not pining for the Metauro, or at least aching to be promised that one day she would go home. Effusions about how

fortunate she herself was to be in Burma again, and how most of the
silly English disapproved of her for always saying that so far as she'd
ever be concerned this country was Home. Really quite nasty about it,
some of them could be.

Then regularly Georgia would fly off at such a tangent that her
godfather couldn't see where the point of contiguity had been. Into
her reading, for instance. In which she was splendidly omnivorous. *The
Arabian Nights* and Robert Louis Stevenson one month. Then Marco Polo
and Ibn Batuta the next, read – for all that you could discern that she had
any method in her tackling of stories – on alternate mornings, with *Moby
Dick* and *Lord Jim* on alternate afternoons.

But it was this free play of her mind in which Charles Lammas rejoiced,
musing on his lonely cliff at night. The more lightly her thought skipped
the better, he reckoned – leaden-thoughted, unconfident.

Now it was Scheherazade. (All very glamorous, being the daughter of
the Grand Vizier of the Indies, or who-have-you. But could Godfather
Charles imagine what it would *really* be like, to have to tell the Sultan one
riveting story after another to stop him having you strangled?) Then it was
the vexed question of the foundation of Malacca. (If the city existed much
before 1400, why did neither Marco Polo, nor the Blessed Oderic, nor Ibn
Batuta, all of whom sailed through the Straits, mention it?) Immediately
after which she reported that Marlow had just gone to visit Stein, to put
before him the troublous facts concerning Jim and ask his advice – so
Lammas knew which story she'd picked up *that* afternoon.

Skip lightly, lightly, his spirit called to her. Don't get bogged down,
like the rest of us. Not yet . . . And he went to sit on a hummock and
look out to sea, conscious that a stirring of the pre-dawn invigoration
he'd known in the old days was visiting him. In old, Italian days, for
example. He chuckled, remembering walking back through Venice after
a dinner party, with Lucrezia Venier to escort, and then the next day at
lunch having to confront Chiara Zanetti's coruscating diamond necklace
and just as coruscating eyes.

Then he got distracted, listening to the dawn chorus begin, thinking
how far you could sail on that sea stretching there. Well, his adventurings
were over. Which was possibly why now invisible presences had charm,
inaudible voices rang fetchingly. He was just banally susceptible – he'd
often told himself so. His life was a succession of beguilements, of
succumbings – as meaningless as that.

Good, though, Georgia's chitter-chatter about the imminent arrival in

Burma of the Commander-in-Chief, Far East . . . *With, of course, you know who, dear Godfather, on his staff*. Damned good, in a pushing and pulling world, the girl's explosions of confidence – she absolutely could *not* bring herself to regret the captain in the Yorkshires, and by way of treating him decently was strewing her girlfriends in his path. Her trillings with the pleasure she'd taken in an invitation to *an awfully posh ball*, in a dawdle through the bazaar or the botanical gardens. Her equally explosive enthusiasms . . . For Roberta Gillway's chances with the Burmah Oil man. For *Lord Jim* – Marlow and Stein should have had her with them at their meditations among the cases of butterflies, *she*'d have helped them save their man.

Her confessions could have their resonance in Lammas' memory too. About how before she'd set off up-country with her father for three months, she'd checked that they'd be back before de Brissac next visited her particular nook of that particular colony. Because she *had* to know, had to hear from him because she didn't trust anyone else, that the rumour which gave him engaged to marry Victoria Armitage was a pack of lies.

Alex Burney's letters to Charles Lammas were short and temperate – not like his daughter's at all. But he had hinted at his amusement at some of the recent proceedings under his roof. And the last time he'd written, he'd mentioned that, really, with de Brissac such a friend of the family these days, such an habitué of the Maymyo bungalow, and Georgia as lightning-struck as ever . . .

Well, Charlie would understand how funny it could be. There was Geraldine's downright idolisation of the poor fellow, whom at the same time she went to embarrassing lengths to compromise with her daughter. Then the way you couldn't walk onto your own verandah and be sure you wouldn't find a nun or two there, or barge in on a discussion of the Holy Ghost.

Mind you, so far as he himself had any views . . . The other week he'd suggested as plainly as he'd felt he could to Christopher that he wasn't to pay a blind bit of attention to either Geraldine or Georgia. Come for a drink or for tiffin or dinner whenever he pleased. Always be glad to see him. Plenty of talk to catch up on.

On the other hand, liking him as he did. If Christopher did ask if he might propose to the girl . . .

To be honest, her father had written, he'd be delighted. But he had a feeling it wouldn't come off.

21

—⁊⁊—

Early in July, word of Jack Lammas reached Edingthorpe. For over a month, his mother had made a point of not always being in the yard or the kitchen when it was the post-boy's time for reaching the Manor. Today it was her husband who from his studio window saw the mail arrive.

The letters were always placed on the oak settle in the kitchen, where everybody could collect their own. By the time Charles had walked there, Mrs Meade and Mrs Fox had already put aside for well-deserved neglect all the envelopes but one. This one lay isolated on the polished wood, with *Red Cross Society* printed along its upper edge, with the two women staring agitatedly at it.

Ellen was twisting her hands in her apron. She had already begun to cry, drawing breath occasionally to gasp, 'Oh Lord! Oh I hope! Oh Master Jack!'

Janet Fox, either because she was made of stronger fibres, or because she had only been with the family for a dozen years and so had not, as Ellen had, actually dandled Jack and bathed him, fed him rusks and scolded him, turned toward Charles Lammas with her blue eyes dry, though her red cheeks were redder than ever. 'Oh Sir. The Red Cross, Sir. They don't . . . If you're dead, they don't – do they, Sir?'

'I don't know, Janet.' At his most impeccably naval, but conscious of his heart suddenly crashing against his ribs more desperately than perhaps it ever had, Charles took the envelope. 'Shouldn't think they'd bother. Let's have a look.'

The letter was short enough to take in at a glance. The women saw his eyes flick down the sheet of paper. For a few moments, he could not speak. But with his mouth pressed suddenly into a very firm line, he nodded a smile at them. And his eyes were brilliant with such a shock of happiness, that they fell sobbing into each other's arms.

He read the letter more attentively.

The paper was headed: War Organisation of the British Red Cross Society and the Order Of St John Of Jerusalem, and bore the emblems of both. It was from the Wounded, Missing and Relations Department. Typed, with spaces left for his name and Jack's to be written with pen and ink, and for the chairman's signature.

Dear Mr Lammas

A communication has been received from Geneva which leads us to believe that Lieutenant J.M. Lammas is a Prisoner of War. Official confirmation of this should be received by you in due course, but we are glad to send you this unofficial statement in the hope of allaying your anxiety.

Please make all further enquiries to: Prisoners of War Department, St James's Palace, London SW1.

Yours sincerely . . .

Charles Lammas stood stock-still, waiting for his heart to thump less dramatically. He kept looking at the piece of paper in his hand. At Geneva, quite recently, they'd had reason to think the boy was alive. The Germans had listed him among those taken alive. No more. No less. Right.

'He's a prisoner of war,' he told Ellen and Janet. 'No mention of his having being wounded, either – though there might not yet be. Here, have a look. Now, I must find his mother.'

Finding Blanche, these days, was not difficult. If she were not in any of her customary haunts about the garden and the house, and if she had not bicycled to Happisburgh to teach her First Aid course, or taken the pony-trap to North Walsham with a load of vegetables and eggs, she would be up in their bedroom. When there was nothing for it. When she had to be alone. On her dressing-table, she had photographs of her brothers. Photographs of Jack and Henrietta in the garden when they were children.

Lammas went upstairs. With their reprieve in his hand, he thought: *Official confirmation of this should be received.* He thought: *Unofficial statement.* But his mouth was dry. The cannonading in his chest was still going on, and it was joyful, merciful heavens it was joyful all right. Blanche my darling, he thought, the boy's alive. Dear God if we can just get through this war. He's alive!

Then he had to stop halfway up the staircase. He stood, with his breath coming very whispery. He dabbed his eyes with his handkerchief.

He went on up, thinking of what a shrine Blanche had made of that dressing-table over the years. Michael in uniform. Jack in uniform. Who now . . . If it could just be true, and stay true. Bits of oriental jewellery her brothers had given her. That watch and chain. These last weeks, she'd taken to carrying them around in the pocket of her skirt or her jacket. You'd see her fingers straying toward them.

Charles walked along the landing, came to their bedroom. Yes, there she was, sitting at her table. She turned, saw his eyes. She stood up, her own lips and eyes suddenly tremulous, the golden chain hanging from her hand.

'He's alive. Red Cross letter. Geneva. London.' Charles made a simple, up and down gesture with the sheet of paper.

'Prisoner of war. We ought to get confirmation in a few days.' Something convulsive happened in Blanche Lammas' throat. But she made no move.

He held the letter out to her. But her new agony of hope, and the blood shaking her heart and her mind, meant that for a minute she simply stood there.

Charles read her the letter. Then, slowly, long quiverings began, in her throat, in her breast. She sat down again, clutching the watch and chain.

'We'll wait,' he said, and smiled into her eyes, which still had not wept. 'We'll wait for the confirmation. But it'll come, my darling. He's alive. You'll see.'

Charles went to her, knelt on one knee by her little embroidered chair. He put the letter on her table, among the brushes and the combs and the boxes, where she could see it.

22

—m—

In the midst of life we are in death, in the words of the Book of Common Prayer. *In the midst of death we are in life* – Anne Daubeney had said that too, not long after her little son's death. Said it to Blanche Lammas, who had come over to Morston with Henrietta in a carry-cot, to ask her if she would be the child's godmother.

Now for three days, Blanche carried those lines in her head. She carried that Red Cross letter folded in her pocket, with the watch and chain which had been Tom Carraway's and now were Jack's. And still she would not give way to belief that he was alive, and she would not give way to tears.

Naturally, the whole neighbourhood knew by then what *official confirmation* they were waiting for at the Manor, and on the third day, when the post-boy had a War Office telegram in his satchel, he biked up the Edingthorpe lane with his face pink and his knees going like pistons. In the yard, he let his precious machine fall to the gravel with a clang and a clatter. (Usually he was punctilious about propping it against an outhouse wall.) He pelted into the kitchen, calling, 'Mrs Lammas! Mrs Lammas!' breathlessly.

She was there, and frowned at his excitement. But this was no time to tell him how silly it was to become jubilant over a message he had not read, and that not all *official confirmations* being delivered daily to houses up and down the land bore welcome news. She opened the telegram.

And when Blanche read, *Information received that Lieut J.M. Lammas previously reported missing now prisoner of war Letter follows Under Secretary of State for War* . . . Then, after holding herself taut and quiet and dry-eyed for so long . . .

She flung up her head, as if in pride, but the tears were already streaming down her cheeks.

Then Charles came striding across the yard, where the flung-down bicycle's wheels were still spinning but more slowly now. When he reached the kitchen, Blanche locked her arms around his neck. She was taking great gulps of air. Through her tears, she murmured wildly, 'Oh Jack my darling boy. Nanny, Nanny, you'd understand, where are you? Oh Michael my darling, why, why? Jack, Jack. Michael, why aren't you here with me now? Why couldn't you . . .? Nanny, he's alive!'

By comparison with the early summer, now messages which seemed to offer irrefutable proof that, somewhere, their son was alive, reached Charles and Blanche Lammas with wonderful frequency.

There was a letter from the War Office Casualty Branch on 9 July which confirmed the telegram of the 5th, and a leaflet all about how to send letters and parcels to prisoners of war. There was a second, much more ample letter from the Red Cross, saying that Lieutenant Lammas appeared to be in a transit camp, and that he was well. They could write to him c/o Agence Centrale des Prisonniers de Guerre, Comité International de la Croix Rouge, Palais de Conseil-General, Genève. When *The Times* arrived on Friday 8 August, in *The Roll of Honour*, after *The Army Council regrets to announce*, and *next-of-kin have already been notified*, Jack's name was listed. Under *Officers, Prisoners of War, R. Armoured Corps*. At the end of September, another War Office letter reported that an official German list of prisoners had been received, which included Jack's name, and recorded his arrival at the end of July at Camp Oflag XC, and said his prisoner-of-war number was 3529.

Long afterwards, they discovered that the transit camp had been at Salonika, and that Oflag XC was at Lübeck, on the Baltic. But already, in those summer months at Edingthorpe – even though each day's newspaper had its *Casualties*, so it was certain that *in the midst of life we are in death* . . . Still, it was impossible not to hope that the inverse might also be true.

Blanche Lammas was not new to not letting yourself believe, and not saying certain things. You never said what you were afraid of, because it was too obvious. There was nothing to be gained by discussions of how life behind Nazi German barbed-wire with machine-guns trained on you all the time might be worse than merely unpleasant. You never said anything that might not be true. No pointless chat about how you were sure Jack was all right, or you were sure the war couldn't last another year – stuff like that. You never spoke of what most you longed for, either – especially not if you had waited and hoped through the old war before this one, and therefore had learned about the vanity of prayer. Longings were too important to voice. And saying it was bad luck.

Even so . . . She couldn't walk in the yard without her mind's eye seeing her son walking across it toward her – and Charles knew she couldn't, he could see her blue eyes following the lad. And Norwich station undid her. The platform where Jack had given her that boyish goodbye hug and kiss, jumped up into the carriage and then leaned out to wave. That she might one day find herself there, and a train draw in, and he'd leap down and come striding toward her. She might be there to fetch him home at last . . . After a couple of years of war, Blanche avoided going anywhere near the station if she could.

The Roll of Honour was the right thing to call it, Charles Lammas knew that. Under the circumstances. Like in the last war. The correct, considerate thing.

But he remembered how you faced up to the chance of being killed and to the chance of being wounded. You faced up to how being killed could be a protracted business, and pain did not cause loss of consciousness. How wounds could not be relied upon to be just a red stain on the shoulder of a man's tunic. You were just as likely to have shell splinters make mince-meat of your face or your stomach or your genitals. But to be taken prisoner . . .

In his experience, you never reckoned that was going to happen to you. And men to whom it did happen could be knocked all of a heap.

To fight through a battle – play your part, in the case of the Battle of Crete, for a week of that. Then to discover that you weren't only beaten, but that the Navy couldn't get through from Alexandria any more, those of you still on the beaches were to be abandoned there. To be told, that night after the last ships had sailed, that in the morning the senior officer remaining would go under a white flag to the enemy.

You were going to be surrendered. That was what they said. Hell of a phrase. To be surrendered. And then to find yourself suddenly possessing nothing but the clothes you stood up in. Utterly powerless. Dependent on the enemy for life itself, for a cup of dirty water, for mercy . . . Jack would try to escape.

His father knew that. Because it was the duty of an officer. But principally because his self-respect would have taken the devil of a belabouring, and he wouldn't feel right till he'd made some pretty dogged attempts to get free. Action! And if the body you were a part of – the army, the battery – was no bloody good any more, then individual action. If together you'd been defeated. If they'd surrendered you . . . And even according to the Geneva Convention, you could be shot in the act of escaping.

Still, now there was hope, and no one at Edingthorpe was immune from it. Charles watched Blanche busy with the Red Cross leaflet about Communication With Prisoners Of War Interned Abroad, and it put new heart into him. He watched her following the instructions about how you had to write KREIGSGEFANGENENPOST at the top left-hand corner of the envelope. He listened to Henrietta and her tirelessly planning what they were going to pack into their first parcel, which apparently it should prove possible to send Jack after three months, and which must not contain certain articles, and must not weigh more than such-and-such.

23

—⁓—

Ever since Japanese armies had been fighting in China, people had known about their torturing and killing of prisoners of war and civilians. But as for German conquests, and their aftermaths . . .

It was true that, ever since the invasion of western Poland a couple of years ago, stories of massacres had seeped through. But nobody knew much about what the Soviet invaders of eastern Poland had been up to that autumn. Not about the murder of five thousand Polish officers at Katyn. Nor about the other ten thousand, whose bodies were never found. And now, two autumns later, with the German invasion of the Soviet Union in full swing . . . A man like Charles Lammas could imagine that the conflict on the Eastern Front would be on a scale and might be of a barbarity not seen in the West. He also knew he had only the vaguest picture of what was going on.

Precious few facts. That the invaders were slaughtering Russian old men and women and children – in Britain, few had any notion of the scale of that. They knew there were labour camps, in which people from all over Europe slaved for Germany. But they did not know the extent to which these wretches were worked to death. Nor that this autumn the extermination camps had begun to function. Nor that the Special Task Forces, called *Einsatzgruppen*, which accompanied the Germany Army, were there in order systematically to exterminate Jews, communist commissars, any prisoners of war who proved recalcitrant or inconveniently sick or difficult to feed. Those two September days, when just outside Kiev the Germans murdered thirty-three thousand Jews, in Norfolk it was good to see the harvest being finished in dry weather. At Edingthorpe, the talk was all about a letter which had just arrived from the man in Jack's troop who'd been his batman, and who had got away from Crete.

He wrote, from the Middle East Force: *Dear Madam, I was your son's servant, and I should very much like to hear if you have received any news regarding him. On the march back over the hills I lost touch with him, owing to darkness and movement of troops, but on the coast I waited for two days looking for any member of our battery. Later I heard that your son volunteered to go back with rations and ammunition for the rearguard.*

That afternoon, they went to walk the dogs at Stiffkey. The tide was low, the sand stretched away. Henrietta remembered it all her life – Mama and Papa and she, and everyone happy because in the same post as the batman's letter had come a postcard from Germany. Addressed in Jack's handwriting. That had been the miraculous-seeming thing.

When you turned the card over, on the back was a printed message with phrases you could cross out, and Jack had crossed out the word *verwundet* and left the phrase that meant you were still more or less in one piece. He had signed it: *Love, Jack.*

A good day, with the three of them at breakfast flicking to and fro in the German dictionary, because otherwise they couldn't make head or tail of the message. A cheerful day – on account of the handwriting. Also because the card offered the alternatives of badly or lightly wounded, and they all agreed that, though if Jack had been half-dead he would have confessed to only lightly wounded, if he announced he hadn't a scratch it was probably fairly true.

24

—∞—

As the morning tide ebbed down Morston creek and the water fell in the Stiffkey river, as the harbour emptied and mud slopes were bared, the bait-diggers came, in twos, in threes. Leaving their black bicycles against thorn trees, on the sea-wall tussocked with marram grass, by pools on the salt marsh where sea lavender spread a purple haze.

They tramped out on the old pilot-path along the south shore of the harbour. Out to the northward also, along what they called the Far Point, which was the promontory of dunes and shell-speckled sandy spits. In boots, in oilskins. Carrying forks and spades over their shoulders, carrying a bucket each. Bringing a pannikin of cold tea, and a bite to eat.

The bait-diggers emerged from the flinty hamlets onto the great sand-bank also, which between Stiffkey and Wells at low water stretched its undulations for miles. Once they were off-shore on the shoal, even if they had come in company they separated. In foul weather, each man vanished quickly into blowing murk or blizzards of rain. But that day, when inland the beech hangers and lime avenues were turning golden, under a windless blue sky tufted with cirrus the exposed sands lay palely gold. The muddier regions were best for finding lug-worms. There each solitary man would work, digging his tumulus, forking through the mire, dropping the worms in his bucket.

When the tide was right out, you could splash across the Stiffkey river without getting wet much above your knees – especially, Henrietta knew, clutching her skirt about her thighs, if you tip-toed. Which was not easy in bare feet on mud and stones, with the quickly rippling current tugging, and when you wanted to keep an eye on the swimming dogs, and wouldn't have minded being able to keep an eye out too for sharp-edged mussels and scuttling crabs.

The Springer spaniels – good, working dogs – were across the river in a trice. Were out on the far bank shaking the water off their fleecy coats in sunlit spangles, and instantly getting their paws caked with mud again. The little Irish water spaniel, rather old and crotchety these days, had to be coaxed into swimming with endearments, with calls of, 'Come on, Honey!' Then, halfway across, she turned round and tried to swim back. So she had to be redirected, and lent a helping hand on the scruff of her neck. Everything, Henrietta hazily felt, was just as you'd expected and therefore just as it ought to be. Happy-making, the card from Jack. Good that she'd got her place at Newnham to read Classics, was off next week to start her first term. Promising, somehow, the seaward distances. Promising, the height of the larks overhead, the length of the warm afternoon.

Charles Lammas watched his daughter splashing through a glinting rivulet on the shoal, he heard her blithely whistling a dog. The next moment she'd remembered that signing a postcard fell a long way short of coming safe home. Her mouth was vulnerable. There was misery in her eyes, and they flinched away from his, and then looked back at him in speechless anguish, as if somehow her father might have been able to do something, might have been able to help.

The dead seal was a pity. That was why the spaniels had to be whistled and called. A rotting carcass on the tideline. Dogs' fascination with carrion.

For a few seconds, striding toward the body, shouting angrily to his dogs, Lammas hoped it was not a dead sailor. Because men were getting washed up along these shores, after engagements between flotillas of small ships, after raids, after attacks on merchant shipping and trawlers. Quite often, his responsibilities had included their collection, recording, burial.

Then he saw it was only a seal. Very different, when you got close enough to be aware of details, a seal and a man when they'd been dead for a fortnight or so – though there were similarities.

Charles Lammas tramped back toward his wife and daughter, cursing his dogs. But he was cursing them affectionately now, and they were trotting at his heels with exaggerated conformity, as if to point out that burst hide and festering flesh might be of interest to riffraff like gulls and maggots and flies, but could never have held charms for them.

Out on the shoal, there were no more larks in the sky, but flocks of oystercatchers took off and wheeled and came sweeping back. The ebbing sea had ruffled the sand, left it flecked with green weed and brown bladderwrack, with shells, with here and there a star-fish, or the big jelly-fish called Portuguese men-of-war.

Unfortunately, evil reports were already being transmitted from Yugoslavia and from Greece, concerning the German invaders' treatment of non-combatants, and of captured and disarmed combatants. Not the full story, by any means. But early rumours. However, just as her father refused to coddle Henrietta with predictions of how all was going to be well, so equally he didn't harp on the horrors being perpetrated. If Jack or Bobbie were killed, there would be time for tears. So as they walked side by side, with Blanche's consonance no less audible for being unspoken,

Charles talked about the Geneva Convention's stipulations regarding the treatment of prisoners – a Convention of which both Great Britain and Germany were signatories, though Russia and Japan were not. And, anyhow, despite the savageries in Warsaw and Belgrade and Athens; despite what was being done in villages from the Baltic to the Aegean . . . The Red Cross knew where Jack was, and reported him *well*. He had signed a card, and crossed out *verwundet*. There was no reason to believe he was not being treated in accordance with international law, and would continue to be so.

A couple of miles' walk out to the old wreck. Did Henrietta remember, her father asked her, about how men had used to come out with horses and carts to break that ship up, salvage what they could? He'd told her that windy day when they'd sailed out to meet *Golden Eye*.

Henrietta said she remembered. A wonderful day it had been. From the bacon sandwiches for breakfast, chugging out down Morston creek, till the dinner with Godmother Anne. Whitebait. And crabs. Caroline had been a bit grumpy. But the rest of them!

So then, because of the strange freedom of walking where soon the tide would come rolling back. Or because even in war time, out there in the briney sunlight and the emptiness you could sense the peace lapping around you. Or because over there a pack of seals had hauled out on the foreshore, thirty of them at least, pale greys and dark greys and mottled greys, and here in the channel sometimes a seal-head broke the surface and seal-eyes gazed . . . Charles Lammas found he was telling his daughter how he'd first come here with his parents and his brother. Mama had first come here with her parents and her two brothers. Then during the last war, he'd known his father and mother were coming here, haunted by their sons, overseas fighting.

He watched her listening to him. Fine local girl, he heard his mind thinking, with her strong rider's legs and her sandy feet, swinging along. She must have patted a muddy dog with the same hand she'd then used to shove her hair back from her eyes, because there was a smear on her forehead which he discovered he hoped she wouldn't wipe off quite yet.

Local girl, dead men's niece, he thought. *The seal's wide gaze* . . . Which poet was that? *The seal's wide spindrift gaze toward paradise.* Not sure paradise didn't rather spoil the line, but the *wide spindrift gaze* was good. There was a sleek head in the tideway now. Gone!

'Then, after that war, Mama and I came here. We talked about our brothers a lot – of course we did. All the time. But we talked about the future too. Made a mighty number of plans always.'

Three, who should have been four. But three was a damned sight better than . . . And there was no loneliness here. Not the bad sort. Not in him. Nor – he was sure of it – in the other two. Just the good loneliness, that hint of freedom. Here, with the present, and the absent, and the dead. And so, since his daughter seemed to know exactly what he meant by hauntedness. Since she listened without perplexity, glancing away seaward, glancing back to meet his look. Since his affinity with this child of his suddenly struck him as a miraculous good which in all these years like a fool he hadn't begun to comprehend . . .

'Then, that windy day we were talking about, I remember coming up this channel in the evening on the first of the tide. Still haunted by the last war's dead. Thinking about Bobbie and Jack, about other young men. And here we are, it's happening. But . . . It doesn't always have to go on like this. The pattern will change. It must, however slowly. Patterns always change, sometimes for the better. So, you see, dear girl . . . Just because you've grown up in a bad time . . .'

One of the spaniels came bounding up, launched its fore-paws and muzzle against her legs in a frenzy of devotion. She stopped, and with both hands rumpled the animal's ears. But she kept her blue eyes on her father. Halted beside her, he finished, ruefully.

'My generation failed to learn the one thing we ought to have learned. We haven't done what needed doing. Haven't been any use. But that doesn't mean that, whatever hellish things are being done now, the same mistakes have to be made again.'

They strolled on, toward the sea. Henrietta picked up a shell, wiped it on her sleeve, looked at it, tossed it down. Then she replied.

'No, of course not. I understand. About Uncle Michael, too, and Uncle Geoffrey. But, Papa . . . Honestly, you don't need to be afraid for me. I'll be all right. Whatever happens.'

25

━ ━

That afternoon was important to Henrietta because, on the eve of setting off to Cambridge for her first term, setting off therefore to be irrevocably grown-up for ever after, her mother's and father's companionship was rather comforting. She liked Papa telling her about before she'd been born. It made her feel the whole coast was peopled with friendly spirits – which she'd known before in a vague sort of way, but it was nice to know it again. And then there was her realisation that she could do something about one of his distresses.

He was anxious about *her* being unhappy. So she said it, straight out: *Honestly, you don't need to be afraid for me.* Knowing, without much thought, that it was the right thing to say. *I'll be all right. Whatever happens.* Because, deep down, it was true.

They went on talking when they reached the sea, and Henrietta liked the feeling of being isolated with her parents out there, a couple of miles offshore, with only the seals and the birds and the blue quietness. No bait-diggers came anything like so far out – they were just a few dots to landward. The sea was calm. They paddled, and Papa read bits of Mario Zanetti's latest letter. Mario was worried that his father in Tuscany was running unnecessary risks, and Papa explained how in Italy being against the government was dicey, even having friends who were against it could be dicey.

Then he went on strolling, and Mama and she sat down on the sand with their feet in the shallowest film of rippling sea. She asked her about Uncle Michael and Uncle Geoffrey, and Mama said: 'Yes, we remember them here. Can't not. Michael . . . I see him everywhere. All the time. But your father's right – what comes next doesn't have to be like what's been. Knowing about who's gone before you is one thing. Being incapacitated by the past is another. So . . . What's to come is yours, my love. Just you remember to enjoy it.'

Afterwards, their isolation together on the foreshore that day remained with Henrietta as what her war had been like. More than the biking around Cambridge, between her lectures and Newnham and the Women's Voluntary Service. More than going to Yarmouth after Saint Nicholas' church had been bombed, and how kicked in the stomach you felt when places you'd loved were destroyed. Had loved, or merely taken for granted. A thump to the solar plexus. Like that time when her horse had come down at a fence and she'd been winded. Just had to lie there, doubled up, surprised by how awful she felt, till it passed.

What her war had been like . . . More than going into Norwich after the bad raids in '42, when Saint Michael at Thorn had been destroyed, and Saint Julian's. Not that she ever liked Norwich during the war. It always seemed to be packed with airmen, drunk or nearly as loutish sober, who whistled at her and shouted. But that time Papa and she went in after the bombing. The whole area between King Street and Ber Street had been gutted by fire. He told her about the mediaeval anchoress Juliana of Norwich, who wrote *Revelations of Divine Love* – 'Not that I've read it, my darling' – and after she was dead was sainted. But her church – a little, fifteenth-century chapel of a place, which the Luftwaffe had just bombed – her shrine had always been called Saint Julian's for some reason.

Isolated, the three of them together, where flights of oystercatchers swept past with their glamorous black and white chevrons brilliant in the sun, and ripples lapped. That was Henrietta's war, to her. With Bobbie away, Jack away, Georgia away. So that, for the first time, she had her parents to herself. So that, in those years when she backed and forthed between Cambridge and Norfolk, the years of Jack being a prisoner of war, and of Mama and Papa and she always thinking about him, but never saying My God it *must* end soon, she became, in many respects, her mother's best friend – or shared the honours with Anne Daubeney.

Became her father's friend too. Not just his tomboyish, adorable daughter, whose resemblance to Blanche could always give a yank to his heart-strings, bring a twist of a smile to his lips. His ally. The war didn't stop them having mighty good times together whenever he came to Cambridge to see her. *Nothing* could have prevented that man, most of their friends agreed, from taking unholy pride in his daughter's academic successes. As for that summer day in '44, when he heard she'd got a First . . . 'Well, really,' Sarah Hedleigh demurred. 'Anyone would think the girl had just accepted a marquis.'

Like his daughter, Charles Lammas remembered that scene because of the three of them being so peacefully islanded out there, with in Blanche's pocket the card with *verwundet* crossed out, with the tiny dunlin and stint which scurried away in front of him on their spindly legs.

He strolled on, glancing back once over his shoulder and thinking how fine his wife and daughter looked together, sitting by the margin of the sea, their heads of brown hair now bent together in conversation, now turned to gaze far away. *I'll be all right*, the girl had said. *Whatever happens.*

Well, maybe she had got not only her mother's extraordinary capacity for love and therefore for suffering, but also her strength, her ability to suffer without letting it disfigure her spirit. And now his mind was alive with ghostlier presences, the living rubbing shoulders with the dead. The living in prison camps in Germany. The living who were quartered very differently, in Cairo. There Bobbie's recent return was evidently, at the Gezira Club and at lesser resorts of hedonism, proving a happy addition to the party-going of a number of his brother officers, most of them in wonderfully smart regiments; and a solid satisfaction to head waiters, dancing girls, go-betweens and – his uncle was much afraid – money-lenders. The living in Italy, and Burma.

Lammas had always liked Mario Zanetti. As a child, when he'd been splendidly adventurous – always climbing impossibly high trees, or getting himself half-drowned when diving with a knife to do battle with an octopus. As a young man, when his father had dispatched him to London, and under Lammas' auspices he'd got his first job, with Colnaghi. Mario had been delightful when invited to lunch at the Travellers', delightful when invited to stay at Edingthorpe. So fortunate, too, that he'd inherited Giacomo's aesthetic sense but not his vast, shapeless head.

Then he had departed to New York, but he and his father's old friend had corresponded, fitfully. About paintings, about family news. And since the war had interposed a silence between Italy and England, they had written more often. Even after the United States entered the war, Mario contrived to receive word from Villa Lucia occasionally, and would pass anything interesting on to Edingthorpe.

Both trans-Atlantic links in this chain were liable to breakages. But the system was a lot better than nothing, and throughout the war it was Charles Lammas' only contact with his Italian friends.

On this occasion, Mario wrote that Emanuela had been on vacation with him. He'd enjoyed squiring her around, spoiling her a bit. As for the Tuscan news . . . Well, Margherita and her husband were all right on their farm near Impruneta, cultivating their olive groves and their vineyards like sensible souls. Keeping their heads down . . . Which commendable policy seemed, thank the Lord, to be working, so far.

It was at Villa Lucia that things might go wrong. Giulio and Raffaella were there a lot, it appeared. He'd been recalled from Vienna to Rome, and Pietro and he were thick as thieves. And of course, Mario wrote, Charles could imagine how pleased his mother was, to have her elder son and her son-in-law such big shots in the regime. Well, hobnobbing with political grandees, and themselves middling grandees on their way up. (Lammas had of recent years been unsure whether Mario Zanetti knew about his affair with his sister. There were fleeting moments in his letters when he suspected that he might, possibly, have preferred him to Giulio Flamini as a brother-in-law.) Of course, it wouldn't normally have been of much consequence, Mario explained, his mother's silly snobbery. The quite innocent pleasure she took in having chauffeured cars rolling into her courtyard, and tipping out the Fascist Party chairman for Tuscany and his smarmy son. Or a general, fresh from some defeat in North Africa, who had managed to leave his men in the lurch and scuttle home. Or the Minister for Lying Newspapers and his mistress; or the Under Secretaries for Pop-guns and Pea-shooters and *their* mistresses. These shennanigans wouldn't have mattered a hang, if it hadn't been for his father, Mario wrote.

His father who, by the way, had instructed him to invite Charles to sell him any recent work he could spare. *Papa mi scrive che* . . . (Mario, like his father, customarily rendered Charles the tribute of Italian.) Any pictures he thought the Zanetti collection might like to acquire. To be paid for in dollars. The same sort of prices they'd been paying before the war.

Of this, more in a minute. To resume . . . The problem was that his father did not appear to have succeeded in remaining indifferent to what was going on in the country. Despite, you might have thought – you might, under the circumstances, have hoped – having lapsed years back into such melancholy as should have precluded the taking of much action. Not, naturally, that his father had written this to him, Mario reported. But – perhaps strangely – Raffaella had. Or perhaps not strangely. At any rate, this habit of using Villa Lucia to harbour enemies of the state, at the same time as other members of the family were using the place to entertain the ruling classes . . .

Still, luckily the estate was a fair size, and the visiting pashas were only interested in dancing with Raffaella – or maybe it was dear old Signora Annunziata's cooking. But Charles would understand. They weren't the pashas whom his mother liked throwing galas for that worried him. It was his brother. And his brother-in-law. Or even, in a country as corrupted with political hatreds as he reckoned his native land was these days, where chicanery was the norm and everybody had scores to settle . . . Even mere bad luck was increasingly likely to be fatal. Accident, or what could be made to appear such. Chance.

Lammas found he had sauntered for hundreds of yards. He turned, walked back, enjoying the picture his wife and daughter made. They were standing in the shallows, idly stirring the ripples with their feet. He glanced at his watch, and thought Yes, the tide was probably beginning to set in over the harbour bar. The first tongues of water would be licking shore-ward up these sands. They must start walking back, soon. In the meantime . . . Awesome, the strength of the affinities you had with a dead brother, with a living daughter. And beguiling too those other haunters, those – what was the phrase? – elective affinities, that was it.

Just like old Giacomo, not to write anything to Mario that might make him fret. Just like him, too, thinking that quite probably in war-time England paintings weren't selling. To have written to Mario telling him to offer to buy canvases neither of them had seen. To pay for them, the letter had specified, even if they could not be shipped to New York till the war was over.

And in the meantime, while the warm blue afternoon lasted . . . Raffaella dancing with her Fascist nabobs, and then going upstairs to write to Mario about their father's sheltering of anti-Fascists about the estate. Geoff walking here, stooping to pick up a shell with just the same motion that Henrietta had used, wiping it so he could see its whorls, chucking it aside. That Cotman watercolour of a harbour mark and sea and gulls – by God that was how you ought to paint. Blanche here when they were engaged. Blanche striding over the sea-bed with tears rinsing down her face, striding and striding, only saying 'Michael' sometimes through her tears. He himself beside her, beginning to think the whole affair was impossible, it was ridiculous, they'd have to call this wedding off. *The seal's wide spindrift gaze*. Time running out, and Far Eastern letters ringing in your head too.

Christopher de Brissac's first letter to Edingthorpe since his return to the East had included a light-hearted account of his dinner at the Strand in Rangoon with the Burneys, and of how the next morning *your charming goddaughter* had been his cicerone on a visit to the Shwe Dagon pagoda. He did not write often. But when he did, *your charming goddaughter*, or *the enchanting Georgiana*, always got a mention.

Nothing to make anything of, much. But then his latest letter – which had arrived the same week as the first of Georgia's – of which you could say that it had passages for which ecstatic was the only word . . .

Standing in his North Sea emptiness, Lammas chuckled. Christopher had begun: *Dear Charlie, I find myself in a really rather curious situation.*

26

—ɯ—

Half a year later, Singapore had fallen and de Brissac was a prisoner of war. At Changi, to begin with.

So, as they learned later at Edingthorpe, was one young man of the Meade cousinage. His Territorial battalion of the Norfolk Regiment had passed a tranquil year preparing to defend Weybourne Hoop. Then they had been among the forces disembarked at Singapore right at the end, about the time the Johore causeway was blown. When robust opinion among the defenders was that it ought to be possible to hold the island indefinitely. Or at any rate for a good six months, which should be long enough, because by then counter-attacks all over South-East Asia would have put the Japanese on the defensive. When less robust opinion, rattled by the sinking of *Prince of Wales* and *Repulse*, rattled by the speed with which the British had been routed out down the Malay Peninsula, was that the campaign had in essentials already been lost.

Very different from Jack Lammas' experience of being a prisoner of war, it transpired, being a prisoner of the Japanese. Jack was half-starved. But only half – and after a few months Red Cross parcels started getting through, so things got a bit better. Later, when twice he escaped, and was recaptured, he was not killed but sent to Colditz, where three hundred or so Allied officers who had proved particularly immune to reason were held, outnumbered by their guards. And already late in 1941 his first letters were arriving at Edingthorpe. Letters made anodyne by the German censorship, naturally enough. Made superficial by his never writing anything that might distress his readers. Yet these stalwartly cheerful messages were proof that he was alive.

Different, for the prisoners the Japanese took. If you were Dutch or Australian, Indian or British, American or Philippino or Chinese . . . Whoever you were. And if you were fortunate enough to survive the business of being captured. If soon after surrendering you were not bayoneted through your chest. Or shot. Or beheaded with a sword. As was generally the fate of the wounded. As was the fate of thousands of fit men taken prisoner. After Hong Kong fell on Christmas Day; and on the other side of the South China Sea, in Sarawak drowsy, verdant little Kuching fell too. After defeats at Bataan and Corregidor. On Malayan beaches, by path-sides. On the islands of Amboina and Timor . . . Wherever Imperial Japanese arms were victorious – and in those months, in the Far East they were victorious everywhere.

Of course, Christopher de Brissac and the other sixty thousand prisoners taken when Singapore surrendered did not know, in those first days when they'd been marched out to Changi and left there, that a third of them would be dead before peace returned. They didn't know that already, back in the city, the conquerors were conducting their first massacre – of five thousand Chinese judged possible trouble-makers. They didn't know that for most of them it was never going to be possible to write home, though some of them began to guess that pretty early on. At any rate, the fact was that no one ever read any later page written by de Brissac. So, in the end, at Edingthorpe that letter of his about how he found himself in a *rather curious situation*, came to have the sad and meagre importance that attaches itself to last things. The letter which at Stiffkey in the autumn of '41 made its recipient smile.

Not that, right up to the fighting in Malaya, the Lieutenant Colonel had not continued his usual correspondence with relatives and friends. But it was remarkable how consistently he'd stuck to his principle of making no allusions, except in that one letter to Lammas, to the real, the inner life he'd been leading in those months.

Not that Christopher and Georgia, in their four months before the Japanese Army finished off their world, did not write to one another during their separations – which were vastly longer than their times together. In their months before the old imperial cobweb was slashed to tatters faster than even Alex Burney had predicted. But – and this was one of the things her godfather learned at the time, when her letters were coming thick and fast right up till the British were defeated in Burma, and she was still in the oubliette when the dungeon door was slammed shut . . . They destroyed one another's letters, by agreement, as soon as they'd read them.

So, at that stage in what Blanche had called the dispersal. With Jack a prisoner of war, but Christopher not yet. With Georgia, who later became a prisoner of war in another sense. With Georgia writing torrentially to her godfather, to the general effect that she was heels over head in love with the magnificent C de B. But, beyond that, in love with every passing minute of every day, with the rice-boats' sails on the Irrawaddy and their reflections, with – everything! Walking after nightfall down by Mandalay Shore, and breathing the woodsmoke from the cooking fires. Picking her way among the puddles and the sleeping cattle by moonlight. Going into temple precincts where the palms rustled. Lingering on the pontoons and the rickety bridges between the clusters of little houses built over the margins of the river, because of the moonlight shimmering in the backwaters, and the sampans tied up, and the peace. With Georgia writing like that – and her father and de Brissac also having written illuminatingly – Charles Lammas began to form quite a clear picture of the state of play between his friends in Upper Burma. A picture that he kept to himself, for a long time. Alex and Christopher addressed themselves only to him. And the family's correspondence with Georgia had for years been his domain. 'A letter from your little favourite,' Blanche would say, handing one to him. Or would ask, without requiring an answer, 'Writing to your youngest sweetheart? Give her my love.' Which he would do.

Not really a clear picture. Countless pictures that kept forming in his mind's miasma, images he could neither substantiate nor banish.

A few facts seemed clear enough. That year when, as it emerged after-wards, in Tokyo strategic thinking veered round toward the southward strike against the colonies of the Western democracies, rather than northward from Manchuria against communist Russia. To establish Japan as the dominant Great Power in Eastern Asia by those means, quickly, and then make peace. Because a long war, say one of more than a year or at most two, would be a lost war, they knew. That year when the assault on Malaya was being discreetly rehearsed on Hainan, recently annexed to the Japanese empire . . . At Maymyo, Alex Burney was delighting in his daughter's company. And he also reckoned that her admirer was an improvement on the common run of hill station conversationalists. With Geraldine and he to all intents become strangers to each other, though when they appeared together at church or at the club their demeanour as man and wife was irreproachable. With Ricky down at Rangoon (where, it formed itself in Lammas' miasma, he on occasion served Georgia as a convenient pretext) and, when he visited his parents, still insufferably callow. So whenever de Brissac's duties brought him to Maymyo, or he had a few days' leave . . . On Burney's verandah, no doubt with a whisky decanter and a jug of ice on the table, they'd talk. Perhaps about the last-ditch negotiations being conducted in Washington. Or about a race meeting, or the teak market. Or, possibly . . . Did they talk about quite a different order of things?

Flickeringly, Charles Lammas saw it. Heard it – muffled, variable. He imagined Alex Burney who, like a lot of men whose jobs required them to pass long periods away from their kind, after a few months in his forests would, if the evening seemed propitious, on occasion unwind surprisingly, for a man apparently so immured in his reserve. Would sit up talking half the night, if the fancy took him.

He brought to mind Alex who had not waited in vain, all those years, for his daughter to come back to him. Who had found in her the kindred spirit he had been dreaming of – said so explicitly, in one letter. Unbent sufficiently to write: *She is a great joy to me.* Which tone of voice brought back to Charles the letter he had written years ago, when Emma died. *She had never been strong . . . Geraldine is desolate.*

Alex who was probably old-fashioned enough never to question the way that Georgia had settled down to living exactly like any other sociable young lady in an out-of-the-way colony. That round of tennis parties and swimming parties and fancy-dress balls. The novels to be read and the letters to be written. The eventual marriage to somebody suitable. (And, indeed, when the girl did finally go in for some lackadaisical training as a nurse, it was, she declared in one of her last letters to reach Edingthorpe, *only because Christopher's words are my commands.*) Alex who was uncommonly prescient when it came to the fragility of British power in the East. Who therefore might be open, mightn't he, to the idea that you should live while you could? Make the most of it. Alex who knew enough about being a soldier, and knew enough about being a servant of empire – or maybe it was being damaged he knew about – to know why you lived by conventions. Knew what they were for . . . And knew that where you really lived was elsewhere, if you really lived at all.

The trouble was, Charles hadn't seen him for seven years. So he'd fall back on more confident imaginings of the Burneys' garden with its japonicas, with its jacaranda tree. The verandah. The talk about things like how it was all very fine Churchill shipping Hurricanes and Spitfires to Russia, but the British cause might have been better served if they'd been brought out to Malaya. The talk about how the Americans sending some of their Brewster Buffalo fighter aircraft instead was of course grand – but they were pretty obsolete, weren't they? Lumpy, unwieldy old crates.

And Christopher? Who was on the staff of the Commander-in-Chief, Far East – right now a post held by an Air Chief Marshal, called . . . Charles couldn't remember his name. Christopher might, on that Maymyo verandah, sip his whisky and remark that his chief was confident the Buffaloes would prevail against the Japanese. Christopher for whom events had always tended to fall out fortuitously. Either that, or the poor fellow was blighted with a strongly developed sense of the chancy. Christopher who had finished by being quite successful at *not* getting married, and who now was in a *rather curious situation.* One that might cause him to chat to Alex Burney in a state of some inner turmoil – or perhaps banal embarrassment, merely. Because the situation turned out to be, when you'd read the letter, that he had wished to ask Alex if he might propose to his daughter. But had not done so. Because the girl had told him not to.

Georgia's letters in those last months of peace in Burma said a lot, and implied more. But Charles Lammas had to wait till after the war, before he got an explanation of this refusal to let the man she was in love with ask for her hand in marriage.

Still, by late '41, Lammas had before his amused mind's eye at least one solid fact which her last months of hectic letters did not spell out but resoundingly confirmed. Which was, that she wasn't just in love with Christopher de Brissac. She was having an affair with him, and was so ecstatic in her happiness that she couldn't scrawl the smallest detail of her existence without this easy triumph of the sensual mind shining through.

Her godfather had written to her about the Home Guard. How Shakespeare would have loved them. Was she looking after the edition he'd given her? Yes, there were honestly times when Bardolph and Poins, Pistol and Nym seemed to be alive again.

She wrote back about how she could just imagine him on Paston cliff with that bunch, and the book had fallen into the fountain at the club but truly wasn't much the worse, and she'd been reading *Much Ado*. Dogberry was a Home Guard character right enough, wasn't he? *Are you, by any chance, dear Godfather Charles, becoming a sort of latter-day Dogberry?*

That was all in the vein of letters received before. Then Georgia wrote about going to Rangoon to stay with Ricky. And it was plain she'd scarcely seen him. It was plain that de Brissac had more occasion to sojourn in the country's capital city than in a hill station, even if it *was* a summer Seat of Government, and there *was* an Army cantonment. It was furthermore plain that anyhow they hadn't spent much time in Rangoon – convenient, there, though the absence of Geraldine's gossipy network must have been.

They'd gone gallivanting off, the girl quite shameless, on the little steamer to Martaban, and up the river Dundami. Then, from Duyinzeik, they'd gone by rail – on a gorgeous, toy railway Georgia wrote – through the forested hills to the ancient city of Thaton, or what was left of it.

Reading, Charles Lammas imagined a bungalow bedroom, somewhere in Lower Burma. Georgia Burney at a cane table, wearing a kimono of some fashion perhaps . . . but writing, writing. And Christopher de Brissac, with a glass in his hand, in a dressing-gown, lounging across the room and coming to stand behind her. Looking down, over her shoulder, at what she was writing. Reading it. Saying something like, 'Good heavens, you aren't sending this to Charlie, are you? He'll be bound to guess.'

SEVEN

1

—๛—

Afterwards, everybody said that the British in Hong Kong and Singapore, in the Malay States and in Burma, had been living in a fool's paradise. Particularly those who had not been there said that.

Like most others who lived through that collapse of empire, Georgia Burney would say Yes. Certainly, she would agree, that's what it turned out to have been. But she never conceded that the defeats and the slaughters had not, by some, been foreseen. Never conceded, either, that though with hindsight it would have been better to have offered independence all round back in the thirties, in those months of the attacks those territories could have been defended. And she had a habit of adding, that at least she'd had her paradise. Of saying: If that was folly, give her more of it.

It was true that half the British in the East spent an unconscionable amount of time complaining about the countries they lived in – which to Georgia appeared a pitiable lack of aliveness to things. After her exile to England, when she came back to Burma she found she hadn't misrecollected all that much. She remembered how to speak Burmese. She could still speak to the Shan countrymen too. She then discovered that the land of her happy childhood's swimming below the waterfalls and jogging into the hills on a pony was only one Burma, and that as a young lady she now had access to further beguilements. Either that, or somehow these days everything she did, everything she sensed, seemed to stop her in her tracks with wonder.

Of course, she had the advantage of being Alex Burney's daughter. He'd done his best to bring his children up to be aware of how they belonged to the line of Westerners in the East – had it from birth, for good or ill, that ambiguity. That being of, and not being of. That having several selves, and not having them. And he'd enjoyed more success with Georgia in his attempt at this education than he had with Ricky – who, like most of the British in the East, knew himself of a caste apart, and preferred another glass of gin to another reminder of an Easternness he frankly didn't feel. More success than with Emma, who walked with a limp, and never learned to talk very well.

Georgia had grown up with stories of the renaissance navigators and merchants criss-crossing in her memory, and since she'd been back in Burma her father and she had picked up their old talk again. All his stories were remorselessly of invasions and counter-invasions, often just

one court butchery after another. In Alex Burney's telling and in Georgia
Burney's understanding, the frailty of political magnificence was plain, and
the cheapness of life was plain. She remembered it, afterwards, when she'd
seen the streets of Mandalay horrible with the dead and the dying, and
seen the British imperium replaced by the Japanese.

Stories, too, of adventurers' grandeur, which startled with how utter
their obliteration had been, startled with the absence of any echoes audible
afterwards. Mergui was an insignificant little port now, with swamps and
wooded islets in the delta behind it. With forty miles back the dilapidated
battlements of Tenasserim, and back again just forest and mountain. But
in the fifteen-hundreds and sixteen-hundreds it was a Siamese possession,
and there was great trade with Malacca and with Bengal. Trade in copper
and quicksilver, in silk and vermilion, in opium and benzoin and musk and
cloves. It was the start of the overland route to Bangkok, and in the 1680s
the Crown of Siam appointed Richard Burnaby as Governor of Mergui, and
appointed Samuel White as Shabander, an office which gave him control
of customs and shipping. Burnaby was a man of harems and drunkenness.
But when fighting broke out between Siam and Golconda, White's ships
brought prize after prize into Mergui, and his power grew. Then in
June 1687, the frigates *Curtana* and *James* anchored there, and Captain
Weltden came ashore with a proclamation, issued at Windsor by James
II, commanding all Englishmen to leave the service of that monarch and
repair to Fort Saint George on the Coromandel Coast.

All a manoeuvre, Burney explained to his daughter. All cooked up by
the East India Company, who had not relished the failure of their Siamese
enterprises (the French were more successful). Had relished even less,
no doubt, the naval and mercantile successes of the interloper Samuel
White. For that matter, the Honourable Company had already begun a
war of reprisals against the Mergui pirates, as they called them, and were
looking for a base on the eastern coast of the Bay of Bengal.

Anyhow, this proclamation was read by Weltden in White's drawing-
room, and all the English seafaring men at Mergui expressed their readiness
to obey the royal command. But the Siamese began staking the river and
mounting batteries of guns, and the British retorted by hauling up the
stakes and declaring they'd spike the guns.

White must have been afraid of an English attack, and complied with the
proclamation simply to make the best of a bad business, Burney supposed.
But possibly it was innocent of Weltden to take his compliance at face
value, when his orders from Fort Saint George had been to blockade
Mergui till the change of the monsoon in October enabled him to sail
back to Madras. Certainly it was innocent of both men to give themselves

up to weeks of debauchery. Because one night, when in the town they were enjoying their drink and their harlots, the Siamese batteries opened fire, and their troops massacred every Englishman they could lay hands on – including the Governor, Burnaby, knifed at his last orgy. The *James* was sunk. White got clear away in his ship *Resolution*, and Weltden in *Curtana*. They ran for shelter among the islands off the Tenasserim coast. And that, said Alex Burney to his daughter, two hundred and fifty years later. That was the end of the English in Mergui, for a long time.

2

—ɯ—

Alex Burney had been licentious in his day, had enjoyed the erotic unashamedly – even if these were not pleasures to be taken, in his case, any more seriously than after a hot day's work he took his bath and his whisky. Not that he ever had the seraglio in one of the remote Shan princedoms with which the Maymyo club wits supplied him. And anyhow, by the time of his conversations with Georgia about Mergui, for instance, right at the end of his life, all that was in the past. He'd even stopped going to visit Doctor Drew in Mandalay.

The first time, they had a gruff exchange along the lines of, 'Is this damned thing what I suspect it is, Drew?' and, 'Well, Burney, you're lucky we don't treat it with mercury any more. Here, let me give you a drink.'

Drew always kept a bottle of Scotch in a cupboard in his consulting room, for when a patient's morale needed to be kept up, or his own did. They sat with the brass fans stirring the heat, which was hot season, plains heat. With bullock carts rumbling by, the other side of the blinds, in the dust and the glare. Drew explained how Burney's chancre and his swollen glands would heal in a few weeks, but that didn't mean the secondary symptoms wouldn't start to show after two or three months, and they were a lot nastier. So the thing was to begin a first course of the treatment soon, before too many of the spirochaetes got into his liver, or the outer lining of his brain, and other places where they wouldn't do him any good and would be difficult to eliminate. What did the beastly little things look like? What *were* they? Well, if you got one of the little buggers under a microscope, it looked like an elongated corkscrew. Now, the secondary symptoms . . . And the treatment – which would be a combination of arsenic and bismuth. Or rather, an arsenical compound known as the Erlich-Hata remedy, or salvarsan . . .

Burney listened, impassive, in the shadowy room. He could hear Drew thinking, *By God he's a cold one*, but he didn't care. He could hear the, *Didn't someone tell me the poor chap had a bad war?* just as distinctly as he could hear the talk about the old days, when it was always anxious work waiting to see whether the mercury bumped off the spirochaetes before it finished poisoning the patient. He heard about the rashes and blisters he was going to get, the fever and the inflamed eyes and . . . *The reward of sin is death*. He smiled, remembering that. He smiled again, to notice the flicker of astonishment on Drew's face, hear his *Damned if I ever met a . . .*

He sipped his whisky, went on brooding that the rewards of lascivious-ness in his particular case appeared to be going to include a sore throat, aching bones, patches of his hair falling out – well, he hadn't got much – and . . . Good heavens, Drew was piling it on a bit, wasn't he? And the side effects of these toxic injections the fellow proposed to give him for weeks and weeks sounded worse than the bloody disease. Shivers and shakes. Twitches and cramps. Diarrhoea, kidney pains, vomiting, sores. God Almighty. *The reward of* . . .

'No,' Burney dryly answered a question he had only vaguely heard. 'There is no possibility of my wife having been infected.'

'Oh. Right. Sorry, old man. Have to ask, you understand.'

'Quite so. Now, listen Drew. If I've grasped what you've been saying . . . Periods of latency and recurrence. Need for course after course of the bismuth and salvarsan or what-have-you. When are we ever going to be sure I'm cured?'

'Well, I'm afraid you've hit the nail on the head, Burney. No need for us to go in for gloomy talk about tertiary syphilis, because if you ever develop that it won't be for ten years or more. But in the meanwhile . . . It's very difficult *ever* to know you've cured it, till the patient dies of something else. And even then . . .'

'I see.' He stood up. 'I'll let you know.'

Concluding at a glance that an offer of another splash of Scotch in his glass was going to be refused, Drew rose too.

'I'd much rather you made an appointment right away to start this treatment. I've explained how it'll make you feel lousy, but . . . Believe me, it's a disease we must stop if we can.'

Burney went through with it, naturally. Went through with all the rewards of lasciviousness which the injections caused. From the first pain to strike, which was in his gums and his teeth, to the skin eruptions he was still getting weeks later. The only easy part of the whole ghastly business was his lying to Geraldine about his symptoms, and about some of his absences from home being in fact stays in Mandalay hospital. For some years, they had spoken to one another more openly in public than when alone, and neither of them ever questioned the other's offered reasons for anything.

Georgia Burney met Drew, later. Not in Mandalay hospital. In the gaol. In circumstances so atrocious that the doctor answered the young lady's questions with almost no hesitation. Told her why her father had sought him out. Told her about the stoical way in which he'd put up with his syphilis and the treatment for it, with a frankness that was not of peace time. Not that she looked like a young lady, when they met for a few minutes in the prison yard, where there was a well with a bucket and a rope. She looked like he did, or nearly as bad. Long, filthy, matted hair. Filthy emaciated body, sores oozing. Black bruises where she'd been beaten. Cuts, festering. And her hands were a mess, where her fingernails had been dug out and pulled out.

This was in an interval of the interrogations. Sometimes, for no apparent reason, prisoners were allowed to drag themselves to that well, let down the bucket, tip water over their flesh. The priest was there too, the Italian priest from the oil-fields. He was a well-known figure then, in Mandalay gaol. The Japanese had tortured him so badly that he had lost his reason, and now they left him in the yard. His vestments were in rags. He stood there, shoving the beads of his rosary into his mouth, trying to chew them. Whenever one of the guards came near him, he made frenzied attempts to renounce his faith, over and over again. But his mind was so destroyed that he could not do even that coherently.

Drew told Georgia that he did not know why, if he were not to be allowed to use his medical skills, he had not yet been killed. Doctors had been murdered when captured at their posts. At Saint Stephen's Hospital in Hong Kong, the Japanese had killed several doctors and nurses, and a lot of patients. At the Alexandra Hospital in Singapore, too, when that island fell. In a few minutes, the place was a slaughter-house. First they butchered the staff. Then, ward by ward, the patients were bayoneted where they lay in their beds. The killers went at it so fast, they even bayoneted some wounded Japanese that the British had been trying to patch up – or maybe it was to reward them for falling into enemy hands. Drew said that other doctors, captured alive, in the prison camps were allowed to do what they could for the sick and the wounded and the maltreated – do what they could, with practically no drugs and no equipment. He had done that. But this interest the Military Police were now taking in him . . . He couldn't account for it. Well, he expected they'd shoot him soon. Often, he hoped they would. Did Georgia know what had become of her parents? Had they got out?

So there, in Mandalay gaol courtyard, Georgia Burney told her fellow survivor of *Kempeitai* interrogation techniques, how they'd got Geraldine a place on one of the last trucks taking civilians down from Maymyo to the airfield here. How she'd persuaded her mother to go, with her jewels stitched into her clothes, and one suitcase – Geraldine, with a single suitcase! – and Blenheim in his wicker cage. She had persuaded her to go, by promising to be on the next truck herself. Had heard almost immediately that some sensible man had said that refugees with parrots were a bloody farce, with space on any form of vehicle at a premium – so Blenheim had been restored free to his native skies while the truck was still grinding down toward the plain. Had heard later that the last flight out of Mandalay had already left, so her mother had set off among the thousands of others who in those weeks attempted the trek out to India.

And her father? the doctor asked. He'd stayed, of course. Burma was his home, by then.

They were not like the Catholic priest, those two, trying to wash their weals, muttering under their guards' scornful supervision. Their brains were still capable of renunciation and betrayal. This respite with their buckets of fresh water couldn't last long.

So Georgia's story of her father's end was hurried. Very brief . . . But Drew could imagine the rest. Charles Lammas could imagine it all, too, when after the war in his Edingthorpe library he read her fragments, her telling of what she had heard and seen. When he brooded on the life and death of his brother's friend.

Oh yes, Burma was Home for Daddy just like it was for her, Georgia told Doctor Drew. So many times, she'd heard him urging her mother to escape while it was still possible, heard him refusing to go with her. And then
Well, a non-combatant of sixty-odd might expect the conquerers to herd him into a camp, or consign him to some form of slave labour. Maybe even leave him be. Ignore him – why not? Depended on the conquerers, of course. And in her father's case it couldn't be a question of standing by his post, because that month his post as a Forestry Officer had ceased to exist. And yet he did, in a sense, stick to his position.

Not the only man in one of the territories being overrun to decide he didn't feel like giving in. Not the only man in the only town where half the people had bolted, and the other half were surrendering as hard as they knew how and changing sides as hard as they knew how, to decide he'd rather get himself shot defending his own house.

Georgia had not been there then. When she had got back to the house, the Japanese soldiers her father had shot in the garden had been carried away for military burial, and the house had been . . . sacked. Defiled. Daddy was still there. Dead. Very dead.

Still, Alex Burney had at least had his rediscovered daughter, those last years. He'd even had, those last months, his discoveries as to her relations with de Brissac, and the even stranger discoveries about himself which these occasioned in him.

Of course, poor Drew knew nothing about that. He scarcely had time to say to his fellow prisoner, 'Typical of your father.' Scarcely had time to add, 'So . . . He did die of something else, before we knew if we'd cured him.' The guards were at them again, kicking, shouting. They were hustled away to their cells. Drew never saw Georgia Burney again – though she saw him, once more.

But Charles Lammas in Norfolk, who had read her letters written in her last months of freedom, knew something of her joyfulness then, and how it had caused new germinations in the mulch of her father's awareness. So that when later he read her war-time scribblings, at least he did not only have those horrors in his head. Though it didn't stop him being haunted until his own death by that hill station with its bomb damage, its officials run away, its people cowed. Those roads where the first Japanese troops were appearing – and they weren't the only danger. In Burma then you were nearly as likely to be killed by a detachment of retreating Chinese, or a band of turn-coat Indians, or a band of dacoits.

Alex haunted him. Alex deciding not to fly out to India. Discovering, then, that this was not a defeat he wished to be part of, he'd rather go down fighting. Not that those soldiers he shot before their comrades shot him were his first kills of the new war. He'd already used that sporting rifle of his when a couple of shifty-looking characters appeared in his street of that lawless town earlier that week, and in a flash he realised they weren't the locals they were dressed as. He was right, too, he found out when they were dead and Georgia was helping him drag them to a slit-trench where they'd be easy to bury. Under their peasant get-up, they wore Japanese Army tunics. It was that brisk struggle to conceal the evidence of that shooting which gave Georgia, a few days later, the idea of what to do with her father's body.

Charles was haunted by that. By few things, in the second war, more than by that scene. The girl who ran through the devasted town to her father's house. Still only a girl, really. Not yet twenty, that week when she saw her first armed Japanese coming toward her. The girl who went with a white face from ruined room to ruined room. Who came out onto the verandah, and cried out at what she saw. Knelt down in horror beside the man riddled with bullets, foul with blood and flies.

She was still too innocent, or too shocked, to reflect at the time that to be shot down like that in what had clearly been, once they'd identified where he was, a terrific concentration of fire, was the best of good fortune. That was the kind of reasoning which her war taught her quickly – but it hadn't yet.

No. She just wept. Knelt beside him, weeping piteously, until she realised that she wanted to bury him. At once. Quickly, before the men came back and perhaps shot her.

She didn't have time, talking to Drew after a couple of years of the occupation, to recall those sorts of details of what she'd felt. But she'd written it down, and afterwards her godfather read it.

I wanted Daddy safe underground. I wanted to be the person who buried him. I wanted to kneel by his grave.

The rains had not yet started, the ground was hard. She didn't know how much time she had. She was new to that bobbing about in the wake of a retreating army, a disappearing way of life. But with the forward formations of the advancing army already there, the deathly hush all around her probably wasn't going to last long. And then she remembered the slit-trench.

It was horrible to her how cold and slimy he was, but she hugged him to her. She half lifted and half dragged him down the steps and through the garden to the trench. She thought of running for the parson, thought of a proper service, a grave beside Emma's. But she wasn't sure who had legged it for India and who hadn't. She thought of a grave under the japonicas right there. How she'd make a wooden cross and paint it white and write her father's name and his dates, and perhaps later she'd plant a rose bush. Then she remembered the ground was hard. And she was beginning foggily to know that the days of decorous burial thereabouts were over for a while. Over, the days of white crosses shaded by frangipanis and japonicas.

She chose a bit of the trench a fair way from where they'd dumped the two spies, and where she'd be able to find it if she were alive after the war. Between two vast rain-trees she'd known all her life (high in one of them, Ricky and she had built a tree-house), on a line with the Maclarens' hedge and . . . Right. She slithered into the trench with her father's body. Gasping, she laid him straight. She scrambled out and went to fetch a spade.

Still no one had come. The piles of earth left by the workers who had dug the slit-trench were still there. The first few spade-fulls, Georgia tipped into the grave as gingerly as she could. As if the soil might hurt him. But when he was covered, she shovelled fast, glancing anxiously this way and that. Then she smoothed the earth down. She took the spade back to the garden shed, went into the house to wash.

She came back to where Alex Burney, who had been raised up from Passchendaele mud, was in Maymyo ground for good. She knelt down. Her hands were shaking, she noticed.

She did not cry for him again. Her time for tears seemed to be passed. She bowed over the soil. She whispered to him.

At least we had our good time at last. She murmured that, she wrote later, and her godfather read later. *Oh Daddy darling, at least we found each other again. We loved one another again. At least I knew who you were.*

3

—⚎—

Their good times they had at last. After Burney had stopped going down
to Mandalay to be what felt like half-killed by Drew's arsenical compound.
When his syphilis was either cured or latent. Times which started being
good when Georgia came back out East, and he refound in her their
old Matter of Burma, a stratum laid down in her consciousness like coal
beneath an ancient forest.

He found other Matters also, strata where the stories were of the West.
She told him about a stained glass window with the Archangel Michael
and a grey destroyer, with Britannia, with swans, with *Heligoland Bight*
and *Dogger Bank* and *commissioned and commanded.* It made him think of a
letter Charlie Lammas wrote about then. *I hope you find her as intriguing and
delightful an emissary to receive as I did.*

Alex Burney found spirits in her, too, which appeared to be innate. Her
rebelliousness . . . Which had come out in her hatred of school, and now
was manifesting itself in all manner of devil-may-care insouciance. Often,
to her mama's consternation, in disrespect for distinguished members of
the colony's upper classes, and in defiance of attitudes which all the
world acknowledged to be correct. Had Georgia generated in herself this
not being impressed, this not accepting, this forming other judgements?
Or was it, her father wondered, just another form of the conventional
jauntiness which in Ricky he found so depressing? Did he himself harbour
a spirit of rebellion – or might he have done, if the Western Front hadn't
. . .? If those months and months of men being killed in the mud, and
then the days of the barrage, and then the torture of his wounds hadn't
somehow . . . So he had been different, since.

But Georgia was such infectious fun to be with, that Alex did not expend
much speculation on whether as a child she had been too steadily happy
to reveal her rebelliousness. Or on whether part of her happiness, now
she was back East again, was the pleasure her autarky afforded her. And
heartening it was, for his acquaintances in Upper Burma, to witness the
way the old fellow let himself be beguiled by his daughter.

Not that his upright, bony figure looked any the less rigidly bolted
together, when you bumped into him as he escorted his wife and daughter
to church or to the club. Or rather, often he escorted only his daughter.
Because although the Burney bungalow was close enough to both these
institutions to make it a pleasant stroll – although the family was securely

hitched to both those pillars of British dominance in the East – these days, even in agreeable weather Geraldine had a tendency to require a tonga or a rickshaw.

Not that Burney's gaunt, sallow countenance altered for the better, either; or that his hats' brims were pulled with less severe formality to shadow his eyes; or that he handled his Malacca walking-stick with unseemly exuberance. No.

In those last years of peace – until the man decided that, after the way the Japanese airforce had been bombing and machine-gunning Burmese civilians in town after town, it was time to stand up and shoot back, or crouch behind your verandah wall and shoot back, pick off as many of the profaners of your peace as you could. Or he decided that, just because organisations were revealing their rottenness, the individual did not have to be defeated. Or something snapped in him at last, and he just felt murderous.

At any rate, that week he took to going around with a loaded rifle slung over his shoulder – so that, when suddenly he didn't trust those two characters skulking up his street, he was in action in a trice, which was lucky for him. And like other men of various races in Burma, and men from Russia to Morocco and Manchuria to Papua, and like quite a lot of women, and many who by rights ought still to have been children . . . He took with him a haul of the invaders which would have impressed blood-thirsty old Ted Eales, stumping his East Anglian marshes, and counting his pairs of nesting redshanks, and growling about how he had plans, these Jerries weren't going to find him a push-over.

In those last years, Georgia's merriment was infecting her father right enough. Those two couldn't so much as sit down at the verandah table for a game of backgammon without ending in peals of laughter. Burney's hats still drew their line of shade across his face – but his shadowed eyes often glittered with amusement. Those eyes that all the Burneys had, with a gleam of concupiscence in them that could be unsettling. And during that last year, when Chistopher de Brissac was not often bodily present in the Maymyo house but was always there, Alex Burney discovered flashes of his daughter's rebelliousness in himself, of her readiness to flout some commonly well-regarded canons of behaviour. Discovered them, for example, when he ambushed himself taking a genial interest, even a mildly wicked pleasure, in the way Georgia was playing fast and loose with Lawrence Cowdrey's affections. Alex knew more than the girl ever suspected about that captain in the Yorkshires' honourable endeavour to become his son-in-law.

Maybe she *had* inherited her boldness from him. Anyway, oddly enough it was a remark of his, a seemingly casual comment he made to her, which possibly lay behind her refusal to become engaged to de Brissac.

4

—∼—

Georgia rejoiced in her power over her father. In greater things – as when she said, 'Daddy, you'll take me with you on your next tour of duty, won't you?' And he did. So that for months up-country she had him practically to herself, and her word was law over him. So that with the courtliest decorum she was introduced to Shan princes with whom over the years he had found it possible to deal amicably. And if, on occasion, in those ramshackle palaces in the back of beyond, there was a faint scent of concubinage in the air, she found it piquant.

In lesser things – such as when toward sunset her father and she would challenge each other to tremendous battles at backgammon. Alex and Georgia Burney would have considered it horribly serious – quite beneath their dignity – to play against the sort of people who betted. But there was between them a magnificent winning and losing of three-masted schooners, Palladian villas, relics of the Buddha from Kandy and pieces of the True Cross from Jerusalem, Shakespeare folios, Cheltenham Gold Cup winners, Ming jars.

Georgia rejoiced, when she found that with her he could take almost anything lightheartedly – even the futility of his marriage to her mother. Or the longing for England which he still often felt. Or what he thought was the parlous state of British power in the East. The precariousness of all this – with his whisky glass in his hand, he would indicate the gloaming – all this peace and privilege and prosperity.

She could make him chime in cheerfully with a lot of her feelings, Georgia found. Once he was rattling the dice-box while he intoned some incantation which was almost guaranteed to result in double sixes, or at least double somethings. And she said, 'Of course, we've got no business to be here.'

He didn't turn a hair. He was having far too jolly an evening. Or he knew how much of what she thought, and enjoyed, about the fools and their Eastern paradise she had imbibed from him.

He went on shaking his dice vigorously, and frowning at the pieces on the board. Said, 'No, my love, indeed we haven't. Better like it while we've got it. Anyway, thank heavens it's not your or my problem. When His Majesty's Government tells us to pull out, we'll pull out. Until then . . . Goddamnit, a three and a two. What's the use of a boring throw like that? Your turn. You want . . .' Screwing up his eyes, to read the board. 'A six and a one wouldn't do you any harm. I must recite my mumbo-jumbo to make sure you don't get it.'

'And if it isn't King George who tells us our time is up out here? If it's the Emperor of Japan, Daddy?'

'Mmm, well. Could find ourselves falling in with his wishes, couldn't we? Hope not. But . . . Last time your admirer was here . . .' Burney looked up from their game, gave her a wink. 'He was saying things that made even me sound like an optimist.'

'I was here too, Daddy, listening. You've forgotten. All that talk about how a lot of Malaya isn't jungle, it's rubber plantations, and perfectly possible for a mechanised army to advance through. You see – I remember perfectly well.'

'My most abject apologies, Georgia. I thought you were just gazing at the Colonel's handsome profile. Now, are you going to throw those dice or aren't you?'

'And about a war a few years ago between two South American countries, I can't remember which, where they used tanks in jungle. How he hoped the Japanese hadn't been studying that war, because far too few of us had. Only there was a man he admired in the Argyll and Sutherland Highlanders, who was training his men in the jungle. And . . . General Percival wouldn't let Brigadier Simson build defences on the peninsula, or lay mine-fields or get bridges ready to be blown up, because it might be bad for everybody's morale. And . . .'

'Stop, stop, my darling! Just roll those dice.'

'You see, I was listening. Double fours!'

When their battles at backgammon were over, Georgia might go on sitting on the verandah with the moths and the peacefulness. Or she might saunter out along the lane under the trees into the orderly town – past other comfortable houses like their own, those Europeans' houses which her father had taught her to regard as the outward form of an inner and outer strength which probably wasn't there any more. A strength that might last her time. (Even that year, most people of most races never seriously imagined it wouldn't.) Might not.

It was June when Alex Burney at the backgammon board made that remark to his daughter about how, 'Last time round, we reckoned those of us who weren't married were luckier.' Continued with, 'And I don't think we were wrong. Your godfather and I, for example. If you've got to fight a war . . . Less to fret about, if you haven't got a wife. Let alone children, for God's sake.'

The remark which had such an effect on the girl. Which to the end of her life she never decided whether her father had dropped into the conversation deliberately or not. It was the rainy season. And she knew that Christopher de Brissac and she wanted to seduce each other. And she knew he would very likely – under the circumstances of the great difference in their ages, and his friendship with her father, and his reputation as a man who did not succumb to marriage . . . He would, almost without doubt, either ask to marry her, or drop her.

So . . . Because it was the rainy season, which meant that even if it were not actually cascading down right then it was, if you were contemplating an after-backgammon saunter, unappealingly humid. And because as often as not the deluge *was* fairly thundering down – Georgia generally confronted her perplexities in a cane chair on the verandah.

Only perplexities was the wrong word for the rejoicing in all things which possessed her that year, so that she hardly cared what ensued so long as she was alive to delight in it. So that she'd sit watching sky-fulls of rain collapsing past the verandah's columns a few feet away, and hearing its pandemonium on the roof and in the monsoon ditches – and she would rejoice. She would think that it didn't matter what happened to Christopher and her – not really – not profoundly. Simply because she was alive, or – she didn't know – but because . . .

Georgia would sit alone, and bunch her knees up and rest her arms across them, and let her eyes linger on the Shan swords hanging on the verandah wall. Or she'd look at the big glamorous moths that circled around the lamp, or at the blackly-silvery crashing rain. Or then, under the monsoon-shaken trees along the lane, she might make out a horse, whose hoofbeats the storm drowned. And a covered tonga with a lantern it seemed impossible the cloudburst should not extinguish at any moment. And the driver, hunched up, with an oilskin cape pulled over his head and shoulders. In the rickety little carriage, there'd be somebody going home after a party. But who? – going from what to what? – thinking what? She'd wonder. She'd make up stories. She'd forget.

The household asleep. The verandah to herself. A lamplit stage, it would seem like to Georgia, and she an actress. The actress of – she didn't know what. A stage which gave onto the whole world, she would think, standing up and walking down toward imagined footlights, to her proscenium arch, and gazing out at the warm night and the monsoon.

Or she might cross to the side-board, and open the ivory box and take out one of the Turkish cigarettes – because these days she was rather enjoying her stylish handling of cigarette-holder and cocktail glass, and stylishness was, well, style could always benefit from a bit of practice.

So she might light a cigarette. She might even – her parents being safely in their separate bedrooms – pour whisky into one of the cut-glass tumblers, and gingerly hold it out into the edge of the warm waterfalling rain, so that her fingers were splattered and her drink diluted. Then she might turn, and command her stage – and whatever she did . . . (But one night of particularly intense actressing and story-telling, she became horribly tipsy, so that her head felt sick.) Whatever she did and however her thoughts pirouetted, she had an excited sense that nothing mattered, nothing would have any real consequences. Like that last English summer, when Jack and she . . . That living an idyll, living a freedom in which nothing followed from anything – though if she was honest she knew that Jack's feelings had been stronger than hers. Posing in the studio; lying awake waiting for your lover's footfalls along the creaking corridor. And now again, more dizzying than ever – it seemed there was a life you could live that was beyond causes and effects. Life as dangerous play you were going to get away with.

Hers was a ridiculously pampered existence, and doubtless quite unjustified, Georgia might confess to the cascading night. But she did not propose to feel a flicker of guilt. Precarious, this way of life? All right, then . . .

Now, where was that *Hopkins* which Christopher had given her? *That Nature is a Heraclitean Fire* . . . But of course it was, she knew that! puffing her cigarette smoke prettily, and picking up a little bronze Siva to toy with. It was also true that everything Christopher gave her to read had a habit of instantly convincing her with its rightness. And when he'd explained a bit about Heraclitus it was clearer. That nature was all those wonderful words like *heaven-roysterers*, like *shivelights and shadowtackle*. That nature was *the bright wind boisterous*, and was *yestertempest's creases*, was *squadroned masks*, was – where was the book?

Caterina was going to be sent down to Moulmein. It was awful, but she just knew she was, from the Mother Superior's tone of voice when she said it was possible. Caterina adored Christopher too, in her way. They were her shy giggles he liked, he said.

Roberta Gillway wasn't a virgin. Not any more. She too . . . *Flesh fade, and mortal trash Fall to the residuary worm; world's wildfire* . . . Would Christopher, if – would he insist on the children being brought up Roman Catholic? Would it matter? No, not a jot. Oh, after the war!

But if there were no war, despite what Daddy and Christopher said? Or if it didn't reach Burma? If normal life went on. Every now and then a wedding or a christening. Amy Foster was Mrs Duff these days, and expecting a baby.

And then Georgia might take pen and paper, write page after page to her godfather in England about Hopkins and about statuettes of Siva, about how glorious it was to have the verandah to yourself at midnight, and rain, and a moth with purple and grey wings which alit beside your writing hand.

Or she might go to bed. Lie under her mosquito net, dreaming of what it would be like to make love with Christopher de Brissac. Deciding to be up at crack of dawn, if the rain had stopped, wander out alone while the morning was still rinsed and glistening.

5

First thing in the morning, the humidity wasn't too bad, and Georgia always thought that the earlier she got up the better the coffee tasted which their Karen maid brought her. If there was a breeze, the recent downpour meant that it brought a faint, fresh coolness in to sway the blinds and the muslin curtains, and she liked that. She liked the lushness of the air after a night's rain, too. The verdancy she could taste in her nostrils, and if she parted her lips she could taste on her palate and tongue.

Then it was the finest freedom in the world to put on her hat, and whistle to the terrier Angus, and go out alone into the dripping avenues. Angus was terribly old now, and half-blind. But everyone agreed that her return had put new vigour into his cantankerous heart, and he always liked to accompany her on her walks.

'Where shall we go, Angus?' she would ask him. 'Is it bazaar day? Or shall we go out to the botanical gardens and see the cannon-ball tree? Or just meander?'

Because all she really wanted were the droplets pitter-pattering from the leaf canopies, and the coils of mist in the valley wreathing among the nobly plumed heads of the palms. And quite often the dog trotted ahead one way rather than another, and she would follow him idly, and end up at the bazaar when it was not bazaar day, so there were only a very few country people there, who had come in to sell their vegetables and their fish, their woven things and carved things and silver things. Or she would find herself near the hospital when no one she knew was there and might like to be visited. And because all she had wanted had been to see a pawpaw with its brilliant yellow gourds spangled with rain-drops. Or because all she had wanted had been to meet an old Shan gardener who was already clipping and raking, and with whom she always exchanged a few cheerful words. Or all she had wanted had been the steam rising from a wooded slope when the sun struck it, and the rainbows which came and went in the dazzling vapour, and *Glory be to God for dappled things*, and the songs the bulbuls sang.

Quite often she sauntered toward the church. Not usually the red-brick one, which was quite large considering Maymyo was a modest place. The older, wooden church, with Emma's among its graves.

It was not that de Brissac or Sister Caterina with their Christianity had made her feel Christian, or even with their Roman Catholicism had made her newly aware of her Protestant upbringing. As she had written to her godfather, she didn't think she was getting religious. But often it was Charles Lammas she thought of, if her dog and she dawdled that way, and she paused to admire – no, almost to worship – a flame-of-the-forest tree with the monsoon mist in it and the first sun on it.

Then as she dawdled on, looking, listening, thinking of *All things counter, original, spare, strange*. Thinking of *Whatever is fickle, freckled* (she was the latter for dead sure, Christopher had teased her, and the former too quite likely). Often she recalled her godfather taking her to Norfolk churches. Recalled what he had said to her once or twice about how he was the kind of man who in any age and any land would have frequented the local temple. Would with a quiet mind have gone through the rituals of whichever the religion happened to be. The rituals that honoured the dead, and paid homage to all that man could never explain or control. Innocent ceremonies that were a stitching together of a community, and a propitiation of the unknown. Godfather Charles walking to Edingthorpe church at Harvest Thanksgiving or on Christmas Day or Armistice Day. Sometimes also going, she knew, when there was no service. Alone. Not to pray. Simply to be there. She escaping Mummy's breakfast conversation by getting up early and coming here with Angus . . . Yes, propitiations, perhaps. Or just peace, and quiet, and solitude. Freedom.

She liked that church. And she liked going there, not with the actressy thoughts of late verandah nights, but with sleep-washed thoughts, monsoon-washed morning thoughts. So she would open the door for her aged, terrier friend, and ask: 'Coming in, Angus? Feeling religious today? According to the Christians, dogs like you haven't got souls, so it won't do you a bit of good. Well, I'll leave the door open, in case you feel like joining me.'

She would go in, thinking her customary mish-mash of thoughts. Maybe what Daddy had said at the backgammon board about the new nationalists, about the Thakins – and how she had once seen a photograph of Aung San and thought him handsome. Or of what he'd gone on to say about British administration here being – just between the two of them, mind you – being in many respects a mess. But at least the neglect was by and large benign neglect.

Then, if she sat down in their usual pew, her meditations were often highly un-church-like. All about how, on the eve of a war, if they were on the eve of a war, it might be a lot more satisfactory to have a love affair than an engagement – however quickly Mummy could be kicked into action to organise the wedding. Indeed, it was one early morning that rainy season on which Georgia Burney, alone in that wooden shrine to Church of England virtues and continuities, formulated her tactics for forestalling de Brissac's probable decision either to confine their relations to the most innocuous flirting or to chuck her while he could, by becoming his lover while she could. Before he . . . Heavens, in Singapore right this minute he was quite possibly deciding between Victoria Armitage and her. Wondering, perhaps, which he might have to marry, and which . . . For that matter, that girl and he might – at a safe distance from quarters where a batman would be laying out this, providing that – might be, under a mosquito net . . . 'Angus! Oh, so you decided you did have a soul.'

So – with the excuse of visiting Ricky, a descent on Rangoon. She must find out if Christopher were coming by ship or aeroplane. Then, on one of the Irrawaddy Flotilla ferries, on the long voyage up the great river . . . If he had anything he wished to say to her, he would have time. They might go ashore at Pagan, and get a rickshaw to go to some of the temples. She would have time . . .

But then, sitting in her pew with her dog flopped at her feet, Georgia might start inconsequentially reading the memorials on the wooden walls, and become aware of the graves outside. Her godfather Charles might come to her – and how she was part of her tradition, of the English in the East, just as he on that North Sea coast was part of his tradition. What he'd said to her about how a church bound you to your past and even, imaginably, to a future. The music, the liturgy, the architecture, the graves. They bound you to other people.

These musings came muddled up with Christopher de Brissac's next arrival in a couple of months, and how the time was ripe, was now, they must act or not act. Muddled up with Roberta's engagement to her Burmah Oil man which was about to be announced. With Daddy's good spirits when conversing with any of the prettier young English wives in Maymyo. (There were extremely few of them, and they led a wonderfully cherished existence.)

But then, also . . . The little, wooden, English church. The dead who were *her* dead. The community of ghosts. The air she breathed of old hopes and justices and injustices. Good things achieved, and things done infamously. Old loyalties, old griefs, and new – new? – she wondered. Anyway, it was hers, this shrine, this air. For better or worse . . . She couldn't step aside from it. Had no other. Was no other.

6

'You won't find Caterina at Maymyo this time. She's been packed off down to Moulmein. Are you sad?'

Christopher de Brissac, with his hat pulled down over the grey which these days was springing up in his brown hair like a crop of wild oats in a wheatfield, stood beside Georgia Burney at the rail as their Flotilla ferry steamed in toward the cliff at Pagan. Or rather, toward the cliff of what eight hundred years ago and a thousand years ago had been that nonpareil of a holy city. Was now dozens and dozens of square miles of low plateau cut by ravines, littered with a few poor hamlets. Littered with several hundred ruined temples, and not so hopelessly ruined temples; with immaculate pagodas; with crumbling-away stumps of pagodas among the copses and fields; and some which now were no more than grassy mounds.

'Sad? I've never *quite* understood why you attributed such a passionate friendship to Sister Caterina and me.' His green eyes smiled at her, mildly sardonic.

It was autumn. The rains had tailed off. The Irrawaddy was high, and today it was glassy, reflecting the blue sky and a few white clouds, and the traders' sails. The cliffs were tawny. From miles out – that river could seem more like a swirling lake – they had seen the first pagodas that crowned the heights. Now they were close enough inshore to see the sandmartins wheeling in front of the bluffs.

'Oh, it's your religion.'

Georgia was pleased so far with what she thought of as her surprise raid on Rangoon. Ricky had swept her up in a terrific social whirl for a few days. Then they had met Christopher at the harbour, and the good sense of their travelling up-country together had been too obvious to ignore, a temptation neither of them had felt like quibbling over. She liked the ferry, with its polished woodwork and brasswork, the other passengers who were English and Indian and Burmese. She was enjoying treating Christopher to her prettiest dresses and her fizziest merriment, and enjoying his knowing this was what she was doing and his liking that. So now she cocked her head slightly sideways, gave him the benefit of her eyes' boldest amusement.

'When I first saw Caterina and you together, I thought, Oh they're so different, being both Catholics won't be a thing you'll notice. And you *are* very different. I mean . . .' She laughed softly. 'I remember a wonderful story she told me about how they'd never worked out what her father had learned at school, because he always got her mother to do any reading or writing that was required. All the same . . . Belonging to that Church of yours is a bit like belonging to the same family, isn't it? If you're in it, it's something you take totally for granted. And the way you both *know* your Church's teaching is right! I can't understand it. Everything is assumed . . . Even if for her it's a matter of going endlessly to mass, and doing everything the Mother Superior tells her to without ever wondering about it, and exhausting herself nursing sick people and teaching small children their catechism. While for you it's a matter of going to mass most infrequently, and sitting up at night reading poetry, usually with the help of a decanter and a cigar. Even so . . . It's a sort of world-wide club you're both members of.'

'A family? Yes . . .' de Brissac said slowly. Thinking that she must have an idea why he was coming to see her parents and her. Allowing himself a few seconds' hesitation – in which his heart thudded with unseemly agitation. Also, he noticed that the moment was far from ideal, because in a minute they would be at the pontoon. 'Or a club, I suppose, if you like. But not an exclusive one. And one which would welcome you, Georgiana, if you were ever to contemplate such a move.'

'Me?' she wondered gaily. 'Poor, wretched, heathen me? Christopher . . . Is that why you've been giving me books by Crashaw and Hopkins and people?'

'Natural enough, surely, to want to share what has given one so much pleasure. Oh Lord – look, we're arriving. Share the poetry one has loved, share that life of the spirit, that beauty, with . . . I say, shall we talk about this when we're ashore? Mind out, we're standing where they want to put the gang-plank.'

He drew her aside a little from the worst of the bustle of fenders being put out and coiled warps being thrown.

'With . . .?' Asked wickedly.

'Oh, well . . .' In humorous despair, he glanced around at the medley of parasols. 'Here we go . . . Share everything with you, Georgiana. With you who I hope one day will marry me. Will you?'

She caught her breath. Her opaque eyes blazed into his.

'Do I have to become a Catholic, Christopher?'

'You don't *have* to do anything. But it would make me very happy.'

Her smile was shamelessly mischievous. 'It'd make things a lot simpler for you – I see that. Poor Mummy! If I ever get married, she'll want it to be in our little church at Maymyo.'

'Georgiana, perhaps we'd better get ourselves and our kit on land. This is a hopelessly ill-chosen moment to ask you. But believe me, I have thought about it for a long time. Now . . . The village with the rest-house is called Nyaungu or something, isn't it? Years since I last stopped here.'

'Yes, that's right. Not much of a place. For a long time, you've been thinking . . .?'

'A very long time, Georgiana. And have you . . . May I hope that one day you may say Yes?'

Her direct eyes were afire with amusement. 'Oh, I've been heels over head in love with you for at least three years. Christopher . . . That time at the Strand, when you told me not to get engaged to anyone, or anyhow not for a good long while. Were you keeping me for yourself, or saving yourself from me?'

He smiled at her, but for a few moments said nothing. Then – 'When we get to Maymyo, I'm going to ask your father for your hand, in a nice old-fashioned way.'

She thought about it, with a quiver on her mouth which afterwards he could never decide had been of victory or of unhappiness.

'No, don't. Because I'd say No.' Then, seeing the hurt jolted into his eyes, she added quickly, gaily: 'Come on, let's go ashore. Heavens, what's the rush? You've got along fine without being married for long enough, haven't you? I'll marry you . . . when the war's over. If you still want me.'

'When the war's over?' He had briskly regained his amusedness. 'But here it hasn't started yet! Why this sudden concern for international relations? And what happens if we're lucky, and the Japanese don't attack?'

'Who knows? Look, that's your trunk they're unloading. Shall we not care too much? Listen, for visiting the temples . . . Much more fun than a rickshaw, would be if we could hire a pair of horses. What do you think?'

As Georgia had said, Nyaungu wasn't much of a place. Like the other scruffy settlements of Pagan, the charm of its wattle and matting houses and its trees and sandy tracks vied with the desolation of what, when King Anawrata ruled, had been the capital of an empire which stretched from the Gulf of Martaban to Southern China, and from the Bay of Bengal to Cambodia.

Still, these days the village had a British magistrate and a wooden Court House, and a post office too, and of course a bazaar. And the Burmese manager of the rest-house had quarters to offer them. A room for the Lieutenant Colonel, certainly. And the best room in the house, which happily was vacant, for Miss Burney, who was please to admire the great tamarind tree outside her window which cast such ample shade.

Reflecting that for a man who had just been refused – had he been? hadn't he been? – he felt unaccountably cheerful, de Brissac went out to see what could be managed in the way of horses. With its cigar-seller, its acacias, its threshing floor . . . Not so sad as all that, the village, he decided. If you didn't dwell too much on the transience of imperial glories which whispered to you from the masonry weathering in every thicket of this countryside. Shacks where the pagoda slaves lived . . . Astoundingly conservative, Burmese society, in some ways. Royal line extinct, empire gone, palaces gone – but families dedicated centuries ago to serve a certain pagoda . . . Still here, still slaves, still in shacks.

Wondering whether the pagoda slaves would outlast the present empire, outlast the twentieth century with its progress and modern warfare, he strode through a gap in a cactus hedge to where he heard whinnying. The architects of old Pagan must have built their houses and palaces out of wood, he supposed. That would be why only monasteries and temples and stupas survived. Oh, and there were bits of defensive walls and earthworks too, if he remembered right, and at least one ruined gateway. Well, there *was* the Court House on a knoll, and a perfectly decent rest-house on another. British power hadn't yet waned, and quite likely wasn't going to.

Oh, I've been heels over head in love with you for at least three years. Smiling to remember that ball at Bure, he chose two horses with tasselled bridles. *When the war's over . . . Shall we not care too much?*

After all these years of not falling in love and not getting married. Just the occasional – what was the right word? – liaison. Then the years of not letting himself fall for her. Telling himself he wasn't bewitched at all, not really. Telling himself that she was too young, and anyhow what was so very different about her? But most of the girls he'd ever met would not in one breath have declared themselves heels over head, and in the next . . . *No, don't. Because I'd say No.*

When the fiercest of the day's heat was past, Christopher and Georgia rode their horses out over that plateau crossed by white sandy ways, by wooded gullies where streams ran sparkling over white sand. They mentioned the Ananda temple and the Thatbyinnyu, and the Shwezigon which was quite close and they could easily have explored. They tried to remember which of the mighty edifices was which, which were of stone or brick, which had famous carvings. But they did not turn their horses' heads toward any of the grander buildings gleaming white or glowing lion-coloured a few miles this way or that. They rode away at a walk among insignificant ruins.

Fields of millet. Acres of blowing grasses – ruffled greens and russets. Goats grazing. Cactus thickets with pink flowers. On the sandy track, a team of oxen plodding homeward to be outspanned and watered. It was when that team had passed, that Christopher reined in his horse, took off his white hat. He leaned from his saddle, pulled Georgia toward him, kissed her.

'Not easy, with your horse a hand higher, and mine restless,' she said. 'Worth it, though. I'll take my hat off too. There. Shall we try again?'

They rode on, and came to a pagoda with overgrown precincts where nobody ever came. There were wild plum trees. Here they tethered their horses. And here they lay down and made love.

When they came riding back in the evening to Nyaungu, the Irrawaddy stretching away to the western shore looked as if it had been glazed and then the sunset had been annealed into the glass. In the foreground, there were the carved sterns of a fleet of river vessels at anchor, and their dark masts and gaffs. Then there lay the great river like a lake of gold and vermilion and rose with beyond it the Tangyi hills in charcoal shadow. And then, beyond again, loomed the Arakan mountains, indistinct with distance and mist, but high enough to be ridged with flame by the last of the sun.

The horses' hooves thudded softly on the sandy road. Fruit bats with leathery wings were flapping about in the tree-tops.

'Don't let's do anything that matters too much, you and I,' Georgia said. 'What do you reckon? Let's just live – like this – doing this sort of . . .' She gestured with her eyes. 'When we can. This Irrawaddy sort of thing. Is that all right?'

'It's extremely all right. Only my temptation to tell your father that I did try to . . . All right! I promise, I won't say a word. Listen – when I get back down to Rangoon, if I still have a few days . . . Do you feel like escaping with me to somewhere obscure, where we'll be wonderfully invisible?'

'Being invisible with you somewhere obscure sounds glorious.'

7

—m—

By the time that de Brissac dined with the Burneys, he was feeling a little more at his ease about seeing Georgia's parents again than he had that day of his discovery that he was acceptable to her as a lover but not as a fiancé. Not much – but a little.

For a start, his return to Maymyo was a return to the Army cantonment there, to days which at once filled up with work. Thank heavens, he found himself thinking. Luckily, also, the first couple of evenings he dined at the mess, as the guest of the Colonel of the King's Own Yorkshire Light Infantry.

Then the next night there was a Charity Ball at the club, which he couldn't very well duck out of. A marquee on the lawn. The fountain floodlit. A special band, lately arrived in Burma from Calcutta, and supposed to be terribly good. Quite a shindig. And anyhow the Burneys were there, so there'd have been no point in going to their house. He caught Georgia's eye across a crowded room, and noted with approval the glister in her glance, and with more approval the distance she kept from him. Her mother was drooping on a sofa when he made his way through the crush to pay his respects to her.

Geraldine had expectations of his present sojourn in the country, Christopher knew – and he was quite sure that his Catholicism would not have been regarded as an insuperable obstacle. Fodder for conversation – of the type to keep twisting back to how fortunate it was that they, the Burneys, were broadminded; and how naturally, if their darling girl's happiness was at stake . . . But not an obstacle. Though the birth of an eventual child would have been the occasion of revived sectarian clamour.

Mrs Burney had, by dint of never dedicating an iota of thought to any lesser concerns, maintained a fair semblance of her youthful shape and pallor. With the help of bodices and diets. With the help of unguents and powders, of hats and veils and parasols – quite often all five at once, and supplemented with the usual awnings, trees, canopies and so on. Nor, although she approved of the Lieutenant Colonel as a suitor for her daughter, was she above larding her remarks to him with 'our generation', and 'at our age'. Though she was ten-odd years his senior. And would, he had never doubted, have taken a betrothal as the right time for much mother-in-lawish embracing, backed up with delicate, relentless badinage.

Now de Brissac felt confident, as he stooped courteously before the sofa where Geraldine Burney sat twitching a little Chinese fan before her powdered cheeks. Because the world of cantonments and club balls was a world the regularities of which had been sustaining and liberating him for years. Because he'd had a few days to mull over the situation – and although an engagement to be married would have been a novelty, he was not new to clandestine love affairs. And because, that night at Pagan, Georgia and he had lain awake late, and talked. So now when her mother with languid fervour complained that it was an *age* since he had last been at their house, (it had been five months, and he had not been in Burma since), and declared that he absolutely *must* come to dinner tomorrow, he accepted cheerfully.

Moonlight on the sleeping village of Nyaungu. Moonlight on the Irrawaddy swirling at the foot of the cliff where the sandmartins were asleep in their burrows. Shadow under the tamarind tree. The light of an oil-lamp, in Georgia's room, on the pale diaphanous swags of the mosquito net, on the pale bed where they made love.

Late, late, and happier than he could remember feeling, Christopher had said something along the lines of how, for pity's sake, of course she didn't have to marry him. Her desire not to was one which he had not the slightest difficulty in sympathising with. Or if she wanted to put it off till the end of a war that hadn't yet started . . .

Georgia had giggled. Well, now she thought of it . . . (Wriggling over silkenly in his arms, and kissing him.) How long, please, did wars generally last? He was a soldier, she trusted he could tell her that.

Or – he had pursued – if she fancied any other excuse for remaining single, naturally that was fine too. But . . . Didn't she think there might be certain advantages if they got engaged, and then got married as few weeks as possible later? For a start, she could come to Singapore as his bride. Whereas otherwise, they weren't going to see much of each other, at this rate. And, if there was a war . . . Well, two things. One was – oh, he didn't know, but – if things got bad, he'd like to think she was his wife. And the second . . . If he were killed, she'd get a small pension.

Georgia's thoughts that night were splendidly higgledy-piggledy, even by her customary standards of the far from monolinear. Then she had to leap out of bed, go to gaze out of the window at how the moonlight glinted on the upper planes of the mighty tamarind, and how inky black was the shadow below. (Go to pose very fetchingly, in the casement, naked, Christopher thought.) Then darting back into their gauzy tent, she unfortunately let a mosquito in with her. So she had to charge around on her knees, clapping her hands till she'd killed it.

Even so, she answered him a bit less skimpily that night than she had as their ferry came in to the pontoon. Obliquely, and with her talk peppered with divagations about how according to Daddy it might not have been Kublai Khan's Mongol hordes who put a finish to the glorious days of Pagan. Possibly an army of feudatory Shan princes' levies had been sufficient to do the job.

Often very obliquely . . . But along with her suggestion that one day he must let her take him to the sacred island of Shwegu, which was a forest of pagodas and her idea of paradise, he got a notion of her sense of precariousness. Derived in part from her father's awareness of imperial fragility. But in Georgia – if you listened to her chatter about how of course the war didn't come into it that much, and she was thrilled about Roberta Gillway's forthcoming wedding. If you heard her saying that everything he said made admirable sense, and he did her a great honour, but could she please just love him madly like this? Saying that even if their world *were* on the brink of dissolution, she was *delighted* that people went sensibly ahead getting married to one another and having babies. She was just stupid enough not to want to herself, to want more of this freedom, these passing moments. In Georgia, Christopher seemed to perceive a state of being in which others' solid facts were, to her, fibres of significance spun infinitely tenuous. Others' truths (his own Christianity among them) were stories so changeable and nebulous they might blow away any minute, you wouldn't be able to listen to them any more.

De Brissac was still puzzling over this while he knotted his bow-tie before an Army looking-glass, preparatory to walking through the town to dine with the Burneys. Or should he take a car? No, a walk would do him good. Georgia with her mind where everything was a vapour that might any moment be dispelled, a story that might be told differently every time. He with the Church. With the regiment.

Frowning at his reflection, he gave his tie a last tweak. Hearing her voice telling him about emperors and water-buffaloes, about pagoda feasts and what were those theatrical performances called, a *pwe*, that was it.

He took up his clothes brush, gave a few perfunctory knocks to the shoulders and sleeves of his dinner-jacket. This would have been the evening he'd have hoped to . . . Oh, hell. All those months of coming round to the conclusion that he *was* in love at last, he *did* want to marry her.

Well, it would be nice to see poor old Alex, whose wife still hadn't forgiven him for having had to sell Rufford.

8

De Brissac was still a couple of hundred yards from the Burney house, when he met Georgia, sauntering, waiting for him.

'I'm so happy!' she exclaimed softly, her eyes flashing, so that for a confused instant he thought he hadn't understood and they *were* engaged; or they were now; or . . . And his heart drubbed with painful exultation, until she went on.

'Can you guess? Mummy and Daddy don't just think it's all right for me to go back to see Ricky again soon. They practically insist I go! Most peculiar. Still, a gift horse . . .'

She laid her fingertips on his cuff. They stood under a rain-tree, in the warm nightfall.

'Do you suppose—' she dimpled – 'it's because in Rangoon there are lots of eligible men? Well, a few more than there are here. Or because they know you're going back there? It can't be because I'm much of a restraining influence on Ricky. Did I tell you about the time when Mr Griffiths wanted him to ride Razzmatazz in the Monsoon Plate? Well, Ricky had sort-of half-promised to ride for somebody else, but Razzmatazz wasn't an offer to be chucked up lightly. So Debbie Griffiths – she's had her eye on that brother of mine for years – Debbie said that if her father sent a case of the club's best champagne round to . . .'

Christopher de Brissac had decided he was not going to so much as mention marriage to Georgia Burney again. Conceivably after the war was over. But that was like saying maybe, sometime, never. If this was how she wanted to play it . . . and who was to say she wasn't shrewd? They'd play it her way.

But her merriment beneath that gigantic rain-tree, its boughs shaggy with creepers and ferns, set up in him such an ache of sadness that for a minute he couldn't speak. And then the gruff friendliness of Alex Burney's welcome . . . Or possibly it was the air seductive with the scents of roses and tobacco plants and jasmine – though with his experience of hill stations he ought to have been resistant to that. Or possibly it was that, since he'd gone from Sandhurst to the Western Front at about the age Georgia was now, Christopher had practically forgotten what family life could feel like; or was now finding desirable that which had never – when staying, for instance, at Bure Hall – appealed to him as something it might be better to witness from the inside rather than from without.

So that even the Burneys, with their coldnesses and sorrows, could on a good evening lap him round with their affections, reminiscences, teasings and jokes, until he found he was thinking that even Geraldine had her good points. Heavens, he knew others who were worse. And one should, if anything, be sorry for her.

At any rate, by halfway through dinner – certainly the Chinese shark's fin soup they started with had something to do with it, and the bottles of well-chilled white Macon – Christopher's melancholy had settled in his chest like a virus. He had to keep telling himself that it was no use dwelling on how much more interesting he'd found Alex of recent years, getting to know him better – because he was never going to be his son-in-law, so that was that. Just another likeable fellow, with whom a few times it had been pleasant to sit at night talking things over. He had to keep on not knowing that he'd wanted Georgiana for his bride. That girl across the table, with her stippling of freckles on her cheekbones, and her laughing eyes which this evening seemed to have tawnyish flecks in them, but no doubt tomorrow they'd appear to be greeny flecks, or there wouldn't be any flecks. He'd wanted her – after all these years of not wanting anyone like that – not as his lover. As his wife. So that the problem now was already beginning to be – and he must never forget that it was his fault for having had too many flings, not hers for being young and free. The problem was going to be: not thinking lightly of her. Not having her just as, not thinking of her as, his mistress. A word he disliked. Probably because he'd had too many brushes with it.

Then the prawn curry arrived, and Alex recalled that the finest one he'd ever tasted had been in Macao, washed down with a Portuguese wine he couldn't remember the name of, but it had been mighty good stuff. Had Christopher ever been to Macao?

He had. And he didn't know if Alex had remarked on the same discreditable fact, but he'd been taken aback by how the first Europeans in the East Indies and on the China Coast, after half of them had perished on that interminable voyage out – shipwrecks, piracy, every disease you ever heard of – when they got there, along with competing for trade with some ferocity, they also . . .

Absolutely, Alex interjected. He knew what Christopher was about to say. The way that, in the fifteen-hundreds and sixteen-hundreds, the English and the Dutch, the Portuguese and the Spanish, took their religious hatreds with them all the way to China. Talk about Christian fellowship. Or merely offering a friendly hand to others who'd survived the same hardships.

So the talk over the prawn curry was all about how both men had noticed that there had only been a Roman Catholic graveyard at Macao. Though the earlier headstones – very primitive, some of them – made sad enough reading. And the disgraceful fact had been, that the Portuguese running that trading station had required that when any Protestant mariner died there, his fellows carried him a few miles inland into the sun-stricken hills outside the settlement, scratched a hole in that stony earth for him where they might.

After dinner, Georgia played her father at backgammon, the best of three games, the winner then to do battle with their guest. She won right at the end, her position having appeared hopeless, by throwing – to her own accompaniment of wild prayers, mock-heroic imprecations, then victory cries – a string of doubles.

So it was that Christopher found himself sitting down at the backgammon board, opposite those dancing eyes. Across from her mouth where the merriment was almost continuous too. Only, occasionally, her lips were sullen. Had a tremor of that unhappiness he thought he'd seen them moved by on the ferry under the cliff at Pagan.

However, Christopher's distractedness was equally due to his quasi-certainty that Alex Burney intuited a fair amount more than he betrayed. About mutations in Georgiana; in him; their relations. Impossible to tell, of course. And the pity of it was, they'd never talk about this. It would go on being Francis Drake dropping anchor at Ternate. Or the first communities of Dominicans and Franciscans and Jesuits at Malacca. Or that suicidal – really, deservedly suicidal – Spanish attempt to acquire Cambodia, which ended in a frightful massacre in 1599. But all the same . . . Goddamnit, it was a *shame* they'd never talk.

So he lost the first game, by miles. Then grappling manfully with his fissile concentration, and aided by a lucky throw or two, in the second game he managed to scamper his pieces off the board while Georgia still had three of hers left.

'Right,' she said, laying out the board for their final contest. 'What are we playing for?'

Christopher had been right. Georgia Burney and he saw extremely little of one another.

He borrowed an apartment in Rangoon, and when he was there she came to him. As he had foreseen, he at once began to find this arrangement distasteful. But there did not seem to be any way of resolving matters differently – unless he ditched her, and he wasn't going to do that. He called her *my darling*, and he thought of her as his darling, and tried not to think of her as his mistress. It was distasteful too that Ricky was in the know. Georgia had recruited him as her ally in subterfuge – rashly, her lover thought, although perhaps it had been inevitable. And anyway, that impeccably aggressive young soldier and raffish socialite was an unattractively lifelike image of himself at that age.

The secrecy of their encounters, which Christopher detested, Georgia seemed to revel in as part of an intoxicating game. It gave her a sense of being detached from the humdrum world where everything mattered so boringly much, she told him. It gave her a sense of floating free, of – oh, surely he knew what she meant. Having your own hidden place was almost as good as having your own time to live in. To be invisible was almost not to be of this world at all – like ghosts. And when de Brissac got three days' leave before he next had to fly to Singapore, she enthusiastically set about plotting their escape to Thaton. Or should they disappear to one of the other ancient Burmese capitals – to Ava maybe, or Amarapura? No, Thaton was more out-of-the-way. The ferry to Martaban. Then up the river Dundami . . .

This was the venture of which she wrote to Charles Lammas so lyrically that her love affair sang out to him from every sentence. And it *was* idyllic, Christopher let himself or made himself feel, watching the reedy river-islands go by, looking at the shore trees, at the blue mountains ahead. Hamlets where the ferry halted, and passengers came out aboard sampans, and others went ashore. Fields of maize and beans. Rice paddies. Patches of chillies, grown in rows. Flocks of white egrets and grey herons that rose up when the ferry came fussing along. A cargo-boat with straining oarsmen creeping up against the current. Another with a reddish sail sweeping down. Idyllic – even if beside Georgia's high spirits he had to keep masking his discontentment, keep deflecting his sharpest thoughts.

So he strolled beside her to visit the pagodas of Thaton, and he concentrated on her story of how nine hundred years ago King Anawrata of Pagan had sacked the city, and from the royal library had borne away five elephant-loads of Buddhist scriptures. He strolled with her to watch the girls weaving silk, and he concentrated on what a pleasant old place Thaton was, with its clumps of bamboo and avenues of betel palms, its shrines and its monks and its schoolchildren. At the Shwezayan pagoda, he concentrated on a gigantic pipul tree of by all accounts fabulous age, and how pretty his lover looked, standing in its shade.

It was in their hideaway in Thaton, that de Brissac thought of Charles and Blanche Lammas more intensely than he had since that week after Charlie had had his stroke, and he kept driving over from Bure to Edingthorpe to sit with him.

Their bedroom had a simple dressing-table, and Georgia was sitting at it, wearing a négligée, brushing her hair. He was idly watching her arms and the movement of the brush, watching the side of her face and her hair which he could see past her shoulder in the looking-glass. 'I've got it,' he said suddenly. 'At last . . . The colour of that hair of yours. Bronze. Slightly tarnished bronze.'

She echoed him: 'Tarnished bronze . . .' thoughtfully. But she didn't smile. And then she did smile, but as if apologetically, and said, 'Christopher . . . Do you remember Jack Lammas?'

'Of course I remember him. Nice lad.'

'I . . . I've just had a letter from Godfather Charles. Well, a couple of weeks ago, actually. He . . . Jack's been taken prisoner. In Crete, in the summer. His father didn't write to me about it till they knew he was alive. He's in a camp in Germany.'

'Good Lord, why didn't you tell me before? Poor chap! Still, I expect he'll be all right.'

'I know, silly of me.' She went on brushing her hair. She was gazing into the mirror past her own head to where Christopher was sitting by the window. 'I should have told you immediately. You're his sister's godfather, aren't you?'

'I am indeed. Georgiana, now I think of it . . .' He smiled. 'That summer I bumped into you at the theatre, and then there was that dance at Bure. Charlie and Blanche's boy . . . An old flame of yours, my darling?'

She was still looking at him in the mirror. She nodded her head slightly, once.

'Much more suitable for you than I am. Why don't you marry *him*, when the war's over?'

'Because it's *you* I'm in love with!' He saw her reflected mouth tremble. She set down her hair-brush with a clatter. Her eyes brimmed with tears. 'For ever and ever, you! Haven't you understood anything?'

That Thaton expedition was a few days before the Japanese attack on Pearl Harbor, and the landings in the Philippines and Malaya. When they got back to Rangoon, Georgia drove Christopher out to Mingaladon airfield in her brother's car.

It seemed like an ordinary parting. When the time came, he said: 'Goodbye, Georgiana, my darling.' She said: 'Goodbye, Christopher.'

He turned, walked away to where his aircraft's propellers were already turning. When he took off into the dazzling blue, she waved her white hat in wide, slow arcs.

Three weeks later, on Christmas Eve, Georgia was still in Rangoon, doing some last-minute shopping for the party Ricky and she had planned for the next day. When she heard the sirens, she imagined it was a practice, but then she looked up. The Japanese bombers were flying in perfect formation, with their escort of fighters. Then she heard the first explosions, and the ack-ack gun on Monkey Point starting to fire.

With her arms full of parcels, Georgia ran back to where she'd left the car. High explosives, incendiaries, anti-personnel bombs. The fuel depôts in the docks were on fire. The wooden houses in the native quarters were on fire. When a bomb landed close enough to Georgia for the blast to knock her flying, after she'd picked herself up she dived into the nearest slit-trench.

In a lull, she got her head up and stared around. The street was littered with mangled bodies. A man near her was still alive. She scrambled out of her trench, and ran to him. An Indian clerk, but his innards had been half torn away. She tried to lift him toward the trench where they would be safer, but he cried out so terribly that she just knelt there.

Then she remembered her nursing lessons. She fumbled under her skirt, pulled off her petticoat, and tried to staunch the man's wound. There were dog-fights in the sky, but Georgia didn't look up except for a hurried glance, and the bombers kept coming back, or maybe they were second and third waves of bombers. The Indian and she were blasted with flying gravel and débris. She cradled his head in her lap. Blood kept welling from his stomach, her petticoat-bandage was no use at all.

When the bombers had finished with Rangoon, they flew on to Mingaladon and attacked the airfield and the Gloucesters' barracks. Stunned by the explosions, filthy with blood and grime, Georgia knelt in the ruined street. After a bit, she realised the bleeding had stopped, she was holding her first dead man. Gently, she laid his head down. She stood up.

9

—m—

Everyone had their own beginning of the end. That was Georgia Burney's. She laid the dead Indian down, and tottered on suddenly unsteady legs over to that slit-trench to see if any of her shopping might be worth salvaging.

Not that the end of British power and prestige in the East had not been coming for a long time. Nor that, just because there'd been an air raid, she thought all was lost.

She found the car, a bit the worse for shrapnel from an anti-personnel bomb. She got in, and with shaky hands tried to start it, and was amazed when the engine seemed unimpaired, she needn't have been dismayed by the holes in the bodywork. Her head felt muzzy. But she had a clearish impression that, if the Japanese could strike that devastatingly at that sort of distance, they were an enemy a lot more formidable than blasé Western opinion had allowed. What was more, Burma's defences clearly weren't all they'd been cracked up to be. And years afterwards, when the territories in the East had been won back, when the power had been restored . . . Though not the prestige. That was gone for good, after those months of defeat after defeat. Afterwards, Georgia remembered that Christmas Eve raid on Rangoon, when the bombing and the fires killed about three thousand civilians. She remembered the next raid on Christmas Day, when she'd already started working as a dogsbody at Rangoon General Hospital. When people had learned not just to stand in their alleys, staring up at the interesting goings-on in the sky, so that casualties were slightly less.

That had been the beginning of her really understanding her end. An understanding which took a harder grip on her flinching consciousness all through those last two months of the old Rangoon she'd known coming apart at the seams.

It was just skivvying, most of the work they gave her to do at the hospital. Occasionally she helped to nurse somebody. She did some driving for the Saint John's Ambulance team at the Town Hall, too, which was less like drudgery, and more fun. But chiefly she slogged away cleaning the wards, washing up in the kitchen, that sort of thing. Hospital staff started melting away right from the start, after those Christmas raids. When the first mobs of refugees set off straggling northward, in cars and in carts, on bicycles, on foot, with bundles, with babies. So those who remained had to turn their hands to all manner of tasks. Georgia made the transition from indulged young lady to nurse-cum-skivvy quite naturally. It was so obviously necessary, she scarcely reflected on it. And she was physically strong, and buoyant of heart. Like her brother. Fantastically tough, both of them, it turned out.

So she buckled down cheerfully to her menial tasks, in those weeks of official announcements about how Burma would know how to defend itself, and there was no question but that Rangoon would be held. In those weeks of news coming that Moulmein had been lost to the Japanese. Of the Army failing to stop the enemy at the River Salween, and then not holding the Bilin either. Those weeks of the civil administration of Burma falling to bits – which it did quickly. Offices from which half the functionaries had run away. Docks with no stevedores. Barricaded shops. Police generally absent by day, and inclined to join in the plundering by night – those who were still in the city at all. Then the banks sent all their money north to Mandalay, and closed. So it became impossible to pay wages.

What law and order there still was in Rangoon by February was maintained by the Gloucestershire Regiment. It was of the rough and ready sort, the justice. They patrolled the streets, shooting fifth columnists and saboteurs and looters. For days, the bloating bodies lay in the dust, worried by dogs and vultures, swarmed over by ants and flies.

Georgia and Ricky were so busy they hardly saw each other. When she did have a few words with him, conversation seemed to have been reduced to the rough and ready too. They swapped stories about people who'd abandoned their posts, who should have known better. Undignified, that scramble for berths on the last ships to Calcutta, seats on the last flights out. People who'd bought, bribed, faked, fiddled.

Georgia got so tired, working long shifts, that sometimes her thinking seemed pretty rudimentary too. At least Upper Burma was still safe, so her parents were all right. When Moulmein was lost, she thought of Sister Caterina in her convent near there. But blurrily . . . as she swabbed floors. She supposed Caterina would be all right. Religious houses were a bit like ambulances with a red cross painted on them, weren't they? People respected them, left them be. As for Christopher, her thoughts of him never left her – but the bad news that kept coming from the Malay States just made her wretchedly aware of how little she knew of his soldiering. Where was he? Doing what? So much of his life she'd never found out about. What did she know about him, when it came down to it? Bony shoulders. Green eyes. His slow drawl, when he said: Georgiana. When he said: sweetheart.

The next time Georgia saw Ricky, he told her they'd recently done a body count in the streets, and a check on their ammunition, and come to the conclusion that the regiment couldn't have accounted for so many marauders, the gangs must be shooting each other. 'Bloody civil war,' he told her – no less jauntily than in peace time he'd said, 'Bloody good show,' when his battalion won a cricket match. All those stockpiles of weapons in the docks, he said, that was the trouble. Too damned easy to swipe. All that Lend Lease gear waiting to go up to China, just lying there with no coolies to shift it. Lorries and guns, medicines and boots.

The fire brigade was as far below strength as the hospital. So when Scott Market caught fire, or was set on fire, it burned to the ground. By the time the battle at the Sittang River had been lost, and Georgia and the other remaining hospital staff were evacuated in buses, by train, in lorries, columns of black smoke were towering up from fires all over Rangoon.

Ricky was still there. By the time the 7th Armoured Brigade was disembarking at the harbour, and a couple of regiments which had been on garrison duty in India, to reinforce the Army trying to throw back the Japanese and keep the Burma Road open, the city was a shambles. Corpses everywhere. So many, that the Gloucesters stopped shooting plunderers, and instead press-ganged them to work clearing away the dead.

The prisons and the lunatic asylums and the leper colonies had been opened. The poor devil of a recently appointed Judicial Secretary gave the order for that – pestered by staff wanting to get the hell out, and reckoning if he didn't, the inmates might starve. After a few days, when he saw the consequences of his decision, he shot himself. There wasn't just thieving in Rangoon in those days. Convicts and madmen, incensed by looted alcohol . . . There were some hideous murders, and rapes. And someone had opened the gates of the zoo. There were alligators on the loose, and boa constrictors, and biggish cats, so there was some big-game shooting. Afterwards, when all the battles had been lost, and Ricky and the other survivors had fought their way out to India. When they'd fought the longest retreat in the history of the British Army – nine hundred or so miles, if you took it from the Sittang disaster, or the carnage of the fighting at Pegu . . . One of the merrier moments in the first letters he wrote from Calcutta concerned his last social encounter at the Strand, when beneath its portico he'd met an orang utan.

But at the time, with detachments of Chinese showing up and removing as much of the Lend Lease stuff as they could, the Gloucesters set about re-equipping themselves for the long fight out. Company by company, they went to the arsenal for trucks, scout cars, armoured cars. With the Japanese getting nearer all the time, and demolition squads preparing to blow up the refineries, and the port authorities sinking anything left that floated.

They helped themselves to what they needed. A couple of launches for crossing rivers, which they hoisted onto lorries. Guns, which they mounted on jeeps. Machine-guns, mortars, rifles. The last time Ricky went to the hospital where his sister had worked, it was to take vaccines from the refrigerators.

10

—᠁—

After devasted Rangoon, when Georgia Burney returned to Upper Burma everything seemed completely unchanged. She had not been able to send word of when or how she was arriving – so her father was not at Mandalay to meet her, as he had always liked to do when he wasn't away in the hills. But up at Maymyo, when she got out of the bus with her suitcase, in a yard a Shan she knew was hosing down his elephant after work, just as he had ever since she could remember. He had Jack-fruit trees in his yard. He played the cool water on the elephant's grey flanks, and the animal stood contentedly, and the water splashed and glinted.

The clock-tower, telling the right time. The man with a pony and cart, who took her home. Everything was the same. And when the next evening she went to the club . . . Bruce Kincaird and Barnaby Melton were guffawing in their chairs, just as they had for years, apparently oblivious that the country was being invaded rather efficiently. They shouted to a boy to bring more drinks, just as they always had. Kincaird waved boisterously to Georgia and called to her to join them, if she fancied; and she called back, 'Not right now,' and Melton ran his slightly disdainful glance up and down her – just as they always had.

But in those months, all over South-East Asia people were having their moments of knowledge of how irrevocably the old peace was being swept away, and how suddenly it did not appear to have been so bad as all that. Of how the new war was going to be unlike anything you'd known.

Whoever you were. If you were Cantonese, and lived in the Hong Kong hinterland, where the Japanese military authorities now declared whole villages to be brothels. If you were English, and had been leading a pleasant existence in Shanghai. If you were there the day the Japanese – fired up, by the news of Pearl Harbor – demanded the surrender of the Western gunboats on the river and in the roadstead. Not much a gunboat could do against an army, with one light cannon on the foredeck and a few tommy-guns. The American commander hauled down his flag. But the fellow on HMS *Peterel* refused; and as the Japanese launch drew away, their troops along the Bund opened up. *Peterel* caught fire, and sank. The dead and the dying drifted down on the tide.

Whoever you were, and however you came suddenly to understand. If you were one of the groups of wounded whom the British and their allies had to leave behind in the retreat down Malaya. They made you as comfortable as they could, in a shady clearing. Gave you a shot of morphine; left you with a full water-bottle, and a packet of cigarettes. So you and your mates lay there, waiting to be taken prisoner. Talking a bit about how near the front line the Jap medical staff would be, following up. And you didn't expect attackers who'd crept up quietly through the trees suddenly to charge, howling like maniacs, stabbing down with their bayonets.

If you were a Malay girl, whom a Japanese platoon abducted from her village. They beat them. They took turns raping them. Packed them off to one of their army brothels. Maybe to Kuala Lumpur, to the Tai Sun Hotel. Or one of the other hotels, which weren't hotels any more. Or to one of the so-called comfort stations, built for the purpose. That was the euphemism. Comfort women, they called them.

If you were one of the American and Philippino prisoners of war the Japanese herded out of Bataan on what came to be called the Death March. Rightly came to be called the Death March. If you were one of the defenders of Singapore, who after a few days corralled up at Changi began to lose their innocence about what captivity was going to be like. The group of senior officers, including Lieutenant Colonel Christopher de Brissac MC, who were required to witness the bungled execution of some of their men who had been caught trying to escape. Or so it was claimed – but Sumatra would have been a long swim. The working parties who were sent down to the shore to carry away and dispose of the hundreds of dead Chinese. The quite soon thousands of dead Chinese. Who were to be found there each day, their wrists roped behind their backs.

If you were one of the party of Dutch and Indonesian nurses whom the Japanese rounded up on a beach in Sumatra, and raped before they murdered. Or if on that other beach that got an evil name, in Malaya, you were one of the soldiers they bayoneted. Or one of the sixty-five Australian Army nurses ordered to march into the sea. As the women waded, Japanese machine-gunners opened fire on them.

Georgia pieced together a lot of stories, afterwards. Pieced together a lot of that disintegration of what had been her world. She even found out later something of what might have occurred in the skulls of Kincaird and Melton, by way of an awakening to altered circumstances.

Her mother and they were in the same party of Maymyo civilians trying to escape. They managed to get aboard one of the last trains from Mandalay north to Myitkyina. After that, there was nothing for it but the trek up the Hukawng Valley. Bullock carts, mules. Bicycles slung with bundles of food, which they pushed through the mud. Nothing like the Burma Road to China, for them. No road over the Naga Hills between Burma and India had ever been built. There were just jungle tracks, and the monsoon had broken. The lorries bogged down, and some of them were pulled out by elephants, but then they bogged down again. And there weren't just hundreds of British refugees. Thousands of Indians too. And camps along the way which you could smell a long time before you reached them, where people lay dying of malaria and smallpox, dysentery and cholera.

Day after day, they dragged themselves through the jungle and the mud and the rain. And the extraordinary thing was, that Geraldine Burney stood out as one of the heroines of that débâcle. That spoiled, despised mem-sahib. Perhaps for the first time in her life she was able to be useful, and that triggered something in her. At any rate, her daughter talked to several survivors of that trek who'd admired her.

That was a lesson for Georgia, all right. A lesson in how little she'd known a person it had never occurred to her she didn't know inside out. 'Oh, Mummy darling, you're so *hopeless!*' Or, 'Oh, Mummy's just like that . . .!' Her own voice haunted her, afterwards. It made her wish she'd tried to get away with her mother. Or that she'd persuaded her to try to stick it out in Maymyo with her. It was a lesson, too, in the unexpected effects which desperate times could have. When Georgia thought of a lot of people who had held positions of authority in Burma; who'd made damned sure they got away while it could still be done comfortably. When she heard stories about her mother. Who when boring Bruce Kincaird couldn't go any farther, sat down beside him. Among the dead animals and dead people. The mud and the excrement and the insects. Sat beside him, in the hot rain. Said the Lord's Prayer, and talked calmly. Said the twenty-third psalm. *Yea, though I walk through the valley of the shadow of death* . . . Until he died. Whereupon she stood up, and trudged on.

She'd taken charge of two Indian children, by then. A girl of about fourteen, whose family had all perished, and whose ears and nostrils were horribly ripped and bloody where a dacoit had yanked away her jewellery. A boy much younger, whose dying mother had given him into the white woman's hands. Apparently Geraldine had just looked into the mother's eyes, and said, 'Yes of course', and picked the child up.

They waded streams in spate. They struggled up mud slopes on hands and knees. Then the looters caught up with them. Deserters from the Frontier Force, deserters from the Military Police. Violent riffraff of all kinds. Armed. One lot one day, and another the next. Melton was one of those who protested, who blustered – and was hacked to death. The looters stole food, they stole money. They took young women and girls. At the rivers, they took the rafts which people were cobbling together. That was how Geraldine lost the last of the Burney rubies and emeralds, which she still had in the hems of her filthy clothes.

Luckily, she managed to pick up a rifle and a bandoleer with some cartridges which someone had abandoned, sling them over her skeletal shoulders. She carried the little boy half the time, too. But after that, he and she and the girl with her torn nose and ears were a little safer. And Geraldine nearly made it out of that deathly valley.

Very nearly. At the end of May, her reduced party reached the banks of the Namyaung River. They clambered through a morass, stood looking down at the gorge where the torrent was raging.

They'd have to wait till the water went down. Or until there were elephants. Or rafts could be made which might cope with those boulders and that white water. But Geraldine was very weak by then. She slumped down pretty much for the last time. When she propped herself up, she picked the leeches off the children, carefully, as she always had. Then she didn't do that any more.

11

—※—

After all the talk about Singapore being an impregnable fortress had died
down, and about how Rangoon was going to be another Tobruk, going to
be held at all costs. After the Japanese air force had bombed Mandalay and
set a lot of it on fire and killed a couple of thousand people. After Burma
Corps had pulled back as far as the River Chindwin, and were shipping
up-stream to begin their retreat through the jungle of the Kabaw Valley.
When Richard Burney at Schwebo, helping to get the wounded and as
many sick and starving refugees as possible onto the remaining transport,
was always looking among the ragged European women for his mother
and his sister . . . In the Shan Hills, a strange hush seemed to have fallen,
after the rout.

At least, in Maymyo and its neighbouring villages, there were days
when Georgia felt she was living in an eerie stillness. When the Japanese
bombers had finished with the place, and the fighters had finished
strafing. The fires had been put out, and the dead buried. When the
last British soldiers had finished blowing up bridges and had gone. Before
the retreating Chinese and the advancing Japanese starting shelling one
another across the hills. When all the talk about sticking to your post had
died down, and almost everyone who'd had much of a post to stick to had
gone – though a lot of them didn't get far. And a lot of those who didn't
end up in unmarked graves or in no graves, ended up back in Maymyo,
or in other towns, interned.

Georgia Burney's staying behind wasn't heroic. She was not like Helen
Rodriguez, in charge of the hospital at Taunggyi, who was told that her
patients and staff would be evacuated, but then the lorries never appeared.
Doubtless they were used for more vital tasks than shifting dozens of
bed-ridden Asians. So she stayed, with her wounded and her diseased,
and with one loyal Shan woman who stuck at it after all the other Burmese
nurses had made themselves scarce.

Georgia merely knew where Home was. She might not be Anglo-
Burmese by blood but she had friends who were, and a lot of them
were staying – a lot of them hadn't much choice but to stay – and she
was Anglo-Burmese by instinct. There were Indians who stayed too, and
Anglo-Indians. Some because they were too ill to be evacuated. Some
because they were unlucky. Some because they were cussed. A very few,
of any race, who quite likely could have got out but chose to stay, in whom

the cussedness came to look like heroism. Such as Miss Rodriguez. Such as Major Seagrim, who remained in the Karen Hills and set about organising resistance to the Japanese. Seagrim who with his Karen guerrillas fought skirmishes so successful that the Japanese occupying forces began to conduct reprisals against villages. To put a stop to which, in the end he surrendered to the enemy, alone, and was killed.

In Maymyo, the Mother Superior and her nuns were still in their convent. Later in the war, that building was used as a barracks. But that April of '42 it was still a religious house, and Georgia's friends the Italian nuns were still imperturbably running the school, cultivating the vegetable garden, nursing the sick. So she asked the Mother Superior if she could come and make herself useful doing the sort of dogsbodying she'd pitched into at Rangoon Hospital. The Mother Superior said Yes, there were always odd-jobs that needed doing. And she added that, if Georgia truly intended to remain now the other English were bailing out, the convent was with any luck as safe a place as any.

Alex and Georgia Burney probably both came into the category of the cussed stayers-behind. He knew she was lying when she swore to her mother that she'd be on the next truck going down to Mandalay, and he didn't complain about that. And when Maymyo became a ghost town, what with most of its old ruling class having bolted. With most people of all races, creeds, classes having decided that discretion was the better part of valour, and a good start would be a bit of hoarding, a bit of barricading, and a lot of keeping your head down. In that last lull, father and daughter stood, you might say, shoulder to shoulder, waiting for whatever was going to come. Or rather, sat on their verandah together. But side by side, waiting. Just as, years before, one summer night on the lawn at Edingthorpe, when Georgia had cloudily conceived that their way of life in Burma might one day come to a disintegration, she had imagined they would confront that end together, on their verandah, side by side.

The Japanese didn't allow them much of a respite – and what time she had, her work at the convent took up most of. Yet in those few days, when she did manage to get across the town to see her father, it was extraordinary the freedom they found in themselves, the freedom with one another they seemed to have emerged into.

Strange shoots germinating in their mulch heads, or something . . . But when they talked about the fall of Singapore, and de Brissac's chances of still being alive, Georgia was sure her father had sensed she'd become his lover. And she marvelled to discover that – though of course nothing was said, thank heavens nothing needed to be said! But her father wasn't outraged. Perhaps he was even glad for them.

She didn't think she was inventing it. At any rate, he understood, he sympathised.

When they talked about what was before them, it was the same, they said very little. Alex made the obvious remarks about how, since she'd been fool enough to hang on here, going to earth at the convent was a sensible move. He gave her quite a lot of money – all he'd managed to extract from a closing-down bank. He reminded her that she had helped him bury the family silver, and she was to dig it up, please, one day. He gave her a small pistol, and some rounds for it. She said, Good God did he expect her to use this thing? He replied, Only if she wanted to, but if a soldier came at her with a bayonet it might suddenly seem a good idea. She wondered whether the Mother Superior would let her into sacred precincts with a firearm. He said that everything he'd ever heard about the Mother Superior gave him to conclude that she was an intelligent woman. But, to be on the safe side, he'd chosen about the neatest little revolver money could buy, so that in her pocket it might pass unremarked.

They said very little . . . And, as with her relations with de Brissac, now with what they each might do under certain circumstances, when confronted with certain stark choices – much that was not said seemed to be communicated silently, and accepted without a fuss.

Georgia was pretty clear that her father was tempted to make a fight of it, and she thought he knew she knew, and was grateful for the lack of squawking. The invaders were his country's enemies – and however derisive of jingoism he might be, he was enough of an old soldier for that to weigh with him. They were Burma's enemies too, even if only half the Burmese had yet worked that out. If lives were to be sacrificed, his was one it would be reasonable to choose. She understood the sort of sense it made to him.

As for the pistol, she was glad to have it. She'd seen Rangoon. If – in conventional, white woman style – she used the thing on herself, to prevent what you were reckoned to consider a worse fate. Or if she didn't. If she used it on others, or she never used it . . . It was a comforting weight in her pocket. She only hoped she could stop people taking it from her.

Alex and Georgia never said a proper goodbye. That was another new, war-time thing, she was finding. Often you didn't say goodbye. Never got a chance.

After he'd shot the two spies, and they'd buried them with their Shan clothes and their Japanese Army tunics and revolvers, they went into the house and cleaned themselves up. He poured himself a couple of fingers of whisky. Then he said, 'Here, I expect you could do with a drop of this.' She said, 'Thanks.'

So he poured a second glass — a more modest one. They collapsed into a couple of chairs, sipping companionably. She said, 'Gosh, Daddy.' He said, 'Good to get the evidence out of sight.' She said, 'Mmmm,' and sipped. That was it. She went back to the convent.

A few days later, she buried him. That time, when she went into the ransacked house, she couldn't find a clean shirt to put on. They'd all been stolen. The china had been smashed. The glass and the pictures had been smashed.

By then, Georgia was getting used to people's homes being desecrated. Even so, the ruin of the order and the charm her mother had taken pride in shocked her — and later it was one of the small miseries that kept coming back. However, at that moment the two lightning flashes in her storm-clouded mind were: that her father was safely underground, and that she *must* have a wash. Daddy was out of it now, he'd got clear away. Whatever his life had been, and his death had been — they had passed. And if water didn't come out of that spout her jangled nerves were going to snap and she would scream. All the Shanghai jars had been smashed. But in the wash-house, by the well and the pump, there was a . . .

She turned the tap. Water came splattering. Georgia rolled up her sleeves. What was more, she'd only been scrubbing for a minute when Angus came trotting in. He thrust his grey muzzle against her shins, he wagged his tail.

Her goodbye to her father she said at the road-side, kneeling by his slit-trench grave. Then she set off to walk back to the convent, her dog at her heels. To walk by alley-ways and garden hedges, not by the main streets, and hope not to run into any Japanese. Nothing like having been a child in a town, for knowing every bridle-path.

Then Georgia couldn't resist it, she turned aside to her old wooden church. It was that humble shrine of the English in Asia she needed to be in. Just for a few minutes. Now that the dissolution of what had been her everything really did seem complete. Now that however much she told herself that the tales of Japanese atrocities were probably just the usual war-time scare-stories, she walked with her heart fluttering, her mouth dry with fright. Still, luckily the lane was deserted.

She sat down in a pew. Angus lay and panted. A minute must have passed, then five minutes . . . But she was too shaken for there to be much in her head except louring thunder-clouds.

Daddy was all right now. She clung to that, and it steadied her a bit — though when she heard a sound at the church door she whipped around with a gasp, her face chalky. Even if shooting and being shot were not most people's idea of all-rightness. But for Daddy, if he couldn't have had anything except defeat, or . . . Yes, he was all right now.

He was the only person she knew anything about. Ricky with the Gloucesters. Lawrence Cowdrey, who'd wanted to marry her, with the Yorkshires somewhere. How were they getting on? Roberta's wedding had been one of the last social events the hill station had seen, while the old society still existed. Had her husband and she escaped? And Mummy? And other people, far away. Jack in Germany, Bobbie in North Africa. Were they still alive? Godfather Charles in his last letter had said Norwich had been bombed again.

The sound at the door had been nothing. But now she knew that the Japanese had arrived, their first troops must be taking over the chief buildings in the town at this very minute, even the quietness was frightening.

Georgia sat, gripping her hands together to stop them trembling. She stared at the painted panelling of the apse without really seeing it. All very fine, knowing that you were going to have to stand on your own two legs. But to sense how lonely and defenceless you were with every quiver of your nerves and your wincing mind . . .

She thought: Christopher, where are you, are you still alive? Wherever you are, just remember that I love you till it burns me away inside, there's nothing left. She thought: My darling, if I never see you again it'll be more than I can bear. But if you survive this war and I don't, come to this church and remember the girl who loved you with all her heart.

Sobs of self-pity clogged Georgia's throat, she forgot the Japanese. Then she pulled herself together. She stood up.

'Right, Angus, we'd better be off. You're going to be a convent dog from now on.'

EIGHT

1

—〰—

It was Christmas Eve 1943, and Caroline Lammas had not seen her husband for four years. The day after Boxing Day it would be exactly four years since he'd left Norfolk to go overseas, she thought for the hundredth time, moving restlessly about her bedroom at Bure Lodge. (The school from the Isle of Dogs still occupied the Hall.)

The Sherwood Rangers had fought, and had had their casualties, at Tobruk and Crete, Alam el Halfa and El Alamein. They had entered Tripoli and fought at Mareth. With the Axis defeat in North Africa complete, they had sailed for Britain, and by the end of the year were in camp near Newmarket, at Chippenham Park.

Leave began, and Bobbie Lammas was expected at Bure any minute now. Phipps had driven to Norwich station to meet his train. Caroline would have gone with him, but she had made a point of not curtailing her Voluntary Service work in the village that afternoon just because her husband was expected – if her husband in any real sense was what he turned out to be.

If it had been summer, Caroline might have allayed her anxieties a little by gazing out of the window at the rooks homing toward the park, black skeins undulating over the farm-land in the opalescent evening sky. But it had been dark for two hours, and she had drawn the curtains, and a North Sea gale was booming around the house.

She felt pent up in the comfortably furnished bedroom where a house-maid had lit a coal fire. (Sir Julian Hedleigh was forthright in his praise of the way his daughter had dedicated herself to war-time tasks which were menial and mechanical – lately she and the other local women had been much involved with Home Guard uniforms. But he would never have countenanced a coal scuttle which she carried upstairs herself, or an ash bucket she carried down.) She felt cooped up between those florally papered walls; and so nervous she had given herself a stomach ache.

If only she could have waited for Bobbie in the room up at the Hall where she had slept all through her childhood, and which was redolent of happy, uncomplicated times. The room cluttered with her girlhood's trinkets, and with its girl's single bed, where nine Christmases ago she had waited for the Lammas contingent to arrive and her engagement to be made official. Better still, if she could have waited for him in the cottage in the Quercy! Under her own roof, even if rented, and however it leaked in rain-storms. Away from her parents. With no one to witness the success or otherwise of Bobbie's and her reunion. She still felt miserable when she remembered their departure from that cottage, how she'd packed away the linen and the crockery for the last time. And the Cahors region had been under Vichy control, and then unoccupied France had been occupied.

Caroline made herself stop fretting about the room, sit down at her dressing-table. She stared at the double bed, with its sumptuous eiderdown. (A far cry from the old travelling rugs and threadbare blankets they'd heaped up to keep themselves snug on winter nights in France.) As the married daughter of the house, her mother had decreed accommodation for her which was almost too solidly, amply, decoratedly – oh, Caroline didn't know, but – but too emphatically conjugal.

Under the circumstances . . . And then she had fussed herself into further wretchedness by being unable to decide whether she wanted a photograph of her husband on her bed-side table. Had ended up by putting one there only because it had occurred to her that Mama and the maids might think it odd if she didn't. So there Bobbie had been, for close on four years. And there he was now. Handsome, all right. Smiling. On their wedding day, wearing a white rose in his button-hole. And Caroline sat with her back very straight, trying with gentle rubbings to soothe the horrible tenseness that had gripped her tummy.

She looked at the bed, imagined Bobbie and her tonight making love there. After all this time . . . He had been unfaithful to her, he must have been, she'd been unable to doubt it, quite unable. How often, and with what satisfactions, she had started by struggling not to imagine too often, and had ended by quite naturally not imagining.

Perhaps they wouldn't want to make love. Perhaps he was in love with some other girl. No, no . . . He was coming to Bure for his leave, after all. Could perfectly well have gone to Edingthorpe. Or to his mother's flat in Pimlico, or his uncle's studio in Kensington. And if Bobbie were having an affair with someone else – that would by no means necessarily prevent him, she knew, from coming to Bure and making love with her.

So she went on nervously rubbing her nervous stomach. Thinking of two or three officers, in particular, of all those she had met these last years. Thinking of flirtations – no, awarenesses was a better word for it – that she'd made sure came to nothing . . . sensibly? timorously? And then that one time in London, after a dance – but it had meant nothing. Afterwards, feeling guilty about how resoundingly she'd enjoyed it hadn't meant much either. And, well . . . Anyhow, she'd done years of lying alone in that bed, and thinking about making love.

With this sea-wind roaring in the winter trees, she wouldn't hear the car in the yard. Should she go down? Wait for somebody to call her? Wait for, 'Caroline! he's here!' She was ready to go down. She had dressed for dinner.

The war had not modified the formality of the Hedleighs' evenings, any more than it had reduced their staff or their income. But tonight this immutability had not calmed Caroline. She had hovered between this dress and that. Between wearing something especially pretty, which would be absolutely right, and overdoing it ridiculously.

She had put on her engagement ring beside her wedding ring, which she had not done for four years, and now smiled to remember Bobbie's story of how Uncle Charles had held out a cheque to him, gruffly ordered him off to Norwich. To Bullen's . . . 'The only place, dear lad. If you want a ring the poor girl can be seen wearing.'

Caroline had slipped onto her wrist Blanche's engraved ivory bracelet. Now she sat twisting it, and turned to give her face and hair a last – but of course it would not be a last – scrutiny in the glass. Thirty, and honestly she reckoned she still . . . Caroline got up, crossed to the full-length mirror. She stood before it, swivelled sideways on. She walked away from her reflection, looking back over her shoulder. Turned, walked toward herself. Posed. No doubt about it, these new high-heeled shoes were a success. Darling Mama. And look at that for a wasp-waist. What with being a bundle of overwrought nerves year after year, and not having had a baby, yet.

But she was sadly adept at jerking that train of thought away from its object. And anyway, this evening she was so jittery she couldn't have concentrated on it if she'd wanted to. Though she knew that her mother hoped that one upshot of Bobbie's leave – he had, after all, by all reports done terrifically well in the fighting in the desert, and been promoted captain – might be the birth of a baby. Mummy had decided she was ready to be a grandmother.

Caroline hurried out onto the landing and listened, because she was almost certain she had heard the commotion of an arrival. But it was Freddie's tread on the stair, and his voice. He was on leave for a few days too, which of course was wonderful. Oh but *why* couldn't Bobbie and she have met in the Kensington studio? Scrambled eggs and a bottle of beer at that paint-stained table. Then lots of glorious love-making on the tatty old ottoman. That would have been all right. Or she could have gone to the French butcher in Soho, and then made that stew with Toulouse sausage and beans and herbs that in the Quercy they'd practically lived on. No she couldn't – not in war time. Anyway, they'd have made love on the studio hearth-rug, on the table, anywhere, everywhere. Just like the best of the old days, like the good times. They'd have worked out quick enough whether they really felt married to each other or not, whether they wanted to be.

Marriages were made and unmade faster in war time than in peace – Caroline had noticed that. Oh God oh God, this meeting him in the drawing-room wasn't going to be much fun. With Mama, whose way of letting society know that she was all set to play the devoted and generous grandmother, was to inform her friends that of *course* it was for her darling *daughter* that she minded so *terribly* much. With Papa and Freddie being jovial, but in fact more interested in their whisky glasses than in Bobbie and her.

Still, with this storm she could hardly go and hang around in the yard. Uncle Charles would have lent them the studio again – she was sure of it. Maybe she *would* go downstairs. Jump out at Bobbie from behind the grandfather clock in the hall, manhandle him into the scullery and lock the door – anything to be like the happy times. Girlhandle him . . . that had been one of their jokes.

Blanche had been sweet, the way she'd rung up a few days ago, and insisted on speaking to no member of the family but her. Nice how she'd issued the invitation to Bobbie and her to dine at Edingthorpe after the Boxing Day shoot, 'and your mother and father too, naturally.' How she'd made it plain that when she spoke of how delighted she was that her nephew was coming home she meant not Edingthorpe Manor, where he'd left all his gear before going to the war, but Bure Lodge, where he had never lived.

Yes, hide in the garage – why not? Get Phipps out of the light smartly. Shove Bobbie into the straw-shed in the dark and kiss him like mad. Only after that decide whether or not they felt like allowing the others a glimpse of them in the drawing-room.

2

—⟶—

Right from his arrival, Bobbie Lammas' high spirits left no one in any doubt that he wished this Christmas to be just like his old Norfolk Christmases. Right from the start – when against the flint wall of the dark straw-shed he kissed his wife with such boisterous vehemence that she was all of a tremble.

Then for a minute she was shudderingly, raspingly tearful. And then he kissed her again, very gently, and she was blissfully tearful. While old Phipps tramped across the stormy yard, carrying a military kit-bag with a shadow of the youthful swagger with which he'd carried his own in Flanders in the last war, and shaking his head and smiling.

In the drawing-room, Bobbie was so charmingly the centre of attention, and at once began to tease half the company and be merrily serious about the war with the other half, and looked so handsome in his uniform and with his face still lightly tanned from the desert sun, that Caroline found she was smiling and smiling. Then in a rush she couldn't tell if it were this Christmas or the magical one of nine years ago. However, it didn't matter, because now as then she had every good excuse for not taking her eyes off him. And now she was in tears all over again. Luckily that didn't matter either. Because with all these people whom she suddenly loved very much, some of them busy cheering her up and others simply smiling and not bothering to cheer her up because they knew she was all right really, you could cry or not cry as you pleased. It being Christmas Eve, and Bobbie after four years being home.

Gloria Lammas was there. The friendly grace with which Sarah Hedleigh had always known how to treat her son-in-law's mother had been noticed over the years by a number of the county's better families. And certainly the poor woman's reunion with her soldier son had been an event to take possession of, stage-manage, almost take the credit for.

Luckily Geoffrey's widow was by that winter too distraught, and had possibly always been too guileless or unimaginative, to sense that Bobbie was to all intents Lady Hedleigh's now, and as such was part of a bounty being extended to her. He had telephoned his mother several times since he'd been back in England, and done his best to be heartening. Unfortunately, the good effects of his sanguine voice had been undone, since her arrival a few days before at Bure, by Sarah's telling her again and again how terrible war was, and how blessed was any woman who lived to clap eyes on her son with his arms and legs still attached where the Lord had put them. She had also told her repeatedly – to the accompaniment of tender smiles, and the raising of a morsel of cambric to the corners of her own eyes – that she must be in an agony of longing to see him. The consequence of which was that Gloria neither ate nor slept properly, and by the time Bobbie appeared could hardly have told you if it were his father or he in whose arms she was sobbing.

Bobbie let her cry, and indeed for a moment he too looked moved. But then he raised his left wrist, while continuing to embrace her firmly with his right arm, and he studied his watch and winked at Caroline. 'Right you are, Mother darling, time's up,' he declared. 'One minute is precisely right for a good maternal weep. Now, I want that drink that Freddie is being damned slow about pouring me.' And at dinner he teased Gloria by asking her about Doctor Freud and Doctor Jung, whom of recent years she had taken tremendously seriously, and telling her about Doctor Fatcake whose research conclusively proved a lot of things – Gloria was flustered not to have heard of him – and Professors Pozzo and Clumph-Pickle who also had theories about what one was not conscious of. Rather risqué theories, some of them, he thought – though of course to be taken with goggle-eyed piety. Now, how was her Rosicrucianism these days, getting along splendidly? Oh, no, her Theosophy of course, how *could* he have got it wrong yet again? The great thing was not to be able to prove or disprove anything – then you could be as earnest as you liked.

It had been Charles Lammas who, years before, had remarked that his nephew's tactics were, once you'd listened to him a few times, really very simple. Gallantry and teasing for the women. Manly good humour for the men. It never varied.

True to this policy, over the roast partridges Bobbie listened respectfully to Julian Hedleigh's assessment of the National Government's perfor-mance, and never by a flicker of an eyebrow intimated that what prattling politicians thought or did not think at Westminster might be of less moment than the actions of fighting men at El Alamein. And he knew exactly how light-hearted to be – they'd got to the apple crumble, and the Burgundy had been replaced by Sauterne – when his father-in-law let fall that, now he'd gone to the trouble of doing up the Lodge so that one might live in it, he rather had the place in mind for Mark after the war was over. But, by the same token . . . Did Bobbie remember a tumble-down old house, not unattractive in its way, called Burnt Haugh? Over by Thorndyke Staithe. He'd been thinking it might do very decently for Caroline and him, one day. That was right, Freddie, wasn't it? (When others were present, Hedleigh was particularly scrupulous about bringing his heir into any discussion of the estate.) So . . . What did Bobbie say to the idea?

Captain Lammas said straight away that it was a jolly generous suggestion, and he was sure Caroline would love Burnt Haugh – and you couldn't tell if he were wondering whether the offer included new weather-proof thatch. He said it with such an off-hand flurry of, 'We'll have to see how things shape up', and 'If the Germans don't succeed in shooting me', that he gave no impression of being eager to accept patronage, or of uncertainty as to his life after the war. The next minute, he was deep in soldierly talk with Freddie about the preparations for the Allied invasion of France, in which they both expected to take part.

Next it was Sarah's turn to be teased. She, he demanded of her, who was invariably the first to know not only about forthcoming Norfolk weddings but about funerals too. She who knew who was about to decamp to farm near Lake Tanganyika; who was going to be on the next Honours List; who hadn't a shilling left. Who knew why Fenby no longer invited Bosky to shoot, and who was going to marry Susanna Fitzwilliam if Myles Grenville hadn't the guts, and why no one would *touch* those Asham girls. She wasn't going to pretend she couldn't tell him . . .

But Bobbie was just getting into his stride when he broke off, and caught his wife's eye.

'Darling, I've been scheming by telephone with my beautiful cousin Henrietta . . . Long may we protect her from Sarah's match-making. Do you fancy skipping the midnight service here, and driving over to Edingthorpe for it instead?'

3

—m—

Charles Lammas suspected some plot was being hatched, from the sparkle in Henrietta's eyes when she insisted her mother and he come with her to midnight carols and holy communion.

He was happy enough to comply. With his moods swinging every-which-way . . . What with being haunted Christmas after Christmas more doggedly than ever by the dead and the far away and the alive or dead. What with at the same time being delighted that Bobbie was getting leave, and delighted to have Henrietta home.

A few days before, Blanche had gone out into the garden with her secateurs. She had cut some strands of ivy, cut some of the red-berried holly and some sprigs too from the rare tree that bore yellow berries. They had bicycled together down the lane to Paston, walked up the path past Mary Oldfield's grave. Blanche had laid little bunches of holly on her family's graves on the landward, sheltered side of the church. They had gone in, and she had put her ivy wreath at the Archangel Michael's feet. Coming away, she had stooped by her old friend's stone and said, 'Let's give Nanny her holly, too.'

So now it was Edingthorpe church's turn. He would trudge through the night to that mediaeval shrine on its knoll very willingly, Lammas thought, putting a guard in front of his fire so that while he was partaking of the ritual his house didn't burn down. Yes, walk up there to honour the passing of old gods and the birth of a new one. Willingly . . . Going through to the gun-room for his coat and his cap. Though this was Jack's third Christmas as a prisoner of war. Blanche had aged, lately, and her hair was turning grey quite fast. His own was white. Though there were times when, with so many friends dead or missing, this new war seemed to be telling on him in a way the other one hadn't – and it had already gone on for longer. He didn't seem to have his old resilience.

Resolutely cheerful, he reminded himself of Bertie Fox, who was ten. It had been a close-run thing, whether the privilege of singing the solo at the beginning of the Edingthorpe carol services this winter would be awarded to Bertie, or to the Grimes' girl Sally whom the other half of the parish favoured.

Charles Lammas had found Janet Fox a job at the North Walsham laundry, when he could no longer afford to employ her at the Manor. She was not unhappy there, and was earning half as much again as she ever had with him. Even so, she still contrived to spend a mighty amount of time in the Manor kitchen, lending a hand and gossiping. And when the parson, after displaying a deplorable streak of indecisiveness and keeping folk on tenterhooks as no Christian would have done, had finally plumped for Bertie as his soloist, that distinguished child's mother made him rehearse his piece before Mr and Mrs Lammas three times.

Going out into the cannonading wind and a few spatters of rain, Lammas smiled to recall how sturdily Bertie had stood before the kitchen range, his arms by his sides as he had been taught, singing lustily at the upper row of plates in the dresser.

Then there had been the problem of the boy's tendency to fall asleep when it was least convenient. The service on Christmas morning should present no insuperable difficulties. But the night before . . . Mercy, the child was normally in bed by eight o'clock, and then you could fire a gun in his room and he wouldn't roll over.

Various drastic methods of keeping the boy conscious had been proposed, and Henrietta had ended in fits of laughter. What about starving him? Because everyone in Edingthorpe knew that if you fed Bertie he went out like a light. But the chorister announced that, if it meant going without his tea, he waren't goin' ter sing, parson nor no parson, even if it that *ware* Henrietta as had the starvin' of 'im.

After the retreat through the Kabaw Valley was over, and then the weeks became months and people who were not accounted for were probably not going to be accounted for, or at any rate not until Burma were reinvaded from India and the Japanese routed out, Richard Burney wrote to his sister's godparents. He was in Calcutta by then, getting fit again. He did not write promptly; and his brevity and lack of comment were those of an officer and a gentleman. But that was how Charles and Blanche were apprised of Geraldine's death. The survivors of her party, who had buried her on the banks of the Namyaung River before the spate subsided sufficiently for them to cross it, had later found Ricky, brought him word.

As for my father and my sister, I imagine they've been interned as enemy aliens, along with the rest of our people who didn't manage to come away in time. We'll go back in and get them all out again, never fear.

Lammas had given up hope for his brother's old Ypres comrade and his own best man very quickly, and almost without distress. When he brought to mind Alex Burney at the Travellers' Club, talking dryly about a few hundred yards of mud which tens of thousands of men had been wounded and killed for . . . *of course.* Alex here at Edingthorpe late at night, growling that naturally there was going to be another German war. While all the humbugging talk about justice and peace and the King Emperor lasted, and the other humbug about vital national interests. Oh and historical destiny, that was a good one. While the jiggery-pokery lasted . . . Charles Lammas could imagine all manner of variations on his theme – but he couldn't imagine Alex surviving the war in Burma. Not with that clipped, hard voice ringing to him. 'It's a curious thing, Charlie. Don't know if you've ever noticed. It doesn't matter who they are: imperialists, communists, nationalists . . . They all like to talk about historical destiny. Makes them feel terrific, having a bloody mission. They don't have to think any more.'

They were the others, who might be alive, for whom Lammas lived in hope, who haunted him always. Who haunted him faithfully, now, as with his wife and daughter he set forth in the teeth of a sea-gale to walk to church. Christopher who had eventually been reported among those captured at the fall of Singapore – but for over a year there had been no further news. Was he in some barracks, or in a sweltering jungle camp somewhere? In a group of ragged prisoners, singing English carols right now, quite likely – if he were still alive. And Stephen Meade, who'd been with the battalions of the Royal Norfolk Regiment captured at the same time. All over the county, there were families with sons now in Japanese prison camps. Stephen whose Aunt Ellen had provided Jack with a simple code – E standing for escape. So that when he wrote home about Ellen's outings, or about Ellen not having been able to get to the sea this year, or not having got as far as the mountains, one understood.

Jack . . . Hope for whom, protracted day and night after day and night, and now for year after year, was telling on Blanche's spirit and on his, Charles knew. So that, gradually, you became less supple, less springy. There was a withering, in time. He remembered his own father and mother.

Jack who, in that Prussian *schloss*, was to be imagined cold and hungry tonight. But who very probably, with his fellow prisoners, was singing carols. 'In the bleak midwinter', that had always been a favourite of his. Or 'The holly and the ivy'. They might easily sing the same words and tunes, tonight, at Colditz and at Edingthorpe. And certainly Jack would be thinking of home. Of his sister, and his parents. Log fires, roast goose. Those sorts of things. Charades. Presents under the tree. Old Christmases.

And Georgia? Whose last letter, written at Rangoon General Hospital and entrusted to the Anderson family who were sailing on one of the last ships to Calcutta, had given the lie to her brother's supposition that she would have tried to get away from the débâcle, from the rude revelation that it was not the historical destiny of the British to enjoy dominion over Burma. Though Charles Lammas, when he had replied to Ricky, had not passed on the girl's exuberant declarations about how if the fighting spread from Lower Burma to Upper she'd take to the hills as a mahout; or dress up in saffron robes like a Buddhist monk; or get herself sold as a pagoda slave, yes, that was an idea. Anyhow, she would invoke the jungle *nats* to protect her. But Mrs Anderson was off this very minute, so she couldn't finish this letter. She sent everybody at Edingthorpe her love – especially the spaniels. And maybe the *nats* would flying-carpet her away to Bengal, who could tell?

The countryside was dark at that hour, the church windows and every cottage's windows blacked-out. They could hear the sea thundering against the cliffs a couple of miles off.

His coat buttoned up to his chin, Lammas gazed with watering eyes into the black blizzard that was crashing ashore over the low-lying coast. Trying not to think of the helplessness of prisoners of war, and trying not to be sentimental about carols sung behind barbed-wire and machine-gun emplacements either, he recalled Hardy's poem about Christmas Eve and the animals in their byres kneeling down.

Jack had liked that poem, when he was a boy – and he could easily be bringing it to mind right now. The old country story, about the donkeys and oxen who remembered that stable in Bethlehem. The poet who knew that if at midnight you took a lantern and went out to your sheds, everything would be as it always was. But even so, the idea . . .

All the things it was useless to go on thinking. But of course you went on thinking them; and it wore you down. Being proud of your son who had revealed himself a determined escaper, and knowing Blanche was proud of him too. Your both knowing that, in that branch of warfare as in many others, casualties were highest among the brave. How hope could buoy you up, momentarily – but in the long haul, hope wore you down. Going on hoping for the same, few, simple outcomes. Jack. Georgia. Till it wore you down, the uselessness of what went on in your heart, the absolute uselessness.

Best simply to be grateful for what had been. Think of the boy who'd read with you by the library fire a good few winters, and tramped up with you to this church a good few times.

Good to hear the bell now, rung vigorously by Sonny Hannant, blown to you in clangy snatches by the storm. No German invasion being imminent – and Christmas Eve being Christmas Eve. Good to notice how, as you approached the churchyard trees, the roaring in their leafless boughs drowned out the distant combers against the cliffs.

Better not think about Giacomo, either. That was new enough still to hurt. Now, what the . . .? Bobbie! How could he have forgotten his guess that Bobbie . . .?

Because as they battled up-hill and up-gale, and began to fall in with other church-goers, Henrietta had hastened ahead, peering into the icily scudding murk. And now a familiar figure – dear heavens, after four of these years a very loved figure indeed – had detached itself from the lych-gate, and come striding toward them. Caroline was there too, hovering behind him.

'Henrietta! Blanche! Lord, who shall I hug first?' And then, 'Uncle Charles, happy Christmas.'

Suddenly enormously happy to have at least one of his war-dispersed voices ringing merrily in his ears once more, Charles Lammas shook his nephew's hand vigorously. Damned fine to have one of them back. Fine, too, the huddle of friendly neighbours at the lych-gate, the calls of, 'Why, tha's Bobbie Lammas!' 'Are you all right, then, lad?' 'Home for Christmas, tha's good.' 'Africa . . .' Salutations whipped away on the wind.

Good the flint-work and thatch of this old coastal bastion, Lammas thought. Good the round tower and the octagonal belfry, the pealing bell to welcome them. Good the grave-humps and the slabs of tilting stone, God's acre where he was lucky they hadn't yet dug a hole for him. The ditches and banks which Jack as a boy had been sure were the remains of Saxon ramparts – and very likely they were. The onshore gale harrying the cloud-rack . . . All satisfactory, tonight.

They hurried up the muddy path, and then beneath the lantern hanging in the church porch Charles could see Bobbie properly for the first time. His grin. One eyebrow cocked in amused enquiry. His eyes flashing back with affection . . . Yes, he was all right. And his voice hadn't changed.

'Well, Uncle . . . You look fairly alive.'

'I'm glad you think so, dear boy.'

They went into the candle-lit nave. The congregation was gathering. People wished one another a happy Christmas. Someone said how pretty the fir tree by the altar looked, decked out with baubles and tinsel. Had Henrietta done that? Yes, she had, with her mother's help, and Ellen Meade's. Someone else shivered, and said you could tell this wind was blowing from Denmark.

Mrs Fox was there, waiting for Bertie's moment of glory, with her red face shining with pride and modesty. Bobbie stepped across to greet her, came back to usher his own party into their pew.

Charles Lammas had always liked those roughly hewn pews, and the great rough-cut beams overhead. He liked the old pulpit and lectern too, and the walls without too many damp patches. Bits of this church might be a thousand years old – but even better was the knowledge that before that other shrines had stood on this site. People had been married and buried here, according to changing rituals, time out of mind.

Lost in this pagan dreaming, Lammas was only distantly aware of the congregation's coughs and sneezes as they waited for the service to begin. Anyway in his own family pew the happy whispering never died away for a second, and now Henrietta was in the grip of such bright-eyed hilarity that her giggles would not be stifled. So her father was left to his habitual contemplation of the rood screen, and of the windows which were of splendid diversity. He'd had fun, years ago, teaching the children which was Decorated Gothic and which was Perpendicular. Piecing together something of the building's history with them. Jack had always liked that sort of investigation, ever since he'd been very little. Jack, who was going to be an architect, when he came home. What was Bobbie murmuring to him?

'Uncle Charles, you're thinking the most unsuitable thoughts, I can tell. Scenes of Venetian debauchery . . . Yes, yes, girls with no morals and no clothes.'

'Oh, not too sinful, by my standards.'

'Thinking of which . . . Any news from Italy? That disgraceful old reprobate Ned . . . Now the Germans have occupied his part of the country, do you suppose he's selling them his Rapallo sea-scapes?'

'I wouldn't be a bit surprised – if he can persuade them to pay for them. Painting portraits of their mistresses too, I hope. No . . . I haven't heard that anything is wrong with Ned – though I might easily not have done. But . . .' Dumped back into his weariness and his bitterness, Charles turned to face Bobbie's smile. 'Giacomo Zanetti is dead.'

'Good God!' Bobbie's voice grated with anger, his eyes glinted. 'Who in hell would kill old Giacomo? Or – or did he simply die? Nearly seventy, I suppose.'

'No, he didn't simply die. I had a letter from Mario the other day. Raffaella had written to him. It seems that for quite a long time he'd been sheltering enemies of the government at Villa Lucia. Hiding people, giving them money, that sort of thing. He'd become an enemy of the government. But he didn't get caught. Either he was clever, or he was lucky, or . . . Well, Mario says that Raffaella played a double game. For

several years . . . And all went well. But then, after Mussolini was out, and
we invaded in the south and the Germans came swarming into the rest of
the country . . .'

The Edingthorpe faithful were getting to their feet. Behind their backs,
around the font, the parson and those eight of his parishioners who, when
surpliced, made up his choir, were getting ready to process up the aisle.

'Go on,' muttered Bobbie. 'Well done old Giacomo, I'd have guessed
he had guts. What happened?'

'What happened seems to have been that the Nazis were more efficient
than the Fascists had been when it came to finding out who their enemies
were. Of course, they'd started carrying out ghastly reprisals, too. And
shooting people merely on suspicion. But in this case . . . He was betrayed.
Or Raffaella finally failed to protect him. Or his luck ran out. They shot
him against a wall of the house.'

In North Africa, Bobbie must have seen a lot of killing, but he was
trembling with anger now.

'The bastards! Christ!' He swallowed. He took a couple of deep breaths.
'And Raffaella . . . Just think, she . . .' But then the twinkle was back in his
eyes. 'You know, Uncle – years ago, I brought her to this service in this
church.'

'I know you did, dear lad.'

Behind them, the shuffling had almost stopped. A prayer-book fell onto
the flagstones. At a quiet command from the parson, Bertie Fox raised his
voice in song.

Once in royal David's city . . .

4

To his uncle's amused perception, there was so much to admire in Bobbie
Lammas' performance that Christmas, that more than once he found
himself on the verge of saying: 'You know, you really are handling this
awfully well.'

There was the gaiety with which, after midnight holy communion was
over, he declined to come to the Manor for a night-cap. For the reason
– of course not so much as hinted at, but utterly unmistakable – that
delightful as it would be to talk by the fire there for an hour, it was going
to be more delightful to take Caroline to bed.

There was the tact behind his declaration that certainly he was going
to attend the morning service at Bure – 'Got to do the thing properly.'
But he'd be over to Edingthorpe directly after that, 'to pick up one or two
things I left here.' So Charles Lammas knew the Hedleighs were going to
get their money's worth. In the church in Julian's park, Captain Lammas
back from fighting in Montgomery's desert victories would be a son-in-law
anyone might be proud of.

Then there was the nonchalance with which, when on Christmas
morning Caroline and he arrived at the Manor, Bobbie dashed upstairs
'to get my shooting things' – and came down again not only with coat
and breeches, but with a couple of suitcases rapidly crammed with clothes
and shoes for all immediately foreseeable occasions. There was the way he
insisted his uncle accompany him to the gun-room when he fetched one
of the pair of Purdeys which had been his father's and his grandfather's.
Because, although Julian would have been happy to lend him a gun,
'There's nothing like shooting with your own.'

Then his re-enchantment of Henrietta . . . Chiefly with his discussion
of how most astutely she should fob off the dozens of passionate admirers
he was quite sure she was beset by, and his complicated stratagems for
protecting her from her Hedleigh godmother's match-making wiles. His
re-enchantment of Blanche – 'Aunt Blanche' half the time, otherwise
'Blanche my darling' – with his stories of Jack before the war had divided
them. And with his never forgetting that, although she was overjoyed to
see him back safe and sound, the object of her deepest love would not be
taking his twelve-bore to Bure this Boxing Day, and not be at the dinner
party at Edingthorpe that night.

In the Manor kitchen, there was already a bustle of preparation for that feast. With the honour of the household at stake, and Bobbie being back, Ellen Meade was determined that it would take more than a world war to cramp her style. Rationing might inconvenience those poor souls who lived in towns. But she, with the resources of Edingthorpe coverts . . . Not to mention the poultry-run, and the vegetable patches, and the pond with its carp and bream.

Janet had come back for the occasion, to help out. She was making mince pies. Onto her third batch, she was. It was at times like this, in Ellen's view, that the difference between having a well-stocked larder and not having one was plain for folks to see. Why, that tub of raisins she'd had since before the war. Laying in victuals ahead of time . . . Knowing how to fill your own stew-pot, so you didn't have to be beholden to no one . . . Them poor souls in towns! All the same, with Sir Julian and his lady coming, it was going to be anxious work, she didn't mind who knew it.

Charles Lammas had fetched up from his cellar some of his last bottles of wine. When he went through to the kitchen to decant them, he found Blanche there – her direction of operations being required. And Bobbie, retelling Timothy Farne's story of the retreat across Crete.

Farne had been one of the two Sherwood Rangers to escape from *the land of Z*, and naturally Bobbie had long since written to Edingthorpe with his account of Jack's and his last days of freedom. But it was splendid, Lammas thought, the way he lolled against the dresser, and told it all again. Because he knew that was what his aunt wished for, and Mrs Fox, and Sidney and Ellen Meade too.

He shot a merry glance at his uncle, went on with his tale. Adding one or two embellishments which had not been in the written version. Adding a few comments with which, as a military man, he was in a position to enlighten his female listeners. Not failing to give old Sidney – visible through the pantry door, where he was plucking and gutting, and listening rather deafly – plenty of opportunities to remind the company that he too had been a soldier.

You would scarcely know it had been a defeat, from the lighthearted rendering Bobbie gave of how Tim Farne and Jack and the rest of B Squadron, or B Battery as they'd been by then, had formed up that last night and moved slowly down a track to the beach. How the hour when the last ship would have to leave came closer and closer. How in the end officers were summoned to the front of the column, and told that the last boats had gone out to the last ship. They were to be surrendered in the morning. They were to go back and tell their men.

Lighthearted and serious at the same time . . . How a bunch of lieutenants at dawn had gone looking for boats to escape on, but found they'd all been machine-gunned and were full of holes. They'd chucked their pistols into the sea.

Lighthearted pure and simple, his story of how then the German bombers had another crack at them, which they hadn't reckoned on after the surrender. How they tramped to the next village to search for any vessel it might be worth putting to sea in, but no luck. Still, they cornered a chicken, and Jack cut its head off with a big Cretan knife he'd bought from a peasant before the battle.

Hard work to pluck. And nasty work, apparently, with that Cretan dagger, to gut – this told loudly, for Sidney's amusement. But in an abandoned house they'd found some potatoes and onions, and some oil left in a bullet-riddled vat. So they shoved it all in a pot, and lit a fire. Five men sharing a chicken, when they'd rather have had two apiece. But it tasted good. And then they looked up, and saw a German soldier pointing a tommy-gun at them. Then a whole platoon appeared – Alpine troops, in green uniforms. Jack yelled, 'Hang on!' to them, in schoolboy German. They finished their chicken.

As for Bobbie's stories of the North African campaign, which were the staple of his conversation that Boxing Day – you'd hardly have known that Rommel had ever won a single battle. His spring campaign in '41, when he advanced from Tripolitania right across Cyrenaica and took Benghazi and reached Egypt. His summer campaign in '42, when he captured Tobruk the day he attacked it, and soon after that was into Egypt again . . .

Or rather, you knew because these achievements put into such admirably dramatic perspective those of Wavell, when earlier it had been *he* who captured Tobruk in only twenty-four hours, and in a couple of months' advance across Cyrenaica the other way destroyed an Italian army six times larger than his. Or it would be the triumphs of Wingate's Ethiopian and Sudanese troops against the Italians. Or Auchinleck, when he took personal command of the Eighth Army and fought the hitherto unstoppable Rommel on the borders of Egypt and beat him.

Charles Lammas had not yet had so much as five minutes alone with his nephew. But he could wait very contentedly, and he knew Bobbie knew he could.

First all these others – to whom Bobbie dished out just the right brief shares of his undivided attention, Charles considered. The Bure gamekeeper, with whom during the shoot he engaged in recollections of the time when, at the Black Horse Wood stand, Jack and Ricky were so intent on their boyish rivalry that they both missed everything that flew over them. And the other time, when Colonel Fletcher brought down about the highest right and left anyone on the estate could remember seeing shot. His mother-in-law . . . Beside whom Bobbie sat at lunch, and whom he beguiled so ruthlessly that by the time the Stilton was being passed round she had already murmured to Lammas that she was going to introduce his nephew to the chairman of Culpeppers, the great merchant bank – a gentleman who had more than once displayed his readiness to be of all possible assistance to dear Julian.

Charles' hour with Bobbie would come, he knew it would. And in the meantime, the modest and jokey way he talked about the Sherwood Rangers' desert fights was excellently judged. Particularly when Frederick asked him about the action at Galal, of which he'd heard tremendous things. And Bobbie said Yes, it had been quite hectic, briefly. But then thank God it had gone their way.

Which was just right . . . For a sharp action which Lammas had heard a fair amount about, as it happened. And which you could call a thundering success, certainly. The regiment had destroyed four German Mark III tanks. They'd also knocked out twenty-two Italian M.13s . . . Which you might be tempted to call a bit of a massacre, those lightly armoured Italian tanks not having a chance in hell against the guns the British could bring to bear on them.

And then, when uncle and nephew might have made an opportunity to talk privately, at first they did not.

It was the day after Boxing Day, and Bobbie had yet again driven over to Edingthorpe. Well, fortunately his father-in-law had more than enough petrol. Bill Meade turned up on his bike, and the three men tramped down across the field with their twelve-bores and their dogs.

They didn't talk, except about how a high wind like this was usually good for pigeon shooting, and about where each of them was going to stand. They left Bill in a spot he'd always favoured, behind some hazels where the stream made a dog-leg, waiting for the pigeon that would fly in toward the plantation of firs. The other two trudged on across the marsh, which was all drenched tussocks of winter-dead rush, and sheets of ruffled grey flood-water with here and there a willow tump. They entered the wood by a ligger over a ditch, and without saying much they separated to stand in different clearings.

Good to have Bobbie back at thirty-five, Lammas thought, in the same wood where when he was ten you'd taught him to shoot. Choosing a place to stand where he'd command a patch of open sky, he glanced to where his nephew had taken up position fifty yards off through the dark brown trees. Oak, ash, alder . . . It was a mixed wood. What keepers called a warm wood, too – meaning that there was a good intermingling of holly and laurel and rhododendron, which gave cover for game even in winter. Entanglements of bracken and bramble, also, so long established that even after weeks of frosts you wouldn't see a pheasant lying low till you nearly trod on it, and the startled bird rose up before your eyes with a clatter of wings.

He turned up his coat collar, to keep the Danish wind from the back of his neck. He loaded, keeping his eyes skinned for the first pigeon to come labouring over the wood against the whole grey sky avalanching the other way. Was that a . . . ? No, seagull.

No moving and no talking, if you wanted pigeon to fly anywhere near you. But good the companionship of standing together in the same familiar wood. Even if this was only a respite, he'd go again. Go into battles which promised to be . . . Yes, yes, but right now he was here.

Giacomo was dead. Bloody Fascist jack-boots stamping on Villa Lucia flagstones. Then bloody Nazi jack-boots stamping, and . . . A lot of shouting no doubt. Hauled out of your own house by foreign soldiers. Stood against your own wall. What earlier in the war he'd thought was quite likely to happen to him, had happened to Giacomo Zanetti instead. Mario had written a very controlled letter about his father's killing. Had Chiara been there? Raffaella? If it was that bastard Giulio Flamini who saw his opportunity of doing Pietro a favour and . . . No, no, impossible. Unfortunately not impossible. Had Flamini found out about his wife's double game? Been blackmailing her for years, maybe, until . . .?

That was a damned lucky pigeon, flying straight over his head without being seen till it was too late.

Concentrate on how wonderful it was to be back doing the old things with Bobbie. To be standing here on sodden ground which was your own ground, standing alive and free with your nephew who was alive and free. Cold fingers on a cold gun. Eyes on the shuddering tree-tops, the tearing cloud-rack. It was like being at the bottom of the sea, standing for pigeon in a wood with a force six blowing – he'd often thought that. With this oceanic roaring in your ears.

Bobbie back doing the old things. Geoff would have understood. Geoff would understand – if any wisp of the spirit endured, after death, for a little while.

Like last night after dinner. He'd gone out with the departing Bure party to their cars, and Bobbie had checked him in the middle of the yard. Had put a hand on his elbow, looked up at where in tatters of the weltering night you could see most of the Plough, and all of Orion with the dog star Sirius at his heels.

Bobbie naming constellations in the yard after dinner – as, when he was a boy, you'd taught him to. Taught Jack, too. And Georgia, and Henrietta.

Look, Uncle Charles, there's Taurus, with Aldeboran good and bright.

A shot. Bobbie had missed. Here came the beginning of a flock, jinking up against the gale, blown sideways. Here was one. He raised his gun.

5

As they were cleaning their guns together, Bobbie said: 'What do you think, Uncle Charles? Shall I let you offer me a drink before I drive back to Bure?'

So here they were, by the drawing-room fire. Both of them still wearing their shooting breeches, though they'd changed their boots for indoor shoes. Bobbie lounging against the mantelpiece, wearing – now he'd taken off his coat, you could see – rather a nice leather waistcoat, which his uncle had a distinct impression of having once owned himself. Bobbie saying, 'Oh . . . winter sherry, Uncle, please. Since that useful father-in-law of mine keeps you so well supplied. Thank you very much. Now, I don't suppose by some rare chance you have a Turkish – one of those fragrant old Turks I used to . . . No, well, never mind. Yes, I *will* liberate one of your cheroots.'

Outside, the first blizzard of the night's rain, which had held off while they were shooting, came whipping almost horizontally over the fields. Unseen in the darkness, in Lammas' wood the pigeons slept in their rocking tree-tops. On the flooded marsh, where grey miniature waves broke against clumps of brown reed, teal and mallard fed. The swollen stream ran high past mirey banks that were pocked where cattle had come to drink, past willows and alders and silver birches, past dykes where moorhens slept.

In the Manor yard, the gun-dogs in their kennel slept, rain drubbing their creosoted wooden roof, rain gurgling in the studio gutters and the outhouse gutters. The rain beat on the rose-bed where, beneath the pruned stubs waiting for spring, Blanche's little spaniel Honey had been buried, the place marked by a small cairn of flints. In the game-larder beside the coal-shed, those pigeons which had flighted in to roost in the wood but had been intercepted by shot, hung by their heads in a row.

In the hall, the grandfather clock ticked. In a draughty bedroom upstairs, where nine winters ago Raffaella Zanetti had sat before a foxed old looking-glass to choose with deliberation her necklace and her earrings, Henrietta Lammas, whose turn it now was to be twenty and at Cambridge, choose her necklace and her earrings. (The dinner party at Bure Lodge that evening was to be for the younger set. Frederick had invited Henrietta, but not her parents.)

Alone in the kitchen, Blanche gazed at the panes between her and the inhospitable night, saw her own lined face and sad eyes looking back at her; looking into Jack's eyes, far away in Colditz castle; looking beyond them, into Michael's eyes. The exhilaration of having Bobbie home, and of having Henrietta home for the Christmas holiday, had ebbed away from her. Though Bobbie had told her that when, at the end of the North African campaign, the famous German 90th Light Division had surrendered, they'd arrived in terrific fettle, and marched in with their band playing. A concert had at once been organised. The German musicians had begun the entertainment, in exactly the right ironical spirit, with *We're gonna hang out our washing on the Siegfried Line*. A football match had been organised, and the German team had won. So maybe, Blanche hoped, when it was the other way round, people treated one another decently.

Blanche stood, hearing the squalls of rain blown against the glass, watching the trickles slithering down. Eyes, eyes . . . The aliveness in them, the thinking.

She turned away, walked like an old woman across the brick-paved floor. She sat down by the range, in the chair which had been Nanny Oldfield's.

In the drawing-room, Charles held out his cigar-case made from *E35's* periscope. The bright enamel birds which Henrietta had perched on the branches of the Christmas tree glinted.

After the Titian studio's Naxos bacchanalia had been sold, Lammas had moved his *Madonna and Child* by Sassoferrato to pride of place on that wall. It was just as beautifully painted, he'd always thought, but of course it was far smaller . . . So he had grouped around it some of his favourite engravings and etchings, till that wall was an absolute Italian mosaic – or a hotch-potch, he wasn't sure which. Prints by Giambattista Tiepolo, by Guido Reni.

Then he'd had to choose something to go where the Sassoferrato had hung before, and since he possessed no comparable oil painting he'd hung one of Piranesi's *Carceri* series there. But it didn't look right. Only he couldn't decide what to replace it with, or where to move it next. Maybe Bobbie would have suggestions. Maybe he'd lend a hand, moving pictures about. They'd done that together often enough. Fiddling with wire and picture hooks. Mumbling to each other because they were holding nails between their lips. Teasing each other about never hanging anything straight. And he could show him that Della Bella *Arabian Horseman* he'd unearthed in one of the solanders.

Bobbie flopped into an armchair. He laid one ankle across the other knee, admired his stockinged shin and calf. He leaned his head on the fingers of his left hand, regarded the older man smilingly.

Looking at the signet ring on that hand, and remembering Passchendaele, Lammas asked: 'Well?'

'Well?' Bobbie amused himself by pretending to be perplexed. 'What do you mean, Well?' But then his steady gaze sparkled. 'Well, you famous old sinner . . . And you're also getting to be quite famous as a painter, did you know that? People are forever asking me if I'm related to the Lammas. Most annoying. Of course, I deny it stalwartly.' His smile widened. 'Well . . . One plays it this way, because it's quite simply the best way to play it.' He sipped his winter sherry. 'You're not going to claim it isn't the best way?'

'Certainly not. I think you're doing everything brilliantly. So, I might add, is your wife.'

'Isn't she just?' he exclaimed. But his arms and legs remained motionless. 'You know, she's quite extraordinary. All this time, I've been having half my Army pay diverted into her account in Norwich. Well, she hasn't spent a shilling of it! The first thing she did on Christmas morning was to offer me a cheque for the total sum. Naturally, I threw it in the fire. All the same . . .'

Charles Lammas' eyebrows, which had risen, came down. 'And . . . In the players' heads?'

'Oh, I . . . Heavens, Uncle, if you want to know what Caroline really thinks – deep down . . . You'll have to ask her. She doesn't – I think very sensibly she doesn't – right now – tell me. There'll . . .' He smiled, wryly. 'There'll be time, I hope.'

Lammas admired his nephew's even-spirited holding in the balance of next year's fighting in France, and his at the moment gallantly conducted marriage. He found his way of saying so.

'I hope so too, dear lad. With all my heart.'

'And if you want to know what the other player feels . . .'

Lightly, Bobbie sprang to his feet. But it seemed that he was too tautly strung, once his poise was broken, to adopt his customary lounging lean against the fireplace. He chucked his cheroot into the flames, went to the drinks tray, tipped another splash of Scotch into his glass.

'If you want to know what the fool thinks about his . . .' He paced from end to end of the drawing-room. Took a second's interest in the sprig of holly stuck to decorate Castiglione's Fame. Swung on his heel. 'Look, I must go. Won't have time to change for dinner, otherwise. I'll take Hetty with me, shall I?'

'Yes, do. Thanks.' Lammas smiled at his nephew who was striding precipitously back down the room, past the fireplace and the looking-glass with its gilt Chinese cranes. 'And, if you remember . . . Bring her back, later.'

'It's all so damned . . .' Bobbie dumped his suddenly emptied glass on the tray, paced back again. 'In fairness to Caroline, I . . . Oh Lord, I never was any use at explaining things. But whatever happens, whatever luck any of us have . . . The thing right now is to live for all you're worth. So that's what we do. The trick is to love her as best I can now, to live for this. And as for what comes . . .'

For an instant he stood still, and faced Charles, and smiled with bitterness but not only with bitterness. 'As I said to you, long ago . . . Truly it hardly matters. Or, anyway, it will matter so superficially, and for so short a time, that I scarcely . . . Goodbye, Uncle Charles. I promise I'll bring the girl back by midnight, or not many hours after it.'

'Goodbye, dear lad. And . . . And good luck.'

The door closed. Lammas stood, feeling very weary, and lonely.

From the hall, he heard Bobbie calling up the staircase: 'Henrietta! I'm off! Are you ready?'

Then he was singing, as he waited for his cousin.

> *Oh I like to go out fishing*
> *In a river or a creek,*
> *But I don't enjoy it half as much as*
> *Dancing cheek to cheek.*

And as her footfalls pitter-pattered down the stairs, and she called 'Here I am!' his voice rose.

> *Dance with me,*
> *I want my arms around you . . .*

6

—〰—

Edingthorpe Manor
7 October '44

My dear Jack

I am afraid we have sad news. Bobbie is dead. They were advancing between Arnhem and Nijmegen, a fortnight ago, when a shell hit his tank. He and the driver, Trooper Farrow, were killed. The others got clear, one of them wounded.

Your mother went up to London immediately, to be with Gloria. I would have gone with her, but since that heart attack I wrote to you about I'm not up to much. Gloria is now here with us for a while. She is still very hysterical, but we are doing our best. Her destruction reminds me of that passage of Matthew. 'From he that hath not shall be taken away even that which he hath.'

I did not see Caroline for the first few days after the news arrived. But then she came to see us. Of course, it is not the kind of thing one ever really recovers from: but her courage is remarkable. And the extraordinary thing is, that she is expecting a baby. I dare say it's foolish of me, but in the midst of our grief this seems to me a marvellous instance of life fighting back against death.

As for Blanche and me . . . Well, you know that Bobbie was practically an adopted son of ours. The way Henrietta comforts your mother is heroic.

And you, dearest boy, who have lost your cousin who was almost your elder brother . . . We think of you all the time. Of Bobbie, and you.

You will be glad to hear that not only were the Sherwood Rangers the first Yeomanry regiment ashore on D Day. Your regiment was also, the week Bobbie was killed, the first British unit of any kind to cross the German border.

With love from your father

Charles.

Jack Lammas had carried that letter in his pocket right through the last winter of the war, when on 19 April he got out of an American Dakota on an airfield in Buckinghamshire. It was a warm, sunny afternoon. And for a minute he was so dizzy with happiness that he just stood there, breathing in his freedom and his home-coming and the verdant air.

More than five years overseas. And here he was, with his feet . . . He glanced down at the pair of Red Cross boots he was wearing, and with a chuckle of sheer joy he tapped one sole on the grass. Here he was, wearing a pair of RAF trousers someone had given him, and the Sherwood Rangers service coat he'd been captured in – the coat he'd worn, for that matter, that blizzardy day at Norwich station when he'd set off for the war. Here he was, with five years of stories weaving and weaving in his mind, and five years of impressions kaleidoscoping in his mind's eye, and his Sherwood Rangers side-cap still on his head. With a blue handkerchief, which had left for the war from Edingthorpe with him that day, knotted round his neck. He raised one hand, touched the cotton. Edingthorpe! Probably not tonight. But tomorrow. Home, by God, after . . . He gazed around at the others. Everyone else seemed to be grinning too. Home!

Upward of five years . . . And the last five days had been as memorable as any, what with the American advance getting closer to Colditz, and some of the guards saying that even if the town did fall the Yanks were going to find they'd liberated three hundred dead men, and then it turned out the commandant had orders from Berlin to march them out to the east.

But the senior British officer, Colonel Tod, refused. The situation was a bit tense for a while, but in the end the commandant surrendered Oflag IV C and the German garrison to Colonel Tod. They undertook not to use their weapons on the British in the castle, or on the Americans, but to remain in position still ostensibly guarding what still appeared to be prisoners. And that worked. It went without a hitch.

The Americans took Colditz with tanks and infantry. The castle was hit once or twice, but no one was hurt. Not much of a defence of the town. Just rifle fire, so far as Jack and the others had been able to see. Some infantry, some of their Home Guard, some Hitler Youth. And, as it transpired, one German officer whose home town it was, back on leave from the Eastern Front. He held the Knight's Cross, and he'd put the ribbon round his neck, and was killed defending his own house with his own rifle.

To be free. To lie in the sun on German spring grass, and eat some of the tinned food the Americans gave them. Couldn't eat much, without making yourself ill, after damned nearly four years of being half-starved. All the same . . . And then these Dakotas, and now . . . And now Buckinghamshire in the sunshine – England must be having an uncommonly early summer, with all this lilac already out. Now these buses which were going to take them to a Reception Camp apparently, but with any luck that wouldn't take long. And then . . .!

Everything was too good to be true, from the lilac flowering in the village gardens to the girls in summery-looking frocks. Fellows in the bus so cheerful they never stopped talking. Other fellows apparently almost too happy to speak. And what was there to say, apart from things like, 'Damned wonderful, eh?' and 'Bloody fantastic!' and 'Just think, a pint of beer!' If only Bobbie had been coming home too, it would have been perfect.

For a moment, jolting along a Buckinghamshire lane, Jack's face clouded over. But he had had five months to get to grips with his cousin's death. And today of all days . . . Today with life and freedom thudding in his veins . . .

He must find out about Georgia. Papa hadn't been able to discover anything about her – but she *must* be alive. And Ricky too. Playing cricket for Winchester, playing cricket for the Gloucesters. Good old Ricky, batting with his cap pulled down over his eyes, cracking the ball through extra cover and hardly beginning to run because he knew it was going for four.

Oh Bobbie. Oh, hell. Still, Caroline wanted him to be Claudia's godfather. That was going to be something he could do for Bobbie, that was going to be his way of loving him from now on. And Georgia . . . He must find Georgia.

At the Reception Camp that evening there were nice women in uniform dishing out food and drink, and everyone was as merry as could be. Even the two Germans they'd brought out with them, because they'd asked to be prisoners of the British rather than the Americans, let alone the Russians, didn't seem as miserable as all that.

The next day was exasperating. Delays while they filled in forms, delays before they were issued with passes. No one knew who they were, and apparently it wasn't enough just to say Lieutenant Jack Lammas, Sherwood Rangers, goodbye. The medical staff assumed they were all lice-infested which they weren't. The officers running the camp seemed to take it for granted that they were all psychological wrecks – which they weren't, just impatient. These three hundred special prisoners the Germans had held in the highest security. These three hundred rough diamonds, bad hats, escapers . . . Clearly they needed special treatment, they needed orders, they needed advice.

By late morning, the rough diamonds were getting restless. Jack was interviewed at what seemed to him insufferable length by a major. Well, he'd never liked majors much. Intolerable rank, he'd always said. And this one, who didn't look as if he'd spent a lot of time lately facing enemy guns, with his idiotic questions only a man sitting snug and ignorant in England could have asked . . . Jack lost his temper. Ended up thumping the major on the chest, yelling at him that he supposed he'd won the bloody war on his own.

Not usual for majors to take that sort of treatment from lieutenants – but this one did. Perhaps he'd believed his own talk about how these wild men who'd been in German cells must be expected to need psychiatric help. And Jack might have been three stone underweight, but he still had those oarsman's shoulders. Anyhow, in the end he and the others had their ration books and their rail passes. Had some money. Had *Instructions To Returned Prisoners Of War (Officers)* which gave them forty-two days' leave.

He'd rung up Edingthorpe. Ellen had answered, and had burst into tears on the telephone, and had wanted to fetch his mother. But he said No, just tell her I'm coming. Is there still a four o'clock train?

Jack had never realised how much he liked Liverpool Street Station, till he was running toward it through bomb damage that he scarcely noticed, and the crowds he only noticed because they kept getting in the way and it was five to four. Then he was in under those grimy Victorian wrought-iron arches, and there was the Norwich train, getting up steam at platform nine just like before the war. He ran to the nearest door, jumped aboard. Then he made his way forward to the front carriage, and the train started.

All the way home, Jack kept planning how he was going to spend his leave. With the weather like this, he'd get *Golden Eye* out. She'd have been laid up in a boat-yard at Ludham or Horning probably. What sort of shape would the old boat be in? Been rather neglected, quite likely. Still, it would be fun doing some maintenance work.

Yes, he'd bike down to Saint Benet's Abbey, just like in the old days. Walk down over the pasture to the river, to *Golden Eye* at her mooring. Just like that last summer with Georgia. If work needed doing on the rigging, Papa would give him a hand. Not with heavy work, after his heart attack. But light things he'd be able to do. It would be companionable, down at the mooring, with the wildfowl, and the river sliding by. He'd tell Papa about his escapes, about walking alone by night and lying up by day. About being recaptured both times, and sent to the cooler.

The countryside through which the train was rushing became Jack's home landscape, and with all his thoughts blurring in delight he just gazed out of the window. This was his landscape all right, where the churches were flint and the skies were wide. A wood-side, with rabbits hopping about in the evening sun. Water-meadows with swans . . . When the train rounded a curve, for a moment he could see Norwich castle on its mound, and the cathedral spire.

Charles and Blanche were on the platform. Jack leapt down from the carriage, strode toward them. But then for an instant he hesitated. His father was leaning on a walking-stick. They both looked grey, and withered, and about a foot shorter than he remembered them.

Blanche Lammas took a few steps forward. She never noticed Jack's momentary wavering, nor the shock that flickered across his eyes.

The next second she was in his arms – which felt amazingly strong, after years of being hugged only by Charlie and Henrietta – not knowing whether she was laughing or weeping with joy, but clinging to him. And for a minute, for her it was as if all griefs had fallen away, as if all losses were revenged, and all loves brought back.

Then Jack was gripping his father's hand with one of his, and clapping him on the shoulder with the other, and Charles was saying, 'Heavens, don't knock me down. Had another heart attack since the one I wrote to you about. Well, well, dear boy. Welcome home.' And even Charles Lammas had to take out his handkerchief, dab his watery old eyes. Then in the milling crowd on the platform he beamed at his gaunt but powerful-looking son, in a way that he had not been in the habit of beaming for many years – except for the day Henrietta got her First.

Holding her son's arm as if it were a hawser that promised great safety, and gazing up into his face as she walked beside him just like a girl with her lover (her husband wondered whether to tease her, but decided it would be unkind, this was an amusement he would keep to himself), Blanche was borne forward on a comber of happiness out of the station to where the car was parked.

'Let's see if I can remember how to do this,' Jack said, and got into the driver's seat.

'My darling boy, you're quite free to kill me now,' his mother declared. 'Any old ditch you feel like tipping us into is fine.'

'Well . . .' He caught his father's eye. 'The great thing is, I'm free. Now, what are these heart attacks you've been going in for?'

Jack had already half-forgotten his impression of how his parents seemed stricken and reduced. Then it was so terrific to be driving the old Austin along familiar lanes, drawing ever closer to Edingthorpe, and Papa's account of his ill-health was so cursory and dismissive, that he was sure all was really as well as you could expect.

After Charlie's first heart attack, Doctor Bennett had told him not to do any climbing or hurrying or lifting, Mama reported. So what had happened? He'd been painting down on the shore at Weybourne, and then had set off up one of the cliff paths, carrying his easel and his paint-box, when . . . It was Giles Whitchurch who found him. Out and about those headlands and foreshores in all weathers and at all hours, Giles – luckily. He'd come upon Charlie, not much more than half alive, where he'd slithered down to a corner of the path and got wedged against a spur, with his painting clobber all scattered where it had fallen.

Jack listened without undue perturbation to his parents making light of the event. Fortunately Giles Whitchurch had come by, and then had fetched a couple of Home Guardsmen with a stretcher and got Papa back to Weybourne Mill and sent for a doctor.

It was really very pleasant recovering there, his father was saying. Except that Giles' ideas of restorative treatment included lengthy bed-side disquisitions on the coins dug up from a Saxon burial site. Each coin, it seemed, had to be discussed.

The typical and ludicrous thing, Mama was butting in to say, had been how Charlie's chief preoccupation had been to get back to where he'd fallen to search for some of his paints and brushes which had not been recovered. Cerulean blue and French ultramarine had both gone missing. Most annoying. Naples yellow, raw umber . . .

A herd of pigs in one of the paddocks, cabbages growing on the tennis court! Well, Jack understood perfectly, of course. But he had not expected these changes, and briefly they seemed odd. And the moment they'd got out of the car in the yard, he'd had it pressed in upon him again how shrunken his father was, how tottery. Apparently he'd had to give up painting out of doors entirely. Though he still managed to do a little work in his studio, sometimes.

The house seemed smaller, Jack thought. And so quiet! Just a few old people creeping about in it. The Meades had aged too.

None of the merriment and liveliness he'd remembered through all these war years. No voices calling with some new plan, no feet hurrying to do something exciting. When had children last rampaged here? Or anyone put on a record, and danced? With Ricky away, fighting in General Slim's Fourteenth Army in Burma. With Hetty at Cambridge – but she was going to get to Norfolk for the weekend of Claudia's christening, Mama promised. With Georgia vanished into thin air, and Bobbie in a military graveyard near Arnhem.

Upstairs, Jack stood in his old bedroom. Everything terribly neat and tidy – trust Mama for that, and trust Ellen. But . . . He opened the wardrobe. It creaked. A smell of mothballs. Beside coats and trousers of his own hanging up, there were some of Bobbie's too. Shutting the wardrobe door, he turned. Saw his cousin there, that last short leave before the Normandy landings. The leave during which he must have conceived his daughter.

The room appeared more modest than he'd remembered. Half a lifetime since Papa had bought this house, and here on the top floor the wallpapers were still the old Victorian ones, tattier than ever now, and the wash-stands were still the same old ones of course. Too pretty to change, perhaps, these walls; or . . .

Back to his regiment, as soon as this leave was over. But then, when peace finally came . . . Back to King's, and then up to London to the Architectural Association, and then – a practice! Buildings! Work! And he'd earn some money, and . . . But Jack couldn't decide whether, when he was earning a salary, he'd redecorate the Manor bedrooms, or leave these old Victorian papers on the walls.

In the silence, he looked around at his boyhood things. A stuffed tanager, with red and green plumage, perched on a barometer. An ostrich egg which had been cut in half, and mounted with a silver stand for the bowl, and silver rims, and as a handle on the lid a silver top-knot. Odds and ends he'd been given. An alabaster chess set from Volterra, which Contessa Zanetti had given him after an expedition there, given him in what suddenly seemed that infinitely long-lost world of before the war – and which reminded him that Emanuela was in America. His father's old Navy dirk. When he'd been a boy of ten, that had been his proudest possession.

He wasn't a boy now. Not after certain things, after certain times. Not after those cattle-trucks crossing Greece under the summer sun. Trucks crammed with prisoners of war. Damn all to eat, and not enough water, day after day with a slop bucket in each truck. The swarms of flies, and being a prisoner.

Not after a lot of things that happened afterwards, in Germany. Alan Purvis when they were escaping from Eichstätt in Bavaria. Sixty of them escaped that night, wriggling along the tunnel they'd spent months digging to get outside the camp perimeter fence, but that poor devil Purvis got claustrophobia and started to scream. Jack remembered the claustrophobic feeling by God, dragging yourself forward in the dark with no air to breathe, and standing in his Edingthorpe bedroom he tried not to remember. And he tried not to remember Alan Purvis right behind him who started to scream, and who had to be silenced before the Germans heard anything, and had to be dragged back and away so the escape could proceed. He remembered how, lying in that mole-run, in desperation he'd kicked Purvis' head till he'd kicked him unconscious, or at least near enough unconscious for the bastard to pipe down and for others behind to haul him out by his ankles.

Not after Mike St Clair at Colditz, either. Mike who was a fanatical escaper. Not just bold. Fanatical. He'd lost the ability to calculate the difference between an outside chance and not having a hope in hell.

The exercise field was a hundred yards or so from the castle in a dell surrounded by trees, where they could walk round and round under guard. That day Jack went up to Mike and asked, had he fixed up to walk round with anyone in particular, or did he feel like company? He looked a bit tense – or maybe it was only now in retrospect that Jack thought that. Anyhow, Mike answered that he hadn't arranged to walk that day with anyone because he felt like a bit of solitude, felt like walking with his own thoughts, if Jack didn't mind.

Jack said he quite understood. There was a high wire fence around that field, and beyond it the German guards strung out with their Alsatians and their automatic rifles. Jack walked, with his thoughts. Mike walked, five paces in front of him. And then he ran. He ran for the fence, and all hell broke loose. Shouted commands, shots. Mike got over that fence in a fury of scrambling, he fell down the other side and picked himself up and ran. Then he went down, and there were more shots.

Everyone had thrown themselves on the ground, because the shooting was coming from all sides. Then the shooting stopped. They got cautiously to their feet again, and were rounded up at gun-point and marched back to the castle. Without Mike St Clair.

Still, those were not the stories he would tell his mother and father at dinner. And this was absurd – he'd not been home for half an hour, and already his spirit had gone back to those camps. He went to the bathroom, washed his hands and face.

But then, on the top floor landing, Jack paused. These watercolour drawings of Grandfather Roly's and Papa's, so familiar on the walls. These floorboards – he'd swear he still knew how to avoid treading on the ones that creaked. He tried. Reached the bedroom which had been Georgia's with all his old soundlessness.

He went in, looked down at the bed. So narrow, so plain. He glanced around at the room. No trace of her remained. It was simply a spare bedroom, as it had been before her English years. Jack looked again at the bed, smiling.

Clattering downstairs, suddenly with a fierce appetite for his dinner, he thought: Georgia. Oh, where are you, Georgia?

8

—⚮—

For hours, Ellen Meade had been in a flurry of activity. Mrs Lammas had told her that Jack wouldn't be able to go back straight away to eating what you might call properly, they'd have to build him up slowly. Ellen had looked astounded, and had sniffed. She had said, 'Yes, Ma'am' – without the slightest intention of being influenced by such talk. *Slowly?* There was going to be nothing slow about the way *she* put new strength into him. The indissoluble trinity of Love and Food and Life, on which alone from eternity the world had most satisfactorily rested, being of a too self-evident truth to discuss.

Ellen's fruit cakes were famous, and when Jack had got out of the car in the yard she had been ready for him, with a massive slice on a plate and a glass of milk, just like he'd always had when he was a child. Now she had baked a loaf of her special bread, which he had always liked. The vegetable soup had been made with the remaining stock from when they'd killed a chicken last week. Bream had been caught and gutted and cooked. A formidable quantity of potatoes had been mashed.

Blanche Lammas said little at dinner, she was so happy just to look at her son. Charles and Jack did the talking. And you would hardly have guessed, from the way they tackled the lighthearted aspects of everything, that it might in fact be exceedingly unpleasant to have a heart attack, or even more exceedingly unpleasant to be a prisoner of war.

Jack told his parents about his first escape, from a camp at Warburg, in the summer of '42, when he was at large for a week and got beyond Bentheim on the Dutch frontier before he was recaptured. Walking by night, lying up in woods by day. Steering by the stars, and by a rudimentary compass – simply a magnetic needle, hung by a thread from its point of balance, but serviceable. Lying up for the best part of twenty hours of daylight, the midsummer nights being so short. Which was all right in fine weather, but one day on that escape it had rained. Still, mostly the weather had been glorious, and he'd skirted the towns and villages, slipping across the starlit countryside westward like a ghost. He'd had a little German money, and when one night he borrowed a skiff on the east bank of the Ems, he left it moored on the west bank with some money on the thwart. The following night, when he crossed a canal by the same method, paddling with a floorboard because the dinghy's prudent owner had removed the oars, he left a payment again.

Jack told them about how most escapers set off in twos or threes for company, but they were always the first to be caught. Naturally you were nearer to silence and invisibility on your own, and he'd headed off alone that time. He'd headed off alone once more the next summer, when he'd got out of the camp at Eichstätt through that tunnel, and was recaptured some days later on the wrong bank of the Danube.

He could still scarcely believe that he was eating bream in the dining-room at home. He'd break off talking, and smile, and gaze around. Yes, there was the old court sword hanging over the door. There was the drawing of a girl's head by Shannon, hanging where it had always hung. Propped up on the mantelpiece, there was that racing-plate of Tofthill's from the time Papa rode him in the Foxhunters' Chase, when he himself must have been, oh, two or three years old. He was home!

So then it was the cheerfullest thing in the world, to describe how the first time, when after a year in a herd of prisoners behind barbed-wire, he'd found himself alone walking in the darkness through hostile country, he'd been horribly frightened and lonely. Damn it, there'd been moments when he was on the point of darting out of his coverts and begging some friendly German to take him to the nearest camp.

But quickly he'd got into the swing of it, and then he'd rejoiced in his solitude. What with the exhilaration of being free, and with every stride making your way toward a greater freedom – represented by the North Sea one time, and Switzerland the next – he'd never, he reckoned, been more alive to the countryside. By God that had been marvellous – walking on fast through the glimmering nights, with an owl swooping past him occasionally, or then a rustle and the fleeting shadow of a fox. Giving even farmhouses a wide berth, so as not to set dogs barking. Keeping on tramping as long into the dawns as he dared, and then finding a snug lair to lie up in.

The first time he'd been recaptured, a guard had jumped out of a hedge and pointed a tommy-gun at his stomach. They had pickets out on both sides of that border. The second time, it had been his unwise choice of a day's lair.

It was strange, telling his escape stories in this room. Here, in this house, where he'd longed to be. Days and nights for long prison years, dreaming of freedom and home. Days and nights of those short escaper's bursts of freedom, when he'd had always flickering in his mind that one idea that now – if he was cunning – if his luck held – you never knew, but he just might . . .! And in the German nights he'd glanced around keenly and listened keenly. He'd lengthened his stride. And it had always been flickering there, the idea of getting home to Edingthorpe on leave before rejoining his regiment, before getting back in the war and hoping to do a bit better this time. The idea of this house, this room, this air . . . And here he was!

So Jack listened to his voice talking cheerfully about that night when he'd come to the banks of the Danube. He put down his knife and fork. Yes, there was the toasting glass, on the sideboard. He heard his voice explaining that when he'd gone scouting along the river shore all the boats had been removed.

Day had broken. He was going to have to lie up, try again the next night. There was no wood nearby, so he'd walked into a hayfield, stepping carefully so as not to damage the crop and leave tell-tale signs. In the middle of the field, he had lain down. He'd eaten a piece of his Red Cross chocolate. Taken a few swigs from his water-bottle.

He had slept. And all would have been well, if that day the mowers hadn't come to cut that field of hay. They saw him, and went to fetch a couple of armed men. He woke up to sunlight and hay and the barrels of guns aimed at him.

He woke up to a vision of what that death would look like, he heard himself telling his parents in the dining-room. Too startled to do anything except blurt out 'Good morning' or something like that – and have that vision of a circle of mowers leaning on their scythes, and a thin ragged soldier lying in a sunshiny harvest field and suddenly smashed into by bullets, so there was blood on him and blood on the stalks of hay.

They were decent people, they didn't fire. They marched him off, with his hands held up over his head, just like the other guard had the summer before near Bentheim, to their village police station. Where the constable turned out to be a perfectly nice man, with a small son. Jack ended up sharing the last of his chocolate with that child.

That first night at home, Jack Lammas was sure he would lie awake for an hour out of sheer happiness. But he fell asleep at once, and didn't wake for ten hours.

At breakfast, he rejoiced Ellen's heart by telling her how often he'd thought of her greengage jam, spread good and thick – so the war-time lack of oranges, which had prevented her from making marmalade, was a matter of complete indifference to him. There wasn't much butter? He'd had no butter at all for four years! That morning, she had without asking poached him not two eggs but three, and toasted great slabs of her bread. He rejoiced her heart even more by eating the lot, and then doing justice to the Manor's honey, and the greengage jam.

Then he went out with his mother to inspect the garden. Not because he had ever been particularly inspired by rose beds or herbaceous borders. Because he knew that showing him her garden would be Mama's happiest way of being alone with him for an hour. And anyway, that day and in the days to come, being about the place again was all he desired.

So he accompanied Blanche to see how well the azaleas down by the pond had grown. He complimented Sidney Meade on the stacked-up logs in the wood-shed. Falling in beside his father's slow step, he went to the orchard to decide about the pruning of the apple trees and pear trees. And all the time, while he was hearing how the Egremont Russets had been cropping splendidly, but last year had been a lean year for pears, neither the Josephine de Malines nor the Emile de Heyst had borne much fruit . . . While he was asking, were these the peacocks he remembered or offspring of theirs, and Papa was telling him how their war-time diet had included roast peafowl once or twice, and very good they were . . . It kept beating away in Jack's brain, how lucky he'd been.

Amazingly lucky . . . Now that news was coming every day from Germany about prison camps liberated, and concentration camps, and extermination camps. Now that it was emerging also that the shooting of prisoners had started right at the beginning of the war.

Not slaughters on the scale of those at Belsen or Auschwitz or Dachau. But right back in the days when the British Expeditionary Force had fought in France . . . A few survivors of massacres were coming home with stories to tell, records to put straight. At Wormhout, near Dunkirk, forty-five men of the Warwickshire Regiment after they had surrendered had been murdered. At Paradis, in the same campaign, a hundred-odd of the Norfolks had surrendered, after they had run out of ammunition. They'd been marched to a long pit in front of a barn, where two machine-guns had been set up. By some miracle, a couple of the men had survived.

Yes, and when Jack thought of those fifty RAF fellows who, after they'd escaped from a camp and been recaptured, had been shot. And when he thought of that foggy day at Eichstätt, and the wryneck migration, and how lucky he'd been . . . So in the orchard he broke off from talking about the D'Arcy Spice, told his father his wryneck story.

He'd had a plan for building ladders to scale the inner fence and then to get across the barbed-wire entanglement to the outer fence and down the other side. There were turrets, with machine-guns and search-lights, of course. But he'd reckoned that when the autumn fogs were at their thickest, real pea-soupers, there was a midway point where the sentries couldn't see much.

A few paces in from the fence, there was a low wire, with a notice saying that any man who stepped over it would be shot. But he'd wanted to get close up to the fence to calculate his ladders. So the next time the fog was so dense he could scarcely make out the turrets, and he hoped the watchers on them couldn't see him, he glanced quickly around and crossed that wire. He approached the fence and the entanglement. On the other side of which, a German sentry patrolling in the murk brought his rifle to his shoulder.

Jack was certain that he would never forget the click of that rifle-bolt. However, yet again he'd been in luck. The man who could have shot him didn't. The camp commandant, to whom he was marched, asked him why he'd stepped over that wire where the notice was plainly legible. Jack said he'd always been an enthusiastic ornithologist, and he'd known the wrynecks were migrating. He'd wanted to get a good look at them.

Like the patrolling sentry, that commandant must have been a good man, not a bloodthirsty man. He could have ordered shooting or God alone knew what, but he didn't. Whatever he thought of the various views of migrating birds which might, in thick fog, be obtained from positions a few yards nearer to or farther from the perimeter fence, he made no comment. Neither did he express surprise at the risks his prisoner seemed prepared to run in order to see a flock of wrynecks, nor disbelief in his story. He dismissed him.

Charles Lammas liked that wryneck story. But these days he couldn't potter much beyond the orchard, so when Jack took the dogs for their walks he went alone. Except that a lot of his father's ideas came with him. They were talking a lot, in those days.

Two Springer spaniels for company. His native lanes and heaths and meadows to wander freely through till evening. The prospect of peace time . . . Jack would walk two or three parishes in one direction or another. To Knapton, to revisit the church which had rows of wooden angels in its roof. The next day, over the common to Ridlington church, and further afield to Crostwight. With his survivor's joy in life welling up in his heart, and his new-found freedom lighting up all the jumbled thoughts in his head . . . And after a fortnight of Ellen's cooking and of long walks, he felt nearly as fit as he'd ever been.

He walked from church to church about that countryside, because when he was a boy his father had taken him to visit churches; and because his love of architecture had started in those tussocky graveyards, and in those tiled or slated or reed-thatched chancels and naves. Then often he'd strike off over a field to find again a spinney where once there'd been a badger's sett, or to follow a favourite stream through a favourite wood.

Half of Burma had already been reconquered, including both Mandalay and Maymyo, and still there was no news of Ricky or of Georgia. With the optimism of his high spirits, Jack assumed that if you had not heard definitely that someone was dead they were probably all right. And then his anxieties would be supplanted by the pleasure of striding once more up the path toward Crostwight's stumpy tower. Or by what his father had said about Giacomo Zanetti's life and his death. Or what he'd said about how the First War had kicked the shit out of a century of meliorism and talk about progress, let alone the refinement of the human spirit; but apparently the class was dim and so a Second War, a repetition of the lesson, had been required – though surely now, with any luck . . . And so all of ten seconds might pass before Georgia came back to haunt him.

Giacomo's death was one of the things that had stricken Papa – it wasn't just the heart attacks he'd had. The way he talked about his old friend's *maremmano* dogs, and his labouring in his orchards, and those malodorous cigars he was inseparable from. Papa had decided that he wasn't ever going back to Italy. But then he'd talk about Giacomo's disenchantment with himself and, after his war, with his fellow men. Yes, how self-dismissive the man had always been . . . And yet he'd known more about Piero Della Francesca than practically anyone alive. And had been at his happiest, perhaps, when taking down paintings off his own walls, and writing on their dusty backs the names of his heir's brother and sisters.

Jack would halt, gaze at a gate and a track leading into a May copse. Would stand so immobile, and gaze so long and so possessedly, that the gnat-swarms in the evening sun would resume their convolutions in the air around his head, and the spaniels, unaccustomed these days to such long walks, would flop down.

Coming back from the war. Coming back, and wanting to stitch old times and new into one fabric. To determine to make a new peace-time life out of the best of the old . . . And to do this knowing that Papa had done much the same after the last war, and was aware you knew you were following in his steps.

This also is vanity and vexation of spirit . . .

And the grasshopper shall be a burden, and desire shall fail, because man goeth to his long home, and the mourners go about the streets:

Or ever the silver cord be loosed, or the golden bowl be broken . . .

Papa had read that to him first the spring that Germany invaded what was left of Czechoslovakia. That spring when he'd been home from Cambridge for what turned out to be his last vac before his last term. And he'd quoted *Ecclesiastes* to him again yesterday. Now Bobbie had gone to his long home, and he was standing here looking at the leafy dappling on a path.

For to him that is joined to the living there is hope: for a living dog is better than a dead lion.

For the living know that they shall die: but the dead know not anything, neither have they any more a reward, for the memory of them is forgotten.

Yes, but there was that other bit too that rang true to him. That bit about . . . And Jack would walk on, and the midges would have their sunny dancing disturbed for an instant, but only for an instant. The dogs would get up, and would trot after him, panting.

He would hear: *Whatsoever thy hand findeth to do, do it with thy might; for there is no work, nor device, nor knowledge, nor wisdom, in the grave whither thou goest.*

And he would think: Cambridge. My final exams. A degree. A job of work to do. Right. Good.

I returned, and saw under the sun . . .

But time and chance . . .

9

—m—

By the time of Claudia Lammas' christening at Bure church, her godfather Jack was surprising himself with the growing strength of his longing to get back to his regiment. The Sherwood Rangers were in Hanover. Unfortunately, the War Office appeared reluctant to send ex-prisoners of war back overseas immediately, and Jack gathered he was in danger of a job at the Ministry of Information. This sounded dreary, and he'd written to Colonel Christopherson in Hanover – but he hadn't yet had a reply.

Not that anything bad had occurred . . . Or only two bad things. The first was that one morning Papa, reading his *Times*, had abruptly said, 'Oh, God.' He'd handed the paper across, folded at the page with the Roll of Honour. Jack had read, in the list of those reported killed in action, the name of Captain Richard Burney, MC, of the Gloucestershire Regiment.

The second bad thing had happened on one of Jack's walks. He'd seen old Brown, who'd fought on the Western Front in the First War, working in a sugarbeet field, so he'd waved and called. The old man had raised his head, but he hadn't said anything. So Jack had called again: 'Good afternoon, Mr Brown!' Brown had stared at him. And then he'd shaken his fist. He'd shouted: 'Yare didn't oughter 'a cum home, yare young varmint!'

That had gone right through Jack. That had spoiled his ramble with the dogs, and spoiled his sleep that night.

Lesser things contributed to his unease too. Mere irritants . . . But maybe he was nervier these days than he'd realised.

It was tiresome to be so regularly informed, invariably by people who throughout the war had not left the British Isles, that all Germans were murdering savages. And no one seemed to want to listen to his stories of individual Germans who often had treated him and other prisoners humanely. Then all these non-combatants who were mighty liberal with their 'We've won the war' jabber. Air raid wardens, farmers, clerks, teachers, nurses, typists . . . A whole smug population of them, all apparently quite convinced that they'd bravely endured the most terrible adversities – and in the great cause of civilisation, what was more, oh naturally. But to Jack's eye they all looked pretty healthy and relaxed. And as for all this gardening chatter in the days before the christening . . .

Jack Lammas was too tough-minded by then not to shrug off, after a rather wretched day or two, old Brown's shaken fist in the beet field, and his cursing him for having let himself fall into enemy hands alive. He went on walking with the spaniels from church to church, in that countryside where the may was coming into white flower, and the sycamores and the horse chestnuts were in full leaf but the alders and ashes were still bare, and the oaks had their first yellowy leaves and tassels of flowers. Often a cold wind blew grey clouds in from the North Sea – but when the sun came out again the meadows were bright with the first buttercups.

To hell with all civilians, he'd think. And he'd scowl as he biked over to Womack Staithe, where *Golden Eye* had weathered the war in a boat-yard under a tarpaulin. Or to Yarmouth, where Tim Farne's younger brother Hugh was a lieutenant on a motor torpedo boat. He'd had quite an exciting time raiding enemy shipping along the European coast, usually at night. Now the German boats were crossing over to the English east coast ports to surrender.

Or Jack's forehead and eyes would be overcast because he'd remembered his cousin was dead. Or because he'd remembered Ricky was dead . . . Which made it more urgent to find Georgia. She must be alive, he must find her.

The dead – *whose love, and their hatred, and their envy is now perished. Neither have they any more a portion forever in any thing that is done under the sun.* The living – *the sons of men snared in an evil time.* The living! In his punchiest high spirits, Jack would decide that there was no reason to believe that they were any longer snared in an evil time. He would summon to mind Caroline and Claudia, and think of how he was going to stand by them, do everything for them he could. He'd think of Henrietta. That Arab harness he'd sent her from Palestine had been two years on the voyage, but then it had reached Edingthorpe safe and sound. Hetty who had apparently promised Papa she'd sit for her portrait this summer. Which was a sweet thing for her to have volunteered. Because Papa's knowing he was just about finished as an artist, and his longing to paint a few last pictures, even *one* truly fine picture, before it was all over, had windlassed a tension in him which . . . Yes, Jack thought, Hetty was a darling, and he'd tell her so.

A bit damned much, though, all this chitter-chatter of Mama's and Sarah Hedleigh's about whose banksia rose was the most magnificent this year. And about what a shame it was that the Bure camelias would have finished flowering before the christening party, though happily the rhododendrons would be at their best.

Jack had always liked the Hedleighs, liked Bure. Yet somehow, these days . . . When he went over there to be with Caroline, who liked to talk to him about Bobbie. When he couldn't get up to the nursery to see the baby and her, without being buttonholed by Sarah with her lamentations of the newly departed schoolchildren's ravages to her property. Or without being brought up to date by Julian as to his preparations for standing down at the next general election in favour of Freddie. Somehow, those two under-gardeners employed to push lawn-mowers endlessly up and down acres of unblemished sward jarred on Jack. However, he discovered that if he went around to the back of the Hall, and in through the servants' quarters, he could go up the back staircase and get to the nursery unwaylaid.

The living! preferably in the form of his regiment. But, in the meantime . . . Going for a pint of beer in a Yarmouth pub with Hugh Farne, and telling him about riding with his brother Tim and some Arab cavalrymen through that defile to Petra. Hearing about Hugh's torpedoes and his six-pounder gun forrard, his two machine-guns on the bridge and his Oerlikon gun aft. How right at the end of the war they'd been equipped with radar – though that hadn't solved their chief problem, which was sea-sickness. Tim's and Hugh's father had played cricket, long ago, with Uncle Geoffrey and Papa and Julian Hedleigh, and then had been killed on the Somme. But Tim and Hugh were both survivors of this war, and so was he, and he was going to find Georgia. Papa had written to the Red Cross. Written to someone who was an Indian civil servant, someone else who was a surgeon in Calcutta.

The living . . . like little Claudia. And, as his mother and Anne Daubeney agreed after the christening, Jack had looked extremely handsome in his uniform, standing at the font beside the young widow, with the tame Bure parson and the other godparents.

Lady Hedleigh's chief anxiety – aside from her viburnums and her tree peonies – was whether Claudia's posthumous arrival might hamper the operations, which she had already instigated, for supplying Caroline fairly briskly with a suitable new husband. But she found time, after tea, to take Jack aside, and confide in him that she was *delighted* that her daughter had asked him to be a godfather. It was – Sarah displayed just enough emotion to offset its control – *precisely* what *darling* Bobbie would have wished.

10

—⊕—

Oh Godfather Charles, Ricky so nearly got to me here! After three years of not knowing if he were alive or dead, but knowing that if he were alive he'd be in the Fourteenth Army. He fought at Imphal, he fought at Kohima. Got an MC. How much about the war in Burma do people in England know? More than we knew in our camp till we were liberated, probably. My nerves are rotten bad these days. I can't think about Ricky without crying. I'm sorry.

They were Gurkhas who got to our camp first. And Ricky was still alive, just think! We were both alive and free, only about fifty miles apart – and neither of us knew it. The battle for Mandalay Hill wasn't over till that day we were freed, and the fighting for the city was still going on. Apparently the last of the Japanese garrison, holed up in the cellars under the Hill, wouldn't surrender and wouldn't surrender. In the end, the British and the Gurkhas destroyed them by rolling drums of petrol down the shafts and igniting the stuff with tracer bullets. The siege of Fort Dufferin was still going on, and they were clearing the city street by street. Ricky was killed by a sniper.

Maymyo had been bombed again and again, and by the end of the fighting there were a lot of dead everywhere. But apparently the carnage in Mandalay after ten days' fighting was horrifying. Like after the first air raids three years ago, which I remember – only now less of the city was left standing. Of course, I wanted to get down there, get to the main body of General Slim's army to try to find Ricky or hear word of him. But at first, when they were still putting out the fires and burying the dead, no jeep-driver had a place for a girl looking for her brother And then, after being lucky for so long, I celebrated my liberation by going down with cholera. On April Fool's Day . . .

Charles Lammas did not read those sentences till the English summer was beginning to wane. It was a long letter, written during the inactive days of Georgia's convalescence. She had written passages about her life during the latter stages of the occupation, in an internment camp – from which it had been possible to sally forth to work in a Japanese military hospital, and thus sometimes pilfer food and medicines for her fellow prisoners. Passages about the campaigns that Ricky had taken part in – written with a fierce sisterly pride which brought tears to Lammas' eyes. Passages about her brother's grave, in a military cemetery at Mandalay. About how stupidly depressed and jittery she was all the time. How she wanted to get away from Burma, begin to forget things a little if she could. Pull herself together . . . In India, she supposed. Go to Europe again, too, she supposed, eventually, though she couldn't really think why.

Lammas' friend the Calcutta surgeon had run Georgia Burney to earth in a clinic in that city earlier in the summer. He had reported her as being *a bit shot about. No question of it, she's had a hellish time. But she'll pull through.* So, after upward of three years, her godparents had known she was alive. Which, what with the war having deprived her of all her next-of-kin, had started to seem an unexpectedly difficult thing to ascertain.

Then that letter came. And although her handwriting was a bit deformed, had momentary scrabbles of – well, you couldn't know what, but possibly hysteria . . . Still, to Charles Lammas her voice rang true. A war-worn Georgia, he thought – but the goddaughter he remembered. Though a Georgia Burney who wanted to get away from her native land was a novelty. Still, on the whole he took heart.

In November, she rang up from London. Blanche answered the telephone, and at once invited her to come and stay at Edingthorpe for as long as she wished to, they'd love to have her. But Georgia said, No, thank-you. And hurt her godmother by the jumpy, almost angry way she said it. As if anyone with a scrap of experience or imagination ought to grasp that such an invitation could only be refused.

But, Georgia announced, she had something for Godfather Charles which she wanted to give him. Might she come down tomorrow? Or she could post her parcel to him if they preferred. Lunch tomorrow? Well – Yes, lunch, all right, thank-you. But truly an hour in the house – less – was all she required.

It was one of those North Sea winter days when it never really gets light. Grey rain was beating heavily on the brown and grey land. Blanche Lammas drove her goddaughter from Norwich station to Edingthorpe. She had quite forgiven Georgia for her telephone conversation, and she was relieved to see that she wasn't too agonisingly thin. But she was in a tremor of pity for the girl whom the war appeared to have turned into rather an elegant young lady, but who glanced about distractedly and wretchedly, who asked such jerky questions about Jack in Hanover and Henrietta in Cambridge.

'Your godfather can't get about much these days,' she said. 'We'll find him in the library.'

They went in. The streaming windows. The dun garden. In the fireplace, three or four logs charring together. Georgia advanced to where she could see bony-looking shanks in knickerbockers protruding from a tall chair.

'My darling girl, so you've arrived,' said an old man's weak voice.

'Godfather Charles, you don't have to get up for me!' She hurried forward to where he was struggling slowly to his feet. As she reached to support his elbows, the package she had been holding under her arm fell with a thud.

'Certainly I do. Not dead yet. Think of Ned, nearly the age my father would be, and still going strong.'

'Edmund hasn't had a heart attack,' Blanche interjected with swift loyalty. And as she stooped to pick up the package, was shocked by the hostile glance which Georgia gave her hands. Still, the girl was clearly in a terrible state, and must be forgiven everything. Blanche laid the string-criss-crossed brown wrapping-paper on a chair, where it could be seen to be unmolested.

Charles and Georgia stood, holding one another's hands. Both shocked by what they saw, after seven years.

'I can't help my eyes, you know,' Georgia said. And to stop him gazing into them, flung her arms around his neck.

He embraced her tight. He kissed her. He could feel her shoulders quivering, so he kept holding her, and he said: 'I've always loved your eyes,' in the gruff voice he always had when he was moved and didn't want to show it too much. 'And I'm much afraid that I can't help looking like . . . You know your Shakespeare well, Georgia – how does it go, the bit about the seven ages of man? The sixth age, in my case, *The lean and slipper'd pantaloon* . . .' Gently, he released her, feeling the moisture on her cheek. Looked again at those colour-changing, murky eyes, which now were pools of hurt. 'Right, let's all have a glass of sherry, and then some lunch. We've got lots to tell you. And then I hope you'll tell us some of your stories.'

'I won't tell you anything!' Georgia Burney's voice cracked. 'I can't! I won't! It's all . . .' She accepted some sherry, but her hand was trembling so she put the glass down abruptly on the mantelpiece. 'It's all in that parcel I've brought you. All here, Godfather Charles.'

She picked up her bundled-together writings, stood clutching them.

'Do sit down, my love,' said Blanche gently. 'It *is* wonderful to have you back. And, please . . . If you can't stay this time, of course I quite understand. But you won't prevent me from insisting that I long for you to come and stay with us, as soon as you can, and for as long as you can. It's so many years since I promised Geraldine I'd be your godmother. And . . . I know you don't think this is your home. But here we are, for you.'

'Oh, I . . .' Georgia stood, cradling her parcel, facing her seated godparents. Her eyes flickered about the room. Not as if hunting. As if hunted. 'Good God, fancy my being back here. No, I shouldn't think I'll come and stay. Only been in England for three weeks, but it's been long enough to discover I can't stand the place. Or, rather, the people.

Thought I might go to Italy, actually. There's someone I want to find out about. Find out if any word of her has come.'

'That jacket and skirt have a London look to them. Don't you think, Charlie, that she's beautifully dressed?'

'The funny thing is,' – but Georgia did not smile – 'I found I have some money. So lucky. A solicitor in Yorkshire got in touch with me. I went up to Hull. Daddy had put funds in savings accounts for Ricky and me. So for a year or two I'll be all right.'

Charles Lammas asked: 'And that is for me?'

'Yes. It is.' She started forward, dumped her bundle on his knees. 'I've been writing to you, all these years.' She laughed at herself. 'Not only to you, but . . .'

'And I went on writing to you, Georgia.'

'Yes, I knew you would.' She jerked her gaze at him. But her eyes would not stay looking steadily anywhere. 'I never got a line. Not till after the war was over. But thanks.' She was talking fast, swivelling on her heels on the hearth-rug. 'Listen – chuck all this in the fire, or read it first and then chuck it. Do what you like. But it's for you – do you understand? Oh, I don't know what I mean. Do you mind if I . . .? Well, it seems I still know where the cigarette box is.'

'Georgia . . .' Charles Lammas began tentatively, imagining the sort of return she might be hoping for. 'If you go to Italy . . . In fact, I have an idea the country is still officially a war zone, so they may not let you in – though that can't last. But, you see . . . Things have changed, among our friends. Giacomo Zanetti has been dead for – oh – it must be two years. And then, right at the end, in what was to all intents and purposes a civil war . . . A gang of communist partisans descended on Villa Lucia. Took Pietro out and hanged him. Took Giulio Flamini, and . . . His wife. Raffaella. Hanged them too. Mario was . . . He'd chucked up New York by then, you know. Well, it appears Mario nearly got there in time to save them. Or try to. It wouldn't have been easy. Warn them, get them away, hide them. But he was too late. I think you'll find him at Villa Lucia now. With his mother, and Emanuela.'

Georgia stared at him with her knowing, nervous eyes. 'Ah! She . . .' Very slowly. 'Raffaella.'

Then with deliberate distractedness she searched for her sherry glass. Found it by the photographs on the mantelpiece. 'Oh, well . . . Where I was, too, we had our problems, with . . . With people being on different sides, and, and that sort of thing. If you do read that stuff of mine, you'd better throw it in the fire afterwards. Pile up your fire till it's blazing a bit more cheerfully than it is now, and – feed it in.'

'Georgia . . .' He held her gaze. At least for a minute, he must stop those wild miserable glances swinging hither and thither. 'But, then, you will come back – won't you? – and talk to me. Come when Jack and Henrietta are here.'

She had sipped her sherry, set the glass down without spilling a drop. She glanced a moment at the picture of Geoffrey Lammas. Then she picked up the one of Jack, looked at it. She turned to her godfather. 'You see, I too . . . Like Jack. I've been in, in enemy h-h-han-han. Oh God, I can't say it again. In enemy. In enemy.'

Shaking, Georgia put the living nephew back beside his dead uncle. She picked up the third image on that mantelpiece, the Winged Victory of Samothrace. And then what remained of her tenuous poise left her. She stared. The photograph of the statue fluttered in her fingers.

'No head! No . . . Christopher!' Her tears clogged in her throat. 'Oh my darling!' Her shriek rose. 'No!'

Georgia went down on her knees on the rug, her neck bowed as if for execution. Screaming in her nightmare, she saw a blade flashing down. 'No! No! No!'

11

In the library again, that evening after dinner, Charles Lammas sat looking at Georgia's crinkled wrapping-paper. It was a bulky package, he could feel its weight on his knee. He caught his wife's eye. Then, peering, fumbling, he began to untie the string.

The knots were tight. Blanche went to his desk, fetched him a penknife. But then, as he laid bare the bundle of writings, she remained on her feet.

'No . . . Georgia brought these for you. Don't read them to me. Later, tell me anything you want to. Or anything she might rather I understood. Or nothing at all. And anyway . . .' Glancing down at the uppermost sheet of paper. 'It looks splendidly illegible.' She smiled at his questioning eyes. 'That girl was always your little favourite. She's been in love with you since she was twelve, bless her – though I've never known if either of you have realised it.'

Blanche put a log on the fire. Then she stood a moment by her husband's chair, her hand on his shoulder. 'It's late, my old darling. I'm going up. Don't get too depressed, reading. She's alive – remember that. Even if she's . . . Well, you'll know more in an hour or two, if you can make head or tail or that stuff. But – even if she's a free-floating mine, poor girl, which could explode at any minute.'

Charles reached up a hand, laid it on hers. 'A bit of a danger to shipping, you reckon?'

'Could be,' she said – and knew he understood she was thinking of their son. 'Good night, Charlie. Or . . . One thing . . . Do you suppose it was a girlish infatuation, or was she really in love with Christopher?'

'Oh . . . In love, I think. Passionately.' Still hearing the girl's cry. Having the library mantelpiece again before his eyes, and still seeing her shaken form there. 'And she still is.'

Left alone, for a minute Charles Lammas did not move. The drawn curtains stirred in a draught from the infirm window-frames. The rain-storm battened on the house, dislodged some caked soot in the chimney which fell down into the fire.

He recollected how, when Blanche had gone through to tell Ellen that she might serve lunch, he had hobbled over to his desk, taken out Christopher de Brissac's last letter about the *rather curious situation*. He saw again Georgia standing by the hearth, taking the letter from him. Saw

her reading it, with that nervous frown between her eyes that was new
and that seemed to be permanent.

He sat, with his lamp lit, listening to the wind and the rain. Then he
picked up Georgia's first sheet of paper.

That was how her war in the East reached him. Nights which he
spent holding up to the light her scribbled-over and again scribbled-over
note-books, scraps of paper, printed odds and ends she'd commandeered.
Trying to decipher her handwriting which got tinier and tinier, trying to
make sense of a sort of shorthand she'd developed. Turning pages around,
when she'd written not only from left to right but then from top to bottom
too. Even resorting to a magnifying-glass, when she'd written very crabbed
between printed lines, or between her own previous lines. Glancing up,
sometimes, to his father's austere self-portrait, or to the old flintlocks on
the chimney-piece. Putting it all down sometimes, and gazing into his
flickering flames.

Georgia had not arranged her writings in any order. Usually it was plain
enough – occasionally it was sickeningly plain – *where* she had written
something. As for knowing *when*. As for trying to fit together the seasons
and the years into one story rather than a patchwork cobbled together
out of wisps of stories . . . Very rarely, you got a date, or some other
clear indication. Generally, her scraps of sense were always fraying. Her
threads twisted, and twisted, and broke.

One of the very first pages her godfather read, she had written in
Calcutta only about three months ago, as far as he could see. So at the
beginning of his night's pursuit of her ravellings, he read about how, once
they'd cured her cholera, she'd set about trying to get word of people.

A lot of names which meant nothing to Lammas. Or which had
cropped up so infrequently in her peace-time letters that they meant
next to nothing.

Her mother. Whom only now she discovered had been buried on the
banks of the Namyaung River three years before.

Sister Caterina. Of whom she could find no trace. But it was early days
yet, and she by no means abandoned hope.

Christopher de Brissac. Who, she found out, as a prisoner of war had
worked on the Burma railway. Or rather, had not slaved on it as tens of
thousands had died doing. He had been one of the senior Allied officers
there – whose particular damnation it had been to have to try to mediate
between the Japanese slave-drivers and their slaves. Try to mitigate a little
the savagery of most of the former, alleviate the sufferings of a few of the
latter. Try to minimise misunderstandings; placate the incensed; defend
the defenceless. He had not died slaving . . . But he had died. The camps

were being freed right then, and the living and the dead recorded in separate lists. (Shortly afterwards, Lammas had read de Brissac's name in *The Times*, under Casualties.) He had been in camps way north-west of Three Pagodas Pass, apparently. Way beyond the Kwae Noi – anyhow by the end. In the camps along the Burmese end of that line, not far inland from where the Gulf of Martaban emerges into the Andaman Sea. Near old haunts of his. Scarcely fifty miles south of Moulmein. Less than a hundred from Thaton.

At first, reading what the convalescent had written only a few months after Maymyo was reoccupied – what she must have written about the time *Indianapolis* docked at Tinian Island with the new weapon on board; what she must have written not long after, when that ship had been sunk and two atomic bombs had been dropped – Lammas hoped the girl's diaries, outpourings, what-have-you, had simply been bundled up in reverse chronological order. Perhaps all he'd have to do would be to turn the heap over, start at the other end.

No such good fortune. The next stained, folded pages were of convent paper. Georgia had written them a night or two after she had buried her father. Buried the man who, her reader recalled, had after 1918 been a lot more bitter against the smugly triumphant British than Jack was now. Who in this had come to be resembled by his daughter – judging by her vitriolic conversation at lunch. Alex Burney with his mockery of patriotic talk, and his mockery of delusions of imperial grandeur, of historical destiny. Which had not prevented him from serving king and country and empire. Had not prevented him – perhaps paradoxically, but not very paradoxically – taking self-contemptuous refuge in such service. Hadn't stopped him taking his self-hatred and one or two other hatreds to their logical conclusions, ducking behind a verandah wall with a rifle in his hands.

Not having imagined that Burney might be alive, Lammas did not grieve for him now he learnt the manner of his death. If anything, as he read, he agreed with Georgia that her father, once buried, was all right at last. And he rejoiced when he read: *At least we found each other again . . . At least I knew who you were.* If anything, he might have repeated to the unlistening air what he had written to Mario Zanetti in his response to news of Giacomo's killing. *When the end came, I don't suppose he minded all that much.* Mario, when he replied, had said he was sure that was so.

12

—◊—

That first night alone with Georgia's war-stained whisperings from enemy-occupied Burma, Charles Lammas began to try to put the fragments in some order. He made separate piles on the library carpet around his feet.

What she had written before and after her time in Mandalay gaol, on either side of his chair – that imprisonment was a watershed. Then subdivisions . . . What she'd written in Rangoon – which was a small heap, because most of it had been lost. But there were also a few comments on that time, written in Maymyo. What had probably been written in that abandoned bungalow on Forest Road, in one stack on the floor. Then what she'd written in the refugee settlement off the road to Lashio, in a second. Her writings in the internment camp, finally, in a third . . . Which gave an approximate chronology.

He didn't get far with his attempt at some semblance of order. And even after many solitary nights, brooding over his goddaughter's oubliette cries . . . And after many other nights, when he didn't read a line of hers. Nor of Bobbie's or Jack's Nor of Alex's or Christopher's or Mario's. When he merely brooded. For that matter, when Georgia came back to Edingthorpe the following year, and they talked by that fire-side . . . There were still gaps and inconsequentialities which even she couldn't explain. References she couldn't explain – or she told him she couldn't.

Charles Lammas might have been badly knocked about by his stroke and then by his heart attacks. His whole spirit might indeed be ailing, might be weary almost to death. But right from that first November night . . . As he read, image after image of war-time Burma formed in the miasma of his mind with a sharpness which his debilities did nothing merciful to palliate. Georgia's voice rang to him as never before.

Villages around Maymyo, where refugees were living in ramshackle huts made of sheets of tin, sheets of corrugated iron, bamboo, palm thatch. After only a few months of the occupation, the men and women all skeletal and most of them apathetic, the children hollow-eyed and pot-bellied.

One settlement only . . . Where Georgia happened to have gone, looking for somebody who was rumoured to have been in Geraldine's party of escapers, and might have news of her. But it gave Lammas by his peace-time fireplace an idea of what it had been like for the thousands of

British and Anglo-Indians and Anglo-Burmese who hadn't got clear away when the invasion occurred.

Half of them hadn't even tried to get away. Knew they hadn't the money for the flight, or the strength for the trek. Or knew they weren't the privileged sort to get one of the last seats on the last aeroplanes. Or couldn't imagine living anywhere except Burma. Hadn't imagined the occupation could be *that* bad. And lots of them in those foul shanties were people who'd tried to escape but had not succeeded. Such as the girl whom Georgia had known as Roberta Gillway. (But this was written on one of the sheets of church music, and written after the convent, after Rangoon, after Mandalay gaol.) Roberta whose wedding to her Burmah Oil man had been one of the hill station's last fashionable occasions before the rout. Then they had been in a contingent of twenty or so civilians trying to trudge out to India, but had only got halfway when the rains broke. They tried to outlast the monsoon in deserted huts in the forest. But after a few months, when the Japanese found them, nearly half had already died of starvation or dysentery or beri-beri.

The Japanese shot the surviving men – including Roberta's bridegroom of the last dry season's last worldly fête. The women, and a couple of girls, ended up back where they'd started, in Maymyo – though not in the elegant and discreetly staffed houses they'd set off from.

When Georgia met her old girlhood friend again, Roberta's arms and legs were festering with sores, and she was . . . Here Georgia had not been able to select a word. She'd scrawled *crazy*, and crossed it out. Scrawled *hysterical* and *broken-hearted*, crossed them both out. At any rate, it appeared that since her capture things had been done before her eyes, and things had been done to her, which someone with more clinical know-how or jargon than Georgia might have called traumatising, Lammas supposed. Later in the war, those two appeared to have seen a fair amount of each other. Had been unlucky enough a number of times to be forced to serve as waitresses in a Japanese officers' mess.

Georgia at the convent, right at the start of her three years immured in war. When the convent was still a convent, though it was jam-packed with fugitives. Every room a bivouac of the homeless and the helpless, with their bundles of what they'd managed to cling on to. Georgia working there – with what her father had called *about the neatest little revolver money could buy* unsuspected beneath her clothes.

It was about then that she started to wear a sari. The Japanese were trying to convince the Burmese they weren't as diabolical as all that – and Georgia hoped that if she dressed like a local and spoke like a local she might, in a crowd, to a casual passer-by . . . It seemed worth trying.

Thank God I'm not a blonde, she'd written. *Christopher you said tarnished bronze.*
It would always be plain she had some European blood. But perhaps other
admixtures too – with her face shadowed or muffled, with her Burmese
sari and her Burmese patter. Any ambiguity, for pity's sake! Anything to
pass unremarked-upon, to glide like a ghost through that tyranny and at
the end come out free – if there ever were an end.

Georgia at Thazi, at the railway junction, so soon after the Japanese
victory that the place was still a shambles. Charles Lammas couldn't work
out from any of her writings what she'd been doing at Thazi. Maybe there
had been an explanation, but it had been among her writings destroyed
in Rangoon. Or in the other batch the Kempeitai took from her, before
they kicked and cuffed her along the corridor in Mandalay gaol to begin
her time in that cell. In that oubliette within the oubliette – *like Chinese
boxes*, she wrote after she came out. In that innermost silence, with half
a coconut of rice a day, and half a coconut of water. With no bed, no
bucket. In the plains heat, with all the biting insects in hell, and the
rags of one sari. Where only her interrogators knew where she was, and
remembered her.

Georgia at Thazi, where the roads were jumbled with the carcasses of
bullocks and horses, of men and women and children. The girl walking
through the stench those bloated and rotting bodies made, through flies
in grey clouds.

Georgia in Mandalay gaol, where the Kempeitai officers were convinced
she was a spy the British had left behind – or they pretended to be
convinced. They shouted at her the names of the others in her spy ring.
Told her they could read the code she wrote in. They had their men
beat her with the flats of bayonets, while they watched, before they
recommenced their questioning of her. They had their men loosen her
fingernails with knives and then yank them out with pliers, while they
watched.

When Lammas, after a few nights' reading, knew his way amongst
his goddaughter's war writings a little, he could pick and choose, to an
extent. But that first night, when every sheet of paper was a revelation
. . . When he was learning for the first time about Doctor Drew, for
instance. Who had tried to cure Alex of syphilis, and had later met
Georgia in the gaol courtyard, and the mad Italian priest from the
oil-fields. Drew whom she had seen once more . . . although he had
not seen her. One of her interrogators' tricks was to have their men
force her face against the small barred window of her cell. In this
way, she saw several groups of people led out into the yard, with
white bandages tied around their heads, and a red spot on each white

bandage. She saw them lined up. Shot. And in one group, she recognised her father's doctor.

That first night, after Blanche had left him alone to read, was the only time when the listener to Georgia's spat-out war confessions and her raging war arrogance was reduced to tears. But even on subsequent nights that winter, when he took that genie of his out of his desk, let free her voice . . .

There were so many dozens of fragmentary journal entries, drafts of letters to Christopher and Caterina and him. So many tirades, invocations, attempts to set the record straight. So many cursings and mockings and grievings. Reading, Lammas never felt he knew where he was going, never felt safe about what he might find on the other side of a page. And the trouble wasn't just the chaos of writings. There was also the chaos *in* her writing, the chaos in her. So that her reader, who maybe had just learned that the Burney bungalow had been destroyed in an air raid, never had the slightest confidence about what the next sentence might not make him know.

It could be about the method of cleansing jungle ulcers with maggots. How the maggots were mighty hygenic when it came to the way they devoured the dead flesh and pus, but you had to be damned sure that when they'd done that you took out of the wound the exact number of maggots you'd put in, and damned sure too that they hadn't bred. And another way of cleansing sores was to stand in the edge of a river. There were fish that would come and nibble away your putrescent flesh.

It could be the unsavoury duties which might – might reliably – be forced upon a prisoner shanghaied to be a waitress at an officers' mess. Quite apart from the torment, when you'd been starved for a couple of years, of politely serving steaks to healthy and drunken oafs.

13

—𝔪—

Other voices sounded in Charles Lammas' head too, those winter nights at the beginning of the new peace time.

Jack at the dining table, with his level eyes and his even way of talking, telling them how, after the herd life of a prison camp, a few days' solitary confinement could come as a relief. The only snag was that in the cooler you were not allowed Red Cross parcels, and back on just German prison rations you got even hungrier. Telling how when he'd been recaptured those two times, of course there was the fear that they might do unpleasant things to you. But they hadn't. And then thirty days alone in a cell wasn't too bad at all.

Or it might be his steady voice telling about how his first winter in Germany, when the deep snows fell, that almost seemed to establish a truce. The next winters it hadn't felt like that, because of the fighting on the Eastern Front. But those first snow-falls had meant there was nothing to do, except stay alive, and plan the escapes that might be possible when more clement weather returned. He remembered the peacefulness of that snow-blanketed country, and the German guards singing 'Stille Nacht'. Though he had been unable not to reflect that a nation whose soldiers sang that well must be almost impossible to defeat.

Other voices. Bobbie as he strode down the drawing-room and wheeled around, saying: *It will matter so superficially, and for so short a time, that I scarcely* . . .

Giacomo Zanetti in the olive grove above Villa Lucia, sitting on that stump, with his hat pulled down over his eyes. Giacomo saying: *What do you reckon, shall we have her marry him?*

The olive trees in the evening light. The easel, with the half-painted picture of the house in its cedars and umbrella pines. Those little blue butterflies flitting. Giacomo's voice. *I don't like the turn things are taking here. Don't much care for the company she's mixing with . . . But if her brother and you and I all said the same thing, we just might, you never know . . .* Yes, on the easel the grey terrace, where the old man had been hauled out. The honey-coloured wall they'd shot him against. Cedars. A branch, with three . . .

I have an idea it's fairly important . . . Thank you. I knew I could rely on you.

Voices, and images. Raffaella's bow mouth. Her wavy, dark brown hair cut short, and the way it bunched on her neck. Her throat . . . How old had she been when they hanged her, thirty? No, thirty-one, more likely.

When at Villa Lucia the last ball for Fascist nabobs had been given, and the last dinner party where the guests had included German colonels and generals. When the Allies had broken through the Gothic Line at last, and partisans were hunting down stragglers and collaborators, and all manner of scores were being settled . . .

Raffaella in a London restaurant, saying she'd dreamed of being married in Ely cathedral. *But, of course, you couldn't be my bridegroom, which was sad.* Raffaella three years later in Tuscany, sheltering from the rain under the loggia. *You've missed the boat. Curious, Charlie. You never used to be one to stand dithering on quays till decisions were taken for you.*

Then . . . If Mario were right, and she really had been playing a double game, on her father's behalf – or even, conceivably, on behalf of her own conscience, though that was mere supposition. Plainly she had not told those communist guerrillas that. She had not cried out that they were about to string up one who for years had risked her life on their side in that civil war. Or Raffaella had cried that – but had not been believed. She had defied Pietro and her husband at last, and cried out that she had been on her father's side all along.

Perhaps Giulio Flamini had known that for some time, but had shouted to their executioners that it wasn't so. Perhaps in her finery, perhaps with her immaculately maintained eyebrows and fingernails, she had not appeared a likely rebel, and so revolutionary justice had been meted out anyhow, just to be on the safe side. Or maybe those liberators had been in such a rush, bashing their victims about a bit, and slinging ropes over convenient branches. Maybe they'd been so intent on the manly business of tying her wrists behind her back, and tying a slip-knot around her throat, that they had not gone in for much discussion. After all – they knew who she was married to. They knew about the galas given in that house. That was why they were there. They knew about the pashas she'd danced with, and probably not only danced with.

Charles Lammas would find that for minutes he'd been gazing into his library fire without seeing it. He would long to have Giacomo and Raffaella back. Have them in the room, alive, to talk to. To ask, to try to explain, to try to understand! Well, maybe Mario would one day succeed in finding out more, and next time he had occasion to be in England would come down to Norfolk and talk to him. But what you really wanted was a conclave of spirits. A chamber of memory – where truths however partial and changeable might go on whispering, not die away quite yet! In the regrettable absence of which . . .

Lammas would struggle to his feet, with the help of his walking-stick. He would set a log on his fire, and as he did so confront his father's melancholy eyes, his hand holding the brush raised in that hieratic gesture. Old believer in disarmament, in education schemes . . . But that self-portrait had been painted after the First War.

Conclaves of spirits, for God's bloody sake! A modest start might have been to seek out his father while the old fellow was still alive. Listen to him. If you couldn't console him, at least leave him with the notion that you were aware of what he'd lived and what he felt.

He had been selfish – naturally. Roland had died unbefriended. And thinking of old truths dying away, and far echoes ghosting back . . .

Charles Lammas would sit down again, take up a sheaf of Georgia Burney's war writings. She, at least, was alive. Blanche had been right to insist on what a miraculous blessing that was. Georgia, if not others of his haunters, would come back here. Come back in flesh and blood. Talk to him with words he could understand.

Georgia's reputation had started to arrive in England after her. Like Mark Hedleigh's had – though his case was lamentably clear-cut. And came at an awkward time for the Hedleighs . . . What with an unaccountable electorate having voted in a Labour Government; and, even worse, a positively delinquent East Norfolk constituency having declined to replace Julian at Westminster with Frederick.

If these occurrences did not signify absolutely the end of the world, in Lady Hedleigh's view they came perilously close to it

However, there were compensations. As soon as Freddie was out of his regiment and back in the City, he resumed the making of such exemplary sums of money that honestly one was tempted to point out that time indulged in as a Member of Parliament – and for that curate's stipend! – would have been time wasted, unless a junior position in government could have been arranged *very* quickly.

Then came the Sovereign's choice of Hugh Fenby as the new Lord Lieutenant, and Sarah had a distinct impression that some of her friends were smiling.

Lammas had been amused by Julian's and Sarah's manoeuvres to get their disgraced second son rehabilitated in society. Ruefully impressed by their success, too. Although there were a few men of Mark's regiment who refused to shake his hand. And finding a new club for him looked like proving tricky. All the same . . . When you reflected that the facts were apparently so plain that nobody had ever disputed them.

It had been during the second Arakan campaign. They were being shelled. And when the order came to attack, Mark Hedleigh refused to come out of his bunker. Crouched there, whimpering. Snarling abuse at his brother officers who came to rouse him out before word got around and worse occurred. He pretended to be ill, he gibbered excuses. So he was going to be court-martialled. Then, luckily for him, a Japanese shell a few days later made such a mess of him that his colonel, out of sheer humanity, had the charge dropped.

Georgia's case was not that straightforward at all. No one had denounced her, officially. Sometimes, as her godfather read by his fire, he found himself thinking that so far as he could make out . . .

Well, there had been a mass of malicious chatter – clearly. Under trying circumstances, people could get damned jumpy – that was clear too. And that often it was impossible to draw a firm line between collaboration on the one hand, and not getting yourself uselessly butchered on the other . . . That faced with two exceedingly unattractive possibilities and two only, a hungry person with good reason to be frightened might take decisions which others . . .

It was all complicated, what was more, by Georgia's so freely expressed contempt for those who had been in authority in Burma, the whole upper echelon in the colony, who had so ringingly declared that everyone must stick to their posts – and had next been observed disembarking from planes in India. It was complicated by the free way she'd taken to saying she reckoned the Burmese nationalists' aspirations were perfectly reasonable, and not difficult to sympathise with.

Not that Georgia Burney did not mock the nationalists too. In her talk. In her jottings-down. She derided them for how briskly they ganged up with the invading Japanese against the British. Derided them for how three years later they briskly ganged up with the reinvading British against their former Japanese masters. For the matter of that, years later she was deriding them for how they'd totally failed to make a new state in which a rat could feel free to live with dignity among other rats.

But these mockeries of Georgia's were of little interest to those of her fellow countrymen who suddenly found themselves recalling how bloody pro-Asian she'd always been. Speaking the language like a native. Hob-nobbing with half-castes. And then going around dressed as a native, passing herself off as a . . . And then . . .

Being raped was one thing. But down in Rangoon, that Burney girl had . . . So they said at the club in Maymyo, as soon as peace-time eating and drinking and bickering had been triumphantly resumed.

Had an affair with quite a senior Jap officer, by God. Or with more than one, probably. The little tart.

No, really?

Yes, positively, old boy. An absolute affair. Major Burridge told me she'd been seen riding around in a staff car down there.

Well, when I think of . . . God Almighty! Tarring and feathering, that's what she needs.

14

—⁂—

My dearest Caterina – if only you knew how often I think of you! If I were a good Christian like Christopher and you, I'd pray for you. But as it is you'll just have to put up with me in my stupid heathen way longing and longing for you to be all right.

A leper colony is the safest place to be – did you know that? So I keep hoping you have lepers in your convent down at Moulmein. In Mandalay, the Mother Superior is brilliant at exploiting the Japanese soldiers' terror of infectious diseases. And when there's no food left, she lets the lepers out and tells them to run after the army trucks, yelling for rice and rupees.

I go on writing, but I don't know if they'll ever get the postal service working again. Or, even more miraculous, let us use it. I suppose they will, if the occupation goes on long enough. If so, you'll get reams of paper from me. Not all the Japanese here are swines. The officer who first appeared at our convent ordered his men not to molest us. And at least one of the journalists here is nice. It was he who found us this house on Forest Road. He's a war correspondent for a Tokyo paper, and he told me that his government hope to expand their empire far enough and fast enough, and hope that then the Allies won't be able to face fighting for donkeys' years to get all their colonies back, so Japan will end up keeping most of the countries they've conquered. In which case, Caterina darling, you and I could be going to be tenth-class citizens under the banner of the rising sun for ages, and I expect they'll get the post functioning again.

I think this house will do fine – if we're allowed to stay here, which may be too much to hope for. Not all the Europeans' houses have been pillaged like ours was. Some of the owners just locked their doors, left everything as it was. So although this house is empty, we've been furnishing it in a simple way with bits and pieces which people left behind. At first, I felt guilty about 'liberating' chairs and things, but under the circumstances it doesn't seem such a crime.

We're an odd bunch. There's old Mr Clay and his Burmese wife and a granddaughter of theirs. He's pretty much an invalid, so he can't help when it comes to foraging for useful things and for food. There's a Shan gardener called Than Tun whose house was bombed and his wife killed. Then Mr Graham, who works at the railway yard, and his wife and their two little boys. Me. Angus. A couple of other dogs. With food getting so scarce, we have to protect the dogs as carefully as we can, but they're always trotting off.

And then, at the turn of a page, blazing out from some chatter about how luckily she still had some rupees left . . .

Oh my God what have I done? Caterina, I've killed a man. Not a Japanese, or I'd have been killed by now too. A Burmese. A dacoit he must have been, I suppose. I don't know who he was. A bad man of some sort.

I must try to be calm, but it was hours ago, and every time I stop shaking I start again, so I can hardly write. I was walking in the forest, hoping to find someone selling vegetables. I realised I was being followed, and then . . .

He grabbed my hair, and he was jabbing at me with his dagger. It was going to be rape first, and then robbery. Whether after that it . . . Caterina, your friend Georgia is a murderess. She, I . . . I have been a murderess since about ten o'clock this morning. It wasn't even difficult. He'd pinned me down on the earth, but I got my right arm free. I took out the revolver Daddy gave me, I fired into his side. He screamed, and rolled off me. I scrambled up, fired two more shots at him I was so frightened, but I shouldn't have done that should I? Because he wasn't dead after the first shot, just wounded Caterina.

Then I ran. I didn't even check he was dead, perhaps he wasn't yet, just bleeding to death. Oh God you see what I've done Caterina, you see who I've become, what I am! I ran and I got here and . . . Everybody has been sweet to me, that's what murderers get, they get tea. Mrs Clay and Mrs Graham put me to bed. Well, on a mat, with a rug over me.

Mr Clay told me I'd done quite right. And the awful thing is, I'm not sorry a bit. I know I ought to pray for forgiveness, I ought to pray for that man's soul. That's what you would say Caterina isn't it, and the Mother Superior would say, and Christopher – but he's a soldier, if he's still alive he's a soldier. That's what the parson at Edingthorpe would say. But it's not what my heart says. Isn't that dreadful? No, that's not dreadful. What's dreadful is that I'm lying when I say I think I ought to feel remorse.

I keep gasping Oh God but that's just blasphemy, that's just a way of saying I don't understand anything or I don't want to understand. Forgive me or not Caterina darling, but I don't see why I should be attacked, I don't see why I shouldn't fight back, and if I win the fight I'm glad. If he wasn't dead after the first shot, I wasn't going to nurse him, he deserved shooting.

As for his soul, if he had one – I saw him in action. And he saw any soul of mine, and we're quits.

Georgia Burney kept her self-hatred for other occasions, Charles Lammas discovered, putting one Maymyo outcry down on his knee. Gazing into his fire. Taking up another sheet of paper.

She kept her self-hatred. Didn't use it up on her Rangoon experience – whatever that was. *About that time in her war she was fierce. Let them say what they damned well like. At least I've kept out of those comfort stations. Let them say what they like, all those members of the Administrative Council who left their Burmese mistresses here when they skipped out to Calcutta. All those wives of unfaithful generals and councillors, wives nobody ever wanted as mistresses.*

No abhorrence, either, for how when in Mandalay they were torturing her she'd pleaded with them, promised anything they wanted. *Luckily I didn't know any names to betray.* She knew you screamed. Didn't need to comment.

No . . . Georgia's loathing was for her younger self. Above all, for her self who'd had that love affair with Christopher de Brissac. In her Forest Road bivouac days, her outpourings of her heart to him were still by and large the jejune stuff you'd expect. But after Rangoon, and then after Mandalay . . . (There was a connection between the two episodes, but Lammas couldn't work it out. Possibly her protector at Army Headquarters had fallen from High Command favour, so her period of grace was over too. Possibly the girl had displeased him – tried to run away, even.) At any rate, her romantic effusions kept being broken into by other tones of voice.

Her godfather read every word that she'd buried in tin boxes and then dug up when the Japanese had gone. Every word – except a few that were illegible – that she'd hidden beneath bungalows' floors when she still had a vestigial liberty. Hidden after that in huts' thatch, in camps' woodwork, in the bamboo haft of a spade they'd dug latrines with. But he found he didn't often reread her love letters – though she'd parcelled them up with the rest, brought them half around the world to dump on his lap.

Delicacy, perhaps. Boredom, perhaps. But by the last year of her war, her rhapsodies had pretty well petered out. And there was a lot more of – *You ought to know how I hate that glib girl you had an affair with. Did you realise how superficial I was? You must have done. You should have told me, truly you should.* Intermingled with – *My God, do you know what I'd give to be your wife?* Which was predictable. As was – *But I am your wife. I whisper that at night, endlessly. Not even knowing if you are alive.*

But then with her next crabbed, crooked sentence, Lammas would be back with – *It's no good, just because this war is being hell, falling back into emotional twaddle like that. When it's over, if we're still alive and I ask you to marry me, you'd better refuse.* Or it wouldn't be the next sentence. It would be a different filthy scrap which he read nights later. *I'm that trite girl who hero-worshipped you because you were so terribly distinguished and so terribly handsome – you don't want her. Not that silly bitch* – the war had done nothing for Georgia's language – *who convinced herself the great passion of her life was for a man she'd understood nothing about. Nothing! And I still haven't a clue who you are.*

15

—m—

*Dear Godfather Charles — who knows, if I find an envelope, and address it to you. If
I scrounge a stamp. Just possibly — after the war is over, and I'm probably dead . . .
Oh if you knew how often I think of your studio! Plays and novels being read aloud,
stories being told, songs being sung. And that blue dress I wore! Our verandah here
was a fine place for stories too, especially after dark with moths fluttering at the lamps.
But the house was burned to the ground, and I was glad, it was horrible there after the
soldiers had been. Charred timbers and ash now. I went past the other day, pushing
this old bike I've acquired. It had rained, the blackened ruins were glistening, the ashy
mud was all puddles. But I marked down where we buried the silver. The soil of Burma
is full of treasure now, people say. The Shan princes had their gold and jewels buried
before the Japanese came — or most of them did, the smart ones did. Regiments buried
their silver. Families like us buried their few bits and pieces. And I stopped a minute at
Daddy's grave, to say goodbye again.*

Or, written on another fragment, in the dry season this time, in a shanty
off the Lashio road. Read on another English winter night.

*So there I was, shoving my bike as usual because both tyres were flat and the
handlebars were laden with bundles. It's been a godsend, that bicycle. It's my mule,
it carries everything. There I went, plodding along the bullock track in the dust and
the sun, thinking of the Edingthorpe studio and you. Telling myself stories, dreaming.
Daddy was alive in that dream, and we were off into the hills again with all our kit
roped onto the pack-elephants, and the syce with our spare horses. Or I was being
carried in a palanquin, I was dressed like the Queen of Golconda herself and treated
like her too, and the spirits of the forest protected us, and we came to an old palace
by a waterfall where . . . I forget the rest. Or Christopher was alive and I was alive
and the war was over. I told him how vapid I'd been not to want to marry him. I had
courage, I told him all the reasons why he ought to hate me. He listened. He said he
did not, he would not hate me. So then I told him that if he had any use for me I was
still his heels over head Georgiana, with her freckles and her tilted-up nose, and my
day-dream was just getting splendidly romantic when I heard that familiar roar in the
sky. I let go of my bike, I yelled to a man with a horse and cart, and the next second
I was in the monsoon ditch. The plane's shadow raced along the road, then there was
a terrific explosion and I was covered with dust. The pilot must have been trying to
wreck the road I think, because there were no jeeps passing or anything. When I crawled
out of the ditch my bike and my bundles were all right, and the road had a big crater in
it, so I thought, Well done the RAF. But the cart had been smashed to kindling, and
the driver and his horse were dead.*

Dreams aren't like they used to be. Godfather Charles, do you remember that day when you were painting my portrait, and you told me about Tolstoy saying that so far as the swarm life of mankind goes we have to obey the laws laid down for us? Biological laws, and social and economic laws, I suppose he meant. But we can be free in so far as our interests are abstract — or something like that. And you said that freedom which was only abstract might indeed be all that was on offer, but you reckoned if so that was pretty disappointing. Thin fare, you said. Watered-down wine, you said.

Well, in these villages turned into refugee camps we live the swarm life of mankind and no mistake. And that's what stories have become to me now. Reminders that freedom is only abstract. Reminders that clouds in my head are only clouds in my head. Of course, I tell myself stories as I always did. More than ever. Or stories tell themselves in my head. Stories Daddy or you told me. Stories from books. Pericles sailing to look for his lost daughter. Drake sailing through the Spice Islands. Lord Jim setting off up that jungle river. And words still echo in my head in the magical way they always have. 'But it's a mild, mild wind, and a mild-looking sky.' Remember? 'And the air smells now as if it blew from a far-away meadow. They've been making hay under the slopes of the Andes, Starbuck, and the mowers are sleeping in the new-mown hay . . . Sleep? Aye, and rust amid greenness, like last year's scythes flung down, and left in the half-cut swathes.' I dare say I haven't got it quite right, but the words go singing themselves over in my head. Then I think of Jack in a prison camp in Germany, and I wonder if he's telling himself a lot of the same stories and poems as I am, and I think he probably is, and I think of you in your studio thinking of him and of me. And all the while . . . The freedom in my head is there — abstract, but it's there. It's there, but only abstract . . . The most nebulous wisps of passions and ideas, clouds which change and change and disperse. But — 'Seeing there be many things that increase vanity . . .' You see what a good pupil I was, Godfather Charles? 'For who knoweth what is good for man in this life, all the days of his vain life which he spendeth as a shadow?' You told Jack and me that in the library, years ago. And now, echoes like that which ring in three heads seem truth of a kind. You ought to watch the people dying in this settlement, then you'd see what I mean. Echoes of old strength of mind which reach me here. Companionship, of a ghostly kind.

And then, the best part of a year later, by her godfather's guess. After Rangoon, after Mandalay. Fragmentary . . . Inextricable, almost, from her internment camp notes about who she suspected was an informant of the Japanese, and who by contrast was an example to them all. For Georgia Burney could write like the recording angel, when she really rolled her sleeves up for the job – and after the liberation, a couple of Englishmen from that camp were tried, convicted, gaoled.

Almost inextricable from her lamentations for her native land, which a malign destiny had chosen for the British empire and the Japanese empire to fight over. Her outcries for the deaths; for the survivors' lives ruined; for the country laid waste. Tangled up among stories of a camp commandant who was a sadist, another who was a perfectly decent man. Her return from Mandalay to Maymyo. Her return alone, victorious. Because to be alive, and sane, was a victory. Only she could hardly drag herself along.

I did it, Godfather Charles! I lived through it, I'm alive! After the heat down in the valley, by the time the Kempeitai had driven me up to Maymyo I was trembling with cold. And of course I knew they could arrest me again whenever they wanted to. All the same . . . I had it blood-beating away in my brain, God damn it I'm out. God damn it, I might just make it.

Luckily, I couldn't see myself. I must have weighed about six stone, maybe. I was weals and sores from head to foot. I had lice in my hair. Mary Graham cut it off. It's growing back now. I could see my fingertips, of course. So could the Kempeitai officer in the military police station in the old cantonment when he gave me a pen, told me to sign a piece of paper with Japanese writing on it. What's this? I asked. It says you have been treated in accordance with international law, he said, and not maltreated in any way. I held the pen with these fingers of mine — they're beginning to look more normal now, but then they were revolting. I looked at him looking at my fingers, and then I caught his gaze and I held it and I liked that, and then I said Right I'll sign.

Next morning, they turfed me out. I could go back to the village they'd taken me from, they said. So I set off to where the Lashio road starts. That sari was more holes than rags by then, but luckily I didn't meet anyone I knew.

It can't be more than five miles to the village, but my legs were so wobbly I kept having to lie down. Almost nobody on the road — too many air raids. I tottered along. I kept myself going by thinking of the Gurkha encampment there, where I had friends. Thinking of the houses where the railway families lived, where the Grahams would still be if all had gone well. John Graham and the other drivers and firemen and mechanics know that if they don't work they'll be shot and their wives and children will starve. So they work, and the Japanese pay them a little, so they have better accommodation and more food than the rest of us. They've always been kind to me. So I thought I'd go there.

I collapsed in a stupor I don't know how many times. Shade. Rest. Dust, ants, flies. So used to being thirsty, that it has to get worse than that before I really mind. Then up again, to stagger on. Thinking, Damn it, alive. Damn it, nearly there.

Reading, Charles Lammas looked up at the Winged Victory. That lifting step, that over-arching pride! That transcender's head would have been worth seeing — he'd often thought that. Those would have been eyes to meet. And now, for a minute, on those stone shoulders he imagined Georgia's dust-caked head as she hobbled into that Shan village. Her face gaunt with starvation, except where it was swollen with insect bites. Filthy, infested hair. Bayonet bruises, bayonet welts. Sores around her mouth. Those shadowy eyes.

Bush telegraph — always fast, always reliable. My friends had come out of the village to meet me. Not Mr Clay, he died last wet season. But the Grahams, and Roberta, and an American girl called Eleanor who's married to a Burmese lawyer only she doesn't know where he is. Even old Mrs Clay had come as far as the bridge, and when I saw her wizened Burmese face smile to see me I burst into tears. I hugged her, and I cried and cried.

Then I had shoulders to lean on. Everyone was saying, Georgia's back.

NINE

1

Of course, the sensible thing to do with the Burney money deposited in that bank in Hull would have been to invest it. After which, it might have been a good idea to look for a job. Not that it was a fortune, by a long chalk – not after the Rufford débâcle. Still, if Georgia had lived moderately it would have lasted her for five years at least.

She did not live moderately. She spent money on fashionable clothes – and her shoes were a marvel. She took a flat in Belgravia. She frequented a classy Knightsbridge hairdresser. Where one day she found herself sitting next to Caroline Lammas, who told her about a nice woman in a Cahors back-street who had used to trim her hair before the war. And with whom she launched into rather a nervy friendship, which involved a lot of intense conversations *à deux*, and a lot of calling each other darling, and going with frenzied determination to parties. Then there were theatres. Georgia declared that she had been so deprived of entertainment that now she'd go to almost *any* show with *almost* anyone. And racing was getting going again, so there were expeditions to Sandown and to Cheltenham. And as soon as the steeplechasing season was over, the flat-racing began, so that was all right.

Georgia Burney was on the razzle – and she was always travelling. The journey from London to Norfolk, which the previous spring Jack Lammas had made with such triumph in his heart, might be one which she did not manage to make. When the next spring came, and she was off with a very festive party to watch the Boat Race, where she cheered the dark blues and the light blues indiscriminately and drank a lot of champagne, she still had not returned to Edingthorpe. But the journey to Paris always seemed to be possible. She was there for ten days in February, and then for almost all of April. Caroline tried a few times to get her to meet Jack, but at the mention of his name Georgia would go stony, absent. If Caroline insisted, gently, she'd scream, 'I told you, *no!*'

2

—⁓—

Charles Lammas had scarcely begun to read that November night, when the longing to have Georgia back there possessed him. He remembered her quivering shoulders in his embrace, he felt again her tears on her hair and on his cheek. He couldn't look at his mantelpiece without seeing her standing there, her whole figure shaken as if with some ague of the spirit, that photograph jerking in her fingers. He couldn't look down at the hearth-rug without seeing her fallen to her knees, crying out in terror against something she saw and others did not see.

The next morning, he wrote her a short, simple letter, begging her to come and talk to him. Or, if she didn't want to do that, then please would she come and listen to him, because he had a lot to tell her.

She didn't reply, and she didn't come, and he didn't feel he could go chasing after her. Anyhow, with the invalidish life he was leading these days . . . He got word of her occasionally by ringing up Caroline, but the news was such as to confirm his fears.

That she had plucked up the courage to bring him her bundle of writings – but had not yet steeled herself to confront the man who had read them. Or she was trying to distract herself – and knew that to talk to him would be to concentrate and to remember. Lammas went over these reasonings till his head ached, and months passed.

That her solitary stumbling along the Lashio road back to the village had been her victory indeed . . . But that to be alive and sane did not mean she wasn't one of the casualties, did not mean prices hadn't been paid.

It was true that the Kempeitai had not arrested her a second time. True that Mrs Graham had nursed her back to some sort of physical health and the beginnings of steadiness of mind, before they were all interned in that camp and things got worse again. That Georgia's malaria had not proved fatal; and she hadn't gone down with cholera till the British were back and medical attention was forthcoming . . . All this was true.

Then Lammas would pick up that Japanese manual about something or other, all over which she had written about her dreams. Her nightmares when male Japanese voices roared orders, and she screamed, but they must have been silent screams and she couldn't wake up. Nightmares when male boots stamped, and male hands took hold of her. When she was back in that officers' mess, and after the men had drunk enough *sake* they'd draw those samurai swords of theirs, have a bit of fun with them making the girls undress while they decided who was going to rape which one.

Georgia was a mine left drifting after the war was over, Blanche had said. A mine that might blow up at any minute. Yes, yes, that was right . . . But it was more right that she'd trusted him with all the truth she'd brought out of that war. After Christopher was dead, and she couldn't find Caterina, and of course Alex was dead, she'd trusted him with who she'd become. With what they'd made of her. With her last spiritual changings . . . No, no, they mustn't be her last. If this was her final metamorphosis . . . Yes, but if she wouldn't come and see him?

The way that by the time she'd been interned, Georgia couldn't write about her pre-war self without using the word *superficial*. Her old life in Norfolk, her old hill station life, her feelings then – it was all *superficial*, the idea seemed to have become an obsession with her. Or *shallow*. When she mentioned her peace-time self, usually in her whisperings to Christopher, that also was a word that came back and back.

The way she wrote about what being *in enemy hands* could really mean. How she wrote about Scheherazade. *God Almighty, when I dressed up for that fancy dress ball, with my head full of romantic slop about being the daughter of the Grand Vizier of the Indies, and the most beguiling story-teller there'd ever been, and the most fascinating woman the Sultan had ever had to deal with, I hadn't imagined I'd really fetch up having to charm for my life. Night after night. Never making a mistake. For a chance of living, of being free one day.*

The way, when she wrote like that about Rangoon, it was not difficult to imagine that some of the British, when the fighting was over, might have been extremely nasty to her. The way that might lie behind her leaving Burma for England. Leaving what had been her childhood paradise, but had then been devastated by two warring empires. Had become where she was tortured by one side, and reviled by the other.

He sent messages through Caroline – but got no response. When Peregrine Bracknell put on his long-promised exhibition, Lammas had Georgia sent an invitation to the private view. He stood among his war pictures, the work he'd been doing right up to his first heart attack. Among coastal scenes such as he had always painted: harbour marks and sea birds, creeks and loneliness – only now the fishing-smacks had machine-guns mounted on their foredecks, and the waves broke along barbed-wire entanglements beginning to rust, barbed-wire where sea-weed snagged at high water, when the tide went down blew drying and tattering. He stood among his pictures of the RAF huts at Ludham, pictures of Hurricanes and Spitfires viewed from curious angles, and curious bits of Hurricanes and Spitfires. Among what he called his RAF still-lives: mechanics' benches, their tools. He leant on his stick, he talked to everyone, and his eyes kept searching the party for Georgia.

Still, he'd been right about one thing, he thought. Years ago . . . When he'd intuited that so far as his marriage was concerned, there'd never be anything new. Nothing strange . . . not of any profundity.

But, if life did have waiting for him one last – what? – bewilderment? A lot more vital than the amorous flings which between the wars the portraitist had indulged in. A responsibility more intriguing than the delight he took in Jack and Hetty – and more difficult, and more urgent, that was for sure. A declining man's last abstract task. A reaching out of his spirit, a perhaps being met halfway by . . . And simply managing to help. Perhaps.

She had brought him her writings. The next move must be his. He just hadn't yet thought of the right one.

Then he lit on David Shaughnessy.

Shaughnessy had known Bobbie Lammas, and in May '46 was in Norfolk for the first time since Munich. When he had danced at the Hedleighs' ball, and been briefly of the conviction that Susanna Fitzwilliam – if by some miracle she could be persuaded to confine most of her attentions to one man – would round off his sentimental education very nicely. In those days, David had been as debonair as most of Bobbie's kindred spirits, Charles Lammas vaguely recollected – instinctively taking to the fellow with black curly hair and merry eyes who had invited himself to Edingthorpe to drink tea with his old friend's uncle and aunt.

'I'm sure you'll remember me when you see me, Mr Lammas.' That was on the telephone. And then, when he had presented himself at the Manor, and had been remembered by Blanche. (She had always extended a generalised affection to all Bobbie's friends, and now cherished their acquaintance with sad love.) After Charles had pretended to recall every detail of a party at Hoveton when they had both been present. 'I can't *tell* you about the way Bobbie talked about the summer holidays he'd spent in this house.'

David Shaughnessy, in his thirties and after three years as a prisoner of war in Thai and Burmese jungle camps, was not as blithe as he had been at twenty, when he had been at Queen's and Bobbie had been at Clare, and they had both laid siege to the same Newnham girls. On one famous occasion, they had match-raced two punts for the honour of taking Clarissa Mallalieu to . . . The details had been obscured by time – but the prize had been consenting; and had kissed the loser too, David

Shaughnessy would recall, when recounting how that devil Bobbie had been ahead by half a length when they shot beneath Magdalene bridge, which was the finishing line.

Perhaps not as blithe as he had been. But cheerful when he talked about how, after years as a prisoner of war, even his dullest work as a barrister was downright fascinating. And cheerful when Charles Lammas asked him if by chance he'd known Christopher de Brissac.

'Certainly I did. Wonderful fellow. Did terribly well, all things considered, right up to the end. Then, he . . . He escaped. Did you know that?'

Lammas put down his tea cup. 'No, I didn't. Tell me.'

'Well . . . As far as I'm aware, no one ever succeeded in getting right away. Nowhere to go, you understand. What could you do? Swim to Australia? Paddle a log as far as India? Stroll over the Yunnan mountains into western China? A few people tried, even so. From Tamarkan, from other camps. They all either died in the jungle, or were recaptured and killed. Can't survive long, walking in those forests, unless you were born to it – especially not if you're half-dead when you set out. And the locals knew any white man must be an escaping prisoner, they'd always sell you back to the Japanese.'

'And Christopher?'

'I don't know how he was recaptured, but he was. We saw him brought back to our camp. That was at a place on the coast, called Thanbyuzayat. The base camp, at the rail-head. We weren't allowed to talk to him. Though . . . Though we protested at that, I can tell you. After a few days of solitary confinement, and . . .' Shaughnessy's eyebrows frowned. 'Interrogation. We saw him taken away in a truck. But they can't have gone far, because the truck was back later that morning. Afterwards, word got around the camp – from a Burmese who'd been out in the forest gathering berries or something. He'd seen this truck turn off the road into his clearing, and he'd hidden behind a tree. They gave Christopher a spade. Pretty standard practice, for those fellows. Told him to dig his own grave. They lounged around, smoking. He dug. Then they had him kneel down on the edge of the pit. One of them . . . You know those damned swords of theirs. One of them cut his head off.'

'I . . . I think I'm beginning to understand something. Look, I have a goddaughter, who . . . It's a long story, and I promise I'll tell you enough of it for our purposes. She was very fond of Christopher, you see, and I'm . . . You've just convinced me that while she was still out East she must have got word of the manner of his death. His being beheaded. Listen, would you do something for me? Meet her. Talk to her. I think you'll be doing her a great kindness. She is . . . very unhappy.'

'Of course I will. Does she ever come to London?'

'She's living in London. But if you don't mind . . . Will you still be in Norfolk tomorrow? If I could get her to come here . . . Lunch any good? Dinner?'

'Can't do lunch, I'm afraid. Dinner would be splendid.'

Charles Lammas went toward the lobby behind the staircase to ring up Georgia. At last! he thought. The right thing to say! So long, he'd held off, not wanting to seem to bully her. But now, surely . . .

But then he thought: No. Give her time to think, poor love. A telegram. The boy would come pedalling into the yard with the afternoon post any minute now. When he went panting back to North Walsham, he could send this invitation off. This right response. Good!

My dear Georgia, David Shaughnessy is here, who knew Christopher at . . . 'How do you spell the place?' *Thanbyuzayat. He knows about his escape and his death. Please come. All my love, Charles.*

3

—✴—

Lammas had been right about the effect his telegram would have. The next evening, when David Shaughnessy arrived at Edingthorpe, Georgia was there. Waiting for him. Knotting and knotting her fingers. Her glances swinging.

Shaughnessy was not the sort of fellow you could imagine deliberately setting out to charm people. But after the first ten minutes at dinner, Charles Lammas could hear Blanche silently deciding that he was the most delightful man she had met for years, and it was just like Bobbie to have had such a friend. As for Georgia, sitting opposite him across the oval table, from his first sentence about that Burma railway he had her enthralled. Occasionally she'd break in with, 'Oh yes, so I've heard.' So it became plain that she had talked to a number of survivors of those camps. Or she might say something about how at her internment camp at Maymyo it had been similar in a particular way, or it had been different.

Shaughnessy talked about the various camps, from Kanchanaburi down near the Gulf of Siam, up to Three Pagodas Pass on the border. Then the other camps, on the Burmese side, which they'd known by the number of kilometres they were from the sea. So Thetkaw was 14 Kilo Camp, and so on, up to 105 Kilo Camp just before the Pass. He talked about a Dutch doctor called Hekking and an Australian doctor called Coates, both of whom had worked heroically and saved a lot of men's lives. Doing all manner of operations with no proper equipment and no anaesthetics. Scraping out tropical ulcers with a spoon which had been honed till it was razory. He talked about the ghastly business of actually building that railway, but how if it was bad for the Allied prisoners of war, it was even worse for the Asian slave labourers. *Romusha*, they called them. Tamils, Malays, Burmese, Thais. Yes, curiously enough the Japanese treated them even more vilely. So they died in even greater numbers.

He talked about what hell it was for officers like Christopher and himself, trying to fend off the worst collisions between the Japanese and the prisoners, and whenever anything went wrong always being blamed by the former and sometimes by the latter too. He answered when asked about Japanese notions of discipline. Not concealing things, but not making a song and dance about what it was too late to do anything about now, in a way Lammas found admirably judged. How the guards beat men with staves, with pick-helves. Beat them to death, sometimes. How men were put in cages where you couldn't stand up or lie straight. Or they made you kneel in the sun all day, or stand to attention all day. Christopher and he had stood to attention for ten hours outside the guard hut in the sun. On account of a work quota which a team of men had not fulfilled, and their having protested that the task set had been beyond human strength in the time given. Standing immobile for hours, men would faint sometimes. Then the Japs would beat you. And there was no asking a passer-by for water, or any nonsense like that. And you really had to stand to attention. If you moved a finger, or they thought you did, they'd be at you with their clubs.

Breaking stone with hammers. Shifting earth with buckets and hods and litters. Not a wheelbarrow on the line, that he'd ever seen. Then the monsoon breaking. How the rain blew in through the open sides of the huts, and the camps flooded. How the monsoon tore away the railway bed, loosened bridge pilings. Then the cholera epidemic, and how they'd made pyres to burn the dead. A layer of bamboo, then a layer of dead men, then a layer of bamboo, then a layer of dead men . . . It wasn't easy to get the wet bamboo to burn.

Lammas liked his sober but cheerful way of letting the facts speak for themselves. He liked his black hair, too, so close-cropped it hardly got a chance to curl. (The painter in him never lying dormant for long, he slightly screwed up his eyes. Started imagining how one might draw that straight nose, that merry smile.) Yes, admirable the way Shaughnessy in the midst of all that horror found things to smile about. A python in the hut one night, and the sudden pandemonium, before the feast. Then Georgia threw her godfather a look of gratitude, and he thought: Poor darling, with her parents and her brother dead. If only, however gradually, she could realise how much Blanche and he – if she could remember . . . What were they saying?

'His plan?' David Shaughnessy hesitated. 'Yes, we talked about it. I was . . . The plan was, that we were going to escape together.' He turned a moment to Blanche, sitting at one end of the polished table, behind her china and her glass, behind her silver candlesticks with their upheld buds of flame. 'You know, Mrs Lammas, this time last year I was still there. And there are moments, even now, when I can hardly . . .' With a flutter of laughter, he gazed around at the pictures, down the table to Charles sitting with his back to the French window and the almost-final darkness fallen in the garden. 'When I can hardly believe in rooms like this. Evenings like this. Let alone' – his eyes twinkling – 'believe in a plate with Cheddar on it.'

But Georgia asked, 'From Thanbyuzayat?' Because her entire soul was bent on that story, on her imagining. So the man who had been Bobbie's friend at Cambridge and Christopher's in Burma faced her directly again. And for the rest of their conversation she held him, gaze for gaze.

'Yes, from Thanbyuzayat. It was one of the camps with a hospital. So-called. A hut just like all the other huts. We were in there. An amazing array of diseases, people were getting. Cholera and dysentery were the worst killers I suppose. But we had men with dengue fever, with malaria. Men with dry beri-beri and wet beri-beri, men with pellagra and scrub typhus and God knows what. Not to mention malnutrition. Our plan was to get as strong as we could down in that hospital hut. Near the coast, it wasn't as bad as it was up the line. We could get an egg to eat occasionally, as well as the little handfuls of rice. Down in the egg belt, we were – that's what they called it.' He chuckled. 'Living off the fat of the land. Christopher and I both had malaria. The trouble was, I didn't get better and he did. Hekking managed to get hold of a little quinine sometimes, though never enough for the number of patients he had. So . . . I didn't get better and I didn't get better. After a bit, Christopher said, Look David, they're going to send me back up the line any day now. I'm going to have to have a crack at it without you. I said, Of course. Yes. You go. Good luck. He said, Right. So long, old lad. Hekking will get you fit in time, don't you fret. And he was right about that. I owe my life to that Dutch doctor.'

'And Christopher's plan?' she asked.

'Our plan had been to try to get up into the Karen Hills. That was the nearest bit of Burma where we'd heard there was any real resistance to the Japanese. Where the people probably wouldn't turn you over to them. Hell of an outside chance, of course. You'd have to get north of Moulmein, and then up the Salween valley. We'd calculated on having to cross a good hundred and fifty miles of country crawling with Japs before we'd get up into the hills, and even then . . . But that was the theory. That was what Christopher set out to try to do. Slip out of the camp at night. That was the easy part. And then somehow turn into a ghost for a few weeks, and keep heading north. But . . .' Shaughnessy smiled. 'A free ghost. And if you ask about his idea . . . The plan was also simply to be free. I expect you can imagine, Miss Burney. After a couple of years of being a prisoner. Being a slave to those fellows. We wanted very much just to get away. To clear out. To go back to being who we'd used to be. Christopher will . . . He'll have been happy just to get out of those camps. Happy to be walking free through the country. Hearing the jungle cocks crow. That sort of thing. Stopping at a stream to drink, and then walking on.'

'Oh, yes,' she breathed. 'I can imagine! I know!'

Silence fell. Then Georgia turned to Blanche, thoughtfully, and then to Charles. Hesitating. Without speaking.

Facing David Shaughnessy again, she asked: 'When you knew Christopher. When you were in that hut together, talking. Did he . . . Did he, ever, mention me?'

'He said once . . .' Pronounced smilingly. So that Lammas observed to his relief that Georgia's burning eyes were not going to consume away that buoyant man's humour. 'We were talking to the doctor. Hekking had a wife and children. Lived to get back to them, I'm glad to say. We were talking about families. I said I wasn't married, thank God. Christopher . . . He told us there was a girl he'd wanted to marry. A hill station girl, he said – by way of explanation. And he told us her name. So since your godfather mentioned you to me yesterday, I've known he meant you. Only he called you Georgiana Burney, not Georgia.'

Her face was a mask. Except for her tears, which slowly welled, and slowly ran down.

Then she said: 'You . . . You must have thought ill of me. No doubt you still do. You're right to do so. I was very shallow, when he knew me.'

Even faced with her weeping, Shaughnessy allowed himself to cock a very slightly amused eyebrow. 'Oh, no. Hekking and I didn't think ill of – of the hill station girl. Why should we? Christopher didn't seem to.'

4

A few weeks later, David Shaughnessy again allowed himself to be used as bait to lure Georgia Burney to Edingthorpe. He really did seem a man sent by Providence, Charles Lammas felt. Either that, or Bobbie's spirit was still exercising a benign influence. Her godfather even momentarily feared that the girl might transfer to de Brissac's last friend the passionate love which, he was increasingly certain, her disabused heart scarcely dared offer to his memory.

However, on his subsequent visit Shaughnessy impressed his host and hostess by mixing-in with his Burmese prison camp stories a lot of cheerful talk about Bobbie before the war. Then he had funny stories about Sarah Hedleigh's difficulties in drumming up a suitor for Caroline whom they both found to their taste. Funny stories, too, about his trepidation when recently he'd had to go all the way to Worcestershire to encounter for the first time his own prospective parents-in-law.

Shaughnessy must be damned tough underneath, Lammas had no doubt. But he was so kind with everyone, and with Georgia was so infinitely sympathetic and patient, always thinking of things about Christopher which she might like to hear, that the older man felt humbled. What with dedicating his life to painting, he'd always been a bit of an egoist. While now, after the most catastrophic war in history, in which – what were the latest estimates? – more than forty million people had been killed. Now, here was a man who had endured three years in one of the most hideous pits in that hell. A man who'd calmly gone back to earning his living as a lawyer. Blessed, clearly, with a formidable physique and no less robust spirit. A fellow with, as it chanced, curly black hair and a straight nose, and a wry way of telling stories about the consternation a python could cause by slithering over sleeping men. Engaged to marry a Worcestershire girl. A fellow of, so far as one could make out, no very marked philosophical or religious tendencies – though doubtless he went to church every now and then, and certainly he was bright. And here he was – not without bitterness, but good at being equable. Here he was, with his great readiness to be kind. Joking away about how, off to brave his darling Tamsin's people in their native shire, the mere sight of a road-sign saying Worcester had nearly been enough to make him turn the car around and flee back to London. Here he was, eating a dish of Edingthorpe strawberries . . . That almost miraculous creature: a good man. Lucky with it, too.

By the time Georgia Burney went to Italy the following winter, she had made several brief visits to her godparents on her own, but she still refused to meet Jack. Nevertheless, they were beginning to be cautiously optimistic about the cobbling back together of her psyche. Or, at least, they were more trustful of her ability to behave calmly when she had decided to. Her ability to perform. 'I'm a lot better with people I scarcely know.' That was the kind of thing she'd say. Or, 'I'm all right when I'm being frivolous.'

With Blanche, she would walk in the garden. Or they'd go together to the kitchen, to talk to Ellen Meade. Georgia might simply be going through the motions, her godmother reported. But that was a considerable improvement on not going through them. And with any luck, in time . . .

With Charles, she would go to the studio. He was really burnt-out as a painter, and he knew it. Henrietta's sitting for him the summer before had gone to waste. After three weeks' work, the picture had so displeased him that he'd given up. It had been leaned with its face to the wall, with others that would probably never be finished.

Still, some breath of Georgia's and his old companionship stole into the studio air, that last time before she left the country, when she went to sit in the little green chair which had always been hers. Among the wooden lay-figures, wearing their bits of finery. With the pictures on the walls; and the White Ensign that had flown on $E35$; and the pike from Marlborough's wars, with its pennant gossamery now. With the rocking-horse, and the Chinese screen.

An enormous roll of canvas had just been delivered from London. Georgia said she remembered how delighted he'd always been when canvas arrived. Dead right, he said – and set to work unpacking it with something of his old zest. He got out some stretchers. Talked about what fun it had always been, deciding on the right size for a composition, deciding how he was going to prepare the canvas. And then the excitement of beginning a new picture!

He did not begin a new picture. Still, he got out a sketch-book, made a few quick pencil drawings of her. She came upon them, after his death. Noticed how vivid they were. Of course, all his life he'd been fishing out those little books of his, noting impressions of what he saw. On his knee in cafés and in people's houses, on the rug after picnics – everywhere. And she noticed too how he had known how to capture her new likeness. Not the portrait in oils of eight years before. But not that girl any more, either. Drawings the size of her hand, abandoned after a few minutes. Yet the new Georgia was there. He'd drawn her flinching eyes. The anxious lines between her eyebrows.

At the time, while her godfather was sketching her, she simply let the peace of that old flint and reed-thatch barn start to seep back into her heart. The peace of being back among those immobile shapes, and the spaces between them. In the lapping quietness. And – she started to know again – in the lapping belief, and love.

So, slowly, they began to talk.

5

When Georgia had first decided to dash off to Italy, it was because she remembered how happy she had been at Villa Lucia when she was sixteen. It had been because, while she was still in Burma, all her efforts to find any trace of Caterina had come to nothing, and she wanted to go to Urbania to find her family, discover if they knew what had happened to her. Above all, because in Italy surely it was impossible that she should bump into anyone who would stare contemptuously at her, and use that word *Rangoon*, and use those other words.

Then it had not been possible, because of Italy still being what they called a war zone. And now, in a rattly bus clanking its way through the foothills of the Apennines, her head was a muddle. And from way back in her, and from way down – from what must be right at the root of her unhappiness, at the root of her – came echoing: *Here comes the Burma girl . . . Here comes the traitor girl . . .*

She was apprehensive, and she felt hot, and too well-dressed. It was nearly Christmas, so she had brought winter clothes. But there was a scirocco blowing, so the sky looked menacing with raggedy black clouds, and the air was unseasonably muggy, and nobody would open any of the bus windows. The other passengers all appeared humble people, and she stood out in her London clothes, and they looked at her. The women were all shorter than she was, and seemed to start wearing black terribly young – some of them couldn't be more than her age.

Her head was a muddle. Not only of horrible things. Godfather Charles in his studio, very frail these days and completely white-headed. But, as he drew, asking her in the most natural fashion what it had been like in Rangoon, when the city was a Japanese colonial capital and looked like remaining one for years, and you had to buckle down to working out how to survive.

She'd jerked up her head. Given him her hard, challenging stare. Because with him she couldn't do the other thing she did, which was to tell a string of lies about being in prison there. He had just gone on looking up at her face, looking down at the sketch-book on his cocked-up knee. So she'd found herself telling him about her high-ranking protector, and how he'd loaded her with rupees. Which had been jolly useful, when she'd escaped back up-country to the village near Maymyo on the Lashio road, where they were all short of just about everything. He'd loaded her with some wonderfully ridiculous presents too, which fortunately could often be turned into rupees. Unfortunately it had been then, when she'd bolted up-country and tried to go to earth . . . When orders had come for her to return; and she had ignored those orders . . . It had been then, that the Kempeitai came for her. But, please, she didn't want to talk about that. He'd read what she'd written.

Her trembling had started again – sitting there, in the green chair. Still in his unruffled manner, Godfather Charles had said that he'd been asking a few people a few questions, and he'd heard that in that Maymyo internment camp she'd been regarded as something of a heroine. Going to work in the military hospital, coming back exhausted, but often with a little food concealed under her sari, or bandages or medicines sometimes. And indeed, at a celebratory dance given soon after the liberation, his goddaughter had been one of the most honoured guests. Absolutely one of the stars of the evening. Danced with General Slim himself. He hadn't been misinformed, had he? She'd said No. And had surprised herself by the calm, worldly voice with which she had added that it was possible to have more than one reputation at once.

Wonderful David Shaughnessy kept cropping up in her muddled thoughts too. In London, he had introduced her to his fiancée. The three of them had gone out to dinner together, and then they'd gone on to the Ritz, and David had danced alternately with Tamsin and her, and it had been fun.

That was a train of thought which led back to . . . Because it was impossible not to compare David with herself. David so undamaged! So whole! David talking merrily about how the Calcutta doctors had performed an initial massacre of the army of parasites who had taken up residence in various dreary regions of his innards, and now the London doctors seemed quite pleased with how their slaughter of the stragglers was proceeding. David so happy with his Tamsin – they'd promised to invite her to their wedding.

Better concentrate on how she was to set about finding Caterina's parents, if they were still alive. Urbania was down in a valley, Godfather Charles had said, on a little river called the Metauro – and the bus was grinding down-hill now. Probably Caterina's brothers and sisters still lived hereabouts, too. Unless they'd all emigrated to America. Or joined religious orders, and been in unimportant settlements in the East when the war came. And afterwards, had been among the thousands and thousands about whom nobody seemed to know anything. The nuns had still been in that convent in the country just outside Moulmein quite late in the war – she'd discovered that. Then the buildings had been requisitioned as barracks or something, just like had happened to the Maymyo convent.

And after that, if the Sisters had been interned; or had been killed; or had managed somehow to go into hiding; or . . .

Better concentrate on what she was going to say. Georgia gazed out of the bus window at black storm-clouds blowing, and slashes of silvery winter sun, and far ahead down in a valley a brown-brick town. She'd looked up a few useful words in the dictionary. The Italian for Burma was Birmania. Right. But the few phrases Emanuela had taught her, and the smattering of the language which Caterina had instilled in her in exchange for English lessons and Burmese lessons, were going to be pitifully inadequate, she just knew they were.

Anything, rather than let the East keep coming back to her. Images from her war. Images from other people's wars. That time in the fringe of the forest when she'd come upon a dead woman, so alive with worms that it had seemed the body was trying to move. Better concentrate on how it was just conceivable that Caterina was here. Just think, in an hour she might be hugging her! Talking about the old times, the happy times! No, it was practically impossible that she'd be here. Yet surely it was possible that she was in a convent somewhere in Italy. If, when the fighting was over, the Church had evacuated some of the nuns, brought them home . . . While she herself had been in hospital with cholera, for instance. That would explain . . . And maybe Caterina had been ill too, had been invalided out.

Anything, rather than the East always coming back. Stories she'd ferreted out. Not the sort she had spoken of either with Godfather Charles or with David Shaughnessy. Though neither of them had illusions about what life had been like during the rise and fall of Japan's famous Co-Prosperity Sphere. What the Asian war had been like. But these were not stories you spoke about.

The bus had stopped yet again. Georgia tried to take an interest in the farmer clambering on board, carrying a brace of bantams with their legs tied together with twine. She remembered how much luckier she had been than a lot of people. Luckier than Beth Montague, who'd survived in Singapore nearly till the end, slaving as a maid in one of the swish hotels. As a maid, and inevitably as a part-time prostitute too. Summoned to the rooms of officers and politicians staying there. The first thing was, you had to give them a massage. Georgia knew all about that.

She'd been luckier than that Dutch girl whose name she didn't know. Who was dragged by her hair onto a parade ground in Java – watched by a herd of Allied prisoners, with machine-guns trained on them. Who was spreadeagled, screaming, with her wrists and ankles lashed to four bayonets stuck in the ground. When that squad of Japanese had all raped her, they hung her up in a tree, to finish her dying there.

Yes – yes – and the East always would keep coming back to her. A year and a half of peace now, and she was still trying to make her peace with it, and she knew she'd be trying till she died. The East she'd been born in. Her father's stories. The war East. The smallest, smallest things could still make her feel shaky. A Japanese soldier had shot Angus, for no reason. On Forest Road, that had been. She'd been walking quickly back to the house, her eyes on the ground like you walked then, and the old dog had been lagging a bit behind. That soldier had raised his gun, and . . .

God this bus was stuffy. Why did that man have to keep staring at her? Two days ago, her train had crossed the border, and still she'd sensed not a spark of the delight in Italy she'd felt before the war. Well, not all that surprising. Didn't feel much joy in anything else either, these days – it wasn't Italy's fault.

Too hot. Far too smartly dressed. Couldn't even gaze out of a damned bus window without feeling obscurely frightened. David Shaughnessy wasn't depressed constantly. Tamsin and he were going to Lake Como for their honeymoon, they'd have a lighthearted time.

She'd understood what he'd said about how Christopher had longed to go free. How he must have rejoiced to be walking across the countryside, however dangerous it was. The joy in birdsong, in every glinting leaf. Jack had said much the same, apparently. Had talked about how intoxicating freedom could be, after a year in a crowd behind barbed-wire.

She understood that – none better. After that pre-war summer in Tuscany and in Norfolk, when the idyll consisted in nothing seeming to have any consequences . . . Or none that mattered. Or none that you couldn't hope to get away with. She understood, because at first when she'd been back East it had still been like that. You acted this part, you acted that part, your thoughts played like a fountain in sunshine, your whole being was lightness itself.

Then the war came, and everything had consequences. A prisoner carrying a hod of rubble slipped and fell, and a guard ran toward him shouting, started bashing him with a club. An escaping prisoner in the forest was seen by a local man, who tracked him for a while and then returned to his village to report that he could run him down. A female prisoner caught the eye of a camp commandant, who . . . But it had got better at the end, when there'd been a comfort station established at Maymyo. With Korean girls, chiefly. Not better for the Korean girls. But better for the white female prisoners.

Strange – Christopher and Jack and she all having been prisoners of war. Behind barbed-wire. Or bamboo. Though in those railway camps they weren't fenced in. The jungle was the prison. Your white skin was the most secure prison of all. Still, all three of them . . . Prisoners of their wars.

6

—w—

When the bus arrived in the square, Urbania did not appear the Arcadian old place Georgia's godfather had told her of, where years ago Giacomo Zanetti and he had stopped during an expedition in search of paintings.

A charming old ducal palace, he had said. A Della Rovere palace, in exactly the right state of dilapidation, with ox-carts lumbering in and out of the courtyard. Willows down by the river, he had said, and gardens.

Getting out of the bus, Georgia was stared at stolidly by thick-set men wearing cloth caps. She had hoped there would be a hotel in the square. However, she heaved her suitcases into a dingy shop, and in her elementary Italian explained that she would like to leave them there, please, while she searched for a lodging for the night. *Un albergo, per favore.* Could they help her? *Una pensione* . . .

In that pokey store, with its low rafters and its Madonna, with its earthen floor and its cobwebs, Georgia felt even more ludicrously elegant. Her hand-bag which she had bought in the rue de Rivoli, her Jermyn Street shoes – she was making an exhibition of herself, simple as that. And now it transpired that the whole idea of a hotel was problematic in this town. So she pitched into enquiring after Sister Caterina, who had gone to Burma maybe ten years ago.

At this point all the men, who had hitherto not so much as taken their cigarettes out of their mouths, came plodding into the shop. Sister Caterina? she asked. Who had gone to Burma, no, sorry, to Birmania. The Church, yes. A Sister. From Urbania. Her friend. Did they know her family?

The men stood around her like small, sturdy bulls, each one more determined than the last that he was the bull to take command of the situation. Georgia remembered Villa Lucia. She thought how different this was from the life the Zanetti family led. How when she'd stayed there she'd scarcely realised what an enclave of privilege the place was. Taken it all for granted, from the escutcheoned doorways to the being waited on at table. While right here, right now . . . Why did they have to crowd around her so closely?

The place unfamiliar, the language unfamiliar – that was all it was, she repeated to herself resolutely. She'd get the hang of things presently. And of *course* no one was going to steal her suitcases. And there *must* be lodgings somewhere in town.

Some of the younger men now seemed particularly convinced that they were going to take charge of the foreign signorina. American? Ah, English. Well, naturally they would solve the problem, it would be a pleasure. What precisely was the problem?

Burma didn't seem to mean a terrific lot to anybody. Georgia tried India. That was better. Language, that was the difficulty, everyone agreed. One young dandy, who was so far from being a bull that the trouble was that he was a gazelle, decided to go for old Giovanni who'd worked for thirty years in Chicago. Then he realised that would be a mistake, so with superb gestures of tyranny he sent one of the stockiest bulls on this errand instead, while himself remaining to direct operations, where he was needed. Then two other men had a particularly vociferous altercation, and Caterina was announced most authoritatively to be dead. The Germans had killed her, the *tedeschi*. No, imbecile, it was the English bomb, that other time.

Only that turned out to be a different Caterina, and the next minute everybody was convinced of something or other, and they were all off together down an alley-way. Georgia thinking, Yes, of course Caterina is dead. It happened not to be the Germans or the English, but what's the difference? Naturally, she is dead. If she'd been alive, she'd have . . . Oh Caterina, what am I doing here? Christopher and you on our verandah, nattering away about Anselm's argument for the existence of God, and the Pope's Swiss guards. I'm mad, why have I come here?

The streets were rutted, there were puddles. With her growing escort of the curious and the opinionated, Georgia was hurried along. The houses all looked poor. And everyone seemed to be wearing black. It made her shiver. Were they all in mourning?

'They heard that she was dead.' This was the old gaffer who had worked in Chicago. 'Her mother and father. They are very sad.'

'Oh, God, I knew it.' Georgia stopped in her tracks. 'My poor darling Caterina,' she whispered. 'You too . . .' She fumbled in her bag for her handkerchief. 'Oh no, I can't bear it. Look, I won't be able to say anything to her parents. I'll just make them unhappy all over again. I . . .'

But it seemed they had arrived. This gloomy yard of damp, crumbling houses was the sunlit playground of Caterina's memory. The haven she had longed to get back to.

This was the door. Solicitous hands took Georgia's elbows, urging her forward into that dark oblong.

She screamed. Furiously, she broke free. They fell back. Not knowing what terrors were released in her by the laying on of hands, by being pushed through doors.

And it wasn't much bigger than a cell, or a bedroom. For naturally she had to grapple her courage to her, and apologise, and go in. Two decrepit old creatures, sitting by a chilly stove. The grey room at once violently filled with shoulders and voices.

The English, the friend of Caterina who went to India. This is her, Grandad. Granny, wake up, this is the friend. Of Caterina, naturally of Caterina.

Yes, Miss, in India. They were told. India, Birmania. Fifteen years, since she joined the Church. Eleven, since they saw her last. Far away . . . In the English empire. The Japanese . . . Ah, war. We too. Here . . .

Georgia thought: If any more human bodies shove into this kitchen I'm going to panic. I know I am. It's precisely the sort of thing I . . . She thought: This is the end of the road all right. This is the end of one road. Still, I must say something to her mother and father. I must!

She had been being introduced to them for what felt like minutes, though it could only have been thirty seconds. But she couldn't make herself heard, and she couldn't understand.

With the inspiration of the desperate, Georgia dropped to her knees before Caterina's mother. This had the merit of getting her face closer to the old woman's and further from all the others'; and it caused a hush.

If these tears in her eyes were the beginning of one of her fits of crying, it would be because her nerves were frayed like hell, not because Caterina was dead. Yes, but never mind about that. And stop thinking that if you don't find a hotel room to lie down in soon and be alone you're going to shriek. Well, maybe if you shriek loud enough they'll find you a room.

So kneeling before that black-bundled old woman, and holding her hands, Georgia began trying to say: Your daughter taught me a little Italian. In Burma, years ago. In my parents' house.

Looking into that scarved, white face, those startled eyes. Hoping she was making herself understood when she murmured about how Caterina was so beautiful, Caterina was of such a sweet nature, and of such gaiety, oh how I loved her, we all loved her.

Caterina's mother was bending forward. Saying something. 'Cara . . .'

Georgia felt the old woman's handkerchief dabbing at the tears on her cheeks. Felt a kiss on her forehead.

She stood up. 'Goodbye,' she said. 'Please, a hotel.'

7

—w—

'Signor Lammas, your guest has arrived. The English signorina . . .'

'La Signorina Burney? Excellent!'

Outside, the Venetian December night had fallen. At his usual table at Harry's Bar, Edmund Lammas RA looked up from his *Corriere della Sera*, saw Georgia at the other end of the room being helped out of her coat by a waiter.

Ned had always had beautiful hands, and as he folded his newspaper he appraised them with his habitual pleasure in taking for granted his own elegance, and approved his creamy cuffs and his gold cufflinks with the same nonchalance. He took off the gold-rimmed spectacles he wore for reading and for painting, put them in his pocket with the precision of one who knows that if he does not punctiliously remember he will dependably forget.

However well into his eighties he might be, Ned stood up to greet Georgia Burney more easily than had his cousin Charles at Edingthorpe the winter before, who would not turn sixty for another year or two. He flicked the silk handkerchief from the breast-pocket of his coat, flourished its softness and its faint aroma of *eau de Cologne* across his face, poked it back into his pocket to resume its pavonian hinting. That suit had been made by a Savile Row tailor before the First War. Dandy of the old school that he was, Ned Lammas would never have worn one from Milan or from Paris. And fortunately his Edwardian wardrobe had been so extensive, that his not having visited England these twenty years was no real inconvenience. He could generally find a coat or a waistcoat that almost nobody would recollect seeing him wear.

A few minutes later, he had ordered two of the driest of dry martinis. 'If, Miss Burney, you will be guided by me. They know how to make them, here. Only place in Italy where they do. So one feels obliged to take the opportunity.'

He had knocked over his Malacca cane, and Georgia had picked it up for him; and he'd then lamented that for years he had no longer been able to believe that his sticks were still an affectation.

He had listened to her misadventures in Urbania, and had seen only the amusing side of everything. 'Oh, these *muddy* little towns. One stays *just* long enough to see if there's *one* picture worth looking at.' Then: 'I know everything, my dear young lady. Well, good heavens, not everything, please don't look alarmed. I mean that, when Charlie wrote, he told me you had lost your parents, and your brother. *So* unfair, the way those who were fond of their relatives always seem to lose them. While I . . . Oh, I was *considerably* older than you are, before I inherited a farthing.' Then: 'Naturally, in an hour we shall dine. But meanwhile . . . Was it dry enough? I think two more, don't you? Truly at my age, and with your looks, we can allow ourselves, we *must* allow ourselves . . . Charlie reasonably cheerful when you last saw him? Blanche either gardening or talking about her garden, or talking about some quadruped or other, you don't need to tell me. Dear Blanche. Though, truly, you must permit an old man to say . . . Whatever else that *ridiculous* war may have done, it has left you very beautiful.'

Georgia was already forgetting how miserable a mid-winter scirocco could make you feel, in a strange town where you knew nobody. A town from which you couldn't bolt till the next bus left in the morning. In a damp bedroom you couldn't sally forth from to look for some supper, because if you did everyone would stare at you, the ones that didn't talk to you and take charge of you. When there was someone you'd have liked to be with, peacefully, for an hour. An old woman who called you *cara* and wiped your tears and gave you a kiss. With her, and with her husband you felt bad about not having spoken to. But it was impossible, because other people would come muscling in. So you lay on your bed, and thought about how dismal Christmas was going to be on your own in . . . Where should she go? Venice?

Ned Lammas had no doubt that it must really have been her anxiety to avoid an English Christmas that had brought her to Italy. And she had no doubt that she had been right to return to haunts of blessed, blessed frivolity. To have sought out Ned with his glittering old eyes, and his adroitly judged superficialities. Ned Lammas with his, 'No, no, *quite* unbearable. Miles and miles of . . .' As so often when he discussed his East Anglian sojourns, his voice sank to a fastidious quaver. '*Sugarbeet* . . . Where one is compelled to stand. For hours, in the rain. *Shooting* things. After which, by way of compensation I suppose – *really*, can you imagine? – one is *dragged* to *church*.'

The old gentleman insisted that he had always made a point of pretending not to have any morals (Georgia got the impression that this was a little speech he had made before); and that, by dint of dogged imitation of the desired state, he had nearly attained it. Yet he plunged into plans for giving her an amusing winter in Venice with what struck her as great kindness. Though he kept breaking off to make self-deprecatory remarks about how he knew he wasn't painting as he had when he was younger, but luckily there were enough buyers knocking around in the sale-rooms who, when they looked at a picture, only understood the signature. Or about how, there in Venice during the First War, he had done his best to console ladies who had lost their admirers or their husbands. Had done his inadequate best. But then, of course, when heroes in uniform turned up, *real* men not artists . . . The drawing-rooms had all been in a flutter. Even Giacomo Zanetti, whom you would never have described as handsome, appeared possessed of formidable consolatory powers.

Ned Lammas was going to introduce her to his friends the Montecchi. Naturally, all his friends were abysmally ancient. Half were so old they were dead – which he did not mind a bit for himself, or for them. He minded for Georgia, who would have found so-and-so absolutely fascinating. And would have known how to listen graciously to dull old what's-his-name, which was the price exacted for getting into that heavenly house and seeing the frescoes.

Still, the Montecchi grandsons and granddaughters were of Georgia's generation; and a wilder, gayer breed it was hard to imagine; and their New Year balls – he would have Marcella Montecchi send her an invitation – were not to be missed. He would also have an invitation to Tiziana Pandolfi's party sent to Georgia's hotel. By the way, she must tell him where she was staying, and then he would tell her where she *ought* to be staying.

He would then, with her permission, introduce her to the French consul and his wife, whom he'd been finding enormous fun recently. And after that in his own flat he would give a small dinner party in her honour. 'Though I shan't invite Benny Shultz, even if he is the most charming of the American idlers here, because the last time . . .! And I'd been innocent enough to think that *I* was meant to be scandalous! Shan't invite Thérèse Jonzac, either. Or Annalisa D'Asolo. Those ladies are both tramps all right. And anyhow, you'll meet them everywhere else.'

Warming to his work, Ned Lammas recalled, years before, introducing his cousin Charles to people he'd hoped the lad might find entertaining. Fresh from the Slade, Charlie had been, and not *too* idealistic.

'And then, when the warm weather comes back . . . No doubt you've already decided to visit our friends in Tuscany. Can't go to the country in winter. *So* boring. In the summer, however, I shall probably show up there too. Tell Mario he's doing it all wrong. Tease Chiara a bit. Darling Chiara, she's one of the last people left alive who knows how to tease me. And, it's curious – one comes to value that.'

He might, as Charles Lammas had long ago suspected, be a man who had never cared much for anything or anyone. And certainly his gaiety was no more impaired by Bobbie's death than it had been thirty years ago by Geoffrey's. And equally certainly one of his favourite stories was about an art historian who, in an unreadably unctuous book – 'I had to look myself up in the index, I'd never have got to myself otherwise' – had written something about how *Edmund Lammas is profoundly interested in* . . . The pomposity or scurrility of *what* he was supposed to be profoundly interested in varied with the painter's listeners. As did his recollection of the exact phrasing of the letter he had written to the man, denouncing his clichés and his platitudes, 'and saying that I was not aware of having ever been profoundly interested in anything in my life.'

But for a moment, with his quartz eyes sparkling as he contemplated his young companion, he appeared to wish to care for her. At least to the extent of deputing someone else to do so.

'Yes . . . Now I think of Villa Lucia, and you . . . A *good* idea. Mario is a sophisticated man, and a nice man, and he has amusing friends.'

8

—ɯ—

Chuck all this in the fire, or read it first and then chuck it. Do what you like. But it's for you – do you understand? Oh, I don't know what I mean.

Unable to find so much as the graves of Sister Caterina or Lieutenant Colonel de Brissac, Georgia Burney when she was back in England had come up with that declaration. And one of Charles Lammas' ways of living up to it had been that he had accepted his wife's offer not to read those Burmese war whisperings. Had admired that offer, and accepted it; and had, as Blanche had suggested, told Henrietta and her what facts of Georgia's war he felt she would be least uncomfortable if they knew without her having to spell them out.

Jack's case was slightly different. In Hanover with the Sherwood Rangers, and now promoted captain, he did not know that Georgia had given his father three years' confessions. In response to his enquiries after her, Lammas wrote back that she had come to Edingthorpe for lunch. He made guarded remarks about how she'd clearly had a vile time during the Japanese occupation; but now, with any luck . . . And the following year he elaborated cautiously, in reply to further requests for news of her. He wrote about Caroline, and the razzle-dazzle time Georgia and she might be surmised to be having – half-hoping this would put Jack off the girl. About David Shaughnessy, and how delighted he was to have stumbled on him. Trying to steer between respecting the girl's confidence, and fore-arming his son a little with some notion of how he might find his old flame altered.

If she ever let him run her to earth. Because when Jack left his regiment, and they overlapped in England, he began to see Bobbie's widow and little Claudia fairly regularly. But when he visited Norfolk, he remarked that Georgia had left word with Caroline that she refused to see him. Oh, one day in the far future of course, but not now, she was sorry, she would not, she could not. And when Jack was back at King's for the autumn term of his last year, and she came to Edingthorpe to sit in the studio and to talk, she didn't mention him.

In May, Jack took time off from preparing for his Finals to write to Chiara Zanetti. He took longer than the ten minutes that might have appeared sufficient to give her some of his news. To enquire after her health. And to say that he hoped to be back in Italy this summer, so would it be possible for him to take up the invitation, left in abeyance during the war years, to visit them again at Villa Lucia? Adding – well tangled-up with other chit-chat – that he'd heard his parents' goddaughter, Georgia Burney, was in Tuscany these days.

The old contessa delegated to her surviving son the task of replying. Mario Zanetti wrote a charming letter, just as friendly as Jack's and much more graceful. So its recipient's first reaction (but that week, he was all taken up with his exams) was that to be so fluently bilingual when you dashed off a letter – it didn't look like a second draft – gave a man tremendous advantages. Why, Mario had even told entertaining stories, and made some jokes. Nice, silly jokes – so it was plain he wasn't trying to be clever, but had simply been in a good mood when he wrote. Jack berated himself for not having remembered that a letter was always improved by a joke or two.

Mario did not write about his father's death, nor his brother's and sister's. Or rather, the sentence, 'I think we're beginning to recover from our war a little', did duty for what might have been more personal, and otiose. After which he related the story of how, during the worst year of the fighting, Signora Annunziata had lost so much poultry to marauding neighbours that she'd taken to daubing her fowls with paint, so they looked like splotchy and squawking tricolours, and were easy to identify in the village hen-runs when she went to commandeer the survivors.

Then there was the matter of the gunsmith's daughter who, when the gunsmith was away serving in Africa, had persuaded Giacomo to let her conceal all the guns in the Villa Lucia attics. So that he, Mario, had been surprised, when the girl had turned up and asked for her father's property, to discover that he'd got racks and racks of firearms under his roof. Surprised, and relieved, too, that it had been the gunsmith's daughter and he, and not either Axis or Allied Military Police, who'd extracted this armoury from behind beams and water-tanks.

Mixed with all of which was the warmest invitation to Jack to come and stay. And the information that Georgia was, indeed, often at the house, and wonderful that was. But sometimes, equally, she was away. Still, he hoped Jack would be lucky, and find her there.

As soon as Jack Lammas had taken his degree, he returned to Norwich for a conclusive conversation with the partners of an architectural practice. Then, a summer holiday before he started work having been agreed upon, he left for Italy.

With, ringing in his ears, his mother's parting injunction: 'That girl doesn't need rescuing, you know. Or rather . . .' Because Blanche was meticulously honest. 'I suspect she *does*. However, that doesn't mean, my darling boy, that you have to try to do it. Or, indeed, that the thing can be done.'

And after a last talk with his father. Who, when it was plain to him that Jack was convinced that his pre-war sweetheart might be in need of his help. Or it was plain he wished to satisfy himself that he would not fall for her all over again. Or he wished to give himself the chance to decide he'd known all along that she was the only girl . . . At any rate, his father had taken Jack a little deeper into his confidence.

Jack had expected not to have his ideas at all straight while his train was steaming through Picardy, and had soothed his mind with the reflection that France was a big country to cross, he would have time at least to come to a few decisions about what he was *not* going to think or feel. But when out of his carriage window he could see the Maritime Alps, his repeated and repeated bracings of his mind for some lucid reasoning were disheartening him.

It was all very well letting his thoughts hark back to Georgia when he and she had sailed *Golden Eye* out for picnic suppers on the river Bure or on Ranworth broad. The summer nightfall late, and endlessly slow. The breeze whispery in the reeds and the willows. Wildfowl on the wing. The smell of fresh water, so different from salt. Then chicken sandwiches and bacon sandwiches, as the old cutter went slipping along with a ripple at her stem, with the creak of her gaff or a moment's flutter at the leech of a sail. A bottle of beer. A slice of Ellen's cake. Then kisses, and sailing back to the mooring in the dusk and the failing wind, and more kisses.

Not difficult to long for that Georgia, the Georgia who meant being innocent and happy together, who came back to him from the old peace time. And then he'd think of other nights that summer, when after dinner at the Manor they'd gone out to the paddock together to catch up a pair of horses. The stars out, and a moon sometimes, and the sound of horses' and ponies' teeth cropping the grass. They'd clipped leading-reins onto the horses' head-collars, and jumped up bare-back. Owls had nested in the stable loft that year, and it was fun sitting your horse in the darkness and watching the fledgling barn-owls come out for their first practice flights.

Far too easy, then, to be tempted by a new peace time that should be like the old one. Then Jack would remember de Brissac in the yard at Bure, that day it snowed, asking him to show him his new sixteen-bore. Christopher de Brissac who'd been Hetty's godfather. The man whose MC had impressed him terrifically, when he'd been a boy. That made

Jack obscurely uncomfortable, now. The man who in the interval of *Twelfth Night* had come to their box . . .

Jack had fought a war since then, and acquired more experience of the ways of men and women. Even so, since his talk with Papa the other evening, he had discovered himself making tremendous efforts to be both manly and worldly when he recalled how, that evening at Wyndham's, Georgia had posed for de Brissac. Now Jack saw it! Now! With her bare arm on that velvet sill. With her new silk scarf Papa had given her carefully arranged across her breast, showing off her breast. Her profile turned to its prettiest advantage, and her eyes dancing.

So she'd fallen in love with him! 'Oh, the real thing, I think,' Papa had said, had been careful to say. She'd had an affair with him, naturally. Though here Papa had been oblique, discreet. Indeed, presumably didn't know. How should he? Just like he'd been discretion itself when he'd said he was afraid one or two Japanese had treated her abominably, and her nerves were still bad. Though his voice had grated with pride when he'd told him how her spirit had withstood God knew what horrors in Mandalay gaol.

It was over a year since Jack Lammas had stood on a Buckinghamshire airfield in April sunshine, and in almost incredulous delight had tapped one Red Cross boot on his native soil. His first euphoria at being a free man once more, when all he had desired had been to walk through familiar lanes with his joy in life and liberty singing itself over and over in his head, had matured into a resolution that he was going to be one of the survivors who really did survive. In his level-headed way, he'd looked around at friends he'd made in prison camps, and right from the start of the new peace he'd seen how, alongside the unlucky men who'd come home with their health ruined, there were others who were finding it impossible to be happy or effective. Simon Harland, who'd been with him on the escape from Eichstätt, was in and out of hospital all the time, having operations on his insides, poor fellow. Archie Hurst, who'd crawled out of the same tunnel that night Alan Purvis got claustrophobia, was running through his inheritance in about as empty-headed a fashion as you could imagine, making a fool of himself with some pretty unpleasant women, offending his old friends, driving his mother to despair. Then, if Jack thought of his mess at Colditz . . . Sam Whitney hadn't got an inheritance to run through, so he was borrowing from banks and from rich friends, running up debts with his half-baked schemes for making a fortune, drinking himself sillier and sillier. Another man had gone to try to make money in Jamaica – but the reports that filtered back were more disgusting than funny. Another had shot himself.

Jack had discovered there were things he mustn't do. Travel by tube, for example. That first leave, in London he'd gone to an underground station. Without thinking. Going down the crowded gallery, he'd begun to feel the horror of it, but he'd told himself not to be an idiot, to keep walking. But the Eichstätt tunnel had come back to him. Wriggling forward in the blackness with no air to breathe. Men in front, men behind. Only an inch or two between your shoulders and the earth, between your face and . . . He'd forced himself to get on the tube when it came, but by the next stop he'd been sitting with his white face down by his knees. Kind people had helped him out, up to the street.

To shrug off the war! For more than a year, every ounce of Jack's mental strength had gone into making sure he was a real survivor, what to himself he called a deep-down survivor. To put certain memories well and truly behind him, so the damned past really stayed in the past. Now, the preeminent thing about all this outliving of the bad past was that Georgia was the reigning spirit of the good past – or perhaps it was that he needed most urgently to know if she had been. To know moreover if she might be the . . . Who was the lucky devil with a yawl that beautiful to cruise in the Gulf of Genoa? Some millionaire. Money. Lots of it. As simple as that. Yes, but – Papa had understood. The other evening, when he'd been talking proudly about Hetty's first book, which was going to come out next year apparently. The way he'd loyally contrasted her hard work and success with Georgia's – what? – her socialite's eddyings. And it was true, Papa *did* rejoice in Hetty, shamelessly. Yet something in the way he'd talked about her scholarly story-telling, her Latin something-or-other, and talked of Georgia who was so different, Georgia with her wisps of legends, all so inconsequential . . . Of course, Papa had been afraid for years that his daughter might be jealous of his goddaughter's position in the family.

Rapallo already! Jack broke off from wondering about how his father had seemed to concede in a veiled way that Georgia might exercise a fascination. He went back to wondering whether he ought to have written to old Cousin Ned – but it wasn't him that he wanted to see! – and then to commanding himself not to be too carried away by feeling sorry for Georgia, if her war had really been as nightmarish as Papa had implied. Though naturally he *would* feel terribly sorry for her – heavens above, he already did – and that couldn't be wrong, could it? And he was still speculating about how Georgia must have been having her affair with de Brissac in – where? well, somewhere in Burma – at about the same time as at Cambridge he'd – no, later perhaps – as he'd had his with Rosie Fanshaw. He was still seeing the images of Jaffa dancing girls, and of the dancing girl of one memorable evening in Tel Aviv when Bobbie and

Tim Farne had disappeared somewhere, and he'd found himself . . . Still remembering how only last spring at Rosie's wedding to that tow-headed chap, he'd met Belinda Lake, and seen her again in London a week later, which had led to . . .

Even coming past Lerici, and seeing the Gulf of Spezia, and thinking that Shelley had been drowned off this coast, didn't impress much order onto Jack's presentation of Georgia to his mind's eye. Knowing that he'd be at Forte dei Marmi any minute now, so truly it was time to marshal a bit of sober sense, or at least to resolve to have a splendid holiday and return home without having got what Mama would call *entangled with any poor girl*. He could hear her voice now. *Dance with all of them, darling boy. Take a different one out to dinner every night of the week. So much safer, and more amusing.*

This coast, where the last summer before the war he'd gone swimming with Emanuela. Would she be at Villa Lucia? Georgia with her stories of the East . . . Well, since riding with the Transjordan Frontier Force, he had his own stories about his own East.

Different . . . The same . . . Like their both having been left behind after defeats. She after the British lost Burma. He after the British lost Crete. Left alone, left standing there, when the organisation you'd belonged to fell to pieces. So it was every man pretty much for himself.

One is one and all alone and ever more shall be so. What childhood rhyme did that come from? Anyway, that was when the individual learned a certain amount about the limited value of organisations. That colonial society of hers had toppled down like a house of cards, and no one was going to put it up again – which, judging by most of what he'd heard, was a damned good thing. Yes, but . . . *One is one and all alone.* That was when – when you were a prisoner jolting along in a cattle-truck toward some loathsome camp . . . That was when the individual knew for dead sure that if he were going to be of any greater value than the organisation had been, he was going to have to prove it by taking individual action. Prove it in his own eyes – they were the ones that counted. Prove it, for example, by escaping. Trying to go free, alone.

But what Georgia's experience of being left behind had really been – her inner experience . . . And who she might be now . . . Eight years! No, nine.

And what was she up to, roosting at Villa Lucia? Was she Mario Zanetti's lover? God, God, maybe this evening they'd tell him they were engaged. Honestly, he must stop inventing things.

Jack stood up, reached his suitcase down from the luggage rack. The sea out of one window. And from the other . . . Pines. And beyond, the white hills of Carrara flushed in the westering sun.

9

Jack Lammas' delight at being back at Villa Lucia – even his delight in Emanuela Zanetti's transformation from enchanting girl to beautiful woman – were subsumed in the welter of feelings released in him by finding Georgia Burney again. Not that, at dinner, he did not pay handsome attention to Emanuela. What with recollections of their old excursions to Florence to look at paintings, and to Forte dei Marmi to go water-skiing. What with the pleasant adjacency of her throat and her lips and her eyes, and how she never seemed to doubt that they'd been terrific friends ever since – did he remember? Since that time they had incautiously lunched in a dreadfully grand restaurant, and when the bill came he'd found he couldn't pay it. So he'd asked her if she had any money, and it turned out she'd left her purse at home.

Besides, Jack found that absorbing Emanuela's attention was a serviceable way of not making it obvious to the whole party that Georgia had instantly reduced him to – what did it feel like? Well, as if he were one of those little tubs of soap-suds – yes, that was about it – into which she was idly dipping a stick with a hoop at its end. And raising up sheeny films, and blowing bubbles that drifted away.

The whole party . . . The most immediately formidable of whom was Chiara Zanetti, wearing a dress of black silk with a turban to match, adorned with pearls. So that her mourning had splendour. And neither age nor grief had reduced the precious metals and precious stones at her neck and her ears, on her wrists and her fingers. They hadn't dimmed the amusement in her sunken eyes, either, Jack discovered when she imperiously questioned him about whether Henrietta took sufficient time off from her books to break a few hearts as a girl of spirit should? 'Naturally, Charlie is besotted with his daughter, and as proud as a lion. Just as my poor Giacomo always was with our three girls. Oh, when I think of what he would have . . . But we will not linger with those sad thoughts. Now, tell me, young man. What are your plans for this summer's amusements, and conquests?' So that Jack could hear her unvoiced: To what, I wonder, do we really owe the pleasure of your company?

Then there was Ned Lammas, paying his annual visit. 'My *villeggiatura*, dear boy.' After which, with an affectation of disapproval: 'Heavens, what a powerful-looking man you have become. The very *sight* of you makes one wish to sink into a chair, and call for a restorative glass of gin.' Ned just as beguiled as his hostess to be an ancient, spectral presence at a dinner party otherwise consisting of the youngish; and the unmarried; and the imaginably entangled, or sparring.

There was Francesco De Angelis, with his shock of chestnut hair. Who appeared to have enjoyed a mild war, most of it passed as a prisoner in Sussex. Who right now was telling Jack what fun it had been to be painted by his father all those years ago. He enquired after the artist's recent show at the Bracknell Gallery, and said he wasn't a bit surprised it had gone well. He added, with the merriest smile, glancing between Georgia and Jack, that what he loved most about his portrait was the English girl who could be seen in the background, sitting in the embrasure, looking out to the garden.

There was Mario Zanetti, sitting at the head of the table opposite his mother, between Emanuela and Georgia. Mario who must be in his late thirties, Jack supposed. Who when driving him up from Forte dei Marmi had spoken in the most temperate fashion about what it was like to have your father murdered by the Right, and your brother and sister by the Left. Had talked cheerfully about how he didn't regret a bit having been practically obliged to abandon New York and his career with Sotheby's. Had described some of his initial struggles – it was going to be a long haul – to make the estate profitable again, and possibly even to have the house's roof put to rights one day.

Mario with his sisters' wavy brown hair, and the most irresistible smile – Jack was acutely aware of his host's good looks. Mario who now at dinner was talking to everyone in the same easy manner, or more often listening. So that Jack, with his thoughts racing around the various possible permutations, for the life of him couldn't make out if Georgia were here so much because of a liaison with the master of the house. Or if Francesco and Mario were rivals. Or if Mario didn't come into it, and Francesco was having an affair with Georgia. Or with Emanuela. There were moments when Jack thought he was going to start blushing, so frustrated was he at not knowing what he supposed almost any of the rest of them could have told him. So suddenly determined was he that, anyway, one or two of the possible courses of events should not ensue.

There was Georgia. There were, at either side of the marble fireplace, the two painted ebony page-boys he recalled from old visits . . . And there was Georgia, in an emerald dress. Who this time had stood her ground, when she had known he was coming. Georgia, who had been sauntering in the box parterre when Mario and he arrived.

She'd stood stock-still, when he came round the corner of the house. He'd had to wind his way in toward her through the knee-high labyrinth which smelled fragrant after the day's hot sun, till he became impatient and stepped over a few of the small green fences. He'd taken her in his arms. She'd said, 'Jack. Oh, Jack.' She'd kissed his cheek. He'd felt that, with a tremor of joy. It had brought back to him the attic bedrooms at Morston. She'd stood back, wiping away her tears. Saying, 'I'm such a fool. These days, everything makes me cry.'

Georgia in a throng would never make heads turn as Raffaella had done and as Emanuela did. Yet there in the parterre Jack had read the unhappiness in her eyes with all his old knowing of her and all his old loving of her. And now, at dinner . . . She didn't dress like the sixteen-year-old he remembered, and for a minute that seemed strange. But, then, he wouldn't have wanted her to. She had aged by more years than had passed, and her manner had a brittleness and an effervescence which made his heart ache.

Mario had asked her about some people in Florence whom they all appeared to know well, and with whom Georgia had been staying for a week. Listening to her describing what a glorious time she'd had, Jack was at once convinced that he would dislike these particular Florentines. A flashy bunch, they sounded, with more money than sense – in his abruptly Puritanical view. So, reckoning that he'd monopolised Emanuela for enough minutes to allow himself now to turn to Georgia, he asked her about Ricky.

Ah, Ricky! Her eyes blazed across the table at Jack. She immediately started talking with un-dinner-party-like vehemence about the Fourteenth Army, which had stopped the hitherto invincible Japanese on the borders of India. That army of men from Britain and Canada and Australia and New Zealand, of Chinese and Indians and Gurkhas. General Slim's army, that had turned the tide. Ricky's army . . .

Georgia's brittleness had snapped, and listening to her fury of pride in her dead brother who'd won an MC, Jack hoped their Italian hosts were not too taken aback by this passion. Yes, surely – after all, she'd been here for months. Some comprehension of why she'd clearly elevated Ricky to be a sort of icon. (He remembered him hitting fifty not out against Sherbourne. He remembered him skating at Hickling.) Why when it came to the army which had won at Kohima and won at Imphal, Georgia would not be quiet. Why, unashamed, she would swing those hot eyes of hers around the company, and talk about that army of Newfoundlanders and South Africans, of Sikhs and Dogras and Madrassis and Assamese, of Karens and Burmans and Kachins. The Forgotten Army, they'd called it, that had won at Meiktila. Her eyes were on Jack alone now, and she hadn't quite finished yet, though he could hear the tears in her voice. An army of

Scots and English, of Negroes from East Africa and Negroes from West Africa, of Pathans and Punjabis and Rajputs and Jats. The army that had won the Battle of the Irrawaddy Shore, and . . . He'd asked about Ricky, hadn't he? Well, she was telling him about Ricky. The army that had won at Mandalay, only – only . . .

Then she had to stop. And Chiara Zanetti asked Edmund Lammas in what language, or in which languages, did he suppose orders had been given and understood? He replied that he believed Urdu was the official language of the Indian Army. So that, and English . . .

Mario remarked on the number of religions those men must have had between them. And the talk turned to the Fourteenth Army company cooks, who had been required to cater for all those diets and taboos.

10

—·m·—

After dinner, Georgia Burney and Mario Zanetti and Jack Lammas went out to the terrace, to the round marble table among the lemon trees in their terracotta urns. Through the drawing-room French windows, you could see the four players at their poker. From their lamps, a cascade of pale gold fell on the flagstones outside, and glittered on the leaves of one of the lemon trees, and flowed over the recumbent form of one of the *maremmano* sheepdogs.

The night was warm, and peaceful if you were not visited by the image of the last master of the house standing with his back to that wall to be gunned down by a German posse. It was too late in the summer for fireflies or nightingales. Too late also to take a lantern, and go searching for orchids in the rough grass – though the Dutch botanist and his auburn-headed wife had survived the occupation of their country, and had been Mario's guests a couple of months before. If you looked away from the lights of the house, you could see the Plough, with Arcturus near it shining good and bright. The cognac which Mario had poured into three liqueur glasses was fire-water of just the right flaminess, Jack thought. And after her outburst at the dinner table, Georgia seemed calm again. Calmer . . . Though there was something restless in the way that emerald dress shimmered. And she was smoking that cigarette as if it were a way of putting off something else.

Mario could not, as his father had done one night nine years before, make the excuse of having to go and see to his dogs. Because they were both drowsing loyally close to his chair. But when he'd finished his drink, and told them the story of the cedar which had been struck by lightning, and what a job they'd had felling the ruined tree without it crashing onto the barn, he stood up.

'If you don't mind, I'll leave you. Several things which I ought to have sorted out today, which if I leave till tomorrow . . . And you'll have lots to talk about.'

His big white dogs got up, patiently padded after him.

'It's all right, I know all that,' Georgia started at once. Crushing out her cigarette in the ashtray with nervous fingers. 'You don't have to say anything. I know, when it comes to Ricky, and Burma, I . . .' She frowned, agitatedly. 'And there are a whole lot of other things you needn't say either. And things I ought to say.'

'My God it's wonderful to see you again,' Jack interrupted her happily. 'Georgia.' He tried the name out again on his lips. Thinking: It's there, the bond between us. I know it is. And she . . .?

She poured herself some more of Mario's fire-water. Glanced apprehensively at the French window, as if she saw the card party issue chattering forth to demand friendliness.

'Wonderful to . . .?' she asked vaguely. And answered, as if it didn't matter what you said because it couldn't matter what you thought: 'Oh, yes.' Then her mind turned another somersault. And what appeared to be much the same essence of the affair, mattered like life and death.

'Listen, I know more or less why you've come here. And I even have a hazy idea of why when I heard you were coming I stayed, this time. Why I waited. No, that's wrong.' The newly cleft lines between her eyebrows puckered. 'I was down in Florence. I mean, I have an idea why I came back up here, to be here when you arrived. I'd been down with the . . . Paquin was there, and Giuliana Feltre, and . . . Listen.'

'I am listening,' Jack said, smiling because he couldn't help it. Thinking how even a war, which had lasted six years in the West and three and a half in the East if you didn't count China and Manchuria, could blow away like a bank of fog. If you were alive. Seeing that brilliant-hued picture of a hay field where mowers leaned on their scythes, and two reservists pointed their rifles at a thin, ragged escaper asleep among the tawny stalks and the mole-hills and butterflies. Then seeing again Georgia's changeable, peaceless eyes fixed on his, and thinking this was right. Seeing her wide, sullen mouth, and thinking that was right too.

'I just want you to know, Jack, that it's no good thinking I'm any use, because I'm not. I mean, I'm all right when I'm being superficial. But that's the only one of my selves that it's all right for me to be.' She sipped. She clumsily shoved another cigarette into her holder, tapped its amber mouthpiece against her teeth. 'There's a whole lot of things you must hear from me. Oh, I know you. You've got your Norfolk to go back to, you're all right. But I haven't got my Shan Hills. You'll have your career, and a nice house, and . . . What you should do is fall in love with a nice girl and marry her and have some nice children. I know you. You'd like that, and you'd do it well.' Talking fast. Fumbling with her gold lighter. Her eyes never leaving his. 'I can't go back to live in Burma. Very right and proper too, I dare say. It just happens to be bad luck on people like me who were born there. It's funny, really, the way . . .' She laughed harshly enough to make Jack glance toward the French window. 'Funny how the men of the Fourteenth Army thought they were freeing Burma, but they were only freeing it from the Japanese. I mean, apart from a few contingents of Chins and Kachins who were fighting for their own paddy fields. Most of the men in that army weren't fighting and dying for a country they and their children were going to live in. Not that the Burmese, when they'd had the Japs for three years, didn't want the British to come and defeat them.' She shook her head, as if maddened by flies buzzing around in it. 'Well, now there's going to be Independence, and the country will be free at last of us and the Japanese, and they won't want people like me there. Daddy ought to have had me by a Shan girl. Then I could . . . But you've got your . . . Why aren't you at Edingthorpe? Why are you here? Oh God, I knew I should have run away.'

'Georgia . . . And if you could refrain from palming me off with some other girl? I know England isn't Burma; but . . .' Irrepressibly cheerful. For truly, this sensation of her lightly blowing soap-bubbles with what had been his being was far from disagreeable. 'There isn't much I can do about that – and there's always Italy. Georgia, my darling . . .' The wobbly sheens drifting away to come to grief against things. 'Will you marry me?'

She was on her feet, staring down at splintered glintings, the trickle of cognac on the marble.

'Oh *Christ*! My nerves make me so angry! And Mario's fond of these glasses.' Then her gaze homed back on Jack, who was on his feet too now, and she began to snarl at him. 'Oh, you don't have to ask me to marry you, you know. Others haven't been so p-p-particular. Haven't been so p-p-polite, by a long chalk, and I . . . Oh, I forgot, I haven't . . .'

Looking wildly around, and taking fright at the French window, Georgia set off down the terrace steps toward the cypress avenue. Rasping out her words all the time, so Jack had to hurry alongside her to hear them.

'I was in love with Christopher de Brissac – did your father tell you that? When times were bad, during the occupation, I'd write to him – or I'd pretend to. I'd start *Dear Godfather Charles* sometimes, like a good girl, and I'd summon him to me and I'd talk to him and he was a good spirit.' Clattering down the stone stair. Crunching headlong across the gravel. 'Yes, I was heels over head in love with Christopher – but I didn't know who he was. He wanted to marry me, and I said No because I felt free, and at first during the war I regretted that passionately. Then I didn't regret it any more, or certainly not passionately. I thought he was lucky to have avoided being hitched to someone as shallow as me. No, but what

I wanted to say was . . . He was the great love of my life, or what in this world passes for such, gets twittered about like that. Are you listening? But I didn't know who he was, and I still don't. His eyes were green, he was in the Coldstream Guards, but apart from that . . . His people came from Northumberland. He'd been seconded to the Commander-in-Chief's staff – Far East, that is. He had bony shoulders, and a bit of a drawl sometimes, and . . . These days, I don't even grieve for him very fiercely. I . . . Oh well, it comes and goes.'

They were off the gravel now, and into the avenue, where their footfalls were almost silent on the dry earth and the years' cypress sheddings. The tall sentinel trees shut out the moonlight. Jack could scarcely see the shadow that was Georgia. He reached out a hand, and found her arm. But she pulled it away.

'I told him about you, once.' She started laughing jaggedly again. But she broke it off, and said as brutally as she could: 'He said I ought to marry you, when the war was over. He said you'd be far more suitable for me than he was. I told him it was him I loved. And then . . . What was the other thing he said?' She stood, muttering to her memory. 'Oh, yes. How everything in his life always seemed to have happened fortuitously. Nothing much had ever gone as he'd planned. He hadn't even gone in, much, for making plans. He'd been who he'd happened to be, and things had just gone on happening. I expect that was how it was, with him, right to the end. Christopher was . . . He was a dignified man, but he had no arrogance. That's what I'd have loved him for, if I'd had any sense. Oh, I was only in love with an ideal, and . . . Jack, I shouldn't have forgotten you. You didn't forget me, I know you didn't. And now since the war has been over I've realised that I never idealised you, and between you and I there was – wasn't there? Is there? Oh God.'

Jack said with dogged courage: 'All that's the fog-bank that's blown away, Georgia. Why do you have to go on seeing it?'

'Yes, yes, I understand what you mean. But . . . That doesn't change the fact that I'm no good, now. I used to delight in the world so happily! Anything that changed – was alive, and went on changing! Down by Mandalay Shore at night, walking on my own I remember. It was safe, in those days. Poor houses, maybe with a kerosene lamp burning. People sleeping on mats, with their doors open. Cattle lying down in the muddy roads.'

'Georgia, you're . . . How old are you? Twenty-five? You can't spend the rest of your life being haunted by the past. You mustn't!'

'Oh, I don't know,' she replied. In her vague voice. Her refusing to consider that it might matter either way voice. And she picked up her thread again.

'I'd wander down to the river's edge, to the houses on stilts and the houses on pontoons. There'd be sampans tied up in the backwaters, and out there that vast flood of the Irrawaddy under the moon, and pagoda islands, and . . .'

The frown must have come back to her forehead. Jack couldn't see it, in the cypress darkness, but he could hear it.

'I had a sense of precariousness, too. Daddy had it, in his way, and I had it in mine, and . . . And I tried to explain it to Christopher, one night. At Pagan, that was. Though I don't know if he ever thought about it, afterwards. Well, my world was just vapour in my mind's eye, all right. And now I . . . I know I can't go on living like this indefinitely, that's another thing you don't need to tell me. No, don't kiss me. I was right – don't you see that's the pity of it? Right about how tenuous these meanings are, these . . . Oh, I don't know. I'm going to bed.'

He heard her quiet footfalls become silent. Heard, tossed over her shoulder: 'To my own bed.'

11

Jack went on walking in the black cypress avenue, with his head a maelstrom of how whatever those Japanese bastards had done to her, he was going to look after her. A maelstrom of how the war had cast adrift its innocent losers and had cast ashore its undeserving winners, and Georgia had lost her patch of Burma but he'd still got his patch of England – so of course he offered it to her. A maelstrom of how it was no use Mama going on telling him to *dance with all of them* like she had years ago when he'd just left Winchester. He was twenty-eight now, and next month he was starting with Rudd and Tench, in Prince's Street, with the prospect if all went well of becoming a junior partner in a few years.

Then in the roiled sea in his head there was Georgia saying Papa was a good spirit, in the war he'd been a good spirit to her. There was his own knowledge, which went right back to when he was a boy who idolised Horatio Nelson and sat up half the night carried away by *The Return of the Native*, that – and what was more, Georgia understood it too – that he was the steady sort of fellow who'd sooner or later want to get married.

The curious thing was, that neither then, pacing with his steps softened by cypress dust, nor lying sleepless in his bedroom, was Jack as discouraged as possibly he should have been. Nor the next morning – he must have slept a bit, because suddenly the sky was radiant – when he went down to breakfast so early that the table in the loggia hadn't yet been laid, so he helped Signora Annunziata do that and then they sat down together. Hardly discouraged at all . . . Because he was pretty sure that Georgia's furious coldness had been, not in her own defence, but to protect *him*. And if, deep down, she loved him that much . . . If that was her instinct . . . He could overcome that.

Signora Annunziata's husband, beside whom Giacomo Zanetti had used to labour in the orchards, had died during the war. But the old cook was made of sanguine stuff, and wore her widowhood with equanimity. For that matter, neither Pietro's and Raffaella's war-time heyday nor their deaths – neither the pride of the mind and the pride of the flesh, nor their humiliation – had made cracks in her stoical Catholicism, or impaired her appetite for breakfast and conversation.

The morning sunlight on the pillars of the loggia, and on the rolling countryside beyond. Coffee and toast. Honey from the estate's hives, peaches from its trees. Jack's heart-strings might be thrumming to strange music, but he still enjoyed his companion's chatter about how she remembered him not only from '39 when Emanuela and he had gone gallivanting off to bathe in the river, but from when he was, oh seven maybe. He and his little sister . . . Heavens how comic they'd been, imitating a cuckoo that had caught a cold, and couldn't cuck and couldn't oo. She remembered as if it had been yesterday. Pretending to be birds with sore throats, streaming noses, sodden handkerchiefs. *Cu-cu-cuck – SHOO!*

Jack smiled. Yes, he would have a third slice of toast. He was pleased to find his rusty Italian seemed to be up to a simple conversation of this sort. He took a nectarine, because the signora told him that to have only a peach was no sort of a breakfast, and anyhow this year the nectarines were a triumph. He thought about Georgia's rage of sarcasm and bitterness last night, and he took courage from thinking that these were wounds in her which love might slowly heal, and took courage from remembering her earlier in the box parterre. No railing about her love affair with de Brissac then – and anyway, for God's sake, it had been five or six years ago! And no running away. For that matter, all her avoiding him last year in England could be interpreted as . . . And yesterday she'd stood her ground. She had wept in his arms. *Jack. Oh, Jack.* And he couldn't really be all that surprised if, when he found her again after nine years, she was having an affair with someone. Yes, Mario was the issue that must be resolved. Right away. This morning. Hearing footsteps, Jack looked up buoyantly, boldly – but it was his cousin Ned, also an early riser. Well, so long as it was an affair, and not too much of a love affair. Yes, but even so . . .

The recognition that during the night he *had* identified his rival was sufficient to bring the blood surging to Jack's grey matter   normally the site of exemplary even-mindedness. Mario Zanetti, whom Papa and Mama had always praised to the skies. Mario with his good looks, with Villa Lucia, with – God damn it, the man was even a count!

By this time, Jack had thanked Signora Annunziata for a splendid breakfast, and they had agreed to resume their reminiscences the following morning. She was going to tell him about Signor Carlo (that was Papa) before he was married. He had splashed his hands and face under the kitchen tap, and the *maremmano* bitch Saba had decided to escort him, and he had struck off at a brisk pace down a track through the wood, to get rid of some pent-up – some pent-up something – just confusion probably. Because already he'd realised that he had no shred of a reason to suppose Mario and Georgia were lovers rather than friends. It was simply his jumpy imagination.

He must be sensible. Last night, Georgia hadn't once mentioned Mario.

Yes – but she wouldn't, would she? Discretion, simply. Leaving her lover his privacy, simply. Leaving him his freedom. Just as there'd been nothing proprietorial in the way Mario had left Georgia and him together to talk. And a Mario Zanetti who had come to mind about what had been done to Georgia during the war in the same sort of way that he minded. A Mario for whom she had been a wonderful discovery Who cared about her. Was gentle with her. Tried to help her forget her war nightmares . . .

Don't imagine it too vividly. It would be sensible instead to decide whether or not he'd been, last night, absurdly precipitate. *If you could refrain from palming me off with some other girl* . . . No – nothing precipitate about it. Georgia and he went back to their childhood. And when he'd asked her, he'd known it was right. And when she replied, and he'd heard the pain in her voice.

Not imagine too vividly. *To my own bed.* Notice, instead, how this far into the summer even the yellow broom on the hillsides was near the end of its season. Indeed, few plants of any kind were flowering, and no trees. Oh, except over there, in a cottage garden, there were clumps of hibiscus, with blue flowers and pink flowers. And try not to think of this landscape as the scene of a love affair – as lit up like that, treasured like that.

Remember how Georgia had fixed her eyes on yours when she'd been talking about Ricky. She swept her gaze all around the company, including Mario – but then it had been to him that she'd talked. About the Fourteenth Army's victories in Burma. Which, come to think of it, if we really were going to dismantle this ridiculous old empire – and with India and Burma and Ceylon getting Independence it looked as if we were going quite a way in that direction – and with Pakistan being invented . . . Those successes in Burma in '45 might turn out to have been about the last great victories of the old empire. After some equally great defeats three years before. Sunnis beside Shi'ites. High Church shoulder to shoulder with Presbyterians and Methodists. Sikhs and Hindus and Buddhists, and those who feared the jungle demons. To him, she'd spoken. Not to any other. To him – with her grief. With that intemperance in her words. That minding with such bitter pride, that there was a whole lower level of life she was beyond caring about.

He'd been Ricky's friend at school. The icon's friend. That was an advantage he had over Mario. Yes, and don't actually think of those two making love. Oh for God's sake, stop forgetting you haven't a clue whether they've ever made love. Good old Ricky, helping to cut down a Christmas tree. He'd have been on his side now, what was more. Tickled to death by the notion of his sister and his old friend . . .

Calling to Saba, and trying not to dwell on how sad it was that Ricky was dead, Jack turned back toward Villa Lucia. The morning was already getting hot, and today was the day for taking the initiative, and – he imagined the lunch party in the loggia, glasses being raised to Georgia.

Good, that resinous tang of cypress trees in summer sun. Good too – he crushed a spray of wild fennel in his fingers, and sniffed it – good all the high-summer scents. Good that today was the day for . . . 'Saba! Come here!' And look, there was a hoopoe, winging away.

Approaching the house again, Jack saw Mario standing in a vineyard with another man. Inspecting the grapes, by the look of it.

Jack hesitated a moment, and then strode that way. Mario saw him, and waved. They met at the corner of the field.

12

—⁂—

'Old Ludovico thinks we're going to be able to make better wine this autumn than last,' Mario said cheerfully, changing at once from his Tuscan Italian to his New England English. 'Been a long way? Glad you took Saba with you. She's been getting frightfully lazy.'

He took off his straw hat, mopped his forehead with his handkerchief. 'Ten o'clock, and it's hot already. You must have been walking fast, or . . .' Mario smiled at his guest, as they fell into step together. 'Has anything happened? You look a bit . . . I mean, if it's something I can ask about. A bit . . . strung-up about something.' And he settled his hat back onto his dark brown hair.

'I . . . Well, since you ask . . . You see – last night, after you left us, I asked Georgia if she'd marry me.'

'Good Lord!' Mario's urbanity was very nearly immaculate, and in a second he had brought his eyebrows back under control. He stopped, and with amusement already in his voice, he wondered: 'And . . . May I know what she said?'

Jack's blood was up, but he couldn't help liking Mario, and admiring him. The two men stood, their wills locked but playful, with the vineyard behind them, and the blue sky.

'She said . . .' He thought back. 'She did her best to put me off the idea. But I want to marry her.' Never – not during this minute of all minutes – would he let the amusement gleam less ironically in his eyes than in Mario's. 'So I'm going to ask her again. Only, so far today I haven't seen her. My fault, for getting up at an ungodly hour, and then charging off across the countryside. You don't, I suppose, know where she is?'

'Well . . .' The crows'-feet at the corners of Mario's eyes crinkled. 'She's not, so far as I am aware, engaged to marry anyone else. *E quindi . . .*' Spoken in his own language, and with a momentary sadness which belied his eyes. '*Dio mio, che . . . Ma no, ma niente.* So . . . I wish you luck. Although Georgia is . . . But you'll know this. Georgia is a free spirit.' As if, faced with a headstrong young man in love, making a point of it – Jack remembered, later. 'Very free. And, yes, to answer your question . . . I believe you'll find her at the cemetery. She told me she wanted to visit my sister's grave. Do you know where it is? Over the little bridge, and through the hazels, and you'll see its wall to your left.'

'Right. Thank you.' And then Jack smiled. 'Unless . . . Unless you'd rather talk to her, first, yourself.'

Mario exhaled a breath of laughter. He thought about it. Then: 'No, no. You go.'

The parish had never been a substantial one. Time out of mind, people had been being buried in that cemetery, but often at the rate of less than one every twelvemonth, and often only commemorated by their low mounds, which subsided after a few years, and by wooden crosses which were even less enduring. So only a few old graves marked by a stone cross or an angel could still be identified, and a few with engraved headstones, and the humbler ones which were recent enough not yet to have disappeared.

Days went by without anyone going near the place, Georgia had discovered, retreating there sometimes to be alone. And today she had been there for an hour, undisturbed. Enjoying the columns of the six or eight cypress trees, and the columns of shade they threw.

In the Villa Lucia garden, she had picked a few of the last roses of the summer, and here in the graveyard she had found a discarded jam-jar, and filled it from the standpipe by the gate. So Raffaella's grave – Raffaella Flamini, it said – now had a modest decoration.

There were quite a few Zanetti graves, and Georgia had paused a minute by Giacomo's, and remembered him encouraging her friendship with his dogs and her consumption of his peaches. Then she had settled by his daughter's place of burial, a few paces off. Had sat down on the short, dusty grass, in the resinous shade. Remembering how years ago, at Edingthorpe, Bobbie had picked up an Italian wedding invitation, and twirled it in his fingers, and asked his uncle: 'Are you going?' Remembering how, though only sixteen, in a flash she had *known*. From Bobbie's voice . . . From the two men's glances . . . From Godfather Charles' voice, when he demurred: 'Oh, no, I don't think so.' And immediately after, from a plethora of recollected signs.

However, Georgia was not so peacefully reflective that she didn't stand up nervously when she saw Jack come through the gate. Although, having wrestled with her Eastern dead last night, and having this morning spoken more mildly with her Western living and dead, her mood was one of new simplicity.

He said, 'Mario told me I'd find you here.' Standing before her, with his straight shoulders, and the clear-cut lines of his face, and his level gaze. Speaking his direct thoughts. 'I . . . I told him why I wanted to find you.

Told him what I'd asked you yesterday, and what I was going to ask you again today. And I . . . I also suggested to him that, if he wanted to, he should come and talk to you before I did.'

Georgia walked away, slowly. She turned by the wall, and came slowly back. She said: 'I'm not Emma Hamilton, you know. You two can't simply hand me between yourselves as you see fit.'

'Good God, I know that. But it's not my fault that you were here when I found you.'

'No, that's true. Oh, by the way . . .' But not uttered with her last night's brutality. 'If you're interested . . . For a year or more the idea of men, the idea of a man . . . I'm getting better, slowly. Though I still have dreams. Oh, and . . . I had a gynaecologist give me a check-up. It seemed a – a good idea. It appears that, although I'm probably half mad, so far as they can tell no l-l-lasting – no d-d-damage much . . . If anyone did want, want to marry me, the doctor said I was n-n-normal enough.'

Jack was blushing. 'Oh, I wasn't thinking about . . . But that's wonderful. Listen, Georgia.' Taking her hands in his. 'Will you marry me?'

She stood straight, still. Her eyes meeting his with perfect clarity. Then, slowly: 'What do you think, Jack?' With a twist of a smile. 'My head full of clouds, and your head where the stories mean a bit more. Is a marriage between them possible? And . . . I've been afraid you might just be sorry for me. You know you mustn't ever be, don't you?'

'Certainly I'm sorry for you. But the reason I want to marry you is more to do with the way you blow soap-bubbles with me.'

'What?' A whisper of laughter. 'Well, that's all right, then. I . . . For me . . . I'm longing to marry you. I only – but I said all that last night.'

Then the blue and white checks of his shirt were all interchangeable in the sunlight and the shade with the blue of hers. And unnoticed by either of them, a butterfly jinked, and a finch flew by.

'Let's get married soon. Right away.'

'Oh – whenever you like. Yes . . . Sooner, later.' She stood back. 'There's still one thing, Jack. During the war, I wrote a lot of nonsense. For your father, as I told you, and for . . . other people. It's all at Edingthorpe. If Godfather Charles hasn't burnt it. You . . . Please . . . You must read it. Then you'll know what sort of a ghost I'll be, to be married to. And then, if you still want me, I'll marry you.'

13

'An *October* wedding, Blanche dearest?' Sarah Hedleigh had taken her surprise at this conjunction of the hymenial with the autumnal no farther than that.

As for Georgia Burney perhaps being a less than ideal choice on Jack's part. Her having in some quarters a reputation which . . . Not to speak of her being, some people had gone so far as to say, an absolute nervous wreck in need of psychiatric help. And silly with it. Having found nothing better to do – and with war-time rationing still in force! – than to fritter away the few thousand pounds her parents had left her. Buying fancy clothes. Leading a jazzy life in London and Paris and Florence. Well, it seemed it would not be the first time, Lady Hedleigh had been informed by Lady Waveney, (still seraphically unaware that half Norfolk knew her as Duchess Sludge) – not the first time that young woman had used her charms to get herself out of fixes she'd got herself into.

However, Sarah did not sympathise too fulsomely with Blanche for the imperfections of her son's fiancée: because she was feeling rather vulnerable on that sort of score herself. Wonderful Frederick had of course done *exactly* the right thing when he'd married that *sweet* girl Lucy Carmichael, whose father had *all* the shares in Banda Oil. And a mine in – was it in the Orange Free State? Well, he had another in the Transvaal, anyway. A mine with *lots* of diamonds in it, apparently.

But poor Mark, who'd lost an arm in the Arakan, darling Mark with people saying slanderous things about him. And Caroline, who had taken *ages* to pull herself together, and stop bursting into tears all the time, and realise that she couldn't just not marry anybody. It was going to be Bill Scott, almost certainly. Well, it *could* have been worse. Scott was *just* a gentleman. (Sometimes, Sarah said he was *almost* a gentleman. It depended who she was talking to.) And to give him his due, considering that his father had started from absolutely nowhere with absolutely nothing, the chap now had a farm at Skyton, and another at Meeting Hill. And there was nothing like land, Sarah had always said. Though the City – and of course Julian and Freddie were both *quite* brilliant . . .

Blanche Lammas never denied that she had felt a shock of disappointment when a letter arrived from Jack in Italy announcing that he was engaged to Georgia, and he would be home shortly to look for a house. She loved Georgia. And, regarded from one point of view, that her son should marry her goddaughter, poor Geraldine's girl – what could be nicer? As for Georgia's reputation, Blanche was guided wholly by her husband, and therefore never gave a second's credence to the vile rumours. If the girl had been forced into hideous situations, and had been treated criminally, Blanche had nothing but compassion for her – laced with sorrow, and anger.

Even so, she was in a passion of anxiety for Jack. That out of boyhood love, out of loyalty, out of feeling sorry for her, he should shackle himself for life to someone who might be innocence incarnate but was also innocence dreadfully injured. A girl who spoke in wild tirades, trembling, stuttering. Who saw things that other people didn't see, and fell to the hearth-rug screaming words you couldn't make head or tail of.

Charles Lammas never wavered. 'Those two love one another,' he'd say. Or, 'I reckon they're right for each other, those two.' Though it was not easy to identify any facts which he might have among the instincts underpinning his contentment with the engagement. Blanche challenged him on that once. He replied that Georgia and Jack, whatever else they might be, were both of such blazing honesty that he'd trust them.

Still, he had a hard time convincing Henrietta. When they were all still children, Georgia had appeared from Burma and taken possession of her brother – that's what she couldn't stop it feeling like to her. And now Georgia had come back from there again to possess him again. After nine years apart, he hadn't been able to see her for twenty-four hours without asking her to marry him! Henrietta knew she ought not to yield to this recrudescence of her old sense of rivalry, ought not to feel displaced – but she did.

It was better when Jack returned to Edingthorpe. And he did not remain long at Villa Lucia. Just time enough for his visit not to appear too obviously a raid. Long enough for Contessa Chiara to confess to her old friend, in the seclusion of the small drawing-room: 'My dear Edmund, you will allow that I may be a tinge relieved? What is more, unless I am much mistaken this will jolt Emanuela and her young man into action.' Long enough for that old Edwardian rake to announce to the betrothed couple that he had no intention of travelling to England for their wedding, but that he would be delighted to offer them his house at Rapallo for their honeymoon.

Jack left his fiancée to wind up her Italian sojourn in her own time. To say goodbye to Mario. But that clearly was a friendship which was going to last. And in the days after their conversation by the vineyard, Jack and he had ridden together, had talked about architecture and painting together, had played backgammon together. To say goodbye to the Tuscan late summer-time – the thunder-storms and the sultry days, the hibiscus time, the wasp time.

As soon as Jack got home, he started work in Norwich. He spent his evenings and his weekends helping his mother with the preparations for the wedding.

This was a happy period for both of them. Because as soon as Blanche saw her son's tranquil eyes and heard his sanguine talk, she began to feel convinced that this marriage was going to be a successful one. What was more, with the bride an orphan, and Charlie so ill with his heart trouble that all he ever did was sit on the terrace when the weather was fine and in the library when it was wet, the task of staging a wedding at shortish notice without spending a fortune fell principally to the bridegroom's mother.

Henrietta helped too. It was one of her ways of deciding that of course she was going to love Georgia as her sister-in-law. It was a way of being especially loyal to Jack, at a season when it had suddenly become of overwhelming importance to her to be so. So the three of them would set forth, in the antiquated Morris which Jack had bought, to scour the countryside for a cottage which he could afford. It was merry, stopping in the familiar villages to ask people, and finding houses they hadn't known about, and disputing the merits of this parish or that.

Money was the problem. As for the wedding itself, Georgia had sent Blanche a cheque for most of the remaining hundreds of her Burney pounds, and Charles had sent one of his last remaining oil paintings up to Perry Bracknell. Of late, he'd only done the occasional watercolour drawing, on days when he felt a bit stronger; and though Bracknell could sell these, they only fetched moderate prices. So Lammas got rid of his more considerable work as infrequently as he could. And he certainly wasn't making enough money to help his son buy a house. A fact which annoyed him, and made him feel humiliated and useless, and did nothing to help the gloomy moods he'd been succumbing to more and more.

At first, Jack thought he would rent a place. His starting salary at Rudd and Tench was modest to a degree, but rents were low. However, Mr Tench pointed out to him that it would be more sensible to pay the instalments on a mortgage, and the firm offered to help him with the initial sum required.

So thus minimally armed, his mother and his sister and he drove from village to village in the warm September evenings. (Honestly, if it continued this blue and golden, an autumn wedding was going to be heavenly, everyone said so.) And in due course they found a cottage for sale in Worstead which they all agreed would do splendidly.

It was a village they'd always liked, with one of the most magnificent mediaeval churches in the county, and only about five miles from Edingthorpe. The cottage was of flint and red brick, with a small garden. Hetty declared herself so enamoured of it that she was ready to sell the Arab harness Jack had sent her from Palestine in order to secure it for him, and if that wasn't enough she'd cut off her hair and sell that too, only please could she not have to cut it off till after the wedding.

It was a hectic month, what with Jack at Worstead getting his cottage painted, and anyhow partially furnished, and immediately going to live in it. What with the Edingthorpe household being plunged into wedding preparations. For if Georgia were not married from the Manor, her godmother demanded, where *could* the poor waif be married from? Her rented flat in London? Most emphatically not! And Blanche remembered a wan, home-sick child of twelve, and a stormy December day at Paston when they'd taken her wreath to lay at Michael's window. An on-shore gale at nightfall she remembered; and herself feeling none too cheerful; and a lonely little girl saying that if she ever got married she hoped it would be at home in Burma.

So Sidney Meade – having made Henrietta promise that when she got married it would be in early summer – was working from morning till night to ensure that even an autumn garden would have its attractions. Ellen Meade – with Janet Fox, returned part-time for a few weeks – was getting ready to feast a hundred-odd guests. (Luckily the party couldn't be much bigger than that, or not all the wedding guests would be able to get into the church.) Mrs Grimes, the farrier's wife, rallied round to help too; and half the men and women of Edingthorpe offered to lend a hand when the great day came.

Then there was the marquee to put up. Not such a palatial pavilion as had graced one of the lawns at Bure Hall when Caroline had been married twelve years ago. A small, slightly weather-beaten marquee; which had for years done service at Aylsham show, and at Bawdeswell point-to-point, and other such rural occasions; and which Bill Meade helped Jack to hire for a most favourable fee.

Jack talked to Mr Miller, the parson, about having the banns read, and about which hymns should be sung. He talked to Sidney about how to decorate a church in autumn without making the place look as if nobody had tidied up after Harvest Thanksgiving.

He asked Tim Farne to be his best man. And suddenly found himself struggling to keep back his tears. Because although Tim was far the best friend he'd made in the regiment, and had been terrific company on that ride through the defile to Petra . . . Bobbie had been in Palestine with them too. And his cousin, Jack knew, would have been the right best man for him.

He asked Hetty if she would read the lesson. He asked Mr Rudd and Mr Tench if he might have next year's holiday this year, so he could take his bride to Rapallo for three weeks – and luckily they agreed.

It was splendid to be installed in his cottage, even if it sometimes felt as if he were perpetually driving or biking between Worstead and Edingthorpe. Then he discovered that his kitchen range smoked whenever the wind blew from the west. Then the pump broke down. And in the thick of all this, Georgia arrived.

14

As far as Jack was concerned, he had been married to Georgia ever since she'd said she would marry him, in the graveyard half a mile from Villa Lucia. Still, he was calmly happy about going through any formal motions his society might require of him. He'd even, before leaving Tuscany, remembered to ask Georgia whether she fancied North Walsham registry office or Edingthorpe church. She had replied that it made no odds to her. Whichever his family would prefer. The church, therefore. And so the matter had been decided.

Even so, the number of things Jack had to attend to in the space of a very few weeks amazed him, and the number of things he had to pay for and how much each of them cost. He had moments of being amazed, too, at the whirl of activity on Georgia's and his behalf which so many other people at once plunged into, apparently all knowing what it was they should do, and doing it quite naturally. And all the time he was buoyed up by the knowledge singing in his head – well, it was almost knowledge – he was buoyed up by the idea that if he threw his energies into doing all these tremendously necessary things he was going to prove to be one of the deep-down survivors, and what was more Georgia was going to be too. If he had anything to do with it . . . If he outlived Alan Purvis' panic in the Eichstätt tunnel, outlived those screams, and he himself become a half-panicked savage animal crashing his boot at that screaming head. If he threw himself into his job, and into getting married to Georgia and loving her . . . She was going to be one of the deep-down survivors too, if it was the last thing he did. Forget the horror of that mole-run. Remember crawling out of the tunnel's mouth into that thicket, with the stars overhead. Remember waiting crouched for the sentry to pass along the perimeter fence behind you, and waiting for the search-light to swing, and remember slipping away into the dark.

Right up to his wedding day, new things he had to do kept cropping up – one of the last being to shoot as many pigeons as he could. Which he had not imagined to be among a bridegroom's duties. But it was. Because Ellen had decided that the principal dish at the wedding lunch should be her famous pigeon pie. Ten of them would be prepared, and cooked on the wedding morning in the Manor's oven and in nine other ovens about the parish. Not to mention all the dishes of vegetables, and the number of loaves of her special bread which Ellen would bake. So it stood to reason that Bill Meade, and Jack, and Grimes the farrier, and old Davey Strike from Smallburgh fen, must in the first week of October shoot a quantity of pigeon which should enable the party to be royally feasted. And it was not surprising that Jack forgot a number of essential things, such as an engagement ring.

However, fortunately Blanche had noticed that particular omission of his, and gave him the ring set with rubies which had been her mother's engagement ring. It was in his pocket when he met Georgia's train at Norwich station.

'Is it all right?' she demanded. Before she would kiss him. Standing on the busy platform, looking at him with fear in her gaze.

'Is what all right? Heavens, Georgia, is something the matter? What on earth do you mean?'

'Oh *God!*' she cried, loud enough to make two porters break off their talk to stare at her. 'Oh God, you haven't read it! I must go back to London, I . . .'

'Oh, that!' Jack would have laughed with relief, if he hadn't seen the despair in her eyes, suddenly shot through with flarings of anger. 'Your war writings. Papa had burned them. Look, if I take your suitcase, and you take my arm . . . Let's get out of the station, shall we? My darling, you're trembling like a leaf.'

'So would you be if . . .! Christ, you could have told me!'

'Didn't I? Lord, what with one thing and another I've been a bit . . . Yes, he'd burned them. I have an idea . . . Here's the car. Of course, I may be wrong. I have a suspicion they existed till quite recently. That he burned them after he'd received my letter saying that we were engaged. And, my darling, from the little he's told me . . .' Jack heaved her suitcase into the car. Smiled at her with that buoyancy of his which had never ailed much, and that month was luckily indomitable. 'If I'd read them, I'd love you even more, if that were possible.'

Silent, quivering, Georgia sat beside him as he drove to Edingthorpe. When they reached the village, she said: 'Jack, I'm . . . I'm in no sort of shape to meet your father and mother right now. Can we . . .? Shall we go up to the church, where we're going to be married? I haven't been there since . . .' She tried to laugh. 'Since that old world before the war. Oh God, my nerves. I've left my flat, did I tell you that? All my kit is in a couple of trunks, they're on their way.' She frowned, marshalling her concentration. 'You know about Caroline giving me her wedding dress, I remember writing to you about that. Only Lady Hedleigh got cross, so I had to give it back, and now Caroline's only lending it to me. It's had to be altered, of course. If you'd had any sense, you'd have gone for a girl with a bosom like hers. But poor old Jack, you've got me. Oh, look, is that Sonny Hannant?' She waved to him, as Jack drove past the Manor gates and on to the track up to the church. 'And I've been to Cambridge, to see Henrietta. I . . . I think she believes me when I tell her how much I . . . She will come to believe. She'll *see* that it's true. Only then I felt such a fool for trying to explain.'

'Well done, going to visit Hetty.' Jack parked by the lych-gate, and jumped out. 'Now, come and see where you're going to be the star of the show.'

'Very strange, the bride being married from the groom's house.' Georgia laughed nervously. 'Still, there are stranger things about this.'

But then they did not go into the church, but strolled on the knoll in the sunshine, with the sea in the distance, and stubble fields all around. The oak trees were greeny gold. A kestrel was hovering.

'So he burned them. He really . . . Are you *sure*? No, of course he burned them. And I've been giving you time to read them! I've been tormenting myself with what you might be thinking of me! I've been expecting you to write to . . . Just Georgia being an idiot again, that's all.' With her laughter at herself coming in fits and starts; but coming. 'You should have seen my hands shaking when I picked up my letters!'

'Look, my darling, I'm *sorry* I forgot to tell you.' Jack grinned at her with cheerful exasperation. 'But surely you know that nothing you could conceivably ever have done or written could make the smallest bit of difference to us? Why, you don't mind Papa throwing the stuff in his fire, do you? He told me you'd said he could. It's just . . . Oh, I don't know, but . . . It's just the fog blowing away. And when it comes to that, *he'd* read what you wrote during the war – and even I only just manage to have a higher opinion of you than he does.'

'Oh, no, I don't mind. But . . .' She faced him, with a wry smile. 'But it was true what I said, about how I'm a bit ghostly. Or – or I've got the sort of head which is all stories and no certainties. Terrible psychological defect, I shouldn't be surprised. I've always been a bit like that, but then the war . . . A head which is all stories being pieced together and then falling to pieces again. And I wanted you to understand what the war had been like in *that* way. About my facts which are always being dispelled, or . . . Half mad – I told you. My stories which are always being told differently, and can't die away without coming back to me, and can't come back without dying away again. Oh I don't know. I'll try to tell you a little, bit by bit, about the mad-woman you're marrying.'

'Tell me what you like, or nothing at all. And I've got a mass of things to tell you. Marvellous story about a wryneck migration. And, Georgia – right now, if you don't mind, I'd rather kiss you than talk to you.'

So kissing, and sauntering, and kissing again, they ended up sitting on a grassy bank by the lych-gate. Where Jack suddenly shoved his hand into his pocket, and exclaimed, 'Heavens, I'd quite forgotten!'

He took out the ruby ring, and put it on her finger. 'Now,' he asked, 'will you agree that the war is over? I mean, as well as agreeing to marry me, and even try to love me a little, and let me love you like crazy, and all that stuff?'

Georgia drew a deep breath. She looked out over the patchwork of meadows and spinnies. 'The war is over. It's – it's in the past.' Then, she nearly cried. But this time her tears did not come. 'And . . . And I'm sorry I've taken so long to succeed in saying it. I love you.'

Then, punctuated by kisses: 'Are you sure you're not going to be terribly bored, living in the country here?' And, 'A survivor like me? An escaper like me? I'm grateful to any society that'll give me a chance. We're fantastically lucky to be alive, Jack, you and I – that's the miracle never to forget. Just catch my eye, sometimes, at dinner parties. Now, how soon are you going to take me to Worstead, to see where we're going to live?'

Followed by: 'Just think – Rapallo!' Kiss. 'Claudia looks adorable in her bridesmaid's dress, but three is awfully young. Still, Caroline and I have been practising her again and again.'

15

—ɯ—

Georgia refused to let Jack be present at her first meeting with Charles Lammas as his prospective daughter-in-law. At the library door, she became agitated again, and muttered, 'No, no, I've got to do this on my own.'

So her fiancé never knew that when his father was greeting her in his most gruff, old Naval officer manner – 'Well, godchild. Congratulations' – and those sea-and-sky eyes of his were glinting with love for her, she broke down completely. Wept and wept. Sitting in the chair beside his, by the fire where he had burned her war, burned her oubliette whisperings. Wept for her mother and her brother whom she'd never really known very well. For de Brissac, whom she had known so little. For her father, whom at the end she had come to know better. For Burma. For herself. Wept, and stammered to her godfather that if he didn't want her to marry Jack she wouldn't. If she was too d-d-damaged. Honestly, she'd break it off, she promised to do whatever he said.

So that Lammas had to summon all his control, and had to play the good-hearted elderly gentleman very consciously indeed for a minute or two. 'Heavens, my dearest Georgia, it's the *right* consummation! Don't *dream* of breaking it off. Good Lord . . .' And he chuckled. 'Don't take this away from me. It's about the only cheerful thought I ever have. Oh, sweet girl, don't cry so terribly. Here, borrow my handkerchief. Quite clean.' And then, meditatively: 'Never did lack guts, though, did you?' And, 'Strange. You're the third person who's wanted me to say whether they should get married or not.'

She dried her eyes. When she had recovered enough strength to refer to her dead, she said carefully: 'Then . . . Then I want to ask you something. With Daddy dead, I haven't got anyone to give me away. I know you're the groom's father, and I expect it's all wrong. But they can't expect me to walk up the aisle all on my own. And you're my godfather. Will you? I'd like it very much, if you would give me away.'

'Oh, I dare say you're right about it being a *little* unconventional to give away a bride to one's own son. But don't let's bother about that for a second. I should be *delighted* to, Georgia. What a happy idea. In the place of my old best man . . . I shall be honoured.' And afterwards, when calm and happy she had stood up to leave him, and was gazing at that Samothracian pride, that step, those wings. In his gruffest manner.

'You're the victrix all right. Well done. Now – off you go to Blanche, to talk about your bouquet and your veil.'

In those last whirligig days before the wedding, Jack was pleased to see how sometimes Georgia would slip away from the bustle to go and sit with his father. He was pleased too by how well his mother and Georgia were getting on.

That week, Blanche Lammas found all her heart astir. Old sorrows and joys came into it . . . Because she couldn't help to prepare Georgia for her wedding to Jack, (the dress still required a few finishing touches, so the North Walsham seamstress had to be enlisted), without remembering her own wedding after the last war, with Tom Carraway dead, and Michael dead. Because from Edingthorpe church if you looked down the long slope you could *see* Paston church . . . If she'd needed any nudging to bring back that day when the sunlight had streamed through her brother's memorial window. Because then she remembered Mary Oldfield – who would have rejoiced in this marriage, Blanche couldn't doubt it. Because the glorious dress, which Georgia was now trying on for what they all hoped would be the last time, while the seamstress tweaked here and pinned there, had been Bobbie's bride's dress, and . . . That was a thought at which Blanche had to gaze firmly out to the garden, and try to think of something exceedingly merry.

Other, newer feelings came to her. After his stroke and his two heart attacks, truly it was practically a miracle that Charlie was alive. But Blanche could not help knowing that she was probably going to be left a widow while she was still in her fifties. And in the shadow of that almost-certainty, her heart could get so turbulent that she could barely speak when she kept noticing how Georgia and Jack were so splendidly enchanted with each other. How determined the girl was to be a good daughter-in-law. How this forthcoming marriage really did seem to bring Charlie flickerings of the sort of happiness which had become rare in him. Although it was disgraceful, how he teased her about longing to be a grandmother. Why *shouldn't* she think it would be nice if Georgia had a baby before too long? Of course, right now she was all chatter about the useful things she was going to pitch into doing the minute they got back from their honeymoon. But after that. *In the midst of* . . . Anne had been absolutely right. *In the midst of death we are in life.*

Blanche was so busy from every dawn till long after dusk, she had little leisure for reflection. What was it Charlie had once said she was? A pantheist, that was right. She'd forgotten what it meant exactly. Anyway, there were the trestle tables for the marquee to see about, and Mrs Morter and Mrs Grimes who wanted to have another consultation about church flowers when she'd hoped everything had been decided. Then the guest list – who was to be placed where on which table at lunch. Poor Georgia had only had about half-a-dozen names to suggest, when they'd been sending out invitations. She'd been all in a fluster till she'd heard that David and Tamsin Shaughnessy had accepted; but apart from them . . . Everyone she'd known appeared to be in other countries, or dead. Then the cases of wine, which the delivery men had just dumped down in the yard – where should Sidney be told to put them? And the extra crockery and cutlery. And the lawns. Which had been mowed – and anyhow, at this time of year . . . Still, Sidney *must* remember to go out with a spade on the morning, because she *refused* to have mole-hills.

In amongst all this happy flurry, Blanche was aware that something of enormous moment was going forward. The knowledge would come to her – imprecise, unmistakable. Would come at the oddest moments . . . When she was reminding Georgia that on the Gulf of Genoa in autumn it could easily rain, so they ought to pack their mackintoshes. Or when Jack was saying that in Norwich he'd remembered to go to Bullen's to pick up the wedding ring, and he'd remembered the tickets from Dover to Calais, but could she remember, what was the third thing he'd meant to do? And she'd be answering, 'I haven't a clue, but don't forget to check that both your passports don't expire next week.' And she would know – it must be bred in the bone, she supposed – that this rite was vital, it was life itself, it was . . . 'Claudia's sash? No – isn't it with her other clothes? Oh, heavens . . .'

Still, it was a relief that Georgia, who'd been dreadfully wrought-up when she'd arrived, had clearly got over whatever the crisis had been. These days, she was merriment itself. Bicycling over to Worstead to tinker with the cottage's furnishings. To get Jack's supper ready, for when he came home from work. To rock to and fro on the swing, which the previous owner had left in the cherry tree. Bicycling back here to Edingthorpe in the evening, to ask what flowers they ought to plant in that little patch of garden of theirs. Her sullen look seemed to have been quite banished, and her eyes were calm – so that promised well, Blanche would think. And she'd go back to reassuring Ellen that pigeon pie and apple crumble were a lunch fit for a king, (nobody wanted fancy dishes, they wanted what they knew they liked), or to helping her ice the wedding cake.

Then she must persuade Jack to try on that morning coat to make sure it still fitted him, because if not the seamstress could be besought to do some last-minute adjusting. Of course, it *would* still fit him perfectly. But it would be nice to see him looking handsome in it, and an excuse to remind him he must wear his gold watch and chain.

Henrietta must have a fuss made over her new dress and hat. She herself was going to have to rustle up something suitable to wear, and . . .

What were Georgia and Caroline giggling about now? Hetty too — tears of laughter in her eyes. The noise those three made, when they were being silly!

Oh, the aisle. Well, yes . . . And Blanche too would begin to laugh.

Because it really did look as if it might be going to be quite funny getting this bride to the altar at all. What with Charlie, who hadn't walked without a stick for three years, but who was insisting he was going to on this occasion. So Georgia had said, 'You can lean on my arm. No one will know.' And he'd said, 'Certainly not! But if I fall down, be a good girl and give me a hand up.' And what with Claudia, who despite repeated instruction only *sometimes* seemed to know what she was supposed to do.

16

—⚬—

That last year of his life, Charles Lammas spent a lot of his time in a twilit zone between waking and sleeping. By his library fire. Upstairs in his dressing-room, with its iris wallpaper. With the framed drawing of a woman by Tissot, which had remained propped against the looking-glass. In shadowy intermittences, sometimes able to order his thoughts a little. Half-seeing, half-understanding.

The night before the wedding, at first when Lammas lay in his bed he felt tranquilly conscious of how lucky he'd been. Nine years, since he'd had that stroke, and had lain here with his right arm out of action, and then had begun to be able to move his fingers along the iris stems. Nine years of life, of luck. And now, with Henrietta doing so well in her postgraduate work at Cambridge. With Jack, with Georgia . . . *Seeing there be many things that increase vanity*. Yes, but this wedding was not vanity. He'd always liked the innocence of wedding preparations. And then the ritual itself . . . Celebrations of the innocence in us. Though doubtless hard-headed fellows like Giacomo and Alex would take a more ironical view. Would have taken. Should he switch his light off now, and hope to sleep?

He imagined the pallor of the marquee, out in the night garden. There'd been a few showers of rain today, so quite likely tomorrow . . . The church, on the upland, among its trees. The dark church swept and bedecked, with the printed service cards laid out ready in the pews. The darkened country, with maybe a fox crossing a field, or a gliding owl. The cliff. Gulls asleep. The sea, lapping.

Lammas must have drowsed, because he saw a wedding invitation where someone had written something in pencil, so you could rub it out. Words from . . . He strained his eyes, but he couldn't read the sentence, or it was in a language he'd forgotten. Meanings which . . . No, he couldn't read it. And now Jack was saying something about Trafalgar weather, only Nicky Muir was there too, on a verandah in the hot Maltese night, and that was strange because hadn't he been drowned before Jack was born? Moist, tender mouth, weak as the eyes. Leaning toward him . . .

Lammas swam, salt water splashing in his face, his lungs heaving. Arms that ached, heart that juddered. It was after him, in that sea where men disintegrated. It. He swam, he swam, but ahead he couldn't make out – he'd never find . . . After him. Gaining. Close behind, now. Glittering murk in his eyes, but there must be a conning-tower, there!

He woke up, gasping, his limbs jerking. God, his heart. No, wait. The light was still on. What was the time? Scarcely one o'clock! He'd got hours of night to go on lying here through. Mustn't go to sleep. Anyhow not for a while. Pyjamas clammed to him with cold sweat. Horrible. Bloody padre, and . . . Looked like the Marmara was going to get him after all, in the end.

Think of cheerful things. Yes, but these were the bad hours, it wasn't easy. These were *the sons of men snared in an evil time*. Stop that.

Think of Jack, sleeping in his cottage, with his morning coat hanging up ready for the morning. With his clean white shirt put out, and his cufflinks, and his tie. Trousers ironed, black shoes polished – all ready for the future.

Think of Georgia, close here, a couple of bedroom doors away. Awake, possibly. Or drifting from dream to dream. Let her not think of Christopher. Let her not cry again for a wooden church in the Shan Hills. Yes, and don't you think of Christopher either, or Geoffrey. We don't want headless men, in the bad hours.

Remember, 'On the starboard bow, Sir.' Remember, 'You there, Lammas?' Remember they came, that time, they raised you up. Yes, but they wouldn't always come.

17

—ɯ—

It was not long before midday, and most of the wedding guests were already in the church. The women eyed each others' dresses and hats, and there was a lot of anticipatory chatter. The men who had been wearing top-hats had placed them on the pews beside them. Some of the smaller children kept clambering up onto the pews to peer back toward the door.

Tim Farne, the best man, was taking his responsibilities extremely seriously. He had been at Worstead early that morning, to make sure the bridegroom ate a proper breakfast. He had been solemnly entrusted with the ring – since which, every quarter of an hour he had again checked that it was safely tucked away in his waistcoat pocket.

Now he was regarding his watch almost sternly, as he decided that he would walk Jack once more around the perimeter of the earthen banks which surrounded the graveyard. If, then, by those firs at the far corner, they paused a moment to admire the sea in the distance, and then proceeded on their circuit, Tim reckoned they'd be up the church path and in through the door at precisely fifteen minutes to twelve.

Jack had once or twice hoiked out an old gold time-piece in a distracted sort of fashion. When it came to soldierly efficiency, Timothy Farne preferred to put his trust in his own watch, which was modern and made of steel. And soldierly efficiency was what was called for, he made no question of that. Lord above, if two old officers of one of the finest tank regiments that had ever gone into an attack – Tim recalled El Alamein, he recalled Normandy, his heart swelled – couldn't get themselves to the church dead on the nail of eleven-forty-five . . . The first British unit to fight its way onto German soil God damn it – Tim had been there, he remembered. And now lucky old Jack was marrying this smashing girl . . . He had been introduced to Georgia yesterday, and her slightly pouting lips, and her tilted nose, and her opaque eyes, had made a profound impression on him.

So the two friends strode around the outside of the churchyard, trying not to get their shoes too muddy. The best man thought the bridegroom could do with a spot of teasing, so he said, 'I bet you'd really rather be back sailing that dhow off Acre.' Jack grinned, and said, 'Well it'd be all right, wouldn't it, if we could have Georgia and the parson on board?'

Then, to show that he was perfectly capable of taking an intelligent interest in other matters, the best man remarked that he supposed these earthworks could easily have been Saxon. Subsided almost completely now. But long ago . . .?

Yes, the groom replied, or even ancient British conceivably. He started talking in an animated but disjointed manner about how it appeared from archaeological evidence that Edingthorpe had been a site of habitation time out of mind.

His friend considered neolithic pottery was a curious subject to launch into at this moment. Still, he listened with a smile to how on the gun-room wall there hung a map of East Anglia which showed prehistoric something-or-other. He interrupted to tell Jack that he was perfectly ridiculous, the way he kept glancing toward the lane from the Manor.

So they completed their circuit, and by the lych-gate halted to wipe the mud off their shoes.

'By the way, Jack old lad, you know that when we walk through that door, every single person in the church is probably going to turn round and look at us?'

'Good God, I hadn't thought of that. How unkind people are! Got the ring, haven't you?'

'Don't be an idiot, of course I've got it. Still, no harm in check-ing. Now, let's have a look at you. Your tie is tied. That white rose in your buttonhole has lent its colour to your face, but . . . You'll do.'

'She's coming! Look!'

Smiling, Jack pointed to where a car had appeared half a mile off near the Manor trees at a corner of the lane.

'I can see a car, yes. But how do you know she's in it? All right, all right, cheer up. Now, here we go.'

Sonny Hannant, who was the verger, was ringing the church bell, with steady heaves at the rope, and reminiscing to George Morter about the night when they'd thought the Germans might invade and Mr Lammas had told him to ring the bell to call out the Home Guard. Frederick Hedleigh and Hugh Farne, who were the ushers, had solved the problem posed by the bride's having no family and practically no friends. They had simply not asked the wedding guests as they arrived, 'Bride or groom?' but had shown people to suitable pews with such cheerful friendliness that almost nobody had noticed this small divergence from etiquette. The only person who was disappointed was Mario Zanetti, who with his sister Emanuela, but not her fiancé, had travelled a thousand miles to represent the Italian connection; and who had been looking forward to declaring 'Bride!' in a ringing voice.

Their task accomplished, the two ushers were lounging in the sunny porch, and agreeing that those little clouds in the offing probably didn't signify rain, or anyway not for an hour or two. They were far more in tune with events than the groom, and much enjoyed telling him that his bride would not be in the car this time. In it would prove to be his mother and his sister, with Caroline and little Claudia. Then Meade was going to drive back to the Manor, to fetch Georgia and her godfather.

However, the ushers were most firm about ordering Jack and Tim off up the nave to make themselves agreeable to the parson in the chancel. Then they settled back on the porch benches, and stretched their immaculately clad legs, and resumed their discussion of who, at this particular wedding, was winning the hat competition. Freddie was afraid that his mama had really rather overdone it this time. But Patricia Bosky's headgear was of an understated elegance which might carry the day. Or his own darling Lucy's hat – but naturally he was prejudiced. While Hugh, who had decided that come what might he was going to kiss Frances Ash before the day was over, praised this hat and that without much rhyme or reason; and without mentioning the one whose brim he intended should touch his own head, in the Manor garden after lunch.

All over the parish, pigeon pies were being conveyed toward the Manor, by people with serious but cheerful expressions, to be kept hot on Ellen's range. In the marquee, Janet Fox and she were giving the tableware a final inspection, and wondering what to do about a robin which had flown in but didn't seem to want to fly out.

Getting out of the car, Caroline knew it was absurd to feel flustered and almost tearful, but she couldn't help it. For a fortnight, she'd been at Edingthorpe at least as much as at Bure, she just didn't seem able to keep away. And now, with Claudia being her pride and joy, but also today a responsibility. With Georgia wearing that particular dress. With Bill Scott being among the guests in the church . . .

She was going to marry him, she knew she was. Very quietly. In a registry office. Or if he preferred, in a tiny chapel somewhere, anywhere, so long as it was a long way from Bure. Wearing everyday clothes.

She was going to say Yes the next time he asked her, because he was a lot nicer than any of her London friends. Mummy could say what she liked, but . . . And his farmhouse at Meeting Hill was between Worstead and Edingthorpe, so Claudia would see her godfather Jack *all* the time.

Even so, waiting on the church path with Claudia, who looked gorgeous in her little blue dress and pink sash, but *would* hold her posy upside-down. Smiling when Freddie and Hugh loyally proclaimed that she was suddenly the favourite in the wedding hat sweepstake, and all other bets were off. With the bell being rung, and Bobbie having been buried for three years . . . She must concentrate on his daughter.

'Now, darling, you must remember. When we go into the church, you follow Georgia and Uncle Charles. I'll be right there too, don't you worry. But you walk behind Georgia, in her white dress.'

On the gravel at the Manor, Lammas stood leaning on his walking-stick – the plan was that he'd leave it in the church porch. Beside him, Georgia too waited happily. She gazed around at the apple trees, their branches bending with the weight of fruit. She put her veil down, and felt wonderfully enclosed and protected, and tried looking at the trees like that. Right now, she had nothing further to say to Godfather Charles, and it seemed he too had nothing more to say. So they stood in quiet consonance, and she looked at the world through her silvery veil.

'Ah, here's Sidney,' Lammas said. 'Ten to twelve. Couldn't be better. Now, dear girl . . . Unless, of course, you've changed your mind? Perfectly all right to duck out, even at the last minute, you know.'

'Godfather Charles! Honestly, after . . .!'

He chuckled. 'Glad to hear it. Only . . . Only you may have to stand there looking beautiful for another moment or two, because there seems to be a hitch of some sort.'

Because old Sidney Meade had hurried from the car with a look of consternation on his face. Had bolted into a shed, come out clutching a spade, and now was almost running past them toward the lawn.

'Sorry, Sir! Mrs Lammas did say, but I forgot. Mole-hills! Won't be a minute.'

18

It was true that Charles Lammas had nothing further to say to his goddaughter, beyond what convention might require or affection casually prompt. But the urgent reason for his quietness was that, after an exhausting and depressing night, he was husbanding all his strength to get through the day.

If he could just keep his aches and his weaknesses at bay till after the cake had been cut, and the newly married couple had left for London. Then, surely, it would be all right for him to shut his library door against the outside world, and collapse into his chair, and possibly sleep – so long as he didn't dream. If throughout the service and then through lunch he could stop his mind from going into a blur, as it so often did, and then he was good for nothing. Mustn't spoil the wedding party by the groom's father suddenly having to be helped to bed.

Thank heavens for rituals like wedding services and lunches, he thought – not for the first time. Thank heavens for things you didn't have to think about too much, like how charming the bride looked, and the prospect of a good lunch.

Yes, that was the trick. Concentrate on the immediate, good things. Georgia blissfully excited beside him at the church door. Sonny Hannant at the bell-rope, his round pink face beaming. Get from one good, simple thing to the next, all day. Caroline's whisper, as she launched little Claudia after them up the aisle. One thing at a time, and keep them very clear, don't let them blur. There was Gloria, with a damned silly, pious expression on her face. Still, he must remember to talk to her for five minutes, during the party. And there was no doubt, in some cases religion could be . . . Bobbie had been the merriest companion he'd ever had. That time they'd sailed down to Aldeburgh, and he'd shinned up the mast to free a jammed halyard.

However, when Georgia and Charles reached the rood-screen, he was tired, and time was breaking up in his head as it had been doing ever since his stroke. For years, increasingly . . . So that the present was sometimes there in his mind, but then it would be dispersed. Still, here they were, at the chancel step, which fortunately he wasn't expected to negotiate. And it didn't matter what went on in his head, so long as he went through all these motions correctly. Nice for Miller to have his church so packed. And sweet the way Georgia on his arm, when they arrived before the parson, whispered, 'Hello Jack.' With flickery glances sideways between them. And he whispered, 'Sweetheart, you look terrific.'

Lammas braced himself to remain on his feet for another minute or two. Luckily, the giving away of the bride happened right at the beginning of the ceremony, and then . . . Claudia was doing fine, that was good. Yes, let him just get these two married to one another, and the next time he came to church they could sing the 'Nunc Dimittis' over him for all he cared. In the old days, he'd had far more ability to control what he remembered and when, what he thought and what he didn't think. Like other people. Oh, well. Just play this part now, play Alex's part, and then . . . *Who giveth this woman to be married to this man?* Alex, buried by these bridal hands, in a slit-trench in Burma. That hand Jack is taking. *I take thee, Georgiana . . .*

Consciousness breaking up in his head, it could feel like, so there were blurry regions where he wasn't really alive, couldn't understand anything. Then images he didn't want would come back to him. So now the sight of Georgia standing before the parson, and saying *I take thee Jack Michael Lammas to my wedded husband*, brought him the same young woman in the rags of a sari. Dragged before interrogators in Mandalay gaol. Where they'd . . . Had she faced the Kempeitai with that sullen, absent look he remembered so well?

To have and to hold from this day forward, for better for worse, for richer for poorer, in sickness and in health. You got decent rhetoric, he'd say that for the Church of England.

That way Georgia would recede deep behind her eyes – beyond finding. Interrogated, with the help of bayonets, and pliers. Her fingertips had gone on bleeding for months after that, she'd written, when in that internment camp they'd ground their rice with stones. Interrogated before that at school. In disgrace after a lacrosse match, was it? And that business with a golf club.

To love and to cherish, till death do us part. Yes, they did you proud, those old writers. *And thereto I give thee my troth.*

Heavens, he'd questioned her himself, gently, about her troubles at school. That way she'd just stood, expressionless. When had it been, recently, he'd remembered burning her school report with her? Oh, yes. Would she ever tell Jack she'd killed a man? About some of the duties of Japanese mess waitresses? Slowly, she'd probably tell him a fair bit. Well, she was free now. How was she going to take to being an English country wife? Oh, she'd be all right. She'd decided. Castaway, after a wreck the other side of the world, come back with her yarns.

They were married now. Better still, Henrietta was going to the lectern to read the lesson, so he could sit down for a few minutes. Good, too, in its way, this having times of Georgia's beating in his head, because . . . Well, because he must be coming toward the end of her visitations. Quite soon he wouldn't be alive to be haunted any more.

Concentrate on one good, simple thing at a time. That was the trick. So he turned to Blanche beside him, who was gazing at their son with love and pride. She met his eyes, and smiled a little tremulously. And he thought what a triumph this wedding she'd organised was and how this evening he'd tell her so. He thought how loyally she'd backed him up all these years as a painter, when if he'd put his energies into almost anything else he'd have made more money. It was over now. But he'd tell her once more: that he knew, he was grateful.

Concentrate on . . . Well, Jack looked very handsome, Blanche was right to be proud of him. He'd been luckier than Christopher. These escapers. And Georgia too . . . Daughter-in-law, now. Victrix, he'd told her, he was glad he'd told her. Got clear away, apart from the echoes in her head. Ever since she was a scrawny schoolgirl, running the muddy fields. Out in front. But not running to be first. Running to be away.

Unimpressed by his ravelling wits, Charles thought of lunch. A glass of champagne would put new heart into him. Tawny, autumn trees. Then the marquee would be a festive scene of exactly the kind he'd always liked. Pigeon pie. Claret. Friends to talk to. Anne Daubeney. Mario Zanetti – and the good thing was, he was staying for a week.

Guy and Marie Rivac, too, over from Bordeaux. Jolly decent of them to come all this way. And a good old chat with Guy about submarines was just the thing which, after lunch, with a cigar . . . Excellent!

Still, that pretty sister of Mario's would remind him of Raffaella. Opening a bedroom window at Rapallo, looking out to the sea. No, it was these two who were off to Rapallo. The Savoy tonight, then the Dover train. Trafalgar weather, Jack had said. Now he remembered clearly. All right if the storm didn't blow till evening, when they'd be having dinner at the Savoy. Well, these church windows had sun in them.

By the end of the service, the blurred regions in his mind were growing like mould. Images came. Words.

He looked at the bride's head. He saw her veil. But through it he saw the Lashio road, and a wraith who dragged herself along. He heard: *God damn it, I'm out. God damn it I might just make it.* He saw her head held up, dust-caked, gaunt with starvation except where it was swollen with bruises and insect bites. Filthy, infested hair. Welts. Sores around her mouth. Those shadowy eyes.